# Public Health Administration

## Principles for Population-Based Management

### Second Edition

*Edited by*

**Lloyd F. Novick, MD, MPH**
*Director*
*Division of Community Health and Preventive Medicine*
*Professor*
*Department of Family Medicine*
*The Brody School of Medicine*
*East Carolina University*
*Greenville, North Carolina*

**Cynthia B. Morrow, MD, MPH**
*Commissioner of Health*
*Onondaga County, New York*
*Assistant Professor*
*Departments of Medicine and Pediatrics*
*SUNY Upstate Medical University*
*Syracuse, New York*

**Glen P. Mays, PhD, MPH**
*Associate Professor*
*Vice Chair, Director of Research*
*Department of Health Policy and Management*
*Fay W. Boozman College of Public Health*
*University of Arkansas for Medical Sciences*
*Little Rock, Arkansas*

**JONES AND BARTLETT PUBLISHERS**
*Sudbury, Massachusetts*
BOSTON    TORONTO    LONDON    SINGAPORE

*World Headquarters*

Jones and Bartlett Publishers
40 Tall Pine Drive
Sudbury, MA 01776
978-443-5000
info@jbpub.com
www.jbpub.com

Jones and Bartlett Publishers
Canada
6339 Ormindale Way
Mississauga, Ontario
L5V 1J2 Canada

Jones and Bartlett Publishers
International
Barb House, Barb Mews
London W6 7PA
United Kingdom

Jones and Bartlett's books and products are available through most bookstores and online booksellers. To contact Jones and Bartlett Publishers directly, call 800-832-0034, fax 978-443-8000, or visit our website www.jbpub.com.

Substantial discounts on bulk quantities of Jones and Bartlett's publications are available to corporations, professional associations, and other qualified organizations. For details and specific discount information, contact the special sales department at Jones and Bartlett via the above contact information or send an email to specialsales@jbpub.com.

**Library of Congress Cataloging-in-Publication Data**
Public health administration : principles for population-based management / [edited by] Lloyd F. Novick, Cynthia B. Morrow, and Glen P. Mays. − 2nd ed.
    p. ; cm.
Includes bibliographical references and index.
ISBN-13: 978-0-7637-3842-6
ISBN-10: 0-7637-3842-5
1. Public health administration.   I. Novick, Lloyd F.   II. Morrow, Cynthia B.   III. Mays, Glen P.
[DNLM:   1. Public Health Administration.  WA 525 P9745 2007]
    RA425.P83 2007
    362.1068−dc22

                                                                        2006037756

6048

*Production Credits*
Publisher: Michael Brown
Production Director: Amy Rose
Production Editor: Renée Sekerak
Associate Editor: Katey Birtcher
Marketing Manager: Sophie Fleck
Manufacturing Buyer: Amy Bacus
Composition: Auburn Associates, Inc.
Cover Design: Kristin E. Ohlin
Printing and Binding: Malloy, Inc.
Cover Printing: Malloy, Inc.

Printed in the United States of America
15  14  13  12  11      10 9 8 7 6 5 4

# CONTENTS

## Chapter 5:   Ethics in Public Health Practice and Management . . . . . . . . . . . . 149
### Ruth Gaare Bernheim

## Chapter 6:   Legislative Relations in Public Health. . . . . . . . . . . . . . . . . . . . . . 161
### Stephanie A. Kennan

## Chapter 7:   Financing the Public's Health . . . . . . . . . . . . . . . . . . . . . . . . . . . . 189
### Perri S. Leviss

## Chapter 8:   The Public Health Workforce . . . . . . . . . . . . . . . . . . . . . . . . . . . . . 225
### Margaret A. Potter, Kristine M. Gebbie, Hugh H. Tilson

# FOREWORD

Public health administrators have many roles. They must hire and supervise personnel who provide services; they must understand the legal, political, and economic climate in which their organizations develop new programs, evaluate existing programs, and make the case for programs to an increasingly attentive constituency; and they must administer a budget to pay for these efforts. *Public Health Administration: Principles for Population-Based Management* provides the tools with which to think through and act on these responsibilities. The information provided in this text is both practical and fully informed by the theory, history, and context of each of its subjects. In the six years since the publication of its first edition, *Public Health Administration* has become essential reading for anyone concerned with improving public health practice.

Today, the U.S. Public Health System is part of a worldwide movement to control and improve the quality of public health services. This movement has several features rooted in business practices: customer service, decentralization, privatization, collaboration, innovation, an entrepreneurial organizational culture, and accountability for results. This movement suggests that public managers devolve authority, plan programs as if they were business ventures, measure performance, innovate, partner, negotiate, contract, and meet "customer" demands, however those are defined. In the light of this systematic reimagining of how public health should operate, public health leaders and managers must constantly negotiate between traditional responsibilities and demands compelled by a new understanding of governmental quality control.

This movement is occurring within the context of a complex array of trends affecting the United States today. These trends include changes in the make-up of the U.S. population; changes in health services delivery and financing; and global political, economic, and environmental developments. Many of these trends are national in scope, yet their effects vary substantially at regional and local levels. Other trends are specific to individual localities and regions, and the political and economic forces that operate within these areas. Every trend affects an administrator's job in multiple ways. A downturn in the economy, for example, increases the number of uninsured or underinsured people a public health agency may be asked to serve; it affects the types of services the agency will be asked to offer as more people use it for their primary care needs; it affects morale in the public health workforce as its members are asked to do more with less; and it makes federal funding of state and local public health programs more fragmented and precarious (thus necessitating the type of entrepreneurial management described above).

*Public Health Administration* gives public health leaders and managers the tools with which to translate what we *know* and *think* about public health administration into what we *do* every day. The pages of this text deal with every aspect of an administrator's responsibilities, defining terms, setting the issues in their historical and political contexts, and giving concrete advice that will help administrators just beginning their tenure as well as seasoned public health professionals facing new challenges or a changing landscape. While much attention has been paid, with good reason, to the need to provide greater access to formal public health training for the public health workforce, less has been paid to systematically providing training in management principles and methods to its leaders and managers. This text helps fill that gap.

We are treated in these pages to an array of writers, both knowledgeable and experienced in the topics they take on. The editors themselves have focused much of their professional attention on improving the public's health through prevention and, in the case of Dr. Morrow, through activity in bioterrorism preparedness and in developing plans for control and prevention of communicable diseases. Dr. Novick, both in his scholarship and in his years practicing the type of management and leadership this book describes, has been instrumental in moving the profession toward a practical and evidence-based approach to public health. In the 1990s, he chaired The Council on Linkages between Academia and Public Health Practice, and was a consultant to the Task Force on Community Preventive Services. The *Guide to Community Preventive Services* stems from that effort, a seminal resource for researchers, policy makers, and public health leaders needing to know what works and what doesn't when planning public health interventions. *Public Health Administration* applies the same type of expertise and insight to managing the people, money, and data that make public health interventions happen.

The assumption behind *Public Health Administration* is that nothing to which public health professionals aspire—no programs or interventions designed to improve and protect the health of the population—can happen without competent, effective leadership. And administration is the means by which effective leadership is translated into effective action. This text helps bring about that translation. It represents an important tool for improving the quality of public health service as it is practiced in every corner of the nation, now and in the decades to come.

*Edward L. Baker, MD, MPH*
Director and Professor
North Carolina Institute for Public Health
Departments of Epidemiology and Health Policy and Administration
University of North Carolina at Chapel Hill
School of Public Health
Chapel Hill, North Carolina

# ACKNOWLEDGMENTS

We thank our families for the contributions they make to our work every day. Without their ongoing support, completion of this book would not have been possible.

LFN, CBM, GPM

# INTRODUCTION

Major events and advances in population health management have reshaped public health practice since the publication six years ago of the first edition of *Public Health Administration: Principles for Population-Based Management.* The field of public health is undergoing remarkable change necessitating the integration of new content throughout this second revision. Public health administration will continue to evolve in response to new challenges and technologies. The population-based approach, the hallmark of public health activities, will retain its importance in future efforts to improve the health of communities.

One area of increased emphasis since the publication of the *First Edition* is the imperative to reduce potentially preventable chronic diseases associated with health behaviors that are influenced by environmental and community factors. The growing "epidemics" of obesity and Type 2 diabetes are health threats that may even reverse progress in extending life expectancy.

Clearly, however, the greatest change to public health occurred after the terrorist attacks of September 11, 2001. These events redefined the role of public health. The ensuing emphasis on preparedness against such terrorist attacks highlighted the role of public health as a "first responder" and a member of the team planning for long-term protection and reduction of hazards to communities. The term "public health infrastructure" came into popular usage to emphasize the need for a basic public health capacity for all communities and to justify the investment of federal and other resources. This infrastructure is to provide protection not only against terrorism (most notably bioterrorism) but for any emerging infectious diseases.

Controversy has accompanied the new preparedness focus of the public health agenda. Does an emphasis on terrorism preparedness reduce investment and dilute commitment to other vital functions?[1,2] While this has indeed occurred, the influence of the new priority of preparedness and the accompanying allocation of funds for that purpose have resulted in major changes for the field which are described in detail in this new edition. The stimulus engendered by bioterrorism has expanded to the threats of emerging disease and natural disasters. The rapid geographic expansion of West Nile Virus infection in the United States, Severe Acute Respiratory Disease (SARS), and the specter of pandemic flu have become concerns since the publication of the *First Edition*.

Similarly, devastating natural disasters, such as the 2004 tsunami and Hurricane Katrina in 2005, have had a major impact on the health of the public. The tsunami was one of the deadliest international disasters ever recorded. Katrina caused the largest displacement of individuals of any disaster ever experienced in the United States. Many of the displaced individuals were impoverished, further emphasizing the public health consequences of this event. The chapters on surveillance, communication, informatics, disasters, public health law, and ethics in this new edition reflect the necessary related changes and advances in public health practice.

The chapters on law and ethics have substantially added content on quarantine and other issues related to public health emergencies. Quarantine, which was not employed throughout most of the 20th century, is now an integral part of preparedness planning. The need for updated laws and regulations related to isolation and quarantine became evident when concerns about the potential for smallpox, hemorrhagic viral fevers, and SARS surfaced. For example, in New York State regulations enabling communicable disease control, including authorization for quarantine, were revised to specifically include these conditions. The Model State Emergency Health Powers Act is described in this text with the basic provisions for preparedness, surveillance, management of property, protection of persons, and public information.

The chapter on surveillance is likewise influenced in part by the new priority of preparedness with the advent of syndromic surveillance and investment of federal preparedness resources that have contributed to electronic disease reporting. Other major changes in this *Second Edition* include more attention to sentinel disease reporting. Emphasis on the problems of chronic disease has led to more content in the surveillance of these conditions and the ascertainment of associated behavioral risks in communities.

Surveillance is one of a series of linked and updated contributions to the acquisition of public health information found in this new edition. The chapter on data updates progress on *Healthy People 2010*. Another information related chapter is on geographic information systems where recent advances are described, not only in newer technology, but in applications in the areas of environmental hazards, exposure assessment, and substance abuse. The chapter on health information systems provides the comprehensive view of health information and its management, providing contemporary concepts on the organization of the most effective systems and the latest technologies available for this purpose. HIPAA and its influence on patient health data and its automated transfer are covered in this chapter.

The Community Health Assessment chapter emphasizes the value of the relatively new tool of state web-based data queries. Of high importance is the development of a process for inventorying and prioritizing community health needs leading to planning for community health improvement. MAPP (Mobilizing for Action through Planning and Partnerships), developed by the National Association for County and City Health Officials (NACCHO), is a major development in this area and a required modality for all departments of health. The term strategic planning has been added to the former title of the community health assessment chapter highlighting both the importance of community participation in planning and the close linkage with assessment of health problems and needs.

Two major aspects of public health practice, described in the *First Edition*, have made remarkable progress and are now treated at length in this new edition. These are accreditation of public health agencies and credentialing of the public health workforce. Often the distinction between these two major terms is misunderstood. Accreditation refers to the local public health agency (there is also movement to accredit state health departments) and is associated with performance measurement of these departments detailed in the chapter on that subject. Credentialing is applied to the public health professional or worker and is based on competencies. The revised chapter on public health workforce, the public health system's most essential resource, provides considerable insights and detail in this area. Clearly, these two elements are related and linked to an adequate public health workforce and capacity of the public health agency.

There have also been notable changes in the organization of public health agencies at the state, local, and federal levels since the initial publication of this text. Changes in local public health departments are described with the recently available NACCHO survey. Regionalization is identified as an important trend in the operation of local health departments. Reorganization of state health departments and agencies within the United States Department of Health and Human Services, including the Centers for Disease Control and Prevention, are included.

Chapters on Community-Based Prevention, Health Education and Promotion, and Public Health Marketing provide updated information on population-based strategies, such as those provided by the Task Force on Community Preventive Services. These chapters focus on developing population-based interventions to influence health behaviors that contribute to the leading causes of morbidity and mortality. Similarly, the chapter on Building Constituencies for Public Health provides updated information from knowledge gained by the Turning Point initiative and other projects. The chapter on legislation also has added content on working at state and local levels including constituents and emphasizes the role of advocacy. The chapter "Financing the Public's Health" includes recent information, not previously published, on the activities of state and local jurisdictions in this area. The chapter on evaluation adds an entirely new section on economic analyses including cost-minimization, cost-effectiveness, cost-utility, and cost-benefit methods. Entirely new chapters in human resources administration and leadership for public health have been contributed by authors associated with the North Carolina Institute for Public Health of the University of North Carolina School of Public Health.

A final development worth noting is the progress toward evidence-based practice in public health and the growing body of evidence produced through the field of public health systems research. Historically, public health research has been viewed solely as an activity of the academic and scientific communities, but more recently, growing numbers of public health agencies and professionals are participating in practice-based research activities in order to learn better ways of organizing, financing, and delivering services. A new chapter on this topic highlights the progress to date and the opportunities and challenges faced by public health administrators who engage in the research enterprise.

Public health practitioners have the opportunity to work in exciting times. Public health practice has achieved increased recognition since the *First Edition* in efforts for preparedness against a possible bioterrorist threat,

SARS, and now pandemic flu. Efforts need to be redoubled to achieve similar recognition and action to counter threats from chronic disease to our nation's continued improvement in health. A recent series in the *New York Times* pointed out the futility of high technology and pharmaceutical interventions for the growing incidence of Type 2 diabetes as opposed to investing in preventive and public health interventions.[3] There are currently 20.8 million people in the United States with diabetes. "Unless something is done to prevent it, diabetes will result in 35 million heart attacks, 13 million strokes, 6 million episodes of renal failure, 8 million instances of blindness or eye surgery, 2 million amputations, and 62 million deaths for a total of 121 million serious diabetes-related adverse events in the next 30 years."[4] The public health approach, outlined in this edition, to addressing health needs of populations is best suited to confront both present and future challenges.

## References

1. Novick L. *The Price of Bioterrorism Preparedness: Are We Compromising the Public's Safety by Diverting Resources from Essential Functions of Public Health?* New York Academy of Medicine, New York: May 28, 2003.
2. Novick L. *Bioterrorism Preparedness: Impact on Local Public Health, American Public Health Association 131st Annual Meeting,* San Francisco: November 17, 2003.
3. In the Treatment of Diabetes, Success Often Does Not Pay. *The New York Times*; 2006: January 11.
4. Rizza R. *Call for a New Commitment to Diabetes Care in America.* American Diabetes Organization, Washington, DC: June, 11, 2006.

Lloyd F. Novick, MD, MPH
Cynthia B. Morrow, MD, MPH
Glen P. Mays, PhD, MPH

# ABOUT THE EDITORS

Lloyd F. Novick, MD, MPH, is Director of the Division of Community and Preventive Medicine at the Brody School of Medicine of East Carolina University. Formerly, he was Professor of Medicine at SUNY Upstate Medical University, where he directed the teaching program in preventive medicine and also served as Commissioner of Health for Onondaga County (Syracuse, NY). He has also previously been Professor and Chairman of the Department of Epidemiology at the University of Albany, School of Public Health. Other past positions include Commissioner of Health and Secretary for Human Services for Vermont, Director of Health Services for Arizona, and Director of the Office of Public Health of the New York State Department of Health. As former Chair of the Council of Linkages between Academia and Public Health Practice, he led their effort to develop evidence-based guidelines for population-based prevention. He continued this interest as a consultant to the U.S. Public Health Service Task Force on Community Preventive Services. He is President of the Association for Prevention Teaching and Research (APTR), formerly the Association of Teachers of Preventive Medicine (ATPM). He is a former President of the Association of State and Territorial Health Officials (ASTHO) and the New York State Association of County Health Officials (NYSACHO). He is founder and editor of the *Journal of Public Health Management and Practice* and editor of the text *Public Health Administration: Principles of Population-Based Management, 1st edition* (Aspen, 2001). Other books include *Health Problems in the Prison Setting* (Thomas, 1977), *Public Health Leaders Tell Their Stories* (Aspen, 1998) and *Community-Based Prevention: Programs That Work* (Aspen, 1999). He has authored more than 80 articles in peer-reviewed publications. He has received numerous national awards including the Special Recognition Award, American College of Preventive Medicine (2006); Duncan Clark Award, Association of Teachers of Preventive Medicine (2004); Distinguished Service Award, Yale University (2003); Excellence in Public Health Administration, American Public Health Association (2001); and Arthur T. McCormack Award, Association of State and Territorial Health Officials (1992). He is a graduate of Colgate University (BA, 1961), New York University (MD, 1965), and Yale University (MPH, 1971).

Cynthia B. Morrow, MD, MPH, is Commissioner of Health for Onondaga County (Syracuse, NY), Assistant Professor of Medicine and Pediatrics at

SUNY Upstate Medical University. Previously, Dr. Morrow worked at the Guam Department of Public Health and was then in private practice in Florida until her family relocated to Syracuse. She serves on the editorial board of the *Journal of Public Health Management and Practice*. Dr. Morrow is a graduate of Swarthmore College (BA, 1987) and Tufts University School of Medicine (MD/MPH 1992).

**Glen P. Mays, PhD, MPH,** currently serves as Associate Professor, Vice Chair, and Director of Research for the Department of Health Policy and Management in the Fay W. Boozman College of Public Health at the University of Arkansas for Medical Sciences (UAMS). He also serves as Director of the PhD Program in Health Systems Research at UAMS, and as Associate Professor of Health Policy in the Clinton School of Public Service at the University of Arkansas. Dr. Mays' research focuses on strategies for organizing and financing public health services, health insurance, and medical care services for underserved populations. He earned an AB degree in political science from Brown University (1992), received MPH (1996), and PhD (1999) degrees in health policy and administration from UNC-Chapel Hill, and completed a postdoctoral fellowship in health economics at Harvard Medical School's Department of Health Care Policy (2000).

# CONTRIBUTORS

Elizabeth A. Baker, PhD, MPH
Associate Professor
Saint Louis University
School of Public Health
Department of Community Health
Saint Louis, Missouri

Leslie M. Beitsch, MD, JD
Florida State University
College of Medicine
Center for Medicine and Public Health
Tallahassee, Florida

Ruth Berkelman, MD
Clinical Professor
Director
Center for Public Health Preparedness
    and Research
Rollins School of Public Health
Emory University
Atlanta, Georgia

Donald J. Berndt, PhD
Information Systems and
    Decision Sciences
College of Business Administration
University of South Florida
Tampa, Florida

Ruth Gaare Bernheim, JD
Associate Professor
Public Health Sciences Administration
University of Virginia
Charlotte, Virginia

Ross C. Brownson, PhD
Professor of Epidemiology
Saint Louis University
School of Public Health
Saint Louis, Missouri

Brad Christensen
U.S. External Communications Director
AMEC
Tempe, Arizona

Leon E. Cosler, RPh, PhD
Assistant Professor of
    Pharmacoeconomics
Albany College of Pharmacy
Albany, New York

Claudia S. P. Fernandez, DrPH, MS, RD,
    LDN
Director
Public Health and Healthcare
    Leadership Institute
North Carolina Institute for Public Health
University of North Carolina
    at Chapel Hill
Chapel Hill, North Carolina

John W. Fisher, PhD
Visiting Assistant Research Professor
University of North Carolina at Charlotte
Charlotte, North Carolina

Kristine M. Gebbie, DrPH, RN
Elizabeth Standish Gill Associate
    Professor of Nursing
Director
Center for Health Policy
Columbia University School of Nursing
New York, New York

Lawrence O. Gostin, JD, LLD (Hon.)
Associate Dean for Research and
  Academic Programs
Professor of Law
Director
Center for Law and the Public's Health
Georgetown University Law Center
Washington, DC

Lawrence W. Green, DrPH
Adjunct Professor
Department of Epidemiology and
  Biostatistics
School of Medicine and Comprehensive
  Cancer Center
University of California at San Francisco
San Francisco, California

Arden S. Handler, DrPH
Professor
University of Illinois
School of Public Health
Chicago, Illinois

Michael T. Hatcher, DrPH, MPH, CHES
Chief
Environmental Medicine and Education
  Services Branch
Division of Toxicology and
  Environmental Medicine (Proposed)
Agency for Toxic Substances and
  Disease Registry
Atlanta, Georgia

Douglas Hirano, MPH
Executive Director
Asian Pacific Community in Action
Phoenix, Arizona

Theresa Hatzell Hoke, PhD, MPH
Scientist
Health Services Research
Family Health International
Research Triangle Park, North Carolina

Stephanie A. Kennan, MA
Senior Health Policy Advisor to U.S.
  Senator Ron Wyden (D-OR)
Washington, DC

Linda Young Landesman, DrPH, MSW
Assistant Vice President
Office of Professional Services and
  Affiliations
New York City Health and
  Hospitals Corporation
New York, New York

Laura B. Landrum, MA
Special Projects Director
Illinois Public Health Institute
Chicago, Illinois

C. Virginia Lee, MD, MPH, MA
Captain
USPHS
Medical Officer
Office of the Director
Division of Health Studies
Agency for Toxic Substances and
  Disease Registry
Atlanta, Georgia

Perri S. Leviss, MPM
Executive Director
Rhode Island Campus Compact
Providence, Rhode Island

Lynne Doner Lotenberg, MS
Social Marketing + Research +
  Evaluation
Arlington, Virginia

Glen P. Mays, PhD, MPH
Associate Professor
Vice Chair, Director of Research
Department of Health Policy and
  Management
Fay W. Boozman College of Public Health
University of Arkansas for
  Medical Sciences
Little Rock, Arkansas

Alan L. Melnick, MD, MPH
Associate Professor
Department of Family Medicine
Oregon Health and Science University
Portland, Oregon
Health Officer
Clark County Public Health
Vancouver, Washington

Cynthia B. Morrow, MD, MPH
Commissioner of Health
Onondaga County, New York
Assistant Professor
Departments of Medicine and Pediatrics
SUNY Upstate Medical University
Syracuse, New York

Ray M. Nicola, MD, MHSA, FACPM
Director
Community-Oriented
Public Health Practice Program
Faculty
Northwest Center for Public
   Health Practice
Senior Consultant and CDC Assignee
University of Washington
School of Public Health and
   Community Medicine
Seattle, Washington

Lloyd F. Novick, MD, MPH
Director
Division of Community Health and
   Preventive Medicine
Professor
Deprtment of Family Medicine
The Brody School of Medicine
East Carolina University
Greenville, North Carolina

Judith M. Ottoson, EdD, MPH
Consultant
San Francisco, California

Janet E. Porter, PhD
Executive Vice President
Chief Operating Officer
Dana-Farber Cancer Institute
Boston, Massachusetts

Margaret A. Potter, JD
Associate Dean and Director
Center for Public Health Practice
Graduate School of Public Health
University of Pittsburgh
Pittsburgh, Pennsylvania

Tausha D. Robertson, DrPH
Director
Health and Productivity Strategy
Icahn Associates Corporation
Fort Lauderdale, Florida

Michael Siegel, MD, MPH
Professor
Social and Behavioral Sciences
   Department
Boston University School of Public Health
Boston, Massachusetts

Benjamin Silk, MPH
Rollins School of Public Health
Emory University
Atlanta, Georgia

Michael A. Stoto, PhD
Senior Statistical Scientist
Associate Director for Public Health
RAND Corporation
Arlington, Virginia

James Studnicki, ScD, MBA, MPH
Irwin Belk Endowed Chair in Health
   Services Research
College of Health and Human Services
University of North Carolina Charlotte
Charlotte, North Carolina

Lee Thielen, BSFS, MPA
Public Health Consultant
Fort Collins, Colorado

Hugh H. Tilson, MD, DrPH
Clinical Professor
Public Health Leadership Program
University of North Carolina
   at Chapel Hill
School of Public Health
Chapel Hill, North Carolina

Bernard J. Turnock, MD, MPH
Clinical Professor and Director
Division of Community Health Sciences
School of Public Health
University of Chicago
Chicago, Illinois

## CHAPTER 1

# DEFINING PUBLIC HEALTH: HISTORICAL AND CONTEMPORARY DEVELOPMENTS

Lloyd F. Novick
Cynthia B. Morrow

## Chapter Overview

Public health practice comprises organized efforts to improve the health of communities. Public health prevention strategies are targeted to populations rather than to individuals. Throughout history, public health effort has been directed to the control of transmissible diseases, reduction of environmental hazards, and provision of safe drinking water. Because social, environmental, and biologic factors interact to determine health, public health practice must utilize a broad set of skills and interventions. During the 20th century, the historic emphasis on protecting communities from infectious disease and environmental threats expanded to counter risks from behaviors and lifestyles that led to chronic disease. Population-based prevention resulted in major gains in life expectancy during the 1900s. In the beginning of this century, public health expanded even further as numerous events necessitated a shift in public health priorities.

## Defining Public Health

Public health consists of organized efforts to improve the health of communities. The operative components of this definition are that public health efforts are *organized* and *directed to communities* rather than to individuals. Public health practice does not rely on a specific body of knowledge and expertise but rather relies on a combination of science and social approaches. The definition of public health reflects its central goal—the reduction of disease and the improvement of health in a community.

In 1920, C.E.A. Winslow provided the following definition of public health practice:

> Public health is the science and art of preventing disease, prolonging life, and promoting physical health and efficiency through organized community efforts for the sanitation of the environment, the control of community infections, the education of the individual in principles of personal hygiene, the organization of medical and nursing services for the early diagnosis and preventive treatment of disease, and the development of social machinery which will ensure to every individual in the community a standard of living adequate for the maintenance of health.[1(p34)]

Almost 70 years later, in 1988, the Institute of Medicine (IOM) published its classic report, *The Future of Public Health,* similarly defining public health as an "organized community effort to address the public interest in health by applying scientific and technical knowledge to prevent disease and promote health."[2(p7)] The mission of public health, then, is to ensure conditions that promote the health of the community.

Population-based strategies for improving community health include efforts to control epidemics, ensure safe water and food, reduce vaccine-preventable diseases, improve maternal and child health, and conduct surveillance of health problems (Exhibit 1-1). In addition to long-standing efforts to protect communities from contagious and environmental health threats, the public health arena is expanding to counter new and contemporary risks: obesity, adolescent pregnancy, injury, violence, substance abuse, sexually transmitted diseases (STD), human immunodeficiency virus (HIV) infection, natural disasters, and bioterrorism. To be successful, however, any approach to improve a community's health must involve both population-based and clinical preventive activities, as presented in Figure 1-1.

Public health differs from clinical medicine by emphasizing prevention and keying interventions to multiple social and environmental determinants of disease; clinical medicine focuses on the treatment of the individual. However, interaction between public health and medicine is necessary be-

Exhibit 1-1   Public Health Activities

- Prevents epidemics
- Protects the environment, workplaces, housing, food, and water
- Monitors health status of population
- Mobilizes community action
- Responds to disasters
- Assures quality, accessibility, and accountability of medical care
- Reaches out to link high-risk and hard-to-reach people to needed services
- Researches to develop new insights and innovative solutions
- Leads the development of sound health policy and planning

*Source:* Reprinted from *For a Healthy Nation: Returns on Investments in Public Health,* Executive Summary, 1994, U.S. Department of Health and Human Services, Public Health Services.

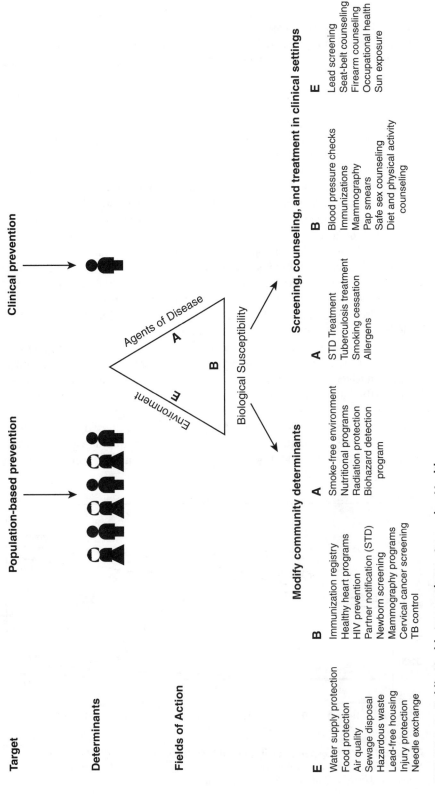

**FIGURE 1-1   Public Health Approaches to Improving Health**
*Source:* Copyright © 2000 L.F. Novick

cause individual health and community health are elements of a continuum. Tuberculosis (TB), HIV infection, STD, lead toxicity, vaccine-preventable disease, and even heart disease and asthma are among the many health problems that are ideally managed in both population and clinical settings.

Ample evidence for the importance of influencing population-based determinants of health is shown by the increase in life expectancy from 45 to 75 years for individuals living in industrialized countries during the 1900s (Figure 1-2). The majority of this gain, 25 of the 30 years, can be attributed to public health measures such as better nutrition, sanitation, and safer housing.[3] Medical care focusing on individual patients, though important, only contributed five years of the gain in life expectancy.

Furthermore, the relevance of public health and clinical collaboration is underscored by estimates that 50% of premature deaths are preventable and influenced by personal behaviors—the abuse of tobacco and other substances, poor diet, and sedentary lifestyles.[4,5] Changes in health status can best be achieved through partnership between clinical efforts focusing on individual patients and community-wide public health interventions addressing environmental and social determinants that place individuals at greater risk of disease.

Both science and social factors form the basis for public health intervention. Successfully eradicating a vaccine-preventable disease from a community requires more than development of an effective vaccine. Acceptance and widespread use of the vaccine in the community is dependent on a successful public health initiative providing public information and facilitating delivery. Too often, scientific advances are not fully translated into community health improvement. For example, in the United States, perinatal transmission of HIV has plummeted in the past 10 years because of aggressive approaches for testing and treatment of HIV during pregnancy and delivery; yet congenital syphilis, while decreasing, has not achieved the same level of success despite the fact that scientific means (penicillin) to eradicate it entirely have been known for many more years. A comprehensive public health ap-

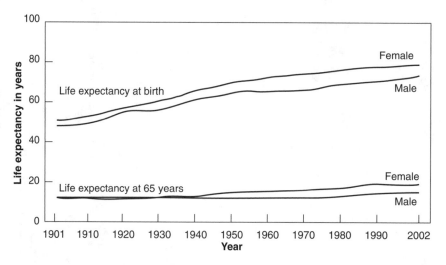

**FIGURE 1-2    Life Expectancy in the United States over the 20th Century**
*Source:* Centers for Disease Control and Prevention, National Center for Health Statistics, *Health, United States, 2005,* Figure 26.

proach, combining science with practical approaches to address cultural and socioeconomic factors important to the improvement of birth outcomes for at-risk women, is essential to eliminate these preventable diseases.

Another example of the important interplay of clinical and public health interventions is that of an outbreak of tuberculosis in a homeless shelter for men in a community in upstate New York in the 1990s. Clinical interventions, including administration of anti-TB medications and sophisticated diagnostic methods, were combined with a broad public health approach to minimize the impact of the outbreak. Outreach efforts and incentives for directly observed therapy were tailored to the social factors associated with this group of men. Risk factors for poor health outcomes included concomitant infection with HIV, alcohol and substance abuse, homelessness, and inadequate ventilation of the shelter. All were determinants of this outbreak. Unfortunately, despite vigorous attempts to engage the individuals diagnosed with active tuberculosis, noncompliance remained a significant challenge, ultimately leading the local public health agency to obtain court orders mandating the hospitalization of several of the men. In addition to ensuring treatment of those known to have active tuberculosis, significant efforts were made to identify, and treat when indicated, hundreds of individuals who were exposed to tuberculosis in this outbreak. This case illustrates a basic tenet of public health: protecting the health of the community, even when these efforts conflict with the individuals' autonomy, involves more than the sum of the treating the infected individuals.

## Early Collective Action to Improve Health in Great Britain and the United States

The evolving definition of public health activity is forged by hazards requiring collective action. Throughout history, attention has been directed to controlling transmissible diseases, improving the environment, and providing safe drinking water. Toilets drained by covered sewers have been found in excavations of civilizations dating to 4000 years ago in the Indus Valley. In 2000 BCE cities, including Troy, had highly developed water supply systems.[6] At the time of Joshua when Israelites settled in the Holy Land, there were rules governing the water supply that dictated that there could not be a cemetery, animal slaughterhouse, tannery, or furnace within 50 cubits (approximately 25 meters) of a village water supply.[7] In the Western Hemisphere, impressive ruins of sewers and baths document the achievements of the Incas in public health engineering.[6]

The Greeks believed that ill health developed from an imbalance between man and his environment, not unlike contemporary public health theories of multifactorial disease causation, in which environment plays a prominent role. In his book, *On Airs, Waters and Places*, Hippocrates summarizes factors important to disease, including climate, soil, water, mode of life, and nutrition.[8] Furthermore, Hippocrates provided guidance to the location of Greek colonies as they expanded eastward to Italy and Sicily. Houses were to be located on elevated and sunny areas, avoiding marshes and swamps with their vector-borne illnesses.[6] The Romans also made the connection between swamps and disease (specifically, malaria), and determined salubrity was an important component of the selection of places for habitation. Ancient terms describing disease are still in use, including *endemic* (background or usual occurrence) and *epidemic* (excessive occurrence).

In the Middle Ages (AD 500–1500), epidemics of infectious diseases spurred collective activities by communities to promote the public's health, presaging the later formation of boards of health and public health departments in the 1800s. The Middle Ages were marked by two major epidemics of bubonic plague—the Plague of Justinian (543) and the Black Death (1348)—with smaller outbreaks of various diseases in the intervening period, including leprosy, smallpox, tuberculosis, and measles.[6] During this period, lepers were considered public menaces and were expelled from the community. This is a stark example of deprivation of individual civil rights in a quest to protect the health of the public. Similarly, the Black Death was regarded as a communicable disease, and the countermeasure employed was isolation of the ill individual. In addition, victims of the disease had to be reported to the authorities, a forerunner of the basic public health functions of disease reporting and surveillance. Quarantine measures were instituted to stop the entry of plague from outside regions. In 1348, Venice, a chief port of entry for commerce from the Orient, was the first city to institute quarantine, requiring the inspection and segregation of ships and individuals suspected of carrying disease. This was expanded in 1423, when a pesthouse or *lazaretto* was erected in Venice as a place to hold detained individuals suspected of harboring infection (*lazaretto* is derived from the name of the Biblical character Lazarus, who was a leper). These detention areas were used for isolation in many types of pestilence.[9] This precedent of isolation and quarantine remains relevant and controversial in contemporary public health practice.

Medieval cities were run by councils who were charged with routine community administration as well as the supervision of disease prevention, sanitation, and protection of community health. Measures were instituted to control the transmission of infections, including food inspections, regulation of waste disposal isolation, disinfection, as well as isolation and quarantine.[6] In another example of early collective public health action, Venice, like other cities at that time, set up a council of men to supervise the health of the city—a forerunner of boards of health that were implemented centuries later.[6] These interactions are diagrammed in Figure 1-3. The collective actions to protect public health that were implemented in the Middle Ages exhibit patterns that are very much in existence in our current public health programs: a population-based focus for interventions, involvement of government, prominence of environmental interventions, and potential for infringement of individual rights to protect the public.

## Collective Activities to Protect Health in the United States

The early American colonists struggled with hunger and malnutrition, scurvy, and infectious diseases such as smallpox, cholera, measles, diphtheria, and typhoid fever.[10] Smallpox was the epidemic disease of the colonies in the 1600s; yellow fever became prominent in the 1700s; and the dread disease of the 1800s was cholera.[9] The major public health function of the colonies was the control of communicable diseases as demonstrated by the enactment of laws

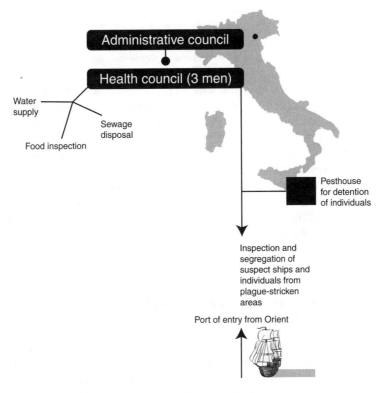

**FIGURE 1-3    Medieval Model for Public Health Practice: Venice, 1300–1500**
*Source:* Copyright © 2000 L.F. Novick

regarding quarantine and sanitation. The colonies consisted principally of a series of seaports connected by ships. In 1699, William Penn, concerned about yellow fever in the colony he had established, passed an "Act to Prevent Sickly Vessels from Coming into This Government."[9] The Massachusetts Quarantine Act of July 1701 required parties bringing infectious diseases within the colony to pay all associated costs and damages and compelled confinement of individuals who were infected with pestilential illnesses. Quarantine laws were enacted in all major towns along the eastern seaboard. Other laws that protected the health of the community included sanitary laws regulating such matters as privies, disposal of wastes, and disposition of animals.

In addition to the passage of these laws, another notable public health intervention of the colonial period was smallpox inoculation. Reverend Cotton Mather, known for his involvement in the Salem Witch trials, provided an account of the smallpox epidemic of 1689–1690 in New England: "In about a twelvemonth, one thousand of our neighbors have been carried to their long home."[9(p22)] The total population of Boston at that time was only 6000. In a smallpox epidemic of Boston in 1721, Mather suggested smallpox inoculation. As with many public health interventions, initially there was considerable controversy concerning smallpox inoculation, but he was able to convince Dr. Zabdiel Boyleston to try the technique. Years later, when smallpox again struck Massachusetts, the death rate was 1.8% in those who were vaccinated, compared to 14% in individuals who were not.[9]

Yellow fever, an acute mosquito-borne viral infectious disease of short duration and varying severity, was the scourge of the 1700s.[11] In 1702, following importation of the disease from St. Thomas, Virgin Islands, New York City bore the brunt of a yellow fever epidemic, although numerous other cities, including Philadelphia, Norfolk, Charleston, New Orleans, and Boston, also fell victim to the disease. Yellow fever epidemics were experienced in cities throughout the century with some cities being hit more than once.[12] A stark example of this is Philadelphia in which nearly 50,000 people were reported to have contracted yellow fever (with 4044 reported deaths) in 1793 only to be devastated by the disease again five years later, when another 3506 deaths were attributed to it.[13] Interestingly, in the northern part of America, the disease was noted to occur only in summer, after ships arrived from ports affected by yellow fever. When the October frost arrived, the epidemics ended. This underscored the importance of the environment in epidemic disease and improved understanding of the opportunity and necessity for public health measures.

## Social and Environmental Factors and Organized Public Health Action

To 19th-century New Yorkers, the word *epidemic* was all too clearly understood and experienced in the form of cholera, smallpox, yellow fever, and typhoid (Table 1-1).[13] In addition to these epidemics, the health of the community was threatened by the constant presence of tuberculosis, the leading cause of death in the United States at that time. In 1890, nearly one out of every four dwellings in New York City experienced a TB-related death. The toll was much higher in poorer neighborhoods, leaving these communities devastated by the disease.[13]

The nature of these contagions or threats to health defines the public health approach to disease as they cannot be countered successfully by addressing only ill individuals. Epidemics transmitted through food and water are best addressed by removing the environmental causes as well as treating the victims. During that time of frequent epidemics, the importance of understanding disease from both a clinical and public health perspective was necessary. In his book, *Hives of Sickness*, David Rosner observes that in the 1800s "while physi-

**TABLE 1-1    The Great Epidemics of New York City During the 19th Century**

| Year | Disease | Total Deaths | Deaths per 100,000 |
|------|---------|--------------|--------------------|
| 1832 | Cholera | 3513 | 1561 |
| 1849 | Cholera | 5071 | 1014 |
| 1851 | Dysentery | 1173 | 221 |
| 1854 | Cholera | 2509 | 395 |
| 1866 | Cholera | 1137 | 113 |
| 1872 | Smallpox | 1666 | 118 |
| 1881 | Diphtheria | 4894 | 266 |
| 1887 | Diphtheria | 4509 | 226 |

*Source:* Bulletin New York City Department of Health, p. 6, March 1953.

cians saw sick patients and sought to identify the cause of disease and treat its symptoms, public health workers addressed the problem of environmental control, developing a perspective that emphasized personal and public hygiene."[13]

Public health activities in both Great Britain and the United States were greatly influenced by growing urbanization and industrialization of the 1800s. London more than tripled in size from approximately 200,000 inhabitants in 1600 to 674,000 in 1700. During the 1700s, London grew only by approximately one third and still had less than one million residents, but between 1800 and 1840, London doubled in size to nearly two million residents.[14] Malnutrition, crowding, filth, and poor working conditions contributed to severe disease outbreaks.[15] Similarly in New York City, the rise of typhus as a significant cause of death was attributed in part to the large increase in the number of immigrants in the 1840s and 1850s. The rise of tenements changed typhus into an endemic slum disorder, but because it affected the poorest group of individuals, it was said to have aroused little public concern.[16]

In 1842, Edwin Chadwick published the *General Report on the Sanitary Condition of the Laboring Population of Great Britain*.[6] This and follow-up reports became classic public health documents, stimulating sanitary awakening and social reforms.[6,7,9,15] Chadwick described the prevalence of disease among the laboring people, showing that the poor exhibited a preponderance of disease and disability compared to more affluent individuals,[9] an observation that remains true throughout the world today. The conclusion of Chadwick's report was that the unsanitary environment caused the poor health of working people. Disease was attributed to miasma and bad odors.[9] Epidemic diseases such as typhus, typhoid, and cholera were attributed to filth, stagnant pools of water, rotting animals and vegetables, and garbage.[14]

As chief administrator of the Poor Law Commission, Chadwick was responsible for relief to the impoverished in England and Wales. He became the champion of sanitary reform, which became the basis for public health activities in both Great Britain and the United States. The "sanitary idea" was public health through public works—prevention of infectious disease through the provision of clean, pure water and sewers for waste disposal. Of note, this theory of public health antedated the germ theory, which did not become dominant until the end of the 1800s.[17]

Chadwick was also the chief architect of the 1848 Public Health Act, which created a general board of health, empowered to establish local boards of health and appoint an officer of health.[6,18] The latter was required to be a medically qualified medical practitioner and inspector of nuisances and sanitary conditions. The board of health incurred the opposition of those with property interests who, for economic reasons, were against proposals for improvement of drainage and water supplies. In 1854, after only five years of operation, Parliament refused to renew the Public Health Act, thereby dissolving England's first national board of health.[6]

Although repealed, the 1848 Public Health Act was instrumental in improving public health and remains relevant to current population-based preventive efforts.[18] The act, based on available morbidity and mortality data, identified all major public health issues of the time and assigned responsibility to national and local boards including inspectors and officers of health.[18] The identified issues included poverty, housing, water, sewerage, the environment, safety, and food. Public health in England and Wales was thus organized with the primary purpose of improving sanitary conditions of the towns. Clearly the drafters of the act were concerned with population health and assigned that responsibility to national and local government.[18]

During this same time period, John Snow, a physician who had provided anesthesia at Queen Victoria's childbirth, investigated London cholera epidemics in 1849 and 1854.[6] He demonstrated through epidemiologic analysis that cholera was transmitted through water contaminated with sewage.[9] Although this theory of waterborne cholera was not fully accepted, the London Board of Health did attempt to avoid disease by obtaining nonpolluted water.[9]

The events in Great Britain shaped the development of public health practice in America as the same concepts of public health were followed in the United States.[9] Early health reformers in the United States, including Henry Griscom of New York and Lemuel Shattuck of Boston, identified environmental improvement to prevent epidemic disease as a moral mission.[19] Shattuck was the foremost American advocate for community action in the area of environmental health. In the report, *Census of Boston*, Shattuck reported on high mortality rates, including maternal and infant mortality rates, with prevalent communicable diseases and TB.[6] He described these findings as directly related to living conditions and low income. In 1850, Shattuck published *General Plan for the Promotion of Public and Personal Health*, describing health and social conditions in Massachusetts and extolling "the sanitary movement abroad."[20] Sewage, refuse, and waste disposal and drainage were identified as priority public health measures; of these, sewage disposal was considered the most important.[21]

C.E.A. Winslow characterized sanitation—ensuring healthful environmental conditions—as the first stage in public health. He stated "To a large section of the public, I fear that the health authorities are still best known as the people to whom one complains of unpleasant accumulations of rubbish in the backyard of a neighbor—accumulations which possess such offensive characteristics which somehow can only originate in a neighbor's yard and never in one's own."[1(p5)]

Early public health interventions in the United States, like those seen in Europe, often required government authority to address environmental factors thought to be compromising the health of communities. Local public health agencies in the United States developed from local boards of health dating to the 1700s.[22] Various claims have been made asserting community formation of the first board of health in the United States with Baltimore, Charleston, Petersburg, New York City, and Philadelphia all contending for the honor. New York City, for example, established a board of health in 1796, which consisted of three commissioners and a health officer. The term *health officer* designated the responsibilities of a quarantine officer. From 1832, repeated cholera epidemics stimulated the creation of boards of health in the eastern United States, and port cities instituted a 40-day quarantine of ships entering harbors.[23] In his 1850 report, Shattuck emphasized the importance of government involvement in public health when he recommended the establishment of a state health department and local boards of health in each town.[20] In 1865, the Association of New York issued a report, *Sanitation of the City*, pressuring New York (both city and state) to organize a Metropolitan Board of Health the following year.[13] The report documented the intimate relationship between social and economic forces creating ill health. A newly organized New York City Department of Public Health followed, focusing on cleaning the streets, regulating sewage and waste disposal, and mandating tenement reforms.[13] It soon became a model for others to emulate.

Subsequent development of local health departments was sporadic until around 1910, when severe epidemics of typhoid fever occurred at a number of locations, including Yakima, Washington, leading to a recommendation from the federal government that full-time local health departments be formed. In the meantime, the New York City Health Department continued to address environmental concerns during the 1900s. In a 1912 annual report, the health department described the removal of 20,000 dead horses, mules, donkeys, and cattle from the streets in addition to nearly half a million smaller animals such as pigs, hogs, calves, and sheep. All told, the disposal of more than five million pounds of spoiled poultry, fish, pork, and beef was accomplished. The report also noted that there were records of 343,000 complaints from the public with respect to poor ventilation and waste disposal and unlicensed manure dumps.[13]

The development and spread of state health departments was similar to that of local health departments. The first state board of health was established by the Louisiana State Legislature in 1855 in response to yellow fever, but this proved not to be a functional organization. The first board of health is thus stated to have been legislated in Massachusetts in 1869 following Shattuck's earlier recommendation.[9,20] Other states quickly followed: California (1870), Minnesota (1872), Virginia (1872), Michigan (1873), Maryland (1874), and Alabama (1875). By 1900, all but eight states had boards of health. With New Mexico forming this organization in 1919, all states had boards.[9]

## The New Public Health Impact of Bacteriology

During the latter part of the 1800s and the early 1900s, scientific advances, particularly in microbiology, ushered in a new dimension for the field of public health.[15] This second or bacteriologic phase of the public health movement was led by the discoveries of Louis Pasteur and Robert Koch and the subsequent "germ theory" of disease. In his studies, Pasteur discovered aerobic and anaerobic organisms and began to consider the possibility of a causal relationship between germs and disease. Koch, a country physician, discovered the bacillus responsible for anthrax and was able to demonstrate that the disease was transmissible in mice. He later discovered other disease-causing bacteria including those that caused tuberculosis and cholera. This new germ theory opened the door for new opportunities to control infectious diseases, including improved diagnosis, understanding of carrier states, and insight into the importance of vectors with respect to transmission of disease. Furthermore, in New York City in the 1920s, the development of antitoxin and immunizations against diphtheria were harbingers of the abilities of organized public health programs to prevent a wide range of communicable diseases.[6] The drastic changes in the distribution of mortality that followed is illustrated in Table 1-2.

The bacteriologic discoveries of Pasteur and Koch became a marker between the "old" and the "new" public health.[24] The association between bacteria and disease causation drew attention away from the sanitary problems of water supply, street cleaning, housing, and living conditions of the

**TABLE 1-2 Mortality from Certain Causes and from All Causes Per 100,000 Population**

|  | Manhattan and Bronx 1873–1875 | Greater New York 1923–1925 | Percent Change |
|---|---|---|---|
| Scarlet fever | 80 | 1 | −99 |
| Diphtheria and croup | 235 | 11 | −95 |
| Diarrhea under five years | 335 | 22 | −93 |
| Diseases of the nervous system | 252 | 39 | −85 |
| Pulmonary tuberculosis | 404 | 84 | −79 |
| All other causes not listed | 874 | 316 | −64 |
| Acute respiratory diseases | 352 | 164 | −53 |
| All causes | 2890 | 1220 | −42 |
| Bright's disease and nephritis | 100 | 69 | −31 |
| Violence | 120 | 85 | −27 |
| Cancer | 41 | 113 | +176 |
| Heart disease | 89 | 255 | +187 |
| Diseases of the arteries | 8 | 61 | +650 |

*Source:* Reprinted with permission from C.E.A. Winslow, Public Health at the Crossroads, *Am J Public Health*, Vol. XVI, No. 11, p. 1077, © 1926, American Public Health Association.

poor.[13,23,24] A disease-oriented approach to public health became important for health officers and local health agencies.[23] Polluted water was demonstrated to be responsible for the transmission of typhoid fever, and methods were developed to measure bacteria in air, water, and milk.[24] Public health professionals continued to emphasize social reform with the realization that disease, even those caused by germs, could not be separated from living and working conditions.[13] By the early 1900s, the stage had been set for the forerunners of our contemporary public health agencies. The initial spurs to community action were threats from the environment, water, and food, resulting in epidemic disease. Options for collective action had been used for centuries, including isolation, quarantine, and waste disposal. The momentum for organized public health activities increased as urbanization and population growth exacerbated outbreaks of disease and unsatisfactory health conditions. The twin models of organized sanitary practices and government structures for public health activities that began in England became of major importance in the United States as was seen with the regulatory authority of the burgeoning public health agencies throughout the country.

## Changing Scope of Public Health Practice and the Accomplishments of Public Health in the 20th Century

In the early part of the 1900s, the public health workforce had gained skills in understanding the impact of the environment on the community's health and was beginning to understand the relationship between bacteria and infectious diseases. Over the next several decades, public health realized tremendous gains with interventions such as improved sanitation, water purity, nutrition, control of infectious disease, and immunization.[25] This translated into major gains in our nation's health over the last 125 years. Life expectancy has increased by greater than 30 years, and the quality of life has remarkably improved. For example, the death rate from all causes in New York City was 31 per thousand in 1824, 41 per thousand in 1851, and 29 per thousand in 1875. By 1925, this rate had dramatically fallen to 12 per thousand. Similarly, in 1879–1880, the average life expectancy in New York City and Brooklyn was 36 years; by 1919–1920, life expectancy had increased to 53 years, an increase of 47 percent in a 40-year period.[26] And as pointed out by Winslow and others, public health activities in reducing environmental and infectious disease threats were responsible: "Our achievements were almost wholly based on the organized application of the sciences of sanitary engineering and bacteriology."[26(p1079)]

Attempts to replicate the successes achieved with infectious and environmentally related diseases have been extended to the contemporary health challenges of nutrition, injury prevention, violence, substance abuse, HIV infection, tobacco-related diseases, and other chronic diseases. As early as 1926, Winslow argued early for this extension in a speech delivered before the American Public Health Association in Buffalo, New York:

> We may . . . say that the health officer should concern himself only with communicable disease. That is a logical position, though a narrow one. Or we may combine this etiological criterion with another based on age and say that the field of the health department includes all the health problems of the infant and the child plus the communicable diseases of the adult. This is a second clear and defensible position and one that approximates current-day practice. Or we may take a still wider view and say that the health program must envisage the whole field of the prevention of disease and the promotion of physical and mental health and efficiency.[26(p1080)]

As Americans began to live longer, the impact of injuries and chronic diseases and the potential for prevention of these health threats became a priority for public health workers, including a substantial decrease in cigarette smoking, decline in the rates of heart disease mortality and motor vehicle-associated fatalities, as well as improved quality of the workplace.[27] The 10 great public health achievements in the United States in the 1900s include advances in both communicable and chronic disease prevention, as seen in Exhibit 1-2.

The public may not recognize many of these gains because it has become accustomed to the accrual of long-standing benefits from communal efforts to protect against hazards to health. Quentin Young, former president of the American Public Health Association, remarked: "Turning on any kitchen faucet for a glass of drinking water without hesitation or peril is a silent homage to public health success, which would not have been possible at the start of the twentieth century."[28(p1)]

It is ironic that the very accomplishments in population-based prevention have probably resulted in decreased visibility for public health activities in our communities. When these protective activities work well, illnesses from water, food, and environmental toxins do not occur. In the absence of clearly visible problems, the public knows little about the methods of assurance, and historically collective support for public health resources and programs has been nominal.

**Exhibit 1-2  Ten Great Public Health Achievements**

1. Vaccines: Few treatments were effective in the prevention of infectious diseases in 1900. Now, smallpox, measles, diphtheria, pertussis, rabies, typhoid, cholera, and the plague are preventable through widespread use of vaccines.

2. Recognition of tobacco use as a health hazard: Since the 1964 surgeon general's report on risks associated with smoking, smoking among adults has decreased, saving lives.

3. Motor vehicle safety: Improved engineering of vehicles and roads plus the use of seat belts, car seats, and helmets have reduced the number of deaths, as has decreased drinking and driving.

4. Safer workplaces: A 40% decrease in fatal occupational injuries (since 1980) has resulted through efforts to control work-related disease such as pneumoconiosis (black lung) and silicosis, which are associated with coal mining, and to improve safety in manufacturing, construction, transportation, and mining.

5. Control of infectious diseases: Efforts to protect the water supply and keep it clean with improved sanitation methods have greatly improved health, particularly curbing the spread of cholera and typhoid. The discovery of antimicrobial therapy has helped to control tuberculosis and sexually transmitted disease (STDs).

6. Fewer deaths from heart disease and stroke: Smoking cessation, blood pressure control, early detection, and better treatments have resulted in a 51% decrease in death rates for coronary heart disease since 1972.

7. Safer and healthier foods: Major nutritional deficiency diseases such as rickets, goiter, and pellagra have been virtually eliminated in the United States through greater recognition of essential nutrients, increases in nutritional content, food fortification, and decreases in microbial contamination.

8. Healthier mothers and babies: Better hygiene, nutrition, access to health care, antibiotics, and technologic advances have helped to reduce infant mortality by 90% and maternal mortality by 99%.

9. Family planning and contraceptive services: These services have altered the social and economic roles of women. Access to counseling and screening has resulted in fewer infant, child, and maternal deaths. Contraceptives have provided protection from human immunodeficiency virus and other STDs.

10. Fluoridation of drinking water: Nearly 150 million people have access to treated water, a safe and effective way to prevent tooth decay. Fluoridation has helped reduce tooth decay in children 40–70% and tooth loss in adults 40–60%.

*Source:* Adapted from Ten Great Public Health Achievements—United States, 1900–1999, *MMWR*, Vol. 48, No. 12, pp. 1–3, 1999, Centers for Disease Control and Prevention.

## Public Health in the 21st Century

A critical issue for public health in this century is the feasibility of the extension of the scope of public health practice to the set of today's public health challenges. In the United States, infectious diseases, although still of critical importance, no longer cause the majority of deaths. One hundred years ago, public health activities were initiated in response to a markedly different pattern of community health, as shown in Figure 1-4. National data show the same transition to chronic diseases (Figure 1-5). Tobacco, alcohol, illicit drugs, firearms, motor vehicles, diet, activity levels, and sexual behaviors are responsible for nearly half the deaths in the United States.[4,5] Monitoring deaths and injuries related to firearms and motor vehicles, studying associations between environmental factors and diseases, surveying sexual and substance abuse behaviors of adolescents, and partnering with other governmental and community agencies to ensure adequate public health preparedness are now staples of local public health activity.

Public health emerged to control communicable diseases related to industrialization and urbanization of the 1800s and 1900s. Epidemics of chronic disease were the next target of public health activities, including atherosclerotic heart disease, cancer, chronic obstructive lung disease, and diabetes. A third group of problems gained attention in the late 1900s: domestic and street violence, substance abuse, and HIV/acquired immune deficiency syndrome (AIDS).[15] Now, several events over the past decade have resulted in a new emphasis on public health preparedness. These events include: (1) the terrorist acts of September 11, 2001, followed by the anthrax attacks through the US postal system; (2) the emerging infectious diseases such as West Nile Virus, severe acute respiratory syndrome (SARS), monkeypox, and most recently the global spread of avian influenza (H5N1); and (3) the havoc caused by hurricanes Katrina and Rita in 2005.

Local and state health departments are on the front line protecting the public health of communities, providing resources, monitoring performance, and providing technical assistance and surveillance. Can the successes achieved in life expectancy and quality of life by public health activities in the 1900s be extended to impact the wide array of contemporary problems?

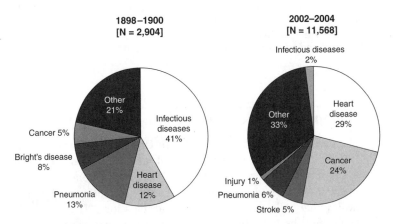

**FIGURE 1-4    Leading Causes of Death in Syracuse, NY, from 1898 to 1900 and from 2002 to 2004**
*Source:* Onondaga County Health Department, 2004, Onondaga County, New York.

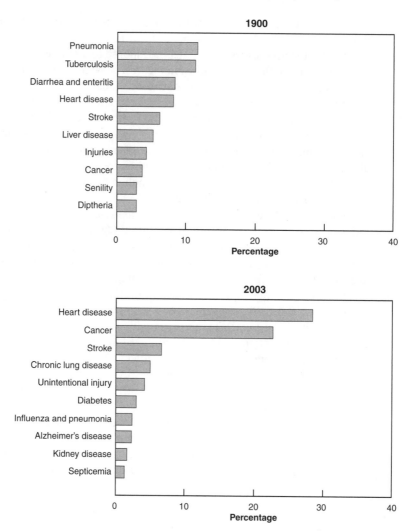

**FIGURE 1-5    Ten Leading Causes of Death as a Percentage of All Deaths in the United States in 1900 and 2003**
*Source:* Adapted from the *MMWR*, Vol. 48, No. 29, 1999, Centers for Disease Control and Prevention, and 2003 data from the National Center for Health Statistics.

## The Contemporary Concept of Health: The Basis for Action

The constitution of the World Health Organization broadly defines health as "a state of complete physical, mental, and social well-being and not merely the absence of disease or infirmity."[29] The IOM Committee on Using Performance Monitoring to Improve Community Health worked with a definition of health that relies on community participation: "Health is a state of well-being and the capability to function in the face of changing circumstances. Health is, therefore, a positive concept emphasizing social and personal resources as well as physical capabilities. Improving health is a shared responsibility of health providers, public health officials, and a variety of other actors in the community who can contribute to the well-being of individuals and populations."[30(p41)]

As discussed earlier, health has multiple determinants. Factors important to health, illness, and injury are social, economic, genetic, perinatal, nutritional, behavioral, infectious, and environmental.[31] Interaction of these factors determines the health of individuals and populations (Figure 1-6). A basic public health and epidemiologic model is that ill health is a product of the interactions between the host, the agent, and the environment. Environment includes physical environment, conditions of living, and the presence of toxic and infectious agents. Social factors of importance include poverty, education, and cultural environments, including social isolation. Biologic factors include genetics and other influences, including behaviors that determine the susceptibility of the individual to disease.

The epidemiologic distribution of disease is determined by factors that influence the host's contact with disease agents and that determine host susceptibility. The availability of the susceptible individual host and the presence of the agent are both influenced by the environment. This fundamental interaction producing ill health is true for infectious agents as well as noninfectious disease. In this model, agents can include nutritional deficiencies or excesses, toxins, substances, firearms, and so forth. The critical contribution of this model is that effects on health are produced by interactions of multiple

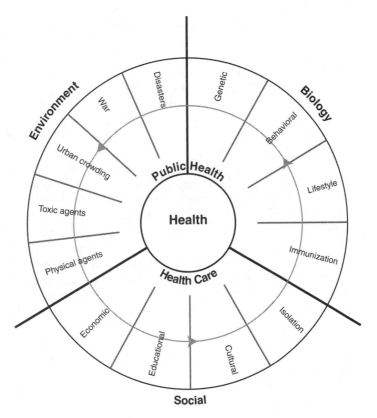

**FIGURE 1-6    Determinants of Health**
*Source:* Copyright © 2000 L.F. Novick

factors, as shown in Exhibit 1-3. In addition, the model demonstrates that there are many opportunities to prevent disease by interrupting any linkage.

A contemporary example of the agent-host-environment model can be seen with the transmission of HIV in a community, which is determined by: (1) infection of individuals with the infectious *agent* HIV, (2) susceptible *host individuals* with risk behaviors related to unprotected sex or needle-sharing drug use (or, in the past, a history of blood product transfusion prior to widespread screening of blood products), and (3) the presence of an *environment* that does not constrain the development of risk behaviors and provides opportunity for interaction between infected and susceptible individuals. The agent-host-environment model facilitates public health intervention because disease can be interdicted by addressing any one of these factors, as shown in Figure 1-7. Reducing the transmission of HIV through a needle exchange program is a successful strategy based on environmental intervention. Successful development of a vaccine would modify host susceptibility. Attempts to change the infectivity of this agent are far more difficult with HIV but have been important in curtailing the transmission of other diseases.

### Physical Environment

Housing, urbanization, overcrowding, and the availability of quality water have been described as being critically important to the health of the public and were a focus of early community efforts. A wide array of problems, including infectious diseases, injuries, and chronic illnesses, can be partly attributed to poor environmental conditions.[32] With the diminished prevalence of infectious diseases as a cause for mortality, there has been a rise in chronic conditions, including cardiovascular disease, cancer, and chronic lung disease. Environmental exposures, including those in the workplace, are important to the increased occurrences of these conditions.[33]

Concern with the environment extends far beyond sanitation. Physical and chemical factors are important in the ecosystem and directly influence health. Air pollution containing potentially hazardous chemicals, biologic and chemical contamination of foods, and environmental carcinogens are all important to the health of the community.[34] Exposures to pesticides may have a major environmental impact, but the health risks from such exposures need to be better understood. Because there can be a long latency period between such environmental exposures and potential effects on mortality and morbidity, developing public health approaches to minimize the impact can be very challenging.

Issues that currently constitute environmental health priorities for action include wastewater treatment, safe drinking and recreational water sources, ambient air standards, childhood asthma, lead toxicity, indoor air quality, food-borne illness, and household and industrial chemicals.[35] In addition to these concerns, since 2001 there has been increased concern for the environment with respect to the potential impact of a radiological or chemical weapon of mass destruction.

The physical environment also includes the structural work and home environment. Advances have been made in improving the safety of the workplace and homes (e.g., laws mandating fences around swimming pools). Conversely, decreased physical activity over the last few decades is attributed

**Exhibit 1-3    Classification of Agent, Host, and Environmental Factors That Determine the Occurrence of Diseases in Human Populations**

| | |
|---|---|
| *I. Agents of Disease: Etiologic Factors* | *Examples* |
| A. Nutritive elements | |
|     Excesses | Cholesterol |
|     Deficiencies | Vitamins, proteins |
| B. Chemical agents | |
|     Poisons | Carbon monoxide, carbon tetrachloride, drugs |
|     Allergens | Ragweed, poison ivy, medications |
| C. Physical agents | Ionizing radiation, mechanical |
| D. Infectious agents | |
|     Metazoa | Hookworm, schistosomiasis, onchocerciasis |
|     Protozoa | Amoebae, malaria |
|     Bacteria | Rheumatic fever, lobar pneumonia, typhoid, tuberculosis, syphilis |
| | Histoplasmosis, athlete's foot |
|     Rickettsia | Rocky Mountain spotted fever, typhus |
|     Viruses | Measles, mumps, chickenpox, smallpox, poliomyelitis, rabies, yellow fever |

*II. Host Factors (Intrinsic Factors): Influence Exposure, Susceptibility, or Response to Agents*

| | |
|---|---|
| A. Genetic | Sickle cell disease |
| B. Age | |
| C. Sex | |
| D. Ethnic group | |
| E. Physiologic state | Fatigue, pregnancy, puberty, stress, nutritional state |
| F. Prior immunologic experience | Hypersensitivity, protection |
|     Active | Prior infection, immunization |
|     Passive | Maternal antibodies, gamma globulin prophylaxis |
| G. Intercurrent or preexisting disease | |
| H. Human behavior | Personal hygiene, food handling, diet, interpersonal contact, occupation, recreation, utilization of health resources |

*III. Environmental Factors (Extrinsic Factors): Influence Existence of the Agent, Exposure, or Susceptibility to Agent*

| | |
|---|---|
| A. Physical environment | Geology, climate |
| B. Biologic environment | |
|     Human populations | Density |
|     Flora | Sources of food, influence on vertebrates and arthropods as a source of agents |
|     Fauna | Food sources, vertebrate hosts, arthropod vectors |
| C. Socioeconomic environment | |
|     Occupation | Exposure to chemical agents |
|     Urbanization and economic development | Urban crowding, tensions, and pressures; cooperative efforts in health and education |
|     Disruption | Wars, floods |

**Occurrence**

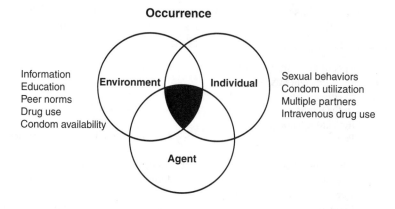

Information
Education
Peer norms
Drug use
Condom availability

Sexual behaviors
Condom utilization
Multiple partners
Intravenous drug use

**Prevention**

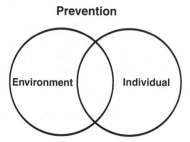

Partner notification / Needle exchange / Safe sex / Condoms

**FIGURE 1-7    Community Prevalence of HIV Infection**
*Source:* Copyright © 2000 L.F. Novick

in part to the changing environment; the development of communities without sidewalks and with long distances between homes, schools, and stores discourages physical activity and contributes to the obesity epidemic.

## Socioeconomic Factors and Disparity

Social and economic factors and their influence on life processes are among the most powerful influences on health.[36] As Chadwick and Shattuck noted in the 1800s, the poor lived shorter, less healthy lives than did the affluent. Despite this early insight into the profound impact socioeconomic factors have on health and despite tremendous gains in public health, disparities persist. In a 2004 editorial in the *New England Journal of Medicine*, Stephen

Isaacs and Steven Schroeder remark on the improvement of health status in the United States over the past 100 years, but they note:

> Any celebration of these victories must be tempered by the realization that these gains are not shared fairly by all members of our society. People in upper classes—those who have a good education, hold high-paying jobs, and live in comfortable neighborhoods—live longer and healthier lives than do people in lower classes, many of whom are black or members of ethnic minorities. And the gap is widening.[37]

Disparities in health outcomes exist when comparing income, levels of education, and race or ethnicity, with each one of these factors being independently associated with health outcomes.

The health disadvantage of those in lower income brackets is not isolated to only one or two diseases, but rather elevated death rates for the poor are evident in almost all of the major causes of death and in each major group of diseases, including infectious, nutritional, cardiovascular, injury, metabolic, and cancers.[36] This effect is graphically noted in Figure 1-8; the adjusted odds ratio for all-cause death is approximately three fold greater for those who earn less than $15,000 per year compared to those who earn more than $70,000 per year.

Heart disease is the leading cause of death in the United States and is one of the areas in which disparities are most evident (Figure 1-9). Unfortunately, these trends in disparities are evident for virtually all diseases and cut across all age groups, affecting even the youngest in our community. An illustration of higher lead levels in impoverished children when compared to children from more affluent families is shown in Figure 1-10.

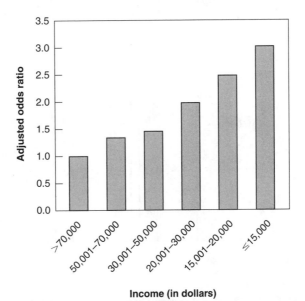

**Income (in dollars)**

**FIGURE 1-8    Adjusted Odds Ratio for Death from All Causes According to Annual Household Income, 1972–1989**
*Source:* Reprinted with permission from Massachusetts Medical Society. S. Issacs et al. Class the ignored determinant of the nation's health, *N Engl J Med,* Vol. 351, pp. 1137–1142. Data are from McDonough et al. The group with an annual household income of more than $70,000 (in 1993 dollars) is the reference group.

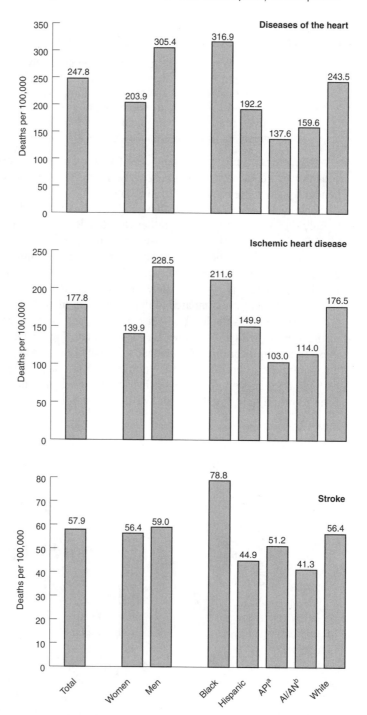

**FIGURE 1-9    Death Rates from Diseases of the Heart, Ischemic Heart Disease, and Stroke, United States, 2001. Age Adjusted to the 2000 US Population.**
*Note:* [a]API = Asian/Pacific Islander    [b]AI/AN = American Indian = Alaskan Native
*Source:* Reprinted with permission from Lippincott, Williams, and Wilkins. From G.A. Menash, et al. State of disparities in cardiovascular health in the United States, *Circulation* Vol. 110, pp. 1233–1241, 2005. Data are from the Centers for Disease Control and Prevention.

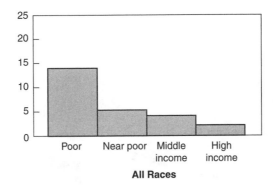

**FIGURE 1-10    Elevated Blood Level Among Children 1–5 Years of Age by Family Income: United States, Average Annual 1988–1994**
*Source:* Reprinted from US Department of Health and Human Services, *Health United States, 1998 Socioeconomic Status and Health Chart Book;* 62.

Life expectancy appears to be more related to income inequalities than to average income or wealth.[38] In a study of the relationship between total and cause-specific mortality with income distribution for households of the United States, a Robin Hood index measuring inequality was calculated and found to be strongly associated with infant mortality, coronary heart disease, malignant neoplasms, and homicide.[39] Despite decreases in mortality, widening disparities by education and income level are occurring in mortality rates. Mortality rates for children and adults are related both to poverty and to the distribution of income inequality.[40] Growing inequalities in income and wealth will likely continue to be a significant determinant of disparities of health in the near future.

The relationship between health status and education for selected causes of death is shown in Figure 1-11.[24] In McGinnis's classic article on the actual causes of death, tobacco was the leading cause of preventable deaths.[4] In the follow-up article by Mokdad, tobacco and physical inactivity/poor nutrition are the most common actual causes of death.[5] Both tobacco consumption and obesity are clearly inversely related to educational status as illustrated in Figures 1-12 and 1-13. The health of mothers and children, another priority target of public health efforts, has also been demonstrated to be associated with educational status. As an example of this, adolescent childbearing rates are seen in Figure 1-14.

Finally, disparities of health outcomes related to race and ethnicity have been extensively studied. Despite the ever-increasing body of knowledge that there is a strong association between race and ethnicity and most health outcomes, disparities persist, and in some cases, are widening. The IOM's 2002 report, *Unequal Treatment: Confronting Racial and Ethnic Disparities in Health Care,* found that one of the factors contributing to these disparities was a "significant variation in the rates of medical procedures by race, even when insurance status, income, age, and severity of conditions are comparable . . . racial and ethnic minorities are less likely to receive even routine medical procedures and experience a lower quality of health services."[41]

When taking into account known, measurable associations between education and income, the impact of racial disparities is markedly reduced, with differences in the relative contribution of educational level to racial disparities

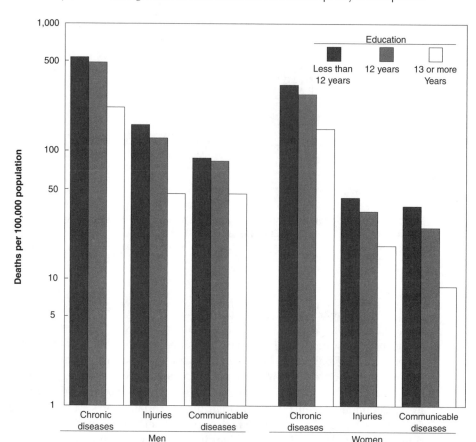

**FIGURE 1-11    Death Rates for Selected Causes for Adults 25–64 Years of Age by Education and Sex: Selected States, 1995**
*Note:* Death rates are age adjusted. Injuries include homicide, suicide, unintentional injuries, and death from adverse effects of medical procedures. Rates are plotted on a log scale.
*Source:* Reprinted from US Deartment of Health and Human Services, *Health United States, 1998 Socioeconomic Status and Health Chart Book*; 91.

varing by disease.[42] Even adjusting for differences in education and income, disparities persist, leading many researchers to believe that stress associated with either being poor or being a racial or ethnic minority in the United States is an independent risk factor for poor health outcome.[37,43]

In addition to the social factors described above, other social factors, including avoidance of social exclusion, are vital to the maintenance of health. Social exclusion results in not only social, but also economic and psychological isolation.[44] Disruptive effects when individuals migrate and change cultures have also been described as having a deleterious impact on health.[45] Social support systems have a positive influence, and persons with extensive networks generally have longer life expectancies.[46]

## Lifestyle

Personal behaviors play critical roles in the development of many serious diseases and injuries.[47] Behavioral factors largely determine the patterns of disease

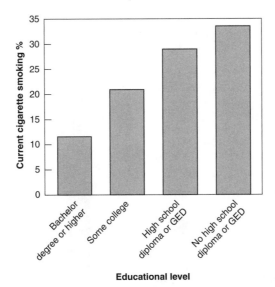

**Educational level**

**FIGURE 1-12    Age-Adjusted Prevalence of Current Cigarette Smoking in 2000 among Persons 25 Years of Age and Older, According to Educational Level**
*Source:* Reprinted with permission from Massachusetts Medical Society. S. Issacs et al. Class the ignored determinant of the nation's health, *N Engl J Med,* Vol. 351, pp. 1137–1142. Data are from the National Center for Health Statistics. GED denotes general equivalency diploma.

and mortality of the 20th-century populations of the United States.[48] The 1964 surgeon general's report, *Smoking and Health,* concluded that cigarette smoking causes lung cancer, chronic bronchitis, and emphysema.[49] Smoking is responsible for almost 20% of premature deaths in the United States.[4,5] The Framingham study showed the role of cigarette smoking, high serum cholesterol, and

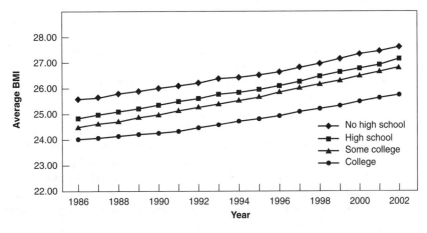

**FIGURE 1-13    Trends in Average Body Mass Index (BMI), by Education: Behavioral Risk Factor Surveillance System 1986–2002.**
*Note:* BMI = body mass index.
*Source:* Reprinted with permission from the American Public Health Association. K.D. Truong et al. Weight Gain Trends across sociodemographic groups in the United States, *Am J Public Health,* Vol. 95, pp. 1602–1606, 2005.

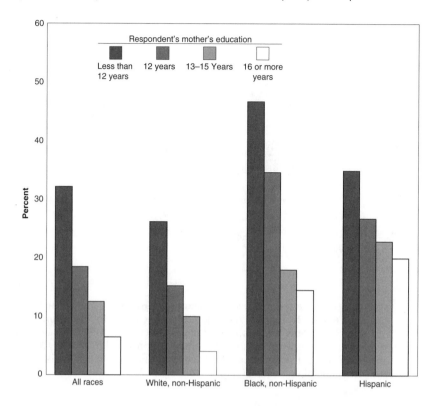

**FIGURE 1-14   Percentage of Women 20–29 Years of Age Who Had a Teenage Birth by Respondent's Mother's Education, Respondent's Race, and Hispanic Origin: United States, 1995**
*Source:* Rerinted from Centers for Disease Control and Prevention, National Center for Health Statistics, *1995 Survey of Family Growth.*

hypertension in ischemic heart disease.[50] Risk factors including smoking, lack of exercise, substance abuse, and consumption of diets high in fat and calories have increased since the early 1900s, resulting in epidemics of cardiovascular disease, lung cancer, chronic obstructive lung disease, and diabetes.[48] *Our Healthier Nation,* a 1998 United Kingdom report presented to Parliament by the secretary of state for health, stated that the causes of ill health were complex and included lifestyle as a predominant factor: "How people live has an important impact on health. Whether people smoke, whether they are physically active, what and how much they eat and drink, their sexual behavior and whether they take illicit drugs—all of these factors can have a dramatic and cumulative influence on how healthy people are and how long they will live."[44(p5)]

Given the previously noted correlations between socioeconomic factors and personal behaviors (e.g., tobacco use, low levels of physical activity), distinguishing the contribution of lifestyle from the contribution of socioeconomic factors is very challenging.

## Population-Based Prevention Strategy: Theory into Action

In the past 30 years, public health practice has necessarily changed to reflect the growing understanding of determinants and the changing concept of public health. The fundamental principle is that the health of the community is dependent on many factors affecting an entire population. Thus the target for public health interventions should be a geographic or otherwise defined population. Because of the broad distribution of most diseases and health determinants, using a population as an organizing principle for preventive action has the potential to have a great impact on the entire population's health. As epidemiologist Geoffrey Rose stated, "A large number of people exposed to a small risk may generate many more cases than a small number exposed to a high risk."[51(p24)] Therefore, widespread problems call for a widespread response, meaning, for a population strategy. For example, the overall burden of heart disease is greater from the many people who are at low risk than from the relatively smaller number who are at high risk. A population-based strategy is directed toward changing the prevalence of risk factors for the entire community, such as a tobacco control program, rather than toward identifying and targeting interventions for high-risk individuals.

A strategy for population-wide prevention based on the interaction between health determinants is shown in Table 1-3. This contract is based on a population-wide target for the United Kingdom—to reduce the death rate from heart disease and stroke and related illnesses among people under 65 years by at least a further third (33%) by 2010 from a baseline in 1996.

The development of a population-based management approach to the prevention of disease and promotion of wellness in the United States has roots in *Healthy People: The Surgeon General's Report on Health Promotion and Disease Prevention,* published in 1979.[47]

Clearly, it takes partnering at all levels to fully realize the impact of any health intervention. Population-based and individual-targeted preventive strategies must be considered to be complementary, not exclusive. Comprehensive population-based prevention strategies may involve screening programs for individuals, such as newborn screening for metabolic diseases, childhood lead testing, colorectal cancer screening, mammography, and Pap smears.

## Healthy People

In 1979, *Healthy People* marked a turning point in the approach and strategy for public health in the United States. Joseph Califano, Secretary of the Department of Health, Education, and Welfare, wrote:

> And let us make no mistake about the purpose of this, the first *Surgeon General's Report on Health Promotion and Disease Prevention.* Its purpose is to encourage a second public health revolution in the history of the United States. And let us make no mistake about the significance of this document. It represents an emerging consensus among scientists and the health community that the nation's health strategy must be dramatically recast to emphasize the prevention of disease.[47(pvii)]

The first public health revolution was the struggle against infectious disease in the late 1800s and early 1900s, which involved sanitation and immunization. The second revolution was spurred by the prevalence of chronic disease, including heart disease and cancer. The key to *Healthy People* was the premise that the personal habits and behaviors of individuals determined

**TABLE 1-3   A National Contract on Heart Disease and Stroke**

| A National Contract on Heart Disease and Stroke | Government and National Players Can: | Local Players and Communities Can: | People Can: |
|---|---|---|---|
| Social and economic | Continue to make smoking cost more through taxation. Tackle joblessness, social exclusion, low educational standards, and other factors that make it harder to live a healthier life. | Tackle social exclusion in the community, which makes it harder to have a healthy lifestyle. Provide incentives to employees to cycle or walk to work, or leave their cars at home. | Take opportunities to better their lives and their families' lives, through education, training, and employment. |
| Environmental | Encourage employers and others to provide a smoke-free environment for nonsmokers. | Through local employers and others, provide a smoke-free environment for nonsmokers. Through employers and staff, work in partnership to reduce stress at work. Provide safe cycling and walking routes. | Protect others from secondhand smoke. |
| Lifestyle | End advertising and promotion of cigarettes. Enforce prohibition of the sale of cigarettes to youngsters. Develop Healthy Living Centers. Ensure access to, and availability of, a wide range of foods for a healthy diet. Provide sound information on the health risks of smoking, poor diet, and lack of exercise. | Encourage the development of healthy schools and healthy workplaces. Implement an integrated transport policy, including a national cycling strategy and measures to make walking more of an option. Target information about a healthy life on groups and areas where people are most at risk. | Stop smoking or cut down, watch what they eat, and take regular exercise. |
| Services | Encourage doctors and nurses and other health professionals to give advice on healthier living. Ensure catering and leisure professionals are trained in healthy eating and physical activity. | Provide help to people who want to stop smoking. Improve access to a variety of affordable food in deprived areas. Provide facilities for physical activity and relaxation and decent transport to help people get to them. Identify those at high risk of heart disease and stroke and provide high-quality services. | Learn how to recognize a heart attack and what to do, including resuscitation skills. Have their blood pressure checked regularly. Take medicine as it is prescribed. |

*Source:* Reprinted from *A National Contract on Heart Disease and Stroke,* presented to Parliament by the Secretary of State for Health, February 1998, © 1998, The Stationery Office, United Kingdom. Crown copyright material is reproduced with the permission of the Controller of Her Majesty's Stationery Office.

"whether a person will be healthy or sick, live a long life or die prematurely."[47(pviii)] The report urged Americans to adopt simple measures to enhance health, including:

- Elimination of cigarette smoking
- Reduction of alcohol misuse
- Moderate dietary changes to reduce the intake of excess calories, fat, salt, and sugar
- Moderate exercise
- Periodic screening (at intervals to be determined by age and sex) for major disorders such as high blood pressure and certain cancers
- Adherence to speed laws and the use of seat belts

In a change from earlier public health approaches, the role of the individual and personal lifestyle choices was emphasized in this report. Geoffrey Rose observed that in the past, "Actions such as the provision of clean water supplies and sanitation were undertaken for people rather than by people. They have been followed in this century by further centrally provided and regulated measures to protect or improve health, including the immunization of infants and children, fluoridation of water, control of food quality and additives, and (limited) cleaning up of the environment."[51(p103)] *Healthy People* recognized that individuals did not have complete control, or responsibility, over their health status in part because of socioeconomic and environmental determinants.[47] Yet, healthy behaviors were seen as an individual responsibility with an important influence (Figure 1-15).

A major thrust of the report was a focus on age-related risk. The health problems that affect children change in adolescence and early adulthood and again in old age. At each stage in life, there are different problems and different preventive actions. Infants are most likely to die from congenital malformations or complications of pregnancy (short gestation or low birth weight). Accidents and violence predominate in adolescence; chronic disease

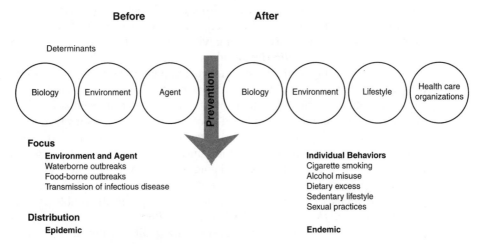

**FIGURE 1-15   Public Health Approach: Before and After *Healthy People Report***
*Source:* Copyright © 2000 L.F. Novick

is the major problem in later adulthood and old age. Public health program planning must be attuned to the age-specific diversity of health problems. *Healthy People* set out five age-specific goals in 1977.[47]

These goals with specific objectives were reformulated by a second report issued by the surgeon general in the fall of 1980.[52] *Promoting Health/ Preventing Disease: Objectives for the Nation* established quantifiable objectives to reach the broad goals of *Healthy People*. This objective-based population preventive strategy continues today with the *Healthy People 2010* objectives (discussed further in Chapter 2). Measurement of some of these goals that were formulated more than two decades ago demonstrates that progress has continued with respect to public health. For example, the infant mortality rate declined until 2001 when 6.8 deaths per 1000 live births were reported. Although this infant mortality rate exceeded the expectations of the original *Healthy People* goals, it falls short of the HP2010 goals. Despite these advances, clearly more work in population-based management of public health needs to be done. In 2002, infant mortality rates increased to a rate of 7.0 infant deaths per 1000 live births. This increase has been attributed to an increase in the number of babies with extremely low birth weights.[53] In addition to the slight but significant increase in infant mortality rates, racial disparities remain deeply concerning. Although infant mortality rates did decrease for both African-Americans and Caucasians until 2002, the proportional discrepancy between African-Americans and Caucasians remained, resulting in a rate among African-American infants that was 2.4 times that of Caucasian infants.[53] As mentioned earlier, public health gains are not equally experienced by all Americans. According to the World Health Organization, in 2002, the United States ranked 28th out of 192 member states with respect to healthy life expectancy (life expectancy adjusted for time spent in poor health), despite spending a higher percentage of the gross domestic product on health-related expenditures than any other major industrialized nation.[54,55] These daunting statistics are presumably in part due to the disparities in health outcomes.

●    ●    ●

Public health as a field of practice has evolved in tandem with historic and contemporary trends in science, disease, and social and environmental conditions. Modern public health practice now extends far beyond the historic focus on infectious disease and environmental threats. The classic IOM report, *The Future of Public Health,* identified the basic challenge for public health as determining methods and implementing activities to resolve a group of health issues that are quite different than contamination of water by a microbial agent.[4] Disparities in infant mortality, emerging infectious diseases, violence, and obesity are examples of contemporary health issues facing the nation's federal, state, and local health agencies. Determinants are a complex mixture of social, environmental, and educational factors. As described in this text, public health methods are being adapted to include new types of collaborative partnerships and community-based prevention that hold the promise of increased effectiveness with our current health problems. The follow-up report, *The Future of the Public's Health in the 21st Century,* emphasizes the necessity of a strong governmental public health infrastructure and community partnerships to ensure an optimally comprehensive and effective public health system.[55]

Abundant examples demonstrate continued challenges that threaten the health of our communities, all requiring vigorous public health action. The line of protection for health hazards can be breached, resulting in significant numbers of illnesses in our community. During 2001–2002, a total of 31 waterborne disease outbreaks associated with drinking water were reported by 19 states. These 31 outbreaks caused illness among an estimated 1020 persons and were linked to seven deaths.[56] Disease outbreaks may be associated with recreational water use as well. In the summer of 2005, over 4000 individuals were reported to have developed a gastrointestinal illness that was associated with a splash park at the Seneca Lake State Park in New York. Cryptosporidiosis was confirmed in over 700 of the cases.

In addition to recurrent familiar threats, the health of the population is challenged by new or emerging threats. In 1999, an outbreak of encephalitis in New York City was identified as being caused by West Nile virus, never previously identified in the Western Hemisphere. This infection, with birds as a reservoir and mosquitoes as a vector, initiated a classic public health response of protection of the community, employing methods of surveillance, information dissemination, and vector control. The five years following the discovery of West Nile virus in the Western Hemisphere were remarkably active for the public health workforce as health threats such as the anthrax attacks in October 2001, the monkeypox and SARS outbreaks in 2003, and the devastating hurricane of 2005, Katrina, challenged public health organization and infrastructure.

To achieve meaningful improvements in population health, contemporary public health organizations engage in a broad scope of activities, many of which now focus on affecting changes in human behavior. The nation's public health system achieved notable improvements in population health throughout the 1900s. Continued progress will likely hinge on the ability of public health organizations and professionals to mount broad-based, multisectoral health interventions that address the diffuse social and ecological pathways to population health.

## Chapter Review

1. Operative components of the definition of public health are *organized* and *community effort.*
2. The majority of the gain in life expectancy in the 1900s (25 of 30 years) can be attributed to public health measures such as better nutrition, sanitation, and housing.
3. Early public health efforts focused on collective action. For scientific advances (e.g., bacteriology) to be translated into community health improvement, the following factors were, and remain, very important:
   - Public information
   - Community acceptance
   - Design of a delivery system for the intervention
4. These early efforts focused on the social and environmental factors of health.
5. Lemuel Shattuck, a strong advocate for public health action in the 1700s, recommended environmental improvement and the formation of public health agencies.

6. Public health activities in both England and the United States were greatly influenced by growing urbanization and industrialization.
7. Scientific advances, particularly microbiology, ushered in a new dimension for the field of public health in the latter part of the 1800s and early 1900s.
8. The changing scope of public health practice was initially concerned with infectious and environmentally related disease but more recently has been extended to nutrition, injury prevention, violence, substance abuse, and tobacco-related and other chronic diseases.
9. The interaction of social, environmental, and biologic factors determines the health of individuals.
10. The public health strategy of prevention begins with the recognition that the health of the community is dependent on an interaction between behavioral and environmental factors.
11. Development and dissemination of *Healthy People: The Surgeon General's Report on Health Promotion and Disease Prevention* established the stage of population-based preventive activities in the United States.

## References

1. Winslow CEA. *The Untilled Fields of Public Health.* New York, NY: Health Service, New York County Chapter of the American Red Cross; 1920.
2. Institute of Medicine. *The Future of Public Health.* Washington, DC: National Academies Press; 1988.
3. Bunker J. Improving health: measuring effects of medical care. *Milbank Q.* 1994;72:225–258.
4. McGinnis J, Foege W. Actual causes of death in the United States. *JAMA.* 1993;270(18):2207–2212.
5. Mokdad A, Marks J, Stroup D, Gerberding J. Actual causes of death in the United States, 2000. *JAMA.* 2004;291(10):1238–1245.
6. Rosen G. *A History of Public Health.* New York, NY: MD Publications; 1958.
7. Kottek S. Gems from the Talmud: public health I—water supply. *Isr J Med Sci.* 1995;31:255–256.
8. Hippocrates. *On Airs, Waters and Places.* von Julius Springer. *Med Classics.* 1938;3:19–42.
9. Smillie W. *Public Health: Its Promise for the Future.* New York, NY: The Macmillan Co; 1955.
10. Duffy J. *Epidemics in Colonial America.* Baton Rouge, La: Louisiana State University Press; 1953.
11. Benenson A, ed. *Control of Communicable Diseases in Man.* Washington, DC: American Public Health Association; 1990.
12. Ellis J. Businessmen and public health in the urban south during the nineteenth century: New Orleans, Memphis, and Atlanta. *Bull Hist Med.* 1970;44(4):346–371.
13. Rosner D. *Hives of Sickness.* New Brunswick, NJ: Rutgers University Press; 1995.
14. Bynum W, Porter R. *Living and Dying in London.* London, UK: Wellcome Institute for the History of Medicine; 1991.
15. Affi A, Breslow L. A maturing paradigm of public health. *Annu Rev Public Health.* 1994;15:223–235.
16. Duffy J. *A History of Public Health in New York City, 1866–1966.* New York, NY: Russell Sage Foundation; 1968.

17. Hamlin C, Sheard S. Revolutions in public health: 1848 and 1998? *BMJ.* 1998;317:587–591.
18. Ashton J, Sram I. Millennium report to Sir Edwin Chadwick. *BMJ.* 1998;317:592–596.
19. Porter E. The history of public health and the modern state, introduction [editorial]. *Clio Medica.* 1994;26:1–44.
20. Shattuck L. *General Plan for the Promotion of Public and Personal Health.* Boston, Mass: Dutton & Wentworth, State Printers; 1850.
21. Kramer H. Agitation for public health reform in the 1870s. *J Hist Med.* 1948;Autumn:473–488.
22. Jeckel J. Health departments in the US 1920-1988: statements of mission with special reference to the role of C.E.A. Winslow. *Yale J Biol Med.* 1991;64:467–479.
23. Fee E. The origins and development of public health in the United States. In: Holland WW, Detels R, Knox G, et al., eds. *Oxford Textbook of Public Health.* 2nd ed. Oxford, UK: Oxford University Press; 1991: 3–21.
24. Fee E. Public health and the state: the United States. *Clio Medica.* 1994; 26:224–275.
25. Kivlahan C. Public health in the next century. *Mo Med.* 1994;91(1):19–23.
26. Winslow C. Public health at the crossroads. *Am J Public Health.* 1926;16: 1075–1085.
27. US Department of Health and Human Services, Public Health Service. *For a Healthy Nation: Returns on Investment in Public Health. Executive Summary.* Washington, DC: US Government Printing Office; 1994.
28. Young Q. Public health: a powerful guide. *J Health Care Finance.* 1998; 25(1):1–4.
29. World Health Organization. Available at: http://www.who.int/about/en/. Accessed January 9, 2006.
30. Institute of Medicine. *Improving Health in the Community.* Washington, DC: National Academies Press; 1997.
31. Omenn G. Health status and its determinants in urban populations. *J Urban Health, Bull New York Acad Med.* 1998;75(2):222.
32. Jackson R. Habitat and health: the role of environmental factors in the health of urban populations. *J Urban Health, Bull New York Acad Med.* 75(2):258–262.
33. Lehman P. Improving the quality of the work environment. In: *Healthy People: The Surgeon General's Report on Health Promotion and Disease Prevention—Background Papers.* Washington, DC: US Government Printing Office; 1979:387–407. DHEW Publication #79–55071A.
34. World Health Organization. The human environment In: *Promoting Health in the Human Environment.* Geneva, Switzerland; 1975:17–29.
35. Lafronza V. The evolution of environmental health. *Transform Public Health.* 1999;2(2):1–4.
36. Wilkinson R. *Unhealthy Societies.* London, UK: Routledge; 1997.
37. Isaacs S, Schroeder S. Class—the ignored determinant of the nation's health. *N Engl J Med.* 2004;351:1137–1142.
38. Wilkinson R. Class mortality differentials, income distribution and trends in poverty 1921–1981. *J Soc Policy.* 1989;18:307–335.
39. Kennedy B, Kawachi I, Prothrow-Stith D, et al. Income distribution and mortality: cross sectional ecological study of the Robin Hood Index in the United States. *BMJ.* 1996;312:1004–1007.
40. US Department of Health and Human Services, Office of Public Health and Science. *Healthy People 2010 Objectives: Draft for Public Comment.*

Washington, DC: US Government Printing Office; 1998. DHHS Publication No. 017=001=00537=1.

41. Institute of Medicine. *Unequal Treatment: Confronting Racial and Ethnic Disparities in Health Care.* Washington, DC: National Academies Press; 2003.

42. Wong M, Shapiro M, Boscardin, J. Contribution of major diseases to disparities in mortality. *N Engl J Med.* 2002;347:1585–1592.

43. Williams D, Neighbors H, Jackson J. Racial/ethnic discrimination and health: findings from community studies. *Am J Public Health.* 2003;93: 200–208.

44. Office of Secretary of State for Health. *Our Healthier Nation.* London, UK: The Stationery Office; 1998.

45. Evans R, Barer M, Marmer T, et al., eds. *Why Are Some People Healthy and Others Not?* New York, NY: Aldine de Gruyter; 1994.

46. Last J. Social and behavioral determinants of health. In: *Public Health and Human Ecology.* East Norwalk, Conn: Appleton & Lange; 1987:211–242.

47. US Department of Health, Education, and Welfare. *Healthy People: The Surgeon General's Report on Health Promotion and Disease Prevention.* Washington, DC: US Government Printing Office; 1979.

48. Breslow L. Behavioral factors in the health status of urban populations. *J Urban Health, Bull New York Acad Med.* 1998;75(2):242–249.

49. Surgeon General's Advisory Committee on Smoking and Health. *Smoking and Health.* Washington, DC: US Government Printing Office; 1964.

50. Last L. Health information and epidemiology. In: *Public Health and Human Ecology.* East Norwalk, Conn: Appleton & Lange; 1987:27–102.

51. Rose G. *The Strategy of Preventive Medicine.* New York, NY: Oxford University Press; 1992.

52. US Department of Health and Human Services. *Promoting Health/ Preventing Disease: Objectives for the Nation.* Washington, DC: US Government Printing Office; 1980. DHHS Publication No. 79-55071.

53. Centers for Disease Control and Prevention. Quickstats: infant mortality rates, by selected racial/ethnic populations—United States, 2002. *MMWR.* 2005;54:126.

54. World Health Organization. Healthy life expectancy, 2002. Available at: http://www.who.int/healthinfo/bod/en/index.html. Accessed January 9, 2006.

55. Institute of Medicine. *The Future of the Public's Health in the 21st Century.* Washington, DC: National Academies Press; 2003.

56. Blackburn BG, Craun CF, Yoder YS, et al. Surveillance for water-borne disease outbreaks associated with drinking water, United States 2001–2002. *MMWR.* 2004;53:23–45.

CHAPTER 2

# A FRAMEWORK FOR PUBLIC HEALTH ADMINISTRATION AND PRACTICE

Lloyd F. Novick
Cynthia B. Morrow

## Chapter Overview

Activities performed by health departments have evolved throughout the last century. A persistent unanswered question has been whether the scope of public health work should include the actual delivery of personal health services. In 1988, a pivotal report of the Institute of Medicine (IOM), *The Future of Public Health*, established recommendations for a new way of organizing public health activities that places expanded emphasis on population-based efforts rather than on personal health care delivery. Three core public health functions were identified: assessment, policy development, and assurance. Several years later, a federally sponsored task force developed another taxonomy of public health activity that centered around the 10 "essential public health services." In 2003, the IOM published a follow-up report focusing on the need to strengthen the government's public health infrastructure while recognizing the need to establish and maintain partnerships to further enhance the public health system. Contemporary public health activities have been shaped not only by efforts to redefine the conceptual basis of public health practice but also by efforts to redefine specific national public health goals as most recently described in *Healthy People 2010*. Recent efforts to improve the processes and outcomes of public health practice have emphasized strategies for increasing the public's quality and years of life, eliminating health disparities, and building infrastructure of public health efforts.

## Public Health Functions

Before 1908, no county in the United States had a full-time health officer with the exception of New York City.[1] In 1910–1911, multiple epidemics of typhoid fever prompted a strong federal recommendation for the creation of full-time local health departments.[2] Rapid growth of these agencies began in the following decade. Between 1908 and 1934, more than a quarter of the counties in the nation had public health services under the direction of a full-time health officer for some part of that period.[2]

In 1933, an American Public Health Association statement, signed by Haven Emerson and C.E.A. Winslow among others,[2] listed two primary goals for public health agencies: the control of communicable diseases and the promotion of child health. Recommendations for specific services that the agencies should provide were also listed, including laboratory services, sanitation, public health education, public health nursing, vital statistics, and research in disease prevention.[3] This basic categorization described the public health role as fundamentally preventive, with a clear separation from the provision of medical care. Emerson went on to further describe six basic functions of a local health department in his 1945 report, *Local Health Units for the Nation,* (Exhibit 2-1).[1]

In 1941, Joseph W. Mountin published the results of a survey of the existing states health agencies, revealing a similar constellation of interests, including vital statistics, communicable disease and tuberculosis (TB) control, maternal and child health (MCH) services, health education, and environmental activities.[4] The role of public health was again targeted to prevention and did not include the provision of medical care, with the exception of treatment for TB and sexually transmitted diseases (STDs) as well as provision of care for the indigent population.

In the latter half of the 1900s, new influences shaped the development of basic public health functions. During this time, a major question for public health surfaced with respect to the merit of provision of a "safety net" for medical care for the indigent population versus the merit of ensuring that medical care for the impoverished be provided within the community. Should prevention and medical care be coordinated but delivered separately? Or, should prevention and medical care be integrated into one comprehensive system?

**Exhibit 2-1    Six Basic Functions of a Local Health Department**

1. Vital statistics, or the recording, tabulation, interpretation, and publication of the essential facts of births, deaths, and reportable diseases
2. Control of communicable disease, including tuberculosis, the venereal diseases, malaria, and hookworm disease
3. Environmental sanitation, including supervision of milk and milk products, food processing and public eating places, and maintenance of sanitary condition of employment
4. Public health laboratory services
5. Hygiene of maternity, infancy, and childhood, including supervision of the health of the school child
6. Health education of the general public so far as not covered by the functions of departments of education

*Source:* Reprinted from H. Emerson, *Local Health Units for the Nation,* 1945, The Commonwealth Fund, New York.

As early as 1949, Terris and Kramer noted that local health departments were moving beyond prevention and into treatment services.[5] New federal programs beginning in the 1960s highlighted the issue of provision of medical care to those at greatest need and influenced the evolution of public health functions. The Maternal and Infant Care (MIC) Program was passed in 1965 (part of Title V of the Social Security Act), as was the Community Mental Health Act. In the same year, additional legislation enacted as part of the "Great Society" included Medicare, Medicaid, and the Children and Youth Program (C&Y), as well as Comprehensive Health Planning (CHP) and Regional Medical Planning (RMP).[2] In some instances, these programs changed the structure of governmental agencies. For example, states were required to designate a single state agency to administer Medicaid, often setting up a dichotomy between public health services and Medicaid activities.[6] Comprehensive health planning legislation resulted in the creation of new planning bodies at state and local levels, also with population-based agendas.

Federal programs of the 1960s did spur growth of health services in local health departments to some extent. Approximately 13% of the neighborhood health centers, nearly 30% of the child and youth projects, and 76% of the maternal and infant care projects were sponsored by local health departments.[7] An increased number of local health departments provided personal health services to indigent individuals. Many local and state public health agencies were providers of last resort for the poor, the uninsured, and Medicaid clients.[5] In many communities with substantial numbers of uninsured residents, public health agencies attempted to provide a "safety net" for health care, but services were often neither adequate nor comprehensive. A 1968 study by the US Public Health Service documented that local health departments were offering medical care services.[8] Local health departments' involvement in providing medical care continued to increase over the following decades with health departments in the Sun Belt, Pacific, and mountain areas being most involved in the provision of medical services.[7]

Despite this local presence, much of the federal funds bypassed state and local government, fostering the growth of community agencies and health centers whose health activities were often not coordinated with local public health agencies. In many places, the role of the local health agencies often was narrowly focused on traditional functions including vital statistics, communicable disease, health education, and MCH activities.[2]

In addition to having a greater focus on the provision of medical care and a narrower focus on population-based management, public health agencies became more fragmented as the health-planning role was now performed by the comprehensive health planning agencies. Furthermore, the local health departments were weakened as many environmental responsibilities were transferred from public health to new state environmental agencies fostered by the creation of the federal Environmental Protection Agency (EPA) in 1970.

## Core Public Health Functions

In 1988, the pivotal report, *The Future of Public Health,* set out recommendations for a new categorization of public health functions.[6] These functions were recommended to counter the attrition of public health vigilance in protecting the public. Lack of agreement concerning mission, politicized decision making, and unsatisfactory linkages with private medicine were cited as underlying difficulties. Little attention to management and the lack of development of leaders were also described as root causes of ineffective public health action. Recommendations included designating central responsibility to state health departments and grouping all primarily health-related functions there. State delegation of this responsibility to local government was foreseen. The IOM report provided a new categorization of public health functions, which has become widely adopted. Functions were denoted as assessment, policy development, and assurance.[6]

## Assessment

The committee recommended every public health agency regularly and systematically collect, assemble, analyze, and make available information on the health needs of the community, including statistics on health status, community health needs, and epidemiologic and other studies of health problems.[6(p7)]

## Policy Development

The committee recommended that every public health agency exercise its responsibility to serve the public interest in the development of comprehensive public health policies by promoting the use of the scientific knowledge base in decision making about public health and by developing public health policy. Agencies must take a strategic approach, developed on the basis of a positive appreciation for the democratic political process.[6(p8)]

## Assurance

The committee recommended that public health agencies assure their constituents that services necessary to achieve agreed-upon goals are provided, either by encouraging actions by other entities (private or public sector), by requiring such action through regulation, or by providing services directly.

The committee further recommends that each public health agency involve lay policy makers and the general public in determining a set of high-priority personal and community-wide health services that governments will guarantee to every member of the community. This guarantee should include subsidization or direct provision of high-priority personal health services for those unable to afford them.[6(p8-9)]

Specific public health activities were identified by state agencies for each of these functions, as indicated in Exhibit 2-2. The categorization of assessment, policy development, and assurance has become a commonly used rubric to describe public health activities and has been adopted by a number of states for the organization of their public health systems. For example, the state of Washington used these core public health functions to develop its public health improvement plan (PHIP). By grouping public health functions into an overall population-based health improvement mission, plans can address specific activities to improve community health status.[9] A difficulty, however, with this type of format is that public health activities are described in general categories but are not readily identifiable, especially to those not in the public health field, such as legislators and the public. A remedy for this can be the concomitant use of examples that point

Exhibit 2-2   Activities of Six State Agencies

| | |
|---|---|
| I.  Assessment | |
|    A. Data Collection | Housing, public lodging, |
|       Vital records            6 |    recreational facility |
|       Morbidity                3 |    safety                          6 |
|       Health facilities        4 |    Health facility safety          5 |
|       Health manpower          5 | B. Licensing |
|       Health system funds      5 | C. Health Education |
|       Health interview surveys 2 |    Education                       5 |
|       Health trends analysis   3 |    Health promotion, disease |
|       Health status assessment 5 |    prevention                      2 |
|    B. Epidemiology | D. Environment |
|       Communicable disease     6 |    Air quality                     3 |
|       Health Screening         6 |    Occupational health and |
|       Laboratory analysis      6 |    safety                          5 |
|    C. Research | Radiation control              6 |
|       Research projects        4 |    Solid waste management          3 |
|       Laboratory research      1 |    Hazardous waste |
| II. Policy Development |    management                     3 |
|    A. Policy |    Public water supply             5 |
|       Goals developed through |    Individual water supply         4 |
|          health assessments    1 |    Sewage disposal                 5 |
|       Standards for local health | E. Personal Health |
|          agencies              5 |    Maternal and child health       6 |
|    B. Health Planning |    Home health                     4 |
|       State health planning    2 |    Immunizations                   6 |
|       Categorical plans        5 |    Dental health                   6 |
|       Certificate of need      5 |    Mental health                   5 |
| III. Assurance |    Alcohol abuse                   5 |
|    A. Inspection |    Drug abuse                      5 |
|       Food and milk control    6 |    Chronic disease                 6 |
|       Product safety, substance |    Inpatient facilities            2 |
|          control               3 | F. Resources Development         6 |

*Source:* Copyright © 1986, Public Health Foundation

to specific activities, such as linking the core assessment function to specific activities (Figure 2-1).

In response to the question of whether a health department should provide assurance of care, acting as a guarantor versus actually engaging in the delivery of medical care, the 1988 report by the IOM strongly recommended the assurance role rather than actual delivery. The responsibility of providing medical care to the poor was seen as draining resources and attention away from disease prevention and health promotion activities that benefit the entire community. It was believed that government had the responsibility to provide access and services, but by another mechanism.[6]

## Health Care Reform and Public Health

Although the core functions described the role of public health activities in broad terms, more specific delineation of public health functions was needed.

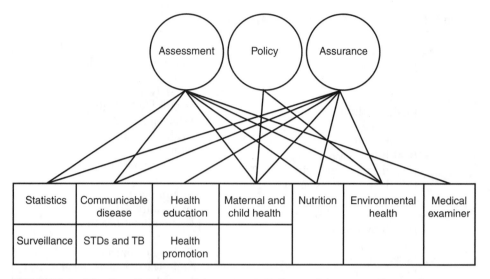

**FIGURE 2-1    The Core Functions of Assessment, Policy, and Assurance Targeted to Specific Areas of a Local Health Department**
*Source:* Copyright © 2000 L.F. Novick

In 1989 the Centers for Disease Control and Prevention (CDC) convened a meeting with public health practice organizations. This brainstorming session resulted in the identification of more than 140 essential activities or functions. At additional meetings, 10 groups of organizational practices were determined.[10] These 10 practices provided a basis for both implementing and measuring the performance of the three core functions. Studies determining the allocation of effort among these functions by local health agencies showed that the assurance function received the majority of time and resources, whereas few resources were being devoted to assessment and policy development.[11]

Further impetus for describing public health activities in more specific terms followed with the introduction of the Health Security Act in Congress in October 1993.[12] This legislation was designed to provide universal access to health services by providing entry to all individuals and their families to a healthcare plan. In addition to medical care, these plans were to provide a schedule of clinical preventive services such as immunization, serum cholesterol measurement every five years, and screening for cervical cancer and mammography for women.[12] This legislation also provided resources to perform these core functions ($750 million by year 2000). A core functions group of the US Public Health Service, chaired by the assistant secretary for health and the surgeon general, vigorously supported the necessary role of public health and population-based programs for a reformed healthcare insurance system in the United States. They emphasized the need to address health priorities and conditions of populations, as distinct from individuals.[13]

Although the Health Security Act ultimately failed to pass, the prospect of this legislation raised a number of questions for public health practice. With provisions for clinical prevention and medical care by managed care plans, these activities would not also be required of public health agencies. Questions were raised concerning a need for public health services under a reformed system of health care, but an important role did remain in the provision of population-based preventive functions. Public health was slotted into assuming responsibility for population-based prevention but not direct provision of medical services (Figure 2-2). Important exceptions or variations to this theme do still exist, including the provision of medical care by a number of health departments, particularly in the Southeast, and by those local health departments participating as providers in managed care plans.

## Essential Health Services

Although the concept of core functions became more widespread in the public health field after 1993, there was inconsistency in the terminology and expectations. In the spring of 1994, Dr. David Satcher and Dr. J. Michael McGinnis chaired a committee to unify public health around these core functions. This led to the development of a uniform set of essential health services that has since become the commonly accepted taxonomy for public health functions.[14] In the fall of 1994, the US Public Health Service (Public Health Functions Steering Committee) issued a vision and mission statement listing these essential health services (Exhibit 2-3). The "10 essential public health services" represent a further development of the previously established core functions and organization practices.

The essential service framework has gained momentum and is commonly used by both public health practitioners and policy makers. Cost studies by the Public Health Foundation have been performed to determine expenditures by function for state and local departments of health.[15] This format provides a common vocabulary and expresses the mission of public health in terms of community-wide health improvement. Although widely accepted, the essential service framework groups activities into categories that may not be immediately recognizable to budget officers, legislators, and the public, all who expect more concrete service activities. A similar difficulty had been previously

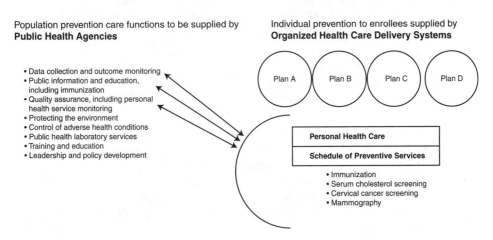

**FIGURE 2-2    Population-Based and Individual Prevention as Proposed in the Health Security Act of 1993**
*Source:* Copyright © 2000 L.F. Novick

**Exhibit 2-3    Public Health in America**

**Vision:**
Healthy people in healthy communities
**Mission:**
Promote physical and mental health and prevent disease, injury, and disability

**Public Health**
- Prevents epidemics and the spread of disease
- Protects against environmental hazards
- Prevents injuries
- Promotes and encourages healthy behaviors
- Responds to disasters and assists communities in recovery
- Assures the quality and accessibility of health services

**Essential Public Health Services**
1. Monitor health status to identify community health problems.
2. Diagnose and investigate health problems and health hazards in the community.
3. Inform, educate, and empower people about health issues.
4. Mobilize community partnerships to identify and solve health problems.
5. Develop policies and plans that support individual and community health efforts.
6. Enforce laws and regulations that protect health and ensure safety.
7. Link people to needed personal health services, and assure the provision of health care when otherwise unavailable.
8. Assure a competent public health and personal healthcare workforce.
9. Evaluate effectiveness, accessibility, and quality of personal and population-based health services.
10. Research for new insights and innovative solutions to health problems.

*Source:* Adopted Fall 1994, Public Health Functions Steering Committee Members (July 1995): American Public Health Association; Association of Schools of Public Health; Association of State and Territorial Health Officials; Environmental Council of the States; National Association of County and City Health Officials; National Association of State Alcohol and Drug Abuse Directors; National Association of State Mental Health Program Directors; Public Health Foundation; US Public Health Service–Agency for Health Care Policy and Research; Centers for Disease Control and Prevention; Food and Drug Administration; Health Resources and Services Administration; Indian Health Service; National Institutes of Health; Office of the Assistant Secretary for Health; Substance Abuse and Mental Health Services Administration.

described with the core public health functions. To address these challenges, the Public Health Foundation prepared a crosswalk matching essential health services with specific service activities (Table 2-1).

In addition to providing an overall structure for public health practitioners, the essential services framework can also be applied to a specific area of public health, as in the dissemination of the document *Public MCH Program Functions Framework: Essential Public Health Services to Promote Maternal and Child Health in America.*[16] Table 2-2 shows the core function and essential services for maternal and child health (MCH). This framework was reported to be useful for public health agencies in Delaware, Maryland, South

**TABLE 2-1    State/Local Health Department Crosswalk of Program Activities to Essential Services**

| Essential Service | Includes but Is Not Limited To | Does Not Include |
|---|---|---|
| 1. Monitor health status to identify community health problems. | • Disease and injury registries<br>• Epidemiology (surveillance, disease reporting, sentinel events), including injury epidemiology, mental health epidemiology, and substance abuse epidemiology<br>• Population-based/community health needs assessments<br>• State/community report cards/development of health status indicators<br>• Vital statistics<br>• Environmental epidemiology<br>• Immunization status tracking<br>• Public Health Laboratory Information System (PHLIS)<br>• Linkages of data sets for population-based applications<br>• Population-based health interview surveys (e.g., BRFSS or other state surveys) | • Management of client-based data systems should be included under #7b. Cost of accessing client-based data systems to evaluate accessibility and quality of care should be included under #9. |
| 2. Diagnose and investigate health problems and health hazards in the community. | • Communicable disease detection (case finding)<br>• Chronic disease detection (case finding)<br>• Injury detection<br>• HIV/AIDS prevention:<br>  –Counseling and testing<br>  –Partner notification<br>• Outbreak investigation and control (including immunizations as part of outbreak control)<br>• Early periodic screening detection or treatment (EPSDT)<br>• Population-based screening services (e.g., cholesterol), including follow-up counseling (e.g., nutrition and exercise)<br>• Contact tracing (e.g., STDs or TB) | • Primary care services<br>• Treatment of STDs, TB, and other communicable diseases<br>• Dental health services (including topical fluoride treatments in schools)<br>• Treatment of diabetes, lupus, hemophilia, sickle cell anemia, epilepsy, Alzheimer's disease, and other chronic diseases<br>• Genetic disease services<br>• Home healthcare services<br>• Purchase and provision of AZT/other drugs<br>• Prenatal/perinatal care<br>• Services for premature and newborn infants and preschool-aged children |

*(continued)*

**TABLE 2-1   (continued)**

| Essential Service | Includes but Is Not Limited To | Does Not Include |
|---|---|---|
| | • Environmental risk assessment <br> • Environmental sampling <br> • Lead investigation <br> • Radon detection <br> • Asbestos detection <br> • Diagnostic laboratory services (e.g., bacteriology, parasitology, virology, immunology, clinical chemistry) in support of population-based health activities <br> • Environmental laboratory services (e.g., environmental microbiology samples, environmental chemistry samples, and occupational safety and health samples) | • Services to children with special healthcare needs <br> • Immunizations, except as part of outbreak control (Note: All the above activities should be included under #7b.) |
| 3. Inform, educate, and empower people about health issues. | • Comprehensive school health education <br> • Population-wide health promotion/risk reduction programs: <br> –Injury prevention education and promotion <br> –Parenting education <br> –Physical activity and fitness <br> –Population-based risk reduction programs <br> –Seat-belt education/ promotion <br> –Sexuality education <br> –Tobacco use prevention and cessation <br> • Nutrition education (e.g., Five-A-Day programs) <br> • Nutrition education as part of WIC <br> • School campaigns (e.g., "Say No To Drugs Day") <br> • Substance abuse prevention <br> • Public education campaigns <br> • Worksite health promotion <br> • HIV education/ information <br> • Educational activities as part of outreach | • Counseling and education as part of personal health services (e.g., nutrition counseling as part of prenatal care [include under #7b]) |

**TABLE 2-1   (continued)**

| Essential Service | Includes but Is Not Limited To | Does Not Include |
|---|---|---|
| | • Educational activities related to enforcement of laws and regulations (i.e., education of tobacco vendors) | |
| 4. Mobilize community partnerships and action to identify and solve health problems (See #5 for planning and policy development activities.) | • Coalition building<br>• Collaboration with outside agencies/ organizations<br>• Forming community partnerships to solve health problems (e.g., task forces, multidisciplinary advisory groups)<br>• Advocacy and budget justification (e.g., testifying at hearings)<br>• Technical assistance to facilitate mobilization of local health agencies or community groups<br>• HIV community planning (include portion, if any, that involves building community partnerships; planning portion should be included under #5) | • Development of legislation, policies, or plans (include under #5) |
| 5. Develop policies and plans that support individual and community health efforts. (See #4 for collaborative activities.) | • Agenda setting<br>• Development of policies and guidelines<br>• Legislative activities (e.g., drafting legislation, developing agency budgets)<br>• Planning (including certificate of need)<br>• *Healthy People 2000* objective-setting activities<br>• APEX *PH* Parts I and II/Healthy Communities/ PATCH/other planning models<br>• HIV community planning (include portion related to planning; portion supporting community partnerships should be included under #4) | • Form partnerships to solve health problems (include under #4). |
| 6. Enforce laws and regulations that protect health and ensure safety. | • Air quality (indoor and outdoor)<br>• Asbestos control<br>• Consumer protection and sanitation | • Construction of facilities and physical plans (this is generally funded through special capital accounts) |

*(continued)*

**TABLE 2-1    (continued)**

| Essential Service | Includes but Is Not Limited To | Does Not Include |
|---|---|---|
| | • Food sanitation<br>• General sanitation<br>• Housing<br>• Public lodging<br>• Recreational sanitation<br>• Shellfish sanitation<br>• Substance control/product safety<br>• Vector/rodent control<br>• Fluoridation services<br>• Hazardous materials management (accidents, transportation spill, etc.)<br>• Occupational health and safety<br>• Radiation control<br>• Lead abatement<br>• Radon mitigation<br>• Waste management—sewage, solid, and toxic<br>• Water quality control (public/private drinking water, groundwater protection, etc.)<br>• Emergency response teams to toxic spills, product recalls, and response to natural disasters (including the maintenance and development of emergency systems)<br>• Medical examiner, toxicology, and other forensic medicine<br>• Enforcement activities related to compliance with youth access to tobacco regulations<br>• Enforcement activities related to the agency's police authority (e.g., quarantine, forcing patients to take medications) | |
| 7a. Link people to needed personal health services. | • Case management/care coordination services<br>• Information and referral hotlines<br>• Outreach services related to linking individuals to personal health services<br>• School health outreach, case finding, and referral services | • Direct healthcare services<br>• School-based clinical services (include under #7b) |

**TABLE 2-1     (continued)**

| Essential Service | Includes but Is Not Limited To | Does Not Include |
|---|---|---|
| | • Transportation and other enabling services<br>• Development of primary care services in under-served communities | |
| 7b. Ensure the provision of care when otherwise unavailable. | • Personal health services, including:<br>–Primary care services<br>–Treatment of STDs, TB, and other communicable diseases<br>–CD4+ testing<br>–Dental health services (including topical fluoride treatments in schools)<br>–Treatment of diabetes, lupus, hemophilia, sickle cell anemia, epilepsy, Alzheimer's disease, and other chronic diseases<br>–Genetic disease services<br>–Home health care<br>–Hospitals<br>–Purchase and provision of AZT/other drugs<br>–Prenatal/perinatal care<br>–Services for premature and newborn infants and preschool-aged children<br>–Services to children with special healthcare needs<br>• Clinical preventive services (e.g., routine immunizations, family planning)<br>• School-based clinical services<br>• Management of client-based data systems that support the services above | • Population-based health services |
| 8. Ensure a competent public health and personal healthcare workforce. | • Required continuing education<br>• Recruitment and retention of health professionals<br>• Professional education and training<br>• Health and environmental professionals licensing<br>• Leadership training/ programs | • Facilities licensing (include under #9)<br>• Quality improvement (include under #9) |

*(continued)*

**TABLE 2-1 (continued)**

| Essential Service | Includes but Is Not Limited To | Does Not Include |
|---|---|---|
| 9. Evaluate effectiveness, accessibility, and quality of personal and population-based health services. | • Facilities licensing<br>• Healthcare systems monitoring<br>• Hospital outcomes data<br>• Personal health services monitoring (including analysis and use of client-based data)<br>• Program evaluation<br>• Data systems related to service availability, utilization, cost, and outcome<br>• Laboratory regulation and quality control services<br>• Regulation of EMS personnel/services<br>• Quality assurance/quality improvement activities (implementation) | • Management of client-based data systems (include under #7b)<br>• Development (vs. implementation) of a quality improvement plan/policy (see #5) |
| 10. Research for new insights and innovative solutions to health problems. | • Biomedical, preventive, and clinical investigations<br>• Health services research<br>• Research and monitoring about the effects of the changing health care environment and unique strategies employed by public health agencies<br>• Demonstration programs<br>• Methods development<br>• Research grants to others<br>• Innovative technologies | |
| General administration | • Stand-alone administration activities (e.g., accounting, legal, or personnel activities)<br>• Office of the health director<br>• Computer support<br>• Maintenance of buildings and grounds<br>• Reporting requirements | |

*Source:* The Public Health Expenditures Project Team, 1998; Public Health Foundation; National Association of County and City Health Officials; National Association of Local Boards of Health; Association of State and Territorial Health Officials; with funding from the Office of Disease Prevention and Health Promotion, Department of Health and Human Services.

Carolina, and Wyoming among others, particularly in reference to communicating public health activities to managed care organizations.[17] The Division of Reproductive Health of the CDC has offered its activities in the assessment and monitoring of MCH status, mobilization of community partnerships, and research for innovative solutions as examples of providing essential services.[18] The success of performance evaluation is tied to uniform measures based on appropriate formats such as essential services.[19]

## Core Functions and Essential Health Services: Implementation

Surveys of state public health agencies in both 1989 and 1996 revealed virtually all respondents adopting and agreeing with the importance of the three core functions described in the 1988 IOM report on public health.[20,21] A high proportion indicated that their operations included performance of these functions: assessment (80%), policy development (49%), and assurance (42%).[20] As recommended earlier by the same IOM report, there was evidence of outreach by state health agencies with increasing legislative activity and relationships with voluntary health agencies.[20] However, the survey also documented an increase in delivery of personal services from 58% in 1989 to 83% in 1996 even though the IOM's recommendations supported the divestiture of public health agencies from direct provision of personal health services.[21] The question was still unresolved. Should the public health entity be the guarantor or the actual provider of medical care? The increase in delivery of services

**TABLE 2-2    MCH Core Functions and Practices Framework**

| Function | Practice | Definition |
|---|---|---|
| Assessment | Assess | Collect and analyze data on demographic, health status, and behavioral characteristics of MCH populations. |
| | Investigate | Investigate health hazards and problems that impact women, children, and youth. |
| | Analyze | Identify determinants and contributing factors to MCH outcomes. |
| Policy development | Mobilize | Develop and support MCH community action programs. |
| | Prioritize | Select key end points for focused intervention activity. |
| | Promote | Initiate and support laws, policies, regulations, and standards that ensure the health and safety of women, children, and youth. |
| Assurance | Link | Triage and refer women, children, and youth to needed population-based and personal health services. |
| | Ensure | Support the competency and quality of MCH interventions at varied community settings. |
| | Evaluate | Systematically examine the effectiveness, accessibility, and quality of MCH services. |
| | Inform | Educate and empower the public and families about MCH to promote positive attitudes and behaviors. |

*Source:* Reprinted from J. Mayer, *J Public Health Manage Pract*, Vol. 3, No. 5, 1997, Aspen Publishers, Inc.

reported by this survey was attributed to an increase in the number of uninsured, with the public health system acting as a safety net.[20]

A similar 1996 survey of local public health agencies demonstrated almost universal agreement with the core functions and an increasing proportion of health departments in which these functions are operative. However, fewer than 50% of those surveyed reported these functions to be currently operative and available in their communities.[22]

An expanding area of interest is the extent to which nongovernmental entities can provide essential healthservices. Private-sector healthcare providers, previously involved with inpatient care, are evolving into consolidated and integrated healthcare systems. Enrollment in health maintenance organizations has rapidly increased. These changes in the healthcare marketplace potentially could lead to interest in providing essential public health services.[23] Listed in Table 2-3 are eight exemplary private-sector entities, all nonprofit health care systems and health plans, that were studied in 1995–1996 to determine if their activities included the three core public health functions and the 10 essential public health services. These eight plans were determined to be conducting 44 activities addressing core functions and essential health services, as shown in Table 2-4. The authors of this study concluded that private-sector organizations are willing to perform public health activities and that local health departments will further their mission by forging collaborative partnerships.[23]

The World Health Organization (WHO) decided to employ essential public health functions (EPHFs) as a tool for implementing "Health for All in the 21st Century."[24] This initiative began in May 1981 when WHO members agreed to pursue health gains for their countries.[25] In 1997, an international Delphi survey, a validated process for attaining anonymous consensus, of 145 public health leaders, managers, teachers, and practitioners was performed.[24] The essential public health categories and functions that resulted from this process are similar to those developed by the US Public Health Services' Public Health Functions Steering Committee, but differ somewhat in format. Exhibit 2-4 displays these functions and also a prioritization as to their importance.

**TABLE 2-3    Case Study Organizations**

| Name | Location |
|---|---|
| Allina Health System | Minneapolis, MN |
| Baptist Health | Little Rock, AR |
| BJC Health System | St. Louis, MO |
| Cambridge Hospital Community Health Network | Cambridge, MA |
| Harvard Pilgrim Health Care | Boston, MA |
| Henry Ford Health System | Detroit, MI |
| Mt. Sinai Health System | Chicago, IL |
| Riverside Methodist Hospitals* | Columbus, OH |

*Merged with its sister facility, Grant Hospital, in September 1995 to become Grant/Riverside Methodist Hospitals.
*Source:* Reprinted from Centers for Disease Control and Prevention, *Private Sector Health Care Organizations and Public Health: Potential Effects on the Practice of Local Public Health,* March 1996, Macro International, Atlanta, Georgia.

**TABLE 2-4    Distribution of Activities by Primary Core Public Health Function**

| Essential Public Health Service (EPHS) | Number of Activities Addressing EPHSs | |
| --- | --- | --- |
| | Predominantly | Total |
| **Assessment** | | |
| Monitor | 6 | 18 |
| Investigate | 2 | 6 |
| **Policy development** | | |
| Inform | 7 | 15 |
| Mobilize | 4 | 9 |
| Plan | — | 6 |
| **Assurance** | | |
| Enforce | — | — |
| Link | 21 | 27 |
| Competent workforce | 3 | 6 |
| Evaluate | 1 | 5 |
| Research and development | — | 2 |
| Total | 44 | 94* |

*Each of the 44 activities could address more than one essential public health service.
*Source:* Reprinted from Centers for Disease Control and Prevention, *Private Sector Health Care Organizations and Public Health: Potential Effects on the Practice of Local Public Health*, March 1996, Macro International, Atlanta, Georgia.

It was strongly agreed by the survey participants that public health functions may be performed by nongovernmental entities, including the private sector. The rationale advanced was that because the determinants of health status are not confined to the health sector, essential health services can be carried out in other areas. More importantly, however, the implementation of EPHFs needs to be monitored by government agencies.[24]

## The Future of the Public's Health

In the United States, a follow-up report by the Institute of Medicine, *The Future of the Public's Health in the 21st Century*, further explored the public health infrastructure and the potential challenges within the public health system that could jeopardize the health of the public. The report outlines the concept of population health and the government's fundamental duty to protect it. Further, it "describes the rationale for multisector engagement in partnership with the government and the roles different actors can play to support a healthy future for the American people."[26(p1)] An illustration of the intersectoral public health system is seen in Figure 2-3. The IOM report, in seeking to address the health challenges facing the American public currently and in the future, identified six areas of change and actions. The six general areas include the following[26(p4)]:

- Using a population health approach (considering environmental, social, and behavioral aspects of public health as described in Chapter 1)
- Strengthening public health infrastructure

**Exhibit 2-4 Essential Pulic Health Categories and Functions (Resulting from the International Delphi Survey of 1997, Rank out of 37)**

1. **Prevention, surveillance, and control of communicable and non-communicable diseases**
   - Immunization (1)
   - Disease outbreak control (3)
   - Disease surveillance (4)
   - Prevention of injury (20)
2. **Monitoring the health situation**
   - Monitoring of morbidity and mortality (2)
   - Monitoring the determinants of health (6)
   - Evaluation of the effectiveness of promotion, prevention, and service programs (10)
   - Assessment of the effectiveness of public health functions (11)
   - Assessment of population needs and risks to determine which subgroups require service (12)
3. **Health promotion**
   - Promotion of community involvement in health (5)
   - Provision of information and education for health and life skill enhancement in school, home, work, and community settings (9)
   - Maintenance of linkages with politicians, other sectors, and the community in support of health promotion, and public health advocacy (14)
4. **Occupational health**
   - Setting occupational health and safety standards (18)
5. **Protecting the environment**
   - Production and protection of, and access to, safe water (7)
   - Control of food quality and safety (8)
   - Provision of adequate drainage, sewerage, and solid waste disposal services (15)
   - Control of hazardous substances and wastes (16)
   - Provision of adequate vector control measures (17)
   - Ensuring protection of water and soil resources (29)
   - Ensuring environmental health aspects are addressed in development policies, plans, programs, and objects (32)
   - Prevention and control of atmospheric pollution (33)
   - Ensuring adequate prevention and promotive environmental services (34)
   - Ensuring adequate inspection, monitoring, and control of environmental hazards (35)
   - Controlling radiation (36)
6. **Public health legislation and regulations**
   - Reviewing formulation and enactment of health legislation, regulations, and administrative procedures (13)
   - Ensuring adequate legislation to protect environmental health (22)
   - Health inspection and licensing (23)
   - Enforcement of health legislation, regulations, and administrative procedures (24)
7. **Public health management**
   - Ensuring health policy, planning, and management (9)
   - Use of scientific evidence in the formulation and implementation of public health policy (21)
   - Public health and health systems research (30)
   - International collaboration and cooperation in health (37)
8. **Specific public health services**
   - School health services (25)
   - Emergency disaster services (27)
   - Public health laboratory services (28)
9. **Personal health care for vulnerable and high-risk populations**
   - Maternal health and family planning (26)
   - Infant and child care (31)

*Source:* Reprinted with permission from D. Bettcher et al., Delphi Study, *World Health Stat Q,* 51, p. 49, © 1998, World Health Organization.

**FIGURE 2-3    The Public Health System**
*Source:* Reprinted with permission from National Academies Press. Institute of Medicine. *Future of the Public's Health in the 21st Century.* Washington, DC: National Academy Press; 2003: 30.

- Supporting and promoting intersectoral partnerships, as seen in Figure 2-3, paying special consideration to meeting the needs of diverse populations
- Developing a systematic approach to ensure the quality and availability of public health services (refer to Chapter 17 on performance management)
- Supporting and promoting evidence-based public health
- Improving communication within the public health system (see Chapter 20 for further discussion of this topic)

The focus on the intersectoral approach is supported in *Healthy People 2010,* which describes, when referring to the 10 essential public health services, "the totality of the public health infrastructure includes all governmental and nongovernmental entities that provide any of these services."[27] *Healthy People 2010* is discussed below.

## National Health Objectives

Prior to the IOM's 1988 pivotal report, national health objectives for the United States grew out of a health strategy initiated with the publication in 1979 of *Healthy People: The Surgeon General's Report on Health Promotion and Disease Prevention.*[28] After preliminary work by US Public Health Service agencies, 167 nongovernmental experts were convened at a conference in 1979 and organized into 15 working groups that developed the draft objectives for the priority areas.[25] This resulted in the 1980 publication of *Promoting Health/Preventing Disease: Objectives for the Nation,* which set 226 goals in 15 priority areas across three categories of preventive health services, health protection, and health promotion.[29] The report was organized into five broad health status goals keyed to the various stages of the life cycle, from healthy infants, healthy children, healthy adolescents and young adults, and healthy adults, to healthy older adults. Examining the risk factors responsible for the preponderance of morbidity and mortality for each age group and also assessing the feasibility of successful public health intervention identified the 15 priority areas. The health promotion effort behind this was based on the theory of multiple determinants of health involving biologic, social, environmental, and behavioral factors. Prevention and risk reduction strategies were aimed at the individual susceptibilities and behavior, agents of disease, environmental factors, and particularly the interaction between these determinations. As discussed in Chapter 1, *Healthy People* emphasized the importance of personal behaviors of the individual in determining health status and also recognized the role of environmental factors.[28]

By 1987, measurement tools showed that nearly half of the objectives had been reached. An additional one quarter of the objectives were not achieved, and data were not available for monitoring the objectives in the remaining quarter. Considerable progress was documented in the priority areas including the control of high blood pressure; immunization; control of infectious diseases; unintentional injury prevention; and control of smoking, alcohol, and drugs. Areas where progress lagged included pregnancy and infant health, nutrition, physical fitness, family planning, STDs, and occupational safety and health.[30] Major declines in the death rates for heart disease, stroke, and unintentional injury during this 1980–1990 period gave hope for progress in succeeding decades, spurring the next installment of objectives: *Healthy People 2000: National Health Promotion and Disease Prevention Objectives.*[30]

### Healthy People 2000

*Healthy People 2000,* based on regional hearings with testimony from more than 750 individuals and organizations, presented a new national prevention strategy, identifying three broad goals. The goals were increasing the span of life, reducing health disparities, and achieving access to preventive services. Objectives were organized into 22 priority areas as shown in Exhibit 2-5. The first 21 of these areas were in three broad categories: health promotion, health protection, and preventive services.[30]

*Health promotion* strategies focused on lifestyle and personal behaviors including physical activity, nutrition, tobacco, and alcohol. *Health protection* strategies included environmental and regulatory activities. *Preventive services* included counseling, screening, and immunization. A special category was established in *Healthy People 2000* for data and surveillance activities (priority area 22). Each priority area was assigned to a government lead agency such as the Centers for Disease Control and Prevention, the National Institutes of Health, and the Health Resources and Services Agency.

*Healthy People 2000* was designed to offer a vision for the new century based on achieving reductions in preventable disability and death. For example, when work on this report began in 1987, a new health threat, human immunodeficiency virus (HIV) infection, had appeared. The devastating impact it had on the nation's health was evident. Given the importance of this new threat, an entire priority area, priority area 18, was devoted to the disease.

Similar to the progress report described for the 1990 objectives, the US Public Health Service has issued midcourse reviews on *Healthy People 2000* with the final review available for 1998–1999. Fifteen percent of the objec-

Exhibit 2-5    *Healthy People 2000* Priority Areas

**Health Promotion**
1. Physical activity and fitness
2. Nutrition
3. Tobacco
4. Alcohol and other drugs
5. Family planning
6. Mental health and mental disorders
7. Violent and abusive behavior
8. Educational and community-based programs

**Health Protection**
9. Unintentional injuries
10. Occupational safety and health
11. Environmental health
12. Food and drug safety
13. Oral health

**Preventive Services**
14. Maternal and infant health
15. Heart disease and stroke
16. Cancer
17. Diabetes and chronic disabling conditions
18. HIV infection
19. Sexually transmitted diseases
20. Immunization and infectious diseases
21. Clinical preventive services

**Surveillance and Data Systems**
22. Surveillance and data systems

*Source:* Reprinted from National Health Promotion Disease Prevention Objectives, *Healthy People 2000*, p. 7, US Department of Health and Human Services, Public Health Service.

tives met the year 2000 targets, with an additional 44% showing movement toward the targets and 18% moving in a direction away from the targets. Eleven percent of the objectives lacked data for measurement. The remainder showed mixed results or no change.[31]

## *Healthy People 2010* Objectives

In 2000, *Healthy People 2010* was released by the US Department of Health and Human Resources. The comprehensive, health promotion and disease prevention agenda was "designed to identify the most significant preventable threats to health and to establish national goals to reduce these threats."[32] Leading federal agencies, informed by an alliance of more than 350 national membership organizations and 250 state health, mental health, substance abuse, and environmental agencies developed the framework for *Healthy People 2010*. The public was encouraged to participate in the process, resulting in over 11,000 public comments on the draft version. The final report had two overarching goals: to increase quality and years of life and to eliminate health disparities. To meet these goals, 467 objectives are organized by 28 focus areas. *Healthy People 2010* has two broad types of objectives—measurable and developmental. The *measurable objectives*, similar to the majority of the preceding *Healthy People 2000* objectives, have baselines and available data for national measurement purposes. *Developmental objectives* represent a desired outcome or health status for which current surveillance systems can not yet provide data. Ten leading health indicators are used to measure progress in the health of the nation. Development of this small set of leading health indicators was seen as critical to improving the planning process and communicating with the public. The 10 leading health indictors cross-referenced with the 28 focus areas is shown in Exhibit 2-6.

### Increase Quality and Years of Healthy Life

This first goal of 2010 is to increase the quality and not just the years of healthy life. A healthy life means a full range of functional capacity throughout each life stage. A range of measures is used for this goal, including morbidity, mortality, and quality. With success in extending life expectancy, more attention is now being focused toward improving the quality of life (QOL). Health-related quality of life (HRQOL) includes both physical and mental health and their determinants.[33] HRQOL has a relationship to individual perception and ability to function. On a community basis, HRQOL includes all aspects that have an influence on health (Table 2-5).

### Eliminate Health Disparities

Eliminating disparities was a goal of *Healthy People 2000,* which had special population targets for some objectives. These targets did not aim at eliminating health disparities by the year 2000. In February 1998, President William Clinton called for eliminating disparities between racial and minority groups in six areas: infant mortality, cancer, cardiovascular disease, diabetes, HIV/acquired immune deficiency syndrome (AIDS), and immunizations. *Healthy People 2010* has the goal of eliminating these disparities during the next decade, with 383 objectives that apply to this goal.[34]

## Public Health Infrastructure

For the first time, *Healthy People 2010* includes a focus area in public health infrastructure, with the goal of ensuring capacity to provide the essential public health services at federal, state, and local levels. Objectives for this area are shown in Exhibit 2-7.

Infrastructure has been described as the basic support for the delivery of public health activities. Five components of infrastructure are skilled workforce, integrated electronic information systems, public health organizations, resources, and research. The need for infrastructure was pointed out by the IOM report in 1988.[6] Keeping pace with information technology, availability of a trained workforce, and availability of resources for local public health problems are infrastructure priorities. This new focus area does not target health outcomes but rather increased capacity to deliver public health services. As such, the objectives currently lack data systems to monitor progress, but are being developed. For example, geocoding is to be incorporated into

**Exhibit 2-6**  *Healthy People 2010,* **Priority Areas by Leading Health Indicators**

| Focus Area | Physical activity | Overweight and obesity | Tobacco use | Substance abuse | Responsible sexual behavior | Mental health | Injury and violence | Environmental quality | Immunization | Access to health care |
|---|---|---|---|---|---|---|---|---|---|---|
| Access to quality health services | ✔ | ✔ | ✔ | ✔ | ✔ | ✔ | ✔ | | ✔ | |
| Arthritis, osteoporosis, and chronic back conditions | ✔ | ✔ | | | | | ✔ | | | |
| Cancer | ✔ | ✔ | ✔ | ✔ | ✔ | | | | ✔ | ✔ |
| Chronic kidney disease | ✔ | ✔ | ✔ | | | | | ✔ | | ✔ |
| Diabetes | ✔ | ✔ | ✔ | | | | | | ✔ | ✔ |
| Disability and secondary conditions | ✔ | ✔ | ✔ | ✔ | | | ✔ | | ✔ | ✔ |
| Educational and community-based programs | ✔ | ✔ | ✔ | ✔ | ✔ | ✔ | ✔ | ✔ | ✔ | ✔ |
| Environmental health | | | | | | | | ✔ | | |
| Family planning | | | | ✔ | ✔ | | | | | ✔ |
| Food safety | | | | | | | | ✔ | | ✔ |
| Health communication | ✔ | ✔ | ✔ | ✔ | ✔ | ✔ | ✔ | ✔ | ✔ | ✔ |
| Heart disease and Stroke | ✔ | ✔ | ✔ | | | | | ✔ | | |
| HIV | | | | ✔ | ✔ | ✔ | | | | ✔ |
| Immunization and infectious diseases | | | | | | | | | ✔ | ✔ |
| Injury and violence prevention | | | | ✔ | ✔ | ✔ | ✔ | | | |
| Maternal, infant, and child health | ✔ | ✔ | ✔ | ✔ | ✔ | ✔ | ✔ | | ✔ | ✔ |
| Medical product safety | | | | | | ✔ | | | | |
| Mental health and mental disorders | | | | ✔ | ✔ | ✔ | | | | ✔ |
| Nutrition and overweight | ✔ | ✔ | ✔ | | | ✔ | | | | |
| Occupational safety and health | | | | ✔ | | | ✔ | ✔ | | |
| Oral health | | ✔ | ✔ | ✔ | | | | ✔ | | ✔ |
| Physical activity and fitness | ✔ | ✔ | ✔ | | | ✔ | ✔ | ✔ | | |
| Public health infrastructure | ✔ | ✔ | ✔ | ✔ | ✔ | ✔ | ✔ | ✔ | ✔ | ✔ |
| Respiratory diseases | ✔ | | ✔ | | | | | ✔ | | |
| Sexually transmitted diseases | | | | | ✔ | ✔ | | | | |
| Substance abuse | | | | ✔ | ✔ | ✔ | ✔ | | | ✔ |
| Tobacco use | | | ✔ | | | | | | | ✔ |
| Vision and hearing | | | | | | | | | | ✔ |

*Source:* US Department of Health and Human Services, Office of Disease Prevention and Health Promotion, *Healthy People 2010.* Available at http://www.healthypeople.gov/

databases so that federal, state, and local entities will have the geographic information system capability to make maps showing disease, risk factors, environmental hazard, and service delivery.[33] Apart from building workforce competency and increasing training and continuing education opportunities, the majority of infrastructure objectives directly address the capacity of state

**TABLE 2-5 Health-Related Quality of Life (HRQOL)**

| "Health" | vs. HRQOL | vs. QOL |
|---|---|---|
| Individual level | | |
| Death | Functional status | Happiness |
| Disease | Well-being | Life satisfaction |
| Community level | | |
| Life expectancy | Environment | Participation |
| | Livability | Sustainability |

*Source:* Reprinted from *Healthy People 2010 Objectives,* Draft for Public Comment, Goal 7, 1998, US Department of Health and Human Services, Office of Public Health and Science.

and local health agencies by calling for increases in the use of technology, scientific disciplines, planning, and improved organization of services. For example, a target of 90% is set for the proportion of state and local public health agencies that use electronic data and online information for data to improve their operations. Another objective targets the availability of individuals with epidemiology skills for local and state public health agencies. In addition to these objectives, state and local public health jurisdictions are expected to develop health improvement plans to monitor and meet performance standards for the essential public health services.

Placement of the infrastructure objectives in *Healthy People 2010* signifies the importance of a core capacity for population-based activities as pro-

**Exhibit 2-7   Public Health Infrastructure**

| *Number* | *Objective* |
|---|---|
| 1. | Competencies for public health workers |
| 2. | Training in essential public health services |
| 3. | Continuing education and training by public health agencies |
| 4. | Use of Standard Occupational Classification System |
| 5. | Onsite access to data |
| 6. | Access to public health information and surveillance data |
| 7. | Tracking *Healthy People 2010* objectives for select populations |
| 8. | Data collection for *Healthy People 2010* objectives |
| 9. | Use of geocoding in health data systems |
| 10. | Performance standards for essential public health services |
| 11. | Health improvement plans |
| 12. | Access to laboratory services |
| 13. | Access to comprehensive epidemiology services |
| 14. | Model statutes related to essential public health services |
| 15. | Data on public health expenditures |
| 16. | Collaboration and cooperation in prevention research efforts |
| 17. | Summary measures of population health and the public health infrastructure |

*Source:* Reprinted from *Healthy People 2010 Objectives,* Draft for Public Comment, Public Health Infrastructure 14-1, 1998, US Department of Health and Human Services, Office of Public Health and Science.

vided by local, state, and federal public health agencies in collaboration with communities and other providers in the public and private sectors. Public health departments responsible for the health of communities need the basic tools: a skilled workforce and the resources necessary for it to perform its task. This noncategorical approach focuses on the skills, manpower, and technology available to these agencies for the array of public health functions, rather than for specific programmatic use.

Creating infrastructure objectives will not lead to their realization without the necessary resources and the commitment to implement them. The resource question is particularly thorny because funding sources are not specified in *Healthy People 2010*. Requests for infrastructure funding of federal, state, or local governments may suffer because they can appear generic or not directly relevant to activities addressing more visible health issues such as infectious disease, maternal and child health, and environmental hazards. Various approaches to this difficulty can be used, such as attaching and integrating infrastructure with program budgets. Unfortunately, no approach to this issue is fully satisfactory, and the availability of resources is the major factor that will determine whether the infrastructure objectives in *Healthy People 2010* will be achieved.

Progress reviews by focus area are available at the Healthy People Web site and show that progress is quite variable. For example, in the focus area of immunization and infectious diseases:

> In 2002, the 2010 target of 90% coverage levels was met or surpassed for four of seven recommended vaccinations of children aged 19 to 35 months—*Haemophilus influenzae* type b (Hib), hepatitis B, measles-mumps-rubella (MMR), and polio. Coverage for pneumococcal conjugate vaccinations (for which no target has been determined) showed a dramatic improvement in 2002 (Obj. 14-22). In general, rates of vaccination coverage for this age group advanced at a rapid pace over the past few years, and disparities among population groups narrowed substantially.[35]

In contrast, the focus area on nutrition and overweight demonstrated a worrisome trend: "Overall, the data on the three *Healthy People 2010* objectives for the weight status of adults and children reflect a trend for the worse. Also, the three objectives for fruit, vegetable, and grain consumption have shown little or no progress in this decade."[36] Considering that dietary factors are associated with 4 of the 10 leading causes of death—coronary heart disease, some types of cancer, stroke, and type 2 diabetes—as well as with high blood pressure and osteoporosis, this is particularly concerning.[36] The progress review of public health infrastructure noted that "In 2004, 50% of major national data systems that track five or more *Healthy People 2010* objectives had the capability to geocode health records of individuals or health care providers by street address or latitude/longitude. The 2010 target is 90% (Obj. 23-3)."[37]

## Governmental and Nongovernmental Aspects of Public Health

Historically, the government's role has been central to the provision of health protection for the community because the genesis of public health activities was in addressing environmental and disease threats. Countering these hazards to health required a governmental presence as manifested by statutory protection, regulation, inspection, and enforcement. In the early development of public health efforts, governmental authority did not act separately from private-sector involvement, including business, medicine, and voluntary associations. As public health practice has evolved with a broader definition of scope extending beyond infectious disease, private-sector involvement in these community preventive activities has grown more important.

The role of governmental activity in public health is not constant but varies with larger political and social trends. Federal activities in public health experienced growth from the 1930s through 1970s as part of Roosevelt's New Deal and Johnson's Great Society. The Shepard-Towner Act of 1922 was the first legislation to provide funding to the states for personal health services by establishing MCH programs. The Social Security Act of 1935 included funding to the states for public health services and training.[6] New programs were funded during the 1960s and 1970s, including Medicaid, Medicare, maternal and infant care projects, family planning services, Head Start, and the Special Supplemental Food Program for Women, Infants, and Children (WIC). But in the 1980s, the new federalism of the Reagan administration shifted the locus of responsibility to the states. Less money for programs was available, and funds of categorical programs were consolidated into the Maternal and Child Health Block Grant and the Preventive Services Block Grant.[38] The MCH block grant consolidated programs for sudden infant death syndrome (SIDS), lead poisoning, and adolescent pregnancy while also imposing an overall reduction in funds from the totals of these programs in previous years. This new federalism has motivated much of the recent effort to refocus the mission of public health toward population-based core functions. Increased state authority to implement mandatory managed care for Medicaid enrollees has led to reductions in demand for clinical services.[39] A substantial portion of the personal healthcare and clinical preventive services now provided by public health departments is being transferred to the private-sector and managed care.[40] This change is being hastened by grants from the federal government to states for the Child Health Insurance Program. A dominant element of public policy with respect to public health activities is devolution—the shift of responsibilities from the federal government to the state and then to the localities and often to private vendors.[41]

The IOM report of 1988, as previously described, characterized the government's role in terms of the functions of assessment, policy development, and assurance.[6] Further, it characterized the official public health agency as "the place where the health buck stops" in making decisions concerning preventive health functions.[6] However, the role of government is shaped by community priorities that often originate in nongovernmental sectors.

In 1991, Daniel Fox pointed to four limitations of government in the public health arena.[42] These heighten the importance of participation by the community, including the private sector, in health improvement. The limitations of government, compromising its role in public health, include a reduced probability of success for interventions, management by crisis, fragmentation, and competing governmental agencies. Many current public health issues and interventions do not inspire governmental action as did the

19th-century threats from diseases such as diphtheria and TB, where the proposed actions had high probabilities of success at limited costs. A second limitation is that public health crises have been associated with public management of the problem but not long-term policy changes. A third limitation is the fragmentation of health responsibilities among a number of different public agencies using separate approaches to public health problems.[42] Fourth, competition for resources between governmental agencies, including welfare, corrections, and police, leaves public health agencies at a disadvantage, particularly because their activities are not perceived as being of similar critical importance to their counterparts.

Contemporary relationships that support core public health functions can be described in four categories: (1) between different health agencies at various levels of government, (2) between health agencies and other public agencies, (3) between health agencies and the private sector, and (4) between private and voluntary organizations.[6] All of these interactions occur regularly in practice so that public health can not be categorized as a strictly governmental or nongovernmental activity. Instead, the public health system is best conceptualized as a network of functions involving both sectors. Relationships between health agencies occur at multiple levels, including, for example, funding and guidance offered by state public health agencies to local health departments. Information and recommendations involve exchanges between these levels, with possible involvement of federal health agencies including the CDC, Human Resources Services Agencies (HRSA), and the Food and Drug Administration (FDA).

Relationships between governmental public health agencies and the private and/or voluntary sector are also manifold. Local health departments work with both nonprofit and investor-owned organizations, including hospitals and businesses interested in promotion of health activities. Voluntary associations such as the American Heart Association and the American Cancer Association act in the private sector, often in cooperation with governmental activities. In the late 1990s, the Turning Point collaborative, initially sponsored by the W.K. Kellogg and the Robert Wood Johnson foundations, demonstrated that the private sector was committed to public health systems improvement with its mission "to transform and strengthen the public health system in the United States to make the system more effective, more community-based, and more collaborative."[43]

## A Community Perspective

As discussed, the domain of public health extends beyond the range of governmental activities. Many individuals, organizations, and other entities are directly or indirectly involved with community health.[44] In addition to public health agencies, stakeholders include individual health providers, purchasers of care, and voluntary and community organizations.[45] Even agencies without an explicit health designation, including schools, businesses, and the media, can have important health-related roles. This broad net of those entities abetting public health purposes is warranted but makes a single definition of public health practice or designation of the public health workforce complex. Edward Baker, former Director of the Public Health Practice Office at CDC and now Director of the North Carolina Institute for Public Health has emphasized this broader approach:

> We present a redefinition of public health practice that extends well beyond the usual government efforts and aggressively seeks out and embraces the skills and resources of many new nontraditional players. While in no way diminishing the importance of public health agencies, we foresee a significantly greater participation by the private sector, particularly the personal medical care system in the future.[46(p1276)]

The interaction between governmental public health agencies and the private sector is currently in flux. The increase in the number of organized healthcare delivery systems, including managed care plans, is making it possible for governmental health agencies to ensure access to care directly rather than to deliver personal health services directly. As reported in the 1996 IOM report, *Healthy Communities: New Partnerships for the Future of Public Health*, there is a question of how many elements of public health can or should be subsumed by the private sector.[45] The number could be considerable. An earlier study described nonprofit organizations performing essential public health services.[23] The 2003 follow-up IOM report further addressed the need of nongovernmental agencies to carry out the three fundamental functions. Although maintaining that governmental public health agencies have a special duty as "the backbone of the public health system," the report provides recommendations for community partners including the healthcare delivery system, employers and businesses, media, and academia.[26]

A range of for-profit and nonprofit organizations are already involved in activities that incorporate public health practices using any definition. Two notable examples include the Henry Ford Health System and Parkland Health and Hospital System.

The Henry Ford Health System (HFHS) is a major comprehensive nonprofit organization serving seven counties in southeastern Michigan. Based in Detroit, the system provides care to the insured and uninsured in areas with high rates of poverty, unemployment, and violence. Principles used in operation include a definition of health as more than the absence of disease, participation in community prevention, and use of the *Healthy People 2000* goals.[47] In 2004, the system provided the community with $127 million in uncompensated care. The system has won numerous prestigious awards for the services it provides in improving the health of the community it serves.[48]

The Parkland Health and Hospital System (PHHS) is one of the nation's largest teaching hospitals and has served as a safety net for Dallas for more than 100 years, serving primarily Medicare, Medicaid, or uninsured clients.[39] With a vision that includes providing "services that improve the health of the community," PHHS is clearly part of the public health system.[49] For example, in 2004 the Community Oriented Primary Care System served more than 450,000 individuals in its 10 centers.[50] Health care is also provided in nontraditional settings, including care for the homeless. Measurements of health outcomes are used to evaluate the program's effectiveness. Health outcomes are calculated using preexisting morbidity based on morbidity and mortality rate data in the served community. The assumption is that the delivery of preventive care will improve the health of the community.[49]

## Medicine and Public Health

Medicine and public health have operated separately in the United States, pursuing different approaches to health improvement. Public health practitioners worked in governmental and social agencies, in contrast to the activities of medicine in the private sector. These activities were focused on the individual, employing a set of biologic disciplines and subspecialties.[51] The Flexnerian reforms in medical education made medical practice more dependent on scientific knowledge and a relationship with hospital settings, resulting in less physician interest in community and preventive activity.[52] Public health focused on populations and determinants of health. The separation of medicine and public health has been associated with conflict. For example, when public health clinics started treating indigent patients in the 1920s and 1930s, it raised the issue of competition with private medicine.[51] Viseltear, a public health historian, has described fundamental differences between the two professions, which have resulted in an "impenetrable barrier" between medicine and public health.[53]

> One difference was based on the economic imperative which held that, as the medical profession was concerned primarily with cure and reimbursed on a fee-for-service basis, the public health profession perforce must be relegated entirely to providing those services in which the private physician had no interest; and the second was the rise of the basic sciences, which led to the emergence of medical specialties and the enthronement of reductionist medicine, upon which the medical schools and medical profession justified as their primary mission sickness and not health, the patient and not the community, cure and not prevention—all principles which are at variance with the public health ethos.[4-53(p148)]

In the 1800s and early 1900s, there was a supportive relationship between physicians and public health, with leaders of the profession playing important roles in community health improvement.[54] Leaders in the two sectors overlapped, and many physicians were actively involved in public health activities.[55] At this time, medical interventions were largely ineffective in treating infectious disease, increasing support for public health measures.[55] But private physicians resisted early 20th-century efforts in compulsory TB reporting and in the role of public health laboratories in testing for diphtheria and antitoxin production.[52,56] Some physicians also resisted development of well-baby clinics, health centers, and immunization programs.[56,57] Physician interest in public health waned with the growth of therapeutic armamentarium and antibiotics later in the 1900s and the growth of reimbursement mechanisms for diagnostic and therapeutic interventions.[55] The medical profession moved from strong support of public health activities to ambivalence or even hostility.[56]

More recently, several factors have emerged that may improve the dysfunctional relationship between medicine and public health. The growth of managed care and the increased recognition of the value of partnerships and collaboration by public health entities has led to efforts by both sectors to bridge this historical separation. In March 1994, the leaders of both the American Medical Association and the American Public Health Association met for this purpose, and a working partnership was established with support of the Josiah Macy, Jr., and the W.K. Kellogg foundations.[51] In March 1996, a historic congress brought together nearly 400 leaders of the professional organizations representing those in practice, education, and research in public health and medicine.[51] The following seven elements were agreed on[51]:

1. Engage the community.
2. Change the educational process.
3. Create joint research efforts.
4. Devise a shared view of health and illness.
5. Work together in healthcare provision.
6. Develop healthcare assessment measures.
7. Create local and national networks.

The American Medical Association and the American Public Health Association have made a long-term commitment to this medicine–public health initiative.

•   •   •

A variety of administrative and policy frameworks now exist to assist public health institutions in defining, organizing, managing, and evaluating their core activities. Nonetheless, important differences remain in how institutions conceptualize and practice public health. A key point of contention involves the role of public health organizations in delivering personal health services. Despite differences of opinion in certain process-related issues, public health organizations appear to be reaching consensus about the larger public health mission, goals, and objectives. A key area of consensus involves core functions that should be performed by public health organizations in both governmental and private settings. Another area of consensus concerns the importance of cooperation between public and private organizations and between medical practice and public health practice. The growing acceptance of these shared goals and objectives promises to improve performance among individual public health organizations and within the public health system as a whole.

## Chapter Review

1. An issue for local health departments is whether their scope of functions should include medical care services in addition to their preventive responsibilities.
2. *The Future of Medicine,* a 1988 IOM report, characterized the functions of public health as *assessment, policy,* and *assurance.* These were designated as core functions and have been widely used to describe the activities of health agencies.
3. In 1994, a listing of 10 essential public health services was developed, representing a further development of the core functions. This is the current taxonomy most often used to describe public health activities.
4. The issue of healthcare reform has crystallized the constellation of functions of public health. With the provision of health services through structured organized plans such as managed care, the functions of the health agency are less in service provision and more in

population-based health protection and promotion, as described in the essential functions.

5. National health objectives for the United States grew out of a health strategy initiated with the publication of *Healthy People* in 1979. Starting with the publication of objectives for 1990 and followed by objectives for 2000, objectives for 2010 are the currently available set.

6. Objectives for *Healthy People 2010* focus on: (1) eliminating health disparities, (2) increasing quality and years of life, and (3) developing infrastructure for public health activities. The set of objectives as a whole constitutes an agenda for health improvement and monitoring progress.

7. The interaction between governmental health agencies and the private sector is currently in flux. With the increase in organized health delivery systems, including managed care, the role of government is moving to assurance rather than delivery of personal services.

8. Recent partnerships between medicine and public health demonstrate a long-term commitment to improve the historically dysfunctional relationship between these fields.

## References

1. Emerson H. *Local Health Units for the Nation.* New York, NY: The Commonwealth Fund; 1945.

2. Jekel J. Health departments in the US, 1920–1988: statements of mission with special reference to the role of C.E.A. Winslow. *Yale J Biol Med.* 1991;64:467–479.

3. American Public Health Association. An official declaration of attitude of the American Public Health Association on desirable standard minimum functions and suitable organization of health activities. *Am J Public Health Yearbook.* 1933:6–11.

4. Mountin JW. Distribution of health services in the structure of state government. *Public Health Rep.* 1941;34:1674–1698.

5. Terris M, Kramer N. Medical care activities of full-time health departments. *Am J Public Health.* 1949;39:1129–1135.

6. Institute of Medicine. *The Future of Public Health.* Washington, DC: National Academies Press; 1988.

7. Miller A, Moos MK. *Local Health Departments: Fifteen Case Studies.* Washington, DC: American Public Health Association; 1981.

8. Meyers B, Steinhardt BJ, Mosley ML, et al. The medical care activities of local health units. *Public Health Rep.* 1968;83:757–769.

9. National Association of County and City Health Officials. *1992–1993 National Profile of Local Health Departments.* Washington, DC: NACCHO; 1995.

10. Dyal W. Ten organizational practices of public health: a historical perspective. *Res Meas Public Health Pract* (supplement to the *Am J Preventive Med).* 1995;6:6–8.

11. Studnicki J, Steverson B, Blais H, et al. Analyzing organizational practices in local health departments. *Public Health Rep.* 1994;109(4):485–490.

12. Health Security Act of 1993, 103rd Cong., 1st sess.

13. Core Functions Project, US Public Health Service. Health care reform and public health: a paper on population-based core functions. *J Public Health Policy.* 1998;19(4):394–419.

14. Harrell JA, Baker EL., Essential Services Work Groups. The essential services of public health. American Public Health Association. Available at: http://www.apha.org/ppp/science/10ES.htm. Accessed January 13, 2006.

15. Eilbert K, Barry M, Bailek R, et al. Public health expenditures: developing estimates for improved policy making. *J Public Health Manage Pract.* 1997;3(3):1–9.

16. Grason HA, Guyer B. *Public MCH Program Functions Framework: Essential Public Health Services to Promote Maternal and Child Health in America.* Baltimore, Md: Johns Hopkins University; 1995.

17. Grason HA. Use of MCH functions framework as a tool for strengthening public health practice. *J Public Health Manage Pract.* 1997;3(5):14–15.

18. Wilcox L. Important directions in public health surveillance and community-based research in maternal and child health: a CDC perspective. *J Public Health Manage Pract.* 1997;3(5):17–19.

19. Gerzoff R. Comparisons: the basis for measuring public health performance. *J Public Health Manage Pract.* 1997;3(5):20–21.

20. Scott H. The future of public health: a survey of states. *J Public Health Policy.* 1990;11(3):296–304.

21. Scutchfield F, Beversdof C, Hiltabiddle S, et al. A survey of state health department compliance with the recommendations of the Institute of Medicine report, *The Future of Public Health. J Public Health Policy.* 1997;18(2):13–29.

22. Scutchfield F. Compliance with the recommendations of the Institute of Medicine report, *The Future of Public Health:* a survey of local health departments. *J Public Health Policy.* 1997;18(2):155–166.

23. Chapel T. Private sector health care organizations and essential public health services: potential effects on the practice of local public health. *J Public Health Manage Pract.* 1999;4(1):36–44.

24. Bettcher D, Sapirie S, Goon E, et al. Essential public health functions: results of the international Delphi Study. *World Health Stat Q.* 1998;51:44–55.

25. McGinnis J. Objectives-based strategies for disease-prevention. In: Holland W, Detels R, Knox G, eds. 2nd edition. *Oxford Textbook of Public Health.* New York, NY: Oxford University Press; 1991:127–144.

26. Institute of Medicine. *The Future of the Public's Health in the 21st Century.* Washington, DC: National Academies Press; 2003.

27. US Department of Health and Human Services, Office of Disease Prevention and Health Promotion. *Healthy People 2010*, focus area 23, public health infrastructure. Available at: http://www.healthypeople.gov/. Accessed January 13, 2006.

28. US Department of Health, Education, and Welfare. *Healthy People: The Surgeon General's Report on Health Promotion and Disease Prevention.* Washington, DC: US Government Printing Office (PHS) 79-55071; 1979.

29. US Department of Health and Human Services. *Promoting Health/ Preventing Disease: Objectives for the Nation.* Washington, DC: US Government Printing Office; 1980.

30. US Department of Health and Human Services, Public Health Service. *Healthy People 2000: National Health Promotion and Disease Prevention Objectives.* Washington, DC: US Government Printing Office (PHS) 91-50212; 1991.

31. US Department of Health and Human Services, Centers for Disease Control and Prevention. *Healthy People 2000 Review.* Washington, DC: US Government Printing Office (PHS) 99-1256; 1998–1999.

32. US Department of Health and Human Services, Office of Disease Prevention and Health Promotion. *Healthy People 2010.* About *Healthy People.* Available at: http://www.healthypeople.gov/. Accessed January 13. 2006.
33. US Department of Health and Human Services, Office of Public Health and Science. *Healthy People 2010 Objectives, Draft for Public Comment.* Washington, DC: US Government Printing Office; 1998.
34. Keppel KG, Percy JN, Klein RJ. Measuring progress in *Healthy People 2010.* In: *Statistical Notes* 25. Hyattsville, Ma: National Center for Health Statistics; 2004.
35. US Department of Health and Human Services. *Healthy People 2010* progress review, immunization and infectious diseases. Public Health Service, 2003. Available at: http://www.healthypeople.gov/data/2010prog/focus14/. Accessed January 13, 2006.
36. US Department of Health and Human Services. *Healthy People 2010.* Progress review, nutrition and overweight. Public Health Service, 2004. Available at: http://www.healthypeople.gov/Data/2010prog/focus19/default.htm. Accessed January 13, 2006.
37. US Department of Health and Human Services. *Healthy People 2010.* Progress review, public health infrastructure. Public Health Service, 2004. Available at: http://www.healthypeople.gov/Data/2010prog/focus23/. Accessed January 13. 2006.
38. Omenn G. What's behind those block grants in health? *N Engl J Med.* 1982;306(17):1057-1060.
39. Wall S. Transformations in public health systems. *Health Affair.* 1998; 17(3):64-80.
40. Lumpkin J. Impact of Medicaid resources on core public health responsibilities of local health departments in Illinois. *J Public Health Manage Pract.* 1998;4(6):69-78.
41. Baxter R. The roles and responsibilities of local public health systems in urban health. *J Urban Health.* 1998;75(2):322-329.
42. Fox D. Accretion, reform, and crisis: a theory of public health politics in New York City. *Yale J Biol Med.* 1991;64:55-466.
43. Turning Point. Mission statement. Available at: http://www.turningpoint program.org. Accessed January 13, 2006.
44. Patrick D, Wickizer T. Community and health. In: Amick B, Levine S, Tarlov A, et al., eds. *Society and Health.* New York, NY: Oxford Press; 1995:46-92.
45. Stoto M, Abel C, Dievler A, eds. *Healthy Communities: New Partnerships for the Future of Public Health.* Washington, DC: Institute of Medicine; 1996.
46. Baker E, Melton R, Stange P, et al. Health reform and the health of the public. *JAMA.* 1994;272(16):1276-1282.
47. Whitelaw N, Warden G, Wenzler M. Current efforts toward implementation of an urban health strategy: the Henry Ford Health System. *J Urban Health.* 1998;75(2):356-366.
48. The Henry Ford Health System. Facts and figures. Available at: http://www.henryfordhealth.org/body.cfm?id=38768. Accessed January 15, 2006.
49. Anderson R, Pickens S, Boumbulian P. Toward a new urban health model: moving beyond the safety net to save the safety net—resetting priorities for health communities. *J Urban Health.* 1998;75(2):367-378.
50. Parkland Health and Hospital System. Who we are. Available at: http://www.parklandhospital.com/index.html. Accessed January 14, 2006.
51. Reiser S. Medicine and public health. *JAMA. 1996;*276(17):1429-1430.

52. Fee E. The origins and development of public health in the US. In: Holland W, Detels R, Knox G, et al., eds. *Oxford Textbook of Public Health.* New York, NY: Oxford University Press; 1991:3–22.

53. Viseltear A. The ethos of public health. *J Public Health Policy.* 1990;11(2): 146–150.

54. Fee E. Public health and the state: the United States. *Clio Medica.* 1994; 26:224–275.

55. Lasker R. *Medicine & Public Health: The Power of Collaboration.* New York, NY: New York Academy of Medicine; 1997.

56. Duffy J. The American medical profession and public health: from support to ambivalence. *Bull Hist Med.* 1979;53:1–22.

57. Council on Scientific Affairs. The IOM report and public health. *JAMA.* 1990;264(4):508–509.

# CHAPTER 3

# ORGANIZATION OF THE PUBLIC HEALTH DELIVERY SYSTEM

Glen P. Mays

## Chapter Overview

A complex array of institutions supports the delivery of public health services in the United States. Both governmental and private organizations factor prominently in the nation's public health system, yet there is no definitive division of labor among the institutions that make up this system. This chapter examines the defining organizational and structural characteristics of the public health delivery system in the United States, with special emphasis given to the intergovernmental and interorganizational arrangements that support this system. Effective management of public health services in any setting requires a thorough understanding of these basic structural elements.

The practice of public health in the United States encompasses a broad and evolving scope of activities. In view of this broad scope, it is difficult to imagine a simple and static institutional structure to support these endeavors. The constellation of organizations involved in delivering public health services is complex and changing, and a clear division of labor among these organizations is not always apparent. Governmental agencies often play leading roles in the public health system, and their responsibilities flow in part from the federalist system of government that defines federal, state, and local governmental authority. Additionally, in many communities nongovernmental organizations contribute substantially to public health activities, including private physicians, hospitals, and other healthcare providers; professional and civic associations; educational institutions; philanthropic and charitable organizations; health insurers; and private businesses. In fact, many public health activities are implemented through the cooperative efforts of multiple organizations and maintained through an array of interorganizational and intergovernmental structures. The organizational landscape of public health activities varies widely across communities and is shaped by the confluence of public priorities and values, available health resources and financing mechanisms, specific political processes and interest groups, and unique historical and environmental conditions.

This chapter examines the defining organizational and structural characteristics of public health activities in the United States. We define a public health system as the constellation of organizations, both governmental and private, that contribute to the delivery of core public health services for a defined population. In some communities these systems are well defined and coordinated, but in other communities the systems are fragmented and diffuse. The effective management of public health programs, services, and organizations in any setting requires a thorough understanding of these systems and their structural characteristics.

## Governmental Public Health Organizations

Governmental responsibilities in public health evolve in response to public needs and demands as well as political will. Economic theory has long provided a rationale for decisions concerning the most appropriate governmental roles in public health service delivery. Those services that represent *public goods* or that generate positive *externalities* are likely to be underproduced by the private marketplace despite the fact that such services are beneficial to society at large. Governmental involvement in the provision of these types of services is therefore essential for social well-being.[1] Services are regarded as public goods when they benefit many people simultaneously because use by one individual does not diminish the ability of others to use the service. For example, public health services that promote clean air and water and safe food produce health benefits for large segments of the community, and it is difficult if not impossible to exclude individuals from benefiting from these services. Services are regarded as having positive externalities when they produce benefits that can be enjoyed even by those individuals not directly involved in producing or using the services. For example, community-wide vaccination programs reduce the transmission of preventable infectious diseases and thereby offer protection even to individuals who are not vaccinated.

The organization of governmental public health activities in the United States flows directly from the limited federalist system of government based on national, state, and local levels of authority. (Refer to Chapter 6 for more detailed discussion.) States occupy pivotal positions within this system because they maintain governmental authority that is not expressly reserved for the federal government through constitutional provisions and legislative power. States, in turn, choose whether to exercise this authority directly or delegate it to local governmental bodies in accordance with state constitutional and legislative provisions. In the domain of public health, the federal government exercises authority primarily through its constitutional powers to tax, spend, and regulate interstate commerce.[2] By comparison, state government agencies typically play even larger roles in public health regulatory activities while also carrying out substantial responsibilities in public health program administration and resource allocation. States often delegate to local governmental agencies the primary responsibilities for implementing public health programs within communities. States vary markedly in the scope of public health activities that they delegate to local governmental control, and both historical and contemporary trends in state–local political relationships contribute to this variation.[3,4] Specific organizational structures used to support public health activities at federal, state, and local levels are examined in the following sections.

## Federal Agencies Contributing to Public Health

Federal agencies are important actors in the public health arena because of their ability to formulate and implement a national health policy agenda and to allocate health resources across broad public priorities.[5] Both executive agencies and legislative institutions engage in federal health policy and resource allocation activities. As part of the policy development and administration process, many federal health agencies provide information and technical assistance to other organizations involved in public health activities, including state and local agencies as well as nongovernmental organizations.[6] In some cases, federal agencies also engage directly in implementing public health activities within specific communities or populations. Direct federal involvement in public health practice typically occurs only for narrowly defined public health activities such as the investigation and control of major health threats, the study of new public health interventions, or the response to major disasters and emergencies. A 1998 study of the nation's largest local public health jurisdictions found that federal agencies were directly involved in implementing public health activities in less than half of the jurisdictions examined.[7] In those jurisdictions having some direct federal involvement, federal agencies were involved in only 7% of the public health activities examined in the study. Federal agencies were most frequently involved in activities concerning adverse health events investigation, public health laboratory testing, and support and communications functions for public health interventions.

Federal agencies undertake public health activities using a variety of policy and administrative instruments. Agencies that are part of the executive branch of federal government use instruments that include regulatory development and enforcement, resource allocation, information production and dissemination, and policy advocacy and agenda setting. The specific set of policy instruments used by a given agency for a given public health issue depends on the authority granted to the agency by Congress, as well as the administrative and political environment in which the agency operates.

## Federal Policy and Administrative Instruments for Public Health

### Regulatory Development and Enforcement

Federal agencies receive their regulatory power either through congressional legislation or, less frequently, through presidential executive order. Often this authority involves a directive to establish the administrative procedures and infrastructure necessary to enforce a specific regulatory provision enacted by Congress. (Refer to Chapters 4 and 6 for more information.) For example, a federal law passed in 1996 charges the US Department of Health and Human Services (HHS) to enforce a regulatory provision requiring health insurers to provide women undergoing childbirth at least 48 hours of inpatient hospitalization coverage following a normal delivery. Alternatively, federal agencies may be empowered to develop standards and regulations within a broad domain of activity, subject to a public review and evaluation process. Many of the environmental health regulations enforced by the US Environmental Protection Agency (EPA), for example, are developed by the agency itself under broad regulatory authority established by federal laws such as the National Environmental Policy Act of 1969 and the Clean Water Act of 1977.

In the domain of public health, federal health agencies make relatively limited use of regulatory powers. The most active federal regulatory activities occur in the areas of food protection, drug and device development, occupational health and safety, and environmental health protection. For example, federal regulations concerning the manufacture, processing, and labeling of food products are carried out as consumer protection activities through agencies such as the US Food and Drug Administration (FDA) and the US Department of Agriculture (USDA). Similarly, federal regulations concerning the development, manufacture, distribution, and marketing of pharmaceutical products and medical devices are extensive, with the FDA requiring rigorous scientific proof of the safety and efficacy of these products in human populations before they are licensed for distribution in the United States. By comparison, the federal government historically has been reluctant to engage in regulatory activities in the field of medical practice and health care financing—preferring to delegate these tasks to state agencies and to the health professions themselves. Federal involvement in this area has increased in recent years as public concern has grown concerning the quality of medical care and health insurance under managed care plans.[8,9] Examples of recent federal regulatory activity include the minimum 48-hour hospital stay provision for childbirth, the requirement that health plans establish equal benefit levels for medical and mental health services (so-called mental health parity legislation of 1996), and the requirement that health plans offer renewable and portable individual health insurance to individuals who lose coverage from a group insurance plan (the Health Insurance Portability and Accountability Act of 1996).[10]

## Health Resource Allocation

Another powerful public health instrument wielded by federal agencies derives from the federal government's power to tax and to spend. Most federal public health programs are not carried out through direct provision of public health services, but rather through financial and technical support provided to state and local public health organizations. Federal agencies allocate financial resources to public health programs through two principal avenues: categorical grants-in-aid and block granting. *Categorical grant programs* are targeted at specific public health services and population groups; *block grants* allocate financial resources to broad domains of activity that are largely determined by the grant recipients. All block grants and many categorical grants are allocated exclusively to state governments, which are charged with disbursing funds appropriately to specific programs and providers. Some categorical grants to states formalize this process by including "pass-through" provisions that require states to allocate resources for specific purposes using a predetermined formula or other mechanism. Categorical grants allow federal agencies to exercise more control over how public health funds are spent than do block grants, which allow greater levels of state discretion in resource use.

*Categorical and Block Grant Programs.* Categorical grants are often criticized as a resource allocation vehicle for their tendency to encourage public health organizations to operate in accordance with federal funding streams rather than in accordance with public health needs and priorities in the populations served. (Refer to Chapter 7 for more detailed discussion on public health financing.) A public health agency might, for example, invest heavily in a cancer screening program in order to draw down federal grant funds, even though population health needs might indicate that priority should be given to maternal and child health (MCH) services. Block grants are often viewed as a strategy for preventing such perverse resource allocation decisions. Critics of block grant strategies argue, however, that these funding vehicles may allow important but low-visibility programs and health needs–including many public health services–to be deemphasized in times of financial crisis. Critics also maintain that block grants can be used to mask overall reductions in federal support for public health activities. Nevertheless, block grants remain important components of federal health financing and include the Preventive Health and Health Services Block Grant, the Maternal and Child Health Block Grant, the Community Mental Health Services Block Grant, and the Substance Abuse Prevention and Treatment Block Grant.

*Entitlement and Discretionary Programs.* Several of the largest federal categorical grant-in-aid programs in the domain of public health confer program benefits to broad classes of individuals and therefore constitute entitlement programs. Both of these programs–Medicaid and the State Children's Health Insurance Program (SCHIP)–provide funds to states for the purchase of healthcare services for low-income families and children. (Another federal entitlement program in health, the Medicare program, does not function through a grant-in-aid process at all but rather is administered directly at the federal level.) Most of the outlays for these programs fund the delivery of medical care, long-term care, and mental health services; nonetheless, these programs are important sources of financing for public health services. The Medicaid program, for example, finances the delivery of clinical preventive services, prenatal care, maternal support and case management services, communicable disease screening and treatment services, family planning services, childhood developmental screening services, and Medicaid outreach and enrollment services for low-income individuals eligible for the program. These programs function as entitlements because funds are allocated to states in amounts based on a proportion of the expenditures incurred by states in serving eligible recipients. Funding levels are therefore determined by program eligibility and utilization, rather than by explicit policy decisions concerning the allocation of federal resources to specific program areas.

Most other grant-in-aid programs that support public health activities are discretionary programs that operate through a fixed appropriation of federal revenue that is subject to periodic updates, adjustments, and revisions. Discretionary programs are generally much more sensitive to political bargaining and governmental financing obligations than are entitlement programs. As a result, many of these programs experience periodic fluctuations in funding levels and scope of authority as they come due for reauthorization and appropriation decisions in Congress. Prominent examples of federal discretionary programs in public health include the following:

- The *Preventive Health and Health Services Block Grant* supports programs in heart disease and stroke prevention, cancer early detection, nutrition, physical fitness, and other areas through grants to state health agencies from the US Centers for Disease Control and Prevention (CDC).
- The *Community Health Centers Program* and the *Migrant Health Centers Program* (Sections 330 and 329 of the Public Health Service Act), both categorical grant-in-aid programs, support comprehensive primary care centers operating in medically underserved areas through direct federal grants to health centers from the US Health Resources and Services Administration (HRSA).
- The *Maternal and Child Health Services Block Grant* supports an array of services involving family planning, maternity support, prenatal care, high-risk pregnancy support, well-child care, and developmental screening through grants to state health agencies from the HRSA.
- The *Special Supplemental Food Program for Women, Infants, and Children* (WIC) funds state health agencies to operate nutritional support programs for low-income pregnant women and children, administered by the USDA.

*Matching Requirements.* Many federal grant-in-aid programs include a requirement that grantees contribute a specified amount of nonfederal funds in order to secure federal funding under the program. Matching requirements allow federal agencies to leverage their limited federal funds in order to secure larger investments of public funds in priority areas. Matching requirements also allow federal agencies and their grantees to share the financial risks associated with investments in public programs—an arrangement that potentially creates additional incentives for the grantee to achieve desirable program performance. Both the Medicaid and the SCHIP entitlement programs include a federal matching component that requires the state grantees to contribute a specified amount of state funds in order to secure federal funds through the program. In Medicaid, the proportion of funds that derive from the federal government varies across states from a minimum of 50% to a maximum of 77% because the state matching requirement is determined by a formula that compares each state's per capita personal income level with the nation's per capita income level. A similar formula is used to determine the state matching requirement under the SCHIP program.

*Competitive and Performance-Based Allocation.* Increasingly, federal agencies are adopting competitive systems for allocating resources to public health activities, including performance-based funding strategies. In one example of this approach, research and demonstration grants are used by federal agencies to develop and test innovative models for public health service delivery that may eventually be suitable for widespread dissemination and use. (Refer to Chapter 17 for further discussion on performance management.) Under these types of grants, federal agencies solicit competitive proposals from prospective grantees and select those proposals that hold the greatest potential for success while also meeting budgetary and programmatic requirements. If successful program models are identified through the initial set of funded projects, federal agencies may allocate resources to additional grantees for replication and expansion of successful program features.

A good example of this resource allocation approach can be found in the Healthy Start Initiative administered by the Bureau of Maternal and Child Health Services within the HRSA. Through a competitive proposal process, the HRSA initially funded 15 community-based projects designed to reduce infant mortality and improve MCH outcomes in communities with high rates of infant mortality and morbidity. All of the selected programs were required to include certain common features such as maternity support and case management services, but all were also allowed to implement additional features based on local needs and capacities. After an initial 3-year demonstration period, the HRSA has begun to support dissemination and expansion programs that are designed to replicate successful program features in other communities. Many other federal agencies that support public health programs also include competitive features as part of their resource allocation processes.

More recently, many federal agencies have moved to adopt performance-based resource allocation systems for public health programs. Under the Government Performance and Results Act of 1993 (GPRA), federal agencies are now required to routinely measure the performance and outcomes of the programs they administer and to demonstrate accountability for the federal funds they use to support these programs. In response to these requirements, federal funds for public health programs are increasingly allocated on the basis of objective performance measures rather than simply on the basis of need or program potential. For example, states that receive funds under the Maternal and Child Health Services Block Grant now report performance measures that document the effects of programs supported under the previous cycle of awards.[11] As part of this initiative, a special panel commissioned by the HHS recently identified performance measures that are appropriate for key public health, mental health, and substance abuse services.[12] This initiative places additional emphasis on the ability of state health agencies to measure public health performance at state and local levels and to demonstrate accountability for federal funds. In a similar vein, the federal Medicare program that provides health care for the elderly and disabled populations has begun to experiment with pay-for-performance (P4P) programs that base payments to hospitals and physicians on objective measures of quality of care.

*Taxation Authority.*    The federal government's power to tax not only generates the revenue to fund federal public health programs, but it also provides an instrument for influencing the health-related activities of individuals and corporations. Tax policy can be used to discourage unhealthy activities by raising the effective "price" of engaging in these activities, such as through federal taxes on tobacco, firearms, and products that degrade air and water quality. Similarly, tax policy can be used to encourage beneficial activities such as tax exemptions for employers that provide workers with subsidized health insurance. State and local governments similarly can use their taxation powers to encourage or discourage health-related activities in the private sector, such as exemptions for housing developers that build sidewalks and designate land for recreational use.

*Information Production and Dissemination*

A third type of policy instrument used by federal agencies involves the production and dissemination of information. In the domain of public health, this information is often produced through federally financed research efforts, surveillance systems, and policy studies. All of the major federal health agencies maintain units devoted to research activities, but the dominant federal agencies for health-related research include the National Institutes of Health (NIH), the Agency for Health Care Research and Quality (AHRQ), and the CDC. Agencies carry out data collection and research efforts both through internal activities and through extramural relationships with universities, professional associations, and contract research organizations. The public health impact of these federal research activities is substantial. For example, biomedical research supported by the NIH leads to the development of new clinical technologies and practices that can be used for health promotion and disease prevention. Genetic information produced through the NIH's Human Genome Project, for example, is fueling the development of new screening and early detection technologies for chronic diseases having an identifiable genetic basis, such as breast cancer. Likewise, health services research supported through the AHRQ and the CDC produces information about effective strategies for encouraging physicians to deliver clinical preventive services and for encouraging healthcare consumers to comply with screening recommendations. Other federal research efforts produce valuable information regarding the cost-effectiveness of public health interventions in areas such as nutrition, physical activity, and environmental conditions. (Chapters 11, 13 and 14 discuss data, health information systems, and surveillance in greater detail.)

The public health impact of federal activities in health information production often hinges on the effectiveness of federal efforts to disseminate this information appropriately. Federal agencies pursue an array of dissemination strategies that includes making data resources available to outside organizations for further analysis and application as well as informing health professionals and consumers about the implications of new research findings. This first approach is actively used by the CDC, because many state and local public health organizations use data from federal birth, mortality, health risk factor, and infectious disease surveillance systems to identify public health needs and evaluate the impact of public health interventions at state and community levels. Similarly, many health researchers and policy analysts make use of data from the CDC's numerous national health surveys for scientific investigations of health status, health behavior, and healthcare delivery.

Several federal health agencies also actively engage in educating relevant organizations and individuals about the public health implications of new health information. In some cases, this approach serves as an alternative to the use of regulatory power by federal agencies. Agencies use the quality of the available information, together with the visibility and authority of their federal office, to educate and influence behavior. The EPA, for example, maintains an array of "industry partnerships" through which it encourages voluntary compliance with strategies to reduce the production and release of harmful pollutants. Similarly, the CDC supports several initiatives to encourage public health agencies, physicians, and other health professionals to voluntarily comply with evidence-based guidelines for delivering community-based preventive services. In some cases, it may be the implicit threat of federal regulation or resource reallocation, rather than the influential power of information and education, that encourages voluntary compliance with such strategies. Nevertheless, federal agencies often are able to use the visibility and authority of their offices to draw public attention to important public health issues, to convene important public health stakeholders around such issues, and to lend credibility to new public health information.

### Policy Advocacy and Agenda Setting

A final policy instrument used by federal health agencies in the public health arena involves policy advocacy and agenda setting in the legislative process. The US Constitution's separation of powers doctrine ensures that agencies in the executive branch of the federal government have no formal legislative authority. Nonetheless, these agencies often play important roles in placing public health issues on Congress' legislative agenda and in garnering support for public health legislative proposals at the federal level.[13] These roles are perhaps carried out most frequently by informing members of Congress and their staff about important public health issues using tools such as legislative briefings, testimony, and conferences. Additionally, federal health agencies often carry out more direct roles in agenda setting by participating in the design of model legislation and by recruiting legislators to sponsor these proposals. Finally, federal health agencies may play roles in garnering legislative support (or opposition) for proposals under consideration in Congress through informal lobbying efforts and direct appeals to professional associations, political interest groups, and members of the public. Through these types of activities, federal health agencies can exert a strong voice in legislative decisions that have implications for public health activities—including resource allocation issues as well as regulatory issues.

The US Congress also has its own internal structures for acquiring information about public health programs, policies, and resource needs. These federal legislative agencies play important roles in public health policy development and implementation at the federal level. The US Government Accountability Office (GAO) is known as the investigative arm of Congress, and it conducts policy analysis, program evaluation, and financial auditing activities for all federal agencies and federally funded programs. Most often, these activities are initiated in response to requests from specific congressional bodies or members of Congress. A division within the GAO specializes in federal public health and healthcare programs and generates periodic reports and congressional testimony on major public health programs. As a source of policy information and evaluation, the GAO plays a critical role in the policy development process and can have an important impact on public health policy decisions. For example, during the 1990s, a series of GAO evaluations of the federal vaccine purchasing program Vaccines for Children led many members of Congress to consider reforms in this program.[14] More recently, an unflattering GAO analysis of federal lead poisoning prevention programs has led legislators to consider policy changes.[15] Other federal legislative agencies that perform important functions in the policy development process include the Congressional Budget Office, which examines the effects of current and proposed policies on federal spending, and the Congressional Research Service, which produces summaries and policy briefs on a wide range of policy issues of interest to Congress.

### Overview of Federal Agencies with Public Health Responsibilities

Many of the federal agencies that contribute to public health activities are organized within the HHS (Figure 3-1). This cabinet-level department in the executive branch of federal government administers programs involving public health services, medical care financing and delivery, mental health and substance abuse services, and social services, including income support and child welfare programs. Several of these agencies within HHS that perform core public health activities are described in the following sections.

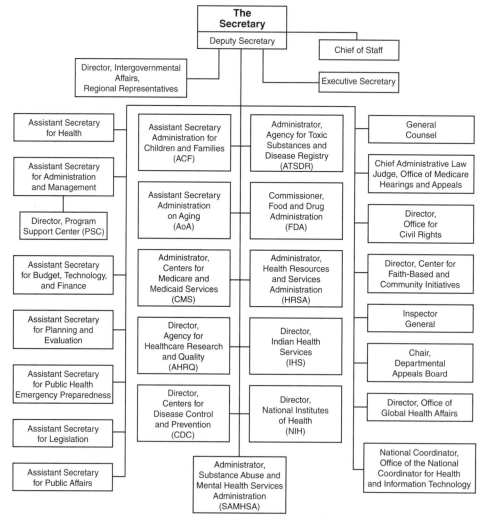

**FIGURE 3-1    Organization of the US Department of Health and Human Services**
*Source:* Reprinted from the Department of Health and Human Services.

*The CDC*

As the federal government's lead public health agency, the CDC administers a range of programs designed to prevent and control specific disease, injury, and disability risks on a national level through epidemiologic surveillance and investigation, research, and program development and dissemination activities. The CDC carries out this mission through a staff of more than 7500 and an annual budget that totals $8.5 billion (FY 2006). The CDC maintains a strong intramural research program that uses state-of-the-art laboratory and field resources to examine disease risks, transmission routes, and intervention strategies for a wide range of public health threats. Additionally, the CDC maintains an extensive extramural research program that uses a broad network of university-based research centers for the scientific investigation of public health risks and opportunities for prevention and control.

Historically, the CDC's research and development initiatives have emphasized laboratory and epidemiologic methods for investigating disease transmission, control, and prevention mechanisms. In recent decades, the CDC's scientific agenda in public health has grown to include an expanded emphasis on the behavioral and social sciences in studying public health issues such as the adoption and diffusion of prevention practices among healthcare providers and populations at risk, the cost-effectiveness of community-level interventions such as health education campaigns, and the adequacy of state and local public health infrastructure. As evidence of this new emphasis, the CDC reorganized its major programs and activities in 2005 under seven broad organizational units designed to address cross-cutting issues in public health research and practice including four coordinating centers, two coordinating offices, and the National Institute for Occupational Safety and Health (NIOSH). The new coordinating centers include an organizational unit for environmental health and injury prevention, health information and services, health promotion, and infectious diseases. Within these coordinating centers, the CDC maintains individual centers and institutes that are organized around specific disease processes and intervention opportunities (Figure 3-2.) These centers include the following[16]:

- The *National Center for Injury Prevention and Control* designs and fields research and intervention programs that focus on the prevention of both unintentional and intentional injuries occurring outside the workplace.
- The *National Center for Environmental Health/Agency for Toxic Substances and Disease Registry* fields research and intervention efforts designed to forestall illness, disability, and death due to human interaction with harmful environmental substances such as indoor and outdoor air pollutants, hazardous wastes, waterborne pathogens and pollutants, food-borne pathogens, and lead exposure.
- The *National Center for Health Statistics* functions as the nation's public health data repository by fielding national surveys of health status, health behavior, and healthcare practices and by maintaining vital and health statistics databases. Among the periodic national surveys and surveillance systems fielded by the center are the National Health Care Survey, the National Immunization Survey, the National Health Interview Survey, and the National Health and Nutrition Examination Survey. The center also maintains efforts for tracking national statistics on prenatal care, births, and deaths through the National Vital Statistics System.

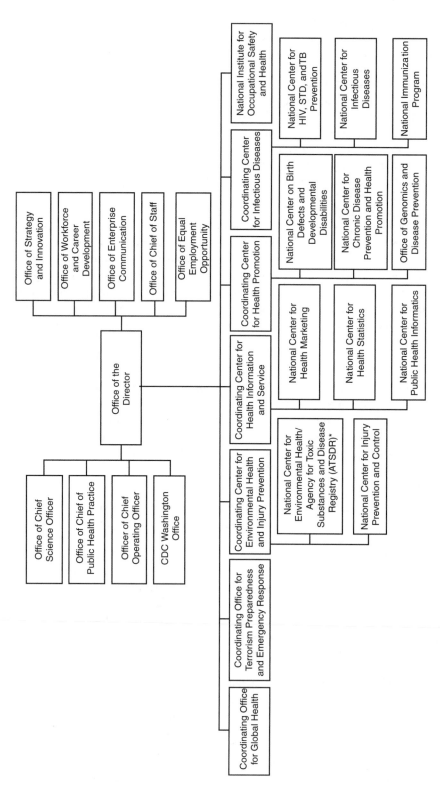

**FIGURE 3-2    Organization of the US Centers for Disease Control and Prevention (CDC)**

*Note:* *ATSDR is a division of operations within DHHS but is managed by a common office of the Director with NCEH.

*Source:* Reprinted from Centers for Disease Control and Prevention, Department of Health and Human Services.

- The *National Center for Public Health Informatics* functions as a resource for the interface between public health and information technology.
- The *National Center for Health Marketing* provides national leadership in the health marketing science and in its application to impact public health.
- The *National Center for Chronic Disease Prevention and Health Promotion* fields research and development activities involving chronic disease prevention and early intervention for health issues such as cancer, cardiovascular disease, diabetes, arthritis, and the special health concerns of maternal, infant, and adolescent populations. Among other activities, this center fields the Behavioral Risk Factor Surveillance System, which collects periodic national and state-level data on adult health risk factors.
- The *National Center on Birth Defects and Developmental Disabilities* provides national leadership for preventing birth defects and developmental disabilities and for improving the health and wellness of people with disabilities.
- The *Office of Genomics and Disease Prevention* provides national leadership in fostering understanding of human genomic discoveries and how they can be used to improve health and prevent disease.
- The *National Center for HIV, STD, and TB Prevention* administers surveillance and disease prevention and control programs that target the transmission of the serious and often interrelated communicable diseases of human immunodeficiency virus (HIV), other sexually transmitted diseases (STDs), and tuberculosis (TB).
- The *National Center for Infectious Diseases* sponsors research and program development activities designed to prevent and control a wide array of existing, emerging, and resurgent infectious diseases— including those that pose unique health threats due to drug resistance or intentional transmission through bioterrorist acts.
- The *National Immunization Program* oversees national and state-based efforts to expand age-appropriate vaccination coverage rates for children, adolescents, and adults. This agency has been heavily involved in the development of immunization registries and tracking systems at the provider level, the community level, and the state level.

The two coordinating offices include the Coordinating Office for Global Health which addresses and supports the role of the CDC in global health activities as well as the Coordinating Office for Terrorism Preparedness and Emergency Response, which provides the strategic direction for the CDC's role in this area. Finally, NIOSH supports scientific investigations of workplace health threats and designs prevention and control programs to improve safety and wellness and reduce health risks within occupational settings.[16]

Among all of the federal health agencies, the CDC is the most heavily invested in intergovernmental relationships with state and local public health organizations. Many of the CDC's initiatives in disease surveillance and control depend on activities carried out by state public health agencies and their affiliated local health departments. For example, the National Notifiable Diseases Surveillance System and the Behavioral Risk Factor Surveillance System depend on data that are collected and reported by state agencies (as well as local agencies in the former case). Likewise, state and local agencies frequently depend on the specialized expertise and technology maintained at the CDC for activities such as laboratory analysis of newly detected unknown pathogens and control of particularly potent infectious disease outbreaks. (Refer to Chapter 14 for more information about surveillance.) To address these mutual dependencies, the CDC maintains a series of efforts to equip state and local public health workforces with the necessary expertise and technology to carry out public health activities of national importance. For example, the CDC assigns trained staff to work in each of the nation's state public health agencies, as well as many local health departments, carrying out disease surveillance and control activities as well as special research and demonstration initiatives. Perhaps the oldest and largest of these initiatives, the CDC's Epidemiologic Intelligence Service (EIS), has placed health professionals in state health departments around the nation since 1951 to carry out 2-year fellowships devoted to epidemiologic investigation. The CDC also maintains a number of workforce development initiatives that range from training and continuing education programs to staff exchange programs—all designed to strengthen state and local public health agency capacities for implementing core public health activities.

Finally, the CDC routinely develops cooperative agreements with state and local agencies as well as professional associations for the development of specific programs and tools to enhance public health capacity. For example, the CDC has worked collaboratively with the National Association for County and City Health Officials (NACCHO), the Association of State and Territorial Health Officials (ASTHO), and other professional associations for more than a decade in developing self-assessment tools for local and state public health organizations, including the widely used *National Public Health Performance Standards Program*.

### Other Agencies of the US Department of Health and Human Services

The CDC effectively functions as the federal government's lead agency for both scientific and practice-based public health activities. Nevertheless, a number of other federal agencies within the HHS carry out critical public health functions that largely complement those of the CDC. These agencies are discussed in the following sections.

*Health Resources and Services Administration (HRSA).*  The HRSA administers $6.3 billion in federal programs designed to expand public access to health care professionals and facilities, particularly in underserved areas. The Maternal and Child Health Bureau within the HRSA administers an array of services and programs designed to increase the timely delivery and uptake of prenatal, infant, and child health services in order to ensure the health of children and their families. The bureau administers grants to states through the Maternal and Child Health Services Block Grant, which supports programs designed to reduce infant mortality, provide comprehensive care for women before, during, and after pregnancy and childbirth, reduce adolescent pregnancy, improve childhood vaccination coverage, and meet the nutritional and developmental needs of children and their families. The bureau also administers categorical grant programs that support the provision of emergency medical services for children and the delivery of abstinence education services to children and adolescents.

*Bureau of Primary Health Care.*   The Bureau of Primary Health Care within the HRSA provides funding and technical assistance to agencies that provide comprehensive primary care services in medically underserved areas, including local health departments as well as nonprofit community health centers. The HRSA's Bureau of Health Professions maintains programs for monitoring and improving the accessibility of health professionals within the United States, including the National Health Services Corps, which sponsors professionals to practice in medically underserved communities. Other initiatives sponsored by this bureau are designed to address training needs and potential workforce shortages and surpluses of health professionals in various fields of specialization and practice settings. A Bureau of HIV/AIDS Services administers funding and technical assistance to programs that provide primary medical care and support services to individuals with HIV and AIDS, and to programs that conduct clinical research on HIV services. Finally, a special programs division within the HRSA manages a variety of health resource programs that include: (1) the Hill-Burton program to ensure that health facilities funded through the federal Hill-Burton Act meet their obligations to provide adequate levels of free and reduced-fee care to low-income populations and (2) the federal Organ Procurement and Transplantation Network that coordinates organ and tissue donation activities.

*National Institutes of Health (NIH).*   The nation's leading agency for funding and administering health research and demonstration initiatives is the NIH. The institutes that compose the NIH conduct intramural as well as extramural research activities in areas of public health importance. The NIH contributes to local public health practice by leading investigations of public health threats, conducting demonstrations of public health interventions, and supporting the public health research interests of local health departments and other community organizations. Consisting of 25 separate research institutes and centers, the NIH is the lead federal agency for biomedical research, and therefore emphasizes both laboratory research and, to a lesser but growing extent, clinical and behavioral research. Medical schools and academic health centers across the country depend on the NIH for most of their research funding because the NIH operates with a total budget of $28.6 billion (FY 2006). One of the single largest NIH research efforts, the Biodefense initiative, focuses on developing effective countermeasures to bioterrorism agents such as anthrax, smallpox, and plague. Additionally, the NIH continues to support genomics research involving human DNA—an initiative that could have profound public health applications through disease prevention and early detection strategies. Other NIH units with a particular public health focus include the National Cancer Institute; the National Institute of Allergy and Infectious Diseases; the National Institute of Child Health and Human Development; the National Heart, Lung, and Blood Institute; and the National Institute of Environmental Health Sciences.

*Agency for Healthcare Research and Quality (AHRQ).*   The Agency for Healthcare Research and Quality (AHRQ) administers a much smaller research enterprise by comparison to the NIH. The agency's sponsored research generally focuses on the organization, delivery, and financing of health services—which includes prevention and public health services but often emphasizes medical care services. Issues of health care quality and accessibility are additional research areas with particular relevance to public health activities. The agency is especially active in the development of clinical practice guidelines and strategies for evidence-based clinical practice grounded in sound scientific research. Through its information dissemination activities, the agency maintains strong relationships with major health profession organizations and health care financing organizations.

*Food and Drug Administration (FDA).*   The FDA functions as the nation's largest consumer protection agency by administering regulatory programs to ensure the safety of food, cosmetics, medicines, medical devices, and radiation-emitting products. Veterinary food and medications also fall under the regulatory purview of the FDA. As specified in the Food, Drug, and Cosmetics Act of 1962 and the FDA Modernization Act of 1997, the FDA's responsibility in drug and device regulation involves ensuring the safety as well as the efficacy of these products. For all of the products monitored by the FDA, the agency ensures accurate labeling, marketing, and consumer information. In carrying out these activities, the FDA inspects food and drug manufacturing facilities, tests products, reviews scientific evidence in support of safety and efficacy claims, and monitors labeling and marketing practices. The FDA enforces its regulatory authority through both governmental influence and legal sanction. The agency frequently encourages manufacturers of products to undertake voluntary corrections or institute voluntary product recalls when problems are identified. When necessary, the agency can obtain court orders to prohibit the manufacture and sale of products or to seize and destroy existing products. The agency can also pursue criminal penalties against manufacturers and distributors.

*Indian Health Service.*   The Indian Health Service administers programs that provide health services to federally recognized American Indian and Alaska Native tribes. This Public Health Service agency provides health services directly and by contract with tribal organizations. Federally operated facilities consist of 37 hospitals, 64 health centers, 50 health stations, and five school-based health clinics. The health organizations supported through Indian Health Service funds provide both medical and public health services to native populations.

*Substance Abuse and Mental Health Services Administration.*   The Substance Abuse and Mental Health Services Administration administers programs for the prevention, treatment, and rehabilitation of substance abuse and mental illness. The agency manages two large federal block grant programs that provide states with funds to implement an array of prevention and treatment programs: the Mental Health Services Block Grant and the Substance Abuse Prevention and Treatment Block Grant. The agency also maintains an extensive surveillance and research portfolio concerning the quality, cost, accessibility, and outcomes of mental health and substance abuse services for prevention, treatment, and rehabilitation. Finally, the agency is actively involved in providing technical assistance and consultation to mental health and substance abuse service providers.

Several other agencies within the HHS play important roles in public health activities although their primary area of operation lies outside the functional domain of public health. Prime among these agencies is the Centers for Medicare and Medicaid Services (CMS), which administers medical care financing programs that include the Medicare program for disabled and elderly individuals, and the Medicaid and SCHIP programs for low-income families and children. As discussed previously, these programs are important financing systems not only for medical care, but also for public health services needed by vulnerable and underserved populations. CMS exercises only partial control over the design and operation of these programs because individual states have flexibility to modify eligibility standards, program benefits, and delivery and payment mechanisms under these programs. Moreover, many states have secured federal waivers in order to institute Medicaid managed care programs that deviate from federal program requirements—such as those programs that restrict a beneficiary's freedom of choice in provider selection.

Because it controls a substantial proportion of the nation's healthcare financing resources, CMS often uses its influence and its purchasing power to effect changes in clinical and administrative practice across the entire US health system. For example, CMS increasingly is using its payment policies to create incentives for hospitals, physicians, managed care plans, and other organizations to engage in quality measurement and reporting activities designed to improve adherence to evidence-based standards of healthcare delivery. CMA also requires healthcare facilities that participate in the Medicare and Medicaid programs to undergo periodic accreditation processes and inspections in order to ensure quality of care in these facilities. These activities are likely to affect the quality of care not just for beneficiaries of federal health programs, but also for the millions of other healthcare consumers who are served by these providers.

Other agencies within the HHS that contribute to public health activities include the Administration on Aging, which administers social and health services programs for older Americans, and the Administration for Children and Families, which operates programs for the social and economic support of children and families. The Administration on Aging's programs that are relevant to public health include those that address the health information and health education needs of the elderly; the nutritional, social support, and long-term care needs of the elderly; the health and social support needs of formal and informal caregivers for the elderly; and the safety, injury prevention, and violence prevention needs of the elderly. By comparison, the Administration for Children and Families' programs that are relevant to public health include the federal Head Start program that provides early educational opportunities and nutritional support to young impoverished children; the Family and Youth Services program that, among other activities, provides health education and counseling services to homeless and runaway youth; programs to prevent and treat sexual abuse among children; and programs that provide health and support services to children and adults with developmental disabilities and mental retardation.

Finally, the HHS maintains several offices at the departmental level that are designed to coordinate public health activities across the major agencies and units within the department. These offices help the department as a whole to realize opportunities for cross-agency collaboration in addressing major public health issues that span multiple areas of operation and expertise. These offices also help the department to achieve a unified voice in communicating public health issues to the public and other major constituencies in health. The Office of the Surgeon General, perhaps the most widely known departmental office, serves as the nation's leading spokesperson for public health issues. The surgeon general also oversees the Commissioned Corps of the US Public Health Service, a collection of more than 6000 federal health professionals who provide first-response intervention in the event of national public health emergencies. The Office of Disease Prevention and Health Promotion works to coordinate federal preventive health programs across the department, including the effort to develop and monitor national health promotion and disease prevention objectives for the nation through the *Healthy People 2010* programs.[17,18] The Office of Emergency Preparedness coordinates health-related disaster preparedness and response activities for the department, and the Office of International and Refugee Health serves as the department's coordinating agency for global health initiatives. Several other department-level offices develop policy, public awareness strategies, and research initiatives for major national health priorities, including the Office of HIV/AIDS Policy, the Office of Minority Health, the Office on Women's Health, the Office of Family Planning, the Office of Adolescent Pregnancy Programs, and the President's Council on Physical Fitness and Sports.

### Other Federal Agencies with Public Health Responsibilities

A number of other federal agencies are not a part of the HHS but nonetheless contribute to public health activities on a national level. These agencies include the following:

- The *Department of Agriculture* sponsors an array of health-related programs involving nutritional support, migrant health, food safety, and the prevention of occupational exposure to pesticides. Among the best-known public health programs administered by this department is WIC.
- The *EPA* develops and enforces a wide array of environmental health and safety programs.
- The *Department of Housing and Urban Development* administers programs to address the health and social problems of populations residing in public housing facilities, homeless shelters, and economically disadvantaged communities.
- The *Department of Education* maintains programs to address the health education and health services needs of students.
- The *Department of Labor* administers programs to promote health and safety in the workplace.

These agencies make important contributions to public health activities through programs and services they administer independently and in cooperation with other federal agencies.

### Federal Oversight, Governance, and Advisory Organizations

To understand the organization and operation of federal agencies in the domain of public health, it is necessary to examine the intricate systems for governance, oversight, and advice under which these agencies function. These oversight systems help to shape the policy and programmatic agendas of federal agencies while also ensuring that the agencies remain accountable to the executive and legislative branches of federal government and responsive to the needs of constituents and the public at large. Among agencies organized within the HHS, all programs and services fall under the jurisdiction of the Office of the Inspector General (OIG) for investigations of potential fraud and abuse cases. Recent enforcement efforts of the OIG in the Medicare and Medicaid programs have resulted in substantial resource recoveries and several cases of criminal prosecution for inappropriate billing practices among providers. The OIG also reviews for inappropriate and inadequate financial management practices among state agencies and other recipients of federal public health and health services grant funds.

Programs and services maintained by the HHS agencies also fall under the purview of the Office of Civil Rights for ensuring equal access to programs and services for all eligible population groups. In recent cases, this office's review and inspection authority has extended to the domain of patient enrollment and provider contracting with managed care plans that participate in the Medicare and Medicaid programs. This office is also involved in ensuring that health facilities funded under the federal Hill-Burton Act provide adequate access to free and reduced-fee health services for uninsured and underinsured individuals and families. Agencies outside the DHHS are not subject to these specific oversight mechanisms, but many of these agencies fall under similar review processes maintained by other cabinet-level executive departments.

All agencies in the executive branch of federal government are subject to the oversight responsibilities of the president. The Office of Management and Budget serves as the president's lead agency for overseeing the programs and activities of the executive branch and for evaluating the effectiveness of agency programs, policies, and administrative procedures. This office is also the lead agency for making funding allocation decisions within the executive branch and for preparing the president's federal budget requests to Congress. In reviewing agency programs and operations, a key area of interest for this office lies in the reduction of unnecessary burdens placed on members of the public. All federal public health research studies and surveillance systems involving human subjects therefore come under the scrutiny of this office, including a review of data collection instruments. The Office of Management and Budget is also the lead agency for the administration of the Government Performance and Results Act of 1993. In compliance with this program, all federal agencies must submit periodic performance plans, program performance measures, and progress reports to demonstrate the effectiveness and efficiency of federal programs and services. This office reviews performance measures, approves performance plans, and assists federal agencies in identifying strategies for performance improvement. In addition to the oversight provided in the executive branch, federal public health agencies are also subject to legislative oversight carried out by the GAO. This office, which has already been described, carries out a broad set of activities in performance measurement, policy analysis, and financial auditing at the behest of Congress.

Federal agencies also make use of a wide array of external advisory committees to help shape their programs and policies in public health as well as in other spheres of activity. Scientific advisory committees consisting of leading researchers and scholars are maintained by agencies such as the NIH, the AHRQ, and the CDC, and carry out a broad mission in public health research and surveillance. Similarly, scientific review committees are assembled by these agencies to review and evaluate specific proposals for research funding.

Review committees are often empowered to go beyond simple advisory activities and play a substantial role in making decisions concerning awards of funding.

Advisory committees made up of healthcare industry representatives and healthcare consumer groups are often empanelled to oversee the regulatory and rule-making activities carried out by federal health agencies. Appointments to these committees are most commonly made by senior officials within the agencies themselves. Although often invisible to external observers, these types of committees can have substantial influence over the organization and operation of federal agencies. These committees may function as catalysts for interorganizational coordination and collaboration because federal agencies often appoint representatives from organizations that currently or potentially act in partnership with the agencies. Advisory committees may also reflect political relationships within the executive branch or between the executive and legislative branches of federal government. For these reasons, knowledge concerning the structure and composition of external governance and advisory committees may be relevant for understanding the roles that federal health agencies play in public health activities.

One final advisory body that provides important assistance in formulating and evaluating federal public health policy is the Institute of Medicine (IOM) within the National Academy of Sciences. Congress established the National Academy of Sciences in 1863 to serve as an external source of research, investigation, and advice for any federal agency requesting assistance. The IOM, which joined the National Academy of Sciences in 1970, conducts health policy studies and reviews on a wide variety of topics in response to federal government requests and in pursuit of information needs identified by the institute's own members. The institute is an independent nonprofit organization that empanels committees of the nation's top scholars and practitioners to study health policy issues and to report findings and recommendations to policy makers, health professionals, and the public at large. The institute has produced many influential studies of public health issues on topics such as emerging infectious diseases, vaccine safety, bioterrorism, medical care quality assurance, community health assessment, and public health performance measurement. The institute's landmark reports on the US public health system—including the original 1988 report on *The Future of Public Health* and its follow-up reports in 1996 and 2003—sparked nationwide efforts to measure, reorganize, and improve the practice of public health not only within federal agencies, but also at state and local levels.[19] The work that Congress and numerous federal agencies perform in the domain of public health is aided immeasurably by the independent analysis and expertise contributed by the IOM.

## State Agencies Contributing to Public Health

Whereas federal roles in public health consist primarily of national policy development and resource allocation activities, state public health agencies are responsible for administering specific public health programs and services on a statewide basis. Part of this responsibility requires agencies to carry out the regulatory and policy objectives outlined in federal public health policies, and part of this responsibility requires the development and implementation of new policies and programs tailored to the specific health needs, resources, and priorities within the state governments. State public health agencies are operational in all 50 states, the District of Columbia, and eight US territories. Federal agencies and the programs they administer have a substantial influence on the structure and function of state health agencies; nonetheless, state agencies exhibit marked diversity in their organization and operation due to the historical and contemporary effects of state-specific political, economic, social, and environmental forces. Understanding this variation is requisite for understanding the larger architecture of public health practice in the United States because state agencies play a pivotal role in shaping the public health activities of local health departments as well as nongovernmental organizations.

## State Health Agencies

The organization of state public health agencies generally follows one of two basic models: a *free-standing agency structure* headed by an administrator who reports directly to the state's governor, or an organizational unit within a larger *superagency structure* that includes other functions such as medical care and social services programs.[20] Approximately half of the states in the United States employ the free-standing agency model for their public health agency, in which the state agency is a cabinet-level unit within the executive branch of state government.[21] For example, the state of Washington employs the free-standing structural model for its public health agency (Figure 3-3). This agency contains administrative units for core public health functions such as epidemiology, health facilities licensing, infectious disease control, MCH services, preventive health care, and environmental health programs. This agency is distinct, however, from the state departments that administer medical assistance (Medicaid) and social services programs.

In the remaining one third of states, the health agency is organized within a superagency structure that also includes agencies that administer medical assistance, social services, and sometimes environmental programs.[22] In these states, the public health agency does not occupy a cabinet-level position within the executive branch of government, but rather the superagency provides cabinet-level representation for public health issues along with other issues within its purview. An example of this organizational model is found in North Carolina's Department of Health and Human Services (Figure 3-4). In addition to its public health division, this agency contains administrative divisions for aging services, blind and disabled services, medical assistance (Medicaid), mental health and substance abuse services, and other social services. A cabinet-level secretary of health administers the entire department, and the state's public health director reports directly to the secretary. These two alternative models of state health agency organization offer clear trade-offs in terms of institutional complexity, governmental authority and power, and visibility within the state government bureaucracy.

Regardless of the organizational model used, most states do not consolidate all public health responsibilities within a single governmental agency. Rather, these functions are typically distributed across an array of separate departments and agencies. For example, state health agencies functioned as the lead environmental agency in only 7 states of 47 state health agencies that responded to a survey in 2001—down from 15 states a decade earlier.[20-22]

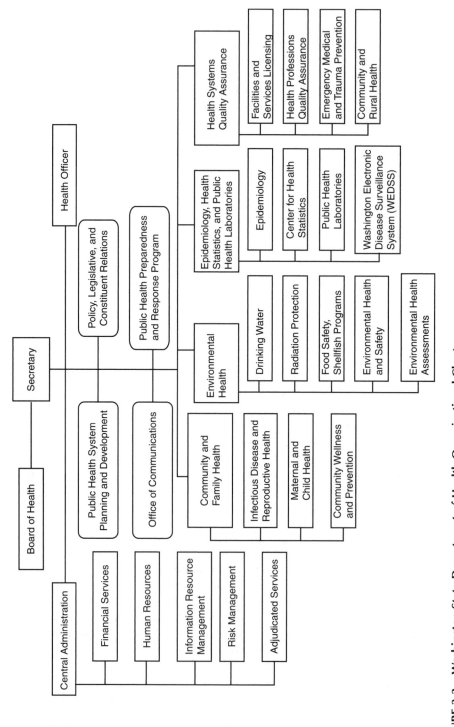

**FIGURE 3-3    Washington State Department of Health Organizational Chart**
*Source:* Reprinted from Washington State Department of Health.

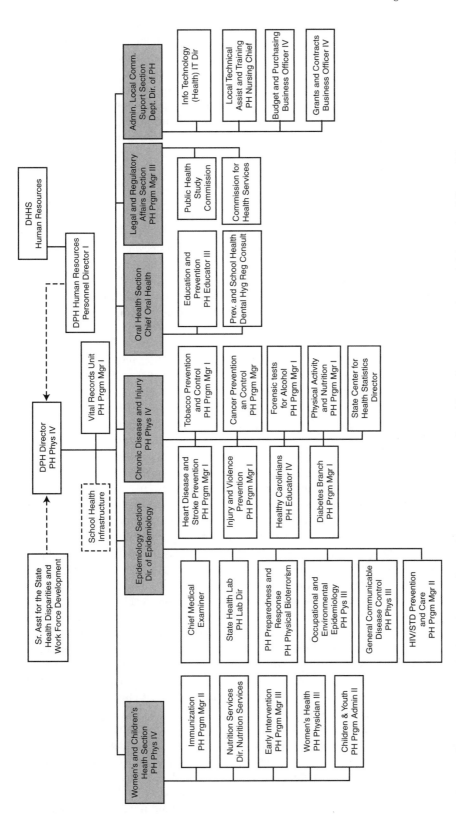

**FIGURE 3-4    Organizational Chart for North Carolina's Department of Health and Human Services Division of Public Health**
*Source:* Reprinted from North Carolina Department of Health and Human Services.

In most of the remaining states, a separate environmental agency carries out this authority, often in coordination with the state public health agency. State public health agencies serve as the designated state Medicaid agency in only 7 states, and as the state mental health authority in only 9 states. Most state health agencies are empowered with the authority for health professions and health facilities licensing and for maintaining programs for children with special health care needs. States that distribute public health functions across multiple governmental agencies often rely on interagency mechanisms to achieve coordination among health-related activities that cannot be consolidated within a single agency's authority.[23]

Consensus has yet to be reached concerning the optimal organizational structure for a state health agency, as states aggregate and disaggregate their state health agencies continually—usually in response to leadership changes at the governor or cabinet levels. For example, in 1996, North Carolina extracted its state public health agency from a superagency framework that also contained agencies for environmental protection and natural resources and combined it with the state human services agency to form a new superagency encompassing health and human services. At approximately the same time, Michigan separated its former superagency of public health, environmental protection, and human services into three separate agencies. More recently, Arkansas consolidated its health department and human services department into a single superagency structure in 2005 in an effort to achieve operating efficiencies and cost savings.

The state public health agencies in 20 states are statutorily required to have a physician as their senior administrator.[20-22] This administrator is appointed by the governor in most states, although a state board of health appoints this official in 4 states and a superagency administrator appoints this official in 7 states. State boards of health exist in 26 states, allowing health professionals and often private citizens to participate in the governance of their agency. These boards have policy-making authority in 10 states, and in the remaining states they function primarily in advisory capacities.

A key feature in the organization and operation of state health agencies is the administrative relationship between the state agency and the local public health agencies that operate within the state.[24] This relationship varies substantially from state to state, depending largely on the governmental powers that are delegated to local governments under state constitutions and state legislation. State health agencies rely heavily on local public health agencies to implement health policies and programs at the local level, but all state agencies do not have strong and direct administrative authority over the operation of these local agencies. Two thirds of the states extend home rule authority to local governments or grant these governments the option of assuming this authority.[20] With home rule authority, local governments can adopt their own local constitutions and exercise a broad range of governmental powers usually reserved for states, such as the levying and collection of taxes to support local programs and services.

State health agencies may have much less administrative control over the operation of local health agencies that function under home rule authority; therefore, in many of these cases, states must rely on other means such as resource allocation and regulatory authority to influence the operations of local agencies. In these cases, state agencies maintain *decentralized administrative relationships* with the local agencies, which operate under the direct control and authority of local government.[24] Decentralized administrative relationships between state and local health agencies exist in 16 of the states.[20] In other states and localities where home rule authority does not exist, state health agencies may directly control and operate local health agencies as centralized administrative units of the state. State agencies may establish operating rules for the local agencies and make key decisions regarding agency staffing, financing, and organization.[24] Such *centralized administrative relationships* exist in 10 states. Three of these states (Delaware, Rhode Island, and Alaska) do not contain any local public health agencies and are therefore served only by the state health agency. In 2 other states (Vermont and Hawaii), the state agency operates regional offices that function as local public health agencies.[20]

Other states operate with a third type of administrative relationship in which local health agencies are subject to the shared authority of both the state agency and the local government.[22] This *shared authority model* exists in 7 states.[20] Finally, in the remaining 16 states, state health agencies maintain decentralized relationships with local health agencies in some jurisdictions within the state while exercising centralized administrative control over agencies in other jurisdictions.[19] This *mixed authority model* predominates among states that extend home rule authority to some local governments but not others. Overall, state public health agencies play a role in supervising local health agencies in 20 states as of 2001.[21]

State health agencies in 20 states organize their jurisdictions into subunits such as districts or regions for the purposes of program administration.[20-22] In these states, district offices often maintain close working relationships with the local public health agencies that fall within their catchment area. In states without such districts, state public health programs are administered centrally, as are relationships with local public health agencies. In most states, a county system of government operates at the local level, with state governments relying heavily on this system for the implementation of state programs and services.[20,22] Even in the presence of county government systems, some state health agencies interact not only with county public health agencies but also with public health agencies organized by other forms of local government such as cities, towns, or special districts.

## Other State Agencies Contributing to Public Health

Because of the diversity of ways in which the official public health agency is organized and empowered at the state level, many state agencies other than this official agency may contribute substantially to public health activities. These contributions may be carried out in concert with the official state agency through an array of interagency relationships, or they may be produced quite independently of the official agency. The predominant public health contributors include the following types of agencies:

- *Environmental protection*—These state agencies are often charged with enforcing federal environmental health regulations as well as state-specific policies. Jurisdiction over water, air, soil, and waste disposal issues are commonly granted to these agencies; whereas, food protection enforcement authority may be retained within the state public health agency. In some states, the environmental protection agency is organized within a larger department of natural resources management.

- *Human services*—In states without superagencies, the human services department often serves as the single-point-of-contact state Medicaid agency. The administrative separation between Medicaid authority and public health authority is disconcerting to some observers because Medicaid programs and public health programs serve many of the same population groups and because of the powerful effects that Medicaid financing policies have on public health programs and services. State Medicaid agencies also maintain jurisdiction for monitoring the quality and accessibility of services delivered by managed care plans that participate in state Medicaid and SCHIP programs. In states without superagencies, the need for coordination between state Medicaid programs and state public health programs is often addressed through interagency coordinating councils and steering committees consisting of representatives from both agencies. State human services agencies also often administer state programs for mental health, substance abuse, and developmental disabilities services.
- *Labor*—State departments of labor often administer programs for workforce safety and wellness. These departments may also have jurisdiction over workers' compensation insurance funds.
- *Insurance*—State departments of insurance maintain regulatory authority over managed care plans and other types of health-insuring organizations. Increasingly, these agencies are called on to establish systems for monitoring the quality, cost, and accessibility of care provided by these types of organizations. These activities are widely regarded as within the purview of public health agencies.
- *Transportation*—State transportation agencies are substantively involved in traffic safety campaigns as well as policy initiatives designed to reduce mortality and morbidity due to automobile crashes.
- *Housing*—State housing departments often contribute to public health activities that address the health needs of public housing clients and homeless individuals. For example, programs to detect and control the incidence of TB and other communicable diseases among homeless shelter residents have become important state agency functions.
- *Agriculture*—Agriculture agencies are increasingly involved in public health activities including health interventions for migrant and seasonal farm workers, programs to ensure the safety of agricultural products, and programs to provide nutritional assistance and support to vulnerable populations.
- *Governor's office*—In addition to cabinet-level state agencies, a variety of state offices focusing on public health issues are often organized within state governors' offices. These offices typically serve to attract public and legislative attention to high-priority health issues, to develop state policies and plans for addressing these issues, and to attract external resources to the state for use in addressing these issues. Examples include executive offices for aging, child abuse and neglect, substance abuse, and violence prevention.

### State Intergovernmental Relationships

A diverse collection of governmental agencies forms the public health infrastructure at the state level. State agency involvement in public health activities tends to focus on statewide program administration and policy development; nevertheless, these agencies are also substantively involved in program implementation at the community level. One survey of the nation's largest local public health jurisdictions found that state agencies were involved in direct program implementation at the community level in nearly all local jurisdictions containing at least 100,000 residents.[7] In these jurisdictions, local public health administrators reported that state agencies were directly involved in performing more than one third of the core public health services undertaken within the jurisdictions. The official state public health agency provided leadership and direction for many of these activities, but other state agencies were often key contributors as well.

One increasingly important vehicle of interaction between state and local public health agencies exists in the form of performance measurement activities. State health agencies face both internal and external pressures to measure the products and outcomes of public health activities undertaken within their jurisdictions. Increasingly, state legislatures are demanding greater accountability for funds spent on public health and other publicly funded services. A growing number of state health agencies are developing performance measurement systems to meet these legislative mandates.[25,26] Similarly, the federal effort to develop "performance partnerships" with state health agencies as a condition of continued grant funding places additional emphasis on the ability of state health agencies to measure the performance of public health activities at state and local levels and to demonstrate accountability for federal funds. State agencies also use performance measurement activities to monitor progress toward their own internal objectives for organizational effectiveness and efficiency.

More recently, the federal government has begun to promote performance measurement activities through the National Public Health Performance Standards Program maintained by the CDC and several other national public health organizations.[27] This program offers a standardized national approach for measuring the performance of core public health activities at state and local levels. A related effort is now underway to develop a voluntary national accreditation program for state and local public health agencies. These initiatives represent increasingly important vehicles for intergovernmental interaction and information sharing in public health. (Refer to Chapter 17 for more information on performance management.)

An additional and perhaps more traditional forum for state and federal intergovernmental relations is the professional organization for state health officials, the Association of State and Territorial Health Officials. Consisting of senior administrators from each state and territorial public health agency, this organization serves not only as a forum for professional exchange among the state health agencies, but also as a powerful voice for state public health issues in the nation's capitol. The association develops consensus statements and policy positions on a broad array of state and national public health issues, as well as model state legislation to assist members in the policy development process within their home states. The association also serves as a vehicle for developing and implementing multistate responses to specific public health issues having a regional impact. Examples of such issues include water and air quality concerns, population migration and development patterns, hazardous waste transport and disposal, natural disaster response and recovery, and socioeconomic trends. Through forums such as this association, state agencies obtain a voice in national public health policy development and maintain mechanisms for intergovernmental communication and coordination.

## Local Governmental Agencies in Public Health

Local governmental public health agencies retain the most direct and immediate responsibility for performing public health activities at the community level. Their prevalence across the nation varies with the definition used to describe them, but recent studies estimate that about 3000 local agencies are operational across the United States when defined as "an administrative or service unit of local or state government, concerned with health, and carrying some responsibility for the health of a jurisdiction smaller than a state."[28] The organizational structures and operational characteristics found among local public health agencies are more diverse even than those observed at state and federal levels. Several explanations for this variation are readily apparent. First, the local governmental entities that sponsor these agencies vary widely in their political authority and jurisdiction—including counties, cities, rural townships, special districts, and state governments. Second, local public health agencies vary widely in the size and composition of the populations they serve. Finally, these agencies show marked diversity in the political, economic, social, and intergovernmental environments in which they operate. Any statistician can confirm that the relative variation in any measure is generally greater across small units of aggregation than across larger units of aggregation. Likewise, public health needs, resources, values, and priorities appear to vary more widely across local public health jurisdictions than across state jurisdictions. The structure and function of local public health agencies are in many ways tailored to these community characteristics.

### Operational Definition of a Local Health Department

"Governmental public health departments are responsible for creating and maintaining conditions that keep people healthy."[29] On November 1, 2005, the National Association for County and City Health Officials (NACCHO) released the "Operational Definition of a Local Health Department" available at the NACCHO Web site. A local health department (LHD) is defined as the public health government entity at a local level including a locally governed health department, state-created district, department serving a multicounty area, or any other arrangement with governmental authority and responsibility for public health functions at this local level. The functions of an LHD are shown in Exhibit 3-1.

There is currently wide variation from community to community in the degree to which the public's health is protected. Standards were set forth by NACCHO to guide the fundamental responsibilities of LHDs (based on governance, staffing patterns, size) recognizing that each LHD may have specific duties related to the needs of the community it serves. The standards are available in the operational definition handbook as well as in Chapter 17, Exhibit 17-6.[29] These standards include the following:

1. Monitor health status and understand health issues facing the community.
2. Protect people from health problems and health hazards.

Exhibit 3-1    NACCHO: A Functional Local Health Department

A Functional Local Health Department
- Understands the specific health issues confronting the community, and how physical, behavioral, environmental, social, and economic conditions affect them
- Investigates health problems and health threats
- Prevents, minimizes, and contains adverse health effects from communicable diseases, disease outbreaks from unsafe food and water, chronic diseases, environmental hazards, injuries, and risky health behaviors
- Leads planning and response activities for public health emergencies
- Collaborates with other local responders and with state and federal agencies to intervene in other emergencies with public health significance (e.g., natural disasters)
- Implements health promotion programs
- Engages the community to address public health issues
- Develops partnerships with public and private health care providers and institutions, community-based organizations, and other government agencies (e.g., housing authority, criminal justice, education) engaged in services that affect health to collectively identify, alleviate, and act on the sources of public health problems
- Coordinates the public health system's efforts in an intentional noncompetitive, and nonduplicative manner
- Addresses health disparities
- Serves as an essential resource for local governing bodies and policy makers on up-to-date public health laws and policies
- Provides science-based, timely, and culturally competent health information and health alerts to the media and to the community
- Provides its expertise to others who treat or address issues of public health significance
- Ensures compliance with public health laws and ordinances, using enforcement authority when appropriate
- Employs well-trained staff members who have the necessary resources to implement best practices and evidence-based programs and interventions
- Facilitates research efforts, when approached by researchers, that benefit the community
- Uses and contributes to the evidence base of public health
- Strategically plans its services and activities, evaluates performance and outcomes, and makes adjustments as needed to continually improve its effectiveness, enhance the community's health status, and meet the community's expectations

*Source:* Reprinted from the National Association of County and City Health Officials. "Operational Definition of a Functional Local Health Department." November, 2005.

3. Give people information they need to make healthy choices.
4. Engage the community to identify and solve health problems.
5. Develop public health policies and plans.
6. Enforce public health laws and regulations.
7. Help people receive health services.
8. Maintain a competent public health workforce.
9. Evaluate and improve programs and interventions.
10. Contribute to and apply the evidence base for public health.

In addition to these standards, there are state-specific standards and National Public Health Performance Standards (NPHSP) for local health systems, as described in greater detail in Chapter 17.

## Organizational Structure

Most local public health agencies are units of county government. A 2005 survey of these agencies indicates that 59% are county departments and another 14% are units of combined city–county government entities (Figure 3-5).[28] Ten percent of the departments are organized as district or multi-county departments—a strategy used by some small and rural local governments to realize economies of scale by combining their health operations. Most of the remaining departments (16%) are operated by cities and towns.

The vast majority of local public health agencies (74%) operate in tandem with a local board of health.[28] These boards vary widely in their structure and function. Most boards contain appointed members only, but nearly a third include elected officials as members.[30] In some cases, a preexisting elected body such as a board of county commissioners or a city council serves as the local board of health. Local boards of health predominate among departments serving small jurisdictions of less than 50,000 residents. More than half of the local boards perform both advisory and policy-making functions for their local public health agency, according to a 2005 survey of local agencies.[30] Policy-making functions may include responsibilities such as reviewing and approving the departmental budget, establishing broad departmental policies and objectives, appointing the department's senior administrative

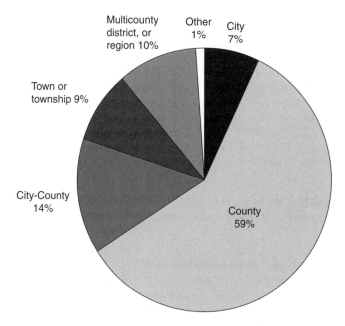

**FIGURE 3-5    Local Public Health Agencies by Type of Organization, 2005**
*Source:* National Association of County and City Health Officials. 2005 National Profile of Local Health Departments. Washington, DC: NACCHO; 2006.

and clinical officials, and evaluating the performance of the department and its leadership. In the remainder of cases, boards provide advice to local health departments but wield no policy-making authority.

Nearly two thirds of the nation's local health departments serve jurisdictions of less than 50,000 residents.[28] Collectively, these departments serve only 10% of the total US population. By comparison, departments serving the nation's largest jurisdictions—those with more than 500,000 residents—make up only 6% of all local health departments but they serve 54% of the US population. (Refer to Figure 3-6.) The remaining 32% of departments operate in jurisdictions of between 50,000 and 500,000 residents and collectively serve 37% of the US population.

### Scope of Public Health Services

The scope of public health services performed by local public health agencies varies markedly across regions and states. These agencies typically adapt their service offerings in order to complement the breadth and accessibility of public health services delivered by other community providers. Nearly all local agencies are involved in communicable disease control activities. A 2005 survey of the nation's local health departments revealed that 90% offered childhood immunizations and 91% offered adult immunizations.[28] More than two thirds of the departments offer testing for STDs, and 64% provide treatment services for these diseases.

The delivery of primary care services by local public health agencies continues to be an issue of much discussion and debate. In some communities, these agencies provide comprehensive primary care services because there are

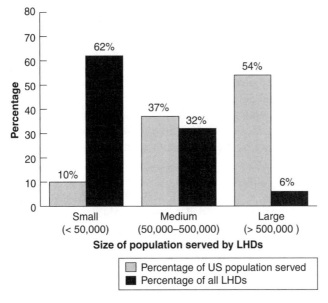

**FIGURE 3-6    Local Health Departments by Size of Population Served**
*Source:* Reprinted from National Association of County and City Health Officials. 2005 National Profile of Local Health Departments. Washington, DC: NACCHO; 2006.

no alternative sources of care for individuals who cannot access private medical providers due to insurance status, financial need, or language and cultural barriers.[1,4] Still, some observers argue that obligations for delivering personal health services detract local public health agencies from their primary mission in performing population-based public health services such as surveillance, health education, and policy development.[19] Despite this unresolved debate, a majority of local health departments are actively involved in delivering well-child care and/or sick-child care—either directly or by contract with other community providers.[4,28] Forty-two percent of these agencies offer prenatal care services, 28% offer home health services, and 14% deliver comprehensive primary care services.

In the area of health promotion and disease prevention activities, 69% of the nation's local health departments are engaged in tobacco prevention programs.[4,28] Nearly three quarters of the local departments provide blood pressure screening, half provide screening for diabetes, 46% provide cancer screening services, and 40% maintain injury prevention programs.[4,28] Obesity prevention programs are offered by 56% of local public health departments.

The vast majority of health departments maintain capacities for epidemiologic surveillance and assessment activities. Eighty-nine percent of local departments conduct surveillance activities for communicable diseases, while 75% perform these activities for environmental health conditions, 41% for chronic diseases, and 24% for injury.[28] Nearly all local health departments are also involved in some type of environmental health protection activity.[4] Some of the most frequently performed environmental activities among the nation's local departments include food safety education and inspection (75%), septic tank and sewage disposal inspection (66%), vector control (54%), and lead inspection (53%).[28]

Over the past decade, some local public health agencies have chosen to privatize the delivery of certain public health activities—most often the delivery of personal health services.[31] A growing proportion of local agencies report providing some types of services through contracts with other organizations rather than directly providing the service.[4] Contracting has become increasingly prevalent for services such as immunization delivery, prenatal care, and child health and developmental screening services. The growth of Medicaid managed care initiatives and SCHIP programs has encouraged this activity in some states because these programs have encouraged larger numbers of private healthcare providers to serve Medicaid recipients and other population groups who historically obtained care from public health agencies.[32]

*Staffing and Financing*

Local public health agencies are sparsely staffed in comparison to many other types of organizations having a comparable scope and scale of activity.[4,33] Half of the nation's local health departments employ fewer than 20 full-time equivalent staff, and one quarter of these departments employ fewer than 8 staff members.[4,28] The average local health department manages approximately 150 staff per 100,000 individuals residing within the jurisdiction. Correspondingly, local health departments operate with relatively modest levels of financial resources. The median annual local department budget totaled $1.02 million in 2005, and nearly one quarter of the nation's departments operated on less than $375,000 during that year.[4,28] On a per capita basis, the median local health department spent $23 per resident per year. (See Chapter 17 for a detailed discussion of financing in public health organizations.)

The largest share of revenue for local public health agency activities derives from local governmental appropriations, which accounted for 29% of the average agency's budget in 2005.[28] By comparison, these agencies receive 23% of their funding from state government appropriations (excluding Medicaid) and 20% from federal sources (excluding Medicare). More than half of the federal funding received by local agencies comes in the form of pass-through funding controlled by the state government. The Medicaid and Medicare programs account for another 9% and 2% of local agency budgets, respectively. Local health departments obtain the remaining funds from private grants and fees assessed for clinical services, permits, and licenses. (Refer to Figure 3-7.) A 15-year longitudinal study of a diverse group of local health departments indicated that fee-based revenue sources have become increasingly important components of local public health financing; whereas, direct federal grants have declined precipitously over the last two decades.[34] State and local funding sources for local public health activities appear to have remained relatively stable over this time period.

The mechanisms through which local health departments obtain state and local revenue vary considerably.[1,34] In some states, local health departments receive a dedicated share of revenue from a specific financing vehicle collected within their jurisdiction, such as a motor vehicle registration tax or a gasoline tax. In other states, most of the state revenue is transferred to local agencies via contracts and grants that are subject to periodic reauthorizations

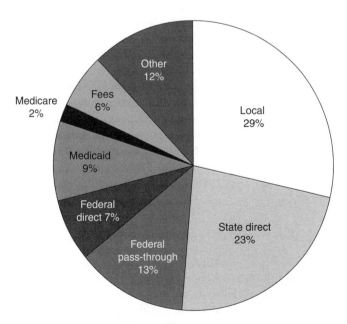

**FIGURE 3-7   Total Local Health Department Revenues by Source**
*Source:* Reprinted from National Association of County and City Health Officials. 2005 National Profile of Local Health Departments. Washington, DC: NACCHO; 2006.

and renegotiations. At the local level, departments may also receive dedicated shares of revenue streams such as property taxes or sales taxes, or they may receive funds through the annual legislative budgeting and appropriations processes. Dedicated revenue streams are often preferred by local public health administrators because these funding mechanisms allow administrators to engage in long-range planning and development activities with accurate projections of future revenues. These mechanisms, however, reduce legislative control over resource allocation decisions and are therefore used sparingly if at all in many states and localities.

### Regionalization

A major trend in the last decade has been the increasing regionalization of local health departments. This has been a functional regionalization rather than one accomplished through statutory change. The impetus for this regionalization is that small health departments serving limited populations do not have enough capacity for many specialized public health functions. Groups of counties banding together voluntarily, sometimes with a larger county in the region serving as the lead, have become increasingly commonplace. The momentum towards regionalization has been encouraged by funding of grant programs and bioterrorism preparedness resources in particular. Small counties, by themselves, would only receive a limited disbursement of bioterrorism funds and would not be able to mount many of the necessary components for preparedness such as surveillance, contact investigations, or provisions for surge capacity. In New York, a number of regions have developed through voluntary association including Western New York, Finger Lakes, Central New York, Capitol, and Mid-Hudson. The Central New York Region's shared public health activities include collaborative preparedness efforts, immunization registry, medical examiner functions, and a uniform approach to a regional community health assessment. Similarly, in North Carolina, eight counties in the eastern part of the state form the Northeastern NC Partnership for Public Health.

This voluntary type of association has many advantages over prior arrangements in some states where formal or statutory arrangements exist to combine several counties into one combined public health jurisdiction. In the voluntary type of association, the county maintains autonomy in determining funding for public health purposes and enforcing laws and regulations. This is important in minimizing the reluctance of county legislators who may otherwise be opposed to relinquishing their prerogatives in such regional efforts.

### Other Local Governmental Agencies Contributing to Public Health

The official local health department is by far not the only unit of local government that contributes to public health agencies in a given jurisdiction. A study of public health activities in the nation's largest local jurisdictions (those with 100,000 or more residents) indicated that the average local public health agency directly provides about two thirds of the public health activities performed within the jurisdiction (Figure 3-8).[7] Other units of local government participate in public health activities in 92% of these large jurisdictions, and these other agencies are involved in an average of 32% of all essential public health activities performed within these jurisdictions (Table 3-1).

Frequent contributors to public health activities include local social service agencies, elementary and secondary public schools, housing departments, fire and police departments, planning offices, parks and recreation departments, public libraries, public transit authorities, waste management agencies, and water and sewer authorities.[34] These organizations often maintain valuable resources for developing and implementing community-wide public health initiatives such as support staff, specialized expertise, building space and equipment, information and communications infrastructure, and public outreach mechanisms. In any given jurisdiction, these organizations are not necessarily units of the same governmental entity. Many local public health jurisdictions fall within multiple, overlapping spheres of local governmental authority, such as those of counties, cities, townships, school districts, transportation authorities, and water and sewer authorities. The extent to which these types of agencies are involved in public health activities varies widely across communities.[7,34] Mechanisms for interagency communication and coordination facilitate the involvement of these agencies in public health activities in some communities. Intergovernmental coordinating councils and interagency planning committees also serve as mechanisms to facilitate multiagency responses to local public health issues.

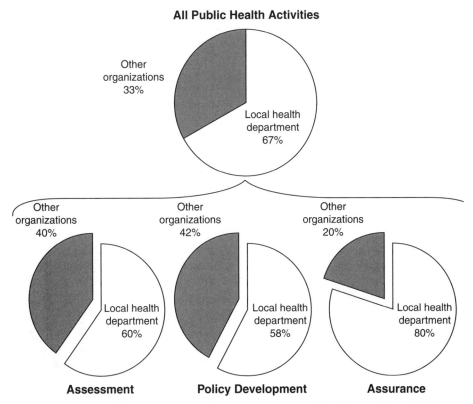

**FIGURE 3-8   Local Health Department Contributions to Local Public Health Activities**
*Source:* Unpublished data from G.P. Mays, P.K. Halverson, and C.A. Miller.

**TABLE 3-1  Organizational Contributions to Public Health Activities in US Local Public Health Jurisdictions with at Least 100,000 Residents**

| Public Health Activity | Percentage of Jurisdictions In Which Selected Organizations Participate In Public Health Activities* | | | | | | | | |
|---|---|---|---|---|---|---|---|---|---|
| | State Agency | Hospital | Nonprofit Agency | Local Agency | Private Physician/Grp. | University | Health Center | Managed Care Plan | Federal Agency |
| Any public health activity | 97.7 | 96.6 | 95.2 | 91.7 | 85.2 | 65.5 | 46.7 | 45.3 | 44.2 |
| Specific types of activities | | | | | | | | | |
| 1. Community health needs assessment | 42.6 | 58.2[b] | 55.4 | 49.1 | 23.3 | 31.8[a] | 19.9 | 14.5 | 6.8 |
| 2. Behavioral risk factor surveillance | 24.5[b] | 22.1 | 19.8 | 17.9 | 5.8 | 15.6 | 5.2 | 5.8 | 4.6 |
| 3. Adverse health events investigation | 82.1[a,b] | 56.3 | 13.1 | 43.8 | 48.0[a] | 12.5 | 11.4 | 7.1 | 21.9[a] |
| 4. Access to laboratory services | 79.5[b] | 49.0 | 4.3 | 17.9 | 25.4 | 9.7 | 4.3 | 5.1 | 15.7 |
| 5. Analysis of health determinants | 36.7 | 46.7[b] | 45.0 | 38.1 | 21.2 | 24.1 | 13.8 | 11.2 | 5.2 |
| 6. Analysis of preventive services use | 15.5[b] | 13.5 | 11.7 | 10.0 | 7.2 | 7.2 | 4.6 | 4.6 | 2.6 |
| 7. Support and communication networks | 47.6 | 66.5[a,b] | 64.2[a] | 62.2[a] | 37.8 | 29.8 | 24.4 | 18.3 | 10.6 |
| 8. Information provision for elected officials | 31.9 | 26.8 | 32.5[b] | 32.2 | 14.8 | 10.5 | 8.0 | 4.0 | 3.4 |
| 9. Prioritization of health needs | 33.3 | 49.6[b] | 47.9 | 45.9 | 25.6 | 25.4 | 15.1 | 11.4 | 5.7 |
| 10. Implementation of public health initiatives | 46.7 | 60.7 | 63.9[b] | 51.0 | 35.5 | 25.8 | 21.5 | 14.0 | 9.7 |
| 11. Community action planning | 20.6 | 34.7[b] | 33.8 | 31.2 | 19.8 | 16.0 | 10.3 | 9.5 | 4.6 |
| 12. Planning for resource allocation | 14.0 | 16.2 | 14.5 | 17.4[b] | 8.0 | 6.6 | 6.0 | 2.8 | 2.3 |
| 13. Resource deployment for priority needs | 27.9 | 35.3[b] | 33.6 | 32.2 | 15.8 | 12.6 | 8.9 | 7.5 | 5.7 |
| 14. Self-assessment of local health dept. | 12.6[b] | 3.4 | 4.3 | 12.1 | 1.4 | 4.9 | 1.1 | 1.7 | 0.6 |

| | | | | | | | | |
|---|---|---|---|---|---|---|---|---|
| 15. Provision of, and linkage to, health services | 44.5 | 57.8 | 59.8[b] | 47.1 | 44.0 | 17.8 | 25.6[a] | 20.4[a] | 8.3 |
| 16. Evaluation of public health services | 21.5[b] | 13.8 | 14.0 | 14.3 | 4.9 | 7.4 | 3.4 | 2.9 | 4.3 |
| 17. Use of process/outcome measures | 27.4[b] | 11.5 | 15.0 | 17.0 | 6.1 | 5.5 | 4.0 | 2.3 | 4.0 |
| 18. Public information dissemination | 47.4 | 48.9[b] | 46.6 | 34.6 | 23.7 | 21.4 | 14.0 | 14.6 | 10.0 |
| 19. Media information dissemination | 37.6[b] | 33.0 | 25.9 | 27.9 | 12.0 | 8.8 | 5.7 | 6.3 | 5.4 |
| Average: Assessment activities (#1–#6) | 46.6[b] | 40.8 | 24.8 | 29.4 | 21.7 | 16.7 | 9.8 | 8.0 | 9.4 |
| Average: Policy development activities (#7–#12) | 32.1 | 42.1 | 42.5[b] | 39.7 | 23.4 | 18.9 | 14.1 | 9.9 | 6.0 |
| Average: Assurance activities (#13–#19) | 31.1[b] | 28.9 | 28.3 | 26.3 | 15.3 | 11.2 | 8.9 | 7.9 | 5.5 |
| Average: All activities | 36.6 | 37.3[b] | 31.9 | 31.8 | 20.2 | 15.6 | 11.0 | 8.6 | 7.0 |

[a] Largest participation measure in the column (activity most frequently performed by the type of organization listed in the column heading).
[b] Largest participation measure in the row (type of organization most frequently reported to perform the activity listed in the row heading).
*As reported by the local health department director.
Source: Unpublished data from G.P. Mays, P.K. Halverson and C.A. Miller.

## Nongovernmental Public Health Organizations

Governmental public health agencies are in many cases the dominant institutions within public health delivery systems. These organizations control much of the human capital and financial resources that are dedicated specifically for public health activities within the United States. Nonetheless, nongovernmental organizations play instrumental roles in the production of public health services, both independently and in concert with governmental health agencies. Nongovernmental efforts in public health delivery include aspects of medical practice that contribute to public health practices and outcomes. Collaborative activities in medical practice and public health practice became more prevalent during the 1990s as the growth of managed health care encouraged hospitals and physician practices to consider the health care needs of defined populations rather than only the needs of individual patients.[35] Other types of nongovernmental organizations maintain a long history of involvement in public health activities such as voluntary associations, philanthropic institutions, and some health professions schools. Some of the most frequent nongovernmental contributors to public health activities are described in the following sections.

### Community Hospitals and Health Systems

Community hospitals have long been important contributors to local public health activities. The federal Hill-Burton program, which financed many hospital construction and capital improvement projects over the past half century, required hospitals that used this funding to provide charitable services. Begun in the mid-1940s, this program established a strong tradition of charity care among community hospitals. As providers of uncompensated acute care services, hospitals continue to play invaluable roles in ensuring access to health care for vulnerable and underserved populations. The charitable missions of many public and nonprofit hospitals motivate these organizations to engage in community health activities that extend beyond the realm of acute care.[36] More recently, hospitals have faced pressures from policy makers and regulators to demonstrate the production of community benefits in order to retain their tax-exempt status. Additionally, the growth of managed care and other cost-containment approaches in many communities during the 1990s created financial incentives for hospitals to engage in public health activities as strategies for reducing costs and encouraging greater efficiency in hospital utilization. For example, hospitals in some areas with large numbers of uninsured residents have become involved in operating ambulatory care clinics for the uninsured in order to reduce the costly utilization of emergency department services.[34] Similarly, some hospitals have expanded their involvement in health promotion and disease prevention initiatives in order to attract the growing numbers of healthcare consumers and purchasers who value these activities.

Hospitals contribute to local public health activities in a variety of ways. In some communities, hospitals participate in directly providing community health services through such efforts as operating primary care clinics for underserved populations, sponsoring community health education programs, and conducting health screening fairs. Hospitals are also major contributors to community health assessment efforts. These contributions are motivated in part by the Joint Commission on Accreditation of Health Care Organizations' decision to require its accredited hospitals to engage in community health assessment processes.[36] Hospitals are important contributors to these efforts because of their unique positions within communities to observe disease effects and identify intervention areas. Finally, hospitals make important contributions to local efforts in public health planning and policy development. In many communities, hospitals wield significant political power through the substantial human and capital resources that they control. Consequently, hospitals can be powerful agents for mobilizing communities around public health issues and for organizing collaborative efforts to address these issues. Hospitals also maintain large administrative data systems that can offer important insight into public health problems within the community, through information such as age- and diagnosis-specific reasons for hospital admissions and emergency department visits.

## Ambulatory Care Providers

Ambulatory care providers also make important contributions to public health in many communities. These providers include private physician practices as well as community health centers supported by federal, state, and local government subsidies. Private physicians often engage in public health activities through local and state medical societies.[34] Medical societies vary widely in the extent of their involvement in public health activities. Some societies maintain only minimal involvement through participation in community health planning and policy development activities. Other medical societies are actively involved in designing and operating community health interventions such as free medical clinics, health fairs, and community health assessments. Private physicians may also contribute to public health activities independently, through such diverse efforts as volunteering in community health clinics, serving on local boards of health, or developing service agreements with local health departments for providing reduced-fee care to the uninsured. Additionally, ambulatory care providers often participate in public health surveillance activities such as the National Notifiable Disease Reporting System. Physicians who diagnose a patient with one or more of the 50 communicable diseases included in this system are required to notify the state or local public health agency that is locally responsible for this surveillance system so that this agency can initiate appropriate disease control activities and transmit the appropriate information to the CDC.

Community health centers provide access to primary care services for vulnerable and underserved populations, and also serve as important sources for health education, counseling, and social support services.[37] These centers include those that receive grants through one of the five federal health center programs administered by the HRSA (community health centers, migrant health centers, homeless health centers, public housing health centers, and school-based health centers), as well as those that are supported through state, local, or private funding. Some of these clinics offer comprehensive primary care services; others specialize in areas such as family planning (i.e., Planned Parenthood clinics), pediatrics, or STD services. In many communities, health centers and local health departments develop reciprocal referral agreements and other collaborative arrangements for targeting health services to vulnerable populations.[36] In some cases, health centers are operated directly by local health departments.

## Health Insurers and Managed Care Plans

Health insurers and managed care plans make important contributions to local public health practice in some communities. For some insurers, these contributions are motivated by altruistic missions of community service; other insurers hope to reduce medical care costs or attract new members through their contributions to public health.[38] Insurers are able to communicate with large numbers of community residents and healthcare providers through extensive networks of members and affiliated physicians and hospitals. Some insurers use this capacity to encourage health promotion and disease prevention practices among their members and to create incentives for affiliated providers to deliver appropriate clinical preventive services to their patients. Insurers may also contribute to community health initiatives that target broad segments of the community population. For example, programs that distribute bicycle helmets to children or child safety seats to new parents have become popular methods for managed care plans to achieve heightened visibility in their service areas.[38]

Insurers also participate in public health activities as strategies for obtaining information about community health risks and disease patterns.[39] Insurers use this type of information to anticipate health risks among their current and potential members. To obtain this information, some insurers participate with other community organizations in community health assessment and surveillance efforts. Other insurers conduct surveillance activities within their own populations of members and contribute this information to public health assessment efforts maintained by other community organizations.

## Nonprofit Agencies

A range of other nonprofit organizations engage in public health activities at local, state, and national levels. Prime among these agencies are the local, state, and national chapters of voluntary health associations such as the American Heart Association, American Cancer Society, American Diabetes Association, and American Lung Association. These organizations implement public awareness campaigns and health education initiatives concerning disease risks and advocate for the public and private support of prevention, treatment, and control interventions. Similarly, social service organizations such as the United Way, the Urban League, and Rotary International are often active in sustaining community-level efforts to identify health risks and to implement community health interventions. Through their active fund-raising efforts, these organizations often serve as important sources of local, nongovernmental revenues to fund public health interventions carried out through a variety of organizations.

In addition to these national affiliates, many communities are served by locally developed organizations that have formed around community-specific needs and resources. These organizations include neighborhood associations, parent–teacher associations, church groups and other faith-based organizations, and local environmental coalitions. These groups often participate in policy development activities such as community health planning activities and advocacy efforts. In many communities, these groups also play important roles in implementing community health interventions, such as church-based and school-based health education programs and local environmental restoration projects.

## Philanthropic Foundations

Important public health functions are also supported by an expanding array of philanthropic foundations and charities. Several large and well-established health foundations maintain a distinguished history of supporting research and demonstration initiatives in public health. These initiatives have helped to develop the public health infrastructure at state and local levels, while also building the public knowledge base concerning how best to organize, deliver, and finance public health activities at state and local levels. Two of the largest and most active national foundations in public health are the Robert Wood Johnson Foundation and the W.K. Kellogg Foundation.

Another type of foundation, which has seen marked growth over the last decade, is the community foundation. Many of these foundations were formed with the proceeds from acquisitions, mergers, and ownership conversions among local hospitals and health insurers.[40] In some communities, these foundations play important roles in developing and financing community health interventions. For example, some foundations sponsor extensive community health assessment activities designed to identify health risks and needs in the local population. Other foundations support the delivery of uncompensated health care to uninsured and underinsured community residents. For example, several large health foundations have been created in California as a result of ownership conversions, including the California Endowment and the California Health Foundation.

## Universities

Universities and other institutions of higher education also make important contributions to local public health practice in many communities. Health professions schools such as schools of public health, medicine, and nursing are perhaps the most common contributors. Faculty from schools of public health often provide technical assistance to local health departments and other community organizations for activities such as conducting disease investigations, community health assessments, and community health planning activities. Additionally, health professions schools often collaborate with community health agencies in developing sites for internships and residencies for health professions students. These types of arrangements provide communities with additional clinical and administrative manpower that can be used to implement new community health interventions. Finally, universities may contribute to local public health practice by developing specialized training and continuing education opportunities for local health professionals. Recent advances in information and communication technology are facilitating the development of these opportunities through distance learning modalities.

Increasingly, university consortia such as the Association of Schools of Public Health (ASPH) and the American Association of Academic Medical Colleges (AAMC) are actively encouraging and supporting university involvement in public health practice activities. The federal government recently has established programs with both of these organizations to develop "academic health departments" that provide a home for practice-based education and research in public health.[41] Through these programs, state and local public health agencies serve as training sites for educational programs and research activities that are maintained jointly by the agencies and their university partners. For example, in 2003 a cooperative agreement from the CDC facilitated the creation of 11 "teaching health departments" through ASPH and seven regional medicine–public health education centers (RMPHEC) through AAMC. The former were partnerships between schools of public health and a state or local public health agency, the latter were partnerships between schools of medicine and public health agencies.[41] In 2006, the AAMC funded 11 regional medicine–public health education centers.[42]

It is important to note that health professions schools are not the only institutions of higher education that contribute to local public health practice. Other types of institutions—including liberal arts colleges, community colleges, and technical schools—also play important roles in contributing technical assistance, training, and educational expertise to community health interventions.

## Other Organizations

A range of other organizations may contribute to public health activities in local communities. In some localities, employers are becoming active in promoting health within their workforces. Employer activities include efforts to reduce worksite health risks, promote healthy lifestyles and behaviors among employees and their families, and assist in the early identification and treatment of diseases. For example, employers may contribute to community health education campaigns in areas such as smoking cessation, physical activity, and nutrition.[34] Similarly, employers may sponsor community health fairs and other initiatives designed to identify and address health risks within the community. Employers may undertake these activities independently or through associations such as business coalitions, local chambers of commerce, and economic development councils. Employers face compelling incentives for engaging in these types of activities given their potential effects on employee productivity and costs incurred for health insurance and workers' compensation benefits.

Other organizations contributing to public health activities include elementary and secondary schools, faith-based organizations, professional associations, labor unions, and other community-based organizations. These organizations vary widely in their involvement in public health issues and in their motivations for doing so. Nonetheless, their potential for making meaningful contributions should not be overlooked within individual communities. Refer to Chapter 16 for further information on constituencies.

## Interorganizational Efforts in Public Health

Interorganizational relationships have become a widely prevalent approach for improving quality, efficiency, and accessibility in public health as in other fields of practice.[43] Much of the collaborative activity occurring to date among health-related organizations has focused on enhancing performance within individual organizations. More recently, health organizations have begun to expand the scope of their collaborative efforts to address health issues that exist beyond the boundaries of individual organizations.[44] These collective efforts strive for health improvement within broad segments of the community population, although they also may offer opportunities for individual organizational gain as well. Examples range from coordinated efforts to increase childhood immunization rates within a neighborhood to jointly sponsored programs that provide health care to uninsured populations.[36] These initiatives, termed *public health partnerships* because of their loose and flexible structures, are defined here as coordinated efforts among public health organizations to address health problems and risks faced by broad segments of a community's population. The term *partnership* indicates that coordination is achieved through loosely structured agreements between organizations that fall somewhere between the two extremes of ad hoc exchange and a consolidated bureaucracy.[45,46] The public health partnerships examined in this chapter are conceptually and operationally equivalent to the phenomenon of *strategic alliances* that has been studied extensively in the business and healthcare fields for more than a decade.[28,45,47]

The organizational motivations for engaging in public health partnerships are varied and range from economic gain to community health improvement.[48] Consequently, a broad array of organizations—both public and private, proprietary and nonprofit—participate in these arrangements. For organizations with an overriding mission of public service and community benefit, partnerships offer strategies for achieving an enhanced impact on community health through pooled resources and expertise. Organizations may also face individual economic incentives for participating in public health partnerships. Partnerships may offer opportunities for addressing community health issues that impose substantial financial or administrative burdens on healthcare organizations—such as uncompensated care costs faced by hospitals or the costs of such preventable diseases as diabetes and obesity that are faced by health insurers. The financial incentives for collaboration may be particularly powerful for organizations that operate under payment systems that reward efficiency and quality in health services delivery.[36]

### Strategic Orientation of Partnerships

Organizations pursue a wide range of interests through public health partnerships. Conceptually, these interests can be distilled into three basic strategic orientations that summarize the organizational motivations behind most collaborative activity.[45] Understanding the strategic orientation of a given public health partnership can assist participating organizations in anticipating and responding to the behavior of their partners.

Some partnerships are developed primarily to allow participating organizations to gain knowledge and expertise in a new field of operation. These types of collaborative arrangements, often termed *opportunistic* partnerships, typically last only long enough for the participating organizations to gain sufficient knowledge to assist them in pursuing their own individual interests.[45] The limited duration and restricted focus of these types of partnerships may cause the arrangement to yield relatively small community-level benefits, although the organization-level benefits may be substantial. However, the community-level benefits that flow from these arrangements may still be substantial if, for example, durable public goods such as service accessibility and quality are expanded as a result of the relatively brief information exchange that takes place between partnership participants.

For example, in one community, a local public health agency and a commercial health maintenance organization (HMO) formed a partnership to develop a managed care plan for serving Medicaid beneficiaries.[34] Through this partnership, the public health agency gained expertise in managed care skills such as prospective budgeting, utilization review, and provider profiling. At the same time, the HMO gained expertise in serving Medicaid beneficiaries—who differed considerably from the HMO's commercial enrollees in their health and social service needs. After several years of operation, the two organizations ended their partnership and developed competing Medicaid managed care plans using the information and experience they gained through collaboration.

Other public health partnerships are formed to provide a resource or service needed by multiple healthcare organizations. These *resource dependency* partnerships are similar to opportunistic partnerships in that the participants use the partnership primarily to pursue individual organizational interests.[38] Organizations form these partnerships to share the costs of a product or service that is needed by different organizations for different purposes. In doing so, public goods are created that contribute to the process of community health improvement. The public goods created by these partnerships range from population-based disease surveillance and health information systems to community-wide efforts in clinical practice guideline development and dissemination. Because these partnerships are formed to address ongoing resource needs, the community benefits produced by them are often less transitory than those produced through opportunistic partnerships. As a consequence, these partnerships often require longer and larger resource commitments by participating organizations.

An example underway in several study communities involves the construction of community-wide immunization registries.[36] These registries are designed to store and retrieve the immunization histories of age-appropriate community residents so that underimmunized children can be readily identified and addressed with appropriate interventions. (For more information, refer to Chapter 13.) In several communities, partnerships consisting of hospitals, physician practices, managed care plans, and public health agencies have formed to develop, finance, and implement these registries. These partnerships offer public health agencies enhanced opportunities for preventing outbreaks of vaccine preventable diseases within their jurisdictions. At the same time, these partnerships offer managed care plans and other private providers the opportunity to track the immunization histories of their individual patient populations. In doing so, these private organizations can avoid the delivery of unnecessary vaccinations, identify alternative sources of immunization services used by their patients, develop targeted interventions for chronically underimmunized patients, and report more accurate measures of patient immunization status to payers, regulators, and accreditation bodies.

A third type of public health partnership involves organizations that pursue a shared mission or set of interests through collective action. In contrast to opportunistic and resource dependency partnerships, these *stakeholder* partnerships are formed by organizations that seek to achieve a common outcome from their collective efforts.[38] This outcome typically involves improvement in one or more areas of community health. To achieve this improvement, stakeholder partnerships often seek participation from the widest possible array of organizations that may contribute to the outcome of interest. Because participating organizations share a common mission rather than simply a common resource need, stakeholder partnerships typically achieve greater levels of organizational commitment and support than other types of partnerships. As a result, these types of partnerships may hold the greatest potential for achieving sustained community health improvement. They also may be the most difficult type of partnership to develop and maintain due to the need to achieve consensus concerning the partnership's core mission and goals.

Most of the stakeholder partnerships observed to date have involved highly visible community health issues.[34,36] For example, one community's high rate of domestic violence motivated a collaborative effort among two hospital systems, a local health department, several social service agencies, and the local law enforcement agency. Each of the participating organizations reported a shared interest in and responsibility for reducing the substantial health and social services costs associated with domestic violence on a community-wide basis. In response, the organizations developed a jointly financed and jointly operated violence prevention program to provide education, case management, and counseling to families exhibiting signs of domestic violence. In contrast to the resource dependency partnership model, these organizations were motivated by a common mission of reducing community violence rather than by a common need for a particular resource or service.

Many public health partnerships do not perfectly fit one of the three strategic orientations described here. Partnerships often derive from a combination of these orientations, with any given partnership occurring closer or further away from a given strategic orientation. For example, organizations may form a jointly operated HMO primarily for opportunistic reasons, but they may also seek to address shared resource needs through the partnership. Therefore, opportunistic motivations may have the strongest influence on this partnership, followed by resource dependencies. By comparison, a partnership to develop an immunization registry may be motivated primarily by resource dependencies (i.e., the mutual need for immunization information), while opportunistic and stakeholder considerations play lesser roles in shaping the partnership. Partnerships may also evolve over time from one strategic orientation toward another. Through the process of partnership participation, organizations gain information about their partners that may motivate them to modify their strategic relationships—for example, to capitalize on newly discovered resources or to limit the risk of loss from newly discovered liabilities in their partners. Despite these complexities, knowledge about a partnership's strategic orientation can assist organizations in anticipating and managing the behavior of their partners.

*Functional Characteristics of Partnerships*

Through public health partnerships, organizations engage in a broad array of activities designed to achieve strategic objectives and enhance community health. Most partnerships can be classified into one of four functional categories: service delivery, planning and policy development, surveillance and assessment, and education and outreach. These categories are described in the following sections.[36]

*Service Delivery.* Collaborative efforts in service delivery are a common type of functional activity performed through public health partnerships. In a recent study of partnerships in 60 diverse public health jurisdictions, more than 40% of hospitals and community health centers participated in public health service delivery activities, compared with 21% of managed care plans and 87% of local health departments.[36] Most of these service delivery partnerships involved joint referral arrangements designed to enhance service accessibility and service coordination at the community level. For example, in one study community, the local hospitals, community health center, and medical society participate in an agreement to refer patients who are at risk for diabetes to a screening and case management program operated by the local health department. Other service delivery partnerships involve joint efforts to finance and deliver community services. Organizations may contribute funding or in-kind resources to these efforts—such as staff time, equipment, supplies, and office space. For example, of the 45 study hospitals involved in the joint production of community services, 75% contribute funding, 42% contribute staff time, and 49% contribute equipment and supplies to these efforts.[36]

*Planning and Policy Development.* A second functional area commonly addressed by public health partnerships involves the development of coordinated plans and policies for responding to health issues. (For more information, refer to Chapter 15.) Through these partnerships, organizations engage in activities such as conducting joint strategic planning and priority-setting sessions to delineate the respective roles of alternative community organizations in addressing health issues; adopting mutually developed service delivery standards, guidelines, and policies; and formulating public health policies and lobbying for their adoption by local, state, and federal legislative bodies. For example, in one study community, a coalition consisting of hospitals, managed care plans, physicians, and a local health department developed restrictive standards for tobacco sales and tobacco use that were successfully adopted by the local board of county commissioners following an extensive lobbying effort.[35] In another community, a partnership consisting of local managed care plans, hospitals, and the local health department developed a standardized form for monitoring and reporting the delivery of developmental screening services to Medicaid beneficiaries.[38] The partnership successfully secured the adoption of this form by all primary care physicians who served beneficiaries enrolled in the community's 10 Medicaid managed care plans.

*Surveillance and Assessment.* A third group of public health partnerships involves collective efforts to identify health risks and diseases within the community and to assess the performance of health organizations and interventions in addressing community health needs.[36] These partnerships include activities such as sponsoring community-wide surveillance efforts to identify behavioral risk factors within the community, conducting community health needs assessments to identify perceived needs for new programs and services, and sponsoring research efforts to assess the effects of health policies, programs, and services on health status within the community. In one community, a managed care plan and local health department sponsored a telephone survey of community residents and health plan enrollees regarding their health behaviors and risks.[38] The organizations used information from the surveillance effort to design both community-wide and organization-specific interventions to address public health issues such as smoking cessation, diet, and physical activity. In another community, a coalition of hospitals, managed care plans, and physicians sponsored a study of community residents who had recently sought care for digestive disorders to determine the appropriateness of treating these residents for the bacteria *H. pylori*.

*Education and Outreach.*    A final group of public health partnerships focuses on educating community residents and healthcare providers about health promotion and disease prevention practices. These efforts include disseminating information on beneficial health behaviors and clinical practices as well as providing outreach to encourage participation in health programs and services. In one of these communities, for example, a coalition of managed care plans and the local health department sponsored an on-site training program in childhood immunization practices that was conducted with all of the pediatricians and family practice physicians operating within the community.[36] In another community, a coalition of hospitals and managed care plans sponsored a breast cancer awareness campaign that included targeted health education messages in the local media and a telephone information and referral line.

Public health partnerships often support activities in several of the functional areas described here. For example, a partnership may include a health education component as well as a service delivery component, as in one community's diabetes awareness and management program.[36] Partnerships may also evolve over time from one functional area to another. Community assessment efforts, for example, often progress into planning and policy development activities. The organizational membership of a partnership may change during this evolution, as may its strategic orientation. These trend effects are described further in the section on partnership life cycles.

### Structural Characteristics of Partnerships

Public health partnerships are maintained through an array of interorganizational relationships that structure the ways in which participating organizations interact. Four basic types of structural relationships are commonly observed in public health partnerships: informal collaboration, contractual agreements, shared governance, and shared ownership. Each of these alternative relationships offers advantages as well as disadvantages in areas such as development and maintenance costs, organizational flexibility, enforceability, and reversibility.

*Informal Collaboration.*    The most informal types of relationships are based on loosely structured agreements between organizations that are maintained by mutual expectations and patterns of behavior. Organizations participating in these informal collaborative groups typically maintain a long history of operating within the same community or market and depend on reputation and peer pressure to enforce the expected behavior of their partners. Shared experiences and repeated interaction enable participating organizations to predict with confidence their partners' actions, thereby eliminating the need for more formal mechanisms of enforcing agreements. Most often, these partnerships focus on collaborative activities that entail relatively little risk to the participating organizations. For activities involving higher levels of risk or resource commitment, participating organizations are likely to demand stronger ways of enforcing the provisions of the partnership.

In one recent study of public health partnerships in 60 public health jurisdictions, local health departments and hospitals were found to participate in informal collaborative groups more commonly than in other types of partnership structures.[36] These types of organizations maintain long histories of operation within their communities compared with other types of healthcare organizations–allowing them to use their reputation as an assurance of behavior rather than using more formalized and costly assurance methods. Only a minority of the managed care plans and health centers that engage in community health partnerships do so through informal structures.

*Contractual Agreements.*    A second, more formalized structural arrangement used in public health partnerships is the contractual agreement. Contracts are used to specify organizational roles and performance expectations within multi-institutional ventures, and to create legal mechanisms for enforcing these expectations. Contracts are particularly important for partnerships involving organizations that lack a shared mission or set of incentives–such as opportunistic and resource dependency partnerships. Moreover, contractual partnerships are often used for collaborative activities requiring substantial financial risk. In these cases, the additional costs entailed in establishing and enforcing contracts are justified by the risk that is avoided or limited through contract provisions.

Managed care plans and health centers appear to rely on contractual partnerships more frequently than other types of structural arrangements.[36] Although most managed care plans do not participate in any type of partnership, nearly two thirds of the plans that do participate rely on contractual agreements. By comparison, 59% of participating health centers rely on contracts, as do 38% of participating hospitals and 24% of participating local health departments.[36] Most managed care plan partnerships involve service delivery functions, which are more likely than other types of partnerships to be carried out through contractual agreements. Partnerships involving service delivery functions often entail substantial risks–including the risk of failing to recover the costs of providing services and the risk of being held responsible for the outcomes of service delivery. Contractual agreements are used in service delivery partnerships to share these risks equitably among participating organizations.

*Shared Governance.*    A third structural model used in public health partnerships involves arrangements for shared governance among participating organizations. Rather than formalizing the content of interaction through contractual agreements, this approach formalizes the decision-making process to be used in developing and implementing collective action. In doing so, shared governance arrangements add flexibility to the partnership structure by avoiding the need to specify fully the nature of collective action and the contingencies for every foreseeable outcome of this action.

Two basic arrangements for shared governance are commonly observed among public health partnerships. In the first arrangement, each participating organization grants membership on its governing board to representatives from partnering organizations. As an alternative to reciprocal board membership, some organizations choose to establish a separate corporate entity to conduct partnership activities, along with a separate governing board for the new entity. Under either model, an organization's degree of power and representation on the governing board is typically commensurate with the organization's resource commitment to partnership activities.

The shared governance arrangement is used in one study community to organize collaborative activities in community health assessment, planning, and health education.[36] A large employer serves as the founding organization for the partnership by establishing a wholly owned subsidiary to house partnership activities. Ten other organizations participate in the governance of the new corporation, including employers, hospitals, medical practices, managed care plans, a community health center, and the local health department. Three organizations—the founding employer, a hospital, and a managed care plan—contribute the majority of financial resources to sustain the effort, and therefore maintain greater representation on the governing board. Community health activities conducted through the partnership include a community-wide survey of resident health status and behavioral risk factors, a comparative study of surgical rates and outcomes at local hospitals, a collaborative effort to develop and disseminate clinical practice guidelines on a community-wide basis to local physicians, and a community-level health education effort to increase age-appropriate mammography utilization.

*Shared Ownership.*   A fourth and final structural arrangement for public health partnerships closely parallels the shared governance model but involves the added dimension of mutual ownership. Under this arrangement, each of the organizations participating in the partnership maintains equity ownership in a separate corporate entity that is formed to administer partnership activities. As a result, each organization shares in the financial liabilities and assets accrued by the new entity. This structural arrangement helps to align the incentives faced by participating organizations and creates a single, shared mission for the jointly owned venture.

The shared ownership arrangement is used in one study community by a group of three hospitals and a network of community health centers to sustain a coordinated care program for serving vulnerable and underserved populations within a 15-county region.[34,36] The hospitals—which include a county-owned facility, an academic medical center, and a nonprofit children's hospital—each maintain one quarter ownership in the corporation, and the network of health centers owns the remaining one quarter share. The shared nonprofit corporation is licensed as an HMO and serves uninsured residents as well as Medicaid beneficiaries.

Taken together, shared governance and shared ownership arrangements are relatively rare within the communities examined in this study.[36] Nonetheless, these arrangements are notable for their ability to sustain multiorganizational, multifaceted community efforts. They appear to accommodate more organizational participants and more functional activities than less formalized arrangements, suggesting a superior ability to manage operational complexity. At the same time, these arrangements are likely to incur larger development costs and necessitate greater sacrifices of individual organizational control than less formalized and less integrated structural models.

*The Life Cycle of Public Health Partnerships*

Public health partnerships evolve over time in response to organizational and environmental changes.[36] A longitudinal study of partnerships identified several alternative life cycle paths for these arrangements (Figure 3-9). Most organizations that participate in partnerships report engaging in either formal or informal processes for evaluating the arrangement on a periodic basis. Through these evaluation processes, organizations assess whether the arrangement is meeting organizational and community expectations regarding its operation and its outcomes. For example, a children's hospital in one community used periodic measures of evening emergency room utilization to evaluate the success of an after-hours community pediatric clinic that was jointly administered with the local health department.[36] The observed declines in utilization that occurred after implementation of the clinic were interpreted as evidence of partnership success in meeting one of the hospital's key internal goals.

In response to both formal and informal evaluations, partnership participants may adopt an array of possible actions. Organizations often choose simply to *maintain* existing partnership arrangements in order to sustain current performance levels or allow additional time for objectives to be met. A 2-year follow-up of public health partnerships operating in eight case study communities suggests that maintenance approaches are used

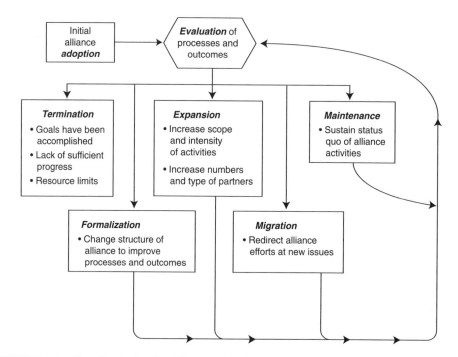

**FIGURE 3-9   The Life Cycle of Public Health Partnerships**
*Source:* Reprinted from *Joint Comm J Qual Improv,* 1998; 24(10):533.

only for relatively brief periods of time.[36] Most partnerships underway within these communities appear to have used one or more active strategies for adapting the partnership during this period in order to meet new or un- fulfilled expectations.

Public health partnerships often undertake a *migration* strategy in which the partnership is redirected at new tasks and goals that are identified by the participants. This is often used once original partnership objectives have been met, or when participants are faced with changes in organizational or com- munity needs. In one community, for example, a partnership that was origi- nally formed to conduct provider education activities regarding childhood immunization practices redirected its efforts to focus on supporting appropri- ate lead poisoning screening practices among community providers.[36] Partnership participants indicated that this migration occurred because the group's immunization objectives had largely been met and because lead poi- soning had become an issue of heightened community concern.

Another possible strategy for partnership adaptation is one of *expansion*, in which participants extend the scale or scope of activities addressed through collective action. With this strategy, partnership participants maintain their original objectives and activities, but they may also adopt new areas of op- eration. Partnerships may expand the volume or range of services delivered, the geographic areas served, or the population groups targeted by their col- lective actions. In doing so, some partnerships also expand their membership to include a greater number or a wider diversity of participating organiza- tions. Expansion activities appear to be used by organizations after smaller successes have been achieved through the partnership.[36] For example, in one case study community, a partnership that initially focused on encouraging age-appropriate women to seek mammography services was expanded to in- clude a component that encouraged community providers to offer appropri- ate mammography counseling and recommendations to their patients.

As a fourth strategy, some organizations attempt to enhance the perfor- mance of their partnership by changing its structure through a process of *for- malization*. This process may entail developing new contract language, governance arrangements, or ownership arrangements in an effort to enforce expected levels of performance. Organizations in one community, for exam- ple, chose to move from an informal collaborative structure to the develop- ment of a jointly owned nonprofit corporation in order to enhance the operation of jointly administered health education initiatives.[36] Participants hoped that this formalization would facilitate their efforts at coordination and joint management of educational programs. Participants also expected that their new structure would enhance their visibility and credibility with exter- nal stakeholders, thereby assisting them in such efforts as securing outside funding and providing outreach to community members.

Finally, some partnership participants choose to *terminate* their initia- tives for reasons including goal fulfillment, insufficient performance, or ex- cessive cost. Partnership termination is not automatically regarded as a sign of partnership failure, however. In fact, most of the terminated partnerships observed in this study resulted from goal fulfillment rather than problems with performance or cost.[36] Partnership termination appears particularly common among opportunistic partnerships and resource dependency partner- ships, where shared interests may be narrowly defined and rapidly achieved.

*Developing and Managing Public Health Partnerships*

In reviewing the experience of public health partnerships across a variety of organizations and communities, several common themes emerge regarding the successful development and management of these arrangements. Drawing on these themes, the following recommendations may help organizations pursue optimal partnership strategies in public health.

*Identify a Boundary Spanner.*   Perhaps most importantly, partnerships appear to require an organization or individual who is able to span the boundaries of multiple organizations and develop a shared vision for collective action. As other studies of partnerships have noted, the role of the boundary spanner is critical in motivating awareness of and interest in collaboration.[28,43,47] In studies of public health partnerships, a wide variety of organizations and individuals have been observed to fill this role. Local health departments served this role in many of these efforts—in several cases assuming the role of a neutral third party in fostering collaborative activity among competing health care organizations. In other communities, private organizations appeared better suited to boundary-spanning roles because of their existing interorganizational relationships or their freedom from cumbersome government regulations in areas such as contracting and purchasing.

In a dramatic example of the former arrangement, the local health department in one community served as the lead agency in an effort to develop a comparative, community-wide report card of health care quality among health plans, hospitals, and other local medical care providers.[34,36] Health plans report that they recruited the health department to serve in this boundary-spanning role because of the agency's scientific expertise and its reputation for neutrality and objectivity.

*Secure Buy-in from Key Stakeholders and Opinion Leaders.*   The successful adoption of any innovation requires the awareness and support of key decision makers. Because the partnerships described here target community-level issues and outcomes, the pool of relevant stakeholders is likely to be large and extend well beyond the set of potential partnership participants. Support from key opinion leaders may be required to ensure the partnership sufficient visibility and acceptance within the community. Furthermore, support from relevant policy and regulatory officials may give the partnership added legitimacy while helping partnership members to identify and anticipate potential legal and regulatory issues. Partnership developers should therefore invest time early in the development process in informing and soliciting feedback from these types of community stakeholders, especially where these stakeholders are not formal partnership participants.

*Recognize and Respond to Participation Constraints.*   It appears critical that individuals responsible for developing partnerships have the ability to recognize the participation constraints faced by potential partnership participants and to devise explicit strategies for addressing these constraints. Organizations face financial, legal, political, administrative, and cultural barriers to participating in partnerships that may or may not be tractable. Some organizations find it useful to devise an explicit participation strategy early on in the partnership development process—one that includes contingencies for key organizations that may abstain from partnership membership. In developing this strategy, it appears important to recognize the opportunity costs faced by potential partnership members and to identify participation incentives that are tailored to these costs. In this way, the participation strategy can be used to secure the sustained involvement of essential partnership participants.

*Keep the Structure Simple.*   Studies reveal a variety of possible structural arrangements, both formal and informal, for sustaining public health partnerships. As with many other managerial decisions, simplicity should be a powerful criterion when choosing an appropriate partnership structure.[28] Many of the public health partnerships observed in this study are based on informal agreements and relatively simple contractual agreements. These structures require relatively little development, management, and maintenance costs when compared to the more formalized shared ownership and shared governance models. Where possible, partnership managers should take advantage of natural participation incentives and shared interests to guide and enforce behavior among organizations, rather than resorting to more formalized and complex interorganizational structures. Ultimately, in making structural decisions, managers must balance the risks entailed in the partnership with the costs of alternative partnership structures. Larger risks justify more costly and complex structural safeguards.

*Ensure Incentive Compatibility among Participants.*   Ensuring incentive compatibility emerges as another critical managerial task in developing and sustaining public health partnerships.[28] Organizations report participating in public health partnerships for a variety of reasons—some of which may not be compatible with overall partnership objectives or with the individual interests of other participants. Successful partnership managers appear able to choose structural arrangements that mediate potential incentive conflicts among partnership participants. In some cases, explicit contractual agreements and risk-sharing provisions are required to counteract underlying incentives for noncooperative behavior among partnership members.

For example, in one community several managed care plans and a local health department jointly sponsored a community-based family planning education campaign that initially entailed incompatible incentives.[36] Health plans faced a clear incentive to refer low-income patients with family planning needs to health department clinics where they could receive free services. Such incentives placed excessive financial burdens on the health department and undermined the continuity of care received by health plan members. To address this incentive compatibility problem, the health department successfully negotiated reimbursement arrangements for family planning services with most of the managed care plans—thereby creating financial incentives for plans to deliver these services themselves. For cases where health plan members continued to use health department family planning services, the agreements included provisions for the health department to share with the health plans information concerning services delivered to their members. As this example illustrates, the ability to address issues of incentive incompatibility effectively appears to hinge on: (1) recognizing the nature of the incompatibility, (2) clearly defining the areas of shared interest, and (3) developing interorganizational arrangements that counteract the incentives for noncooperative behavior without eliminating the incentives for collaboration.[28]

*Ensure Effective Communication and Information Flows among Participants.*   The task of managing communication and information flows among partnership members also appears as an essential element of successful public health partnerships. Many partnership participants reported that the efficient flow of information among organizations was often critical for enabling service coordination and integration to occur. Achieving this flow requires the development of effective protocols for interorganizational communication, explicit policies for information sharing, and reliable systems for data exchange. Adding to the challenge, partnership participants reported that information protocols and policies must be sufficiently flexible to address individual concerns about: (1) the proprietary nature of some types of organizational information and (2) the need for confidentiality in patient-specific health information. Achieving interorganizational consensus about these issues appears far from automatic in many cases.

Partnerships observed in several communities addressed both confidentiality and proprietary concerns by establishing a separate, private corporate entity to collect, process, and manage shared information among participating organizations.[36] This approach was used in the development of a community-wide immunization registry in one community and in the development of a community health information and assessment system in another community. Partnership participants indicated that the corporate entity shields proprietary information from being disseminated inadvertently or in response to public-sector information requests under the federal Freedom of Information Act statutes. The entity also enforces confidentiality requirements and ensures the compatibility and quality of data from multiple institutions.

*Develop an Explicit Evaluation Strategy.*    Partnership managers face the important task of developing appropriate processes for monitoring organizational and community performance. Many of the partnerships examined in this review appeared to fall short in this task, relying primarily on informal evaluation processes maintained by individual organizational participants. Clearly, an effective evaluation process hinges on the existence of adequate communication and information flows across participating organizations. Partnership managers must take the additional step of establishing processes for developing and disseminating appropriate measures of performance from this information. These processes ensure that optimal decision making can occur among partnership participants at all stages of the partnership life cycle. In doing this, performance measurement activities must keep pace with changes in partnership structures, processes, and outcomes.

An ideal evaluation strategy focuses both on organization-specific outcomes and on community-level outcomes.[49] Measuring organization-specific outcomes is likely to be essential for the ongoing support and assistance of key internal stakeholders. However, from a public health perspective, the effects on community health outcomes are of primary importance. The ability to demonstrate these community-level effects to key external stakeholders may prove essential in securing ongoing community support and assistance and in recruiting an expanded pool of partnership participants.

*Maintain Momentum through Stages of Success.*    Finally, public health partnerships can build momentum by progressing through stages of success.[50] Small successes early on in the partnership process can build confidence among partnership participants and provide motivation for subsequent accomplishments. As participants gain experience in working successfully within the partnership structure, increasingly complex and difficult objectives can be undertaken. Managers should therefore follow an explicit plan to achieve stages of success beginning with that small and easily accomplished task and progressing to more complex and far-reaching objectives. In turn, the partnership evaluation strategy should be designed to provide timely feedback concerning each of these objectives.

Public health partnerships vary markedly in their objectives, structures, and functions. On the whole, this variation appears healthy rather than problematic. Public health administrators require many degrees of freedom in designing multi-institutional arrangements to fit specific community needs and organizational capacities. Administrators must also ensure that these arrangements remain flexible and adaptive to changing needs and priorities over time. The challenges entailed in forming and maintaining public health partnerships should not be underestimated; administrators must strike a balance among diverse organizational interests and complex community needs. It is equally important, however, not to undervalue the opportunities for public health improvement created by collaboration.

•   •   •

This examination of the public health delivery system in the United States reveals the enormous complexity of the system. No clear division of labor emerges among different types of organizations involved; nonetheless, the scale and scope of activity that is produced by the system is considerable. Governmental health agencies factor prominently in this mix of institutions, reflecting the federalist system of government from which they derive. Nongovernmental organizations are also active participants and often leaders in public health delivery at local, state, and national levels. Many public health activities are now carried out not within institutions but between them, through interorganizational and intergovernmental partnerships. The number and variety of organizations that participate in these relationships is encouraging. Evidence from a growing number of communities suggests that partnerships are addressing complex public health issues that cannot be managed effectively by any one organization acting alone. By pooling the resources and skills of multiple organizations within the community, these efforts offer promising strategies for improving the public health delivery system in the United States.

## Chapter Review

1. Government authority in public health is generally distributed in the following ways:
   - Federal authority is carried out primarily through policy development, public health financing, and broad regulatory enforcement.
   - State authority extends to specific public health regulatory functions, as well as responsibilities in public health resource allocation and program administration.
   - Local government responsibilities focus on implementing public health policies and interventions within communities.
2. Many of the federal agencies with public health responsibilities are organized within the US HHS, including the CDC, HRSA, NIH, AHRQ,

FDA, the Indian Health Service, and the Substance Abuse and Mental Health Services Administration.

3. Wide variation exists in how public health responsibilities are organized within state health agencies. State agencies typically follow one of two general structural models:
   • The free-standing agency model
   • The superagency model

4. Administrative relationships between state and local public health agencies assume one of four basic forms:
   • Decentralized relationships
   • Centralized relationships
   • Shared authority relationships
   • Mixed authority relationships

5. An increasing amount of public health activity occurs through inter-organizational relationships, often termed *partnerships*. Key elements of these relationships include their strategic orientation, their structural design, and their functional characteristics.

## References

1. Arrow KJ. The organization of economic activity: issues pertinent to the choice of market versus non-market allocation. In: Arrow KJ, ed. *Collected Papers of K.J. Arrow.* Vol. 2. Cambridge, Mass: Harvard University Press; 1969:147–185.

2. Gostin LA. *Public Health Law: Power, Duty, Restraint.* Berkeley, Calif: University of California Press; 2000.

3. Turnock BJ. *Public Health: What It Is and How It Works.* Gaithersburg, Md: Aspen Publishers; 1996.

4. Rawding N, Brown C. An overview of local health departments. In: Mays GP, Miller CA, Halverson PK, eds. *Local Public Health Practice: Trends and Models.* Washington, DC: American Public Health Association; 2000.

5. Lee PR, Benjamin AE. Health policy and the politics of health care. In: Lee PR, Estes CL, eds. *The Nation's Health.* 4th ed. Boston, Mass: Jones and Bartlett; 1994:121–137.

6. Litman TJ. The politics of health: establishing policies and setting priorities. In: Lee PR, Estes CL, eds. *The Nation's Health.* 4th ed. Boston, Mass: Jones and Bartlett; 1994:107–120.

7. Mays GP, Halverson PK, Baker EL, Stevens R, Vann JJ. Availability and perceived effectiveness of public health activities in the nation's most populous areas. *Am J Public Health.* 2004;94(6):1019–1026.

8. Roper WL. Regulating quality and clinical practice. In: Altman SH, Reinhardt VE, Shactman D, eds. *Regulating Managed Care: Theory, Practice, and Future Options.* San Francisco, Calif: Jossey-Bass; 1999:145–159.

9. Moran DW. Federal regulation of managed care: an impulse in search of a theory. *Health Affairs.* 1997;16(6):7–33.

10. Fuchs BC. *Managed Health Care: Federal and State Regulation.* Washington, DC: Congressional Research Service; 1997.

11. US General Accounting Office. *Performance Budgeting: Past Initiatives Offer Insights for GPRA.* Washington, DC: GAO; 1997.

12. US Department of Health and Human Services, Panel on Performance Measures and Data for Public Health Performance Partnership Grants. *Assessment of Performance Measures for Public Health, Substance*

*Abuse, and Mental Health*. Washington, DC: National Academies Press; 1997.

13. Rochefort DA, Cobb RW. *The Politics of Problem Definition: Shaping the Policy Agenda*. Lawrence, Kan: University of Kansas Press; 1997.

14. US General Accounting Office. *Vaccines for Children: Reexamination of Program Goals and Implementation Needed to Ensure Vaccination*. Washington, DC: GAO; 1995. PEMD-95-22.

15. US General Accounting Office. *Lead Poisoning: Federal Health Care Programs Are Not Effectively Reaching At-Risk Children*. Washington, DC: GAO; 1998. HEHS-99-18.

16. Centers for Disease Control and Prevention. About CDC: CDC organization. Available at: http://www.cdc.gov/about. Accessed August 2, 2006.

17. US Department of Health and Human Services. *Healthy People 2000: National Health Promotion and Disease Prevention Objectives*. Washington, DC: US Government Printing Office (PHS) 91-50212; 1991.

18. US Department of Health and Human Services. *Healthy People 2010*. Conference ed. Washington, DC: US Government Printing Office; 2000.

19. Institute of Medicine. *The Future of Public Health*. Washington, DC: National Academies Press; 1988.

20. US Centers for Disease Control and Prevention, Public Health Practice Program Office. *Profile of State and Territorial Public Health Systems: United States, 1990*. Atlanta, Ga: 1991.

21. Beitsch LM, Brooks RG, Grigg M, et al. Structure and functions of state public health agencies. *Am J Public Health*. 2006;96(1):167-172.

22. Maralit M, et al. *Transforming State Health Agencies to Meet Current and Future Challenges*. Washington, DC: National Governors Association; 1997.

23. Kaluzny AD, Zuckerman HS, Ricketts TC. *Partners for the Dance: Forming Strategic Alliances in Health Care*. Ann Arbor, Mich: Health Administration Press; 1995.

24. DeFriese GH, Hetherington JS, Brooks EF, et al. The program implications of administrative relationships between local health departments and state and local government. *Am J Public Health*. 1981;71(10):1109-1115.

25. Nelson DE, Fleming DW, Grant-Worley J, et al. Outcome-based management and public health: the Oregon benchmarks experience. *J Public Health Manage Pract*. 1995;1(2):8-17.

26. Griffin SR, Welch P. Performance-based public health in Texas. *J Public Health Manage Pract*. 1995;1(3):44-49.

27. Halverson PK, Nicola RM, Baker EL. Performance measurement and accreditation of public health organizations: a call to action. *J Public Health Manage Pract*. 1998;4(4):5-7.

28. National Association of County and City Health Officials. *2005 National Profile of Local Health Departments*. Washington, DC: NACCHO; 2006.

29. National Association of County and City Health Officials. Operational definition of a local health department. Washington, DC: NACCHO; 2005:1-9. Available at: www.naccho.org. Accessed November 26, 2006.

30. National Association of Local Boards of Health. *National Profile of Local Boards of Health, Centers for Disease Control and Prevention*. Washington, DC: NALBOH; 1997.

31. Halverson PK, et al. Privatizing health services: alternative models and emerging issues for public health and quality management. *Qual Manage Health Care*. 1997;5(2):1-18.

32. Wall S. Transformation in public health systems. *Health Affairs*. 1998;17(3):64-80.

33. Gerzoff RB, Brown CK, Baker EL. Full-time employees of the US local health departments, 1992–1993. *J Public Health Manage Pract.* 1999;5(3): 1–9.

34. Mays GP, Miller CA, Halverson PK. *Local Public Health Practice: Trends and Models.* Washington, DC: American Public Health Association; 1999.

35. Roper WL, Mays GP. The changing managed care–public health interface. *JAMA.* 1998;280(20):1739–1740.

36. Nelson H. *Nonprofit and For-Profit HMOs: Converging Practices but Different Goals?* New York, NY: Milbank Memorial Fund; 1996.

37. Lipson DJ, Naierman N. Snapshots of change in fifteen communities: safety-net providers. *Health Affairs.* 1996;15(2):33–48.

38. Halverson PK, Mays GP, Kaluzny AD, et al. Not-so-strange bedfellows: models of interaction between managed care plans and public health agencies. *Milbank Q.* 1997;75(1):1–26.

39. Mays GP, Halverson PK, Stevens R. The contributions of managed care plans to public health practice: evidence from the nation's largest local health departments. *Public Health Rep.* 2001;116(suppl 1):50–67.

40. Lewin T, Gottlieb M. In hospital sales, an overlooked side effect. *New York Times.* April 27, 1997:1.

41. Novick LF. The teaching health department. *J Public Health Manage Pract.* 2004;10(4):275–276.

42. Maeshino R. Public health practice and academic medicine: promising partnerships regional medicine public health education centers: two cycles. *J Public Health Manage Pract.* 2006;12(5):493–495.

43. Kanter RM. Collaborative advantage: the art of alliances. *Harvard Bus Rev.* 1994;72:96–108.

44. Kanter RM. Becoming PALs: pooling, allying, and linking across companies. *Acad Manage Exec.* 1989;3:183–193.

45. Mays GP, Halverson PK, Kaluzny AD, et al. Managed care, public health, and privatization: a typology of interorganizational arrangements. In: Halverson PK, Kaluzny AD, McLaughlin CP, eds. *Managed Care and Public Health.* Gaithersburg, Md: Aspen Publishers; 1998:185–200.

46. Scott WR. Innovation in medical care organizations: a synthetic review. *Med Care Rev.* 1990;47(2):165–192.

47. Mays GP, Halverson PK, Kaluzny AD, et al. Collaboration to improve community health: trends and alternative models. *Joint Comm J Qual Improv Health Care.* 1998;24(10):518–540.

48. US Centers for Disease Control and Prevention, Committee on Community Engagement. *Principles of Community Engagement.* Atlanta, Ga: Public Health Practice Program Office, Centers for Disease Control and Prevention; 1997.

49. Mays GP, Halverson PK, Miller CA, et al. Assessing the performance of local public health systems: a survey of state health agency efforts. *J Public Health Manage Pract.* 1998;4(4):63–78.

50. Halverson PK. Strategies for managing the public's health: implications and next steps. In: Halverson PK, Kaluzny AD, McLaughlin CP, eds. *Managed Care and Public Health.* Gaithersburg, Md: Aspen Publishers; 1998:350–363.

# CHAPTER 4

# PUBLIC HEALTH LAW

Lawrence O. Gostin

## Chapter Overview

Laws are enacted to influence healthy behavior, respond to health threats, and enforce health and safety standards. Public health law is principally concerned with government's assurance of the conditions for the population's health—what government may, and must, do to safeguard human health. Federal, state, and local governments exercise public health powers derived from the complex legal relationships among these levels of government. Protecting and preserving community health is not possible without an effective legal framework to guide a wide range of private endeavors.

Preservation of the public's health is among the most important goals of government. The enactment and enforcement of law, moreover, is a primary means by which government creates the conditions for people to lead healthier and safer lives. Law creates a mission for public health authorities, assigns their functions, and specifies the manner in which they may exercise their authority. The law is a tool for public health practice, which is used to influence norms for healthy behavior, identify and respond to health threats, and set and enforce health and safety standards. The most important social debates concerning public health take place in legal fora—legislatures, courts, and administrative agencies—and in the law's language of rights, duties, and justice.[1] It is no exaggeration to say that "the field of public health . . . could not long exist in the manner in which we know it today except for its sound legal basis."[2(p4)]

The Institute of Medicine (IOM), in its foundational 1988 report, *The Future of Public Health*, acknowledged that law was essential to public health, but cast serious doubt on the soundness of public health's legal basis. Concluding that "this nation has lost sight of its public health goals and has allowed the system of public health activities to fall into disarray," the IOM placed some of the blame on an obsolete and inadequate body of enabling laws and regulations.[3(p19)] The IOM recommended:

> states review their public health statutes and make revisions necessary to accomplish the following two objectives: (1) clearly delineate the basic authority and responsibility entrusted to public health

agencies, boards, and officials at the state and local levels and the relationship between them; and (2) support a set of modern disease control measures that address contemporary health problems such as AIDS, cancer, and heart disease, and incorporate due process safeguards (notice, hearings, administrative review, right to counsel, standards of evidence).[4(p10)]

The IOM reiterated its call for public health law reform in its 2003 report, *The Future of the Public's Health in the 21st Century*: "Public health law at the federal, state, and local levels is often outdated and internally inconsistent. This leads to inefficiency and a lack of coordination and may even pose a danger in a crisis."[5(p4)] The IOM commended the "pioneering work" of two model public health statutes: (1) the Model State Emergency Health Powers Act, drafted at the CDC's request following the terrorist attacks of 2001, which provides public health agencies with powers in a declared emergency; and (2) the Turning Point Model State Public Health Law, a Robert Wood Johnson Foundation project, which provides a comprehensive structure for the mission, powers, and duties of public health agencies. Both model laws are considered in more detail later in this chapter.

This chapter reviews the state of public health law in the United States. First, a theory and definition of public health law is offered. Second, public health powers within the constitutional design are explained. Third, the current structure of federal, state, and local health agencies is examined. Finally, the future of public health law is considered, explaining the deficiencies in state public health statutes and proposing guidelines for law reform.

## A Theory and Definition of Public Health Law

Public health law is often used interchangeably with other terms that signify a connection between law and health, such as *health law, law and medicine*, and *forensic medicine*. Despite the similarity of these names, public health law is a distinct discipline capable of definition. I have defined public health law as:

> the study of the legal powers and duties of the state, in collaboration with its partners (e.g., health care, business, the community, the media, and academe), to assure the conditions for people to be healthy (e.g., to identify, prevent, and ameliorate risks to health in the population) and the limitations on the power of the state to constrain the autonomy, privacy, liberty, proprietary, or other legally protected interests of individuals for the common good. The prime objective of public health law is to pursue the highest possible level of physical and mental health in the population, consistent with the values of social justice.[6]

Public health law has at least five characteristics that help separate it from other fields at the intersection of law and health: government, populations, relationships, services, and coercion.

### Government's Essential Role in Public Health Law

Public health activities are the primary (but not exclusive) responsibility of government. The importance of government in ensuring the conditions for the population's health is demonstrated by its constitutional powers and its role in a democracy. The Preamble to the Constitution reveals the ideals of government as the wellspring of communal life and mutual security: "We the People of the United States, in Order to form a more perfect Union, establish Justice, insure domestic Tranquility, provide for the common defense, promote the general Welfare, and secure the Blessings of Liberty to ourselves and our Posterity, do ordain and establish this Constitution. . . ." The constitutional design reveals a plain intent to vest power in government at every level to protect community health and safety. Government is empowered to collect taxes and expend public resources, and only government can require members of the community to submit to regulation.

The role of government in a democracy also helps explain its importance in advancing the public's health. People form governments precisely to provide a means of communal support and security. Acting alone, individuals cannot ensure even minimum levels of health. Individuals may procure personal medical services and many of the necessities of life; any person of means can purchase a home, clothing, food, and the services of a physician or hospital. Yet, no single individual, or group of individuals, can ensure his or her health. Meaningful protection and assurance of the population's health requires communal effort. The community as a whole has a stake in environmental protection, hygiene and sanitation, clean air and surface water, uncontaminated food and drinking water, safe roads and products, and the control of infectious disease. Each of these collective goods, and many more, are essential conditions for health. Yet, these goods can be secured only through organized action on behalf of the population.

This discussion does not suggest that the private and voluntary sectors are not important in public health. Manifestly, private (e.g., managed care), charitable (e.g., the Red Cross), and community (e.g., human immunodeficiency virus [HIV] support) organizations play roles that are critical to public health. Nevertheless, communal efforts to protect and promote the population's health are primarily a responsibility of government, which is why government action represents a central theoretical tenet of what we call public health law.

## Serving the Health Needs of Populations

Public health focuses on the health of populations rather than on the clinical improvement of individual patients. Generally, public health focuses on communal health, whereas medicine focuses on the health of individuals. Classic definitions of public health emphasize this population-based perspective: "As one of the objects of the police power of the state, the 'public health' means the prevailingly healthful or sanitary condition of the general body of people or the community in mass, and the absence of any general or widespread disease or cause of mortality."[7(p721)] Public health services are those that are shared by all members of the community and are organized and supported by, and for, the benefit of the people as a whole. Thus, whereas the art or science of medicine seeks to identify and ameliorate ill health in the individual patient, public health seeks to improve the health of the population.

## Relationships between Government and the Public

Public health contemplates the relationship between the state and the population (or between the state and individuals who place themselves or the community at risk) rather than the relationship between the physician and the patient. Public health practitioners and scholars are interested in organized community efforts to improve the health of populations. Accordingly, public health law observes collective action—principally through government—and its effects on various populations. The field of public health law similarly examines the benefits and burdens placed by government on legally protected interests. This is in direct contrast to the field of health care law, which concerns the microrelationships between healthcare providers and patients as well as the organization, finance, and provision of personal medical services.

### Population-Based Services

Public health deals primarily with the provision of population-based health services rather than personal medical services. The core functions of public health agencies are those fundamental activities that are carried out to protect the population's health:

- *Assessment*—the collection, assembly, and analysis of community health needs
- *Policy development*—the development of public health policies informed through scientific knowledge
- *Assurance*—assurance of the services necessary for community health

Activities regarded as essential public health services include efforts to monitor community health status and investigate health risks; inform, educate, and empower people about health; mobilize community partnerships; regulate individual and organizational behavior; evaluate effectiveness, accessibility, and quality of personal health services; and pursue innovative solutions to health problems. Moreover, the public health community is increasingly interested in scientific methodologies to monitor the efficacy of services.[8]

### Demand Conformance with Health and Safety Standards

Public health possesses the power to coerce individuals for the protection of the community and thus does not rely on a near-universal ethic of voluntarism. Although government can do much to promote public health that does not require the exercise of compulsory powers, it alone is authorized to require conformance with publicly established standards of behavior. The degree of compulsory measures necessary to safeguard the public's health is, of course, subject to political and judicial resolution. Yet, protecting and preserving community health is not possible without the constraint of a wide range of private activities. Absent an inherent governmental authority and ability to coerce individual and community behaviors, threats to public health and safety could not be reduced easily.

Having defined public health law and distinguished it from other fields, it will be helpful to examine the public health law in our constitutional system of government.

## Public Health in the Constitutional Design

No inquiry is more important to public health law than understanding the role of government in the constitutional design. If public health law is principally about government's assurance of the conditions necessary for the population's health, what must government do to safeguard human health? Analyzing this question requires an assessment of duty (what government must do), authority (what government can, but is not required to, do), limits (what government can not do), and responsibility (which government— whether federal, state, or local—is to act).

The US Constitution is the starting point for any analysis concerning the distribution of governmental powers. Although the Constitution is said to impose no affirmative obligation on governments to act, provide services, or protect individuals and populations, it does serve three primary functions: (1) it allocates power among the federal government and the states (federalism), (2) it divides power among the three branches of government (separation of powers), and (3) it limits government power (to protect individual liberties). In the realm of public health, then, the Constitution acts as both a fountain and a levee; it originates the flow of power—to preserve the public health— and it curbs that power—to protect individual freedoms.

If the Constitution is a fountain from which government powers flow, federalism represents a partition in the fountain that separates federal and state powers.[9] By separating the pool of legislative authority into these two tiers of government, federalism preserves the balance of power among national and state authorities. Theoretically, the division of government powers is distinct and clear. The federal government is a government of limited power whose acts must be authorized by the Constitution. The states, by contrast, retain the powers they possessed as sovereign governments before ratification of the Constitution.[10] The most important state authority is the power to protect the health, safety, morals, and general welfare of the population. In practice, however, the powers of the federal and state governments intersect in innumerable areas, particularly in areas of traditional state concern, like public health.

Federalism functions as a sorting device for determining which government (federal, state, or local) may respond legitimately to a public health threat. Often, federal, state, and local governments exercise public health powers concurrently. Where conflicts among the various levels of government arise, however, federal laws likely preempt state or local actions pursuant to the supremacy clause: the "Constitution, and the Laws of the United States . . . and all Treaties made . . . shall be the supreme law of the Land."[11]

In addition to establishing a federalist system, the Constitution separates governmental powers into three branches: (1) the *legislative* branch, which has the power to create laws; (2) the *executive* branch, which has the power to enforce the laws; and (3) the *judicial* branch, which has the power to interpret the laws. States have similar schemes of governance pursuant to their own constitutions. By separating the powers of government, the Constitution provides a system of checks and balances that is thought to reduce the possibility of governmental oppression.

The separation of powers doctrine is essential to public health. Each branch of government possesses a unique constitutional authority to create, enforce, or interpret health policy. The *legislative branch* creates health policy and allocates the necessary resources to effectuate that policy. Some believe that legislators are ill-equipped to make complex public health decisions. (Refer to Chapter 6 for a detailed discussion.) Yet, as the only "purely" elected branch of government, members of federal or state legislatures ultimately are politically accountable to the people.

The *executive branch,* which enforces health policy, has an equally significant role in public health. Most public health agencies reside in the executive branch and are responsible for implementing legislation that may often require establishing and enforcing complex health regulations. The executive branch and its agencies are uniquely positioned to govern public health. Public health agencies are designed and created for the purpose of advancing community health. They have sufficient expertise and resources to focus on health problems for extended periods of time. Agencies, however, may occasionally suffer from stale thinking, complicity with the subjects of regulation, and the inability to balance competing values and claims for resources.

The *judicial branch,* which interprets the law and resolves legal disputes, also has an important role concerning public health. Courts can exert substantial control over public health policy by determining the boundaries of government power and the zone of autonomy, privacy, and liberty to be afforded individuals. Courts decide whether a public health statute or policy is constitutional, whether agency action is authorized legislatively, whether agency officials have sufficient evidence to support their actions, and whether governmental officials or private parties have acted negligently. Although the exercise of judicial power may serve public health, courts may fail to review the substance of health policy choices critically. Federal judges, once appointed, are politically less accountable (though state judges may be elected). Courts, bound by the facts of a particular case or controversy, may be overly influenced by disfavored expert opinions and may focus too intently on individual rights at the expense of public health protections.

The separation of powers doctrine is not a model of efficiency. Dividing broad powers among branches of governments significantly burdens governmental operations, which may actually thwart public health. The constitutional design appears to value restraint in policy making: legislative representatives reconcile demands for public health funding with competing claims for societal resources; the executive branch straddles the line between congressional authorization and judicial restrictions on that authority; and the judiciary tempers public health measures with individual rights. As a result, the possibility of strong public health governance by any given branch is compromised in exchange for constitutional checks and balances that prevent overreaching and foster political accountability.

A third constitutional function is to limit governmental power to protect individual liberties. Governmental actions to promote the communal good often infringe on individual freedoms. Public health regulation and individual rights may directly conflict. Resolving the tension between population-based regulations and individual rights requires a trade-off. Thus, although the Constitution grants extensive powers to governments, it also limits that power by protecting individual rights and freedoms. The Bill of Rights (the first 10 amendments to the Constitution), together with the Reconstruction Amendments (13th, 14th, and 15th Amendments) and other constitutional provisions, create a zone of individual liberty, autonomy, privacy, and economic freedom that exists beyond the reach of the government.[12] Public health law struggles to determine the point at which governmental authority to promote the population's health must yield to individual rights and freedoms.

Understanding and defining the limits of public health powers by the federal, state, and local governments is an integral part of our constitutional system of government. In the following sections, the constitutional authority and exercise of public health powers by each of these levels of government are explored.

## Federal Public Health Powers

The federal government must draw its authority to act from specific, enumerated powers. Before an act of Congress is deemed constitutional, two questions must be asked: (1) does the Constitution affirmatively authorize Congress to act, and (2) does the exercise of that power improperly interfere with any constitutionally protected interest?

In theory, the United States is a government of limited, defined powers. In reality, political and judicial expansion of federal powers through the doctrine of implied powers allows the federal government considerable authority to act in the interests of public health and safety. Under the doctrine of implied powers, the federal government may employ all means "necessary and proper" to achieve the objectives of constitutionally enumerated national powers.[13] For public health purposes, the chief powers are the powers to tax, to spend, and to regulate interstate commerce. These powers provide Congress with independent authority to raise revenue for public health services and to regulate, both directly and indirectly, private activities that endanger human health.

The taxing power is a primary means for achieving public health objectives by influencing, directly and indirectly, health-related behavior through tax relief and tax burdens. Tax relief encourages private, health-promoting activity; tax burdens discourage risky behavior. Through various forms of tax relief, government provides incentives for private activities that it views as advantageous to community health (e.g., tax benefits for self-insured health-care plans).

Public health taxation also regulates private behavior by economically penalizing risk-taking activities. Tax policy discourages a number of activities that the government regards as unhealthy, dangerous, immoral, or adverse to human health. Thus, the government imposes significant excise or manufacturing taxes on tobacco, alcoholic beverages, and firearms; penalizes certain behaviors such as gambling; and influences individual and business decisions through taxes on gasoline or ozone-depleting chemicals that contribute to environmental degradation.

The spending power provides Congress with independent authority to allocate resources for the public good or general welfare without the need to justify its spending by reference to a specific enumerated power.[14] Closely connected to the power to tax, the spending power authorizes expenditures expressly for the public's health. The grant of such expenditures can be conditioned on a number of terms or requirements. The conditional spending power is thus like a private contract: in return for federal funds, the states agree to comply with federally imposed conditions. Such conditions are constitutionally allowed provided the conditions are clearly authorized by statute and a reasonable relationship exists between the condition imposed and the program's purposes.[15,16]

The need for federal public health funds effectively induces state conformance with federal regulatory standards. Congress and federal agencies use conditional spending to induce states to conform to federal standards in numerous public health contexts, including direct health care, prevention services, biomedical and health services research, public health regulation and safety inspection, and workplace safety and health.

The commerce power, more than any other enumerated power, affords Congress potent regulatory authority. Congress has the power to regulate: (1) all commerce among foreign nations and Indian tribes, and (2) interstate commerce among the states.[17] Although the scope of the interstate commerce power has been judicially limited during the course of our constitutional history, the current conception of Congress' commerce powers is extensive, although not unlimited.

The Supreme Court's modern construction of the interstate commerce power has been described as "plenary" or all-embracing, and has been exerted to affect virtually every aspect of social life.[18] The expansive interpretation of the commerce clause has enabled the national government to invade traditional realms of state public health power, including the fields of environmental protection, food and drug purity, occupational health and safety, and other public health matters. Thus, the commerce clause gives national authorities the power to regulate throughout the public health spectrum.

Any legitimate exercise of federal taxing, spending, or commerce power in the interests of public health may be determined to trump state public health regulation. By authority of the supremacy clause, Congress may preempt state public health regulation, even if the state is acting squarely within its police powers. Federal preemption occurs in many areas of public health law, such as with cigarette labeling and advertising regulations and occupational health and safety.

As a result of broad interpretations of its supreme, enumerated powers, the federal government has a vast presence in public health. It is nearly impossible to find a field of public health that is not heavily influenced by US governmental policy. Public health functions, including public funding for health care, safe food, effective drugs, clean water, a beneficial environment, and prevention services, can be found in an array of federal agencies.

## State Police Powers

Despite the broad federal presence in modern public health regulation, historically, states have had a predominant role in providing population-based health services. States still account for the majority of traditional public health spending for public health services (not including personal medical services or the environment). The 10th Amendment of the Constitution reserves to the states all powers that are neither given to the federal government nor prohibited by the Constitution. These reserved powers, known as the police powers, support a dominant role in protecting the public's health.[19]

The police powers represent the state's authority to further the goal of all government, which is to promote the general welfare of society. Police powers can be defined as:

> the inherent authority of the state (and, through delegation, local government) to enact laws and promulgate regulations to protect, preserve, and promote the health, safety, morals, and general welfare of the people. To achieve these communal benefits, the state retains the power to restrict, within federal and state constitutional limits, private interests—personal interests in liberty, autonomy, privacy,

and association, as well as economic interests in freedom of contract and uses of property.[20]

This definition of *police power* reflects three principal characteristics: (1) the government purpose is to promote the public good, (2) the state authority to act permits the restriction of private interests, and (3) the scope of state powers is pervasive. States exercise police powers for the common good, that is, to ensure that communities live in safety and security, in conditions that are conducive to good health, with moral standards, and, generally speaking, without unreasonable interference with human well-being.

Government, in order to achieve common goods, is empowered to enact legislation, regulate, and adjudicate in ways that necessarily limit, or even eliminate, private interests. Thus, government has inherent power to interfere with personal interests in autonomy, liberty, privacy, and association, as well as economic interests in ownership and uses of private property. The police power affords state government the authority to keep society free from noxious exercises of private rights. The state retains discretion to determine what is considered injurious or unhealthful and the manner in which to regulate, consistent with constitutional protections of personal interests.

Police powers in the context of public health include all laws and regulations directly or indirectly intended to reduce morbidity and premature mortality in the population. The police powers have enabled states and local governments to promote and preserve the public health in areas ranging from injury and disease prevention to sanitation, waste disposal, and water and air pollution. Police powers exercised by the states include vaccination, isolation and quarantine, inspection of commercial and residential premises, abatement of unsanitary conditions or other nuisances, and regulation of air and surface water contaminants, as well as restriction on the public's access to polluted areas, standards for pure food and drinking water, extermination of vermin, fluoridization of municipal water supplies, and licensure of physicians and other healthcare professionals.

## Local Public Health Powers

In addition to the significant roles that federal and state governments have concerning public health law in the constitutional system, local governments also have important public health powers. Public health officials in local governments, including counties, cities, municipalities, and special districts, are often on the front line of public health. They may be directly responsible for assembling public health surveillance data, implementing federal and state programs, administering federal or state public health laws, operating public health clinics, and setting public health policies for their specific populations.

Although states have inherent powers as sovereign governments, localities have delegated power. Local governments in the constitutional system are subsidiaries of their states. As a result, any powers that local governments have to enact public health law or policies must be granted either in the state constitution or in state statutes. Sometimes state grants of power are so broad and generic that they afford cities home rule. For example, if the state constitution expressly affords a city the power to protect the health, safety, and welfare of local inhabitants, this is an important guarantee of home rule.

Absent constitutionally protected delegations of power to local governments, however, states may modify, clarify, preempt, or remove "home rule" powers of local government.

## New Federalism

Since the founding of the United States, the division of federal and state governmental powers has been an important and highly controversial part of our federalist system of government. The Supreme Court, at least since Franklin Delano Roosevelt's New Deal, has liberally interpreted the federal government's enumerated powers, leading to an unprecedented expansion of national public health authority. More recently, however, the Rehnquist Court had emphasized that there exist enforceable limits on Congress' powers. Known as new federalism, federal courts have begun to hold that federal police powers should be circumscribed, with more authority returned to the states.

The Supreme Court has narrowed the scope of the commerce power, holding that the federal government cannot regulate purely intrastate police power matters. In *United States v. Lopez,* the Court held that Congress exceeded its commerce clause authority by making gun possession within a school zone a federal offense. Concluding that possessing a gun within a school zone did not "substantially affect" interstate commerce, the Court declared the statute unconstitutional.[21] The Court continued to narrow the scope of the commerce power in *United States v. Morrison* when it struck down the private civil remedy in the Violence Against Women Act.[22] The act created a civil rights remedy, permitting survivors to bring federal lawsuits against perpetrators of sexually motivated crimes of violence. Congress proclaimed that violence impairs women's abilities to work, harms businesses, and increases national health care costs. But the Court, reiterating its arguments in *Lopez*, found no national effects.

In addition to *Lopez* and *Morrison*, the Court has held in a series of recent cases that Congress, even if empowered to act for the public good, must exert its authority in ways that do not excessively intrude on state sovereignty. In *New York v. the United States*, the Supreme Court struck down a federal statute providing for the disposal of radioactive waste as violating the 10th Amendment.[23] The Constitution, stated the Court, does not confer upon Congress the ability to "commandeer the legislative processes of the States by directly compelling them to enact and enforce a federal regulatory program."[23(p175)] The Supreme Court used the same reasoning to overturn provisions in the Brady Handgun Violence Prevention Act, which directed state and local law enforcement officers to conduct background checks on prospective handgun purchasers.[24]

In this era of new federalism, some federal public health laws may be vulnerable to state challenges. National environmental regulations are particularly at risk because they invade core state concerns and are being challenged in the court system.

In summary, a highly complex, politically charged relationship exists between various levels of government regulating for the public's health—federal, state, tribal, and local. The Constitution ostensibly grants the federal government limited powers, but these powers have been construed in ways that have facilitated an enormous growth of national public health authority.

The Constitution does not grant states any power because, as sovereign governments that predated the Republic, the states already had broad powers. Known as the police powers, states may act to protect the health, safety, and well-being of the population. Local governments, as subsidiary entities of states, possess only those public health powers delegated by the state. In an era of new federalism, the Supreme Court has gradually limited federal public health powers and returned them to the states. Even so, the vast majority of public health functions currently exercised by the federal government are likely to survive constitutional scrutiny.

## The Modern Public Health Agency

The deep-seated problems of modern society caused by industrialization and urbanization pose complex, highly technical challenges that require expertise, flexibility, and deliberative study over the long-term. Solutions cannot be found within traditional governmental structures such as representative assemblies or governors' offices. As a result, governments have formed specialized entities within the executive branch to pursue the goals of population health and safety. These administrative agencies form the bulwark for public health activities in the United States. Public health agencies are found at all levels of government—federal, state, and local.

### Federal Public Health Agencies

The modern role of the federal government in public health is broad and complex. Public health functions, which include public funding for health care, safe food, effective drugs, clean water, a beneficial environment, and prevention services, can be found in an array of agencies. The Department of Health and Human Services (HHS) is the umbrella agency under which most public health functions are located. Under the aegis of the HHS, various programs promote and protect health. The Health Care Financing Administration (now the Centers for Medicare & Medicaid Services) was created in 1977 to administer the Medicare and Medicaid programs. The Centers for Disease Control and Prevention (CDC) provides technical and financial support to states in monitoring, controlling, and preventing disease. The CDC's efforts include initiatives such as childhood vaccination and emergency response to infectious disease outbreaks. The National Institutes of Health (NIH) conducts and supports research, trains investigators, and disseminates scientific information. The Food and Drug Administration (FDA) ensures that food is pure and safe and that drugs, biologicals, medical devices, cosmetics, and products that emit radiation are safe and effective. (Refer to Chapter 3 for more discussion on the organization of public health.)

The Department of Labor (DOL) administers a variety of federal labor laws, some of which pertain to workers' rights to safe and healthy working conditions. Specifically, the Occupational Safety and Health Administration (OSHA) develops occupational safety and health standards and monitors compliance. In 1970, the Environmental Protection Agency (EPA) was created to control and reduce pollution in the air, water, and ground. The EPA develops national standards, provides technical assistance, and enforces environmental regulations. In 2002 the Congress established the Department of

Homeland Security (DHS), which consolidated 22 agencies unifying a variety of security functions in a single agency.

### State Public Health Agencies

The state's plenary power to safeguard citizens' health includes the authority to create administrative agencies devoted to that task. State legislation determines the administrative organization, mission, and functions of public health agencies. Contemporary state public health agencies take many different forms that defy simple classification. (Refer to Chapter 3 for a more detailed discussion.) Before 1960, state public health functions were located in health departments with policy-making functions residing in a board of health (e.g., issuing and enforcing regulations). As programs expanded (e.g., increased federal funding for categorical programs and block grants), certain public health functions were assigned to other state agencies (e.g., mental health, medical care financing for the indigent, and environmental protection). Currently, 55 state-level health agencies (including the District of Columbia, American Samoa, Guam, Puerto Rico, and the US Virgin Islands) exist, each of which may be a free-standing, independent department or a component of a larger state agency.

The trend since the 1960s has been to merge state health departments with other departments—often social services, Medicaid, mental health, and/or substance abuse—to form superagencies. Under this framework, the public health unit is often called a *division* of health or public health. Another common framework is to assign public health functions to a cabinet-level agency. Under this framework, the public health unit is often called a *department* of health or public health.[25-27]

The trend has also been to eliminate or reduce the influence of boards of health. These boards, once ubiquitous and highly influential, are now often replaced or supplemented with specialized boards or committees established by state statute to oversee technical or politically controversial programs (e.g., genetics, rural health, expansion of healthcare facilities).[28] The chief executive officer of the public health agency—the commissioner or, less often, the secretary—is usually politically appointed by the governor, but may be appointed by the head of a superagency or, rarely, the board of health. Qualification standards may include medical and public health expertise, but increasingly, chief executives with political or administrative experience are appointed.

### Local Public Health Agencies

Local government exercises voluminous public health functions derived from the state, such as air, water, and noise pollution; sanitation and sewage; cigarette sales and smoking in public accommodations; drinking water fluoridation; drug paraphernalia sales; firearm registration and prohibition; infectious diseases; rodents and infestations; housing codes; sanitary food and beverages; trash disposal; and animal control. Local government also often regulates (or owns and operates) hospitals or nursing homes.

Municipalities, like the states, have created public health agencies to carry out their functions.[29] Local public health agencies have varied forms and structures: centralized (directly operated by the state), decentralized (formed and managed by local government), or mixed.[30] Local boards of health, or less often, governmental councils, still exist in most local public health agencies with responsibility for health regulation and policy. The courts usually permit local agencies to exercise broad discretion in matters of public health, sometimes even beyond the geographic area if necessary to protect the city's inhabitants (e.g., during a waterborne disease outbreak).

Local public health agencies serve a political subdivision of the state such as a city (a municipality or municipal corporation), town, township, county, or borough. Some local public health functions are undertaken by special districts that are limited governmental structures that serve special purposes (e.g., drinking water, sewerage, sanitation, or mosquito abatement).

## Rule Making, Enforcement, and Quasi-Judicial Powers

Public health agencies are part of the executive branch of government but wield considerable authority to make rules to control private behavior, interpret statutes and regulations, and adjudicate disputes about whether an individual or company has conformed to health and safety standards. Under the separation of powers doctrine, the executive branch is supposed to enforce law, but not enact or interpret it. Nevertheless, the lines between law making, enforcement, and adjudication have become blurred with the rise of the administrative state.

The courts, at least theoretically, can carefully scrutinize legislative grants of power to public health agencies. Conventionally, representative assemblies may not delegate legislative or judicial functions to the executive branch. Known as *nondelegation*, this doctrine holds that policy-making functions should be undertaken by the legislative branch of government (because assemblies are politically accountable), whereas adjudicative functions should be undertaken by the judicial branch (because courts are independent).

The nondelegation doctrine is rarely used by federal courts to limit agency powers. The doctrine, however, has received varying interpretations at the state level—some jurisdictions liberally permit delegations whereas others are more restrictive. In 1987 New York State's highest court, for example, found unconstitutional a health department prohibition on smoking in public places because the legislature, not the health department, should decide the "trade-offs" between health and freedom. "Manifestly," the court said, "it is the province of the people's elected representatives, rather than appointed administrators, to resolve difficult social problems by making choices among competing ends."[31(p1356)] By 2003 however, the people's elected representatives did resolve this issue when the Clean Indoor Air act (Public Health Law, Article 13-E) was passed prohibiting smoking in virtually every workplace including bars and restaurants. The law also allowed that "Localities may continue to adopt and enforce local laws regulating smoking. However, these regulations must be at least as strict as the Clean Indoor Air Act."[32]

### Rule Making

Although public health agencies possess considerable power to issue detailed rules, they must do so fairly and publicly. Federal and state administrative procedure acts (as well as agency-enabling acts) govern the deliberative processes that agencies must undertake in issuing rules. (Unless specified by statute, state administrative procedure acts generally have been held not to apply to local governmental agencies.) Administrative procedure acts often require two different forms: (1) *informal*, simple and flexible procedures often consisting of prior notice (e.g., publication in federal or state register), written comments by interested persons, and a statement of basis and purpose for the rule; and (2) *formal*, more elaborate procedures often requiring a hearing.

## Enforcement

Health departments do not possess only legislative power. They also have the executive power to enforce the regulations that they have promulgated. Enforcement of laws and regulations is squarely within the constitutional powers of executive agencies. Although legislatures set the penalty for violations of health and safety standards, the executive branch monitors compliance and seeks redress against those who fail to conform. Pursuant to their enforcement power, health departments may inspect premises and businesses, investigate complaints, and generally monitor the activities of those who come within the orbit of health and safety statutes and administrative rules.

## Quasi-Judicial Powers

Modern administrative agencies do not simply issue and enforce health and safety standards. They also interpret statutes and rules as well as adjudicate disputes about whether standards are violated. Federal and state administrative procedure acts and agency-enabling legislation often enumerate the procedures that agencies must follow in adjudicating disputes. Rarely, these laws require *formal adjudications*. Formal adjudications typically are conducted by an administrative law judge (ALJ), followed by an appeal to the agency head. Formal adjudications usually include notice, the right to present evidence, and agency findings of fact and law as well as reasons for the decision. Even in the absence of statutory requirements, federal and state constitutions require procedural due process if the regulation deprives an individual of property or liberty interests.

In summary, modern administrative agencies exercise *legislative power* to issue rules that carry heavy penalties, *executive power* to investigate potential violations of health and safety standards and prosecute offenders, and *judicial power* to interpret law and adjudicate disputes over violations of governing standards. Agency powers have developed for reasons of expediency (because of agency expertise) and politics (because specialists are presumed to act according to disinterested scientific judgments).

Although ample agency power is critically important for achieving public health purposes, it is also troubling and perplexing in a constitutional democracy. One important problem is that commercial regulation may simply transfer wealth from one private interest group to another rather than promote a public good. For example, licenses can exclude competitors from the market, or regulation of one industry may benefit another providing comparable services (e.g., coal, electrical, or nuclear energy). A related problem is that agencies may be unduly influenced, or "captured," by powerful constituencies or interest groups. Agencies, over the long-term, may come to defend the economic interests of regulatory subjects. Finally, agencies may operate in ways that appear unfair or arbitrary, inefficient or bureaucratic, or unacceptable to the public. The very strengths of public health authorities (e.g., neutrality, expertise, and broad powers) can become liabilities if they appear politically unaccountable and aloof from the real concerns and needs of the governed. This is why governors' offices, representative assemblies, and courts struggle over the political and constitutional limits that should be placed on agency action that is nominally intended for the public's health and safety.

# Public Health Law Reform

Effective public health protection is technically and politically difficult. Law cannot solve all, or even most, of the challenges facing public health authorities. Yet, law can become an important part of the ongoing work of creating the conditions necessary for people to live healthier and safer lives. A public health law that contributes to health will, of course, be up-to-date in the methods of assessment and intervention it authorizes. It should also conform to modern standards of law and prevailing social norms. It should be designed to enhance the reality and the public perception of the health department's rationality, fairness, and responsibility. It should help health agencies overcome the defects of their limited jurisdiction over health threats facing the population. Finally, both a new law and the process of its enactment should provide an opportunity for the health department to challenge the apathy about public health that is all too common within both the government and the population at large.

The law relating to public health is scattered across countless statutes and regulations at the state and local level. Problems of antiquity, inconsistency, redundancy, and ambiguity render these laws ineffective, or even counterproductive, in advancing the population's health. In particular, health codes frequently are outdated, built up in layers over different periods of time, and highly fragmented among the 50 states and territories.

## Problem of Antiquity

The most striking characteristic of state public health law and the one that underlies many of its defects is its overall antiquity. Certainly, some statutes are relatively recent in origin, such as those relating to health threats that became salient in the latter part of the 1900s (e.g., environmental law). However, a great deal of public health law was framed in the late 1800s and early to mid-1900s and contains elements that are 40–100 years old (e.g., infectious disease law). Certainly, old laws are not necessarily bad laws. A well-written statute may remain useful, effective, and constitutional for many decades.

Nevertheless, old public health statutes that have not been altered substantially since their enactment are often outmoded in ways that directly reduce both their effectiveness and their conformity with modern standards. These laws often do not reflect contemporary scientific understandings of injury and disease (e.g., surveillance, prevention, and response) or legal norms for the protection of individual rights. Rather, public health laws use scientific and legal standards that prevailed at the time they were enacted. Society faces different sorts of risks today and deploys different methods of assessment and intervention. When many of these statutes were written, public health (e.g., epidemiology and biostatistics) and behavioral (e.g., client-centered counseling) sciences were in their infancy. Modern prevention and treatment methods did not exist.

At the same time, many public health laws predate the vast changes in constitutional (e.g., tighter scrutiny and procedural safeguards) and statutory (e.g., disability discrimination) law that have transformed social and legal conceptions of individual rights. Failure to reform these laws may leave public health authorities vulnerable to legal challenge on grounds that they are unconstitutional or that they are preempted by modern federal statutes such as the Americans with Disabilities Act. Even if state public health law is not challenged in court, public health authorities may feel unsure about applying old legal remedies to new health problems within a very different social milieu.

### Problem of Multiple Layers of Law

Related to the problem of antiquity is the problem of multiple layers of law. The law in most states consists of successive layers of statutes and amendments—built up in some cases over 100 years or more in response to existing or perceived health threats. This is particularly troublesome in the area of infectious diseases, which forms a substantial part of state health codes. Because communicable disease laws have been passed piecemeal in response to specific epidemics, they tell the history of disease control in the United States—for example, smallpox, yellow fever, cholera, tuberculosis, venereal diseases, polio, and acquired immune deficiency syndrome (AIDS). Through a process of accretion, the majority of states have come to have several classes of communicable disease law, each with different powers and protections of individual rights: those aimed at traditional sexually transmitted diseases (or venereal diseases), including gonorrhea, syphilis, chlamydia, herpes; those targeted at specific currently or historically pressing diseases, such as tuberculosis and HIV; and those applicable to "communicable" or "contagious" diseases, a residual class of conditions ranging from measles to malaria whose control does not usually seem to raise problematic political or social issues. There are, of course, legitimate reasons to treat some diseases separately. Nevertheless, affording health officials substantially different powers, under different criteria and procedures, for different diseases is more an accident of history than a rational approach to prevention and control.

The disparate legal structure of state public health laws can significantly undermine their effectiveness. Laws enacted piecemeal over time are inconsistent, redundant, and ambiguous. Even the most astute lawyers in departments of health or offices of the attorneys general have difficulty understanding these arcane laws and applying them to contemporary health threats.

### Problem of Inconsistency among the States and Territories

Public health laws remain fragmented not only within states but also among them. Health codes within the 50 states and the US territories have evolved independently, leading to profound variation in the structure, substance, and procedures for detecting, controlling, and preventing injury and disease. In fact, statutes and regulations among American jurisdictions vary so significantly in definitions, methods, age, and scope that they defy orderly categorization. Ordinarily, a different approach among the states is not a problem and is often perceived as a virtue; an important value of federalism is that states can become laboratories for innovative solutions to challenging health problems. Nevertheless, there may be good reason for greater uniformity among the states in matters of public health. Health threats are rarely confined to single jurisdictions, but pose risks within whole regions or the nation itself. For example, geographic boundaries are largely irrelevant to issues of air or water pollution, disposal of toxic waste, or the spread of infectious diseases.

Public health law, therefore, should be reformed so that it conforms with modern scientific and legal standards, is more consistent within and among states, and is more uniform in its approach to different health threats. Rather than making artificial distinctions among diseases, public health interventions should be based primarily on the degree of risk, the cost and efficacy of the response, and the burdens on human rights. A single set of standards and procedures would add needed clarity and coherence to legal regulation and would reduce the opportunity for politically motivated disputes about how to classify newly emergent health threats.

## The Model State Emergency Health Powers Act

Following the anthrax attacks in October 2001, the CDC asked the Center for Law and the Public's Health (CLPH) to draft the Model State Emergency Health Powers Act (MSEHPA).[33] As of July 2006, the MSEHPA has been adopted in whole or part in 44 states, the District of Columbia, and the Northern Marianas Islands.[34] The Model Act is structured to reflect five basic public health functions to be facilitated by law: preparedness, surveillance, management of property, protection of persons, and public information and communication. The preparedness and surveillance functions take effect immediately upon passage of the Model Act. However, the compulsory powers over property and persons take effect only once the governor has declared a public health emergency, defined as the occurrence of imminent threat of an illness or health condition caused by bioterrorism or a novel or previously controlled or eradicated infectious agent or biological toxin. The health threat must pose a high probability of a large number of deaths or serious disabilities in the population.

The Act facilitates systematic planning for a public health emergency. The state Public Health Emergency Plan must include: coordination of services; procurement of vaccines and pharmaceuticals; housing, feeding, and caring for affected populations (with appropriate regard for their physical and cultural/social needs); and the proper vaccination and treatment of individuals in the event of a public health emergency.

The act provides authority for surveillance of health threats and continuing power to follow a developing public health emergency. For example, the act requires prompt reporting for healthcare providers, pharmacists, veterinarians, and laboratories. MSEHPA also provides for the exchange of relevant data among lead agencies such as public health, emergency management, and public safety.

MSEHPA provides comprehensive powers to manage property and protect persons to safeguard the public's health and security. Public health authorities may close, decontaminate, or procure facilities and materials to respond to a public health emergency; safely dispose of infectious waste; and obtain and deploy healthcare supplies. Similarly, the Model Act permits public health authorities to: physically examine or test individuals as necessary to diagnose or to treat illness; vaccinate or treat individuals to prevent or ameliorate an infectious disease; and isolate or quarantine individuals to prevent or limit the transmission of a contagious disease. The public health authority also may waive licensing requirements for healthcare professionals and direct them to assist in vaccination, testing, examination, and treatment of patients.

Finally, MSEHPA provides for a set of postdeclaration powers and duties to ensure appropriate public information and communication. The public health authority must provide information to the public regarding the emergency, including protective measures to be taken and information regarding access to mental health support.

### The Turning Point Model State Public Health Act

The Turning Point National Collaborative on Public Health Statute Modernization seeks to transform and strengthen the legal framework to better protect and promote the public's health. Funded by the Robert Wood Johnson Foundation as part of its Turning Point Initiative, the collaborative is a multidisciplinary group comprising representatives from five states, nine national organizations and government agencies, and experts in specialty areas of public health.

Released on September 16, 2003, after three years of development and a national commentary period, the Turning Point Model State Public Health Act (MSPHA) is designed to serve as a tool for state, local, and tribal governments to use to revise or update public health statutes and administrative regulations.

Consistent with findings from the Institute of Medicine (IOM) in *The Future of the Public's Health in the 21st Century* (2003), the act adopts a systematic approach to public health powers and duties. It focuses on the provision of essential public health services and functions. The act presents a broad mission for state and local public health agencies to be carried out in collaboration with public and private entities within the public health system. Much of the substance of the act concerns traditional powers of state or local public health agencies (e.g., contagious disease control, nuisance abatement, and inspections). These powers are articulated within a framework of modern jurisprudence and public health science that balances the protection of the public's health with respect for the rights of individuals and groups.

### Guidelines for Public Health Law Reform

Based on the MSEHPA and the MSPHA, the following should guide the process for public health law reform:

1. *Define a mission and essential functions. Take responsibility for ensuring the conditions of health.*
   State public health statutes should define a cogent mission for the health department and identify a full set of essential public health functions that it should, or must, perform. Broad, and well-considered, mission statements in state public health statutes are important

because they establish the purposes or goals of public health agencies. By doing so, they inform and influence the activities of government and, perhaps ultimately, the expectations of society about the scope of public health.

2. *Provide a full range of public health powers.*

Voluntary cooperation is the primary way to obtain compliance with public health measures. However, where voluntary strategies fail, public health officials need a full range of powers to ensure compliance with health and safety standards. At present, public health officials in many states have a sterile choice of either exercising draconian authority, such as deprivation of liberty, or refraining from coercion at all. The temptation is either to exercise no statutory power or to reach for measures that are too restrictive of individual liberty to be acceptable in a modern democratic society. As a result, authorities may make wrong choices in two opposite directions: failing to react in the face of a real threat to health or overreacting by exercising powers that are more intrusive than necessary. Public health authorities need a more *flexible* set of tools, ranging from incentives and minimally coercive interventions to highly restrictive measures.

3. *Impose substantive limits on powers (a demonstrated threat of significant risk).*

Whereas public health authorities should have all the powers they need to safeguard the public's health, statutes should place substantive limits on the exercise of those powers. The legislature should clearly state the circumstances under which authorities may curtail liberty, autonomy, privacy, and property interests. At present, a few state statutes articulate clear criteria for the exercise of public health powers; others provide vague or incomplete standards; still others leave their use partly or wholly within the discretion of public health officials. Although public health authorities may prefer an unfettered decision-making process, the lack of criteria does not serve their interests or the interests of regulatory subjects. Effective and constitutionally sound public health statutes should set out a rational and reliable way to assess risk to ensure that the health measure is necessary for public protection. Most importantly, public health authorities should be empowered to employ a compulsory intervention only to avert a significant risk based on objective and reliable scientific evidence and made on an individualized (case-by-case) basis.

4. *Impose procedural limits on powers (procedural due process).*

There are good reasons, both constitutional and normative, for legislatures to require health authorities to use a fair process whenever their decisions seriously infringe on liberty, autonomy, proprietary, or other important interests. For example, if health authorities seek to close a restaurant, withdraw a professional (e.g., physician) or institutional (e.g., restaurant) license, or restrict personal freedom (e.g., civil confinement), they should provide procedural due process. Procedural protections help to ensure that health officials make fair and impartial decisions and to reduce community perceptions that public health agencies arbitrarily employ coercive measures. Where few formal procedures exist, public health officials risk rendering biased or inconsistent decisions and erroneously depriving persons and businesses of their rights and freedoms. Although public health authorities may feel that procedural due process is burdensome and an impediment to expeditious action, it can actually facilitate deliberative and accurate decision making.

5. *Provide strong protection against discrimination.*

Throughout the modern history of disease control, the stigma associated with serious diseases and the social hostility that is often directed at those with, or at risk of, disease has interfered with the effective operation of public health programs. The field of public health has always had to consider issues of race, gender, sexual orientation, and socioeconomic status carefully. Persons who fear social repercussions may resist testing or fail to seek needed services. As part of any effort to safeguard the public's health, legislators must find ways to address both the reality and the perception of social risk. Public health statutes should have strong nondiscrimination provisions.

6. *Provide strong protection for the privacy and security of public health information.*

Privacy and security of public health data are highly important from the perspective of both the individual and the public at large. Individuals seek protection of privacy so that they can control intimate health information. They have an interest in avoiding the embarrassment and stigma of unauthorized disclosures to family or friends. They similarly have an interest in avoiding discrimination that could result from unauthorized disclosures to employers, insurers, or landlords. At the same time, privacy and security protection can advance the public's health. Privacy assurances can facilitate individual participation in public health programs and promote trust between health authorities and the community. Public health laws, therefore, should have strong safeguards of privacy to protect these individual and societal interests.

## The Future of Public Health Law

This chapter explores the varied roles of law in advancing the public's health. The field of public health is purposive and interventionist. It does not settle for existing conditions of health, but actively seeks effective techniques for identifying and reducing health threats. Law is a critically important but perennially neglected tool in furthering the public's health. To achieve improvements in public health, law must not be seen as an arcane, indecipherable set of technical rules buried deep within state health codes. Rather, public health law must be seen broadly as the authority and responsibility of government to ensure the conditions for the population's health. As such, public health law has transcending importance in how we think about government, politics, and health policy in America.

## Chapter Review

1. Public health law has at least five characteristics that help separate it from other fields at the intersection of law and health:

- Government
- Populations
- Relationships
- Services
- Coercion

2. Political and judicial expansion of federal powers through the doctrine of implied powers allows the federal government considerable authority to act in the interests of public health and safety. For public health purposes, the chief federal powers are the powers to tax, to spend, and to regulate interstate commerce.

3. Police powers provide a dominant role for the states by affording authority to promote the general welfare of society. The state and, through delegation, the local government enact laws and promulgate regulations to protect and promote health.

4. The Supreme Court has narrowed the scope of the commerce power, holding that the federal government cannot regulate purely intrastate police power matters. Some federal public health laws may be vulnerable to state challenges.

5. Public health agencies are part of the executive branch of government but wield considerable authority to make rules to control private behavior, interpret statutes and regulations, and adjudicate disputes. Health departments also have the executive power to enforce the regulations they have promulgated.

6. The most striking characteristic of state public health law is its *antiquity*. Public health laws use scientific and legal standards that prevailed at the time they were enacted.

7. The recently developed Model State Emergency Health Powers Act and the Model State Public Health Act provide guidance for public health reform and thus a more uniform approach to different health threats.

## References

1. Gostin LO, Burris S, Lazzarini Z. The law and the public's health: a study of infectious disease law in the United States. *Columbia Law Rev.* 1999; 99(1):59–128.

2. Grad FP. *Public Health Law Manual.* 3rd ed. Washington, DC: American Public Health Association; 2005.

3. Institute of Medicine. *The Future of Public Health.* Washington, DC: National Academies Press; 1988.

4. Institute of Medicine. *The Future of Public Health.* Washington, DC: National Academies Press; 1988.

5. Institute of Medicine. *The Future of Public's Health in the 21st Century.* Washington, DC: National Academies Press; 2003.

6. Gostin LO. *Public Health Law: Power, Duty, Restraint.* 2nd ed. Berkeley, Calif: University of California Press; In press.

7. *Black's Law Dictionary.* 7th ed. New York, NY: West; 1999.

8. Durch JS, Bailey LA, Stoto MA, eds. *Improving Health in the Community: A Role for Performance Monitoring.* Washington, DC: Institute of Medicine; 1997.

9. Hodge JG Jr. Implementing modern public health goals through government: an examination of new federalism and public health law. *J Contemp Health Law Policy.* 1997;14:93–126.

10. *Gibbons v Ogden,* 22 US 1 (1824).
11. US Constitution, art. 6, cl. 2.
12. Griswold v Connecticut, 381 US 479 (1965).
13. *McCulloch v Maryland,* 17 US (4 Wheat.) 316 (1819).
14. *United States v Butler,* 297 US 1 (1936).
15. *Pennhurst State School and Hospital v Halderman,* 451 US 1 (1981).
16. *South Dakota v Dole,* 483 US 203 (1987).
17. US Constitution, art. 1, sec. 8, cl. 3.
18. *United States v Darby,* 312 US 100 (1941).
19. *Jacobson v Massachusetts,* 197 US 11 (1905).
20. Gostin LO. *Public Health Law: Power, Duty, Restraint.* 2nd ed. Berkeley, Calif: University of California Press; In press.
21. *United States v Lopez,* 514 US 549 (1995).
22. *United States v Morrison,* 529 US 598 (2000).
23. *New York v United States,* 505 US 144 (1992).
24. *Printz v United States,* 521 US 898 (1997).
25. Turnock B. *Public Health: What It Is and How It Works.* Gaithersburg, Md: Aspen Publishers; 1997:145–156.
26. Gebbie KM. Steps to changing state public health structures. *J Public Health Manage Pract.* 1998;4(5):33–41.
27. Gossert DJ, Miller CA. State boards of health, their members and commitments. *Am J Public Health.* 1973;63(6):486–493.
28. Miller CA, Gilbert B, Warren DG, et al. Statutory authorization for the work of local health departments. *Am J Public Health.* 1977;67(10): 940–945.
29. National Association of County and City Health Officials. *Profile of Local Health Departments, 1992–1993.* Washington, DC: NACCHO; 1995.
30. Mays GP, Halverson PK, Miller CA. Assessing the performance of local public health systems: a survey of state health agency efforts. *J Public Health Manage Pract.* 1998;4(4):63–78.
31. *Boreali v Axelrod,* 517 N.E. 2d 1350 (1987).
32. New York State Department of Health. A guide to the New York State Clean Indoor Air Act. Available at: http://www.health.state.ny.us/nysdoh/clean_indoor_air_act/general.htm. Accessed June 21, 2006.
33. Gostin LO, Sapsin JW, Teret JP, et al. The Model State Emergency Health Powers Act: planning and response to bioterrorism and naturally occurring infectious diseases. *JAMA.* 2002;288:622–628.
34. The Center of Law and the Public's Health at Georgetown and Johns Hopkins Universities. Model state public health laws. Available at: http://www.publichealthlaw.net/Resources/Modellaws.htm#MSEHPA. Accessed July 20, 2006.

## CHAPTER 5

# ETHICS IN PUBLIC HEALTH PRACTICE AND MANAGEMENT

Ruth Gaare Bernheim

## Chapter Overview

In their roles as leaders and managers in public health systems and organizations, public health professionals must address increasingly complex ethical conflicts in day-to-day practice. Ethical questions arise not only about the appropriate *scope of public health* (e.g., should the focus of public health include socioeconomic conditions, such as homelessness, and unhealthy behaviors, such as unhealthy eating) but also about the justification for particular *public health interventions* (e.g., when is it ethical to take actions that infringe the interests of one or some individuals for the benefit of others). Although law provides the foundation for public health authority to act, it is often broadly framed, leaving much room for administrative discretion about when and how to use public health authority. Ethics plays an important complementary role in helping public health officials determine and justify the appropriate course of action.[1]

Adding to the challenge for managing the ethical issues in public health is the expansion of the concept of the public health system and who should be involved in the decision-making process. Although the landmark 1988 Institute of Medicine (IOM) report on public health focused on strengthening federal, state, and local government agencies (as they had primary responsibility to protect and promote the health of the public),[2] the 2003 IOM report, *The Future of the Public's Health in the 21st Century*, describes the public health system as a "complex network of individuals and organizations that have the potential to play critical roles in creating the conditions for health."[3] The actors in the public health system include community groups, businesses, and the media, as well as academics, healthcare providers, and many others. This means that not only do public health professionals now often work in large organizations or agencies, but they also are expected to work in partnerships and collaboratively with communities, stakeholder groups, and citizens—who have widely varying values that often shift over time as the political and social context evolves. Public health managers then are called upon to involve many stakeholders in the process of addressing ethical conflicts.

Public health ethics is a field of study that can enrich and support real-world public health decision making and management of ethical conflict. It is receiving increasing professional and scholarly attention, as public health agencies struggle with emergencies such as Hurricane Katrina, biopreparedness planning for pandemic flu, and chronic disease concerns arising with growing obesity. Recent reports from national public health associations point out the need for public health officials to develop competencies in public health ethics,[4] and public health leaders have developed a code of ethics for professional practice.[5] The goals of this chapter are to provide an overview of ethics in public health and to present ethics tools—the Public Health Code of Ethics and a framework to guide ethical deliberation in public health. The tools can be used by public health managers both to integrate ethics into the public health agency's regular management activities and to facilitate deliberation about particular cases. A brief introduction to ethics is provided first.

## What Is Ethics?

It is helpful to begin the discussion of public health ethics by clarifying the terms *ethics* and *morality*, which are often used interchangeably. Although the terms are closely related, they have different meanings. The key difference is that ethics refers to the discipline that *examines* what is good conduct, the moral standards of a society, and what, all things considered, we should do in a particular situation or when faced with a decision. Morality, on the other hand, refers to our *shared beliefs* about what is good and bad, right or wrong. Morality is thought of as a social institution that is passed along through generations. People grow up with a basic understanding of moral norms, such as truth-telling, keeping promises, and not killing or harming innocent persons. Morality encompasses moral norms, principles, rules, and standards of conduct adopted in society about right and wrong, and as such, it provides reference points for our ethical decision-making process.

What is the source of morality? Throughout history, many religious traditions and philosophical theories have offered perspectives on morality and have contributed to an understanding about what constitutes right and wrong human conduct and about what moral norms should guide human decision making. As new situations occur, such as innovative medical treatments brought about by scientific advancements, new ideas about what is "right conduct" are considered and eventually some are widely accepted in society as part of our common morality. Moral norms then evolve, and our understandings of what is right and good action are interpreted and enriched over time.

Although some norms are universal (e.g., we must not lie), other moral norms are particular for professions or religious groups (such as medical confidentiality for the medical profession). For professions, codes are created in part to lay the foundations for trust with those that they serve and to establish the profession's particular identity. The Code of Ethics for Public Health is a list of moral norms of public health professionals. Moral norms are not absolute, and in particular circumstances it is justified to override one moral norm when it conflicts with another—as when lying can be justified to save someone from being killed. Justifying an action entails presenting sufficient grounds or reasons for overriding one moral norm in order to comply with another.

## Approaches to Ethics in Public Health

In public health management, there are at least three ways to approach ethics, which include focusing on: (1) the agent or public health professional, (2) the organization or public health agency, and (3) the action or public health intervention (i.e., reasoning about the right action to take).

An approach to ethics that focuses on the character of the agent, in this case the public health manager, can be traced back to Aristotle, who emphasized the cultivation of virtues. In a contemporary "virtue ethics" approach to business management, Robert Soloman suggests that the list of important virtues includes honesty, loyalty, sincerity, courage, reliability, trustworthiness, and benevolence, to name just a few.[6] He emphasizes that important considerations for management, among others, are the cultivation in managers and executives of excellence (expertise), integrity (the integration of one's roles, responsibilities, and values), and judgment (practical wisdom).

Organizational ethics, on the other hand, focuses on the mission, values, and systems within an agency that create a climate for ethical behavior, practices, and policies. It has received attention in health care since 1995 when the Joint Commission on Accreditation of Healthcare Organizations (JCAHO) promulgated standards that explicitly require healthcare organizations to have programs and practices that address institutional ethics.[7]

Public health professionals have recognized the importance of organizational ethics for the practice of public health and have developed a code of ethics to guide public health professionals and agencies that addresses the relationship between public health institutions and the populations they serve. The Public Health Leadership Society (PHLS), in consultation with public health practitioners from across the nation, promulgated the "Principles of the Ethical Practice of Public Health" (Code),[8] which was formally adopted by the American Public Health Association executive board in 2002 and has subsequently been either adopted or endorsed by at least six other national organizations. The current principles are broad statements that will be updated over time to incorporate lessons learned from practitioners. The code is provided as a reference for practitioners in clarifying among themselves and with the public the values and purposes of the public health profession.

### The Principles of the Ethical Practice of Public Health

1. Public health should address principally the fundamental causes of disease and requirements for health, aiming to prevent adverse health outcomes.
2. Public health should achieve community health in a way that respects the rights of individuals in the community.
3. Public health policies, programs, and priorities should be developed and evaluated through processes that ensure an opportunity for input from community members.
4. Public health should advocate for, or work for the empowerment of, disenfranchised community members, ensuring that the basic

resources and conditions necessary for health are accessible to all people in the community.

5. Public health should seek the information needed to implement effective policies and programs that protect and promote health.

6. Public health institutions should provide communities with the information they have that is needed for decisions on policies or programs and should obtain the community's consent for their implementation.

7. Public health institutions should act in a timely manner on the information they have within the resources and the mandate given to them by the public.

8. Public health programs and policies should incorporate a variety of approaches that anticipate and respect diverse values, beliefs, and cultures in the community.

9. Public health programs and policies should be implemented in a manner that most enhances the physical and social environment.

10. Public health institutions should protect the confidentiality of information that can bring harm to an individual or community if made public. Exceptions must be justified on the basis of the high likelihood of significant harm to the individual or others.

11. Public health institutions should ensure the professional competence of their employees.

12. Public health institutions and their employees should engage in collaborations and affiliations in ways that build the public's trust and the institution's effectiveness.

The consideration and adoption of a statement of broad ethical principles, like this code of ethics, is only a first step for organizations in developing an ethics program. Public health agencies must also encourage managers and their staffs to integrate ethics into training, management, and decision-making processes. This process requires both a bottom-up and top-down process of active participation and discussion by professionals throughout the agency. For public health agencies, this code of ethics can provide important guidance and a foundation for ethics discussions about all public health activities, from disease surveillance and outbreak investigations to determining appropriate interventions to conducting research and program evaluation. The most important impact of adopting this code may be that it can serve as a catalyst for management and staff reflection and deliberation about the ethical dimensions of their day-to-day activities in public health and about ways they can continually improve their practices and policies to reflect ethical values.

A third dimension of ethics in public health is the ethical analysis of particular actions or dilemmas. Public health ethics offers a systematic approach to balancing competing moral considerations and stakeholder interests, making trade-offs, and justifying decisions. It asks: All things considered, what is the right action to take in this situation, and why? Balancing the competing moral claims is similar to the process officials use in understanding and making public health cost-benefit trade-offs. The difference is that instead of weighing and balancing "quantifiable" health gains or losses, public health ethics focuses on identifying, weighing, and balancing moral interests at stake in a particular situation.[9] Consider the following case from public health practice.

## Case: With Whom to Partner?

The health department in a poor community with major dental healthcare needs is invited by a local fast-food restaurant to be a partner on a dental health project. The restaurant, with support from its soda vendor, proposes to donate $100,000 a year toward a health department free dental clinic. In exchange, the restaurant wants only to have its name and the name of the soda listed in very small print on health department educational material on dental health distributed to the community. Two health department officials, including the nutritionist directing the obesity program, believe such a partnership is unethical. What should the health commissioner do?

In a study of ethical issues in public health,[10] public health officials identified public–private partnerships (PPPs) like the one described in this case as examples of the challenges arising in day-to-day practice, given limited public resources, the opportunities that collaborations and partnerships create for additional resources, and the funding requirements of many grantors and policy makers for multidisciplinary, community collaborations. Public health practitioners felt the need to address and understand potential ethical issues arising from the different cultures, different values, and different governance structures of potential partners in the private sphere. Some practitioners felt that the potential partners were more powerful, in a sense, than their public health organizations, and that this created ethical tension.

In approaching a case about public–private partnerships, one health director suggested consideration of the following factors:

1. Congruency of goals for the project and mission of the different partners and collaborations—Are the missions and goals of the partners consistent with that of the local public health agency?
2. Conflicts of interest—Is there a perceived or real conflict of interest in the partnership?
3. Conflicts of obligation or accountability—To whom and to what are local public health agencies accountable?
4. Ethical values and moral claims—What values are local public health agencies balancing in the decision? Who are the stakeholders involved in this case, and what are their moral claims? What values should public health officials protect? What is the role of the public health professional?[11]

This case illustrates that ethical analysis for a public health decision involves weighing the ethical considerations at stake *in the particular context*, such as what are the goals and potential benefits of *this* partnership; what is the harm or perceived harm of such collaboration; do *these* partners have a history of working together for the public good; what are the moral claims of the vulnerable populations who may not have other options for dental care; how are those most affected involved in the decision making, and so on?

Whatever the ultimate decision in this case, justification to the public is indispensable. Accountability to and transparency with the public requires that reasons, explanations, and justifications can be provided. Justification requires that public health managers state, "We have decided to enter into this partnership because. . . ." Justification is required because all members of society are stakeholders—constituting the collective patient of public health. Justification plays such a key role in public health because public consent is the source of moral authority and legitimacy for public health decision making in a democratic political order. As one political theorist emphasizes, public authorities have the responsibility to take into account the moral understanding of the group in whose name a decision is being taken because moral judgments, unlike scientific judgments, are "everyone's job" in society.[12] Ethical decision making involving transparency and validation lays the foundation for public involvement, cooperation, and trust, which are particularly important for public health leaders who must rely not on force but on persuasion and collaboration.

Numerous groups have distinguished public health ethics from medical ethics and identified ethical principles and moral considerations that grow out of public health's population focus. In a study of public health professionals in practice,[10] the ethical principles identified by public health officials included producing population benefits; avoiding, preventing, and removing harms for the population; producing a maximum balance of benefits over harms; and distributing benefits and burdens fairly. Ensuring public participation also emerged as a key principle in public health ethics, as did respecting autonomous choices and actions, protecting privacy and confidentiality, keeping promises and commitments, and speaking honestly and truthfully. Transparency and building and maintaining trust also were key moral considerations for practitioners.

What does the field of public health ethics offer public health managers? It provides vocabulary, concepts, and frameworks to analyze the ethical dimensions of cases and policies. General ethical principles and moral considerations can provide starting points to guide ethical deliberation and to clarify reasons or justifications for particular decisions. The following categories of reasons and major ethical themes, based on influential ethical theories, have emerged in contemporary public health discourse:[13]

- Utilitarianism—Judges actions on the basis of their consequences (i.e., maximize net utility for all parties affected by the decision)
- Liberalism—Focuses on individual interests and human rights
- Communitarianism—Emphasizes communal values, visions of common good, traditional practices

## Ethical Analysis in Public Health Practice

Public health decisions in practice generally are made in public health agencies and reached through or after group deliberation and reflection. The public health ethics framework in this chapter is not intended to be a simple formula, but is rather a series of questions designed to provoke rigorous deliberation in public health agencies or ethics advisory groups. It draws on numerous approaches in contemporary ethics:

1. One approach, often called *principlism*, orders discussion of cases around ethical principles, such as justice and beneficence. This approach is often identified with the foundational work of Tom Beauchamp and James Childress in medical ethics, called *Principles of Biomedical Ethic*.[14]
2. Another approach is *casuistry*, which is a case-based method that emphasizes a pragmatic analysis of the particular details and context of each case.

3. Yet another approach is *virtue ethics*, which calls attention to the character and moral traits of the actor, such as honesty and transparency.

The questions in this framework invite reflection about public health cases and decisions from all of these perspectives. The goal is to facilitate ethical reflection and deliberation in order to reach the best possible resolution, all things considered. And perhaps just as importantly, another goal is to foster an imaginative process that helps forge professional and stakeholder consensus around public health issues. Ethical deliberation in public health can facilitate social learning about how to make ethical decisions collectively and build a community of stakeholders willing to work together for the public's health.

The following sections discuss these topics further.

---

### Framework for Analysis and Deliberation about Ethical Issues in Public Health[9]

1. Analyze the ethical issues in the situation.
   - What are the public health *risks and harms of concern in this particular context*?
   - What are the public health *goals*?
   - Who are the *stakeholders*, and what are their moral claims?
   - Is the source or scope of legal *authority* in question?
   - Are *precedent cases* or the historical context relevant?
   - Do *professional codes of ethics* provide guidance?
2. Evaluate the ethical dimensions of the various public health options.
   - Utility—Does a particular public health action produce a *balance of benefits over harms*?
   - Justice—Are the benefits and burdens *distributed fairly* (distributive justice), and do legitimate representatives of affected groups have the *opportunity to participate* in making decisions (procedural justice)?
   - Respect for individual interests—Does the public health action *respect individual choices* and interests (autonomy, liberty, privacy)?
   - Respect for legitimate public institutions—Does the public health action *respect professional and civic roles* and values, such as transparency, honesty, trustworthiness, keeping promises, protecting confidentiality, and protecting vulnerable individuals and communities from undue stigmatization?
3. Provide justification for one particular public health action.
   - Effectiveness—Is the public health goal likely to be accomplished with this option?
   - Proportionality—Will the probable benefits of the action outweigh the infringed moral considerations?
   - Necessity—Is it necessary to override the conflicting ethical claims in order to achieve the public health goal?
   - Least infringement—Is the action the least restrictive and least intrusive?
   - Public justification—Can public health agents offer public justification for the action or policy that citizens, and in particular those most affected, can find acceptable?

### Analyze the Ethical Issues in the Situation

As a first step, public health officials need to explore the particular context, and identify the goals and potential harms of the public health action. In the case described previously, from the perspective of the health department officials, what are the key public health goals in this situation? To provide care for vulnerable populations, to maintain community relationships and trust, and so on? What is the harm or potential risk of harm and the ethical issues of concern? Is there a professional conflict of obligations, given that the health department regulates and inspects restaurants? A focus for this case discussion is the range of stakeholders, which is defined as those in the community who are in any way affected by the decisions. For each stakeholder, the ethical analysis should identify the stakeholder's interests, goals, and concerns; power and reputation in the community; and likely preferred outcome. In addition, the framework invites consideration of previous cases, because an analysis of the situation's relevant similarities and differences from precedent cases often provides an important starting point or presumption in case deliberation.

### Evaluate the Ethical Dimensions of the Various Public Health Options

Ethical deliberation should include an imaginative exploration of the various options for public health action in the situation. Take, for example, the options available for HIV prevention among adolescents and young adults. Some reports suggest that half of all new HIV infections in the United States are among those between the ages of 10–24 and approximately 50% of those infected have not been tested.[15] Options range from routine HIV screening for all young adults who visit physician offices to targeted testing for those among the young adult population at highest risk. Ethical deliberation might focus on the following questions: Does the option of testing only those at high risk produce a balance of benefits over harms? Are the benefits and burdens distributed fairly? These are complex questions given the 25-year history of the AIDS epidemic that includes discrimination, stigma, and socioeconomic harms for those diagnosed with the disease. It may be that both options are ethically defensible, meaning that ethical justifications can be made for both options, and then the question becomes how does one choose and justify one option over another? Part 3 of the framework poses questions to help public health decision makers justify a particular option.

### Provide Justification for a Particular Public Health Action

Six justificatory conditions provided in the form of questions guide deliberation and decisions about whether choosing one option that promotes one value (e.g., utility or public health benefit) warrants overriding other values (e.g., individual liberty or justice). The justificatory conditions require public health officials to consider whether any proposed program will likely realize the public health goal that is sought (effectiveness), whether its probable benefits will outweigh the infringed general moral considerations (proportionality), whether the policy is essential to realize the end (necessity), whether it involves the least infringement possible consistent with realizing the goal that is sought (least infringement), and whether it can be justified.

A comparison of different HIV screening programs illustrate ways that screening programs can meet or fail to meet some of the justificatory conditions. For example, mandatory screening programs of donated blood clearly meets all of the justificatory conditions, as does the screening of individuals in some settings where they can expose others who can not protect themselves. For each of these circumstances, screening is effective and necessary to achieve the public health goal. In contrast, mandatory screening programs for all those seeking a marriage license do not meet the justificatory conditions, given that mandatory screening is neither necessary, impartial, nor the least intrusive means to identify and protect sexually active individuals in the larger population.

Ethical justifications for HIV screening programs for pregnant women have evolved over time. In the mid-1980s the CDC recommended that pregnant women in high-risk groups be "offered" the HIV test, despite some calls for mandatory screening of pregnant women in high-risk groups. Voluntary, selective (high-risk) screening, and not mandatory or routine screening, was justified because no treatment was available for HIV infection at the time. Mandatory screening of high-risk women would have been an unjustifiable violation of autonomy and justice. In 1995, after treatment by zidovudine (ZDV) was shown to reduce perinatal HIV transmission, the CDC and the American Academy of Pediatrics (AAP) recommended universal voluntary counseling and HIV testing for pregnant women to allow for prophylactic use of ZDV. The shift from targeted to universal, voluntary counseling and screening, however, did not eliminate perinatal transmission. Given the subsequent continuing perinatal transmission, an Institute of Medicine report in 1999 recommended universal HIV screening of pregnant women, with patient notification and the option for patients to opt out of testing. In subsequent years, a universal opt-out approach was endorsed by health professional organizations and the CDC. The shift from universal voluntary screening to a routine, opt-out approach was justified, given the evidence demonstrating that it was necessary in order to achieve the goal of eliminating perinatal transmission. Challenges still exist in 2006, and on the basis of CDC estimates that in 2002 between 144 and 236 HIV-infected infants were born in the United States, even further screening is justified. Given recent evidence that HIV transmission occurs during pregnancy in women who tested HIV-negative early in pregnancy, the CDC now recommends a routine second HIV test during the third trimester for women known to have elevated risk for HIV infection and in areas with elevated HIV prevalence among women of childbearing age.[16] Again, this targeted second screening of pregnant women is justified because of the potential significant harm to the neonate that can be avoided through medical interventions before and during birth.

The following case provides an example of how ethical deliberation, guided by the ethics framework, might enrich public health decision making.

## Case: Newborn Screening and Parental Consent

The state legislature is considering a law that would require parental consent for newborn screening. Parental consent currently is not required, although newborn testing is not conducted over parental objection. Currently only a few states require consent. The health department has been asked to take a position on the pending legislation. What position should the health department take?

This case illustrates the appropriateness of ethical analysis when the questions are, should there be a law, and, if so, what should the law be? The goal of ethical deliberation is to analyze and provide reasons for a public health decision that are grounded in moral norms and that take into account the ethical dimensions of the issues at stake for various stakeholders. Key questions are: Who are the stakeholders, and what are their positions? Are precedent cases and the historical context relevant? What are available options? Options include: mandatory screening without consent; routine screening with advance notification (opt in); routine screening without advance notification (opt out), which includes screening and testing unless objection is raised; voluntary screening, which requires full consent and might also include a pre- and postcounseling session with each new mother.[17]

Some arguments offered against requiring consent from parents focus on the fact that the benefits of screening are obvious and substantial, relative to potential harms; that no "reasonable" parent would refuse screening; that obtaining consent from each parent is difficult, costly, and an unwarranted expenditure of time and money; and that the history of newborn screening has led to the current social acceptance of newborn screening as routine.

Some arguments raised for requiring parental consent are that parental consent is necessary because refusal of newborn screening is not unreasonable, given the increasing list of diseases included in the battery of newborn tests and the low probability of many of them; newborn screening can have adverse consequences, such as psychological harms associated with false positive tests; long-term parental caretaking is enhanced when parents are included in all clinical decisions about their children; and the process of obtaining consent does not have to be time consuming or burdensome but rather can be part of an educational process that enhances the health professional–patient relationship.

In considering their position, public health officials might look for guidance from professional organizations. The American Academy of Pediatrics, for instance, addressed the issue of informed consent for newborn screening in its 2001 policy statement, "Ethical Issues with Genetic Testing in Pediatrics."[18] The report provides the following ethical analysis (footnotes within the quote have been deleted):

> A persistent ethical issue in newborn screening is whether screening should be voluntary or mandatory.
>
> The principal ethical justification offered for mandatory screening is the claim that society's obligation to promote child welfare through early detection and treatment of selected conditions supersedes parental prerogatives to refuse this simple medical intervention. An opposing argument maintains that parents traditionally have broad discretion for making healthcare decisions for their children.
>
> With continued broad public support, approaches involving informed consent (that is, parental permission) may fulfill the important goals of the programs and enhance program quality while respecting traditional parental prerogatives to be informed participants in healthcare decisions for their children. In a study of newborn screening in Maryland involving informed consent, the majority of women

preferred that permission be asked before screening, and the informed refusal rate was only 5 per 1000 infants.

The policy regarding newborn screening is an example of a case about which there are competing ethical values and stakeholder claims. For public health managers, an important feature of the public health agency's approach is setting in place an ethics process whereby stakeholders, community groups, professionals, and all concerned would have the opportunity to participate. Public health requires a process of public accountability. At a minimum, accountability involves "transparency in openly seeking information from those affected and in honest disclosure of relevant information to the public."[1(p174)] For issues about which there is ethical disagreement, public health ethics requires a fair process, which—as defined by Norman Daniels in a different context—includes: (1) transparency and publicity about the reasons for a decision; (2) appeals to rationales and evidence that fair-minded parties would agree are relevant; and (3) procedures for appealing and revising decisions in light of challenges by various stakeholders.[19]

This chapter presents an introduction to the ways ethics can be incorporated into public health practice and management. It emphasizes that ethics in public health has at least three dimensions: the character and virtues of the agent or decision maker; the integration of ethics throughout an organization; and a systematic process for deliberation about particular cases or ethical dilemmas. It emphasizes that for all dimensions, ethics in public health requires an ongoing process of reflection about such ethical questions as, What are the virtues of a public health professional? What are the goals and ethical responsibilities of the public health agency? What, all things considered, is the ethical action in a particular case, given the stakeholders' interests and moral claims and the responsibilities of the public health professional?

## Chapter Review

1. Ethical questions arise about the appropriate *scope of public health* and about the justification for particular *public health interventions.*
2. Ethics in public health has at least three dimensions: the character and virtues of the decision maker, the integration of ethics throughout an organization, and a systematic process for deliberation about particular cases or ethical dilemmas.
3. The Code of Ethics for Public Health is a list of moral norms of public health professionals.
4. Steps in approaching an ethical issue include (1) analyze the situation; (2) evaluate ethical dimensions of various public health options; and (3) provide justification for a particular public health action (benefits and harms).

## References

1. Childress JF, Faden RR, Gaare RD. Public health ethics: mapping the terrain. *J Law, Med Ethics.* 2002;30:170–178.

2. Institute of Medicine. *The Future of the Public Health.* Washington, DC: National Academies Press; 1988:28.

3. Institute of Medicine. *The Future of the Public's Health in the 21st Century.* Washington, DC: National Academies Press; 2003.

4. Institute of Medicine. *Who Will Keep the Public Healthy; Educating Public Health Professionals for the 21st Century.* Washington, DC: National Academies Press; 2003.

5. Thomas JC, Sage M, Dillenberg J, Guillory VJ. A code of ethics for public health. *Am J Public Health.* 2002;92:1057–1059.

6. Solomon RC. Corporate roles, personal virtues: an Aristotelean approach to business ethics. *Bus Ethics Q J Soc Bus Ethics.* 1992;2. In: Donaldson T, Werhane PH, eds. *Ethical Issues in Business.* Upper Saddle River, NJ: Prentice Hall; 1999:81–93.

7. Spencer E, Mills AE, Rorty MV, Werhane PH. *Organization Ethics in Health Care.* Oxford, UK: Oxford University Press; 2000:6.

8. Public Health Leadership Society. Principles of the ethical practice of public health. Available at: http://www.phls.org/products.htm. Accessed June 11, 2006.

9. Bernheim RG, Nieburg P, Bonnie RJ. Ethics and the practice of public health. In: Goodman RA, ed. Law in Public Health Practice. 2nd ed. Oxford, UK: Oxford University Press; in press.

10. Bernheim RG. Public health ethics: the voices of practitioners. *J Law, Med Ethics.* 2003;31:S104–S107.

11. Reich MR, Hershey JH, Hardy GE, Childress JF, Bernheim RG. Workshop on public health law and ethics, I & II: the challenge of public/private partnerships (PPPs). *J Law, Med Ethics.* 2003;31(4, suppl):90–93.

12. Nagel T. Moral epistemology. In: Institute of Medicine; Bulger RE, Fineberg HV, eds. *Society's Choices: Social and Ethical Decision Making in Biomedicine.* Washington, DC: National Academies Press; 1995:201–214.

13. Roberts MJ, Reich MR. Ethical analysis in public health. *Lancet.* 2002; 359:1055–1059.

14. Beauchamp TL, Childress JF. *Principles of Biomedical Ethics.* 5th ed. Oxford, UK: Oxford University Press; 2001.

15. Nguyen TQ, Ford CA, Kaufman JS, et al. HIV testing among young adults in the United States: associations with financial resources and geography. *Am J Public Health.* 2006;96:1031–1034.

16. Centers for Disease Control and Prevention. Achievements in public health: reduction in perinatal transmission of HIV infection—United States, 1985–2005. *MMWR.* 2006;55(21):592–597.

17. Gostin L. *Public Health Law.* Berkeley, Calif: University of California Press; 2000:193–195.

18. Committee on Bioethics, American Academy of Pediatrics. Ethical issues with genetic testing in pediatrics. *Pediatrics.* 2001;107(6):1451–1455.

19. Daniels N. Accountability for reasonableness. *BMJ.* 2000;321:1300–1301.

## CHAPTER 6

# LEGISLATIVE RELATIONS IN PUBLIC HEALTH

Stephanie A. Kennan

## Chapter Overview

The federal government plays a significant role in public health through the enactment of legislation that creates, authorizes, and funds programs. States, in addition to their own legislative roles, are often responsible for implementing federal health programs and regulations. The federal budget and appropriations processes determine which public health programs become national priorities and which resources become available to states in carrying out these functions. In understanding these processes, public health organizations can better determine when their expertise and knowledge would be most effective in the lobbying arena and when to anticipate changes to programs.

## Overview

The public health legislative process reflects the federalist system of government from which it derives. States have traditionally been responsible for performing regulatory health functions such as provider licensure, insurance regulation, and promulgation of public health standards for ensuring safety. The federal government establishes national health priorities by creating and authorizing public health programs and by allocating federal funds to these programs. Increasingly, states become the regulators and implementers of health programs, standards, and regulations established through federal legislation. Local public health organizations tailor these larger programs and initiatives to specific communities and populations.

Understanding the steps of the federal budget process; the appropriations process which stems from the budget process; and the roles of the president, Congress, and the states can help public health organizations know at what points they can be most effective in providing information and expertise. This knowledge also helps inform organizations when to look for potential changes in programs and how to shape priorities.

A hypothetical example illustrates the importance of such knowledge: Congress creates a program to assist states in creating or enhancing trauma programs, authorizing such a program to operate for five years. However, in year four Congress does *not* provide funding for the program through the annual appropriations process, effectively ending the program and making reauthorization a more difficult task.

## The Federal Budget Process

When applied to the federal government, the term *budget process* actually refers to a number of processes that have evolved separately and that occur with varying degrees of coordination. In its most elemental form, the federal budget is a comprehensive accounting of the government's spending, revenues, and borrowing. Ultimately, however, the budget and the appropriations processes also represent the country's priorities by what is funded, how it is funded, and by how much.

Article 1 of the US Constitution grants the "power of the purse" to Congress, but does not establish a specific procedure for the consideration of budgetary legislation. The Budget and Accounting Act of 1921 established the statutory basis for an executive budget process by requiring the president to submit to Congress annually a proposed budget for the federal government.[1] It also created the Bureau of the Budget (reorganized as the Office of Management and Budget [OMB] in 1970) to assist the president and the General Accounting Office (GAO) to assist Congress as the principal auditing agency of the federal government. The General Accounting Office was renamed the Government Accountability Office in 2004.

The Congressional Budget and Impoundment Control Act of 1974* established a statutory basis for a congressional budget process and provided for the annual adoption of resolutions on the budget as a mechanism for facilitating congressional budgetary decision making.[2] It also established the House and Senate Budget Committees and created the Congressional Budget Office (CBO) to provide budgetary information to Congress independent of the executive branch.

The key terms in federal spending are *budget authority*, *obligations*, and *outlays*. Congress enacts *budget authority* in law. Budget authority allows federal agencies to incur *obligations*, such as entering into contracts, employing personnel, and submitting purchase orders. *Outlays* represent the actual payment for these obligations, usually in the form of electronic transfers or checks from the Treasury Department. Typically, budget authority is provided in legis-

---

*The Congressional Budget and Impoundment Control Act of 1974 has been amended several times. The full authority is listed as 2 U.S.C. 601-688 (1988 & Supp. IV 1992); PL 93-344 (88 Stat. 297); amended by the Balanced Budget and Emergency Deficit Control Act of 1985, PL 99-177 (99 Stat. 1037, 1038); further amended by the Balanced Budget and Emergency Deficit Control Reaffirmation Act of 1987, PL 100-119 (101 Stat. 754); further amended by the Budget Enforcement Act of 1990, PL 101-508 (104 Stat. 1388-573 to 1388-630); further amended by the Omnibus Budget Reconciliation Act of 1993, PL 103-66 (107 Stat. 312); and further amended by the Budget Enforcement Act of 1997, PL 105-33 (111 Stat. 251).

lation authorizing or creating the program. Annual appropriations, on the other hand, generally provide funding, which is often lower than what is authorized in the authorizing legislation.

Within the budget, there are two categories of spending: mandatory spending and discretionary spending.[3] Mandatory spending includes interest, entitlement programs, and programs funded by permanent appropriations. Spending for mandatory programs is based on benefit levels or other factors that have been established by laws that created the program rather than through the appropriations process. Changes in spending for these programs can only be altered through changes in substantive law. Medicare, Medicaid, and Social Security are examples of mandatory spending and are entitlement programs. Discretionary programs' spending levels are established by Congress through 12 general appropriations bills and other appropriations bills, such as emergency appropriations bills that occur during the annual appropriations process.[4]

For fiscal year (FY) 2004, mandatory spending and net interest payments accounted for almost 61% of total outlays, while nondefense discretionary spending accounted for 19.3%. Nondefense discretionary spending represented less than $1 out of every $5 the federal government spends.[5] Therefore, vital programs such as research, immunizations, and drug abuse and prevention compete for dollars within the federal budget with other programs such as Head Start; the Special Supplemental Food Program for Women, Infants, and Children (WIC) feeding program; and other priorities of government in a relatively small part of the federal budget.

For FY 2002, the 15 largest mandatory programs accounted for 51.1% of total federal outlays; the 11 largest discretionary spending activities account for 22.8%. The top three mandatory spending programs were Social Security (old age and survivors insurance), Medicaid, and Medicare Part A (hospital insurance).[6]

The amount of federal funds available for discretionary programs is minimal. This explains why Congress continues to worry about the growth of Medicare and Social Security as the baby boomers age. Growth in entitlements, if not slowed or reformed, will squeeze the amount of funds available for other worthwhile priorities.

## Steps to Creating the Federal Budget

The Congressional Budget and Impoundment Control Act of 1974 as amended establishes the congressional budget process, which coordinates the legislative activities on the budget resolution appropriations bill, reconciliation legislation, revenue measures (taxes), and other budgetary legislation. Section 300 of this act provides a timetable so that Congress may complete its work on the budget by the start of the fiscal year on October 1. If the budget and appropriations bills are not completed by October 1, the federal government could shut down. However, Congress often employs short-term mechanisms to avoid a shutdown.

### Preparing the President's Budget Submission

As required by the Budget and Accounting Act of 1921, the president prepares and submits a comprehensive budget to Congress by the first Monday in

February.[1] Due to the size and complexity of the federal budget, however, the president must rely on the departments and agencies to bear the primary responsibility of formulating their budget requests.

Federal agencies typically rely on their own internal process to prepare their initial budget requests, with the agencies usually beginning work on the budget approximately 10 months before the president submits his budget to Congress (approximately 17–18 months before the start of the fiscal year). This means that at any given point, each agency and department in the federal government is working on three budgets: implementing the current budget, defending the proposed budget, and preparing a future budget.

To prepare a budget submission, agencies estimate the resources necessary to continue the existing programs at current levels for the next fiscal year. This includes spending estimates for personnel, equipment, and other program expenses. Then, agencies include estimates for new initiatives funded with any available incremental resources. In addition, OMB will inform an agency of any presidential initiatives to be incorporated into its initial budget. All the lower-level budget requests are then consolidated into an agency-wide budget to be submitted to the OMB.

The agency-wide budget requests and performance plans are reviewed by OMB. During this review process, agency officials clarify policy and technical questions with OMB staff. The OMB director makes decisions on the budget requests and performance plans, and agencies are notified of these decisions through what is known as the OMB "passback." Agencies are then given an opportunity to appeal if they disagree with aspects of the passback.

Once final decisions are made by the president, federal agencies must revise their budget requests and performance plans to conform to these decisions. The materials prepared for the president's budget submission to Congress include program descriptions, the requested spending levels, and the proposed appropriations language for each "account." This information is contained in the appendix volume of the president's budget submission each year.

Therefore, while the president delivers a comprehensive examination of federal revenues and spending to Congress, the budget submission reflects the priorities the executive branch has placed on programs.

### Congressional Action Begins with the Budget Committees

Within six weeks of the president's budget submission, congressional committees prepare their "views and estimates" of spending and revenues within their respective jurisdictions to the House and Senate Budget Committees. These views and estimates, along with information from other sources, are then used by each budget committee in drafting and reporting a budget resolution to its respective body. CBO also "reestimates" the president's budget. CBO and OMB often use different budget assumptions about economic growth and cost of programs. This difference is often a source of friction between the legislative and executive branches.

After hearings, each budget committee chairman creates an individual budget proposal known as the "chairman's mark" and presents that proposal to the respective committee. This proposed budget is usually developed in consultation with other members of the political party and leadership. In recent years, this has not been a bipartisan effort and also has in many instances ignored the president's proposed budget. In addition, it is possible for the House Budget Committee chairman and the Senate Budget Committee chairman to have very different approaches and views of what should be accomplished through the budget, including differences on spending growth and tax cuts.

Next, each committee meets and amends the chairman's proposal of the respective committee. This is known as markup, because the proposal is literally marked up and changed. Because the budget resolution created in committee deals with aggregate numbers, it is important to understand what assumptions go into the creation of the budget. The assumptions are not spelled out in the legislation. For example, a proposed budget resolution could state that Medicaid spending should be reduced by $20 billion over the next five years. The budget committee makes assumptions about where the reductions will be made but the committee of jurisdiction over Medicaid could ignore those assumptions and create other policies to comply with the spending reduction requirement. This part of the process is known as budget reconciliation.

### Passing the Budget Resolution

Once a budget resolution has been passed in committee, it goes to the full body for consideration. The full House and Senate then have the opportunity to amend the resolution that their respective budget committee has created. When the House and Senate pass their respective budget resolutions, they are then "conferenced" just as any other legislation would be. This means that representatives of the Senate and House Budget Committees meet to resolve differences in the resolutions passed by the House and Senate. The final resolution that is the product of this conference is then passed by both the House and Senate without the opportunity for it to be amended. Because it is not a law, the budget resolution serves as a blueprint for establishing budget priorities and defines the parameters for all subsequent budgetary actions for that year. The spending, revenue, and public debt laws necessary to implement decisions agreed to in the budget resolution are subsequently enacted separately as part of the "budget reconciliation" process or as part of the appropriations process. In 2004, Congress was unable to pass a budget resolution. The Congressional Budget Act provides for a backup process so that the appropriations process can begin should this occur.

### Budget Reconciliation

Often, but not always, budget resolutions contain what are known as budget reconciliation instructions, but the resolutions do not have to provide instructions. These are instructions to the committees of a jurisdiction concerning the spending of programs in their jurisdiction. This should not be confused with the appropriations process. In some years, instructions are limited to specific issues such as reducing taxes, and in other years they can touch upon almost every authorizing committee. What the instructions represent in reality is a spending number to the committee of jurisdiction by which the programs under that committee's jurisdiction must have their spending reduced. The committee of jurisdiction could choose to ignore the assumptions in the budget resolution.

For example, the FY 2006 budget resolution assumes spending reductions in Medicaid. However, the reconciliation instructions are in essence a target for reducing spending in the health programs under the jurisdiction of the US Senate Finance Committee. The committee could follow the budget resolution assumption and make the full cut from Medicaid or decide to reduce spending in Medicare and Medicaid, both of which are under its jurisdiction. What matters in the end is that there was a $10 billion reduction in spending for the health programs under the committee's jurisdiction.[7]

This also means that if the committee wanted to make programmatic changes that cost rather than save money, they could do so as part of reconciliation. However, they would have to find additional cuts in order to pay for those changes so that the committee reports out a bill that meets the spending reduction requirement in the resolution. For example, hypothetically, if the committee wanted to make changes to mental health services in Medicaid that were estimated to cost an additional $100 million a year, the committee would have to cut something within Medicaid or Medicare to make up that $100 million while still meeting the overall spending reduction target of $10 billion.

Reconciliation is often how programmatic changes are made in Medicare, Medicaid, and other entitlement programs. Because reconciliation legislation usually passes, it provides an opportunity for interest groups and members of Congress with specific legislative ideas to tack them onto reconciliation to assure passage. Under reconciliation, these changes are packaged into one measure, which is then considered under expedited procedures that limit debate and place restrictions on amendments.

## The Appropriations Process and Health Programs

### The Relationship Between Authorization and Appropriations Measures

Authorizing legislation is legislation that establishes, continues, or modifies agencies or programs. For example, the Older Americans Act authorizes a number of programs to assist the elderly. Authorization legislation usually specifies the maximum amount that can be spent on a program and for how long. For example, authorizing legislation could create a program to be funded at $18 million for each of three years.[8] At the end of three years, Congress would have to decide to reauthorize the program or end the program. If Congress decided to renew the program, it could increase or decrease the maximum amount authorized to be appropriated for the program. The appropriations process would decide how much money would actually be spent per year. For example, even if a program has been authorized at $18 million for a given year, the appropriations committee could decide to provide no funding or funding at a lower level. Programs rarely receive appropriations at the maximum amount authorized.

### Appropriations

Whether or not a budget resolution contains budget reconciliation instructions, it does contain instructions to the appropriations committees concerning the amount of funds they will be able to allocate among programs. The passage of 13 appropriations bills is necessary to assure the funding for the federal government by the beginning of the new fiscal year, October 1. A reorganization of the appropriations committee consolidated what were 13 subcommittees into 12 in 2005. It is not unusual for Congress to fail to complete action on all appropriations bills by October 1. In theory, a program not funded by October 1, will be shut down. However, Congress may also provide funding through a "continuing resolution" (CR). A CR permits Congress to continue funding for programs at current levels through a specified time period to keep the government, or that part not yet funded, operating. This device is often used if Congress feels that it needs a few more days or weeks to finish its work.

The bulk of the discretionary spending of all functions of the government is subject to the annual appropriations process. This process is overseen by the House and Senate Appropriations Committees. Each committee is divided into subcommittees. Each committee has a subcommittee that has jurisdiction over public health funding. In the House and Senate, that subcommittee is known by the same name: the Subcommittee on Labor, Health and Human Services, and Education. These subcommittees produce the bill that becomes the vehicle for funding programs in the Department of Labor, the Department of Health and Human Services (HHS), and the Department of Education. Funding for veterans' health programs is overseen by the Subcommittee on Veterans Affairs and Housing and Urban Development for each committee. It should be noted that some health research is funded through the Department of Defense and its appropriations.[9]

As noted earlier, the amount of discretionary funding as part of the overall budget is relatively small. Therefore, the Appropriations Committees have to make difficult decisions about which programs to fund and by how much. These committees hear from interest groups, government agencies, and other members of Congress regarding specific funding levels for each program. These committees are the focus of many interest groups that want funding for disease-specific issues or by other members of Congress looking for funding for specific projects in specific locations. Not only is what is funded at question, but what the funding levels are in the final package is key to determining the nation's priorities. A frequent lobbying strategy is to ask members of Congress to sign on to a letter of support for a particular funding level for a program to demonstrate broad, bipartisan support to make the funding a national priority.

## Earmarks

By the end of March or early April, members of Congress submit to the appropriation committee of their respective body, lists of local or special projects they wish to see funded through the appropriations process. Members' "wish lists" are based on requests from constituents including individuals, state governments, businesses, and institutions such as universities and libraries. This kind of funding is known as an earmark. Earmarks provide funding for a specific local project such as funding for a specific hospital's health information technology project, renovating a community health center, or a local outreach program. Members are asked to attach priorities to these requests. Each year the individual appropriations subcommittees decide how they want to handle member requests, including the format and information needed for the request and when the information is due. If a request is important from a state perspective, a frequent lobbying strategy is to not only ensure that an individual member places a project on their individual list, but to also ensure the entire congressional delegation, including House and Senate members, includes the request on their wish lists.[10]

## Conference and Report Language

Should Congress begin to run out of time to consider each of the 13 bills separately on the floor of the Senate or House, it is not uncommon for the leadership to put together several bills and create an "omnibus appropriations" bill.

After each body has passed its version of an appropriations bill, or an omnibus, it goes to conference so that members of the House and Senate can resolve differences. The final product is known as the "conference report." This report is then sent back to each body for final passage. Conference reports cannot be amended on the floor of the House or Senate and must be voted up or down by a simple majority. Generally, before the House considers a conference report on an appropriations measure, it adopts a special rule waiving all points of order against the conference report and its consideration. The rule usually does not provide for amendments either.[11,12]

A conference report contains more than the legislative language of a bill. It also contains an explanation of what Congress' intent was in specific provisions. Although report language does not hold the force of law, it is useful in establishing a legislative history. In addition, report language serves as a useful tool in providing specific directions to the agencies that will have to implement the budget or new program.

## Health Appropriation Anomaly

Most federal domestic health programs are administered through or in consultation with agencies that are under the Department of Health and Human Services (HHS). This includes the Food and Drug Administration (FDA). However, the FDA is the only agency within HHS that does not receive its appropriation from the Labor-HHS-Education appropriations bill. The FDA once was part of the US Department of Agriculture (USDA). Because the appropriators never moved jurisdiction of the funding of that agency to the Labor-HHS-Education subcommittees, the FDA and all of the programs it oversees still receive appropriations as part of the agriculture appropriations bill.[13]

## Legislating on Appropriations Bills

Technically, appropriations bills are charged specifically with determining spending levels for programs rather than with delineating programmatic changes. In fact, the Senate and House have rules that prohibit legislating—or making changes in policy—on an appropriations bill. By attaching a "rider," a provision that does not affect the spending level but changes policy, a member can bypass the committee legislative and hearing process. What is considered legislating on an appropriations bill, however, can be the subject of debate. In the Senate, a point of order can be brought against a provision by a member who believes that a provision is legislation on an appropriations bill.[13] The point of order is subject to a ruling by the parliamentarian and a vote by the Senate on whether or not the provision violates the rules, if a member chooses to raise the rule. In the Senate, if no one raises the point of order, then the rule is not invoked. The House of Representatives has its own rules that also in theory prohibit legislating on an appropriations bill.[14]

What is considered legislating on an appropriations bill may be simply a measure of expediency. For example, within the agriculture appropriations bill for the FDA for FY 2000, the House version attached a provision prohibiting the use or research of the controversial drug RU486, a drug that is primarily used as an abortifacient. This provision did not impact the FDA's program spending levels, but was a prohibition on certain agency activities concerning the agency's role in overseeing the safety and effectiveness of drugs. Such a prohibition could be considered legislating on an appropriations bill because the proposal was aimed at eliminating the availability of RU486. However, it could be argued that the actual language was only a directive concerning how the FDA organizes its spending priorities. Because similar language was not included in the Senate version, it would be left to conference to determine if that provision made it into the final conference report, which would not be subject to amendment and would have to be voted up or down. This is also an example of how a social issue can impact spending allocations and priorities.

## Creating Health Programs—Authorizing Committee Jurisdictions

Healthcare issues can be considered in any number of committees depending on how the legislation or issue is crafted. The usual breakdown for health legislation falls among four committees within the House and Senate.

In the Senate, Medicare and Medicaid are within the jurisdiction of the *Senate Finance Committee*. The Senate Finance Committee also has jurisdiction over Social Security issues. In the House of Representatives, Medicare Part A and B, both benefits and spending issues, are under the jurisdiction of the *House Ways and Means Committee*. Like the Finance Committee, this committee also has jurisdiction over Social Security. However, Medicare Part B benefit issues also fall under the jurisdiction of the *House Energy and Commerce Committee,* which also has jurisdiction over Medicaid. This split jurisdiction of Medicare Part B has meant that House budget reconciliation proposals have contained policy changes that are very different within the same bill and are left unresolved until the conference with the Senate.

Public health programs are under the jurisdiction of the *House Energy and Commerce Committee* and the *Senate Health, Education, Labor, and Pensions Committee*. These committees deal with such issues as FDA reform, NIH research, medical data privacy, the Public Health Service Act, health professional training, and so forth.[11,13]

There are times, however, in which the political leadership can assign health issues that may cut across several committees' jurisdiction to one committee. For example, in 1998, when Congress was considering a global tobacco settlement, the tobacco issue could have cut across several committees. However, this would have slowed down the consideration of such comprehensive legislation. In the Senate, the leadership decided to allow the Senate Commerce Committee to have jurisdiction over the entire issue even though this committee had no usual jurisdiction over traditional public health programs. The Commerce Committee also has a Subcommittee on Science, Technology, and Space. It is not uncommon for this subcommittee to hold hearings on issues related to health technology or research depending upon the interest of the chair of the subcommittee.

## How a Bill Becomes a Law—Really

The Constitution requires that bills that raise taxes start within the House of Representatives. Otherwise, any bill can begin in either body by first being introduced by a member and then being referred to a committee that holds hearings. After hearings, a committee holds a markup in which committee members can offer amendments. The bill is then "reported" to the full body for consideration, where it can be subject to further amendment. Then the same thing happens in the opposite legislative body. When the two versions are completed, they are then conferenced and a conference report is sent for final passage in the House and Senate. After final passage, the bill is sent to the president for his signature or veto. If the president vetoes a proposal, the bill is sent back to the House and Senate to be voted on again. Three fourths of the House and three fifths of the Senate are needed to override a veto. See Exhibit 6-1 for an explanation of the rule-making process.

As referred to in instances in this chapter, the House and Senate have different rules for the consideration of different kinds of legislation. It is important to note that a little-discussed committee in the House controls what amendments are offered to legislation on the floor of the House and in fact scripts the consideration of bills before the full body. This committee, known as the House Rules Committee, is one of the most powerful committees in the House.

All legislation in the House must go before the House Rules Committee before it can be considered on the floor of the House. If a bill has been referred to and considered by different committees within the House, those different

Exhibit 6-1    The Rule-Making Process

- Congress has passed a law, and it has been signed into law by the president.
- A federal agency proposes rules or regulations to implement the law.
- The proposal is cleared through the agency and the department.
- The proposal is sent to the Office of Management and Budget (OMB) for clearance concerning budget impact.
- Once cleared through the OMB, the proposal is published in the *Federal Register* for a public commentary period.
- Public comments are received and considered.
- Revisions to the proposed regulations are made.
- The revised regulations are cleeared through the agency and department.
- The OMB provides final clearance.
- The revised regulations are published as final regulations in the *Federal Register*.

versions can be pieced together into one proposal by the House Rules Committee. The committee also decides the length of time for consideration of a bill and what amendments will be permitted to be considered. This makes ensuring that specific issues and interests are addressed at the committee with jurisdiction level that much more important because if an issue is not addressed and a floor amendment is needed, there is always the possibility that the House Rules Committee can block a floor amendment. Before each bill is voted on in the House of Representatives, the House votes to adopt the rule. It is in the debate on the rule that members can make the case for defeating the rule if the House Rules Committee has proposed a rule that blocks the consideration of an amendment that the majority of the House thinks should be considered.[15]

The Senate does not have a committee with the same authority as the House Rules Committee.[13] Instead, the Senate operates under a set of rules designed to protect the rights of the minority and reflects that the Senate is a smaller body than the House. The Senate leadership of both parties can work together to develop a time agreement for the consideration of a specific bill. A time limit can specify how many amendments can be offered. That agreement is usually adopted by unanimous consent. Should a time limit not be agreed to, then other rules in the Senate can be used to close debate if two thirds of the body agrees.

Unanimous consent is frequently used in the Senate for the passage of noncontroversial bills without taking up debate time on the floor. Therefore, if a bill contains a provision that is particularly onerous, interest groups will often seek out a member to object should a unanimous consent agreement on that bill be offered. It takes only one member to object in such instances.

The Senate also has a mechanism whereby an individual senator can block the consideration by the full body of a bill or nomination. This process is known as a hold. This process still remains somewhat secret, so that it is difficult to discover who had placed a hold on a bill. Placing a hold means that even if a bill has passed the committee with jurisdiction, it cannot be considered as a free-standing bill or as part of a unanimous consent.

The Senate also has rules that allow members to filibuster.[13] This is an example of how the Senate rules protect the rights of the minority. Filibustering is more than simply holding the floor and talking as some Hollywood movies portray it. It can be a series of parliamentary procedures that slows the process down, preventing the Senate from consideration of other legislation. Using such procedures to slow the process requires members to be on the floor, throwing off the Senate schedule and delaying other members' ability to get work done.

## Legislation and Regulation

Federal agencies are authorized to issue regulations by their authorizing statutes, statutes establishing new programs, and statutes amending and extending the duties and responsibilities of those agencies. Most regulations are issued under the notice-and-comment procedure established by the Administrative Procedure Act (APA).[16] Less commonly, some agencies are required to add such elements of adjudicatory proceedings as cross-examination and rebuttal witnesses to the notice-and-comment requirements when promulgating regulations. These agencies include the Federal Trade Commission, the Consumer Product Safety Commission, and the Occupational Safety and Health Administration.

It is important to note that to challenge the federal authority of a regulation, thorough research must be done beyond the legislation creating the program, but must include all the enabling legislation of the powers and duties of the department.

## Informal Notice-and-Comment

### Rule Making

The informal notice-and-comment rule-making process requires that an agency publish a notice of proposed rule making in the *Federal Register;* afford all interested parties an opportunity to participate in the proceeding through the submission of written comments, or, at the discretion of the agency, by oral presentations; and when consideration of the relevant matter presented is completed, incorporate in the final rules "a concise general statement of their basis and purpose."[17] A final rule must be published in the *Federal Register* not less than 30 days before its effective date. Interested persons have the right to petition for the issuance, amendment, or repeal of a rule.[18] The APA does not specify a minimum period for public comment. However, Executive Order 12866, which was issued on September 30, 1993, requires a period of no less than 60 days.[17] An agency may extend or reopen the period for public comment at any time. Agencies are also free to grant additional procedural rights to interested persons. Much of the bare-bones rule-making requirements in the APA have been fleshed out in detail by federal court rulings that have sought to make the rule-making process more accessible to the interested public and to ensure fair and meaningful input.

Approximately 75% of all regulations are issued by agencies over which the president exercises considerable oversight and supervision and are subject to Executive Order 12866.[19] These agencies are also the ones issuing the more costly social regulations. They include the Environmental Protection Agency (EPA), the Occupational Safety and Health Administration and the Mine Safety and Health Administration (both in the Department of Labor), the FDA (HHS), the Department of Energy, the Department of the Interior, the Department of Agriculture, and the Department of Transportation.

### The Federal Register

The *Federal Register* is much like an executive gazette, published each work day, consisting of public documents issued by the president and federal agencies that announce and describe actions, either taken or proposed, that affect or will affect the public. Each document, depending on the subject matter, is printed in one of four sections of the *Federal Register*. The four sections include a rules and regulations section, a proposed rules section, a notices section, and a presidential documents section. In addition, the *Federal Register* contains a corrections section and a jumps and blanks section.

The number of pages and documents in the *Federal Register* that are devoted to regulatory actions constitutes only a small number of the total pages and documents printed in that publication. It is difficult if not impossible to determine precisely the number of federal regulations issued each year. Regulatory action taken by an agency may involve issuing a new regulation, revising or abolishing an existing regulation, or a combination. Moreover, each regulatory action may create several new regulations or affect a number of existing regulations.

The rules and regulations section of the *Federal Register* contains regulatory documents announcing and describing final regulatory actions taken by the federal agencies. Some of the documents have general regulatory applicability and legal effect and are listed in the *Code of Federal Regulations (CFR)*. The *CFR* is the annual codification of the general and permanent rules published in the *Federal Register* by federal departments and agencies. Its purpose is to present the official and complete text of agency regulations and thereby provide a comprehensive and convenient reference for those regulations. The documents in the rules and regulations section are the documents having the greatest regulatory impact on the public. The section also contains two other types of rule documents. One type of document, termed *ministerial* and *informational/administrative*, does not affect regulations. These documents include notices of meetings, notices that proposed regulatory action is being terminated, corrections of previous rule documents, and changes in comment periods and similar matters. These documents deal with such matters as airworthiness directives, quarantine actions and related measures to prevent the spread of animal and plant pests and diseases, and similar ongoing regulatory activities.

The proposed rules section contains notices to the public of regulatory actions proposed by the federal agencies. The purpose is to give the interested public an opportunity to participate in the rule-making process.

Except for one section, the remaining four sections of the *Federal Register* generally have little to do with federal regulations. The *notices* section is the largest of the sections and contains material (other than rules or proposed rules) that is applicable to the public. Included in this section are notices of hearings and investigations, committee meetings, agency decisions and rulings, delegations of authority, filing of petitions and applications, and agency statements of organization and functions.

The *presidential documents* section contains such documents as proclamations, executive orders, and similar instruments of national interest. Occasionally, an executive order may impact the regulatory process. For example, Executive Order 12291, issued in February 1981, established the policy of requiring agencies to conduct a cost-benefit analysis on regulations imposing yearly costs of $100 million or more, and centralized the review of regulations in the OMB.[20] Executive Order 12866, issued in October 1994, revoked the earlier order, but continued the requirement for cost-benefit analysis of major regulations and review by the OMB.[17]

The *corrections* section consists of corrections to previously published information, and the *jumps and blanks* section consists of pages left blank to enable the agency to maintain the integrity of an accurate page count of the other sections.

## Accountability of Federal Agencies

Contrary to what many members of the public may believe, federal agencies are not independent entities free of external constraints and oversight. Most of the agencies are under the supervision and direction of the president. All are subject to congressional oversight and dependent on Congress for their statutory authority and usual appropriations. Almost all of their regulatory actions are subject to judicial review. Federal agencies act only under authority that is delegated to them by specific laws or by presidential directives. In addition, the APA establishes the framework under which the agencies engage in rule making and subjects that rule making to judicial review.

Since 1981, regulatory action of federal agencies has been closely monitored by the OMB. The OMB, which is part of the executive office of the president, reviews and clears the most important regulatory actions to ensure that, in general, among the various alternatives, the regulatory action is most likely to achieve its goals with the least cost and burden to the public.

In addition, congressional review of regulations is required. The Congressional Review Act of 1997 requires agencies to send their final regulations to Congress for review 60 days before they take effect.[21] A regulation may be rejected within the review period if Congress passes a joint resolution of disapproval and the president signs it, or, if he vetoes the resolution, Congress overrides the veto. Since the law's enactment, seven joint resolutions of disapproval have been introduced, but not one has been passed.

More often what occurs is that members of Congress are contacted by interest groups or state governments to point out that a particular proposed regulation is unfavorable. Members of Congress frequently write agencies asking for changes in regulations as members of the public during the public comment period.

### Judicial Review of Rule Making

The APA subjects agency actions to judicial review except where a statute precludes such review or "where agency action is committed to agency discretion by law."[16] Any person adversely affected by an agency action "within the meaning of the relevant statute" may challenge that action.

## The Department of Health and Human Services

The HHS is the principal agency within the federal government with the responsibility for protecting the health of all Americans and providing essential human services. The HHS includes more than 300 programs covering a variety of activities, including the following:

- Medicare and social science research
- The prevention of outbreaks of infectious disease, including immunization services
- Food and drug safety assurance
- Medicare (health insurance for elderly and the disabled)
- Medicaid (health insurance for low-income individuals)
- Financial assistance for low-income families
- Child support enforcement
- Maternal and infant health improvement
- Head Start (preschool education and services)

- Child abuse and domestic violence prevention
- Substance abuse treatment and prevention
- Services for older Americans including home-delivered meals
- Comprehensive health services delivery for American Indians and Alaska Natives
- National health data collection
- Homeland security

HHS programs are administered by 11 HHS operating divisions (see Chapter 3 for more detailed discussion). The HHS is the largest grant-making agency in the federal government. The HHS must work with state and local government because many of the HHS-funded services are provided at the local level by state or county agencies, or through private-sector grantees.

## HHS Operating Divisions

US Public Health Service operating divisions include the National Institutes of Health (NIH), the FDA, Centers for Disease Control and Prevention (CDC), the Agency for Toxic Substances and Disease Registry (ATSDR), Indian Health Service (IHS), the Health Resources and Services Administration (HRSA), the Substance Abuse and Mental Health Services Administration (SAMHSA), and the Agency for Healthcare Research and Quality (AHRQ).

- The NIH is the world's premier medical research organization, supporting more than 35,000 research projects nationwide in diseases such as cancer, Alzheimer's, diabetes, arthritis, heart ailments, and AIDS. The NIH includes 17 separate health institutes. It was established in 1887 as the Hygienic Laboratory. Its main campus is outside of Washington, DC, in Bethesda, Maryland.
- The FDA ensures the safety of foods and cosmetics as well as the safety and efficacy of pharmaceuticals, biologic products, and medical devices—products that represent 25 cents of every dollar in US consumer spending. Originally established in 1906, it is headquartered in Rockville, Maryland.
- The CDC maintains national health statistics and works with states and other partners to provide a system of health surveillance to monitor and prevent the outbreak of diseases. The CDC also provides for immunization services and guards against international disease transmission, with CDC personnel stationed in more than 25 foreign countries. In addition, the CDC supports research into disease and injury prevention. Originally established in 1946, it is headquartered in Atlanta, Georgia.
- The ATSDR works with states and other federal agencies to prevent exposure to hazardous substances from waste sites. The agency conducts public health assessments, health studies, surveillance activities, and health education training in communities around waste sites on the US EPA's National Priorities List. The ATSDR has also developed toxicologic profiles of hazardous chemicals found at these sites. Founded in 1980, it is headquartered in Atlanta, Georgia.
- The IHS has 37 hospitals, 60 health centers, 3 school health centers, and 46 health stations. It also assists 34 urban Indian health centers. Services are provided to nearly 1.5 million American Indians and

Alaska Natives of the 557 federally recognized tribes through a work-force of approximately 14,500 employees and an additional tribal and urban Indian health workforce of approximately 10,000. Annually, there are approximately 90,000 hospital admissions and 7 million out-patient visits, 4 million community health representative client con-tacts, and 2.4 million dental services. Established in 1924 as part of the Department of the Interior, the IHS was transferred to the HHS in 1955. It is headquartered in Rockville, Maryland.

- The HRSA helps provide health resources for medically underserved populations. A nationwide network of 643 community and migrant health centers, plus 144 primary care programs for the homeless and residents of public housing, serve 8.1 million Americans each year. The HRSA works to build the healthcare workforce and maintains the National Health Service Corps. The HRSA also provides services to people with AIDS through the Ryan White CARE Act programs and over-sees the organ transplantation system. It also oversees the National Practitioners Data Bank, which contains reports on physicians and other providers who settle malpractice suits or lose clinical privileges or their license to practice. The HRSA was established in 1982 and is headquartered in Rockville, Maryland.

- The SAMHSA oversees programs concerning the quality and availabil-ity of substance abuse prevention, addiction treatment, and mental health services. It provides funding through block grants to states for direct substance abuse and mental health services, including treatment for more than 340,000 Americans with various substance abuse prob-lems. This agency also helps improve substance treatment through its Knowledge Development and Application Grant Program. It was estab-lished in 1992 and is headquartered in Rockville, Maryland.

- The Agency for Healthcare Research and Quality (AHRQ, formerly the Agency for Healthcare Policy and Research [AHCPR] supports research on healthcare systems, quality and cost, and the effectiveness of med-ical treatments. It was established in 1989 and is headquartered in Rockville, Maryland.

## Human Services Operating Divisions

Three divisions within the HHS administer human services. These agencies are the Centers for Medicare and Medicaid Services (CMS), the Administration for Children and Families (ACF), and the Administration on Aging (AOA).

- The CMS administers two entitlement programs, Medicare and Medicaid, which provide health care to approximately one in every four Americans. Medicare provides health insurance for more elderly and disabled individuals. Medicaid, a joint federal-state program, pro-vides health coverage for low-income persons. CMS also administers the State Child Health Insurance Program (SCHIP). CMS was originally established as the Health Care Financing Administration in 1977 and is headquartered in Baltimore, Maryland.[22]

- The ACF is responsible for more than 60 programs that provide ser-vices and assistance to needy children and families. Some of the programs this agency administers include the state-federal welfare program, Temporary Assistance to Needy Families, National Child Support Enforcement System, and the Head Start Program. Programs under this agency assist low-income families with child care funds and support state programs to provide for foster care and adoption assistance. Its programs also fund child abuse and domestic violence prevention programs. Established in 1991, the agency brought together several existing programs and is headquartered in Washington, DC.[22]

- The AOA supports a nationwide aging network, including programs authorized by the Older Americans Act, and provides policy leadership on aging services.[22]

## Bioterrorism Preparedness Functions of the HHS

The Public Health Security and Bioterrorism Preparedness and Response Act of 2002 (PL 107-188) was passed in response to concerns about bioterrorism attacks and was intended to improve the nation's ability to respond to bioterrorist threats and other public health emergencies. The act builds upon the programs and the authorities established in Title III of Public Health Service (PHS) Act by the Public Health Threats and Emergencies Act of 2000 (PL 106-505, Title I). The 2002 legislation authorizes spending for five years for the secretary of HHS to upgrade and renovate facilities at the CDC; purchase smallpox vaccine; expand the national stockpile of drugs, vaccines, and other emergency medical supplies; and provide grants to state and local governments and hospitals to improve preparedness and planning. The secretaries of HHS and of the USDA also are required to regulate facilities that handle potentially dangerous biological agents.

Among the provisions of this legislation are provisions to protect the nation's food and drug supply and enhance agriculture security, including new regulatory powers for the FDA to block importation of unsafe foods. To protect the drinking water supply, the act requires community water systems to conduct vulnerability assessments and develop emergency response plans.[23]

## Block Grants and Funding Programs

There is no legal definition for the term *block grant*, but block grants are characterized by a federal-state or local relationship in which there is considerable discretion in grant administration within a broadly defined program area. Typically, block grants have less "red tape" in their applications and administrative requirements. They apply to broad purposes such as public health rather than to narrow (categorical) purposes such as lead poisoning or rodent control. They consolidate a number of existing narrowly based programs into one grant instrument. They frequently are associated with budget reductions, although that is not necessarily the outcome.

Block grants blend the characteristics of categorical grants and general revenue sharing. This blending of attributes and expectations associated with each type of grant leads to a constant tension, and is a major factor explaining why block grants are sometimes characterized as "unstable." There are almost always compromises—the products of trade-offs made in the process of enactment.

The debate over block grants has historically focused on design, implementation, and evaluation as a part of the larger debate about what role the federal government should play in domestic government and where responsibility should be shared among the various levels of government and the private sector, including decision-making authority.

Some believe that block grants are a more efficient and effective mechanism for achieving federal purposes. Some proponents of block grants also view categorical grants as an instrument of an overreaching national government and block grants as a devolving of power to subnational governments. The objective, then, would be to not make the federal government work more effectively, but to get the federal government out of the picture.

Opponents of block grants fear that financial support for blocked programs will diminish, as it is thought to be more difficult to get support for broad purposes. In addition, many fear that the absence of social targeting requirements means that some groups would not benefit. Still others believe that the government that collects the taxes should be the government that determines how the money is spent.

Today, many view block grants as a synonym for budget cuts, in large part because of the experiences during the Reagan administration, when funds for newly created block grants were reduced by 13% from the previous year's (FY 1981) total appropriation for 57 categorical grants. This 13% reduction was lower than the 25% saving the Reagan administration had sought to achieve through its block grant proposal.[24]

In 2005, it was widely thought that the Bush administration would propose block granting Medicaid because of a desire to provide more state flexibility and to slow federal spending for this program. This did not occur, but the administration did propose block granting the federal portion of state administrative costs for Medicaid.[25]

The Substance Abuse Prevention and Treatment (SAPT) block grant is an example of this shared federal-state responsibility using funding as the lever. SAPT is administered by the SAMHSA and is the primary tool the federal government uses to support state substance abuse prevention and treatment programs. Funds go directly to states, which have broad discretion to decide how to use them, within federal guidelines. Funds are allocated to states under a formula reflecting several factors: state personal income data, state financial resources, state population estimates, and the cost of providing services in each particular state. States must meet other requirements to get full funding. States must have a law providing that it is unlawful for any manufacturer, retailer, or distributor to sell tobacco products to individuals under 18. States must also have a mechanism for measuring compliance with its requirement and for reducing noncompliance to specified levels. States are required to maintain a level of spending on substance abuse prevention and treatment programs that is at least as high as the average spending for two years preceding any particular year. If a state does not meet this requirement, it will lose a portion of its grant funds.

In addition, these funds are then subject to what is known as the Synar amendment. This amendment, passed in 1992 as part of the Alcohol, Drug Abuse, and Mental Health Administration Reorganization Act,[26] requires states to enforce their tobacco minimum-age-of-sale laws or risk losing substance abuse block grant funds. The Synar amendment is administered by SAMHSA and has been an important catalyst for the passage of state tobacco-control legislation. Under Synar, state officials are supervising random, unannounced visits to retail outlets by minors as a means of monitoring retailer compliance. Retailers caught selling tobacco to minors may be fined or have their tobacco licenses suspended. So although this block grant is not directly aimed at tobacco smoking prevention, additional federal legislation has established a health priority by using the loss of federal funds as the hammer to get the state to establish reduction in youth smoking as a state priority.

## Medicaid

Medicaid is the largest joint federal-state entitlement program and is not subject to the annual appropriations process. It is a means-tested entitlement program. It provides primary and acute care as well as long-term care to over 50 million Americans at a cost to federal and state governments of approximately $276.1 billion in FY 2003. Of all federally supported social programs, only Medicare comes close to this level of spending and only Social Security costs more. Each state designs and administers its own Medicaid program under broad federal guidelines. States that want to go beyond the guidelines or do less than the guidelines, must apply for waivers. State variability in eligibility, covered services, and how those services are reimbursed make understanding Medicaid a complex challenge. Medicaid can be thought of as three distinct programs: one program funds long-term care for the chronically ill, disabled, and aged; another program provides health insurance for low-income children and families; and the Disproportionate Share (DSH) Program assists hospitals with the cost of uncompensated care.

Each state establishes its own eligibility within broad federal guidelines. States must cover certain population groups such as recipients of Supplemental Security Income (SSI), that is, the aged, blind, and disabled, and have the option of covering others. Historically, Medicaid eligibility for poor families (generally women with dependent children) was linked to the receipt of cash welfare payments. The historical link between Medicaid and welfare benefits was severed in the creation of the Temporary Assistance for Needy Families (TANF) Program in 1996. That legislation did allow states to maintain the link as an option.[27]

Medicaid does not cover everyone who is poor. Eligibility is also subject to "categorical restrictions"; benefits are available only to members of families with children and pregnant women and to persons who are aged, blind, or disabled. Beginning in 1984, Congress expanded eligibility for pregnant women and children. Partly as a result, the number of beneficiaries grew by 60% over the next 10 years.

Special eligibility rules apply to persons who receive care in nursing facilities and other institutions. Many of these persons have incomes that are well above the poverty level but qualify for Medicaid because of the high cost of their care. Medicaid has thus emerged as the largest source of third-party funding for long-term care. It is also a major source of federal support for programs to serve individuals with mental retardation or developmental disabilities.

As budget pressures increase because long-term care costs escalate, states often take the lead in trying to find new healthcare delivery systems and arrangements to decrease costs while assuring quality of care. This has included the move to managed care for Medicaid beneficiaries and increasing use of home- and community-based care waivers to meet long-term care needs.

States are often concerned when Congress enacts legislation that establishes unfunded mandates. Unfunded mandates are responsibilities or duties imposed by the federal government on state and local governments without providing funding for the costs incurred. Advocates of mandates that may incur costs at the state and local levels contend that such mandates are often designed to address problems that are found nationwide. They argue that regulations set uniform standards for all localities, and that requiring localities to pay at least some of the costs motivates them to cease violations. State and local government officials, on the other hand, have expressed alarm at the increasing cost of complying with the mandates.

### State Children's Health Insurance Program

The State Child Health Insurance Program (SCHIP) was created in 1997 by the Balanced Budget Act of 1997 (PL 105-33). In general, SCHIP provides federal matching funds for states to expand health benefits coverage for modest-income children through Medicaid, a separate state program, or a combination of both. It has been suggested that many currently uninsured children are actually eligible for coverage under SCHIP, but are not enrolled. As of April 2005, of the 50 states, the District of Columbia, and the 5 territories, 17 had used Medicaid expansions, 18 used separate state programs, and 21 used a combination approach. Approximately 6.2 million children were enrolled in SCHIP during FY 2004. In addition, eight states reported enrolling about 646,000 adults in SCHIP through program waivers.[28]

## Long-Term Care

With the increased life span of Americans, the aging of our society, and a growing number of individuals living with one or more chronic illnesses or disabilities, long-term care is becoming more of a pressing issue at the state and federal levels of government. Although Congress had debated different approaches for changing the way in which these services are financed, the cost of expansion of long-term care coverage under public programs has been the central focus of the debate. In 2002, $157 billion was spent on long-term care services for persons of all ages, with almost half of that sum expended through Medicaid.[29] This figure does not include the amount of informal caregiving provided by families.

In FY 2003 both federal and state sources paid about $83.8 billion, more than two thirds of which was for services in institutions and the rest was for services in home- and community-based settings. Because so much of the long-term care dollars are now coming from Medicaid, states have been in the forefront of studying and experimenting with innovative ways in which to provide cost-effective long-term care. In addition, in 2000, Congress authorized a new state grant program under the Older Americans Act to assist family caregivers. For FY 2005, the program was provided $163 million.[29]

## State–Federal Interface in Public Health

The current role of states in public health is a mixed set of signals in which the state may choose its priorities and has more flexibility but is facing a demanding economic environment with many priorities competing for funds.

States have traditionally held the authority to regulate insurance and to provide state licensure to qualified providers. Yet even in these areas, actions on the federal government can have impact. For example, in state licensure, many states have moved to provide authority for non-MD health providers to act more independently. However, Medicare's conditions of participation do not recognize these differences. For example, a classic fight continues between certified registered nurse anesthetists (CRNAs) and anesthesiologists over Medicare reimbursement. Although many states permit CRNAs to have independent practices, Medicare does not recognize this. Therefore, Medicare policies can impact not only the reimbursement, but also the growth of specialties and non-MD health providers who often provide access to care in rural areas. Another example is that nurse practitioners under some state laws can order hospice services for patients. However, the Medicare program does not recognize this authority for the Medicare hospice benefit.

The relationship of the states and the federal government has been characterized by many shifts over the history of the United States. In 1964, the federal government sought "creative federalism" in which the Johnson administration's Great Society programs sought to end the national government's role in meeting the administration's goals to achieve socially desirable goals in reducing poverty and the elimination of hunger. Medicare and Medicaid were created during this time. In the 1970s, presidents tried to respond to the concerns raised about the intergovernmental grant system, particularly duplication, fragmentation, overlap, and confusion.[29] The administrations of Richard Nixon and Gerald Ford attempted to redirect the relationship of the federal government to the states. The administrations' principal tools were revenue sharing and consolidating federal aid programs into six special revenue-sharing programs. The intent was to shift funds, authority, and responsibility to states and local governments in an effort to manage the intergovernmental grant system more effectively.

With the Reagan administration, new initiatives stimulated the debate on the appropriate roles of federal, state, and local government. President Reagan sought to restructure the system of governance fundamentally. In 1981, Congress passed the Omnibus Budget Reconciliation Act, which consolidated a number of social programs into nine block grants, allowing for greater state and local autonomy and flexibility in the fashioning of strategies to address federal objectives and local needs. The administration was not successful in the second phase, which would have reallocated federal-state responsibility and resources for welfare, food stamps, and Medicare, and would have turned back revenue sources to the states.

The Clinton administration's initiative of reinventing government and the House Republicans' Contract with America, resulted in the passage of federal legislation that required the federal government to assess the cost-benefit impact of federal legislation on states, local governments, and the private sector and prompted consideration of how to reform the regulatory process.

So where does that leave the states when it comes to establishing public health policy and implementing new and innovative strategies for meeting the health needs of populations within the states' and localities' borders? In the current climate, states have options that they might not have had in the 1960s and 1970s. At the same time, states face the continued challenge of managing reductions in funds from both federal and state governments and meeting other requirements placed on them from the federal level.

For example, more states are seeking waivers from Medicaid and Medicare to find different ways of providing care for dual eligibles, and many states have sought Medicaid waivers to either expand or operate Medicaid programs differently. Some states are looking at waivers from programs that would permit them to address the needs of the disabled and to assist them in getting back to work without losing healthcare coverage.

Because long-term care is becoming a larger Medicaid burden for the states, some states are looking at the use of state dollars for different types of services. For example, assisted living has been pioneered in the state of Oregon, which now leads the country in the amount of state dollars used to provide home- and community-based care services.

In addition to trying to address state and local needs, states are also charged with more responsibility in their role as agents for the federal government. For example, states are under criticism because of the way in which they have acted to ensure the quality of nursing homes under federal quality standards. States, in turn, charge that the resources given to them by the federal government to do the job of quality surveys are not enough to ensure quality.

The passage of the SCHIP also showed a willingness on the part of Congress to provide states with flexibility even while trying to require that more children be covered. States were free to design plans within guidelines. Most began to design plans that were either an expansion of state Medicaid programs or stand-alone components. A growing number of states explored statutory options provided under SCHIP to include family coverage. Many states examined how to develop innovative outreach strategies to provide families with applications and program information.

Other examples of recently passed health legislation show less flexibility for the states. The Mental Health Parity Act of 1996, for example, mandated private insurance coverage requirements concerning mental health services.[30] The Health Insurance Accountability and Portability Act of 1996 also placed requirements on health insurance coverage that the states must oversee.[31] In this legislation, however, it specified that if the state does not provide adequate oversight, the CMS would be authorized to become the entity that ensures that requirements of the act are followed.

Economic downturns force states to reevaluate spending for healthcare expansions to cover more of the uninsured undertaken in periods of better economic growth and limit the amount of state funds for assisting in renovations and upgrading of public health programs and facilities. Whether or not the federal government can be counted on to assist financially depends upon what priorities are created in the federal budget. Federal health programs are often at risk in the federal government's need to address budget deficits, and often federal reductions in spending come when states also have fewer resources. Those dependent on federal and state grants to run programs, and state and local government dependent on federal funding to ensure the continuance of specific programs, have to be aware of what economic conditions will mean for the funding sources.

## State Legislation

Legislative authority is operative in both federal and state government. For the states, government authority is based on "police power" to provide for the health, safety, and welfare of the population.[32] In terms of public health, police powers include all laws and regulations that improve morbidity and reduce mortality of the community. (For more detailed discussion, see Chapter 4.) These powers cover the wide range of areas that enable public health agencies to pursue their most fundamental missions of protection from communicable disease transmission, requiring immunization for school entry, ensuring confidentiality essential to preventive programs, and implementing environmental protections including those for air, water, and waste disposal. As illustrated in Chapter 4, although legislation serves to protect health, it is sometimes in conflict with private interests. For example, it is state legislation that provides for the detention of individuals with active pulmonary tuberculosis who refuse to take medications, and who thereby endanger the community with risk of transmission of this disease.

Legislation to protect from injury is also enacted at the state level, including requirements for bicycle helmets. Again, state legislation is critical to an agenda to improve population health and also can be controversial, balancing public and private interests in areas such as HIV reporting and partner notification and immunization requirements that can exclude unimmunized children from school. Public health administrators require skills in both fostering and advocating for legislators who advance this agenda and conversely resisting legislative attempts at the state level, which can compromise their objectives. This principle was emphasized in the 1988 IOM Report *Future of Public Health*.[33] Duties of the state were enumerated including the assurance of an adequate base for health activities.

Legislative priorities culminating in the enactment of state statutes are the result of a concerted effort by a number of involved parties. Public health agencies formulate legislative priorities and work with executive staff of the chief executive office (governor), legislators and legislative staff, advocates, and other interested individuals. Legislative support or nonsupport of public health does not occur by accident or spontaneously. Ascertaining the impact of the proposed bill on the spectrum of those persons affected and the associated costs is a necessary part of this preparation. In considering or crafting new legislation, an ongoing partnership between the public health specialist and the lawyer or legislative draftsman must be formed early. Also, a decision may need to be made if a new statute rather than new regulation is needed to accomplish the objective.[32] These efforts should best begin long before the opening of the legislative session.

In advocating for legislation, public health proponents need to relate to legislators and often, more importantly, to more accessible legislative staff. It is often more effective to make a point with legislators by encouraging other individuals and interests in the community to make their views known to legislators rather than rely on state health staff. State staff are providing information and "educating" legislators. Generally, state law or regulations prohibit all public officials from engaging in political activities or lobbying. As Grad pointed out, "It has never been held under any state 'Hatch Act' that a public health officer or employee may not bring the need for legislation to the attention of the appropriate legislative officers."[32]

If the legislative proposal is of importance, the program may be included in the governor's annual message. When the draft legislation has been prepared by the state health department or governor's office, an interested legislator can introduce it into the legislative process. By a similar route, outside groups can get health legislation introduced into the system. It is the public health director's (or staff's) responsibility to take a position and be available for testimony on the proposal.[32]

Using New York State as an example, a bicameral legislature (like most states) has 150 members of the Assembly and 61 members of the Senate. All are elected in even-numbered years; members of both houses serving 2-year terms.[34] Major players are the governor (and executive staff), the majority party in each house, and its leadership. The Speaker of the Assembly and Senate Majority Leader wield enormous power and also appoint all chairpersons of committees. There are 36 Assembly and 34 Senate Standing Committees. In both houses, Assembly and Senate, after introduction, the bill is referred to the Rules Committee. This committee assigns the bill to a committee. Health bills will be considered in Health Committee, but may be considered in other committees as well because of split jurisdiction of the subject or need for fiscal review. A bill must pass both houses. If the Senate and Assembly pass different versions, a compromise must be worked out by a conference committee and approved by each house before it can be sent to the governor. The governor must sign or veto the bill within 10 days. Also, budget bills are enacted by the legislature after the governor presents a proposal two months before the end of the fiscal year. In New York State, specific items added to the budget by the legislature are subject to the governor's approval. The budget process is key to state public health agencies because of the resources appropriated, and also because the accompanying language is statute and can commit the agency to new or varied courses of action.

In New York and other states, county or municipal legislatures can also enact legislation of importance to public health. This is particularly important in areas such as the prohibition of indoor smoking often leading state legislative action in this area. Local legislatures can enact ordinances important to environmental inspections, animal control, public safety (e.g., mandating the use of helmets for skateboarding) and in various other areas. In general these local laws can not contradict or preempt state legislation. In some cases, state legislation can be enacted precluding local legislation from superseding state-legislated specific provisions.

## The Role of Advocates

Advocates are important at the federal, state, and local level. News articles refer to various interest groups either helping or defeating specific legislative issues. Armies of well-heeled paid lobbyists are often pictured in the halls outside important committee meetings. This is a major factor in the federal and state legislative process. However, advocacy goes on every day in the form of letters and conversations with federal and state officials and their staff by ordinary citizens.

Officials can only know from the people they serve what the concerns of their communities are going to be, and this information helps officials determine priorities. Providing information to officials can not be underestimated in helping both the official and the staff who advise them in understanding the needs of localities. Whether the information is describing a problem, or simply letting them know of a program's success, providing an idea of how to improve the administration of a program, the value of information directly from those using or administering programs can not be underestimated.

It is important to understand the funding process at the federal level—and what latitude states can have through block grants and waivers to redirect health priorities into what is needed in state and local communities. If a federal health program can make a significant impact on a state or local community, it is important to know when to contact a federal official for help. For members of Congress, it is the funding issues that drive the process. Knowing that funding is needed for a project in June for the next fiscal year instead of in early March makes the official's job harder if it is determined that this should be a priority.

Testifying before a congressional committee, city council, or state or county legislature health committee is important to educate and influence policy makers with jurisdiction over public health programs and funding.[35] An oral presentation should be presented briefly with several major points, concise documentation, and key recommendations. This should be accompanied by more detailed written testimony to be left with the committee and the presenter's contact information to provide further information.

Meetings with legislators should follow the same principles of making a specific request in a concise presentation. The value of legislative staff and the importance of meeting with them and developing a relationship on public health issues should not be underestimated. Networking with other advocates and identifying supportive constituents of the legislator is another strategy for success. Finally, speaking at public meetings and keeping media informed are other important approaches that public health officials can take to influence legislation.

•    •    •

Because the federal government can set so many priorities by what it chooses to fund, and at what level it chooses to fund programs, the federal government plays an instrumental role in determining what a state must do concerning health policy. The states, on the other hand, enjoy enormous flexibility in meeting health policy goals, while at the same time acting as the federal government's agent in overseeing many more programs. Public health organizations increasingly find it necessary to become actively involved in health policy development in order to shape federal, state, and local public health priorities. Knowledge of legislative processes and legislative relationships at the federal, state, and local levels is requisite for developing a policy environment that supports population health improvement.

## Chapter Review

1. The federal budget is a comprehensive accounting of the government's spending, revenues, and debts.

2. Within the budget, there are two categories of spending: *mandatory* and *discretionary*. Most public health programs fall into the discretionary category.

3. The budget resolution serves as a blueprint in establishing budget priorities for that year. The spending, revenue, and public debt laws necessary to implement decisions agreed to in the budget resolution are subsequently enacted separately as part of the budget reconciliation process or as part of the appropriations process.

4. The appropriations process is overseen by the House and Senate Appropriations Committees; each has a subcommittee with jurisdiction over public health spending.

5. Except for tax bills, which must begin in the House of Representatives, any bill can originate in either body after it is first introduced by a member. After referral to a committee and hearings, the bill is reported to the full body for consideration. After the same thing happens in the other legislative body, the two emerging versions are brought to a conference, and a final conference report is voted on by the House and Senate.

6. Federal agencies are authorized to issue regulations by their enabling statutes, statutes establishing new programs, and statutes amending and extending the duties and responsibilities of those agencies.

7. The federal government plays an instrumental role in determining what a state must do concerning health policy by setting priorities for funding. The states serve as the agent of the federal government in overseeing federally legislated programs. In addition, states enact their own legislation, which shapes a broad scope of public health activities.

## References

1. Budget and Accounting Act of 1921, 42 Stat. 20.
2. Congressional Budget and Impoundment Control Act of 1974, Pub L No 93-344 (88 Stat. 297).
3. Congressional Budget Office. *The Economic and Budget Outlook: Fiscal Years 2000–2009.* Washington, DC: US Government Printing Office; 1999.
4. Keitih R, Schick A. *Manual on the Federal Budget Process.* Washington, DC: US Library of Congress, Congressional Research Service; 1998. CRS Report 98-720 GOV.
5. Esenwein G, Winters PD. *The Option of Freezing Non-defense Discretionary Spending to Reduce the Budget Deficit.* Washington, DC: US Library of Congress, Congressional Research Service; 2005.
6. Heniff B, Jr. *The Largest Spending Programs in The Federal Budget: FY 2002 Outlays over $10 Billion.* Washington, DC: US Library of Congress, Congressional Research Service; 2003.
7. House Concurrent Resolution 95, as agreed to on April 28, 2005.
8. Balanced Budget Act and Emergency Deficit Control Act of 1985, Pub L 99-177, (codified at 2 USC 901).
9. US Senate Committee on Appropriations. Available at: http://appropriations.senate.gov/subcommittees/subcommittees.htm. Accessed .
10. Streeter S. *Earmarks and Limitations in Appropriations Bills.* Washington, DC: US Library of Congress, Congressional Research Service; 2004.

11. *US House of Representatives Rules and Manual.* House Rule XXII, clause 9. H.R. 105-358, 1998.
12. Senate Rule XXVII, *Senate Manual*, Senate Document 104-1 (1997).
13. Senate Rule XVI, *Senate Manual*, Senate Document 104-1 (1995).
14. House Rule XXI, *House Practice: A Guide to the Rules, Precedents and Procedures of the House of Representatives.* 104th Cong, 1st Sess (1996).
15. *House Practice: A Guide to the Rules, Precedents and Procedures of the House of Representatives.* 104th Cong, 2nd Sess (1996).
16. Administrative Procedure Act, 60 Stat. 237, (codified at 5 USC 701-710).
17. Executive Order 12866, *Federal Register*, 190 (1993).
18. 5 USC 553.
19. Congressional Research Service. *Federal Regulatory Reform: An Overview.* Washington, DC: US Library of Congress, Congressional Research Service; 2000:3. CRS Issue Brief IB 95035.
20. Executive Order 12291, 46 *Federal Register*, 13193 (1981).
21. Congressional Review Act of 1997, 5 USC 801-808.
22. Department of Health and Human Services: HHS agencies. Available at: http://www.hhs.gov/about. Accessed June 27, 2005.
23. Pub L 107-188. Available at: http://www.fda.gov/ocbiogterrorism/nioact.html. Accessed August 24, 2005.
24. American Enterprise Institute for Public Policy Research. *Rethinking Federalism: Block Grants and Federal, State, and Local Responsibilities.* Washington, DC: American Enterprise Institute for Public Policy Research; 1981.
25. Wachino V, Schneider A, Ku L. *Medicaid Budget Proposals Would Shift Costs to States and Be Likely to Cause Reductions in Health Coverage.* Washington, DC: Center on Budget and Policy Priorities; 2005.
26. Alcohol, Drug Abuse, and Mental Health Administration (ADAMHA) Reorganization Act of 1992, Pub L 102-321.
27. Personal Responsibility and Work Opportunity Reconciliation Act of 1996 (PWORA), Pub L 104-193.
28. Herz EJ, Fernandez B, Peterson CL. *State Children's Health Insurance Program (SCHIP): A Brief Overview.* Washington, DC: US Library of Congress, Congressional Research Service; 2005.
29. O'Shaughnessy C, Lyke B. *Long-Term Care: What Directions for Public Policy.* Washington, DC: US Library of Congress, Congressional Research Service; 2005.
30. Mental Health Parity Act of 1996, Pub L 104-204, Title VII.
31. Health Insurance Accountability and Portability Act of 1996, Pub L 104-191.
32. Grad F. *The Public Health Law Manual.* 2nd ed. Washington, DC: American Public Health Association; 1990:1-137.
33. Institute of Medicine. *The Future of Public Health.* Washington, DC: National Academies Press; 1988:1-225.
34. Stock E. *The Citizen Lobbyist.* Albany, NY: The League of Women Voters of New York; 1999.
35. American Public Health Association. *APHA Legislative Advocacy Handbook.* Washington, DC: American Public Health Association; 2005:1-65.

# CHAPTER 7

# FINANCING THE PUBLIC'S HEALTH

Perri S. Leviss

## Chapter Overview

Approximately 3% of the nation's total health expenditures in 2004 were devoted to public health activities.[1] Of the funds spent by public health departments, a considerable amount is spent for personal health services. New participants in providing public health services include community-based providers, hospitals, and managed care organizations. Local health departments (LHDs) are now forced to share limited funding sources, identify nongovernmental funding streams, and develop new alliances. Additionally, public health departments now must expend significant effort to evaluate the costs of providing their services.

Public health departments across the country are responsible for ensuring the health of the public. The discussion of these responsibilities often appears in the form of legislative mandates, regulations, executive orders, and public mission statements. But how does anyone know if public health departments are adequately funded to achieve this daunting mission? Additionally, with the billions of dollars spent on healthcare services each year nationally, what is the right amount of monies allocated to public health?

The financing of public health services is complicated by the unique organization of public health delivery within each state and locality. Some states have active LHDs that receive significant funding for the provision of comprehensive preventive and primary care services; others have no organized local governmental units and the majority of governmental public health funding resides with the state health departments (SHDs). More recently, nongovernmental players in the health system have taken growing responsibility in providing some public health services as a cost-effective way to prevent disease, morbidity, and mortality. This chapter will first explore the history and the current trends for financing public health services and then discuss the critical business tools necessary to deliver public health services effectively in the 21st century.

## Why Look at Public Health Financing?

Understanding the financing of public health services is critical for private and nonprofit health providers as well as public health departments. However, the body of literature on this subject is slim compared to the available sources on healthcare financing. This is consistent with how the majority of Americans view public health services. Many do not understand the difference between public health and healthcare services; some do not know they even have a governmental body that oversees public health activities; and others equate public health with research. In an era of shrinking government services and an aging population, it is increasingly important to evaluate who is delivering public health services and how the services are financed in order to maximize the "bang for the buck" that Americans get for their health dollar. In addition, reviewing how public health services are financed in different parts of the country provides public health departments operating at national, state, and local levels the necessary information to support future funding and organizational decisions. Finally, if governmental public health departments want to continue to participate actively and help steer health policy in collaboration with other parts of the health system, the departments must pay critical attention to the costs of the services that they deliver as well as the funding streams that support these services.

There are a number of states that have taken it upon themselves to address the financing issues in public health in innovative ways without the dedicated leadership of the federal government. Washington state identified financing as an important issue in several public health improvement plans (PHIP) that were published in the 1990s, and the state committed to developing a stable and sufficient system of financing public health at that time. The PHIP's financing committee was then charged to evaluate the financing system and develop policy recommendations. In the Washington state 2000 PHIP, the committee identified three overall problems facing the state's public health system: (1) the lack of established financing principles and the wide variation in the level of public health investment, (2) the complexity of funding formulas and the lack of flexibility in financing today's public health priorities, and (3) the absence of information about outcomes from investment in public health. The financing committee then completed a detailed study of the revenues and expenditures of local and state public health departments and worked with local public health officials to develop a guiding philosophy for financing public health. The issues identified by Washington state are applicable to most other states.[2]

The state legislature in Washington then directed local and state health officials to draft standards for public health (a basic set of public health services that should be available to all) and determine the costs for the services. The process for calculating the costs of providing public health services involved using the standards for public health in Washington state and, for each activity, identifying the cost drivers (e.g., population) and the labor costs needed to provide the service. The final reports determined that the public health programs in the state were underfunded and that the existing public health system in Washington had only about one third of the resources it needed to provide basic public health services. As part of its more recent objectives for the 2003–2005 PHIP, the financing committee proposed to (1) publish a white paper on financing models for public health that would be considered by state policy makers and (2) estimate the costs of achieving public health standards systemwide that would identify areas for increased investment while being cognizant of system accountability, efficiency, and performance. The products of the work completed by Washington state provide important examples of what can be achieved by other states if the methodology of the work is widely disseminated and adequate resources are provided for training.[3]

## Public Health Versus Personal Health Expenditures

Compared to most other industrialized countries, the US government expends the least amount of public funds on health services as a percentage of total expenditures. At the same time, the United States spends a much larger proportion of its gross domestic product on healthcare services than most other industrialized countries. Additionally, unlike other industrialized nations, the United States has historically placed a greater emphasis on hospital services than on primary and preventive care services; other industrialized countries have historically allocated a greater percentage of health dollars to ambulatory care services.

The US government invested significant resources into building the acute care/hospital-based infrastructure in the post-World War II period. In 2004, the US government spent over 30% of its total expenditures on hospital care, compared to less than 3% spent on government public health activities.[1] The history of hospital-based spending in the United States began in the turn of the 20th century as the combination of many factors, including increased urbanization, industrialization, and immigration; new medical discoveries (e.g., anesthesia, vaccines); and the production of new medical equipment (e.g., radiographs), gave rise to large healthcare institutions to treat Americans. With more people involved in health care, and more permanent physical structures to support the delivery of services, hospital-based healthcare workers began organizing themselves and created significant lobbying forces over the years that have directed additional funding to support these acute care institutions as well as the workers themselves.[4]

As this medical enterprise grew throughout the early half of the 1900s, public health was left out of the healthcare formula. At this point, health care and public health split, with health care being relegated substantially to the private sector and public health being directed as largely a governmental responsibility. And equally as important, the health insurance system (both publicly and privately funded) provided incentives for hospital-based care and for diagnostic and therapeutic procedures, rather than for clinical preventive services (e.g., immunizations, screening tests).[5] It was only with the onset of managed care in the 1990s that some of these clinical preventive services became covered services. Finally, research-oriented funding streams encouraged biomedical research instead of population-based and behavioral studies. In her book, *Medicine and Public Health: The Power of Collaboration,* Roz Lasker surmises, "Reflecting public demand for biomedical advances (in the post-World War II period), funding was considerably less generous for population-based public health programs than for medical care; for health departments than for hospitals; for epidemiological and social science investigation than for clinical studies and basic science research; and for the education and training of public health professionals than for those in medicine."[5(p19)] The combination of these factors has led to a public health infrastructure that is underfunded and undervalued; yet public health only services have added 25 of the additional 30 years to our life spans at the same time that direct medical care services only contributed 5 of these additional years.[6] (Refer to Chapter 1 for more detailed discussion.)

## History of Public Health Financial Data Collection

Over the past 40 years, public health expenditures have accounted for between 1% and 3% of the nation's total health spending. In 2004, approximately $56.1 billion was spent on public health; the nation's total health expenditures were $1.88 trillion.[1] On a per capita basis, it is estimated that Americans spend $4000 each year for personal medical care compared to $44 per year for population-based public health services.[7] Routinely measuring how much is spent on public health services is a difficult task. Over the years, there have been a variety of local and national studies on the subject (Exhibit 7-1). However, there is no system to capture these data points comprehensively or longitudinally. The following sections cover a select number of activities that have taken place over the past century in order to measure the revenues and expenditures of public health services.

The Public Health Service (PHS) collected data on cities and programs in the early 1900s.[8] In 1923, the American Public Health Association's (APHA) Committee on Administrative Practice (CAP) collected data from 83 city health departments on expenditures, organization, and public health practice. In 1943, the CAP published the *Health Practices Indices,* charts that included the range of services provided at LHDs as well as budgetary information.[9]

In the late 1940s, states that received federal funding as part of the Hill-Burton Act were required to report the staffing levels for public health departments. The PHS often examined these data in combination with other expenditure information provided by state health agencies.[8]

Beginning in 1960, the Health Care Financing Administration (HCFA) has used a combination of Census Bureau data and other local and state data sources to develop an estimate of public health expenditures in its reporting of national health expenditures.[8]

In the 1970s, the National Public Health Program reporting system (otherwise known as the Association of State and Territorial Health Officials [ASTHO] reporting system) was developed and funded by the PHS to provide longitudinal public health expenditure data by categorical public health programs. Under contract with PHS, the Public Health Foundation developed and administered the system. The most comprehensive and expensive system to date, the ASTHO reporting system was intended to provide accountability for its members' spending of federal grants and contracts and other public funds. Although the system captured data on numerous federal funding streams, the main impetus for developing the system was to track spending for the public health services block grant, which at the time was administered by the Department of Health, Education, and Welfare (HEW) under Section 314(d) of the Public Health Service Act. Additionally the system was used as a resource

**Exhibit 7-1    Timeline for Public Health Financing Data Collecton Activities**

---

1923    The American Public Health Association (APHA) Committee on Administrative Practice (CAP) collects expenditure data from 83 city and local health departments.

1943    The APHA CAP publishes *Health Practice Indices* that include budgetary information.

1960    The Health Care Financing Administration begins estimating public health expenditures based on census data and other local/state data sources.

1970    The National Public Health program Reporting System is developed to collect longitudinal public health expenditure data.

1990    The National Association of City and County Health Officials (NACCHO) publishes estimates of national public health expenditures as part of the first *National Profile of Local Health Departments*.

1991    The Centers for Disease Control and Prevention (CDC) begins a study to estimate expenditures on health promotion and disease prevention activities.

1992    The Public Health Foundation issues an inventory of the block grant expenditures for state health departments.

1993    The CDC and NACCHO conduct a second survey of local health spending.

1994    The Public Health Foundation begins a series of studies to track expenditure data for state and local health departments.

1995    A second study by the Public Health Foundation, in collaboration with the Public Health Service, focuses on state health expenditures.

1996    Urban Institute's *Assessing the New Federalism Project* evaluates the public health system and its financing in 13 states.

1997    The Public Health Foundation, in collaboration with the NACCHO and the National Association of Local Boards of Health, evaluates local health spending.

---

for the federal government, state and local departments of public health, Congress, state legislators, schools of public health, researchers, and the press. The data system included information on state and local health department expenditures by revenue streams and by major program category. The system included a uniform classification system that allowed similar programs to be compared across states. The system also inventoried state spending on a standard list of federal funding sources, which allowed one to compare contributions by the federal government to contributions by state and local governments. In 1992, the reporting system was changed considerably to provide more impact-related data focusing on nine broad public health problems. Data for the new system was collected for FY 1991 to FY 1993, but the outputs were never published as PHS defunded the project in 1995 due to concerns about the comparability of data and difficulty in quality control.[10]

In 1990, the National Association of County and City Health Officials (NACCHO) published the *National Profile of Local Health Departments,* which provided limited financial as well as programmatic data on local public health for the year 1989. This study was undertaken in part to support the *Assessment Protocol for Excellence in Public Health (APEXPH)* project. This study was later revised to include more financial data and other modifications and reissued once again in 1995 under the title *1992–1993 National Profile of Local Health Departments.*[9]

In 1991, the Centers for Disease Control and Prevention (CDC) began a study, National Expenditures for Health Promotion and Disease Prevention Activities in the US, to estimate health promotion and disease prevention activities nationally. The results demonstrated that in 1988, there was approximately $32.8 billion devoted to these activities, which represented 3.5% of the total national health expenditures. However, the CDC recognized that the study lacked clear definition of public health expenditures.[8]

In 1991, the Public Health Foundation (PHF) issued *Public Health Agencies 1991: An Inventory of Programs and Block Grant Expenditures,* which compiled financial and programmatic data on state health department expenditures and funding sources. The data compiled from the study indicated that more than $118 billion was spent in 1989 for public health by both state health agencies and LHDs ($77.5 billion in direct state dollars, $17.5 billion in pass-through grants to LHDs, and $23.0 billion in additional LHD expenditures). The study reported that in FY 1989, state funds accounted for 53.7% of state health agency expenditures, federal grants/contracts 36.5%, local funds 1.9%, fees and reimbursements 5.1%, and other sources 2.8%. SHDs spent approximately 75% of their funds on personal health services, with smaller amounts for environmental health, health resources, and other public health functions. Nineteen percent of the state health organizations' expenditures were directed at LHDs. Personal health services are those programs that involve the direct clinical care of a patient (e.g., adult primary care, child health clinics, TB/STD/HIV clinics) as opposed to population-based services that are aimed for a population (e.g., restaurant inspections or an antismoking campaign). Additionally, the study reported that 28.1% of the LHDs' expenditures came from state funds, 33.6% from local funds, 15.5% from federal grants and contracts, 12.9% from third-party reimbursements, 2.3% other, and 7.6% unknown. More than 50% of LHD expenditures were for personal health services. Finally, the study evaluated the health organizations' spending for two of the largest federal block grant programs and found that the majority of the $434 million in Maternal and Child Health Services (MCH) block grant dollars and $84 million in prevention block grant dollars were spent on personal health services (95.4% for MCH and 63.7% in prevention).[11]

In 1992–1993, the CDC, along with the NACCHO, collected data through a national mail survey on the spending characteristics of LHDs. The *1992–1993 National Profile of Local Health Departments* study found that the average annual per capita spending for LHDs was $32. Additionally, the data showed that there was a wide range of spending among LHDs, and that the size of the population was the greatest predictor of the amount spent on local health services. According to the NACCHO survey, in 1992–1993, 13% of LHDs reported that they spent less than $100,000, 53% reported expenditures greater than $500,000, and 34% reported expenditures greater than $1,000,000. Other factors that explained variability in expenditures included the number of staff, the number and types of programs provided, and the available funding sources. Additionally, the study captured data similar to that of the PHF's earlier study, but in this case, the data indicated that LHDs rely more heavily on state funds and less on federal sources. The study also found that as population size increases, the percentage of an LHD's funding from state and local sources increases and the percentage from Medicaid and Medicare decreases.[9]

Beginning in 1994, a series of studies were funded by the PHS (performed in coordination with the PHF and other bodies) to establish and track a comparable set of expenditure data for public health services. These studies involved the collection of expenditure data on the federal, state, and local levels from 1993 to 1998. The first of these studies involved a sample of health departments in Connecticut, Iowa, Missouri, Oregon, and Rhode Island, and later Illinois, Texas, and New York. The study resulted in a set of guidelines describing and distinguishing core public health activities and detailing the expenditures of government agencies (public health agencies, mental health agencies, environmental health agencies, and substance abuse agencies) on public health services. Results from the study indicated that the eight states reported spending $2.8 billion or $44 per capita (ranging from $31 to $57) on core public health services (not including personal health services). This figure was significantly higher than that from the earlier NACCHO study, which reported an average of $32 per capita. Additionally, the study concluded that core public health services accounted for only 27% of the total expenditures by these government agencies.[8]

In 1995, a second study was undertaken by the PHS in collaboration with the Public Health Foundation and a group of other federal agencies and national associations to improve on the original study methodology. This study included six of the original states that had participated in Phase I (Illinois, Iowa, New York, Oregon, Rhode Island, and Texas) with the addition of Arizona, Louisiana, and Washington. Additionally, the study included data from local governmental agencies as well as their state counterparts. Results from this study indicated that $8.8 billion was spent in 1995 on essential or core public health services, but of this, $6.1 billion (or 69%) was spent for the provision of personal health or primary care. On a per capita basis, the study concluded that $137 (ranging from $51 to $219) was spent on average for health services (now including population-based health at $42 per capita and personal health services at $95 per capita). The study identified that a number of public health services were being delivered by organizations other than the public health departments. The study also demonstrated that state sources accounted for 50% of expenditures for population-based health services, local sources (tax levy appropriations and fines/fees) accounted for 16%, federal funds for 32%, and Medicaid and other funds accounted for 2% in the nine participating states.[8]

In 1996, as part of the Urban Institute's *Assessing the New Federalism Project,* the public health system was evaluated in 13 selected states. This study demonstrated the wide range of state public health funding that is controlled and administered on the local level. Of all the study states, Wisconsin had the greatest percentage (79.1% in 1994) of state and local public health dollars that were locally administered; Massachusetts had just 7.4% of the dollars administered locally. Additionally, the study found that the sources of funds for LHDs varied tremendously. In Massachusetts and New Jersey, more than 85% of the LHDs' funding came from local revenue sources, with the remainder being spread between states, federal, Medicaid, Medicare, and other sources. Contrasting data were gathered from Alabama and Florida, where the largest percentage of revenues came either from the state (in Florida's case) or from Medicaid and Medicare (in the case of Alabama). The study observed that the ways in which LHDs secure and spend their dollars was related to their individual organizational structures or that in some cases the financing structures had supported the development of specific organizational structures. Through evaluating the intersection between how LHDs obtain their revenue and how they expend dollars, the Urban Institute scholars developed four categories of states:

1. States where LHDs receive the majority of revenues locally, but the majority of spending statewide is controlled at the state level
2. States where LHDs receive a large percentage of revenues locally and spending is also locally controlled
3. States where the largest percentage of revenues come from nonlocal sources and spending is controlled by the state
4. States with low levels of revenue from local sources, but a relatively high degree of spending is controlled locally[12]

The third study by the PHS was jointly conducted by the NACCHO, the National Association of Local Boards of Health (NALBOH), and the PHF in 1997–1998 and involved three case studies of Onondaga County, New York; Northeast Tri-County, Washington; and Columbus, Ohio, in order to test the ability of LHDs to use a standard data tool for collecting public health expenditure information and to compare the expenditure patterns of the three localities. The study results showed that, on average, approximately 21.4% of the LHDs' expenditures were for personal health services, 67% were for population-based services, and 11.6% were for administration and other services. However, the range among the three participating counties was very wide.[13]

The final and most recent public health expenditure study conducted by the Public Health Foundation was released in March 2000. The report, titled *Statewide Public Health Expenditures: A Pilot Study in Maryland*, was the first statewide study of public health expenditures.[14]

In April 2003, the Millbank Memorial Fund, the National Association of State Budget Officers, and the Reforming States Group announced a large expansion to the *State Health Expenditure Report* to consistently measure expenditures for population or public health services. The *2000–2001 State Health Expenditure Report* began to capture national spending on population-based health services by splitting public health into two categories: direct public healthcare expenditures and population health expenditures. The *direct public health care expenditures* include monies spent on TB treatment, HIV/AIDS treatment, Phenylketonuria (PKU) testing, cancer treatment, chronic disease treatment, medically handicapped children's programs, WIC programs, pregnancy outreach and counseling, emergency health services, and others. The *population health expenditures* includes monies for prevention of epidemics and the spread of disease, protection against environmental hazards, injury prevention, promotion of chronic disease control and encouragement of healthy behavior, disaster preparation, disaster response, and health infrastructure. In the report, the authors acknowledge increased attention and new funding beginning in 2002 for public health resulting from the tragic events of September 11, 2001. Therefore, while this issue of the report does not capture the increased funding in this area, the authors have created a baseline methodology to measure population-based expenditures nationally. The population health expenditures category includes state spending for environmental health, surveillance, promotion of healthy behavior, as well as the public health components of disaster preparation and disaster response. In June 2005, the latest addition of the report was released, which includes expenditure data from 2002 and 2003. Trends in population health spending can be measured for FY 2000–FY 2003.[15,16]

In 2005, the United Health Foundation issued its report *America's Health: State Health Rankings–2004 Edition*. This report included new indicators on the percent of health dollars for public health and per capita public health spending. The percent of health dollars for public health measures the percentage of total health expenditures in a state that are targeted for public or population health programs. The 2004 ranks are based on 2001 data (prior to any bioterrorism funding) and ranges from a high of 34.5% of the state health budget (Alaska) spent on public health to a low of less than 2% (Georgia, New Jersey, North Carolina, Connecticut, Idaho, and Louisiana) being spent on public health. On average, the percentage of health dollars spent for public health has risen over the last few years to a high of 6.1% in 2004, from 5.5% in 2002.[17]

In June 2005, the National Association of County and City Health Officials (with the Public Health Foundation under contract) began the 2005 National Profile of Local Public Health Agencies Study. The profile questionnaire was distributed to every local health department in the country (except the state of Rhode Island) and gathered information on public health infrastructure and finances (see Chapter 3 for details).

In the last several years, there have been a number of states that have tried to measure the public health expenditure and revenue trends as well as the costs of providing public health services. In some cases, this exercise was precipitated by a potential reduction in public health funding or a state legislative mandate was the catalyst. In all cases, the benefits to conducting the fiscal analysis have been great, but at a tremendous cost in terms of human resources. The few states that have dedicated energy to this endeavor include California, Georgia, New York, Massachusetts, Missouri, New Jersey, and Washington, but in each case the process was homegrown and tailored to that jurisdiction. Additionally, the federal government has done little to generalize the methodology employed and promote the process among other jurisdictions.

- During the 1990s, the Georgia Division of Public Health worked with a private medical practice firm to conduct a cost accounting analysis of public health services in order to negotiate Medicaid reimbursement rates for public health services. Using and adapting standard Current Procedural Terminologies (CPT) codes for the medical care field and adopting relative value units (RVUs) with the associated procedures, Georgia was able to measure and weigh the relative intensity of public health services by type of service. The analysis provided public health officials with information about the costs of services, the productivity of the services provided, and the cost-benefits of the services. The process of conducting the study required state and local public health officials to adopt a standard set of defined public health services.[18]

- The State of Missouri has been collecting information on financial conditions and trends from local health agencies since the early 1990s. The State Department of Health and Senior Services publishes aggregate and county specific data on local health department revenues, revenue sources, financial solvency, and expenditures. The data are easily accessible through the state's Web site and can be used for policy and research endeavors (see www.dhhs.mo.gov).

- In 1995–1996 the California Center for Health Improvement conducted a study of public health expenditures at the state level. The study included funds from the state public health agency as well as the Air Resources Board, the Integrated Waste Management Board, the Department of Education, and the California Youth Authority. The study found that county spending on public health was difficult to break out from state spending and that prevention-related services and clinical services were categorized inconsistently from one jurisdiction to another, which affected the validity of the data collected in these programs.[19]

- In 2000, the Forums Institute of Public Policy developed a background briefing document titled *New Jersey Public Health Financing in a Changing Environment: Implications for Policy Makers.* Included in the report was a series of cited analyses of New Jersey local health department expenditures and revenues for 1994, 1997, and 1998. The authors found that during this period, public health expenditures were relatively evenly distributed among five major categories of public health (administrative services, environmental health, communicable disease, maternal and child health, and adult health). During the three years reported, a consistent trend appeared that over 70% of revenues were supported through local taxes.[20]

- During the last months on calendar year 2002 and into calendar year 2003, New York State used a methodology similar to that employed by the Public Health Foundation to capture expenditures and revenues in all of its 58 local health departments over a 3-year period. The data output from the analysis was used to successfully lobby the New York State governor's office to restore public health funding. The fiscal survey collected data on expenditures (total and by program), revenues (total and by revenue source), and staffing patterns. Actual ratios that were collected included: total expenditures (mean and median), per capita expenditures, per capita expenditures by public health program, percentage change in total and per capita expenditures, program-specific public health spending as a percentage of total expenditures, total aid received by LHDs, mean and median state aid revenue contribution, state aid as a percentage of total revenues, local tax levy as a percentage of total revenue, per capita state aid funding, and mean and median per capita state aid funding.[21]

- In 2004, the Massachusetts Health Policy Forum issued a report titled *Funding Cuts to Public Health in Massachusetts: Losses over Gains* in response to statewide public health funding reductions. In the report, the authors go one step further by tracking the changes in state funding for public health programs/services from FY 2001 to FY 2004 and then identifying the changes in health indicators that have resulted from the funding changes. The study's authors reviewed several key public health areas, including children's health; family planning and teen pregnancy prevention; infant mortality and low birth weight; chronic disease prevention and treatment; environmental health; community health centers; public health infrastructure; tobacco control; HIV/AIDS, STDs, and hepatitis C; substance abuse, and domestic violence and sexual assault, and used them as examples of the devastating results that come from budget reductions.[22]

Although the studies listed above are numerous, most have not been published in scholarly journals, and there has been few if any attempts to organize the financial data and evaluate the processes for collecting data locally and nationally. However, the data gathered and the methodologies used through the studies provide a benchmark and a lens through which to evaluate the allocation of public health dollars among the different range of health services. In summary, the national trends appear to be the following:

- Public health services continue to represent a small percentage of the total amount spent on health care.
- Of the funding spent on public health services, a considerable amount is expended for personal health services.
- There is a significant variation in the amount spent as well as the financing sources for local public health services.
- There is a wide range of organizations that deliver public health services (both population-based and personal health services).

All the data collection activities thus far reemphasize the need for a routine and consistent methodology of capturing public health expenditure data and an evaluation of how differences in public health expenditures may impact health outcomes. The need for this type of system was recognized nationally with the development of the *Healthy People 2010* goals that included Goal 23-16: Increase the proportion of federal, tribal, state, and local public health agencies that gather accurate data on public health expenditures, categorized by essential public health service.[23]

## Benefits and Challenges in Collecting Public Health Finance Data

There is a wide variety of direct and indirect benefits to collecting national public health finance data and to maintaining an electronic data base of the data. Additionally, there are a number of diverse constituency groups which may want access to the data. Public health departments need the data for their day-to-day organizational management and to support funding decisions. Lawmakers need reliable public health financing data to make informed decisions when allocating funds for new or existing programs.[22(pi)] Although public health's foundation lies in the collection and analysis of data, there is a notable absence of financial data sets. In a recent review of the Web site for Partners in Information Access for the Public Health Workforce, there are hundreds of national, state, and local data sets listed, but the only financial data sets relate to medical expenditures, not population-based services.

Many challenges exist in the collection of national public health fi-nance data, including the lack of uniformity in public health programs and services, the absence of common financial reporting standards for public health departments, and a lack of basic financial expertise across local and state health departments. Additionally, because most local health depart-ments follow accounting standards of the individual locality, how dollars are counted and what accounting rules are followed differ by jurisdiction. One significant impediment in collecting public health finance data is the lack of uniformity in the way in which public health is organized and de-livered. Some states have a centralized structure for the delivery of public health services, others have a decentralized structure involving the counties or localities, and some have a system that may involve a combination of both. However, based on the outcomes of the few states that have conducted statewide fiscal surveys of public health, the upfront resource requirements in survey design and administration would diminish over time as the survey process is institutionalized. The process of conducting fiscal surveys would force state and local health departments to devise one common list of pub-lic health services.

The following are several basic rules to follow when collecting public health finance data:

1. Have a pilot jurisdiction (state, county, or town) test the financial sur-vey instrument before it is more widely distributed.
2. Identify the appropriate staff person(s) to collect the financial data. Provide training to those collecting the data at the local levels.
3. Choose a base year when there were no large-scale program or policy changes that could skew the data. Collect data for multiple years so that trends can be identified and evaluated.
4. Use common data sources. If collecting fiscal data from multiple juris-dictions, mandate the data source that all participants should use. This could be an adopted budget, a state mandated report, or some other source.
5. Look for ways to categorize different organizations of public health: by size of jurisdiction, by type of community (rural, suburban, urban), by region of the country, or by scope of services (full service versus partial service). Create analysis plans for each subgroup.
6. Produce common data tables that the public can learn to consistently expect year after year. Reach out to constituency groups, including local political leaders, to get input into what data they would like to review. Some suggested data tables are total expenditures, per capita expenditures, program-specific expenditures (e.g., expenditures for HIV treatment), total revenue by source, and per capita revenue by source.
7. Develop a practically oriented resource guide to identify the best prac-tices for collecting and managing public health financial data.

In September 2003, the Management Committee of ASTHO identified several issues that should be evaluated prior to any development of a new expenditure reporting system. Most importantly, the committee recom-mended deciding what the expenditure data would be used for (e.g., advo-cacy, general information) and what the most important priorities would be for the data collection effort (e.g., accurate data for each state, a national estimate, trend data). Additionally, one must decide what level of expenditure data should be collected, by program, by category of services, and so on. Finally, the ASTHO committee concluded that the surveyors should predetermine what types of public health organizations should be included in the survey. There are many different types of organizations that deliver public health services, including government organizations (departments of health, human services, environmental health, and mental health), nonprofit entities, hospitals, and community primary care organizations. Which agencies are included in the survey will determine what level of data is captured. Answers to these questions will help determine what the expenditure reporting system will look like. Additional questions that would help shape the next reporting system include issues of data input and access, meaning how the data would be collected and who would have what level of access to the data.

## Organization of Public Health Financing

The way public health is financed follows the structure of public health delivery. The federal agencies that distribute public health funding and provide oversight of the funding are fragmented and at times uncoordinated. State and local public health departments receive federal public health dollars from a combination of agencies under the Department of Housing and Urban Development, the Department of Agriculture, the Environmental Protection Agency, the Department of Education, and the US Department of Health and Human Services (HHS), including:

- Food and Drug Administration
- Indian Health Service
- Agency for Healthcare Research and Quality
- Office of the Assistant Secretary for Health
- Public Health Service
- Centers for Disease Control and Prevention
- Health Resources and Services Administration
- Substance Abuse and Mental Health Services Administration
- Centers for Medicare and Medicaid Services
- National Institutes of Health

In addition, the organization of public health at the state level differs across the country. Usually, there is one central government body that oversees public health services in each state; however, in some cases, the agency may have more or less expansive programmatic responsibilities. In recent years, the power of public health at the state level has been diluted as many state public health agencies have either merged with human services/social service agencies or mental health agencies. Other public health functions have been fractionalized as the responsibilities were split up among many different state organizations. A 2001 survey of states modeled after a similar 1990 survey conducted by the CDC found that 25 (55.6% of reporting) states that responded to the questionnaire had free-standing or independent public health agencies, and in 20 states, the public health agencies were located within a superagency along with other health care and social service entities. Additionally, this study found that states employ a variety of governance models with their local health departments. Of the states reporting, 11 (24.4%) noted that the state health department guided efforts at the local level (centralized control), 10 (22.2%) states relied completely on their local communities for control (decentralized control), and 24 (53.3%) reported a type of mixed or shared control. Even with all these different organizations participating in public health, the last part of the 1900s brought important new participants to public health. In addition to governmental organizations, community-based providers, hospitals, and managed care organizations began to participate actively in providing and overseeing public health services. With the addition of these new participants, LHDs were forced to share limited funding sources, identify nongovernmental funding streams, and develop new strategic alliances in order to ensure the public's health.[24]

There are a variety of factors that have affected how public health funding is organized locally and nationally. Public health has never "made it" to the public agenda. Although some categorical public health issues have received local and national attention (e.g., cholera, tuberculosis [TB], human immunodeficiency virus [HIV]/acquired immune deficiency syndrome [AIDS], *E. coli*) because of large outbreaks of disease or public health emergencies, public health is not a high-priority public policy issue for Americans. Even with the rash of public health-related events over the first few years of this century, including smallpox, anthrax, Severe Acute Respiratory Syndrome (SARS), West Nile virus, and even today's threat of pandemic flu, the press and the general public do not routinely speak of public health. Many circumstances contribute to the lack of public attention surrounding public health, including the large number of diverse programs and services included under the auspices of public health and the absence of advocacy and lobbying groups who work on public health (most public health advocates are organized around a specific population or disease). As opposed to other social issues, such as welfare, foster care, and education, there has been little comprehensive or national planning to address the public health system, and therefore little financing associated with building the public health infrastructure. Federal and state funding has continued to follow specific programs and services, and state and local public health agencies have continued to operate in reactive as opposed to proactive modalities.

An added intricacy in the organization of US public health finance is the large differentials that exist among the more than 3000 local health departments in terms of both funds and scope of services. There is also a new category of city health departments; these are local health departments of the largest metropolitan areas. Although these large health departments—coined metropolitan health departments (MHDs)—are not states, their financing structure is usually different than most of the small local or county health departments around the country. The CDC and other federal agencies have begun to recognize the differences in financing the larger health departments and in several cases have provided direct grant funding to the three largest MHDs (New York, Chicago, and Los Angeles) in selected grant programs including the bioterrorism program, Healthy Start, and Ryan White. Additionally, many national philanthropies fund projects at MHDs. The alternative funding streams available to MHDs has meant that these health departments have had an added opportunity to develop innovative programs; however, in many cases, the funding has been categorical and limited to only a few years, which has created instability in some of these MHDs. Finally, many of the MHDs are large providers of home health care, emergency medical services, and direct primary care services to the indigent and incarcerated populations. These services have separate funding streams outside of core prevention and population-based health, and MHDs face new challenges as to how to access these complicated revenue streams at the same time that they retain core funding for population-based services. When considering a national financing strategy for public health, one must look at MHDs as a separate functional group that must be considered in the model of protecting our public's health.[25]

## Federal Funding Streams and Expenditures

The movement toward organized public health services began at the end of the 1800s and continued at a fast pace throughout the 1950s and 1960s. In this period, state and federal funding streams were developed to support local health services. During the early part of the century, federal funding was only made available on a special case-specific basis in order to conduct research and demonstrations in sanitation fields. In these programs, the federal government funded the salaries for these activities directly and did not flow the monies through the state or local governments. In 1918, the first federal "grant" program was created through the PHS for venereal disease control services, but the funding stream quickly dissipated a few years later. However, it was the 1935 passage of Titles V and VI of the Social Security Act that provided institutional funding for public health activities. The Social Security Act created "general health grants" that supported state and local public health services; special grants for maternity, child health, and disabled children were approved soon afterward in 1936. A flood of specialized and categorical programs were created through the late 1930s and through the 1940s around issues of venereal disease, emergency maternity and infant care, TB, cancer, heart disease control, mental health, and industrial waste studies. Grants for capital construction of health facilities were also created during this boom (post–World War II) period.[26]

After the initiation of federal public health financing, there was significant variability in the amount and comparable percentage that states received for public health services. In a 1955 article published in the *American Journal of Public Health,* Jay Haldeman wrote, "There is considerable variation among the states in the proportion which federal grant funds constitute state and local expenditures for public health purposes. Although variation in state wealth has narrowed since health grants were first instituted, the state having the highest per capita income is still more than twice as well off financially as the state with the lowest per capita income."[8(p967)] In 1953, federal contributions ranged from 9% of the state's total public health expenditures in California and New York compared to 54% in Arkansas and 55% in Wyoming. In the median state, federal grants consisted of 28% of the total expenditures, with the low-income states still contributing a larger percentage of their own resources to public health services than the wealthier states.[26]

Federal grants totaling more than $63 million reached a relative high during the early 1950s. With the Korean War, grant dollars were diminished for public health services, and the trend toward federal financing of hospital-based acute care services began and continued for many decades. At the same time that federal funding was declining, state and local appropriations for public health services began increasing. From 1946 to 1955, the ratio of state and local health appropriations to federal grants rose from 2:1 to 6:1. However, even through this growth period, public health advocates maintained that public health services were underfunded and that the federal government had an obligation to support the assurance of the public's health.[26(pp968-970)]

From the 1950s through today, the financing of local public health services has become more and more of a regionally based decision, resulting in part from historical relationships between individual states and localities. The federal government continued to finance categorical public health programs based on the emergence of new diseases or threats (e.g., HIV/AIDS, bird flu), the priorities of Congress, and the needs of individual localities. Although many advocates were and continue to be supportive of state and local government determining the local health needs and programs for its own communities, the lack of a standard structure for local public health and the absence of a mandated set of national public health programs have over the years led to a fragmented public health infrastructure that differs from community to community and state to state.

The majority of discretionary federal funds for states and localities are allocated through a combination of block grants, formula grants, and categorical programs that are overseen by the US Department of Health and Human Services. One of the largest public health programs throughout the 1970s was the public health services block grant. The public health services block grant served as the foundation for many other categorical and block grant programs that followed in the 1980s and 1990s. Block grants are a type of mandatory grant in which the recipients (normally states) have substantial authority over the type of activities to support, with minimal federal administrative restrictions. The basic premise is that states should be free to target resources and design administrative mechanisms to provide services to meet the needs of their citizens.[10]

Formula grants distribute funds to states and localities based on a mathematical formula. Usually formula grants rely on disease incidence/prevalence or population figures as a democratic way for monies to reach those areas that demonstrate the greatest need. One of the most widely known formula grants is Title I and Title II of the Ryan White Care Act. Categorical grants distribute funds based on public health need for a specific disease or program. The CDC provides a large percentage of its funding through categorical grants for diseases such as TB, HIV, STDs, and other chronic diseases. Usually, categorical grants are very restrictive in terms of what activities are allowable under the grant, and the proliferation of categorical grants in the 1980s and early 1990s created a silo effect in which related diseases or programs became fragmented due to differing funding streams.

During the Reagan era new federal dollars for public health services were limited, and existing funding streams were not secure. Many public health programs were either reduced, eliminated, or combined in the form of block grants. It was during this period that the MCH block grants and other block grants were developed, phasing out dozens of categorically based programs. It was not the block granting itself that reduced public health funding; rather, combining the public health programs allowed lawmakers to make future reductions to the block grants without constituents being able to attach a specific public health program to the dollar losses. It is difficult to develop a constituency for a "block grant" as opposed to an advocacy group for a low birth weight prevention program. In 1989, the largest federal grants supporting state and local public health activities were the MCH block grant, Family Planning (Title X), Preventive Health and Health Services block grant, HIV/AIDS (Ryan White), and the Immunization Action grant. In the 1990s and through the Clinton administration, the federal government continued to "block grant" much of the available public health funding.[11] It is concerning that President George W. Bush's budget proposals have repeatedly called for the elimination of the Preventive Health and Health Services block grant, although to date, Congress has restored most of the block grant funding. (For further discussion of block grants, see Chapter 6.)

There have been several efforts to reform the federal grant structure. These efforts for grant reform have stopped and started many times; at this stage, the changes have not provided LHDs with what they need to finance core public health programs. Most recently, the federal government claimed that block granting some programs would reduce the administrative burden of some federal grants and provide greater flexibility to localities. The Bush administration also identified grant reform as a priority in order to increase state flexibility and to direct monies at the state and local levels. The Institute of Medicine and its Committee on Assuring the Health of the Public in the 21st Century has identified the federal financing structure of public health as a priority issue to be addressed, and the committee specifically recommended that the "federal government and states renew efforts to experiment with clustering or consolidation of categorical grants for the purpose of increasing local flexibility to address priority health concerns and enhance the efficient use of limited resources."[27]

States, however, continue to rely heavily on federal grant funding to support their public health departments and services. In many states and cities, federal grants make up a large percentage of their operating budgets. Due to their budgetary prominence, federal grants drive programmatic policies and priorities at the state and local levels. In some states, federal dollars have compensated for diminishing state support in certain public health areas. The Special Supplemental Food Program for Women, Infants, and Children (WIC) Program and other related nutrition programs make up the largest percentage of SHD budgets. Other large federal grants today include the MCH block grant, the Family Planning (Title X) grant, and the Prevention block grant.[12]

At the turn of the century there was much hope that public health departments would receive a windfall of funding from the state tobacco settlements. Originally envisioned as a large funding pot for public health campaigns, public health departments appeared to lose control over the tobacco settlement funds, and the monies were in some cases diverted to cover shortfalls in state budgets. In response to the events of September 11, 2001, and the increased attention on bioterrorism and disaster management, the federal government introduced one of the largest public health funding streams to state and local governments in FY 2002. The bioterrorism federal grant program (administered by the CDC) distributed $1.1 billion to states in 2002 and $1.5 billion in 2003 for health departments to develop the capacity to manage bioterrorism and other related emergencies. This has proved to be a mixed bag for public health as health departments have been forced to spend much of their limited resources on disaster preparedness and long-standing public health problems such as chronic diseases continue to be underfunded. Additionally, just at the time that the bioterrorism funds were distributed, public health departments were faced with other issues such as smallpox and SARS, which drained limited resources. Therefore, it has been a continued game of catch up for public health moving from one epidemic or emergency to another without sufficient funding for core programs.[27]

The consistent use of categorical funding for public health over the last century has in part led to the development of an inadequate public health infrastructure. Most state and local health departments have organized programs and services around funding streams, and there have been few dollars allocated to basic infrastructure needs such as information technology, communications, and so on. In the last several years the Institute of Medicine and several other nationally prominent organizations have called for enhancements in the vulnerable public health infrastructure, but up to this day there have been little or no federal dollars to support the need. Additionally, over the years, there has been a systematic shift in responsibility for public health services from the federal level down to the states and, now, the localities for carrying out critical public health functions.

## Medicare and Medicaid

Over the years, two of the largest federal health programs (Medicaid and Medicare) have provided varying support to state and local health departments. Congress did, however, expand Medicaid coverage to pregnant women and children in the late 1980s, which provided some additional revenue for traditional public health providers.[28] However, most recently, the small amount of revenue that came from these programs has begun to disappear. With the predominance of Medicaid managed care, Medicaid revenue has been declining for many LHDs as patients obtain services with providers who are in a network and local public health agencies discontinue some of the Medicaid-reimbursable clinical services they have historically provided. Additionally, many states have reduced their share of Medicaid financing, therefore limiting this reimbursement stream for local and state health departments.

Medicaid was enacted in 1965 as part of the War on Poverty programs to provide healthcare coverage for the poor. Over the past 30 to 40 years, Medicaid has provided a small but important revenue stream for many LHDs. Encouraged by the passage of the Omnibus Budget Reconciliation Acts of 1986 and 1987, many states expanded traditional Medicaid coverage for pregnant women and infants with incomes that were at or above poverty. With this expansion, maternal health and family planning-related public health activities obtained a new funding source. Since its inception, Medicaid has provided increased access to personal and public health services for these designated populations. Many public health departments that are providers of personal health services (including primary care, MCH services, and home health services) have historically depended on Medicaid revenues to help support other population-based public health programs or to help reduce local tax levy contributions for public health. The introduction of and emphasis on Medicaid as a funding stream for public health services have in some ways contributed to public health's ongoing identity battle about whether or not it is a personal healthcare provider or a population-based care provider. Medicaid dollars have supported many personal health services that public health departments have and continue to provide as safety nets for vulnerable populations. (Refer to Chapter 2 for more detailed discussion.)

The advent of medical managed care presented both an opportunity and a threat for local health departments. Managed care organizations (MCO) were interested in providing primary and some preventive care services to the same patients currently served by the local public health department, which presumably allowed public health departments to focus their energies and resources on more population-based services. Additionally, since both MCOs and LHDs had similar interests, they could structure collaborations to encourage joint planning and patient services. While in the late 1990s and early 2000s, many public health departments developed both formal and informal relationships with managed care departments, many of these relationships have been problematic and have not produced the innovations that many predicted or hoped. Less than a decade after the concepts of public health and managed care were introduced, it appears that in some cases, public health and managed care were competitors rather than collaborators and the Medicaid managed care plans have found difficulty in maintaining profitability.[29]

Medicare has not provided significant funds to public health organizations nationally, in part because many of the personal health services that health departments provide are not geared to the Medicare-eligible population. Additionally, Medicare recipients have many other options for receiving personal health services and do not choose to go to the LHDs or SHDs for care. Historically, many public health departments have operated home health agencies; in some cases, these departments collect Medicare revenue. Recently, many of the public health departments that did own and operate home health agencies have either privatized or contracted out these services, and the small amount of Medicare dollars flowing to public health departments has declined. In some cases, public health departments may have developed other public health programs that Medicare will finance, but these are few and far between. For the most part, those population-based public health services directed at the elderly population (such as an elderly falls prevention program) are not reimbursable by Medicare.

## State Funding Streams and Expenditures

Massachusetts formed the first state health department in 1869 and by the early 1900s, more than 40 states had health departments established to control and prevent infectious diseases. SHDs provide both categorical grant funding and base funding for the provision of public health programs. The amount of funding provided by states to localities, the form of the funding, and the requirements of the financing differ among states. In 1996–1997, the New York State Association of County Health Officials, the New York City Department of Health, the New York State Department of Health, and the New York Academy of Medicine, with the assistance of the Association of State and

Territorial Health Officials, conducted 25 open-ended telephone surveys with representatives from SHDs nationwide. Eligibility criteria for survey participation were aimed at identifying those SHDs that had embarked on a formal process to evaluate the roles of state and local health units in providing and ensuring public health services in the eight years prior to survey administration. In the majority of states contacted ($n = 18$), public health services were provided exclusively or primarily at the county or multicounty level. Four states had a large number of municipal public health units; in three states, the SHD was responsible for the provision of all public health services.[30]

Among the participating states, significant variation existed in the level of state funding and in the method used to distribute state funds to the local health departments. Funding, for the purpose of this study, referred only to discretionary or base funding of local health units and did not include pass-through contracts or state and federal categorical grants. From the surveys, funding patterns were categorized into seven core methodologies that were employed across jurisdictions. The history of how one financing mechanism was chosen over another was in many cases influenced by the history of the relationship between the state and the locality, the makeup of the legislative and executive branches, and the baseline funds that were available for local distribution. Brief descriptions of these different financing methods are included in the following paragraphs: [30]

- *Combination funding: The use of more than one funding mechanism to fund LHDs.* Usually, this involves some per capita funding for basic public health services and specific grants for discrete local activities or staff.
- *Contract funding: The use of a negotiated contract to fund the public health services provided at the local level.* Usually, LHDs submit a funding application annually to the SHD to receive funds available through the local health maintenance fund.
- *Formula funding: The distribution of funds to local health units based on a formula that incorporates variables that correlate with the health status and the financial resources of the population.* The formulas may include different variables, such as per capita income, assessed land value, and disease rates, in an attempt to account for differences in localities' resources and population-level health indicators.
- *Local funding: The almost exclusive use of locally collected funds and grants to support the public health services provided by the local health department.* LHDs in these states are usually funded primarily through local taxes, inspection fees, and categorical and outside grants.
- *Per capita funding: The distribution of state funding to local health units based solely on the population base served by the local health department.* In some states, per capita funding is not available to part-time health departments, but full-time municipal health departments are eligible for a sliding level of per capita funding depending on the size of the health department. The goal of the funding differential where most health departments are currently organized at the municipal level is to encourage the consolidation of municipal health departments while simultaneously increasing the capacity of LHDs.
- *Reimbursement funding: LHDs are reimbursed for a specific set of services based on the expenditures associated with providing the services.*

The types of services that are allowable for reimbursement are usually preestablished by the state, and a complete programmatic and financial documentation of expenditures is required in order to process the reimbursement. The SHD usually requires the LHDs to predefine the set of services and strictly ensures that the localities are performing the said services described in the plan.

- *State funding: The LHDs are extensions of the SHDs and the state is responsible for funding and providing all the public health services at the local level.* This usually occurs in smaller or more rural states, where there are less formally organized governmental units.[30]

The past several years have brought significant revenue shortfalls for states. These shortfalls have had a direct effect on public health as state legislatures and governors have been forced to scale back government health and human services. In a paper issued by ASTHO in September 2003, the Management Committee stated that discussions with states illustrated several common trends: (1) states were being forced to balance large federal grant investments in emergency preparedness with state budget shortfalls, which put pressure on other core public health programs; (2) states were experiencing cutbacks in the Medicaid program; (3) states were struggling to maintain their tobacco settlements funds for public health programs; and (4) states were experiencing a loss of their experienced public health workforce.[31]

### Local Funding Streams and Expenditures

In addition to federal and state funding, most LHDs receive varied amounts of local support to carry out basic public health functions. Local funding usually comes in the form of tax levy contributions from residents and businesses that reside in the community and therefore are the "users" of services. The amount of funds chiefly depends on the local tax base (in essence, the makeup of the locality that is served), its taxing policies, and the level of importance local governments place on public health programs and services.[12] These funds are appropriated by the local legislative and executive branches through a routine and formal process that usually occurs annually, at a minimum. LHDs usually have an opportunity to request additional local tax levy dollars for new programs, mandated services, or other emergencies. Tax levy funds may also be reduced because of budget issues in any given jurisdiction. Many communities rely heavily on local tax revenue and economically disadvantaged communities may have a more difficult time providing a full array of public health services due to the absence of an expansive taxable base. According to the National Association of City and County Health Officials' 2001 *Chartbook of Local Public Health Agencies,* local public health departments get an average of 44% of funding from local government appropriations, 30% from the state, 19% from fee-based revenues, and 3% from direct federal appropriations.[32]

### Permits, Licensing Fees, and Fines

Many of the larger LHDs rely heavily on the fees and fines that they may collect directly from their regulatory activities. Fees and fines result from inspections, permits, and licensing, largely from environmental health activities. Specific programs and activities that typically generate fees and fines include day care, lead poisoning prevention, inspections (food, water, camps, and beaches), and vital records. Usually fees are based on costs established by each jurisdiction individually.

### Patient Services Revenue

Over the past decade, many public health departments have begun to implement sliding fees to support the continued operation of their programs. Sliding fees usually assess a copayment based on a client's reported income as well as family size. In cases where the patient can not pay, the fee slides down to zero to ensure that everyone receives the health services that he or she needs. For public health departments that have not routinely collected fees, the shift in both thinking and process required by the implementation of fee scales has meant significant time and effort in training staff and installing new billing systems. However, if public health departments want to remain cost competitive, they must be able to collect patient revenue effectively while maintaining their strong mission-driven organizations.

### Indigent Care and Charity Care Pools

Some public health departments obtain reimbursement for uncompensated clinical and primary care services through indigent care pools, although the availability of these funds has diminished over the years. The eligibility criteria, structure, and amounts available for and from these pools differ state to state, but some LHDs have been able to access these pools to support their personal health or "safety net" services.[33]

### Private Foundations and Corporations

Public health departments have only recently joined the crowd of organizations seeking new sources of funding (other than governmental sources). Foundations, philanthropies, and corporations provide alternative financing options for local public health services. However, the drawbacks to these funding sources are that they are usually time sensitive and they are dedicated to a specific new program, not for basic public health infrastructure. Additionally, some localities may not look favorably at financing core public health services through nongovernmental means, further limiting the types of programs that would be appropriate for this funding stream. However, private foundations or corporations provide an ideal testing ground for new programs in order to generate a proven track record so that the program can eventually receive local, state, or even federal funding.

## Key Financial Operations in LHDs

LHDs are facing difficult decisions about their programs and services. As health care has become more and more business-like, LHDs are being forced to enhance key financial capacities to operate more efficiently and effectively.

There are several basic areas of content knowledge that public health departments and professionals must have in order to successfully compete in today's healthcare environment.

## Strategic Financial Planning and Budgeting

Public health departments must develop an integrated program planning and financial process to ensure that fiscal issues are incorporated into the organization's planning activities. The staff in the fiscal office should be involved in programmatic development from the initial stages and not as an afterthought. To support this integrated process, LHDs should place their financial staff and office in prominent positions. Budgeting should be a proactive, routine, and comprehensive process that begins at the program level and works its way up centrally. The process for developing and monitoring LHD budgets should be clear and concise, with a few designated review points along the way. Capital budgets should be considered in coordination with the operating budgets. The budgeting process should be completed annually in conjunction with a department's strategic planning activities so as to enable the LHD to define its internal and external priorities and shift dollars to support these activities. Finally, the budget process should account for and monitor all activities of an LHD, including those funded by grant dollars.

The Mississippi State Department of Health (MSDH) uses strategic financial planning processes as part of its budget and resource allocation planning. The county planning model (CPM) is a multidecision model that ranks counties in the state according to established criteria using financial data, demographic data, and mortality data. The scoring system for the CPM consists of 20 weighted variables grouped into four categories. The weighted variables were chosen based on the CDC's health status indicators, the Institute of Medicine's priority areas for national action, as well as other sources. The four major categories of model variables are populations at higher risk of disease and/or death, access to health care, quality of care, and health outcomes. All counties are ranked based on CPM score and then the scores are divided into quartiles (25th, 50th, and 75th), which allows for the grouping of counties in an easy to understand format. Using CPM analysis within the budget process allows public health officials to understand the potential costs of providing a new public health service across counties and calculates the costs associated with improvement in CPM score or relative state rank. It also determines the amount of funding that is required to have a desired public health outcome. Counties within a state can be compared against a statewide mean. Using the CPM model allows the State of Mississippi to align scarce resources with its programmatic public health priorities and proactively determine the effects it desires with limited public health resources.[34]

## The Budget Process

The budget should be developed initially by each of the major program areas within the LHD with the technical assistance of the finance staff. In small LHDs, the budget may be developed more centrally. The program budgets should each be submitted in a uniform format (preferably in an electronic format). Within the program budgets, there should be two distinct types of requested dollars:

those for existing programs and those for new programs. Dollars requested for existing programs should detail the percentage increase or decrease based on last year's funding allocation and explain the change (e.g., there was a sharp increase in the costs of asthma drugs, or fewer patients came to the TB clinic). Dollars requested for new programs should be accompanied by a detailed description of the following items: reason for the request (e.g., new federal mandate or an emergent public health need), requested funding source (tax levy or grant dollars), description of the request, 5-year budget projections (including both revenues and expenses associated with the request), and an impact statement if the funding request is denied. Along with the requests for new funds, programs should be required to submit a list of activities that could be reduced or eliminated if necessary. This information should be submitted to a central committee in the LHD for consolidation and review. The public health director or health commissioner should be intimately involved in the review and approval of the LHD's budget (as well as the LHD's personnel and finance directors). The executive staff of the LHD should communicate the department's final recommendations to key program staff before the budget is submitted to any outside party. In some jurisdictions, the budget should be submitted to the local board of health for approval as well.

Typically, the budget that has been developed by the LHD is then submitted to the budget or finance office of the executive branch. The negotiation between the LHD and the executive branch is usually a back-and-forth processes that may involve the development of supplemental materials to support a budget request, telephone conversations between the parties, and sometimes even face-to-face meetings. During this period, politicking becomes fierce, and LHDs may call on advocates, the research community, or other supporters to lobby their cause. Once the budget or finance office approves the LHD's budget, it is submitted to the jurisdiction's chief executive (e.g., mayor, county executive) for consideration. Usually, the LHD will have an opportunity to present its budget to the chief executive, but this depends on the jurisdiction. Once the chief executive has approved the budget, it is submitted to the legislative branch of government for consideration. Usually, part of the legislative review involves meetings with the LHD to discuss the budget submission. The legislative and executive branches may have different budget priorities, and this is the time when they must reach consensus. It is during these negotiations that the LHD may find items added, deleted, or modified in its budget based on the priorities of the legislative branch.

When the two branches of government reach consensus, a final budget is passed, and the LHD is notified of its final spending authority. The adopted budget is usually published and made available for public review. The LHD can then begin implementing new programs or eliminating activities in accordance with what was included in the budget. Usually during the budget year, there are several scheduled opportunities for external modifications in the budget (meaning that the LHD can obtain new dollars or can lose existing dollars based on the decisions of the legislative and executive branches of government). The frequency of these changes depends on the individual locality. Additionally, the amount of internal flexibility that an LHD has to modify its own budget (shifting dollars among and between LHD programs) during the budget period is also dependent on the jurisdiction. Larger health departments may have a higher ceiling on the amount of dollars they can shift without obtaining approval from the executive branch.

There are many different types of budgeting techniques. The type of budget that an LHD uses most likely depends on the budgeting system in operation for the entire local governmental structure. Some different types of budgets include performance-based budgets, zero-based budgets, line-item budgets, and program budgets. A jurisdiction may also employ a combination of types. Additionally, most LHDs usually have both an operating budget and a capital budget that follows the process that is described above. The *operating* budget funds those items that are required to maintain the daily operations of the LHD, including the staff, materials, and supplies. The operating budget includes both the revenues and the expenses associated with the health department's activities. The *capital* budget finances equipment purchases and facility construction. For equipment to be capitally eligible, it usually has to last for a certain number of years and be worth more than a certain dollar amount. The exact requirements are set by the individual locality.

The cycle for developing the LHD's budget follows the cycle that has been established for the local government. In most counties and cities, the budget cycle is annual, although in some small jurisdictions, it may be longer. The budget cycle follows the jurisdiction's fiscal year so that a new budget is adopted prior to the beginning of the new fiscal year. The dates of fiscal years also differ by jurisdiction, with most following either the calendar year (January 1 to December 31) or another set of dates determined by the local government.

## Expenditure and Revenue Monitoring

In addition to developing the budget, the LHD must routinely monitor its spending and revenues (both tax levy and grant dollars) to ensure that its public health programs stay within their allocated spending limits and that the LHD is collecting anticipated revenues. Developing a central system for systematically monitoring expenses and revenues is critical for any LHD. In many cases, the LHD will use a system that has been centrally designed for all government agencies within its jurisdiction, but in other cases, the complexity in the LHD's funding streams may require that a system be designed specifically for the LHD. Additionally, as with any arm of government, the LHD must monitor its budget to be accountable to the taxpayers. Any monitoring system that is developed must have both central control by the LHD's finance office as well as decentralized access to the system by program staff. Actual spending and revenue collections should be reconciled against the budget on a monthly basis to ensure early detection of problems. As part of the monitoring process, the LHD may have some of its grant programs audited by outside organizations, or the LHD may choose to audit some of its subcontractors. In either case, the LHD should see the audit as an opportunity to get its financial data in order and help plan for future public health programs.

## Revenue Generation

When developing new programs or evaluating old programs, LHDs should evaluate how they can generate revenues associated with the public health service. Many health departments are constrained from generating any profits. In many cases, the health departments are not currently able to recover their costs. Additionally, health departments should look for new customers to purchase existing or new public health services. This may include for-profit corporations, hospitals, community-based organizations, managed care organizations, individuals, and many others.

Historically, many public health departments have not charged for their services based in most part on a belief that cost sharing may have a detrimental effect on the patients continuing to come to public health departments to receive care. However, in today's environment of new safety-net providers, the implementation of Medicaid managed care, and declining public health resources, public health departments should establish fees for a variety of clinical and nonclinical services. LHDs may choose to set fee schedules for a unique range of services based on the services provided, the services chargeable under law, the local political environment, and a variety of other factors.

### Billing, Collections, and Other Financial Systems

Many public health departments have antiquated systems that support the collection and monitoring of financial data. To compete in the new health environment, public health departments must have more advanced information systems and staff to support these systems in order to capture advanced financial as well as billing-related data. The development and maintenance of these systems are complicated by the fact that LHDs often have a number of funding sources, each with different cycles of allocating dollars and different reporting requirements. Additionally, public health departments must change the attitude of their workforce to integrate billing and fiscal monitoring activities into routine workflow processes.

## Public Health Financing Challenges

Public health departments are being forced to reinvent themselves because of a variety of confounding environmental and political factors coming together at one time: increased activities for bioterrorism and disaster planning, fewer dedicated public health dollars for infrastructure, new infectious diseases and the reemergence of old diseases thought long eliminated, and public demand for less government. In the 1990s, public health departments across the country spent an enormous amount of time financially evaluating which services they should continue to provide, which they should expand, which they should minimize, and which they should eliminate. Now these same departments must once again go through a metamorphosis of sorts in order to "brand" their services and compete in today's financially competitive marketplace. This will require public health departments to evaluate themselves on standard financial models and to more universally measure the cost-benefits and the cost-effectiveness of their services and communicate this information to the general public and lawmakers alike.

The challenge for public health as it decides what it wants to look like throughout this century is to develop a financing methodology that consistently and securely supports core activities. Although the financing structure for public health services is fragmented at best; historically, there have been dollars to support specific categorical public health services that have cross-subsidized some of the core population-based services. However, many of these funding streams are disappearing, or the departments are no longer providing the services that received funding. It is the core population-based public health services such as disease surveillance, outbreak investigations, emergency response programs, and environmental health services that need to be financed nationally and locally.

## Stable Funding for Public Health Infrastructure

The Institute of Medicine released the report *The Future of the Public's Health in the 21st Century* in 2003, written by the Committee on Assuring the Health of the Public in the 21st Century. This follow-up to the 1988 report *The Future of Public Health,* identifies the need for a national expenditure reporting system based on the framework of the essential public health services and the recently adopted National Public Health Performance Standards Program. The development of this type of system would provide much of the data required to estimate the financial investment required in order to appropriately fund public health. Specifically the committee recommends that

> HHS be accountable for assessing the state of the nation's governmental public health infrastructure and its capacity for providing essential public health nationally. The assessment should include a thorough evaluation of federal, state, and local funding for the nation's governmental public health infrastructure and should be conducted with state and local officials. The assessment should identify strengths and gaps and serve as the basis for plans to develop a funding and technical assistance plan to assure sustainability. The public availability of these reports will enable state and local public health agencies to use them for continual self-assessment and evaluation.[29(p150)]

Additionally, as part of the report, the committee recommended that Congress mandate the establishment of a National Public Health Council. The National Public Health Council would meet annually to work on a variety of activities including financing strategies for public health. Specifically, the National Public Health Council would

> advise the secretary of HHS on financing and regulations that affect the governmental public health capacity at the state and local levels; and provide a forum for overseeing the development of an incentive-based federal-state-funded system to sustain a governmental public health infrastructure that can assure the availability of essential public health services to every American community and can monitor progress towards this goal.[29(p169)]

## Capturing the Complete Picture—Who Delivers Public Health Services Anyway?

Although many public health services are delivered by the federal government, state governments, and local governments, a significant amount of public health activities are delivered by a multitude of small, community-based and faith-based organizations around the country. In many cases, the types of organizations involved in public health activities is a local decision, and even large philanthropies such as the United Way may have more or less of a hand in public health in a specific community. The addition of these new players in public health has added resources to protect and promote the public's health; however, it has made it even more difficult to track the expenditures and revenues associated with public health. Even within government, public health services are not consistently provided by the department of health. In some jurisdictions, public health and social services are provided by a common agency, and the provision of environmental health services is sometimes provided by the public health department, but also often by the department of environmental protection. Therefore any national reporting system for public health financing must be flexible enough to allow for multiple models of data entry and the inclusion of nongovernmental organizations into the mix.[35]

## Privatization of Public Health Services

In reaction to the climate endorsing a limited role for government, many health departments privatized public health services over the last decade. The privatization of public health services has taken many different forms across the country. Some health departments have contracted out entire personal health programs (e.g., child health, dental health, primary care) to other public or private-sector providers or even networks of providers (e.g., local hospitals, community-based organizations); others have contracted out the clinical parts of personal health programs and maintained a monitoring, oversight, or quality assurance role for the programs; and others have eliminated the programs altogether. As health departments reduce their spending, it is critical that they invest resources (both financial and personnel) in identifying revenue to support those remaining public health services. Additionally, privatization presents an opportunity for LHDs to develop new partnerships for the provision of public health services. Although the LHD may not have the funding to provide the public health service itself, it may play an important role in coordinating the activity or developing the public health policies supporting the activity.

## Financial Skills in the Public Health Workforce

The absence of public health finance as an area of study has led to a public health workforce without sufficient training in financial management. When reviewing the curriculum of most schools of public health, there is a noticeable absence of coursework in finance, accounting, or business principles that is directly applied to public health settings. Instead, schools of public health offer courses in *healthcare* finance (mostly hospital based) and general nonprofit accounting to their public health students. Additionally, there are not any national fiscal competencies for public health workers. Each local and state public health department has a team of fiscal administrators, but the training and experience of these individuals varies widely.

The lack of analysis, research, and academic and workforce training in the field of public health finance has produced a cyclical and dysfunctional relationship where (1) there is no financial system to document the financial contributions of public health activities (including the costs and benefits of providing public health services), and the amount of funds necessary for a well-functioning public health system is not documented systematically;

(2) the public health workforce is not trained and proficient in financial management; and (3) there is little structured academic teaching on public health finance, and there is no standard set of curricula on the topic. In 1993, the CDC and the Health Resources and Services Administration (HRSA) formed a collaborative group to develop competencies for public health graduates. The competencies included seven areas with one being financial planning and management skills, the others were (1) orientation to public health, (2) analytic skills, (3) basic public health sciences, (4) communications/cultural skills, (5) policy development/program planning skills, and (6) computer skills. Under the area of financial planning and management skills the following competencies relate directly to finance:

- Developing and presenting a budget
- Managing programs with budgetary constraints
- Developing strategies for determining budget priorities
- Monitoring program performance
- Preparing proposals for funding from external sources[36]

Since this time there have been several other groups who have worked on competency issues for public health, but none have given a prominent role to financial management. To address this complex issue, the Committee on Assuring the Health of the Public in the 21st Century recommends the "CDC, in collaboration with the Council on Linkages between Academia and Public Health Practice and other public health system partners, develop a research agenda and estimate the funding needed to build the evidence base that will guide policy making for public health practice."[29(p161)]

In November 2003, researchers from Saint Louis University began a study to assess the competencies needed by public health managers in the area of public health finance. By developing a list of 60 competencies acquired by students in programs of health administration, the researchers then were able to send this list to 12 individuals in various public health administrative positions around the state to evaluate which of these competencies are related to public health finance. The study found that the public health administrators believed that the majority of the health administration competencies (geared to more private-sector institutions) were applicable to public health finance and that public health managers require a broad range of competencies.[36]

Given the lack of national guidance, some states have taken it upon themselves to develop innovative training programs that could be easily replicated across the country. The Florida Department of Health (FDOH) is one of several health departments that has recognized the need for a highly skilled public health workforce in the area of financial management and beginning in 1997 has worked with the Florida Association of County Health Department Business Administrators on a variety of training programs for business managers in the state's local health departments. The association developed a business manager mentoring program that links experienced workers in public health finance (who volunteered for the program) with newly hired business managers in county health departments. Matches were made based on the size of the county health department, the type of community (urban/rural location), and overall budget size. In addition, the FDOH and the association hired a field financial trainer who works directly with county health departments and coordinates regional trainings in public health finance.[37]

## Research on Public Health Finance

There is little available research on public health financing issues or dollars available for this type of research. As Dr. Moulton states in a September 2004 article in the *Journal of Public Health Management and Practice,* "Public health finance is an embryonic field that lacks basic concepts, data, measures, and practice guidelines as well as terminological, conceptual, and methodological consensus."[19(p377)] In a 2005 query of the *American Journal of Public Health* database, only 10 articles had the word *Finance* in the title when searching all archived articles from 1982 to 2005. Most of the articles found in the literature search were about the financing of a specific service such as mental health, home care, prenatal care, or vaccination programs.

Some of the few public health activities that have a body of literature focusing on fiscal issues are immunization or vaccination programs. During the 1990s and into the most recent decade there has been increased attention about the costs and benefits associated with vaccination programs and about how limited federal resources should be spent stockpiling drugs or developing intricate distribution programs. This research on immunization financing could be conducted on many similar public health functions to determine what programmatic and policy changes could be enacted nationally and locally.[38]

## Cost Competitiveness

As arms of government, public health departments generally have not spent significant energy evaluating the costs of providing public health services. Many governmental public health departments develop program-based budgets (not budgets based on the unit costs of services) and evaluate the costs only for those services that they charge for. As part of the process of reinventing themselves, health departments must have data on the costs of their services. Although there is no oversight or regulatory body that requires this information, understanding the costs of all public health services has significant value for public health departments as an internal management tool, as a way to negotiate more funding, and as a public relations opportunity. By knowing what an individual unit of service costs an organization to deliver and quantifying these services, public health departments can accomplish the following:

- Compare themselves to similar organizations.
- Compare the cost of one type of public health service to another within the organization.
- Comprehensively evaluate the components (both personal services and other than personal services) of cost to identify areas of efficiency and inefficiency.
- Analyze their internal organization and infrastructure.
- Understand the range and demand for services delivered.
- Lobby local, state, or national organizations for the reimbursement of discrete public health services.
- Demonstrate the value of public health services to the public.

Some states and localities have systems to measure the costs of public health services, but most of these systems are not widespread and are not consistently used among states and localities. Furthermore, there is no federal mandate that requires public health departments to capture this data. Two examples of states using a form of cost analysis are Florida and Georgia. The county health departments in Florida all use a contract management system (CONMAN) that reports monthly financial and service data for each of the major public health programs. County health departments are required to enter into an annual contract with their local county government that details the amount of services to be delivered and the expenses and revenues associated with the services. The CONMAN system is used as a contract monitoring tool, but it has also provided county health departments with data to develop service-specific unit cost analysis and to develop program-based budgets across counties. The data from CONMAN is used by the public and policy makers alike and the state, and the localities all have a mutual interest in evaluating and using the data for planning.[37]

As part of its cost study analysis, Georgia developed a model for collecting the costs of its services (cost per procedure). In addition to providing information for reimbursement discussions with local Medicaid providers, the data and the process of collecting the data has allowed Georgia's public health departments to compare productivity and costs among sites and make management decisions regarding the allocation of resources.[18]

## Information Technology Innovations

Public health departments are the collectors and analyzers of data. Over the past decade or two, organizations have begun to use new technology to support these activities, but in many cases, the systems that were built were ad hoc and not central to the daily operations of public health departments. For public health organizations to participate actively as leaders in promoting and protecting the public's health, they must invest significant dollars in building local, state, and national systems to support information exchange. Many other health organizations are implementing computer-based patient records; installing sophisticated systems for billing, management, and data tracking; using handheld tablets for field work; and developing Internet strategies for routinely accessing and monitoring health data. Public health departments must be active designers and purchasers of technology and be committed to expending the necessary resources to update their operations to current technology standards. Public health should look to related industries such as health care and higher education that have developed model systems for national data collection that could be adopted by public health. The costs up front for technology may pose a challenge for departments because much of the technology will only show returns after several years, but it is a worthwhile investment.

### The Business of Public Health

Public health departments have not thought of themselves as businesses and therefore have not acted accordingly. This has meant that public health departments have not focused energy or resources on understanding their customers, marketing services to their customers, actively collecting revenues for their services/programs, or maintaining a productive and happy workforce—some of the key tenets of any business. But health is one of the largest business sectors in the United States and in the world, and has gained significant prestige and market share over the past century. If public health departments want to survive as an important force in the health arena, they need to be prepared to change attitudes as well as shift resources in order to support some core business-related activities.

Public health departments have the unique challenge of trying to inform the general public about what they routinely do to protect the public's health. Many of the public health services that are provided by government go undetected unless there is an emergency. Most Americans would not know that a public health department's surveillance activities are used to identify encephalitis-carrying mosquitoes or to link reports of disease activity to a common food source like contaminated meat. Public health departments must take this opportunity to identify the erosion of the public health infrastructure as an issue that needs public support and one that requires national financing standards. Only when these issues reach the policy agenda will the development of a secure and comprehensive financing mechanism for public health be realized.

Additionally, public health must produce and then distribute basic financial information and cost-benefit data for the general public and for policy makers. Most industries including health care and public education have a standard set of formulas for the evaluation of their services. The lack of financial data on public health makes the argument for increased funding more difficult because people want to know the "bang for the buck" they are getting in public health and up to this point, no one has been able to consistently provide this information. In the Nov/Dec 2005 issue of the *Journal of Public Health Management and Practice*, an article by Warren Williams, David Lyalin, and Phyllis A. Wingo, argues that business modeling could and should be applied to public health programs in order to formally conduct systematic analysis of the operations and financing of public health services. The article presents examples of how business modeling can be used to improve performance and to generate cost savings. However, using business modeling represents a shift in how public health programs have historically seen themselves, and using business models will require a culture shift for public health practitioners.[39]

Some states such as Washington have been diligently working over the years to change the long-established mindset of policy makers and the general public about the business of public health, but this challenge has not been easy. Some of the recommended steps that Washington state has already taken or plans to take over the coming years provide excellent examples of what can be done in other states to develop stable and sufficient funding for public health. These include the following:

1. Identify a basic set of state and local public health services, estimate the costs to deliver the services, and evaluate how the basic services will be funded.
2. Adopt a consistent cost model, and analyze the cost of public health services routinely
3. Develop financial incentives for efficient state and local public health departments.

4. Establish and distribute funding principles that identify what is paid by the state and what is paid by the localities to help guide programmatic decisions.

5. Identify ways to make revenue sources more flexible, and ensure that revenue is allocated using established funding principles.

6. Create clear and frequent modes of communication among funding agencies, the public, state and local health department staff, and elected officials.[2]

•   •   •

Understanding the financing structure of public health services is an important and difficult task that is complicated by the lack of literature on the subject. Although there are volumes of texts published on healthcare financing, there are no books and few scholarly journal articles that have been dedicated to the financial structure of public health services. The disorganization and the haphazardness of the public health financing structure nationally present significant risks to the future of public health. Without institutionalized and consistent financing systems for public health services, these activities can be eliminated without significant public attention. Additionally, the lack of organized systems for public health financing prevents the collection of comprehensive and national data sets on public health activities. With financial data in hand, public health advocates may be able to develop stronger arguments in support of enhanced public health activities, but the collection of the financial data requires national funding support. As public health continues to compete with healthcare services for funding and public attention, it is essential that public health arm itself with as much information as it can about its programs and services. By financially accounting for its activities, public health practitioners can demonstrate the true bargain that public health really is.

Public health must devote concerted attention to financing and financial management over the next decade as its infrastructure and workforce ages, federal funding for public health is squeezed, and state governments continue to experience budget shortfalls. To comprehensively address fiscal issues in public health, national organizations working with the health officials must develop a national strategy for public health financing that includes:

• *Research*—Build consistent formulas and processes for financial data collection and analyses, and disseminate important findings among national, state, and local public health practitioners.

• *Education and training*—Develop a standard public health finance curriculum taught at schools of public health, and develop basic finance training for those already in the field.

• *Performance standards*—Devise core competencies of financial management that public health departments can use to measure their performance.[19]

## Chapter Review

1. The financing of public health services is complicated by the unique organization of public health delivery within each state and locality.

2. There is no existing system that can comprehensively measure the amount of spending on public health services or evaluate how differences in public health expenditures may impact health outcomes.

3. The financing of local public health services varies and is related to historical relationships between states and their localities.

4. Under President Reagan, many public health programs were combined into block grants followed by reductions in overall funding; they were no longer explicitly tied to an individual and recognizable public health problem.

5. Public health departments must develop an integrated program planning and financial process. The budget process should be completed annually in conjunction with the organization's strategic planning activities to enable the public health department to define priorities and shift its resources accordingly.

6. The public health department must monitor its spending and revenues to ensure that programs are within allocated spending limits and that the organization is collecting anticipated revenues.

7. As states continue to implement Medicaid managed care, public health departments are faced with continuing declines in revenues because of decreasing numbers of Medicaid-eligible visits.

8. Public health financing challenges include identifying a financing mechanism for infrastructure and the core population-based health services.

9. Public health organizations must gather data on the costs of providing services to identify areas of efficiency and inefficiency and demonstrate the value of public health to the public.

# References

1. Centers for Medicare and Medicaid Services. *Table 2: National Health Expenditures Aggregate Amounts and Average Annual Percentage Change, by Type of Expenditure: Select Calendar Years 1960–2004.* Centers for Medicare and Medicaid Services, Office of the Actuary, National Health Statistics Group.

2. Washington State Department of Health. *2000 Public Health Improvement Plan.* Olympia, WA: Washington State Department of Health; 2000:29–30.

3. Washington State Department of Health. *2002 Public Health Improvement Plan: A World of Threats and Opportunities.* Olympia, WA: Washington State Department of Health; 2002:23–26.

4. Anderson GF, Maxwell S. The organization and financing of healthcare services. In: Taylor RJ, Taylor SB, eds. *The AUPHA Manual of Health Services Management.* Gaithersburg, MD: Aspen Publishers; 1994:87–101.

5. Lasker RD. Committee of Medicine and Public Health. *Medicine and Public Health: The Power of Collaboration.* New York, NY: The New York Academy of Medicine; 1997.

6. US Public Health Service. *For a Healthy Nation: Returns on Investment in Public Health, 1993.* Washington, DC: US Public Health Service; 1994.

7. Eibert K, et al. Measuring expenditures for essential public health. *Public Health Foundation.* 1996; November.

8. Eibert K, et al. Public health expenditures: developing estimates for improved policy making. *J Public Health Manage Pract.* 1997;3:1–9.

9. Centers for Disease Control and Prevention, National Association of County and City Health Officials. *1992–1993 National Profile of Local Health Departments.* Washington, DC: Centers for Disease Control and Prevention, National Association of County and City Health Officials; 1995:7–19, 21–23, 31–37.

10. Barry M, Bialek R. Tracking our investments in public health: what have we learned? *J Public Health Manage Pract.* 2004;10(5):383–392.

11. *Public Health Agencies 1991: An Inventory of Programs and Block Grant Expenditures.* Washington, DC: Public Health Foundation; 1991:3–5, 115.

12. Wall S. Transformations in public health systems. *Health Affairs.* 1998; 17(3):64–80.

13. Barry M, Centra L, Brown, C, et al. Where do the dollars go? Measuring local public expenditures. Paper presented at: Office of Disease Prevention and Health Promotion, Office of Public Health and Science, US Department of Health and Human Services; March 1998; Washington, DC.

14. Atchison C, Barry MA, Kanarek N, et al. The quest for an accurate accounting of public health expenditures. *J Public Health Manage Pract.* 2000;6(5):93–112.

15. Milbank Memorial Fund, National Association of State Budget Officers, the Reforming States Group. *2000–2001 State Health Care Expenditure Report.* Milbank Memorial Fund, National Association of State Budget Officers, the Reforming States Group; 2003.

16. Milbank Memorial Fund, National Association of State Budget Officers, Reforming States Group. *2002–2003 State Health Care Expenditure Report.* Milbank Memorial Fund, National Association of State Budget Officers, Reforming States Group; 2005.

17. *America's Health: State Health Rankings—2004 edition.* Minnetonka, MN: United Health Foundation; 2004:23–24, 100.

18. Hadley CL, Feldman L, Toomey KE. Local public health cost study in Georgia. *J Public Health Manage Pract.* 2004;10(5):400–405.

19. Moulton AD, Halverson PK, Honore PA, et al. Public health finance: a conceptual framework. *J Public Health Manage Pract.* 2004;10(5):377–382.

20. Forums Institute for Public Policy. *New Jersey Public Health Financing in a Changing Environment: Implications for Policymakers.* Princeton, NJ: 2000.

21. Leviss P, Novick L. Examining public health financing in New York state: a methodology for evaluating local and national public health data. *J Public Health Manage Pract.* 2004;10(5):393–399.

22. Kurland J and Klein Walker D. *Funding Cuts to Public Health in Massachusetts: Losses over Gains.* Waltham, Mass: Massachusetts Health Policy Forum; 2004.

23. US Department of Health and Human Services. *Healthy People 2010.* 2nd ed. Washington, DC: US Government Printing Office; 2000.

24. Beitsch LM, Brooks RG, Grigg M, et al. Structure and functions of state public health agencies. *Am J Public Health.* 2006;96(1):167–172.

25. Plough A. Understanding the financing and functions of metropolitan health departments: a key to improved public health response. *J Public Health Manage Pract.* 2004;10(5):421–427.

26. Haldeman J. Financing local health services. *Am J Public Health.* 1955; 45(8):967–971.

27. Barrett K, Greene R, and Mariani M. The Government Performance Project: Public Health. Public health: the costs of complacency. *Governing Magazine.* 2004;February.

28. Jones L. State by state approach to public health. *Am Med News.* 1995; 38(8):1–2.

29. Institute of Medicine. *The Future of the Public's Health in the 21st Century.* Washington, DC: National Academies Press; 2003:150–153.
30. New York State Association of County Health Officials, et al. *Public Health Assessment Project Final Report.* Albany, NY: New York State Association of County Health Officials; 1997.
31. Public health finance: an examination of the topic by the management committee of ASTHO. Association of State and Territorial Health Officials, September 2003.
32. Mays GP, McHugh MC, Shim K, et al. Getting what you pay for: public health spending and the performance of essential public health services. *J Public Health Manage Pract.* 2004;10(5):435–443.
33. Brown ER, Dallek G. State approaches to financing health care for the poor. *Ann Rev Public Health.* 1990;11:377–400.
34. Fos PJ, Miller DL, Amy BW, et al. Combining the benefits of decision science and financial analysis in public health management: a county-specific budgeting and planning model. *J Public Health Manage Pract.* 2004;10(5):406–412.
35. Gebbie K. Ways to think about money. *J Public Health Manage Pract.* 2004;10(5):428–430.
36. Gillespie KN, Kurz RS, McBride T, et al. Competencies for public health finance: an initial assessment and recommendations. *J Public Health Manage Pract.* 2004;10(5):458–466.
37. Napier MJ, Street P, Wright R, et al. The Florida Department of Health and the Florida Association of County Health Department Business Administrators: a model of successful collaboration to sustain operational excellence. *J Public Health Manage Pract.* 2004;10(5):413–420.
38. Institute of Medicine. *Calling the Shots: Immunization Finance Policies and Practices.* Washington, DC: National Academies Press; 2000.
39. Williams W, Lyalin D, Wingo PA. Systems thinking: what business modeling can do for public health. *J Public Health Manage Pract.* 2005;11(6):550–553.

## CHAPTER 8

# THE PUBLIC HEALTH WORKFORCE

Margaret A. Potter
Kristine M. Gebbie
Hugh Tilson

## Chapter Overview

The public health system's most essential resource is its workforce. The US public health workforce consists of individuals from a wide variety of professions, technical disciplines, and educational backgrounds. This diversity both challenges and motivates efforts to define and assess the composition of the workforce. By understanding workforce skills, training needs, and practice settings, public health decision makers can design programs and policies that make optimal use of this resource.

This chapter defines and describes the current public health workforce, considers what influences the demand for and the supply of public health workers, reports on current estimates of the workforce size and distribution, and examines strategies for educating and training those who provide essential public health services to the nation's communities. This chapter closes with challenges and opportunities facing this diverse group of professionals in the immediately foreseeable future.

## Who Are Public Health Workers?

A management focus on population-health requires a broadly inclusive definition of the public health workforce. Its composition includes those working in an official voluntary or not-for-profit public health agency as well as in community-based private organizations, health care organizations, and businesses. Hence, an inclusive definition can be stated as:

> The public health workforce is composed of individuals whose major work focus is delivery of one or more of the essential services of public health, whether or not those individuals are on the payroll of an official, voluntary, or not-for-profit public health agency.[1(p4)]

For any practical application, this inclusive and encompassing approach to defining the public health workforce requires some limitation. There are many individuals whose work contributes only incidentally to the population's health. These might include the intensive care nurse who appropriately reinforces the reduction of tobacco use by limiting smoking by a patient's visiting family members or the highway patrol officer who reduces injuries by enforcing speed limits on interstate highways. Although the contributions of these persons to public health is important, it is nevertheless secondary to the main responsibilities of their employment; rarely are public health goals considered in the plans for their day-to-day work.

Various alternative definitions emphasize one or another aspect or characteristic of the public health workforce. A report by the Centers for Disease Control and Prevention (CDC) identified workforce competency as being the first of three foundational components of the nation's public health infrastructure.[2(piii)] An Institute of Medicine (IOM) committee focused on the combination of educational background and work site, defining a public health professional as "a person educated in public health or a related discipline who is employed to improve health through a population focus."[3(p4)] A national blue-ribbon committee excluded work site, or "the nature of the employing agency," from among the factors that define the public health workforce.[1(pv)] A study of local public health agencies counted workers in 27 occupational classifications; it distinguished them by employment status, including direct employees, contract employees, volunteers, and others.[4] The following sections provide further explanation for each of these characteristics.

## Competencies

As a foundation for professional definition, so-called competency sets are used to develop educational curricula and to establish standards for professional certification. Well-established competency sets exist for preventive and occupational medicine, dental public health, health education, law, and many other specialized areas.[5(App.I)] A recent revitalization of the public health field began with an Institute of Medicine report in 1988 that launched a decade-long effort to define professional competencies.[6] The first set of core competencies for public health was published by a national committee called the Faculty Agency Forum[7] and later revised and sustained by the Council on Linkages Between Public Health Practice and Academia.[8] In addition to these practice-oriented competency lists, educational competencies for the master of public health degree have been proposed by the Association of Schools of Public Health.[9] In their report, *Who Will Keep the Public Healthy,* a later Institute of Medicine report addressing education for the field proposed the addition of eight competency domains including informatics, genomics, communication, cultural competence, community-based participatory research, global health, policy and law, and public health ethics.[10]

The Council on Linkages competencies are the most recently published and validated (see Table 8-1). Here, the competencies are grouped by *domain*—or major category of knowledge or skill. This entire set has been analyzed and scored by type or level of worker to whom each competency applies.[8] The competencies describe what professionals in the field as a group should be able to do, rather than the abilities or attributes of separate profes-

**TABLE 8-1    Council on Linkages Competencies by Domain**

## Analytic/Assessment Skills

- Defines a problem
- Determines appropriate uses and limitations of both quantitative and qualitative data
- Selects and defines variables relevant to defined public health problems
- Identifies relevant and appropriate data and information sources
- Evaluates the integrity and comparability of data and identifies gaps in data sources
- Applies ethical principles to the collection, maintenance, use, and dissemination of data and information
- Partners with communities to attach meaning to collected quantitative and qualitative data
- Makes relevant inferences from quantitative and qualitative data
- Obtains and interprets information regarding risks and benefits to the community
- Applies data collection processes, information technology applications, and computer systems storage/retrieval strategies
- Recognizes how the data illuminates ethical, political, scientific, economic, and overall public health issues

## Policy Development/Program Planning Skills

- Collects, summarizes, and interprets information relevant to an issue
- States policy options, and writes clear and concise policy statements
- Identifies, interprets, and implements public health laws, regulations, and policies related to specific programs
- Articulates the health, fiscal, administrative, legal, social, and political implications of each policy option
- States the feasibility and expected outcomes of each policy option
- Utilizes current techniques in decision analysis and health planning
- Decides on the appropriate course of action
- Develops a plan to implement policy, including goals, outcome and process objectives, and implementation steps
- Translates policy into organizational plans, structures, and programs
- Prepares and implements emergency response plans
- Develops mechanisms to monitor and evaluate programs for their effectiveness and quality

## Communication Skills

- Communicates effectively both in writing and orally, or in other ways
- Solicits input from individuals and organizations
- Advocates for public health programs and resources
- Leads and participates in groups to address specific issues
- Uses the media, advanced technologies, and community networks to communicate information
- Effectively presents accurate demographic, statistical, programmatic, and scientific information for professional and lay audiences

### Attitudes

- Listens to others in an unbiased manner, respects points of view of others, and promotes the expression of diverse opinions and perspectives

## Cultural Competency Skills

- Utilizes appropriate methods for interacting sensitively, effectively, and professionally with persons from diverse cultural, socioeconomic, educational, racial, ethnic and professional backgrounds, and persons of all ages and lifestyle preferences
- Identifies the role of cultural, social, and behavioral factors in determining the delivery of public health services
- Develops and adapts approaches to problems that take into account cultural differences

### Attitudes

- Understands the dynamic forces contributing to cultural diversity
- Understands the importance of a diverse public health workforce

*(continues)*

**TABLE 8-1 (continued)**

### Community Dimensions of Practice Skills

- Establishes and maintains linkages with key stakeholders
- Utilizes leadership, team building, negotiation, and conflict resolution skills to build community partnerships
- Collaborates with community partners to promote the health of the population
- Identifies how public and private organizations operate within a community
- Accomplishes effective community engagements
- Identifies community assets and available resources
- Develops, implements, and evaluates a community public health assessment
- Describes the role of government in the delivery of community health services

### Basic Public Health Sciences Skills

- Identifies the individual's and organization's responsibilities within the context of the Essential Public Health Services and core functions
- Defines, assesses, and understands the health status of populations, determinants of health and illness, factors contributing to health promotion and disease prevention, and factors influencing the use of health services
- Understands the historical development, structure, and interaction of public health and health care systems
- Identifies and applies basic research methods used in public health
- Applies the basic public health sciences including behavioral and social sciences, biostatistics, epidemiology, environmental public health, and prevention of chronic and infectious diseases and injuries
- Identifies and retrieves current relevant scientific evidence
- Identifies the limitations of research and the importance of observations and interrelationships

**Attitudes**
- Develops a lifelong commitment to rigorous critical thinking

### Financial Planning and Management Skills

- Develops and presents a budget
- Manages programs within budget constraints
- Applies budget processes
- Develops strategies for determining budget priorities
- Monitors program performance
- Prepares proposals for funding from external sources
- Applies basic human relations skills to the management of organizations, motivation of personnel, and resolution of conflicts
- Manages information systems for collection, retrieval, and use of data for decision making
- Negotiates and develops contracts and other documents for the provision of population-based services
- Conduct cost-effectiveness, cost-benefit, and cost-utility analyses

### Leadership and Systems Thinking Skills

- Creates a culture of ethical standards within organizations and communities
- Helps create key values and shared vision and uses these principles to guide action
- Identifies internal and external issues that may impact delivery of essential public health services (e.g., strategic planning)
- Facilitates collaboration with internal and external groups to ensure participation of key stakeholders
- Promotes team and organizational learning
- Contributes to development, implementation, and monitoring of organizational performance standards
- Uses the legal and political system to effect change
- Applies theory of organizational structures to professional practice

*Source:* Public Health Foundation, 2001. Access to full competencies lists at www.trainingfinder. org/competencies/index/html

sions or occupations. Thus, the usefulness and importance of workforce competencies appears in the following discussions of credentialing and training.

## Educational Background

No single degree or professional credential defines all public health workers or all public health professionals. Rather, the public health workforce includes individuals from almost every discipline and profession associated with health services as well as from numerous professions outside of the health arena. Each of these brings to public health a special combination of knowledge, skills, abilities, and, perhaps most importantly, world view. This diversity is essential to the vitality and success of public health efforts.

The master of public health (MPH) degree is the one most closely associated with expertise in public health practice. It may be earned at any one of the many schools of public health or at a program of community health, health education, or community or preventive medicine—many of which receive national accreditation from the Council on Education for Public Health.[11] Only a small fraction of those in the workforce have attained the MPH degree, in part because the capacity of the nation's schools and programs in public health is insufficient.[12] Only one quarter to one third of the membership of the American Public Health Association is reported to have an MPH degree,[13] and most public health careers begin with some other educational course. These include any one of a numerous array of academic degrees (such as basic or applied science, statistics or mathematics, information science, and the social or behavioral sciences) or professional degrees (such as dentistry, engineering, law, medicine, nursing, social work, and veterinary medicine).

The MPH degree includes a basic introduction to epidemiology, biostatistics, environmental health, behavioral science, and management. Graduates can also specialize in one of these fields, or in a program area such as maternal and child health (MCH), international health, or public health laboratory science. A large proportion of those seeking the MPH have had some work experience in a public health organization and expect to return to a position of greater responsibility. Others follow the MPH with study for the doctor of public health (DrPH) or the doctor of philosophy (PhD) in a field of science related to public health—training that provides an opportunity for deeper specialization and development of research skills. The DrPH is a practice degree, supporting a higher level of leadership or innovation in service organizations; its role in relation to occupational categories is not specific. The field currently has a limited number of such graduates. Most schools describe the role of the PhD as preparing students for academic careers.

The single largest group of professionals in public health practice is nursing, and most of them do not have an MPH degree. To be considered a public health nurse, graduation from a bachelor's degree program is considered essential. Nursing schools also offer graduate degrees in public health nursing and community health nursing. These programs include much content that is similar to that offered in the MPH, but they may omit key topics such as environmental health. Other disciplines such as environmental engineering, social work, and nutrition offer graduate degrees that are highly relevant to public health. However, the amount of general public health content of these programs varies widely. The graduates of these programs are well equipped to fill specialized positions in public health and will learn on the job about public health. Many of those seeking graduate degrees may have begun work in public health with less training, and they use formal education as a strategy for career advancement. The employing agency must assess the amount of on-the-job training or continuing education needed to ensure that these specialists have sufficient public health orientation to collaborate effectively with all partners.

### Professional Certification

There is, at present, no governmental or private organization that licenses or certifies public health as a separate and distinct profession. Some public health professions (medicine, nursing, dentistry) require licensure to practice in every state, and offer some form of certification as a public health specialist. Other professionals, such as sanitarians, are licensed in some states, certified or registered in others, or left to voluntary standards in still others. Public health educators may be certified by the Society for Public Health Education, though in most areas, this is not required by state law.

There is growing support to establish a uniform certification standard and procedure for all public health professionals. The concept has received numerous endorsements, including those of distinguished practitioners and academicians.[12,14,15] Such a professional credential would distinguish practitioners as having special expertise, qualifying them for hiring and promotion into defined positions of technical importance or leadership, and perhaps as meriting improved compensation and status within public and private employment systems.

A few states have implemented certification programs for a subset of the workforce: health agency directors or officers in leadership positions. Such programs are either voluntary or mandatory and typically specify education or professional background, or years of relevant experience and competencies demonstrated through successful practice.[16] The National Environmental Health Association (NEHA) provides certification as a Registered Environmental Health Specialist or Registered Sanitarian (REHS/RS) as well as other credentials for individual professionals in that field including wastewater, food safety, hazardous substances, radon, and others.

The Association of Schools of Public Health (ASPH) and the American Public Health Association (APHA) have spearheaded the formation of a National Board of Public Health Examiners. Its purpose is to ensure the competence of public health graduates through a national credentialing examination. The examination will be voluntary and based on competencies developed by the ASPH Education Committee. Members of the board are to be drawn from ASPH and APHA as well as the Association of State and Territorial Health Officials, the National Association of County and City Health Officials, the Association for Prevention Teaching and Research (formerly called the Association of Teachers of Preventive Medicine), and private-sector representatives. The examination is projected for launch in 2008.[17]

## Occupational Classifications and Employment Status

Occupational classifications and job titles define public health workers by what work performance is required of them. Any number of such classification systems exists among governments and private-sector employers.

The national system of listing and categorizing the employed workforce is the Standard Occupational Code (SOC) System of the US Department of Labor, Bureau of Labor Statistics (BLS).[18] SOCs classify workers into occupational categories for the purpose of collecting, calculating, or disseminating uniform national data to employers, educators, and others interested in documenting or tracking employment numbers and trends. The SOCs create a comprehensive occupational framework within four levels of aggregation: 23 major groups, 96 minor groups, 449 broad occupations, and over 820 detailed occupations. As listed in Exhibit 8-1, at least 55 SOC titles designate some aspect of public health work, as used in a recent workforce enumeration study.[19]

**Exhibit 8-1   Classification Scheme for Public Health Occupations as Developed by Columbia University Center for Health Policy & US Bureau of Health Professions**

**Administrative**
Health Administrator

**Professional**
Administrative/Business Professional
Attorney/Hearing Officer
Biostatistician
Clinical, Counseling, and School
  Psychologist
Environmental Engineer
Environmental Scientist & Specialist
Epidemiologist
Health Economist
Health Planner/Researcher/Analyst
Infection Control/Disease Investigator
Licensure/Inspection/Regulatory
  Specialist
Marriage and Family Therapist
Medical & Public Health Social Worker
Mental Health/Substance Abuse Social
  Worker
Mental Health Counselor
Occupational Safety & Health Specialist
PH Dental Worker
PH Educator
PH Laboratory Professional
PH Nurse
PH Nutritionist
PH Optometrist
PH Pharmacist
PH Physical Therapist
PH Physician
PH Program Specialist
PH Student
PH Veterinarian/Animal Control
  Specialist

Psychiatric Nurse
Psychiatrist
Psychologist
Public Relations/Media Specialist
Substance Abuse & Behavioral
  Disorders Counselor
Other Public Health Professional

**Technical**
Computer Specialist
Environmental Engineering Technician
Environmental Science and Protection
  Technician
Health Information Systems/Data
  Analyst
Occupational Health and Safety
  Technician
PH Laboratory Specialist
Other Public Health Technician
Investigations Specialist
Other Protective Service Worker
Community Outreach/Field Worker
Other Paraprofessional

**Clerical/Support**
Administrative Business Staff
Administrative Support Staff
Skilled Craft Worker
Food Service/Housekeeping
Patient Services
Other Service/Maintenance

**Volunteers**
Volunteer Health Administrator
Volunteer PH Educator
Volunteer Paraprofessional

*Source:* Bureau of Health Professions, National Center for Health Workforce Information & Analysis. *The Public Health Workforce, Enumeration 2000.* Washington, DC: US DHHS, Health Resource & Services Administration; December 2000.

Not all workers counted among the occupations listed in Exhibit 8-1 in the BLS's periodic surveys would meet even the inclusive definition stated above for the public health workforce. For example, an individual counted as an epidemiologist might work in a health care setting such as a hospital studying outcomes of surgical procedures and as such would not necessarily be delivering an essential public health service. Whether all individuals included in the listed public health occupations should be counted as members of the public health workforce depends on the purpose: employers assessing workforce supply and demand for population-health agencies and organizations would need a count more narrowly focused on those work settings than the currently configured SOC data can provide.

Employment status can affect the representation of public health workers in national labor statistics based on SOC codes. The inclusive definition stated above recognizes that contractual workers and volunteers comprise important groups who contribute to the delivery of essential public health services. Public health efforts are often the result of a mix of volunteers, paid individuals, professionals, and lay persons. This is in no way a detriment and, in fact, is one of public health's major strengths. Particularly as public health efforts become more focused on the socioeconomic and behavioral determinants of health, this blending becomes more important to the success of public health programs. Nevertheless, the BLS's methodology for surveying employers includes full and part-time wage and salary workers, omitting contractors and volunteers.

Finally, public and private employers use job titles designed for or adapted to their respective needs. Each state government (and many local governments) use civil service job titles and descriptions that emphasize educational, technical, scientific, and/or military criteria to recruit and employ workers across many types of agencies; therefore, these titles may lack any specification of population health qualifications or responsibilities. Thus, for example, a "statistical specialist" in a state civil service system might be employed in a state agency that monitors insurance rates as well as in one that monitors health trends. Similarly, private community-based organizations, health care firms, and other businesses may maintain job titles that require public health competencies or that define population health responsibilities; but, if such titles differ from SOC codes, the incumbent individuals could be omitted from national labor statistics.

## Implications of the Inclusive Definition

A broad workforce definition implies that workforce improvement plans must not overlook training for all staff levels, including support and administrative personnel. If the relationship between a public health organization and the community it serves is to be healthy and helpful, it is important that the person who answers the phone, the one who opens the door, the one delivering specimens to a laboratory—in other words, everyone—all have a sense of the mission of public health and of the way his or her tasks and the tasks of others contribute. A mishandled phone call alerting health officials to a possible case of food poisoning may be just as much a contributor to an unnecessarily large outbreak as a misdiagnosis under the microscope or a poor epidemiologic analysis. A rude janitor can do more to drive a tuberculosis (TB) patient away from completing therapy than the overly insistent disease control specialist or the poorly prepared visiting nurse. Clerks in the vital records office, outreach workers, drivers, and volunteers all can contribute to a healthier public. Although their needs may not be elaborate, they, and ultimately the community, will benefit from the regular receipt of information on priorities and issues, on the way their work contributes, and on ways that their own behavior serves as a model for public health in the community.

Further, public health concerns vary over time and without the luxury of time to recruit new, specialized staff for each event. A range of public health expertise, represented by a staff inclusive of at least epidemiology, medicine, nursing, health education, environmental health and legal skills, allows for combining and recombining problem-solving teams as the community's needs shift among communicable disease outbreaks, chronic chemical exposures, child health, facility safety, or emergency preparedness.

## Work Sites

The public health workforce is found in both population-based and institutional services, as illustrated in Figure 8-1. The wide distribution of these workers throughout both the public and the private sector rests on contemporary realities of the US public health system. Governmental resources will always be limited relative to needs, making essential the ongoing role of private-sector workers. Further, population health depends on expert performance in six functional areas: infectious disease control, environmental safety, injury prevention, behavioral health risk-avoidance, disaster response and recovery, and assurance of health care services.[1(App.B)] Each of these areas has its own resource bases, stakeholders, and scientific, socio-political, and professional institutions.

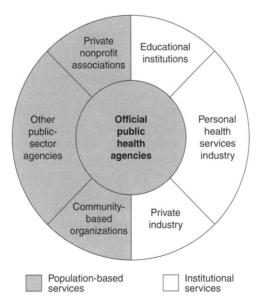

**FIGURE 8-1    The Professional Public Health Workforce: Major Work Settings**
*Source:* Reprinted from Kennedy VC, Spears WD, Loe HD, et al. Public health, workforce information: a state-level study. *Public Health Manage Pract.*1999;5(3):12.

*Public Agencies*

The core of public health workers lies in the federal agencies of the public health service (see Chapter 3 for further discussion) and in the designated agency of every US state and many local jurisdictions having responsibility for public health functions. Other public-sector agencies at the federal, state, and local levels share responsibility for the various functional areas affecting population health, and thus they too employ a portion of the public health workforce. For example, public health-related programs exist in departments of environment, agriculture, labor, education, natural resources, social welfare, transportation, and policy—in other words, nearly every department of federal and state governments. At the local level, there are apt to be fewer distinct agencies, with local health agencies working collaboratively with multiple state or federal authorities.

The major federal work site for public health personnel is the Department of Health & Human Services (HHS), which employs nearly 60,000 individuals. There are eight operating divisions within the HHS:

- Agency for Healthcare Research and Quality
- Agency for Toxic Substances and Disease Registry
- Centers for Disease Control and Prevention
- Food and Drug Administration
- Center for Medicare & Medicaid Services
- Health Resources and Services Administration
- Indian Health Service
- National Institutes of Health
- Substance Abuse and Mental Health Services Administration

The Center for Medicare & Medicaid Services should be included among public health agencies because of its concern for the policies and financing of health care for the elderly and the poor. Among the eight divisions, the two largest employers are the Indian Health Service and the National Institutes of Health, which together account for just over half of the total HHS workforce. Most HHS employees are employed in either clinical research or clinical service settings. Approximately one third of all HHS employees are in medical or health-related occupations, and another 11% are biologists or chemists.[20]

The job titles, qualifications, and duties of public employees are defined by civil service personnel systems at the federal, state, and local levels. (See Chapter 9 for a detailed discussion.) These personnel systems reflect a variety of public policy interests including fair employment practices, equal employment opportunity, military service, and job security—above and beyond educational background and job-related competency. This and the typically slow pace of change in governmental systems make it difficult to update job specifications on a regular basis with particular attention to the evolving needs of public health practice. For this reason, *Healthy People 2010* Objective 23-8 calls for public health agencies to incorporate essential-service-based competencies into their personnel systems.[21]

*Private Organizations and Businesses*

Public health workers are also employed in numerous settings outside the government, including both for-profit and nonprofit enterprises. In the personal health services, many individuals work to promote community health, gather and report health statistics, track nosocomial infections, and plan health-promotion and health-education programs. In many hospitals and community health clinics, they also implement and evaluate community-based programs.

In profit industries throughout the economy, many corporations have come to recognize the impact of health on productivity and profitability and therefore have undertaken public health initiatives such as health promotion and education. Although often focused on employee populations, some such businesses have extended these initiatives to entire communities. Workers in labor unions often monitor health impacts or threats to health and inform their members about health issues.

Some for-profit industries in the health field employ public health professionals as essential to their core business. They work in pharmaceutical companies developing and testing vaccines and drugs, in health insurance and health maintenance organizations monitoring the health status of enrolled populations, developing programs and policies aimed at sustaining good health, and evaluating the quality and effectiveness of programs of disease prevention and health promotion.

Private nonprofit associations, such as the American Cancer Society, the American Diabetes Association, and the American Heart Association, have sizable workforces that monitor the target disease in the population, provide education, and evaluate treatment options. These associations often collaborate with governmental health agencies. Personnel in some of these national associations as well as in their local chapters substantially contribute expertise to carrying out population health functions. Examples include the American Red Cross in disaster response and recovery and the United Way in funding and evaluating personal health services. Today's tobacco control efforts in the United States benefited directly from the combined efforts of the American Lung Association, American Cancer Society, and American Heart Association.

Communities receive public health services from a vast array of community-based organizations (CBOs). In some rural and underserved areas, the presence of these organizations may match or exceed that of official governmental public health agencies.[22] Some CBOs have regular full-time staffs, others rely on volunteers, and many combine both professional and volunteer staffs. Often, CBOs are affiliated with local charity, religious, or political institutions. Some CBOs address a specific health or other social problem; others are more concerned with the general health and well-being of the community. Partnerships between formal health agencies and CBOs are essential to the public health mission and have benefited from increased recent attention from research and demonstration projects.[23]

The elementary, secondary, or college school setting, with a concentrated population of children or young adults, presents both challenges and opportunities to public health. Spread of communicable diseases may happen more quickly, but there is access to enforce immunization requirements and to teach essential health information. At the high school level, the direct provision of personal health care has also been developed with school-based health and dental clinics. In some jurisdictions the local health agency provides nurses for some or all K–12 school settings. In many others, including colleges and universities, these nurses and other health professionals are employed by the school and should be considered a part of the public health workforce.

*Major Professional Groups*

A number of professions predominate in the public health system because of either expertise, numbers, versatility, or a combination of these characteristics. A survey taken of local health departments in 1999–2000 revealed that the most common services they provide are immunizations, communicable disease control, community assessment, community outreach and education, environmental health services, epidemiology and surveillance programs, food safety, health education, restaurant inspections, and tuberculosis testing.[24] Workers associated with these services are especially important participants in the public health workforce. Figure 8-2 illustrates that nurses—a particularly versatile group of professionals in terms of the positions they hold—comprise the largest number of staff positions in local health departments regardless of population size of the jurisdiction served. Administrators, sanitarians, and environmental health specialists are the next largest categories of staff throughout the jurisdiction sizes.

As shown with greater detail in Table 8-2, the specialization of health department staffs tends to increase with jurisdiction size: those job classifications with few or no full-time employees in the smaller jurisdictions are better represented in the larger jurisdictions. Thus, generalists able to fulfill many roles play a particularly significant role especially in the many health agencies serving small local populations.

## Occupational Classifications

In the following paragraphs, the characteristics of some of the most important public health occupations are summarized.

*Epidemiologists and Biostatisticians*

Epidemiology is the study of the distribution and determinants of health-related states or events in specified populations and the application of this study to the control of health problems. By this definition, nearly all people who work in public health may be epidemiologists in some sense, but those considered to be experts in public health's core science generally have a graduate degree in epidemiology and focus their work on the surveillance of health problems and the effectiveness of interventions. Epidemiology can be the primary specialty for a graduate or postgraduate degree, generally an MS, MPH, or PhD. It can also be a graduate specialization added to initial preparation in medicine, nursing, or another health field. Although epidemiologists previously were concerned exclusively with infectious and vector-borne diseases, some now specialize in other areas such as occupational and environmental hazards, violence and injury, and chronic diseases.

The federal investment in enhancing the preparedness of state and local populations after September 11, 2001, led to increased employment of epidemiologists. (Refer to Chapter 23 for further discussion of disaster preparedness.) The Bureau of Labor Statistics reported 2480 epidemiologists working in 2000 and approximately 4000 in 2002, and it projects their rapid increase

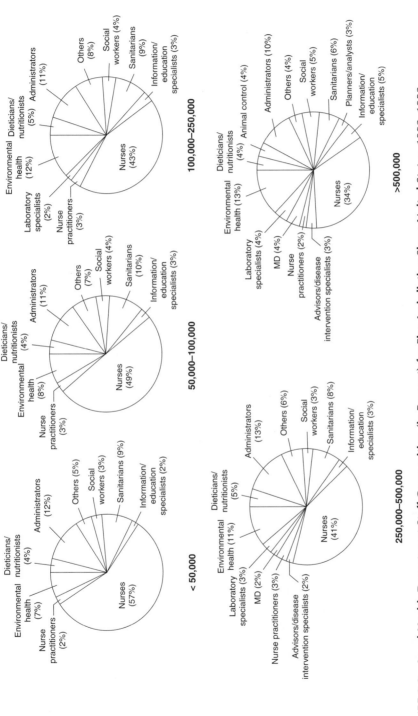

**FIGURE 8-2   Local Health Department Staff Composition (in Percent) for Five Jurisdiction Sizes: United States, 1992–1993**

*Note:* Each circle represents 100% of the responding staff for local health departments in the population category noted below the circle.

*Source:* Reprinted from Gerzoff RB, Brown CK, Baker EL. Full-time employees of US local health departments 1992–1993. *J Public Health Manage Pract.* 1999;5(3):5.

**TABLE 8-2** Percentage of Local Health Departments (LHDs) Having at Least One Full-Time Employee in the Listed Job Classification: United States, 1992–1993

| | Population Category (in Thousands) | | | | | |
|---|---|---|---|---|---|---|
| | < 50 | 50 to 100 | 100 to 250 | 250 to 500 | > 500 | All |
| Number of LHDs | 1209 | 334 | 203 | 80 | 66 | 1892 |
| Percent of LHDs | 64 | 18 | 11 | 4.2 | 3.5 | 100 |
| Nurses | 86 | 91 | 95 | 96 | 97 | 89 |
| Administrators | 57 | 77 | 84 | 90 | 88 | 66 |
| Sanitarians | 36 | 56 | 49 | 51 | 53 | 42 |
| Environmental health specialists | 27 | 43 | 60 | 68 | 64 | 36 |
| Dieticians/nutritionists | 17 | 41 | 67 | 76 | 89 | 32 |
| Public information specialists/ health educators | 12 | 42 | 62 | 66 | 94 | 27 |
| Nurse practitioners/physician assistants | 12 | 34 | 57 | 64 | 85 | 26 |
| Social workers | 11 | 27 | 42 | 61 | 73 | 21 |
| Physicians | 4 | 16 | 37 | 54 | 77 | 14 |
| Laboratory specialists | 2 | 15 | 37 | 51 | 73 | 12 |
| Animal control specialists (non-DVM) | 5 | 12 | 18 | 20 | 41 | 10 |
| Dental assistants/hygienists | 2 | 12 | 25 | 39 | 68 | 10 |
| Public health advisors/disease intervention specialists | 3 | 8 | 21 | 39 | 53 | 9 |
| Epidemiologists | 3 | 3 | 18 | 28 | 67 | 8 |
| Dentists | 1 | 5 | 14 | 23 | 52 | 6 |
| Planners/analysts | 0 | 3 | 11 | 19 | 67 | 5 |
| Toxicologists | 0 | 0 | 0 | 3 | 6 | 0.3 |
| Industrial hygienists | 0.2 | 0.3 | 3 | 4 | 20 | 1 |
| Veterinarians | 0.3 | 0.9 | 0 | 6 | 17 | 1 |
| Other | 56 | 61 | 61 | 69 | 55 | 58 |

*Source:* Reprinted from Gerzoff RB, Brown CK, Baker EL. Full-time employees of US local health departments 1992–1993. *J Public Health Manage Pract.* 1999;5(3):1–9.

in the workforce at 21–35% from 2002 to 2012.[25] Epidemiologists have typically worked in public-sector agencies and academia but are increasingly now employed by managed care organizations and in hospitals, medical centers, and hospital systems in programs to control nosocomial infections. Some are employed in the private sector in consulting firms and other corporations. These positions may be in conducting research, consulting, or providing oversight on scientific investigations.

The work of epidemiologists frequently overlaps with that of biostatisticians. Although also an undergraduate area of concentration, biostatistics education also occurs at the MS, MPH, and PhD levels in schools of public health. In such graduate programs, biostatisticians focus primarily on statistical theory, techniques, and methods to identify and analyze health problems, to evaluate the effectiveness of health services, and to analyze data for planning and policy development. Many are employed in the research divisions of pharmaceutical companies and academic medical centers as well as in specialized federal public health agencies.

## Educators and Behavioral Scientists

The public health workforce also needs to include an adequate number of individuals with skills in education and behavioral sciences. (See Chapter 21 for a detailed discussion.) The more that is known about human behavior, the more important becomes the application of behavioral tools for disease prevention and intervention. For example, efforts to control STDs frequently address human sexual behavior and decision making. In efforts to prevent chronic disease, behavioral science drives program planning for promoting increased exercise, changing individual eating patterns, and reducing stress. All of the public- and private-sector organizations engaging in health promotion, health education, and risk communication for general or special populations employ social and behavioral scientists and professionals.

## Environmental Health Specialists

Environmental health specialists ensure a safe and healthy environment through the control and management of air and water quality, food safety, toxic substances, solid wastes, and workplace hazards. Job titles for individuals working in environmental health are extremely varied, but include scientist, engineer, geologist, hydrologist, toxicologist, risk assessor, industrial hygienist, and sanitarian.

The lead national agency that employs environmental health specialists is the Environmental Protection Agency. However, environmental specialists are found in almost all federal offices. Within state governments, environmental workers are frequently employed in departments of environmental quality, environmental health, or environmental protection. Locally, environmental specialists work in local health departments and in the environmental agencies of some large cities.

Environmental health workers are also employed by private consulting and engineering firms whose clients need help in assessing environmental risks and complying with environmental regulations. All organizations associated with the preparation of food products—from mills and bakeries to meat-packing houses and restaurants—use a variety of sanitarians and environmental health specialists.

## Nurses

Public health nursing in the United States originated with the work of Lillian Wald at the Henry Street Settlement House in New York City, established in 1895. Wald and her colleagues targeted a wide range of disease prevention and health promotion efforts at vulnerable immigrant populations.[26] Since then, public health nurses have remained distinct from other nursing specialties by their focus on populations rather than individuals and on disease prevention rather than acute or chronic care. Although public health agencies often employ nurses with a diploma or associate degree, a public health nurse generally has a bachelor's degree. In larger agencies, nurses with public health education and experience work in community-based programs or hold leadership positions. Other nurses are limited to clinical or more support positions. Public health nursing covers most aspects of public health but is most visible in infectious disease control programs such as directly observed therapy for tuberculosis, maternal and child health programs, and immunizations. Newer programs in which nurses have been active include lead poisoning identification and abatement, tobacco control, injury prevention, and mental health services. The role of nurses in school health has been discussed earlier. In addition, two key areas of practice are occupational health and hospital infection control. Both of these require public health perspectives for effective practice, though are often not thought of in a quick listing of public health nursing positions.

## Physicians

Physicians practicing in public health come from almost every specialty of medicine but mainly the primary care specialties including pediatrics, obstetrics, internal medicine/infectious disease, emergency medicine, and pathology. Physicians have traditionally held leadership positions in public health agencies at all levels of government as well as in public health academia. Public health programs require physicians' knowledge of human health and disease as well as their advanced education and leadership skills. Often physicians learn about public health on the job in community- and population-based programs. It is likely that many physicians leading health agencies lack any formal public health training.[27]

Some, however, are certified specialists in population health. Postgraduate medical education in the form of structured preventive medicine residencies is provided for three specialties: general preventive medicine/public health, aerospace medicine, and occupational medicine. Board certification in preventive medicine requires three years of formal post-MD training including a year in clinical care, a year in public health education (an MPH or its equivalent), and a year in formal accredited practicum (one of the 76 residency programs approved by the American Council for Graduate Medical Education). The cost of supporting this extensive training has led to the decreasing number of residencies. Federal funding for preventive medicine programs was $1.4 million in 2004, down from $2 million two years earlier. The number of board-certified preventive medicine physicians stood at 7518 in 2004, down from 9208 in 1949; and similarly, preventive medicine residents represented 0.8% of the physician workforce in 2002, down from 2.3% in 1970.[28]

Recent years have also seen some movement away from physician-focused leadership in public health. The number of local health department directors who were physicians fell from virtually all in 1945 to only 32% in 1995.[27] One state, persistently finding it difficult to recruit a physician as secretary of health, recently rescinded the statutory requirement of a medical degree for that position.[29] Current staffing trends recommend leadership of the public health agency by a team that includes the high-level competencies of public health, including preventive medicine, but not necessarily a physician director.

## Nutritionists

Given the influence of dietary habits on health outcomes, it is no surprise that nutritionists are part of the public health workforce. Nutritionists plan and supervise the preparation and service of institutional meals, assist in the prevention and treatment of illnesses by advising on healthy eating habits, and evaluate dietary trends in the population. Major areas of nutritional practice are clinical, community, management, and consultancies.[30] The advent of the US Department of Agriculture's (USDA's) Special Supplemental Food Program for Women, Infants, and Children, commonly known as WIC, demonstrates the value of nutritional interventions as one of the nation's most successful public health programs. A substantial proportion of the *Healthy People 2010* goals for the nation require nutritionists' skills in the design and development of relevant programs.[31]

Cultural competence plays a unique role in public health nutrition. Although cultural competence is an asset and requirement of any public health program, the need for culturally competent nutritionists is perhaps greater than for any other public health specialty. The continued flow of immigrants from around the globe means that most communities must regularly update food-related activities and information to accommodate the habits and preferences of those from other cultures.

### Maternal and Child Health Workers

Rather than being a single occupation, the category of maternal and child health (MCH) worker encompasses a number of professions and skills. MCH programs are often staffed by physicians, nurses, health educators, nutritionists, social workers, and others interested in the health of mothers and children. Physicians may be specialists in family medicine, pediatrics, or obstetrics and gynecology. Similarly, MCH nurses may specialize as midwives, women's health care practitioners, or pediatric nurse practitioners.

MCH is also an area of public health education, with many schools of public health offering it with a specialized MPH degree. This education includes family planning, comprehensive maternity care, growth and development, comprehensive pediatric care, and genetics including inborn errors of metabolism (e.g., phenylketonuria). Work with families of children with special health care needs, homeless families, and families receiving services following reported abuse may often include health workers with MCH expertise as well as mental health expertise.

### Health Service Administrators

Managing public health programs is a unique challenge; funding streams are usually complex, and the programs are not easily analyzed using the tools appropriate for the private sector. With every resident of the service community as a client, analysis of cost-benefit and investment payoffs do not fit a sales or customer model. Many of those served by public health may not know that they have been served or may not be happy about the experience (e.g., a restaurant forced to close temporarily because of a food-handling problem).

Because public health recruits managers not only from public health training programs but also from business settings and public administration training programs, public health leaders need to ensure that the new recruits are adequately oriented to a public health perspective. That said, it is also important for public health managers to listen to and learn from those trained in settings such as industrial administration, business management, human resource management, information technology, and other business management specialties. To cross-fertilize managerial perspectives and expertise, public health organizations can exchange staff with other national, state, and local agencies and institute a variety of training strategies. Recent trends in continuing education for administrators have been reflected in a collaborative effort, the Management Academy for Public Health,[32] in which interdisciplinary teams are trained in both principles of administration and the science of public health.

## Dental Health Workers

Many public health agencies employ dentists and dental hygienists in both preventive and restorative roles. In addition to supporting the fluoridation of public water supplies, public health agencies promote children's dental health through education, the application of sealants, and the application of topical fluoride in areas without fluoridated drinking water. Those agencies with clinical services may also provide dental examinations and restorative dentistry as a part of ensuring care for those individuals without other sources of care.

## Generalists and Specialists

Current dialogue in public health often begins with an affirmation of a view of health as the product of a complex interaction among multiple forces rather than the linear result of the treatment of individual diseases with singular causes.[33] Also suggesting an integrative, multidisciplinary approach to public health is the "ecological" model, which takes into account a nested set of factors beginning with individual genetics and moving through concentric layers including personal behavior, the functional status of families and communities, the immediate and global physical environments, and the social environment.[34(pp51–71)]

Thus, many public health workers are generalists, trained and experienced in a variety of perspectives and capable of functioning across a broad array of day-to-day public health services. The lone public health nurse in a small local agency may, for example, provide immunizations, give advice on elder health, conduct prenatal education, administer directly observed TB therapy, counsel those at risk of HIV infection, and interpret vital records reports and infectious disease summaries. Generalists must recognize when to call for consultation by a specialist and require support by a system of regular updates and refreshers on public health topics.

Most programs benefit from specialized staffs that are able to devote their knowledge and skills full time to single areas of public health concern, especially when dealing with larger populations. Such areas can be defined as a single kind of threat to health (vector control), a single disease area (STDs), a single health resource (outreach and access to care), or a single public health skill (epidemiology, microbiology, or health education). Finding the right number of specialists, providing them with the resources necessary to fulfill their potential, and linking them appropriately with each other and with generalists is one of the enduring challenges for public health leaders and managers. With the growth of new knowledge concerning health and the determinants of health, it is likely that the need for specialists will continue to grow and that their numbers will increase throughout the public health workforce.

## How Many and What Kind of Workers Are Needed?

As with much of public health systems, the question of need for public health workers lacks a definitive or prescriptive answer based on a body of research. (Refer to "Needed: An Evidence Base for Workforce Policy" later in this chapter.) At present, history and observation form a basis for identifying the variety of factors that appear to influence the need for public health workers and that tend to change over time. These include prevailing health threats to the population, the availability of complementary health care resources, and the social and political allocation of responsibility for health between government and the private sector. Associated with the latter factor is the question of funding for public health services, much of which is shared among federal, state, and local tax bases. (Refer to Chapter 7 for a complete discussion of public health financing.) Still evolving is a performance-based standard for establishing optimal numbers and qualifications of public health workers at the state and local levels.

### Health Priorities

An historical perspective reveals that major population trends in morbidity and mortality have influenced the perception of need for public health workers having particular backgrounds and skills. At the founding of the nation's public health services, Lemuel Shattuck's 1850 *Report of the Massachusetts Sanitary Commission* called for physicians who would keep records of vital statistics and patient contacts as well as for nurses and sanitary scientists.[35] (For further discussion, refer to Chapter 1.) In the early decades of the 1900s, infectious diseases were the predominant cause of mortality. In 1922, the Committee on Municipal Health Department Practice prescribed the workforce needed to staff a city health department serving a population of 100,000: a health officer, physicians to lead divisions of epidemiology and communicable diseases, nurses for clinical and preventive functions (one nurse to each 2000–2500 persons), and sanitary and nuisance inspectors (one for approximately 25,000 people).[36] The bacteriologic revolution and an increased acknowledgment of the depth of knowledge needed to effectively protect the public's health brought further breadth and specialization to the public health workforce. By 1945, the list of recommended personnel included health educators and differentiated statistical clerks from other clerks, health officers from other administrative medical personnel, and engineers from sanitarians.[37]

Since the latter half of the 1900s, shifts in morbidity and mortality have changed the priorities for public health work from infectious diseases to behavior-related conditions such as cancers and cardiovascular disorders, thus increasing the need for health educators and behavioral scientists. With research advancing the understanding of environmental health factors—such as lead paint in houses, air quality, and waterborne pollutants—the need for workers with engineering and technical backgrounds has risen as well.

In the mid-1990s, an expert panel in Washington state estimated the number and job titles of personnel needed to carry out the 10 essential services of public health[38] as 21.25 full-time equivalent employees for every 50,000 persons in an agency's jurisdiction.[39] The panel recognized that the selected population size was fairly arbitrary and that many other factors could legitimately influence the estimated need for personnel.

## Availability of Healthcare Services

The needed numbers, distributions, and skill sets of the public health workforce depend on the availability, affordability, and quality of health care resources. First, an essential service of public health is to ensure that individuals are linked to needed care. When healthcare services are widely accessible and affordable, the responsibility of public health agencies to provide direct service—and thus to employ clinical personnel—is minimal. Second, the quality of health care services directly influences population health and thus the demands upon public health agencies and workers. For example, high-quality perinatal services improve a population's maternal and child health indicators, and health care providers' vigilance and aggressive prevention of hospital-acquired or nosocomial infections prevents the spread of treatment-resistant bacteria in the larger community.

Shifts in healthcare policy and funding can also impose burdens on public health agencies without a corresponding increase in their resources to maintain adequate personnel levels. An example of this effect occurred with the Medicaid program reforms of the mid-1990s.[40] Prior to reforms, local health agencies had often fulfilled their responsibility to provide direct care for those unable to afford private health services by maintaining primary care clinics. (See Chapter 2 for more information.) An important source of revenue for such clinics was the fee-for-service payment from state Medicaid programs. Relying on these clinics were the poor and uninsured in local communities, for some of whom the reforms limited or eliminated Medicaid eligibility. Simultaneously, the reforms were moving Medicaid eligibles into private-contractor managed care plans, stopping the flow of fees on a per-service basis and typically disqualifying health agencies as Medicaid providers. (For more on Medicaid Managed Care, refer to Chapter 7.) The result was to reduce income to support primary care clinics while doing little to reduce the demand for their services.

## Allocation of Responsibility Between Government and the Private Sector

To the extent that various functions and services of public health are staffed by workers in nongovernmental entities, the "public" portion of the public health workforce may have fewer numbers, different skill sets, and/or different distribution patterns. The 1988 Institute of Medicine report asserted that the core functions of public health—assessment, policy development, and assurance of services—are essentially the responsibility of government: "These functions correspond to the major phases of public problem-solving: identification of problems, mobilization of necessary effort and resources, and assurance that vital conditions are in place and that crucial services are received."[6(p43)] In the view of this report, government might well delegate, contract for, or otherwise allow nongovernmental entities to carry out these functions; but it should, nevertheless, retain ultimate accountability for them.

The rationales for transferring responsibility for health services from public agencies to the private sector—increased efficiency, flexibility in response to changing demands, and a desire for programmatic innovation—are weighed against concerns associated with such transfers, such as loss of public accountability, decreased accessibility, and inequitable distribution of resources.[41] An appropriate balance of efficiency and accountability would, for example, require that a local agency contracting with a private clinic to provide prenatal services to low-income uninsured populations would have to retain responsibility for quality assurance and monitoring. The reduction of clinical personnel in such an agency might have to be offset by an increase in workers skilled in contract writing, management, and supervision and those able to foster collaborations and resolve conflicts between organizations with diverse and often conflicting missions.

So-called privatization of services and programs is common in public health. (Refer to Chapter 3 for detailed discussion.) Workers who provide personal care services (e.g., nurses, physicians, and social workers) are most often the target of privatization efforts. In many areas, visiting nurse associations and home health and maternal/child health services are now contracted by local governments rather than being part of the governmental system. Health clinics are often outsourced to area hospitals or private practice groups. In some areas, entire local health departments have been turned over to local hospital corporations.[41-45] Keane et al[46] reported that, based on surveys with 347 local agency directors, commonly privatized services included: primary care (28%), communicable disease (27%), health education (27%), chronic disease screening and treatment (19%), and immunizations (19%). These researchers also found that the agency directors viewed some services as not appropriate for privatization, including communicable disease (27%), environmental health (24%), and regulatory or enforcement functions (21%).

It is not clear whether or to what extent privatization of public health services might affect the public health workforce. Keane et al found that, when privatization occurred, the majority of contractors were for-profit organizations.[46] Nevertheless, there has been no reported attempt to correlate agencies reporting high levels of private contracting with those reporting low levels of direct employment.

## How Many and What Kind of Workers Are There Now?

From 1923 to 1946, the US Public Health Service bulletins regularly included reports that summarized the public health workforce.[47,48] From 1946 until the mid-1960s, the US Public Health Service continued to gather and report data on local health units and their employees using a standardized report of public health personnel.*[49] Local jurisdictions wishing to receive state or federal monies were required to provide workforce data, and under a variety of titles, survey results were reported nearly every year. Recognizing their importance

---

*Similar reports with other titles can be found going back to1946. Many were authored by Clifford Greves and Josephine Cambell.

to the public health system, government officials conducted a separate census of public health nurses nearly every year between 1940 and 1960.[50] But in the late 1960s, legislative changes brought an end to the public health workforce surveys, and no consistent, longitudinal assessments of the public health workforce were conducted for the remainder of the 20th century. Between the 1970s and the 1990s, a series of reports to Congress on the status of health personnel in the United States continued to develop estimates based on old data. One such report stated that the nation had approximately 500,000 public health workers—250,000 public health workers in the primary public health workforce and another 250,000 ancillary workers.[51]

At the state level, the public health workforce is estimated at approximately 130,000 full-time equivalent positions.[52] The highly variable staffing patterns across state health departments reflect the diversity of services and functions for which each department is legally responsible and the health priorities it seeks to address. This is not unlike the situation for LHDs. Compared with local districts, however, states, because of their fiscal, regulatory, and policy-setting responsibilities, have a larger proportion of their employees in managerial and oversight positions and fewer providing direct services. Surveys of the public workforce have been motivated by specific legislative or policy initiatives. In Washington state, for example, training needs of the workforce needed to be assessed.[53] In Texas, the state health department had a general need for information so they could conduct workforce planning.[54] The Texas study was noteworthy because it took a statistical survey sampling approach and examined not just the official public health agencies but also the numerous other agencies that provided public health services. In Wyoming and Idaho, a federal desire to understand rural local health systems led to a detailed investigation that compared the states' local public workforces. Despite both states being rural and in the same region of the country, the authors reported large differences in both workforce structure and organization.[55]

**Enumeration 2000**

The most recent national study to enumerate the public health workforce was commissioned and carried out in the late 1990s. The findings of that study, titled *Enumeration 2000*,[19] was based on existing state and local reports and on nationally available federal employment information. It yielded the often-quoted figure of 448,244 workers, or one for every 635 persons in the United States. The efforts of these employed workers are augmented by nearly 3 million volunteers. The distribution of workers across levels of government illustrates the concentration of professionals with research and analytic skills at the national and state levels and of professionals with direct service skills at the local level. Figure 8-3 and Table 8-3 illustrate these findings.

*Enumeration 2000* might be challenged for lacking original data or failing to meet the inclusive definition of a public health worker. But its shortcomings are attributable to systematic deficits of definition and data sources as well as inconsistency in counting the public health workforce over many decades. Recognizing these issues, the Association of State and Territorial Health Officials subsequently convened a study, yielding insights to guide future enumeration strategies for future description, monitoring, forecasting, planning, and advocating for the public health workforce.[56]

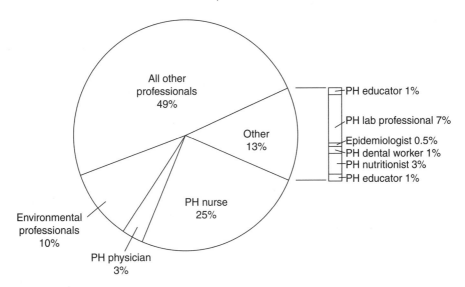

**FIGURE 8-3    Estimated Public Health Professionals by Selected Occupational Title: National Summary**
*Source:* Bureau of Health Professions, National Center for Health Workforce Information & *The Public Health Workforce, Enumeration 2000.* Washington, DC: US DHHS, Health Resource & Services Administration; December 2000.
*Notes:* "Environmental professional" includes environmental engineers and environmental sanitarians & specialists. "All other professionals" includes professionals in other titles and professionals unidentified by title. Percentages may not add to 100% due to rounding.

## Future Trends in Workforce Demand and Supply

It is reasonable to expect that the demand for public health workers will grow. US local health departments reported 6% of their budgeted positions as unfilled.[49] Up to 45% of state public health workers will be eligible for retirement between 2005 and 2010.[57] Growth rates for the number of nurses employed in a variety of community settings have been more than 20% for the past several years.[58] The federal investment in preparedness for public health emergencies and disasters is increasing FTEs in state and local health departments,[59] and this trend is likely to continue so long as does the federal investment.

Nurses, the numerically dominant profession in the public health workforce, are in short supply in the health workforce generally, and this makes their recruitment and retention into public health work particularly problematic. The National Sample Survey of Registered Nurses documents the continuing trend in the aging registered nurse (RN) population in 2000. In 1980, the majority (52.9%) of the RN population was under the age of 40, while in 2000 less than one third (31.7%) were under 40. The major drop was among those under the age of 30.[60(p7)] These data suggest that it will be difficult to fill the ranks of retiring public health nurses in the years ahead.

In the current decade, health agencies are considering the workforce implications of increased surveillance for infectious diseases, not only naturally occurring but also as a tool of terrorism. Further driving this concern is the emergence of infectious pathogens newly threatening to human populations, including SARS, monkeypox, and avian influenza. As previously noted,

**TABLE 8-3   Estimated Public Health Workers by EEO-4 Occupational Category and Setting: National Summary**

| Category | Federal Agencies | Voluntary Agencies | State and Territorial Agencies | Total |
|---|---|---|---|---|
| Officials and Administrators | 1,152 | — | 14,768 | 15,920 |
| Professionals | 58,897 | 8,012 | 133,116 | 200,025 |
| Technicians | 11,695 | — | 29,815 | 41,510 |
| Protective service | 429 | — | 841 | 1,270 |
| Paraprofessionals | 1,236 | — | 18,342 | 19,578 |
| Administrative support | 11,841 | — | 40,071 | 51,912 |
| Skilled craft | 17 | — | 1,166 | 1,183 |
| Service/maintenance | 44 | — | 4,676 | 4,720 |
| Category unreported | 443 | 7,373 | 104,320 | 112,136 |
| Volunteers | — | 2,864,825 | 5 | 2,864,830 |
| Total w/ volunteers | 85,754 | 2,880,210 | 347,120 | 3,313,084 |
| Total w/o volunteers | 85,754 | 15,385 | 347,115 | 448,254 |

*Source:* Bureau of Health Professions, National Center for Health Workforce Information & *The Public Health Workforce, Enumeration 2000.* Washington, DC: US DHHS, Health Resource & Services Administration; December 2000.

employment of epidemiologists has increased since 2000, and this increase is projected to continue through 2012.

As mentioned earlier, the 2003 IOM report, *Who Will Keep the Public Healthy?* recognized eight fields of expertise newly growing in importance for public health practice: informatics, genomics, communication, cultural competence, community-based participatory research, global health, public health policy and law, and public health ethics.[3(p62)] Although not all of these fields are likely to require large numbers of additional workers, they do predict areas of expertise that public health agencies are likely to need in the foreseeable future.

## What Strategies Can Enhance Workforce Capacity?

Despite government's primary responsibility for core public health functions, the private sector may have an advantage in the competition to hire skilled workers and therefore to deliver highly technical or specialized services. Public health agencies may be disadvantaged by the broader policy interests of civil service hiring systems, the lower compensation levels, and the lower perceived prestige or status of public-sector employment. One approach to countering these disadvantages is the credentialing of public health workers. Other approaches are targeted to increasing educational programs at both graduate and undergraduate levels for entry into public health work, to maintaining and enhancing the skills of currently employed workers, and to providing career development opportunities.

### Graduate Education

The continuing interest in public health has led to the growth in schools of public health and graduate programs offering the MPH degree. In 2006, there were 36 accredited schools, 6 pre-accredited schools, and 64 accredited graduate programs—some of which are preparing to seek school-level accreditation. Faculty for these schools and programs are often scholars with limited experience in the practice of public health. This may be problematic, as noted in *Who Will Keep the Public Healthy?*, as schools need both research-oriented and practice-focused faculty members.[3(p127)] Changes needed for the immediate future include the development of faculty with practice expertise, increased student involvement in public health agencies for field work, and active efforts to provide continuing education to the already-employed workforce.

## Undergraduate Public Health Education

The 2003 Institute of Medicine report on the public health workforce strongly recommended that at least some public health courses be offered to undergraduate students as a way of increasing the public health literacy of the population and of attracting students to graduate study in public health.[3(p144)] Such workers could provide much needed entry-level field staff for public health programs and services, particularly at the local level; certainly, baccalaureate nursing programs have been and will likely continue to educate entry-level public health workers. However, the Institute of Medicine committee was silent on whether increasing the number of public health workers with undergraduate training (other than nurses) is desirable. There has been little attention to the contributions of those baccalaureate graduates already employed, and there has been no assessment of their impact on the public's health in the public or the private sector. Nevertheless, a number of schools of public health as well as other colleges and universities have introduced undergraduate courses and degree programs.[61]

## Training for Employed Public Health Workers

Public health workers arrive on the job with diverse educations and experience. Much of this educational preparation is specific to a single professional practice area and may or may not include specific public health content. Thus, many workers need not only on-the-job and technical/vocational training for a specific task, but also general orientation to public health. Even with an appropriate public health background, staff development and continued learning opportunities are a necessity. Public health organizations have begun to explore strategies for developing a readily available core of public health knowledge that could be tapped as a part of new employee orientation or existing workforce updates.

Efforts are underway to identify the core content for meeting these needs.[62] Basic content includes an orientation to the values, history, and world view of public health. Other content areas correspond with the major domains of professional competency including assessment and epidemiology, analytic thinking, effective communication skills, community development, policy development, politics, and organizational effectiveness.

For public health workers with professional credentials (such as medical, nursing, dental, health education, and so on), maintaining state-issued licensure or certification often requires earning continuing education credits. Typically, continuing education-accredited courses are made available through profession-specific meetings and conferences as well as by professional schools. Such sources may not, however, emphasize public health applications and topics and thus may miss the mark for professionals who are public health workers. On the other hand, public health associations' may not always choose to go through the often tedious process of obtaining each separate profession's continuing education accreditation for meetings and conferences. The American Public Health Association does now offer continuing education in all of the major professional areas. If the development of credentialing in public health moves forward, a specific program of continuing education units in public health may also be established.

Mode of delivery is a major consideration in training employed public health workers. Although many are in urban areas with extensive resources and short distances to educational centers, many others work in small and isolated agencies. There may be no one to take a worker's place when training is at another site. One day of training may require a 3-day trip. Managers must be sure that workers have both the money and the time needed to attend these training opportunities. Job responsibilities must be covered and adequate resources provided. Distance learning technologies help to relax these constraints. There is increasing availability of training content via the Internet and satellite television.

### Worksite-Based Training Programs

Beginning in the late 1990s, the US Health Resources and Services Administration and the Centers for Disease Control and Prevention introduced workforce development programs designed to enhance access by working professionals. In 1996, the CDC awarded competitive 3-year grants to schools of public health to develop distance-accessible MPH programs for the agency's field assignees as well as other interested students. The success of those programs enabled employed workers—even those from out of state—to earn the advanced degree while maintaining their regular employment. In 1999, HRSA piloted another workforce development approach: this one to develop a competency-based training curriculum suitable for distance media and providing a series of short courses. In the next two years, HRSA awarded six grants to fund 14 Public Health Training Centers in schools of public health, which currently provide training programs through a variety of media in 42 states.[63] Beginning in 2002, the CDC funded schools of public health to launch Centers for Public Health Preparedness, a program that now includes 42 grantees nationally and that emphasizes training and education in preparedness competencies.[64]

### Online Inventories of Training Resources

Internet technology has made courses and lectures widely available, often without fees or copyright restrictions. The quality of content is determined either by users' ratings or by a Web site's sponsors. Several online inventories either provide direct access to training resources or direct users to access points.

The original example of Web-based learning resources is the Supercourse developed by LaPorte and others and offered through the Global Health Network. The Supercourse provides online access to the lectures of master teachers in a wide array of public health sciences and disciplines.[65] Its contributors agree to post slides with the intention of making them available to other teachers and to learners without charge, and users provide evaluations of the content. The Supercourse Web site currently lists and indexes over 2400 courses by over 20,000 faculty contributors from 151 countries.[66]

The Public Health Foundation has supported online access to training resources since early 2001. Its Trainingfinder system used Council on Linkages' competencies to index courses produced and offered by numerous educators and trainers. The federal investment in state-level preparedness training and education drove many states to explore the use of learning management systems (LMS), developed in the 1990s for corporate training and defined as "the platform for [an] . . . online learning environment . . . enabling the management, delivery and tracking of blended learning (i.e., online and traditional classroom)."[67] State preparedness directors envisioned the use of LMS to deliver uniform training to regular personnel as well as surge-capacity volunteers and to maintain records of course completion and mastery. About half the states developed or adopted their own LMS, and the other half combined resources to subscribe to the Public Health Foundation's TRAIN, an LMS that built upon the earlier Trainingfinder system.[68] Nonsubscribers lack access to TRAIN's management and tracking capabilities but can nevertheless access its course inventories.

Member public health schools of the national network of CDC-funded Centers for Public Health Preparedness contribute courses and materials to a resource center, which is maintained by the staff of the Association of Schools of Public Health.[69] The resource center provides online access to an index of public health and emergency response training materials in a variety of formats including CD-ROM, Web cast, manuals for exercises and drills, and course outlines. It is intended for learners as well as teachers. The resource center directs users to developer and delivery points. Having been developed under a cooperative agreement with federal funds, these learning resources are often subject to only minimal copyright restrictions.

The leadership council of HRSA-funded Public Health Training Centers (PHTC) developed a national curriculum inventory of distance-accessible learning resources. The inventory is based on the Council on Linkages' core competencies for public health professionals and includes the products of PHTCs over the course of six years.[8,63]

## Career Development

Succession planning and individual career development are understood in the private sector as essential to a business success plan. *Who Will Keep the Public Healthy?* strongly suggested that all agencies and all individual public health professionals accept responsibility for such efforts.[3(pp145–167)] The New York State Department of Health, for example, has developed a strategic plan for workforce development that includes an analysis of recruitment and retention concerns at the state and local level, succession planning for key leadership positions at the state level, and increased partnership with schools of public health to assure that needed competency education is available across the state.

The national and regional leadership institutes have provided an important impetus to this effort. Rather than teaching specific techniques for managing individual programs, these creative programs have emphasized the leadership skills needed to move the public health enterprise forward and have made the commitment to lifelong personal growth an explicit expectation of scholars. The network of alumni of these institutes has sustained many state and local agencies through policy change and belt-tightening and can be expected to continue to do so. These programs have also been the stimulus to seek additional higher education for at least some participants.

## Considerations for the Future of the Public Health Workforce

The need for public health workers is growing even as many in the existing workforce near retirement age, and the number of accredited schools and programs for public health education is growing as well. The question is whether graduates will choose to work in the field that continues to offer relatively low compensation, to restrict hiring with little regard for public health competency, and to endure a relatively low perception of status. Credentialing of public health professionals is seen as at least one aspect of a solution to this dilemma. By introducing a national standard of competence, the credential could be easily assimilated into states' existing civil service systems. By articulating a nationally standardized definition of unique competence, the public health credentialing examination could arguably raise prestige as well as compensation levels. Nevertheless, controversy remains around the recognition of experience and expertise among public health workers whose education would predate any newly introduced credentialing process.

To the public health community, the need for more public health workers and enhanced training is self-evident and unquestionable. To those in government who make and pay for resource allocation decisions, the needs may not be so consistently obvious. The current investment in workforce development appears to be motivated largely by concerns for terrorist-sponsored biological attacks and by the threat of pandemic influenza. Funding for training programs have for the past decade been annually eliminated by federal executive-branch budget makers, only to be reinstated by congressional appropriators—a process that is fraught with risk and that tends over time to drive down the amounts approved. Compelling arguments for public health workforce development can be made, but the evidence must first be gathered in research directed toward establishing the current size and structure of the public health workforce.

### Needed: An Evidence Base for Workforce Policy

The gaps in scholarly research upon which to form evidence-based policy recommendations for the future of the public health workforce are substantial. These gaps stem, in turn, from equally serious gaps in knowledge about the public health system in general. Recent efforts to address some of the most serious of these gaps underscore their importance. For example, the Council on Linkages Between Public Health Practice and Academia, with staffing from the Public Health Foundation and strategic partnerships with the CDC and several national associations, has proposed a research agenda for public health systems.[70] The Robert Wood Johnson Foundation has funded a 3-year program to conduct research and policy development in public health systems, with a particular focus on financing—the quid pro quo for workforce support.[71] In addition, one focus of the foundation's Health Care Financing and Organization initiative is "improving the strategic use of information and accountability measures by leaders to enhance performance and raise the visibility and impact of public health."[72]

For a successful national (and state and local) workforce policy, decision makers need to know how many workers of which types working together in which configurations across which programs and components of the public health system constitute the most effective and efficient workforce. But the evidence to address such questions is largely lacking. Indeed, in its deliberations regarding the *Future of the Public's Health,* the Institute of Medicine's Committee on Assuring the Health of the Public for the 21st Century concluded that, while it would have preferred to make recommendations regarding the precise allocation of resources including workforce across the system, the evidence based upon which to do so could not be found.[34(p149)]

A public health workforce initiative was convened by the CDC as the so-called Callaway Gardens effort, named for the rural Georgia location for some of its deliberations. This effort resulted in a logic model for understanding information needs for workforce policy, which is reproduced in Figure 8-4.[73]

The logic model includes major components for generating and training a competent workforce that entail effective efforts at the "inputs": recruitment, education and training tied to documented competency and performance, and training methods for lifetime learning that are effective. The major components for fielding this workforce into the public health "process" involve: defining an appropriate delivery system into which workers might be recruited, deploying an appropriate number and mix of workers for the agreed highest priority tasks at hand, and creating a workplace conducive to worker retention and continuing growth. And, finally, these efforts must be brought effectively to bear on the "outputs": programs, efforts, and services of the proper mix in a community (or for a population) in a way that health status is improved.

The Callaway group also surveyed the available science (or, better said, the lack of such science) with which to answer these questions. In a series of four expert panel workgroups convened between November 2000 and February 2003, the Callaway process nominated a set of top priority items of most urgent attention to build the needed evidence base—forming an agenda for public health workforce research with five top-priority elements:[64]

1. *Predictive relationship*—Determine the relationship between performance indicators for workforce systems and health outcomes controlled for community context.
2. *Competency development*—Identify effective methods for building individual competency.
3. *Workforce performance*—Determine the best indicators for measuring workforce performance.
4. *Workforce monitoring*—Establish a system to track and monitor data about the public health workforce.
5. *Labor market forces*—Describe the components of the system for employment in public health . . . and its influences on recruitment and retention.

No less vital to address these issues will be the establishment of the field of public health workforce research as a credible and funded component of

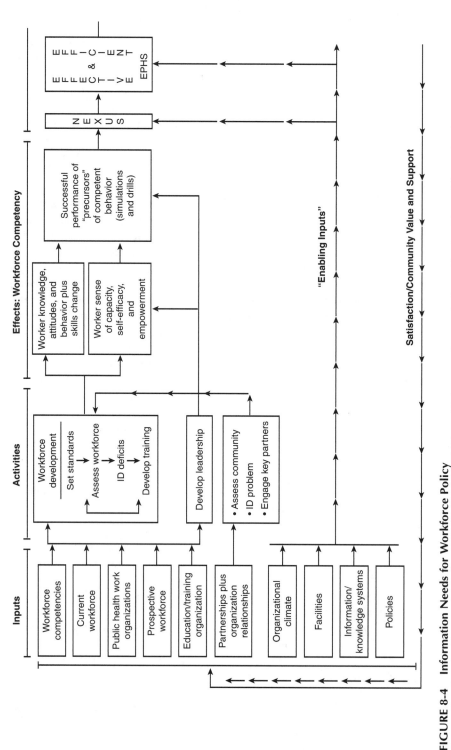

**FIGURE 8-4   Information Needs for Workforce Policy**
*Source:* Reprinted with permission Cioffi JP, Lichtveld MY, Tilson H. A research agenda for public health workforce development. *J Public Health Manage Pract.* 2004;10(3):186–192.

academic public health. Achieving recognition for the scholarly appropriateness of such science (e.g., for promotion and tenure of faculty members within academic centers) and developing a critical mass of funding to sustain academic centers of excellence are vital for progress in this underattended field of research.

## Chapter Review

1. An inclusive definition of the public health workforce recognizes all individuals whose major work focus is the delivery of one or more of the essential services of public health, whether or not those individuals are on the payroll of an official, voluntary, or nonprofit public health agency.
2. Public health workers may also be characterized as possessing a unique set of competencies; having varied educational backgrounds, work sites, and occupational classifications; and including direct employees, contracted employees, and volunteers.
3. The public health workforce encompasses numerous professions, including large numbers of nurses, administrators, sanitarians, and environmental health specialists. Other professionals include epidemiologists and biostatisticians, educators and behavioral scientists, physicians, nutritionists, maternal and child health workers, and dental health workers.
4. The optimal distribution of public health workers between generalists and specialists depends on the size and complexity of the populations served. This distribution is likely to shift toward specialist training as public health knowledge and technology becomes broader and more complex.
5. The number and type of the public health workers needed depends on such factors as the health priorities of the population, the availability of health care services, and the social and political allocation of responsibility between government and the private sector—all of which tend to change over time.
6. As of the year 2000, it was estimated that the number of public health workers at all levels of government and including some private-sector employees is 450,000—about half of whom are professionals.
7. Current strategies to enhance the capacity of the public health workforce build upon the longstanding and growing base of graduate education programs by adding undergraduate degrees in public health, by increasing attention to career development opportunities, and by investing in training programs.
8. To meet the future demand for a highly qualified and effective public health workforce, leaders are advocating for the pursuit of a rigorous agenda for research to support workforce policy.

## References

1. Public Health Functions Project. *The Public Health Workforce: An Agenda for the 21st Century.* Washington, DC: US Department of Health and Human Services; 1997.

2. Centers for Disease Control & Prevention. *Public Health's Infrastructure.* A status report prepared for the Appropriations Committee of the US Senate. Washington, DC: US Department of Health & Human Services; 2001.

3. Gebbie K, Rosenstock L, Hernandez LM, eds. *Who Will Keep the Public Healthy? Educating Public Health Professionals for the 21st Century.* Washington, DC: National Academies Press; 2003.

4. National Association of County and City Health Officials. *Local Public Health Agency Infrastructure: A Chartbook.* Washington, DC: NACCHO; 2001.

5. Gebbie KM. *Competency-to-Curriculum Toolkit: Developing Curricula for Public Health Workers.* Rev ed. New York, NY: Center for Health Policy, Columbia University School of Nursing, Association of Teachers of Preventive Medicine; 2004.

6. Institute of Medicine. *The Future of Public Health.* Washington, DC: National Academies Press; 1988.

7. Sorensen AA, Bialek RG, eds. *The Public Health Faculty/Agency Forum. Linking Graduate Education and Practice. Final Report.* Bureau of Health Professions, Health Resources and Services Administration, Public Health Practice Program Office, Centers for Disease Control. Gainesville, Fla: University Press of Florida; 1994.

8. Public Health Foundation. Competencies for public health professionals. Available at: http://www.trainingfinder.org/competencies/index.htm. Accessed December 2, 2005.

9. Clark NM, Weist E. Mastering the new public health. *Am J Public Health.* 2000;90(8):467–468.

10. Institute of Medicine. *Who Will Keep the Public Healthy?* Washington, DC: National Academies Press; 2003.

11. Council on Education for Public Health. Available at: http://www.ceph.org. Accessed 19–.

12. Moore F. *Analysis of the Public Health Workforce, Final Report.* Washington, DC: HRSA; 1985. No. HRSA 85–266P.

13. Carpenter ES. *Proposed Credentialing System for Public Health Professionals: What Would It Mean for Schools of Public Health.* Ann Arbor, Mich: Association of Schools of Public Health; 1990.

14. Turnock BJ. Competency-based credentialing of public health administrators in Illinois. *J Public Health Manage Pract.* 2001;7(4):74–82.

15. Sommer A, Akhter MN. It's time we became a profession. *Am J Public Health.* 2000;90(6):845–846.

16. New Jersey Administrative Code: Title 8, Chapter 7. Licensure of Persons for Public Health Positions, as amended December 7, 1998.

17. Mahan C. Credentialing graduates from accredited schools of public health and programs. Paper presented to: Annual Meeting of the Deans, Association of Schools of Public Health, Philadelphia, PA, December 2005.

18. US Department of Labor, Bureau of Labor Statistics. Standard Occupational Classification. Available at: http://www.bls.gov/soc/home.htm. Accessed September 24, 2005.

19. Gebbie KM, et al. *Enumeration 2000.* Health Resources and Services Administration Web site. Available at: http://www.cumc.columbia.edu/dept/nursing/research/ResCenters/chphsr/pdf/enum2000.pdf. Accessed on January 3, 2006.

20. US Department of Health and Human Services. *HHS Employment Profile and HHS: What We Do.* Washington, DC: DHHS; 1999.

21. US Department of Health and Human Services. *Healthy People 2010.* Objective 23-8. Available at: http://www.healthypeople.gov/document/ HTML/. Accessed December 2, 2005.

22. Meit M, ed. *Bridging the Health Divide. The Rural Public Health Research Agenda.* Available at: http://www.upb.pitt.edu/crhp/. Accessed January 20, 2005.

23. Padget SM, Bekemeier B, Berkowitz B. Collaborative partnerships at the state level: promoting systems changes in public health infrastructure. *J Public Health Manage Pract.* 2004;10(3):251–257.

24. National Association of County & City Health Officials. *Local Public Health Infrastructure: A Chartbook.* Washington, DC: NACCHO; 2001.

25. US Bureau of Labor Statistics. 2000 national occupational employment and wage estimates. Available at: http://stats.bls.gov/oes/2000191041.htm. Accessed December 29, 2005. O*Net Occupational Information Network. Summary report for 19-1041.00—epidemiologists." Available at: http://online. onetcenter.org/link/summary/19-1041.00. Accessed on December 29, 2005.

26. Mason DJ, Leavitt JK. *Policy and Politics in Nursing and Health Care.* 3rd ed. Philadelphia, Pa: W.B. Saunders; 1998.

27. Gerzoff RB, Richards TB. The education of local health department top executives. *J Public Health Manage Pract.* 1997;3(4):50–56.

28. Bronta P. Associate Director for Policy and Government Affairs, American College of Preventive Medicine (undated).

29. 71 Penn Stat § 1401.

30. Bureau of Labor Statistics. *1998–1999 Occupation Outlook Handbook.* Washington, DC: US Government Printing Office; 1999.

31. US Public Health Service. *Healthy People 2010: Objectives for the Nation.* Washington, DC: US Government Printing Office; 2000.

32. Management Academy in Public Health, University of North Carolina, Chapel Hill. Available at: http://www.maph.unc.edu/. Accessed .

33. Amick BC, Levine S, Tarlov AR, et al. *Society and Health.* New York, NY: Oxford University Press; 1995.

34. Institute of Medicine. *The Future of the Public's Health in the 21st Century.* Washington, DC: National Academies Press; 2003.

35. Shattuck L. *Report of the Sanitary Commission of Massachusetts, 1850.* Cambridge, Mass: Harvard University Press; 1948.

36. Winslow CEA, Harris HL. An ideal health department for a city of 100,000 population. *Am J Public Health.* 1922;12(11):891–907.

37. Emerson H, Luginbuhl M. *Local Health Units for the Nation.* New York, NY: The Commonwealth Fund; 1945.

38. Public Health Functions Steering Committee. Public health in America. Available at: http://www.health.gov/phfunctions/public.htm. Accessed January 21, 2006.

39. Libbey PM. Correspondence of February 13, 2002, and enclosed unpublished 1994 Washington State Public Health Improvement Plan Capacity Standards, Resource Estimate, and Technical Advisory Committee's Narrative Description of Its Assumptions, Cost Estimate Calculations, and the Cost Estimate of the Minimum Staffing Pattern (cited with permission).

40. Gebbie K-M. Follow the money: funding streams and public health nursing. *J Public Health Manage Pract.* 1995;1(3):23–28.

41. World Health Organization. *Evaluation of Recent Changes in the Financing of Health Services.* Geneva, Switzerland: WHO; 1993. WHO Technical Report Series 829.

42. Kertesz L. Public facilities going private. *Modern Healthcare.* 1996; 9:32–41.

43. Keener SR, Baker JW, Mays GP. Providing public health services through an integrated delivery system. *Qual Manage Health Care.* 1997;5(2):27–34.

44. Pierce JR. Transformation of a local health department from primary care to core public health. *Public Health Rep.* 1998;113:152–159.

45. Wall S. Transformations in public health systems. *Health Affairs.* 1998; 17(3):64–80.

46. Keane C, Marx J, Ricci E. Services privatized in local health departments: a national survey of practices and perspectives. *Am J Public Health.* 2002;92(8):1250–1254.

47. Mountin JW, et al. *Ten Years of Federal Grants in Aid for Public Health: 1936–1946.* Washington, DC: Superintendent of Documents; 1949. Public Health Bulletin No. 300.

48. Treasury Department, US Public Health Service. *Report of the Committee on Municipal Health Department Practice.* Washington, DC: US Government Printing Office; 1923.

49. US Department of Health, Education, and Welfare, Public Health Service. *Public Health Personnel in Local Health Units.* Rev. ed. Washington, DC: US Government Printing Office; 1967. Publication No. 682.

50. US Department of Health and Human Services, Public Health Service. *Nurses in Public Health.* Washington, DC: US Government Printing Office; 1960.

51. US Department of Health and Human Services, Public Health Service, Health Resources Administration. *Public Health Personnel in the United States, 1980.* Washington, DC: US Government Printing Office; 1992. HRP-0904085.

52. Public Health Foundation, State Health Agency Staffs. *1991 Final Report of a Contract with DHHS-PHS-HRSA.* Washington, DC: Public Health Foundation; 1992.

53. Northwest Center for Public Health Practice. *A Profile and Training Needs Assessment of Community/Public Health Professionals in Washington State.* Seattle, Wash: Northwest Center for Public Health; 1998.

54. Kennedy VC, Spears WD, Loe HD Jr, et al. Public health workforce information: a state-level study. *J Public Health Manage Pract.* 1999;5(9);10–19.

55. Richardson M, et al. *Local Health Districts and the Public Health Workforce: A Case Study of Wyoming and Idaho.* Seattle, Wash: Center for Work Studies, University of Washington; 1999. Working Paper 56.

56. Association of State and Territorial Health Officials. *Strategies for Enumerating the Public Health Workforce.* Available at: http://www.astho.org/pubs/WorkforceEnumerationReport.pdf. Accessed January 20, 2006.

57. Council of State Governments, Association of State & Territorial Health Officials, National Association of State Personnel Executives. *State Public Health Employee Worker Shortage Report. A Civil Service Recruitment and Retention Crisis.* Washington, DC: ASTHO; 2004.

58. Division of Nursing, Bureau of Health Professions, Health Resources and Services Administration, US Department of Health and Human Services. *The Registered Nursing Population.* Washington, DC: Division of Nursing; 1997.

59. Association of State & Territorial Health Officials. Issue report. The organization of preparedness in the states: a public health case study. Available at: http://www.astho.org/pubs/PreparednessCaseStudy-Organization.pdf. Accessed June 5, 2006.

60. Spratley E, Johnson A, Sochalski J, Fritz M, Spencer W. The registered nurse population: findings from the National Sample Survey of Regis-

tered Nurses. Washington DC: US Department of Health and Human Services, Health Resources and Service Administration, Bureau of Health Professions, Division of Nursing; 2000.

61. Riegelman R, et al. Undergraduate education in public health. Paper presented at: 131st Annual Meeting of the American Public Health Association, November 18, 2003.

62. Gebbie KB, Hwang I. *Preparing Currently Employed Public Health Workers for Changes in the Health System.* New York, NY: Columbia University School of Nursing; 1998.

63. Public Health Training Centers. Available at: http://www.asph.org/document.cfm?page=780. Accessed January 21, 2006.

64. Centers for Public Health Preparedness. Available at http://www.asph.org/acphp/. Accessed January 21, 2006.

65. LaPorte RE, Akazawa S, Hellmonds P, et al. Global public health and the information superhighway. *BMJ.* 1994;308:1651–1652.

66. Supercourse. Epidemiology, the Internet, and global health. Available at: http://www.pitt.edu/~super1/. Accessed December 30, 2005.

67. Hall J. Assessing learning management systems. Available at: http://www.clomedia.com/content/templates/clo_feature.asp?articleid=91&zoneid=29. Accessed December 30, 2005.

68. Public Health Foundation. TRAIN National. Available at: https://www.train.org/DesktopShell.aspx. Accessed December 30, 2005.

69. ASPH's Resource Network of CPHP materials and courses.

70. Public Health Foundation, Council on Linkages Between Public Health Practice and Academia. Public health systems research. Available at: http://www.phf.org/Link/tools.htm#PHSR. Accessed on December 28, 2005.

71. Robert Wood Johnson Foundation. Active grants: public health. Advancing the field of public health finance through public health systems research. Available at http://www.rwjf.org/portfolios/resources/grant.jsp?id=052643&tiaid=141. Accessed December 28, 2005.

72. Robert Wood Johnson Foundation. Changes in health care financing and organization. Available at: http://www.rwjf.org/applications/program/cfp.jsp?ID=19274. Accessed December 28, 2005.

73. Cioffi JP, Lichtveld MY, Tilson H. A research agenda for public health workforce development. *J Public Health Manage Pract.* 2004;10(3):186–192.

# CHAPTER 9

# HUMAN RESOURCES MANAGEMENT

Janet Porter
Tausha D. Robertson
Lee Thielen

## Chapter Overview

The purpose of human resources management is to select and maintain a workforce capable of meeting organizational and community goals. Personnel management consists of a variety of functions including job analysis, recruitment and selection, compensation, coaching, and performance appraisal. Workforce planning, diversity, mentoring, and training are integral components of a successful human resources strategy.

Successful human resources management motivates workers and results in enhanced organizational effectiveness. Research has consistently demonstrated that optimally deploying human resources is essential to organizational success. The employees of any organization determine its failure or success, its strengths or weaknesses, its accomplishments, and its disappointments. Over the last 25 years, the Gallup Organization has interviewed over a million employees. They discovered that the strength of a workplace can be simplified to the following 12 questions:[1]

1. Do I know what is expected of me at work?
2. Do I have the materials and equipment I need to do my work right?
3. At work, do I have the opportunity to do what I do best every day?
4. In the last seven days, have I received recognition or praise for doing good work?
5. Does my supervisor, or someone at work, seem to care about me as a person?
6. Is there someone at work who encourages my development?
7. At work, do my opinions seem to count?
8. Does the mission/purpose of my company make me feel my job is important?
9. Are my coworkers committed to doing quality work?
10. Do I have a best friend at work?

11. In the last six months, has someone at work talked to me about my progress?
12. This last year, have I had opportunities at work to learn and grow?

This chapter addresses how organizations can put systems in place so that employees respond positively to these core questions, which are linked to improved organizational outcomes. Basic principles that human resources systems need for success are reviewed.

Public health administrators often place emphasis on the management of financial resources and information resources, but often the most important determinant of institutional success is how well human resources are managed. Personnel management includes all of the functions and activities that allow an organization to manage its workforce. In addition, it is through personnel management that organizational procedures, policies, and values related to the workforce are determined and implemented. Although core personnel management activities are usually organized in a designated human resources office, all managers and all supervisors engage in personnel management every day. These midlevel managers rely on a centralized human resources office to provide information, guidance, and support with difficult personnel issues.

Most organizations hire and staff a human resources or personnel office with professional staff members. Qualified staff understand both the theory and the practice of personnel management, but they must also understand current employment law and the practices and policies of any parent organization, such as the county or state government. These individuals also require strong interpersonal and technical skills to develop and implement human resources strategy. Because of the many laws governing employment practices, record keeping requirements and advancing information technologies often drive the kinds of new skills needed to staff a successful human resources office.

Staff in human resources offices require a basic understanding of employment law, personnel selection, counseling, mediation, position classification, compensation, and information management. The office should be positioned in a central part of the organization, such as directly reporting to the public health director or to a director of administration. For an organization to accomplish its mission and objectives, the practices and policies of human resources must support the organization's direction (Figure 9-1). In addition, the human resources office must work closely with the accounting, budgeting, and payroll functions of the organization so that all units can accomplish their objectives.

Human resource activities can be viewed as a cycle that includes workforce planning; job analysis; recruitment and selection; socialization and motivation; training and development; coaching and performance appraisal; and promotion, transfer, or termination (Figure 9-2). This chapter is organized to provide useful information that will guide managers through these processes.

## Workforce Planning

Human resource experts should be integrally involved in developing an organization's strategic plan. After all, without skilled staff, the plans cannot be

**FIGURE 9-1    Relationship of HR Strategies to Organizational Strategies**

executed. And for most public health organizations, 80% of the budget is personnel. The strategic planning process should be iterative with various scenarios developed, workforce and other expenses calculated, and estimates as to impact on the community and budget determined.

As Figure 9-1 illustrates, after the organization's strategic plan is developed, human resources must identify strategies and tactics to support the strategic plan. Human resources progress on those strategies should be reviewed at least quarterly so that adjustments in the plans or schedule can be made. The human resources plan is essentially a workforce plan that identifies

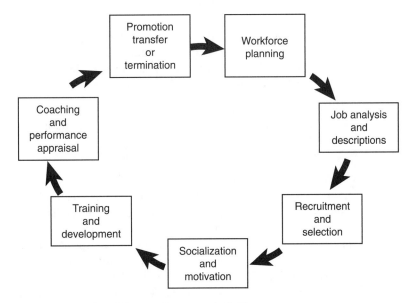

**FIGURE 9-2    Cycle of Human Resource Activities**

**Public Health Human Resources Challenge**

Current workforce trends indicate that the US public health is aging, with many workers retiring or near retirement. For example, the average age of the public health nurse, an integral part of the public health workforce, is 49.5 years.[18] In addition, up to 43% of the state public health department will retire or be eligible for retirement by 2006.[19]

To counteract this growing crisis, public health leaders have begun discussing potential strategies to do the following:[20]

- Strengthen the skills and competence of the existing workforce to fill the experience void left as workers retire.
- Effectively prepare and recruit students and professionals from other disciplines to enter and remain in the practice of public health to ensure adequate numbers of workers, in the right places, with the right skills to protect and improve the health of the American public.
- Examine the working environment of public health agencies in order to formulate changes that could bolster retention and recruitment.
- Coordinate recruitment and retention efforts to reduce duplication and maximize efficiency and effectiveness.

the number and types of qualified personnel necessary along with the expected salary and benefits necessary to fully staff those positions.

## Job Analysis and Job Description

The primary building block for any human resources department is job analysis. Before you can recruit and select candidates there must be a serious consideration of the organizational needs related to the position. This process requires two steps, job analysis and job description.

Job analysis refers to separating the whole into its parts in order to examine and interpret each part.[2] To conduct a job analysis, human resource departments must collect data from a variety of sources determined by the following:[3]

- *Job content*—Identifies and describes activities such as tasks and duties
- *Job requirements*—Outlines the knowledge, skills, and attributes (KSAs) a candidate should possess
- *Job context*—Identifies the purpose, responsibilities of the employee, working conditions, and supervision arrangements

Using this information, a job description can be created. The job description should begin by listing the job title, department, grade or classification, and supervisor title. The next section of the job description includes a job summary, which is a brief paragraph outlining the specific duties performed in the job. A well-written job summary can be utilized in subsequent recruitment materials. The final portion of the job description is a job task section that identifies all of the tasks required for the job. It can be helpful to organize these tasks into categories that represent important areas of the work performed. This provides a clear overview of the work expectations. The job analysis and job description can be useful tools in the performance appraisal process discussed later in this chapter.[3]

## Recruitment

The ease in recruiting public health workers is heavily dependent on issues such as salary, the supply of workers with the needed skills, the strength of the private sector, the responsiveness of the personnel system to changes in the marketplace, the reputation of the organization, the morale of the current workforce, and the skill of those charged with recruiting. The most difficult person to recruit is usually the organization's senior administrator. A local or state health official is ideally a doctoral-level professional, with either an MD or a PhD in another health profession. Experience in public health practice and public-sector administration is often helpful to administrators in these positions. Significant public health experience may offset the need for extensive academic training. The ability to offer tenure in office, such as a contract for a specified period of appointment, promotes continuity and increases the supply of qualified applicants willing to serve in these high-level positions.[4]

A large proportion of the public health workforce falls into five professional groups. (Refer to Chapter 8 for further discussion.) These groups include physicians, nurses, environmental professionals, administrators, and health educators. These professions are in high demand in the private sector as well as the public sector, making recruitment and retention important to the success of the public health organization.

Many of the limitations imposed by merit systems and comparable civil service systems are not always under the control of the public health organization, but some are. For example, the supply of workers with the skills needed may be limited, so the challenge lies in how to increase the supply. One way is to develop relationships with academic institutions and their faculty to help channel referrals to the organization. Another technique is to recruit internally and create opportunities for existing staff to increase their skill level within the organization. A third example is to pay for employees to enhance their professional and technical skills through external education and training, perhaps even paying the tuition for graduate programs.

Managers should never assume that personnel systems are unchangeable. They are only unchangeable if the managers never seek flexibility or improvements. An important role for senior administrators and other high-level managers is to develop relationships with decision makers that allow input into the process of developing rules, procedures, and laws that govern the personnel systems of the organization. For example, following difficult recruitment efforts by one state health agency for a high-level regulatory manager, the agency suggested that out-of-state moving expenses be included in the state's fiscal rules. At the next hearing for changes in fiscal rules, that change was made for the state. This effort was appreciated by all of the state agencies. Managers of other agencies simply had not thought to ask.

Another creative solution includes the incorporation of private-sector techniques for recruitment. In the past, these techniques might have been viewed as foreign to the public sector, but in fact they allow greater success in recruiting difficult-to-find talent. They include signing bonuses, pay matching to allow a counteroffer when an employee or potential employee is being recruited by others, referral awards to existing staff for helping recruit hard-to-fill positions, and temporary pay differentials to compensate for such responsibilities as acting duties or special projects. These types of incentives in the public sector are fairly recent phenomena and are driven by talent shortages that can occur in such areas as nursing and computer specialists.

Asking employees to assist with recruitment is especially useful because staff will often have a developed network of contacts in their field and enjoy being part of the promotion of the agency.

Recruitment may be targeted or broad reaching. Traditional recruitment techniques have included newspaper ads, professional organizations' job lines or newsletters, and the posting of announcements through bulletin boards. Another approach involves Internet-based recruiting, especially on the Web site of the organization or related institutions. Most governmental agencies now include Internet announcements as a way to notify potential applicants of opportunities. Job fairs may be helpful for certain types of recruitment, and using internships to identify talented individuals who are still in training is an excellent technique that allows both the intern and the organization to see if there is a good fit. Recruiting broadly or even targeting specific minority groups is critical to diversifying the workforce.

Minimal information to include in any job announcement includes a brief and accurate job summary, minimal qualifications, salary range, how to apply for the position and receive additional information, and a closing date for applications. It is also helpful to open the announcement with a positive description of the agency that creates the image of an exciting place to work.

## Diversity in the Workplace

Customers to public health organizations include people of myriad languages and cultures. In addition to issues of ethnicity, religion, color, sexual orientation, and culture, a well-balanced organization includes a broad range of age levels and people with disabilities. The recruitment, testing, and selection of staff needs to be designed to reduce any potential adverse effects on protected classes. Adverse effects are defined as using a "selection process for a particular job or group of jobs that result in the selection of members of any racial, ethnic, or sex group at a lower rate than members of other groups."[5(p197)] Agencies and organizations that work proactively to encourage diversity incorporate fair selection practices, targeted recruitment, and employee training in diversity. They also use an employee-manager committee to encourage diversity in the workforce and appoint a staff member to function as an equal opportunity counselor. Furthermore, some of the laws governing equal opportunity and affirmative action include Title VII of the Civil Rights Acts of 1964 and 1990, Executive Order 11246 (amended by Executive Order 11375), the Equal Pay Act of 1963, the

Age Discrimination in Employment Act of 1967, the Americans with Disabilities Act, and state and local laws.[6]

## Selection of Applicants

The most important decisions that any manager makes are those of selecting and promoting employees. Unfortunately, the personnel selection process is too often hurried, incomplete, and inappropriate, resulting in huge costs in productivity and morale, as well as potential legal actions. The selection process in any organization is usually governed by specific rules and laws. The intent in the public agency is to maintain a system that is based on merit or the meeting of minimal qualifications. Most agencies will use a combination of reviewing résumés, testing for knowledge or skills, role playing, and checking references prior to interviewing the final candidates. The human resources office will usually wish to partner with the program manager or senior administrator to determine the best techniques to match the candidates with the job requirements.

The basic principles of psychology—primacy and recency—apply to communication with prospective employees. Primacy means that people form a lasting first impression based upon the first contact, or the first few minutes of an encounter. Thus, the employees whom prospective candidates meet first—receptionists, secretaries, human resources staff—have tremendous impact on candidates' impressions of the professionalism of the organization. Conversely, people may form lasting impressions from their last encounter or final few minutes with an organization. A manager must spend time making sure that the job description is professionally presented, that the address for mailing resumes or applications is correct, and that the person answering questions is knowledgeable and welcoming to candidates.

Interviewing candidates for employment is key to wise selection. The interview process is most effective if the hiring manager has clarity about the job expectations and has established a systematic process during the interviews for garnering information from the candidates. The interview process is usually limited to the final few (usually three) candidates who have been selected through the initial screening process. A manager may select the final three candidates or involve a formal or informal search committee to assist with the review and selection of candidates. It is usually advisable to invite peers to interview candidates. This can help to clarify for the candidates what the job really is and peers can provide insight into candidates' fit with the position. Perhaps a team of stakeholders and others with whom the applicant must work and interact can provide input to the appointing authority. The appointing authority is defined as the individual who has the authority to make the actual offer of employment. The appointing authority should be the direct supervisor of the new hire. This may be a department head, a program manager, or perhaps the senior administrator or health officer.

A good interview is conducted in a comfortable setting and includes introductions to all the parties involved, along with an explanation of why they have been asked to participate. Questions have been prepared ahead of time and are consistently asked of all the candidates. Questions should be experientially based ("Tell us about your experience") and open ended. Many questions can not be asked, and the human resources office should have guidance regarding the questions to avoid.

The Mountain States Employers Council, Inc., has identified the following 10 common errors made when interviewing candidates:[7]

1. *Failing to establish rapport with the applicant*—There are two excellent reasons to put the applicant at ease. First, he or she will respond better to the interview and provide a clearer representation of talents and experience. Second, while the interviewee is marketing him- or herself to the organization, the interviewer is also marketing the agency as a good place to work. Having the applicant think positively about the interviewer and the organization is important for successful recruiting. Some ways to ease into the interview are to offer the applicant a cup of coffee, or to show the candidate the office, laboratory, or site where the candidate will be working.

2. *Asking direct instead of open-ended questions*—Applicants will offer more information if they are asked questions that can not be answered with yes, no, or a similar brief statement. For example, "Have you ever investigated a disease outbreak?" is less useful than, "Tell me what experience you have had with disease investigations."

3. *Asking questions that are too general*—Questions that are too general provide too little useful or specific information to assist in the selection process. Requiring an answer that lends itself to specific time frames, experience, skill, events, and so forth will yield more useful information. For example, "Tell me about your nursing career" may reveal less than, "Please discuss your last position as a visiting nurse for a local health department."

---

### Hiring the Best

It is theorized that most job failures can be prevented by looking beyond the resumes and references and concentrating instead on identifying a candidate's work habits.[21] "Eighty-five percent of all job failures have to do with a lack of appropriate work habits, not technical skills," said Still. "Technical skills are very easy to identify. On the other hand, how the person does the job and what kind of habits they bring in is in many cases more important to identify than technical skills."[22] A candidate's ability to perform well in your organization can best be assessed by exploring that person's past work behaviors and habits. It is not enough to ask candidates what they did during their previous employment, but rather, how they did it.[22]

Asking behavior-based questions places the interviewer in the role of an analyst. One example of a behavior-based question is asking the candidate to describe an incident in which he or she had a disagreement with a coworker. Human relations experts suggest that this method allows candidates to reveal aspects of their personalities obscured by other interviewing techniques. Based on their answers, the interviewer gets a history of the candidate's ability to work with others, a key indicator of future success.[21]

4. *Asking multiple questions*—If lengthy and complex questions are asked, the applicant is likely to answer only a portion of the question or answer the question as he or she interpreted its meaning.
5. *Failing to ask reflective questions*—If an answer is not clear or seems incomplete, the interviewer should ask for additional information. For example, if asked why he or she left a previous position, a brief answer of "There were layoffs due to reduced funding" might not provide sufficient information to evaluate the reasons why the individual left. By adding another question such as "Tell me more about the agency's decision to terminate your position," additional information may be obtained regarding the termination.
6. *Asking leading questions*—Too much information included in the question can lead the applicant in the direction that will yield the most acceptable answer. However, that answer may not be indicative of how the applicant really feels about the topic. For example, the question, "Our agency is very interested in keeping abreast of the latest technology. How do you feel about learning new software when we upgrade our computers?" can bias the applicant toward a positive response.
7. *Not allowing enough time for the applicant to respond to questions*—The interviewer should avoid rushing the applicant. Providing sufficient time to give a complete answer is important.
8. *Asking questions that identify or single out a candidate's protected group status*—Only questions that are related to the job should be asked. Questions that tend to identify or discuss a person's race, religion, sex, age, disability, or national origin should not be mentioned.
9. *Spending too much time talking*—The purpose of the interview is to hear from the applicant, not the interviewer. A good rule of thumb is that the applicant should be talking approximately 80% of the time.
10. *Failing to demonstrate active listening*—The interviewer should provide both verbal and nonverbal messages that show whether he or she is listening, attentive, and interested in the answers.

## Reference Questions

A key part of the selection process includes the verification of previous employment and the discussion that occurs with previous employers or other references. Applicants might typically provide three or more references, with two of them from previous direct supervisors. Applicants should be asked for written authorization to contact previous employers and references. Many agencies or companies have a policy to release only the dates of employment and the titles of the positions held. Questions asked of references should include how the individuals know the applicants and how they might have worked together, as well as questions that will indicate the work ethics and skills of the applicant. One way to elicit useful information is to describe the qualities and skills sought and then ask if the applicant has those qualities and skills. Objective questions are useful, such as "Did the applicant use Excel spreadsheets in his work in your office?" Work attendance history may be useful to indicate work practices. It is sometimes useful to ask the individuals whether they would hire the applicant themselves, and, if so, why. Just as in an interview, any questions that appear to indicate an attempt to determine religion, race, age, sexual orientation, or national origin should be avoided.

## Socialization and Motivation

### Socialization

After the newly recruited employee becomes a member of the organization, preparation is needed so that the former applicant learns and becomes committed to the organization's goals, objectives, and operations.[8] Organizational commitment involves three factors: (1) belief in the goals and values of the organization, (2) willingness to exert considerable effort on behalf of the organization, and (3) desire to continue work with the organization. This concept is not limited to organizational loyalty, but rather it reflects a desire by the individual to further the success of the organization. Better work performance is correlated with the employee's commitment to the organization.[9] There is also a positive relationship between organizational tenure and job commitment.[10] High levels of organizational commitment are associated with low levels of employee turnover.[11]

What enhances employee commitment to organizations, including public health organizations? The attachment the employee brings to the organization on the first day of work correlates with the employee's propensity to develop a stable attachment and long stay with the organization.[7-9] The implications for astute recruitment and employee orientation are evident.

The organization needs to spend time thinking about the orientation of all new hires. Often organizations see that as a time to review policies and procedures when, in fact, it should be a time to orient new hires to the organization's values. If a core value is customer service, have a customer come to talk; if a core value is teamwork, have a team come and talk about how they work together. Again, the concept of primacy means that new hires will long remember their first day at work.

### Motivation

Human resources are especially important to the public health organization because staff are undoubtedly the most important asset in achieving improvements in population health. A chief priority of both senior and middle managers within the organization is to excel at the motivational challenge to increase employee participation and production at work. Managerial approaches to motivation are examined in this chapter, including employee development, mentoring, job training, quality management, and recruitment. Additionally, human resource systems and processes frequently encountered by public health managers are examined, including merit systems, job classification systems, labor relations processes, and contract development processes.

Patterns of managerial motivation are shown in Table 9-1. According to the Porter and Lawler model, employee effort is determined by two factors: (1) the value placed on certain outcomes by the individual, and (2) the extent to which the person believes that his or her effort will lead to attainment of these rewards.[12,13] Other theories of successful managerial motivation also emphasize

TABLE 9-1   General Patterns of Managerial Approaches to Motivation

| Traditional Model | Human Relations Model | Human Resources Model |
|---|---|---|
| **Assumptions** | | |
| 1. Work is inherently distasteful to most people. | 1. People want to feel useful and important. | 1. Work is not inherently distasteful. People want to contribute to meaningful goals that they have helped establish. |
| 2. What they do is less important than what they earn for doing it. | 2. People desire to belong and to be recognized as individuals. | |
| 3. Few want or can handle work that requires creativity, self-direction, or self-control. | 3. These needs are more important than money in motivating people to work. | 2. Most people can exercise far more creative, responsible self-direction and self-control than their present jobs demand. |
| **Policies** | | |
| 1. The manager's basic task is to closely supervise and control subordinates. | 1. The manager's basic task is to make each worker feel useful and important. | 1. The manager's basic task is to make use of "untapped" human resources. |
| 2. He or she must break tasks down into simple, repetitive, easily learned operations. | 2. He or she should keep subordinates informed and listen to their objections to his or her plans. | 2. He or she must create an environment in which all members may contribute to the limits of their ability. |
| 3. He or she must establish detailed work routines and procedures, and enforce these firmly but fairly. | 3. The manager should allow subordinates to exercise some self-directions and self-control on routine matters. | 3. He or she must encourage full participation on important matters, continually broadening subordinate self-direction and control. |
| **Expectations** | | |
| 1. People can tolerate work if the pay is decent and the boss is fair. | 1. Sharing information with subordinates and involving them in routine decisions will satisfy their basic needs to belong and to feel important. | 1. Expanding subordinate influence, self-direction, and self-control will lead to direct improvements in operating efficiency. |
| 2. If tasks are simple enough and people are closely controlled, they will produce up to standard. | 2. Satisfying these needs will improve morale and reduce resistance to formal authority—subordinates will "willingly cooperate." | 2. Work satisfaction may improve as a "by-product" of subordinates making full use of their resources. |

*Source:* Adapted with permission from Miles RE, Porter LW, Craft JA. Leadership attitudes among public health professionals. *Am J Public Health.* 1966;1990–2005.

the role of individual expectancy with respect to the assigned job. If people are assigned to tasks for which they lack capability, their expectancy for accomplishment and resulting performance will be low. Human resources managers sensitive to the importance of these self-efficacy beliefs in job performance typically rely on the following four methods to strengthen employee confidence:[13]

1. Performance successes strengthen a person's perception of his or her capability. Building experience through stages of success can help to overcome limitations in training, supervision, and mentoring.

2. Modeling ideal performance using other employees can convey to observers effective strategies for responding effectively to different work situations.
3. Social persuasion, including realistic encouragement, can increase individuals' beliefs that they possess the necessary capabilities to do the job.
4. Reducing job stress levels using stages of successes, performance models, and social persuasion can improve performance over time.

The foundation of the human resources model is positive reinforcement of employee performance, rather than use of punishment for undesirable behaviors, and concentration on building strengths. Positive reinforcement is a widely recommended strategy that is supported in both the scientific and professional literatures on human performance. Positive reinforcement enhances an individual's commitment to the organization and can be achieved by fulfilling the individual's core professional needs for job security, social support, and achievement.

Guidelines for positive reinforcement include the following:[14]

- Don't reward every worker in the same way; differentiate rewards based on performance.
- Do something. Nonaction by managers also influences employee behavior, but there may be negative consequences to nonaction on performance.
- Tell the individual worker what he or she can do to receive positive reinforcement.
- Tell the worker what he or she is doing wrong.
- Do not correct the worker in front of others.
- Make the consequences equal to the behavior; reward good workers and counsel employees with unsatisfactory performance.

It is important to think about how the team functions effectively and to reinforce positive team behavior over time. Team motivation is a function of leadership, individual drive, clear goals, resources to do the job, and rewards for positive behavior.

## Training and Development

Professional development of employees pays off in two key ways. First, such development leads to greater job satisfaction by the employees, improved morale, reduced turnover, and enhanced performance. Second, the organization benefits from a staff with a breadth of skills, knowledge, and attitudes. Creativity and ownership in the success of the organization come from enhancement of the quality of the workforce. Employee development includes training and education, mentoring programs, and employee involvement in organizational improvement and decisions. Public health organizations are often at a competitive disadvantage in the pay and working conditions that they are able to offer employees relative to other employers. However, the intrinsic satisfaction that can come from making a difference in the community is a highly motivating characteristic of public health work. Employees who

---

**Teamwork**

Because public health is an amalgam of disparate disciplines—environmental health, nursing, nutrition, epidemiology—glued together by a common mission of improving community health, effective team work is necessary.[23] Every member of the team has to appreciate that each person's role is equally important. For example, in a workshop to challenge staff to think about creating their vision for the future, a receptionist stood up and presented drawings illustrating her view of the team. One of her three drawings was of machinery with interlocking cogs and wheels—all different sizes but obviously interdependent. She simply stated, "We all need to operate like a well-oiled machine. Like all machines, some parts are bigger than others, but all are equally important for even if the smallest cog breaks, the machine stops. And, the oil that lubricates our working parts is the love we have for each other and for the communities we serve." With her hand-drawn pictures she eloquently described that everyone was equally important to the overall functioning of the team no matter how seemingly insignificant their tasks.[23] Fostering the sense of team and respect for all positions is a cornerstone for effective human resource management in public health.

---

feel valued and see tangible investments in their growth will often develop a commitment to the organization that is as powerful a motivator or more powerful than compensation.

Every organization needs a training budget that is recognized as being just as important as other expenses, such as utilities and equipment maintenance. A common error in organizations is to assume that the training budget is discretionary and thus subject to reduction during difficult budgetary times. Each employee needs a personal development plan that includes both specific skills and personal growth components. This plan should be negotiated during each annual work planning session and updated to reflect changing roles in the organization and new technologies. For example, clinical responsibilities within an organization may be declining as these responsibilities are assumed by private-sector managed care plans, but the need for community health assessment may be growing. This shift in organizational and community needs should be reflected in the skills that management makes available to staff through training opportunities.

Training initiatives must also reflect the evolving competencies required of public health professionals, such as designing and interpreting health status indicators or surveillance data for specific risk factors and disease outcomes and crafting and monitoring service contracts to achieve specific results consistent with the rules and laws of the local jurisdiction. These examples of professional competencies may be quite different from the tasks that were expected of staff in the recent past, when more clinical services were directly provided by public health organizations. As the role of public health organizations changes, staff must be transitioned to new responsibilities. New technologies create a constant need for new skills as information tools and scientific options evolve. A developmental plan for each employee needs to recognize these changes.

## Coaching and Performance Appraisal

Employees are most likely to be successful if an organization recognizes the following:

- Performance improves most when clear goals are mutually established.
- Coaching is at the core of every interaction every day.
- Coaching comes from supervisors, peers, and direct reports.
- The key element of organizational learning is individual learning, and individual learning comes from many sources, one of which is coaching.

Coaching occurs regularly between individuals working together in organizations to improve performance. However, at least annually, organizations require a formal performance appraisal—a review of the employee's performance relative to goals.

Although most managers will eagerly agree that personnel management is a key responsibility, many do not relish the tasks and roles required for effective performance management. Formal performance appraisals are an important part of supervisory responsibilities in most organizations. Appraisals are for the benefit of the organization, and ideally, for the benefit of the employee. They are used to inform organizational decisions that determine salary, promotions, transfers, layoffs, demotions, and terminations. They also provide the mechanism and opportunity for employees to receive useful coaching and suggested changes in behavior, attitudes, knowledge, and skills. However, if left to their own devices, many managers and supervisors would never administer a performance appraisal. Therefore, the organization usually creates prescribed procedures with common forms and other tools. However, the formal appraisal process should not provide information to the employee about their performance that is new; with regular coaching the employee has gotten feedback all year long about their performance and is attuned to strengths and areas for improvement.

Successful performance appraisal systems take time to implement, and yet most supervisors spend only four to eight hours a year per employee in performance management, including preparation, paperwork, and discussion.[15] It is, therefore, not surprising that most employees do not see a link between their performance and their pay.

Many options are available to an organization regarding the instrument used for appraisals. These can include a numeric rating scale or a nonnumeric rating. For example, the instrument may be developed with a maximum number of points set at 100. Other instruments may focus on categories of performance such as *exceeds objectives, fully meets objectives, partially meets objectives,* and *unsatisfactory.* One agency uses *unsatisfactory, fully competent,* and *peak performer,* which also match numeric ranges. Some instruments focus on behavior; others focus on traits and skills. Factors evaluated, such as communications, leadership, or problem solving, may be weighted so that some are recognized as more crucial than others. The instrument itself is less important than how it is administered and how plans are developed against which the employee is evaluated.

An organization is more likely to have successful performance management if: (1) both supervisors and employees are trained regarding the appraisal process and how to develop meaningful objectives and work plans, (2) supervisors are trained to be coaches and mentors, and (3) performance management is seen as a meaningful mechanism for development. Performance management starts with the job, not the form, and both parties have a responsibility regarding its success.

The phases of performance management include the following:[7(p21)]

- Performance planning, where objectives, standards, competencies, and a development plan are mutually determined
- Performance execution, which involves the actual work being accomplished
- Performance assessment, which includes both parties independently assessing how the plan was achieved
- Collection of data from other parties, such as subordinates, peers, or customers
- Performance review, where the results are discussed
- The renewal of the agreement or contract for the following performance period

Typically, a performance appraisal should include four parts:

- The employees' self-assessment of their performance ("How do you think things are going?")
- The supervisors' feedback on the employee ("Let me provide you feedback on how you are doing relative to your goals.")
- The employees' feedback on working more effectively with the supervisor ("What can I do to make you more successful in your position?")
- The development of a plan for performance improvement ("So this is your development plan for next year.")

The employee needs commitment to the objectives and goals, solicitation of feedback from others, communication that is open and regular with the supervisor, the collection of performance information or data, and preparation for the review. The supervisor is responsible for creating an environment that encourages open communication and motivation, observing and documenting performance, updating and revising objectives and standards, explaining the relationship between the overall goals of the organization and the employee's objectives, creating developmental paths, and reinforcing effective behavior. The employee's work plan should reinforce and integrate with a unit or program work plan. Objectives at both the program and the employee level should be specific, measurable, achievable, results oriented, and timely.

Some of the most common errors in performance management include the following:[15]

- *Contrast effect*—The employee is compared with another employee or employees.
- *First impression error*—An initial observation rules the supervisor's thinking even though it is no longer applicable.
- *Halo or horns effect*—One aspect of the employee's performance is generalized to the entire performance.
- *Like me effect*—The supervisors may rate employees who are similar to him or her higher than others.
- *Skews to the center, negative, and positive*—The supervisor has a tendency to rate employees in the middle, or at the high or low end of the scale.

- *Attribution bias*—The supervisor has a tendency to attribute failing to factors that are under the control of the employee and successes to outside causes.
- *Recent effect*—The supervisor remembers the most recent event instead of the full performance period.
- *Stereotyping*—The supervisor ignores the individual and generalizes across groups or work units.

Some organizations directly link pay to performance, others do not. In governmental agencies, salary increases are often based more on seniority than on performance. In unionized organizations, union rules and contracts may dictate salary levels to a greater extent than the supervisor. The success of performance management does not require a link to pay, although that link may make both employees and supervisors more aware of the importance of appraisals and planning activities. The need to include as much objectivity as possible in appraisals increases with the link to pay. If there is no obvious linkage, supervisors may have a tendency toward "grade inflation" or leniency in ratings. Supervisors generally find it more comfortable to discuss positive ratings and results than to focus on areas where objectives are not being met. This tendency leads to a sense of unfairness in the workforce and discounts the opportunities that performance planning and appraisal provide.

A successful performance appraisal occurs when a supervisor and employee reach a better understanding of the employee's performance level and develop a plan to further improve performance.

## Transfer, Promotion, and Termination

Evaluations can be helpful in determining the strengths and areas in need of improvement for employees. The evaluation process can also yield information that assists the human resources staff with decisions related to the most useful placement of employees. One of the most important functions of a human resources department is identifying the best position fit for employees. Effective transfer and promotion strategies are an essential component of this process. Transferring and promoting exiting employees allows individuals to grow within the organization. The opportunity to progress within the organization is a major factor in retaining productive employees.[16]

Human resources personnel must also recognize situations in which the best move for the employee is out of the organization. Though this is the most difficult component of human resources, it is necessary and crucial for success of the organization. Failure to address problem employees can limit organizational effectiveness.

Human resource departments have traditionally focused on schedules and benefits and pay structure and grievance procedures. Yet, a great opportunity exists for human resources to impact the effectiveness of the organization by working with managers to match employees with the position or work that needs to be done. And, perhaps more importantly, to address those employees who are not suited to the position or the organization.[17]

### Dealing with Difficult Employees

While in training at the University of North Carolina at Chapel Hill, Public Health Leadership Institute Scholars from across the United States had 1158 peers, superiors, subordinates, and clients complete the Center for Creative Leadership's (CCL) Benchmarks assessment to evaluate their skills in meeting job challenges, leading people, and respecting self and others. The results over the three cohorts were remarkably consistent. For all three, the number one leadership deficit was in; "confronting problem employees."[24] You might say this is not a leadership skill; this is a basic personnel management skill.

Leaders in public health will say they are rated poorly at confronting problem employees because they work within civil service systems, with unions and government bureaucracies that limit their flexibility. However, the 88,731 private-sector respondents who have evaluated their leaders with the CCL's Benchmarks instrument, also have identified "failure to confront problem employees" as the number one deficit for over 10,000 leaders who work in Fortune 500 companies, associations, non-profits, the military, and the government.[24] Clearly, we in public health are not unique in not having the skills—or the incentives or support systems—to address problem employees.

## Personnel Policies

Policies that implement basic rules of the organization and provide management intent are important to successful personnel management. At a minimum, an organization should have specific agency or organizational policies on such topics as affirmative action, violence in the workplace, the use of drugs and alcohol by employees, outside employment, use of the various types of leave, work hours, disability accommodations, employee grievances, and sexual harassment. Many of these policies are determined by the need to clarify how the agency or organization will respond to legal questions and challenges. With specific policies in place, an organization is better equipped to deal with employee behavior issues and lawsuits. It is important that each employee has a copy of the current policies. These should be provided at a new employee orientation and followed with periodic issuance of policies to all staff members. Policies should be signed by the top-level manager to illustrate that they are organization-wide policies and decisions. Policies should cite relevant law and other directives such as state or local rules.

## Chapter Review

1. The foundation of the human resources department is built upon job analysis and developing effective descriptions. It is difficult to make appropriate recruitment and selection decisions without clear direction.
2. Although personnel management responsibilities are the overall responsibility of the human resources office, all managers and all supervisors deal with personnel management every day. The human

resources office provides guidance and direction with the various personnel functions and deals with the most difficult personnel issues.

3. Diversity is encouraged to yield skills and experience in the workforce that are appropriate for the populations served.

4. Human resources staff must work with managers to determine the best fit within the organization. This is an ongoing, iterative process that contributes to the overall effectiveness of the organization.

5. Personnel policies should spell out the basic rules of the organization, including those pertaining to affirmative action, violence in the workplace, the use of drugs and alcohol, outside employment, employee grievances, work hours, various types of leave, and sexual harassment.

## References

1. Buckingham M, Coffman C. *First, Break all the Rules.* New York, NY: Simon & Schuster; 1999:27–28.

2. Hornsby JS, Kuratko DF. *Frontline HR: A Handbook for the Emerging Manager.* Mason, OH: Texere; 2005:43–60.

3. Hornsby JS, Kuratko DF. Human resource management: critical issues for the 90s. *J Small Business Manage.* 1990;28:9–18.

4. Thielen L, et al. *A Guide for the Recruitment, Selection and Retention of a State Health Officer.* Washington, DC: Association of State and Territorial Health Officials; 1993.

5. Shafritz JM, et al. *Personnel Management in Government, Politics and Process.* New York, NY: Marcel Dekker Inc; 1986:28–30.

6. McConnell CR. *The Effective Health Care Supervisor.* 4th ed. Gaithersburg, Md: Aspen Publishers Inc; 1997:461–471.

7. Mountain States Employers Council. *Top Ten Errors Made by Interviewers.* Denver, CO: Mountain States Employers Council Inc; 1999.

8. Neale MA, Northcraft GB. Factors influencing organizational commitment. In: Steers RM, Porter LW, eds. *Motivation and Work Behavior.* 5th ed. New York, NY: McGraw-Hill; 1991:290–297.

9. Steers RM. Antecedents and outcomes of organizational commitments. *Admin Sci Q.* 1977;22:46–56.

10. Koch JL, Steers RM. Job attachment, satisfaction and turnover among public employees. *J Vocational Behav.* 1978;12:199–228.

11. Angle H, Perry J. An empirical assessment of organizational effectiveness. *Admin Sci Q.* 1981;26:1–14.

12. Miles RE, Porter LW, Craft JA. Leadership attitudes among public health officials. *Am J Public Health.* 1966;56(12):1990–2005.

13. Pinder CC. Valence-instrumentality-expectancy theory. In: Steers RM, Porter LW, eds. *Motivation and Work Behavior.* 5th ed. New York, NY: McGraw-Hill; 1991:144–164.

14. Hammer WC. Reinforcement theory and contingency management in organizational settings. In: Steers RM, Porter LW, eds. *Motivation and Work Behavior.* 5th ed. New York, NY: McGraw-Hill; 1991:61–87.

15. Grote D. *The Complete Guide to Performance Appraisal.* New York, NY: Amacon; 1996.

16. Fried BJ. Recruitment, selection, and retention. In: Fried BJ, Fottler MD, Johnson JA, eds. *Human Resources in Health Care: Managing for Success.* 5th ed. Washington, DC: AUPHA; 2005:163–204.

17. Buckingham M, Coffman C. *First, Break All the Rules*. New York, NY: Simon & Schuster; 1999:99–105.
18. Association of State and Territorial Health Official, Council of State Governments, National Association of State Personnel Executives. *State Public Health Worker Shortage*. Washington, DC: ASTHO; 2004.
19. Council of State Governments, National Association of State Personnel Executives. *The Trends Alert: State Employee Workforce Shortage*. Lexington, KY: Council of State Governments; 2002.
20. Council on Linkages Between Academia and Public Health Practice. *Evidence-Based Forum on Effective Recruitment and Retention Efforts*. Washington, DC: Council on Linkages; 2004.
21. Still DJ. *High Impact Hiring: How to Interview and Select Outstanding Employees*. Dana Point, Calif: Management Development Systems; 2001: 27–53.
22. Siering M. Interview techniques can separate prime candidates from 'wannabes.' *Denver Business Journal*. November 14, 1997.
23. Porter J, Baker EL. The management moment: management is a team sport. *J Public Health Manage Practice*. 2004;10:564–566.
24. Porter J, Baker EL. The management moment: the coach in you. *J Public Health Manage Pract*. 2004;10:472–474.

## CHAPTER 10

# LEADERSHIP FOR PUBLIC HEALTH

Tausha D. Robertson
Claudia P. Fernandez
Janet Porter

## Chapter Overview

The changing landscape in public health requires rapid responses to emerging crises and long-term attention to necessary system changes. Agencies and organizations must lead by having individuals with the appropriate skills tackle such lofty tasks. As a result, leadership training, support, and development must become a high priority. This chapter will review several leadership theories and applications in public health. Essential skills and leadership development for public health leaders will also be addressed.

The case of a public health leader is typically one of being thrust into the leadership spotlight despite little or no training in leadership, per se. At times these leaders find themselves being promoted, because of technical expertise, into positions requiring additional skills that they have yet to develop. Even those who do not seek positions of leadership can find that the spotlight of leadership is thrust upon them by chance or circumstance as public health issues emerge. The need for effective leadership to help manage changing and turbulent times brings up many questions. Participants in our public health leadership retreats and fellowships often ask:

- Are leaders born or made? Is it nature or nurture?
- What are the essential skills of public health leadership?
- How does one lead in a changing landscape?
- What is the difference between leadership and management?
- What is transformational leadership all about? Do I need to transform my organization to be an effective leader?
- How do I measure my leadership growth and development?

## The Nature vs. Nurture Debate

Leadership has been a topic of discussion for thousands of years. Aristotle taught that from birth, some are marked for subjugation and others for command. Philosophers heralded this "Great Man" (or "Great Woman") theory for millennia, with the idea that only "great people are worthy."[1] Of course, it is easy to identify great leadership in hindsight when history has the end of the story recorded. However, it is far more challenging to predict the future. Theories about predicting and teaching leadership have abounded for the past 100 years.

In the perpetual nature vs. nurture argument, trait theories clearly fall into the nature camp.[2] Early theories of leadership postulated that certain personal characteristics, such as mental, physical, or cultural attributes, separate great leaders from followers or unsuccessful leaders,[3] and hence became known as the "Great Person" theory of leadership. More recent research suggests that the traits that contribute to effective leadership include drive, leadership motivation, honesty and integrity, self-confidence, cognitive ability, ability to motivate others, knowledge of the business, and ability to create a strong sense of shared values.[4-15] Although these traits seem to lend themselves to leadership, research has failed to reveal any individual traits that predict leadership effectiveness or success or to even separate leaders from followers.[2,4,16]

There are no known ways to teach the traits attributed to "great" leaders.[1] It may be that possessing these traits helps the individual acquire the experience and skills necessary for successful leadership. The concept that certain individuals have particular gifts which make them more suited to the role than others "contrasts sharply with the mundane, practical, and yet important conception that leadership is really managing work that other people do."[1] It may be that a combination of leadership traits and management skills serve to create "great public health leaders." Possession of a specific trait does not guarantee leadership success; rather, it is the behaviors employed by an individual that have the greater impact on their leadership performance.[1,2,17]

## Essential Skills and Competencies for Public Health Leadership

Vast arrays of skills have been identified as necessary for leaders, including decision making, risk taking, building internal capacity, creating sustainable vision and translating that to a mission,[11,12,14] communicating, and learning from experience, among others.[12,14] Table 10-1 provides a listing of leadership skills gleaned from a wide variety of leadership research.[10-12,14,18-20]

The National Public Health Leadership Development Network has developed a framework to provide standards for professional development and to measure leadership performance in public health.[21] Skills are listed in four leadership practice categories: transformation, legislation and politics, transorganization, and team and group dynamics.

Transformation requires that leaders engage in systems thinking. Rarely are public health issues resolved within an organization. It usually requires change to the overarching systems that impact the health of the public. Systems thinking utilizes both analytical and critical thinking processes. Leaders should be able to envision what the future may hold by conducting a tactical assessment of the changing environment and key indicators. The

**TABLE 10-1  Leadership Skills**

| | | |
|---|---|---|
| • Self-awareness | • Self-confidence | • Persuasion |
| • Creating sustainable vision and translating that to a mission | • Learning from experience | • Creating partnerships/ fostering collaboration |
| | • Continuous quality improvement (CQI) | • Developing others |
| • Decision making | • Risk taking | • Building internal capacity |
| • Problem solving | • Priority setting | • Negotiation |
| • Creative thinking | • Maintaining credibility | • Delegating |
| • Strategic thinking | • Teaching | • Creating organizational slack |
| • System thinking | • Building teams within the institution | • Forming teams and coalitions |
| • Entrepreneurial ability | • Marketing | • Management techniques |
| • Building trust | • Building relationships | • Sensitivity |
| • Working effectively in social systems | • Communicating | • Building infrastructure (e.g. improve information system capabilities) |

goal should be to develop long-term strategic plans rather than narrow short-term solutions to immediate issues.[21]

Legislation and politics challenge a leader to adapt to changing political climates and agendas in order to push forward with necessary change. To do this, one must be skilled in negotiation and able to collaborate with others in the political landscape. Leaders who are able to navigate in the political realm may be more effective, since public health is heavily affected by legislation and policy at the local, state, and national level.[21] Public health issues traverse a wide variety of organizations, communities, and agencies. Effective leaders must possess the ability to work beyond the confines of their organizations. Organizations that operate in a silo are unlikely to produce widespread impact on the health of the public.

Managing teams and groups dynamics is a necessary skill for leading in public health. Emerging and existing issues require cooperation between individuals and groups to reach a common goal. Effective leaders are able to build team capacity and strengthen their capabilities to complete the task at hand.[21]

The National Public Health Leadership Institute (PHLI), a year-long continuing education program for senior leaders offered through a partnership between the University of North Carolina School of Public Health, Kenan-Flagler Business School, and the Center for Creative Leadership, echoes the need for similar skills. Table 10-2 outlines the leadership skills and competencies addressed in the program.[22]

## Situational Leadership

Depending on the situation, the particular health department, and its community partners, a public health leader may have a great deal of influence over

## Communication

Whetton and Cameron interviewed employees in North America to learn the most effective behaviors leaders and managers can employ in their organizations. Their findings have relevance for public health leaders as well. According to the study, effective communication ranked number one in terms of the behaviors attributed to successful leaders.[49] As public health leaders are faced with a greater number of issues that are increasingly more complex, health literature illuminates a set of communication skills that include:[11,50,51]

- Making one's intentions and positions clearly known
- Consistency in what is communicated
- Surfacing, managing, and negotiating conflict through communication
- Giving feedback and encouragement
- Persuasion
- Creating meaning and understanding or sense making
- Effective writing and reporting
- Reflective listening
- Interpersonal relating
- Facilitation skills

It is important to note that many of these skills are embedded in the Public Health Leadership Competency Framework developed by the National Health Leadership Network.[21]

the environment, or very little. The situational or contingency-style leadership models may hold some promise of guidance for public health leaders as they acknowledge the complex, evolving world within which these executives work and the diverse groups with whom they work.

With growing evidence that different leadership styles are called for in different organizations and under different conditions, research theory focuses on what is called situational leadership style. This theory emphasizes the importance of adaptability of the traits and behaviors on the leader's part as a central component of his ability to be effective.[2,4,23–26] The very nature of change within organizations and their climate underscores the importance of a leader possessing a variety of leadership skills from which she can choose as situations demand.

Some consider situational leadership as a theory that attempts to integrate what is known about leadership into a comprehensive model.[2] Three

**TABLE 10-2  PHLI Key Leadership Skills and Competencies**

1. Use systems thinking to lead innovation and change.
2. Partner effectively with communities.
3. Negotiate relationships with partners and stakeholders.
4. Communicate effectively in crisis and high-risk situations.
5. Reflect and act upon personal leadership strengths and weaknesses.
6. Envision the public health future, and develop and lead teams to create it.

basic factors form the core of this theory, including the amount of task-oriented behavior, leadership-oriented behavior, and the readiness level that organizational members exhibit in performing a task, function, or objective.[2,25]

Blanchard's situational leadership model translates four main skills into four behaviors or orientations of leaders towards followers: directing, coaching, supporting, and delegating.[25] Applying this theory to public health leadership, one would suspect that delegation of responsibility to the organization's workforce is a commonly employed style.

However, situations may arise where a public health leader must exert directing behaviors, particularly when unpopular decisions must be made and enforced. If a public health leader relies on a portfolio of leadership skills to suit different situations, it is imperative that the leader knows when and where to use them.

Recent research by the Hay/McBer firm indicates that flexibility of leadership skills and the leader's emotional intelligence are associated with positive changes in organizational climate. In studying a random sample of 3871 executives, they found six distinct styles of leadership including the coercive, authoritative, affiliative, democratic, pacesetting, and coaching styles. In this study, climate refers to six key factors that influence an organization's working environment: flexibility, responsibility, standards, rewards, clarity, and commitment. They concluded that leaders who have greater diversity of leadership styles, or basically those who have more flexibility, are more successful. In their study, the most positive effect on climate was associated with the use of the authoritative, affiliative, democratic, and coaching styles, which masterful leaders have the flexibility to switch between seamlessly when needed.[3]

## Management vs. Leadership

The development of the transformational theories of leadership stimulated a reconsideration of the concepts of *leadership* and *management* and initiated drawing distinctions between the two. These differences have not been entirely clear, as there has been great confusion in terminology, and these distinctions may be largely academic rather than practical in nature. Many authors seem to use the words almost interchangeably at times while others are quick to illustrate the distinctions between management and leadership as if it represents a litmus test of the truly effective executives.[1,2]

Although there do seem to be a set of practical and important tasks that fall under "management" and a set that belong under the heading of "leadership," some actions that have passed for leadership in health systems, organizations, and in the literature really represent management skills. Before refocusing on leadership skills, it is important to note that some management aspects of a public health practitioner's work can not be exchanged for leadership. There is great inherent value to enabling people and ideas to interact to "establish strategies and make decisions." It is not leadership alone that makes public health systems function. Although the distinction is primarily an academic one, the difference between leadership and management behaviors raises many questions. The context itself may contribute much to the evaluation and categorizing of behaviors; some fall more cleanly into the two groups.

**Effective Partnerships**

The complexity of major public health problems extends beyond any single stakeholder group, community, profession, organization, or agency. As such, the ability to create successful partnerships is a critical leadership skill.[21] These partnerships need to transcend the public health issue of the moment or latest funding stream or personal connection between two leaders and need to be deep-seated organizational commitments to diligently work together on intransigent issues.[52]

Without question the key to a good partnership lies in careful partner selection. Even then, many times it is clear that there are dominant organizations in the community that must be partners in order for an initiative to get off the ground. It is critical that the partners selected balance your agency, bring resources, expertise, political connections, and bring past experience—especially in the areas where you are lacking. Leaders must have an honest sense of their organization's strengths and vulnerabilities in order to select a partner that will fill in skill or asset gaps. Select partners who provide balance, complement your organization, and provide political strength, resources, or the credibility necessary to get the job done.[52] Once the selection process has occurred, the literature indicates that there are key steps to implementing effective partnerships. One such example is the Childs and Dobbins three-stage model of partnership implementation called The Developmental Process of Successful Partnership Working.[53] The formative phase includes the identification of champions in the partner organization to kick-start the process, develop a vision, and create a climate of equality for the entities involved. The second phase outlines achieving agreement that entails identifying additional champions in the partner organization, designating personnel to carry out partnership duties, communicating openly to foster goodwill and commitment, and establishing clarity about each partner's contribution and expectations. The final phase is sustaining the partnership. Partnerships are sustained when they have ownership and commitment at the highest levels of the organization. In addition, both organizations must demonstrate value to the other in order to justify continuing the relationship.[53,54]

In essence, management holds a primary allegiance to the organization and fulfills certain roles because they are attached to the position. Managers may set production goals for an organization, assign workloads, and ensure that workers have the requisite skills and materials necessary to complete their assigned tasks. Leadership, on the other hand, is the way managers get things done by inspiring the best performance and building the internal capacity of an organization in sometimes nontangible ways.[2] Although a central role of administration, leadership is merely one role of management. However, the peril is that public health leaders will engage only in management and not in leadership because of lack of training and experience or because of organizational constraints. Although a public health leader may benefit from leadership skills, he or she must not simultaneously relinquish his or her management duties. An ability to seamlessly execute both when necessary is a skill that is vital to successful public health leaders.

The current academic thinking holds that while management talent is an important component of administration, it is quite different from those of leadership. Traditional management follows a transactional model, in which work is exchanged for rewards.[2,4,17,26,27] Here, the leader works to maintain the status quo and preserve the current working criteria. Playing within the rules, maximizing personal rewards, and providing incentives commensurate with performance are thought to support only ordinary performance in organizations.[2] In transformational leadership, however, upsetting the status quo to create new rules that optimize the system using an interdependent structure are proposed to create extraordinary results. Table 10-3 lists the functions and orientations that fall under each task domain.[1,2]

Kotter draws even further distinctions between management and leadership skills.[28] According to Kotter, management copes with complexity while leadership copes with change. An important management skill is to plan and

**TABLE 10-3    Transactional vs. Transformational Leadership: Differences Between Managing and Leading**

| | Transactional Leadership or Management Skills | Transformational Leadership or Leadership Skills |
|---|---|---|
| Performance: | Considered by leadership writers to produce ordinary performance | Considered by leadership writers to produce extraordinary performance |
| Goal: | To maintain the status quo by playing within the rules | To change the status quo by changing the rules |
| Goals arise out of: | Necessity, are reactive, and respond to ideas. They are deeply imbedded in the organization's history and culture | Desires; they are active, shaping ideas; may be a departure from organization's history and culture |
| Emphasis: | Rationality and control, limits choices, focuses on solving problems | Innovation, creativity to develop fresh approaches to long-standing problems, and open issues to new options |
| Attitudes towards goals: | Impersonal, if not passive attitudes | Personal and active attitude |
| Incentives: | Based on exchange of needs (i.e., "tit for tat") | Based on the greater good |
| Locus of reward: | Maximize personal benefits | Optimize systemic benefits |
| Requires: | Persistence, tough-mindedness, hard work, intelligence, analytical ability, tolerance, and good-will | Genius and heroism |
| View work as: | Enabling processes, ideas, and people to establish strategies and make decisions | Creative, energizing, and emerging |
| Tactics employed: | Negotiate and bargain, use of rewards, punishment, and other forms of coercion | Inspire followers, create shared vision, motivate |
| | Strive to convert win-lose into win-win situations as part of the process of reconciling differences among people and maintaining balances of power | Strive to create new situations and new directions without regard to reconciling groups or power |

budget, while the leadership counterpart is to set a direction. Managers use organizing and staffing to achieve the institutional plan while leaders align people to achieve organizational objectives. Controlling and problem solving skills are employed by managers to ensure that plans are accomplished while leaders motivate and inspire people to achieve the mutual vision.

## Transformational Leadership

Trait-based theories of leadership have seemingly reemerged as transformational leadership. These theories acknowledge the power and influence of an individual with the gift for more than just leading their organizations—but rather transforming them. According to Burns, transformational leaders and followers are intimately intertwined and need to raise each other to higher levels of motivation and morality.[29] Values and evolving interrelationships characterize this type of leadership that is supposed to continually evoke motivation from followers "in a ceaseless process of flow and counterflow."[4] This theory focuses on three key dimensions of leader behavior that are heralded in an almost magical way: envisioning, energizing, and enabling.[4]

More contemporary theorists Bennis and Nanus,[30] writing in the mid-1980s, also studied the nature of transformational leadership and provided a list of steps for individuals to follow in their pursuit of becoming transformational leaders of their organizations. Bennis and Nanus suggest that individuals do the following:[30]

- Develop a clear and appealing vision.
- Develop a strategy for attaining the vision.
- Articulate and promote the vision.
- Act confident and optimistic.
- Express confidence in followers.
- Use early success in small steps to build confidence.
- Celebrate suggestions.
- Use dramatic, symbolic actions to emphasize key values.
- Lead by example.
- Create, modify, or eliminate cultural norms.
- Use rites of transition to help people through change.

Many of these strategies appear in later theories by other leadership gurus promoting total quality management,[31] continuous quality improvement,[32] models of driving down decision making and learning and teaching behavior,[14,33] chaos theory,[34] knowledge organizations,[35,36] and systems thinking.[37,38]

Leaders transform their organizations by creating and communicating a strategic image of the future that excites their followers. They create the language of the organization that makes it an informed, aware, communicating whole, or in other words create a conversation "flow."[39] To transform public health, it is suggested that leadership must enable followers by empowering them through the use of personal-oriented leadership traits, such as the ability to express support, empathy, and confidence in followers, to empower them to face challenging goals on their own.[4,40,41]

While transformational leadership was the buzzword of the 1990s, it was not without its critics. In 1995, John Kotter noted several reasons why transformation efforts fail, citing eight errors organizations commonly make that undermine their ability to create, implement, and sustain the vision that guides the transformation.[42] Many of these errors fall within a leader's sphere of influence: keeping a vision alive, refraining from declaring victory too soon, and assuring that there are small victories along the path of change to keep employee motivation.

One of the greater challenges to transformational leadership is the tendency to revert back to the known culture, an effect separately described by Robert Fritz and John Kotter.[42,43] According to this theory, over a matter of just a few years the institution can "forget" the transformational process if it is not constantly reinforced by management. Fritz also suggests that staff turnover may play an important role in transforming organizational culture, as loss of personnel tends to erase or erode institutional memory. Being a successful transformational leader in public health presents a difficult challenge indeed.

## Measuring Leadership Growth and Development

One question most good leaders ask is "How am I doing as a leader?" To address this it is important to understand how leadership is measured. Due to the influence of situational factors, the progressive and repetitive nature of learning, and the time it takes to move from a theory one espouses to a theory one puts into use, it can be difficult to assess how far one's leadership needle has moved. Several psychological assessment instruments can help with leadership development and self-insight. The primary focus of these tools is to help the leader understand him- or herself better, to promote self-reflection, and to apply knowledge about him- or herself and others into leadership practice. The goals of development using such instruments are to help the individual appreciate the contributions of others; to understand effective communication styles with a variety of people; to gain insight into creating and sustaining an organizational culture that allows for normal differences in perspectives, types, and temperaments; to motivate and empower one's self and others; and to understand how one's own behavior can be interpreted or "read" by others in organizations.

It is estimated that at any given time about 2300 leadership assessment instruments are available, yet only 3–5% of these have scientific validity or reliability testing to support them.[44,45] Although instruments that do not have scientific rigor might help start an interesting conversation about leadership, there is a distressing tendency for individuals to self-label after receiving instrument feedback, thus such nonscientifically grounded instruments should be used with caution. Table 10-4 lists a sample of scientifically sound leadership instruments and the topic areas for which they may be useful. This is not a comprehensive list of the 140 or so quality instruments available, but it does survey some of those most respected and broadly used.

It is vital to note that leadership assessment instruments are designed to inform learners about their behaviors, perspective, biases, and beliefs in relation to the larger world around them. These instruments should be administered and debriefed (counseled) by a professional with the appropriate background, usually certification in the instrument. Instruments are not intended to be used for decisions about hiring, work load assignment, downsizing, and so on, as

**TABLE 10-4    Leadership Assessment Instruments and Applications**

| Instrument | Instrument Focus: Provides feedback on | Areas of Application |
|---|---|---|
| **360° Instruments** A variety of instruments exist that examine skill sets by industry, level of seniority, etc. Example: A public health-specific 360 is available from Discover Learning (Discovery Learning.com) | Specific set of organizationally desirable behaviors from boss, superiors, peers, direct reports | Provides a "snapshot" of leadership performance along many domains |
| **180° Instruments** Example: The Kaplan Leadership Versatility Index180 assesses the capacity to strike balances across the opposite types of leadership. (www.kaplandevries.com) | Provide feedback on specific domains of skill from boss/ superiors and peers | Balance in skills and assessment of overleveraging of skills in areas of natural tension (e.g., forceful and enabling leadership) |
| **Personality Inventories** Example: Myers Briggs Type Indicator (MBTI) | Personality type preferences for interacting with others, gathering information, evaluating information, and lifestyle choices | Organizational culture, understanding others, communication |
| **Behavior Inventories:** Example: Fundamental Interpersonal Relationships Orientations-Behavior (FIRO-B) | How behaviors are read by others in organizations | Communication, leading others, motivating others |
| Example: California Psychological Inventory 260 (CPI 260) | Benchmarks 26 behavior sets against "ordinary people" | Leading others, gaining insight into how one's behaviors are similar or different to others |
| Example: CPI 260 Coaching Report for Leaders | Benchmarks 20 behavior sets against those of senior leaders and managers from the CCL database | Leading others, gaining insight into how one's behaviors are similar or different to other successful leaders |
| **Change Inventories** Example: Change Style Indicator | Approach to change: originator, pragmatist, or conserver | Dealing with change, understanding how others approach change, communication around change, adapting to situational change |
| **Emotional Intelligence** Examples: Bar-On EQi and the Mayer-Salovey-Caruso Emotional Intelligence Test (MSCEIT) | Ability to solve emotional problems and perform tasks either by subjective assessment of perceived emotional skills or by ability-based skill measures | Dealing with people skills, soft skills, and areas that require "noncognitive" intelligence. Communicating with others, creating organizational culture, motivating others |

**TABLE 10-4    (continued)**

| Instrument | Instrument Focus: Provides feedback on | Areas of Application |
|---|---|---|
| **Thomas-Kilman Conflict Mode Instrument** | Methods of dealing with conflict, including competing, collaborating, compromising, avoiding, and accommodating | Dealing with conflict, anger, and relating to others |

they are generally not skill-based inventories. Because many of these are self-report instruments, it is essential that the individual completing them understand that they are (1) confidential between the coach/counselor and themselves; (2) for their personal use, insight, and leadership development; (3) are not intelligence tests; and (4) are not skill-based assessments and thus have no right or wrong answers. Leadership instruments help individuals objectively view and understand the impact of their behavior on others, both positively and negatively. Thus, they help the individual to make informed choices about how they interact with others.

These psychological assessment instruments are not designed to be implemented in a test-retest fashion, as if to imply that a different score would be more desirable. Statistical test-retest validation studies actually examine the stability of the instrument. Furthermore, the importance of context can not be underemphasized. Context is one of the primary tasks of the coach to explore during the debriefing process. When objectives such as a "higher score" are a part of the assessment, the quality and truthfulness of the answers must be called into question. For example, if a job candidate who completes the Myers Briggs Type Indicator (MBTI) believes that someone with an extraverted personality is desired for the position, she might answer falsely in order to appear as a stronger candidate for the position, rather than for what is her true preference. Continuing with this example, applying leadership assessment tools to hiring decisions also inaccurately implies that someone who prefers an introverted style could not execute the job equally well as someone with an extraverted personality preference. There is no relationship between scores on an instrument such as the MBTI and skill at implementing tasks commonly associated with the preferences. There are other skill-based inventories that do measure intelligence, mathematical ability, logical deductive reasoning, and so on. Although these may be used in hiring decisions, they are not used in leadership development and are not addressed here.

The cornerstone instrument for many programs is a 360° feedback instrument.[46,47] These tools provide a snapshot of current leadership performance as assessed in the individual's current work environment by direct reports, peers, and superiors (some versions of these instruments are "180°s" and do not include feedback from direct reports). It is quite insightful for leaders to have 360° feedback as they consider the information from other leadership instruments which may be used. Although psychological assessment instruments have some limitations, participants generally find them invaluable as

---

**Using 360° Feedback in a Local Health Department**

The City of Milwaukee Health Department (MHD) evaluated the use of a 360° feedback system as a component of their ongoing total quality improvement program. The use of such instruments has been limited in public health while widely utilized and accepted in corporate settings. The pilot program in Milwaukee was well received and deemed valuable by the organization's leadership. Interviews with the health commissioner and health operations director yielded comments such as:[55] "It was an effective mechanism to not only introduce, highlight, and assess key skills for managers, but also to help them improve those skills." "It changed our managerial climate and managerial expectations." As a result of the positive evaluation results, Swain et al concluded that 360° feedback systems could benefit public health agencies.[55]

---

part of their leadership development, particularly when between three and seven instruments are used over a period of time and the participant is able to work confidentially with a coach to examine the threads or themes in the instruments. It is often helpful to administer/debrief no more than 3 instruments in one leadership session (e.g., during a week-long leadership retreat) and to allow for many months of ongoing consideration and reflection as part of a leadership development program. For all instruments, the coach and the leader should discuss how the insights and items assessed play out in the leader's day-to-day leadership experience.

Although it might seem tempting to readminister a 360° assessment to measure leadership growth, research has shown quite disappointing results caused by response shift bias. Education on any topic typically results in one having a far greater appreciation of their previous ignorance on a topic, and leadership is no different. The same holds true for external observers as well: repeatedly asking stakeholders to rate performance results in lower ratings over time primarily because of their increased attention on the attribute—regardless of the actual changes in performance on the candidate's part. Furthermore, these assessments are time consuming in organizations, which can also impact the quality of the feedback when used sequentially. When outcomes are used to reward, penalize, or judge, it is doubtful the leader will be able to complete the instruments with the openness and honesty required for them to serve a useful purpose. Finally, it is inappropriate to use leadership assessment instruments other than how they were designed as the statistical and validity measures that support them do not apply outside of the design parameters.

## The Importance of Mentoring

A common core to leadership theory is that great leaders are made by experience, by the work of insight, by personal growth, and by learning from mentors.[1] Thus, it is imperative that public health invest in developing its leaders through leadership training, support, coaching, and mentoring. All too often individuals are promoted based on their technical expertise and come to leadership positions unprepared for some of the delicate tasks that lay before them. Their leadership potential can be enhanced by careful nurturing of and reflection on the perspective, biases, and beliefs that are the underpinning of how they exercise their skills.

## Chapter Review

1. Possession of a specific trait does not guarantee leadership success; rather it is the behaviors employed by an individual that has the greater impact on their leadership performance.
2. The skills linked to effective leadership can be learned. The National Public Health Leadership Institute utilizes the following as key leadership skills and competencies:
   • Use systems thinking to lead innovation and change.
   • Partner effectively with communities.
   • Negotiate relationships with partners and stakeholders.
   • Communicate effectively in crisis and high-risk situations.
   • Reflect and act upon personal leadership strengths and weaknesses.
   • Envision the public health future, and develop and lead teams to create it.
3. The very nature of change within organizations and their climate underscores the importance of a leader possessing a variety of leadership skills from which he or she can choose as situations demand.
4. Leadership skills must be continually refined and developed. Numerous leadership assessment instruments are available to assist with this process. It is important to work with trained professionals to select a well-rounded leadership development program that will serve the needs of your organization.

## References

1. Zaleznik A. Managers and leaders: are they different? *Harvard Business Rev.* 1992;March–April:126–135.
2. Pointer DD, Sanchez JP. Leadership: a framework for thinking and acting. In: Shortell SMK, Arnold D, eds. *Health Care Management: Organization Design and Behavior.* 4th ed. Albany, NY: Delmar, Thompson Learning; 2000:106–129.
3. Goleman D. Leadership that gets results. *Harvard Business Rev.* 2000: 78–90.
4. Bowditch JL, Buono AF. *A Primer on Organizational Behavior.* 4th ed. New York, NY: John Wiley & Sons; 1997.
5. Cocowitch V. Introduction to leadership. In: PUBH 300 Leadership class S, ed. Chapel Hill, NC; 2000.
6. O'Brian WJ. The soul of corporate leadership: guidelines for values-centered governance. *Innovations In Management Series.* Waltham, Mass: Pegasus Communications, Inc; 1998.
7. Farkas CM, Wetlaufer S. The ways chief executive officers lead. *Harvard Business Rev.* 1996;May-June:110–122.
8. Manz CC, Sims HP. *Super Leadership: Leading Others to Lead Themselves.* New York, NY: Prentice-Hall; 1989.

9. Kouzes JM, Posner BZ. *The Team Leadership Practices Inventory (TEAM LP): Measuring Leadership of Teams, Participant's Workbook*. San Francisco, Calif: Jossey-Bass Pfeiffer; 1995.

10. Kouzes J. Finding your leadership voice. In: Hesselbein F, Cohen PM, eds. *Leader to Leader*. San Francisco, Calif: Jossey-Bass Publishers; 1999.

11. Kouzes J, Posner B. *The Leadership Challenge: How to Get Extraordinary Things Done in Organizations*. San Francisco, Calif: Jossey-Bass; 1988.

12. Van Velsor E, McCauley C, Moxley R. Our view of leadership development. In: McCauley CDeaE, eds. *The Center for Creative Leadership Handbook of Leadership Development*. San Francisco, Calif: Jossey-Bass; 1998.

13. Labarre P. Do you have the will to lead? *Fast Company*. 2000:222–230.

14. Pfeffer J, Sutton R. *The Knowing-Doing Gap: How Smart Companies Turn Knowledge Into Action*. Boston, Mass: Harvard Business School Press; 2000.

15. Rowitz L. *Public Health Leadership: Putting Principles into Practice*. Gaithersburg, Md: Aspen Publishers Inc; 2001.

16. Lord RG. An information processing approach to social perceptions, leadership and behavioral measurement in organizations. In: Cummings LL, Staw BM, eds. *Research in Organizational Behavior*. Greenwich, Conn: JAI Press; 1985.

17. Van Vleet DD, Yukl GA. A century of leadership research. In: Rosenbach WE, Taylor RL, eds. *Contemporary Issues in Leadership*. Boulder, CO: Westview Press; 1989:65–90.

18. Upshaw VM, Sollecito WA, Kaluzny AD. Leadership in public health. In: Novick LF, Mays GP, eds. *Public Health Administration*. Gaithersburg, Md: Aspen; 2001:567–584.

19. Labarre P. Do you have the will to lead? An interview with Peter Koestenbaum. *Fast Company*. 2000;March:222–230.

20. Warden GL. Reflections and projections. Presented at: PUBH 395 Leadership Seminar; 2001; Chapel Hill, NC.

21. Wright K, Rowitz L, Merkle A, et al. Competency development in public heath leadership. *Am J Public Health*. 2000;90:1202–1207.

22. About the National Public Health Leadership Institute. Available at: http://www.phli.org/aboutPHLI/index.htm. Accessed December 19, 2005.

23. Hersey P, Blanchard KH, Johnson DE. *Management of Organizational Behavior: Utilizing Human Resources*. 7th ed. Upper Saddle River, NJ: Prentice-Hall; 1996.

24. Hersey P, Blanchard KH. *Management of Organizational Behavior: Utilizing Human Resources*. Englewood Cliffs, NJ: Prentice-Hall; 1977.

25. Blanchard K. *Situational Leadership: The Article*. Escondido, Calif: The Ken Blanchard Companies; 1994.

26. Hersey P, Blanchard KH. *The Management of Organizational Behavior*. 2nd ed. Englewood Cliffs, NJ: Prentice Hall; 1984.

27. House R. A path-goal theory on leader effectiveness. *Admin Sci Q*. 1971; 16:321–338.

28. Kotter JP. What leaders really do. *Harvard Business Rev*. 1990:43–50.

29. Burns JM. *Leadership*. New York, NY: Harper & Row; 1978.

30. Bennis WG, Nanus B. *Leaders: the Strategies for Taking Charge*. New York, NY: Harper & Row; 1985.

31. Kim DH. Towards learning organizations: integrating total quality control with systems thinking. *Innovations in Management Series*. Waltham, MA: Pegasus Communications; 1997.

32. James BC. Implementing practice guidelines through clinical quality improvement. *Frontiers of Health Serv Manage*. 1993;10(1):3–37.

33. Tichy NM, Cohen. E. *The Leadership Engine: How Winning Companies Build Leaders at Every Level.* New York, NY: Harper Business, HarperCollins Publishers; 1997.
34. Wheately M. *Leadership and the New Science.* San Francisco, Calif: Berrett-Koehler Publishers; 1992.
35. Argyris C. Teaching smart people how to learn. *Harvard Business Rev.* 1991;May–June:99–102.
36. Drucker PF. The new society of organizations. *Harvard Business Rev.* 1992;Sept–Oct:95–104.
37. Senge PM. *The Fifth Discipline.* New York, NY: Doubleday; 1990.
38. Senge PM, Ross R, Smith B, Roberts C, Kleiner A. *The Fifth Discipline Fieldbook—Strategies and Tools for Building a Learning Organization.* New York, NY: Doubleday; 1994.
39. Isaacs W. *Dialogue and the Art of Thinking Together.* New York, NY: Random House; 1999.
40. Tichy NM, Devanna MA. *The Transformational Leader.* New York, NY: John Wiley; 1986.
41. Tichy NM, Devanna MA. The transformational leader. *Train Dev J.* 1986;July(a):27–32.
42. Kotter JP. Leading change: why transformation efforts fail. *Harvard Business Rev.* 1995;March–April:59–67.
43. Fritz R. *Corporate Tides: The Inescapable Laws of Organizational Structure.* San Francisco, Calif: Berrett-Koehler Publishers; 1996.
44. Pearman R. In: Fernandez CP, ed; 2005.
45. Buros Institute of Mental Measurements. Available at: http://buros.unl.edu/buros/jsp/search.jsp. Accessed November 15, 2005.
46. Lepsinger R, Lucia AD. *The Art and Science of 360-Degree Feedback.* San Francisco, Calif: Pfeiffer; 1997.
47. Chappelow CT. 360-degree feedback. In: C.D. M, ed. *The Center for Creative Leadership Handbook of Leadership Development.* San Francisco, Calif: Jossey-Bass; 1988.
48. Rohs FJ. Response-shift bias: a problem in evaluating leadership development with self-report pre-test post-test measures. *J Agricult Educ.* 1999;20:4.
49. Whetten DA, Cameron KS. *Developing Management Skills.* 4th ed. New York, NY: Addison-Wesley; 1998.
50. Farrell J, Robbins M. Leadership compentencies for physicians. *Healthcare Forum.* 1993;36:39–42.
51. Beckham J. Tools for staying ahead in the nineties. *Healthcare Forum.* 1991;34:84–90.
52. Porter J, Baker E. The management moment: selecting partners and setting the stage. *J Public Health Manage Pract.* 2005;11(4):369–372.
53. Childs J, Faulkner D. *Strategies of Cooperation: Managing Alliances, Networks and Joint Ventures.* Oxford, UK: Oxford University Press; 1998.
54. Wildridge V, Childs S, Cawthra L, Madge B. How to create successful partnerships—a review of the literature. *Health Info Libr J.* 2004;21(Suppl 1):3–19.
55. Swain GR, Schubot DB, Thomas V, et al. Three hundred sixty degree feedback: program implementation in a local health department. *J Public Health Manage Pract.* 2004;10(3):266–271.

# CHAPTER 11

# PUBLIC HEALTH DATA ACQUISITION

C. Virginia Lee

## Chapter Overview

Data in public health are needed for community health assessment, strategic planning, and evaluation. Attribute data include demographics, socioeconomics, health expenditures, disease prevalence, and mortality. Behavioral risk and environmental information are also key to appraising the health communities. Data are available from federal, state, and local sources. Many of the different organizations within the Department of Health and Human Services (HHS) have different data systems that can be applied to population-based health managers. Of these, the Centers for Disease Control and Prevention (CDC) is a major federal source of data for community health planning and measures of preventive effectiveness. State sources of data include vital statistics, disease registries, and Medicaid reports. Local data are available from disease reporting, special surveys, and, increasingly, managed care sources.

A major use of data in public health today is to perform community health assessments and enhance community planning by providing the information needed to use tools adequately such as Mobilizing for Action through Planning and Partnerships (MAPP) developed by the National Association of County and City Health Officials (NACCHO) and the CDC.[1] Assessment and performance measures are discussed in greater detail in Chapters 15 and 17 respectively. In this chapter, several categories of data are examined, including demographics, socioeconomics, health care expenditures, healthcare resources and utilization, environmental hazards, as well as specific health indicators such as mortality data, years of potential life lost, and disease prevalence. This chapter reviews federal and state sources of data for use in community health planning and the geographic level for which the data are available. Additionally, local health surveys are discussed and the use of managed care data is reviewed. The chapter concludes with some important issues to consider when using data, such as access and confidentiality.

## Historical Perspective on Data Collection

Governments have found it useful to collect statistics on the population, animals, and objects under their jurisdiction since the beginning of civilization. The ancient Babylonians made tabulations of agricultural yields and commodities. Around 600 BCE, the ancient Greeks used censuses as a basis for taxation. The Roman Empire was the first government to make extensive documentation of the land it controlled and the populations residing on that land. Registration of deaths and births began in England in the 1500s.

### Census of the Population

The first census of the population in the United States was conducted in 1790 when US marshals collected the data with the help of hired assistants. The first census consisted of six questions.

1. Name of head of household
2. Number of free white males 16 years of age and older
3. Number of free white males under 16 years of age
4. Number of free white females
5. Number of other free persons
6. Number of slaves

The form of the census stayed essentially the same for the next 50 years. In 1840, the government expanded the scope of the census to cover agriculture. By 1860, there were six separate questionnaires with 142 questions. Among the topics covered in the various questionnaires were population, health, mortality, occupation, income, and agriculture. In 1880, Congress created a temporary civilian census office to handle the data collection. The US Bureau of the Census as a permanent organization within the government was established in 1902. The 1950 decennial census was the first in which computer technology was used to tabulate the data.

### Vital Statistics

The legal authority to register births, deaths, marriages, divorces, fetal deaths, and abortions lies with the states and territories.[2] Virginia first enacted a registration law in 1632, followed by Massachusetts in 1639. Early in the 1800s, the decennial census contained questions about births and deaths. However, the results were inconsistent. In 1902, when the Census Bureau was established as a permanent agency, it was authorized to obtain annual copies of records that were kept by state vital statistics offices. In 1880, a national death registration area was established. Later in 1900, a standard certificate of death was recommended. The national birth registration area was established in 1915. By 1933, all states were registering live births and deaths to an extent that national birth and death statistics could be produced.[3] In 1946, responsibility for collecting and publishing national-level vital statistics was transferred to the US Public Health Service.

### Reportable Diseases

In the United States, the first collection of data on selected diseases was for diseases in other countries for the purposes of quarantine. In 1878, Congress authorized the US Marine Hospital Service to collect morbidity reports on cholera, smallpox, plague, and yellow fever for US consuls overseas.[3] In 1893, the authority for data collecting and reporting was expanded to include state and municipal data. Legislation enacted in 1902 required that the surgeon general provide forms for the collection of data at a national level in an effort to provide uniformity to the system. The first notifiable diseases annual summary in 1912 had data from 19 states, the District of Columbia, and Hawaii. By 1928, all states, the District of Columbia, Hawaii, and Puerto Rico were participating. Data were reported for 29 specific diseases.[3] In 1961, the CDC assumed responsibility for the collection and publication of data concerning nationally notifiable diseases.

## Present National Uses of Data

The *Healthy People* series is a nationwide public health planning tool that identifies the most significant preventable threats to health and focuses public- and private-sector efforts to address those threats. *Healthy People* is based on scientific data and is designed to be used for decision making. The first set of national health targets was published in 1979 in *Healthy People: The Surgeon General's Report on Health Promotion and Disease Prevention.*[4] This set of five challenging goals, to reduce mortality among four age groups—infants, children, adolescents and young adults, and adults—and increase independence among older adults, was supported by objectives with 1990 targets that drove action.

*Healthy People 2000: The National Health Promotion and Disease Prevention Objectives* was released in 1990.[5] It is a comprehensive agenda organized into 22 priority areas, with 319 supporting objectives. Three overarching goals are to increase years of healthy life, reduce disparities in health among different population groups, and achieve access to preventive health services. In the *Healthy People 2000 Final Review*, 21% (68 of 319 unduplicated objectives) met the year 2000 targets and an additional 41% showed movement toward the targets. Data for 11% showed mixed results, and 2% showed no change from the baseline. Only 15% showed movement away from the targets. The status of 10% could not be assessed.[6] In the priority focus area of mental health and mental disorders, significant reversals were seen specific to objectives involving interventions in high-risk environments (prisons, adults not taking steps to control stress) and suicide attempts among adolescents. In the priority focus area of diabetes and chronic disabling conditions, several of the objectives moved away from their targets (most related to prevalence of diabetes and its complications). The full final report for *Healthy People 2000* is available at www.cdc.gov/nchs/products/pubs/pubd/hp2k/review/review.htm.

*Healthy People 2010 (HP2010)* began to be developed in 1996 at a meeting of the Healthy People Consortium—an alliance of 350 national membership organizations and 300 state health, mental health, substance abuse, and environmental agencies. At that meeting, consortium members discussed the year 2000 framework, goals, objectives, and improvements needed to make the 2010 agenda relevant to the first decade of the 21st century. From that meeting and a series of other meetings and forums, a number of focus areas have been identified for *HP2010*. (See Chapter 2 for a detailed discussion.) Table 11-1 shows those focus areas and the federal agency or office within the HHS that is responsible for the lead on each area. In 2005, there was a midcourse review that recommended modifications in some of the objectives. Those recommendations went out for public comment in the fall of 2005. For a full listing of the recommendations and the public comments, go to www.healthypeople.gov/data/midcourse/default.asp.

## Federal Sources of Data

The federal government has been moving towards providing data, services, and information over the Internet. In 2000, in keeping with the movement towards electronic government (e-gov), a government-wide portal (FirstGov. gov) was launched online. FirstGov.gov is an interagency initiative administered by the US General Services Administration. FirstGov.gov is the official US gateway to all government information. The Reference Center of the FirstGov.gov Web site provides links to data and statistics from most government agencies.

In the 1970s, the federal government sponsored several studies examining mapping activities among government agencies. Those studies generally confirmed that there was widespread duplication of effort. In 1983, the Office of Management and Budget (OMB) began to address these problems when it issued a memorandum establishing a formal committee with the specific charge of coordinating digital cartographic activities among federal agencies. This committee, known as the Federal Interagency Coordinating Committee on Digital Cartography (FICCDC) was chaired by the Department of the Interior and included representatives from the Departments of Agriculture, Commerce, Defense, Energy, Housing and Urban Development, State, Transportation, Federal Emergency Management Agency, and National Aeronautics and Space Administration. The FICCDC was specifically charged to "improve the use of digital cartographic base data within the federal government and to provide a framework for its proper management." Throughout the 1980s, the use of geographic information systems (GIS) increased markedly as they were found to be cost-effective ways of handling large volumes of data to assist decision makers. (Refer to Chapter 12 for further discussion of GIS.) The OMB directed the FICCDC to examine its mission and the expanded spatial data coordination role to address these changes. OMB issued a revised Circular A-16 on October 19, 1990, formally establishing the Federal Geographic Data Committee (FGDC). The committee, chaired by the Secretary of the Interior, involved federal, state, and local governments, as well as private sector entities concerned with spatial activities. The FGDC was directed to develop the National Spatial Data Infrastructure (NSDI). The NSDI is viewed as a series of actions (such as standards creation) to bring about improved collection, sharing, and use of geographic information. It provides a base or structure of relationships among data producers and users, and a foundation for data applications, services, and products.

The Department of the Interior sponsors an intergovernmental project, the Geospatial One Stop, which builds upon its partnership with the FGDC to

**TABLE 11-1** *Healthy People 2010* **Focus Areas and Their Lead Federal Agencies**

| Focus Area | Agency/Staff Office Lead/Co-Lead Responsibility |
|---|---|
| Access to quality health services | Agency for Healthcare Research and Quality, Health Resources and Services Administration |
| Disability and secondary conditions | Centers for Disease Control and Prevention, Department of Education/National Institute on Disability and Rehabilitation Research |
| Educational and community-based programs | Centers for Disease Control and Prevention, Health Resources and Services Administration |
| Environmental health | Agency for Toxic Substances and Disease Registry, Centers for Disease Control and Prevention, National Institutes of Health |
| Family planning | Office of Public Health and Science, Office of Population Affairs |
| Food safety | Food and Drug Administration |
| Health communication prevention and health promotion | Office of Public Health and Science, Office of Disease, Centers for Disease Control and Prevention |
| Heart disease and stroke | National Institutes of Health, Centers for Disease Control and Prevention |
| Injury/violence prevention | Centers for Disease Control and Preventionn |
| Kidney disease | National Institutes of Health |
| Maternal, infant, and child health | Health Resources and Services Administration, Centers for Disease Control and Prevention |
| Medical product safety | Food and Drug Administration |
| Mental health and mental disorders | Substance Abuse and Mental Health Services Administration, Centers for Disease Control and Prevention |
| Nutrition | Food and Drug Administration, National Institutes of Health |
| Occupational safety and health | Centers for Disease Control and Prevention |
| Oral health | Centers for Disease Control and Prevention, National Institutes of Health, Health Resources and Services Administration |
| Physical activity and fitness | Office of Public Health and Science, President's Council on Physical Fitness and Sports, Centers for Disease Control and Prevention |
| Public health infrastructure | Centers for Disease Control and Prevention, Health Resources and Services Administration |
| Respiratory diseases | National Institutes of Health, Centers for Disease Control and Prevention |
| Sexually transmitted diseases | Centers for Disease Control and Prevention |
| Substance abuse | Substance Abuse and Mental Health Services Administration, National Institutes of Health |
| Tobacco use | Centers for Disease Control and Prevention |

*Source:* Reprinted from *Healthy People 2010, Understanding and Improving Health,* Vol. I, US Department of Health and Human Services.

improve the ability of the public and government to use geospatial information to support the business of government and facilitate decision making. Individuals can access spatial data and find links to data for significant events such as Hurricane Katrina at the Web site for the project (www.geo-one-stop.gov/).

## United States Geologic Survey

As part of any community health assessment, it is essential to define the community or target population. The United States Geologic Survey (USGS) is a science organization that focuses on biology, geography, geology, geospatial information, and water in the study of the landscape, our natural resources, and the natural hazards. Among the data sources that the USGS provides is leadership on the National Map project (http://nationalmap.gov/index.html). The USGS provides access to the geospatial data in the National Map. Through the Seamless Data Distribution System, USGS provides free downloads of national base layers, as well as other geospatial data layers. These layers are divided into the following framework categories:

- Places
- Structures
- Transportation
- Boundaries
- Hydrography
- Orthoimagery
- Land cover
- Elevation

The data available in this survey may be useful for both community health assessments and strategic planning.

## The Centers for Disease Control and Prevention (CDC)

The mission of the CDC is to promote health and quality of life by preventing and controlling disease, injury, and disability. The CDC is considered the primary prevention agency within the federal government. As such, it is one of the primary sources of data for community health planning and monitoring prevention effectiveness. The National Center for Health Statistics (NCHS) at the CDC provides a central resource for population-based managers. The center collects data from "birth and death records, medical records, interview surveys, and through direct physical exams and laboratory testing."[7] Table 11-2 shows examples of vital statistics data that are useful for healthcare planning as well as selected sources of that information.

### National Center for Health Statistics

There are numerous programs within the NCHS. For example, The National Health and Nutrition Examination Surveys consist of a series of surveys that were undertaken by the NCHS. The purpose of these surveys was to estimate the national prevalence of selected diseases and risk factors, to estimate na-

**TABLE 11-2    Data for Community Health Planning: Perinatal Indicators, Mortality, and Years of Potential Life Lost (YPLL)**

| Category | Source | Data Set Name | Small Geographic Unit |
|---|---|---|---|
| Perinatal indicators (e.g., total live births, teenage live births, prenatal care, low body weight live births, live births with mortality or birth defects) | 1. National Center for Health Statistics | 1. National Vital Statistics Program (birth and fetal death certificate) | 1. County |
| | 2. Centers for Disease Control and Prevention | 2. Abortion services statistics | 2. States |
| | 3. State or local registries | 3. Congenital malformation or birth defect registries | 3. County Limited Local |
| Mortality (e.g., leading causes or mortality by age and population subgroups) | 1. National Centers for Health Statistics | 1. National Vital Statistics Program (compressed mortality file) | 1. County |
| | 2. State vital statistics | 2. State vital statistics | 2. Street |
| Years of potential life lost (YPPL) | 1. State vital statistics | 1. YPPL statistics are derived from age of death on death certificate | 1. County |

*Source:* Reprinted with permission. Lee CV, Irving JL. Sources of spatial data for community health planning. *J Public Health Manage, Pract.* 1999;5(4):9–13, Table 1.3.

tional population reference distributions of selected health parameters, and to investigate reasons for trends in selected diseases and risk factors. The first National Health and Nutrition Examination Survey (NHANES I) was conducted from 1971 to 1974.[8] The purpose was to measure indicators of the nutrition and health status of American people through dietary intake data, biochemical tests, physical measurements, and clinical assessments for evidence of nutritional deficiency. The target population was the civilian, noninstitutionalized population, 1–74 years of age, living in the coterminous United States. Native Americans residing on reservations were not included. NHANES II was conducted from 1976 to 1980 and expanded the nutrition component.[9] The medical components of primary interest were diabetes, kidney and liver functions, allergy, and speech pathology. The target population was expanded to include those persons 6 months to 74 years of age, including people in Alaska and Hawaii. There was oversampling of those persons aged 6 months to 5 years, those aged 60–74 years, and those living in poverty areas. NHANES III was conducted from 1988 to 1994 and included those persons 2 to 6 months of age in the target population.[10] There was oversampling of children aged 2 to 35 months, persons over 69 years of age, Black Americans, and Mexican Americans. Table 11-3 includes data from CDC surveys as well as those of other agencies. In 1999, NHANES became a continuous annual survey rather than a periodic survey. Data from the surveys are released every 2 years. Since 2003, the content of the survey questions has been kept constant for the 2-year data release cycles. Data files for 1999–2000 (interview sample size

**TABLE 11-3    Data for Community Health Planning: Hospitalization, Ambulatory Medical Care, and Estimated Prevalence of Disease**

| Category (Examples) | Source | Data Set Name | Smallest Geographic Unit |
|---|---|---|---|
| Hospitalization (e.g., leading causes of hospitalization by age and population subgroup) | 1. National Center for Health Statistics<br>2. Health Care Financing Administration<br>3. Dartmouth Center for Clinical Evaluative Services<br>4. Medicaid Data System | 1. National Hospital Discharge Survey<br>2. Medicare Statistical System<br>3. Dartmouth Atlas of Health Care | 1. Census regions<br>2. State<br>3. Hospital referral region |
| Ambulatory medical care | 1. National Center for Health Statistics | 1. National Hospital Ambulatory Medical Care Survey<br>2. National Ambulatory Medical Care Survey | 1. Four national regions<br>2. Four national regions |
| Estimated prevalence of disease | 1. National Center for Health Statistics<br><br>2. Centers for Disease Control and Prevention<br><br>3. National Institutes of Health<br><br>4. State cancer registries | 1a. National Health Interview Survey<br>1b. National Health and Nutrition Examination Survey<br>2a. National Notifiable Diseases Surveillance System<br>2b. AIDS surveillance<br>3. Surveillance, Epidemiology, and End Results (SEER) Program<br>4. Cancer and tumor registries | 1. National<br><br><br>2. State<br><br><br><br>3. County<br><br>4. County, ZIP code, limited street |

*Source:* Reprinted with permission. Lee CV, Irving JL. Sources of spatial data for community health planning. *J Public Health Manage Pract.* 1999;5(4):9–13, Table 1.3.

9965), 2001–2002 (interview sample size 11,039), and 2003–2004 (interview sample size 10,122) have been released.

The National Health Care Survey (NHCS) provides results of surveys of a variety of health care providers. There are many specific surveys including those involving inpatient care, long-term facilities, and outpatient care. For example, the National Health Provider Inventory (National Master Facility

Inventory) is a comprehensive file of inpatient health facilities in the United States. There are three categories of facilities in the inventory: hospitals, nursing and related care facilities, and other custodial or remedial care facilities. Hospitals must have at least six inpatient beds, and other facilities must have at least three inpatient beds to be included in the inventory. The inventory is kept current through reports from state licensing and other agencies for all newly established facilities. In addition, there is a yearly survey of hospitals and periodic surveys of other facilities. The National Hospital Discharge Survey is a continuing nationwide sample survey of short-stay hospitals in the United States. Before 1988, lengths of stay greater than 30 days were excluded. Presently, the only exclusions are discharged newborn infants and discharges from federal hospitals. Abstracts of patient records are prepared from the sample of selected hospitals. Similarly, the National Home and Hospice Care Survey is an annual national survey of home health agencies and hospices that was begun in 1992. A sample of current and discharged patients is conducted by staff that is familiar with the type of care being received. With respect to outpatient care, the National Ambulatory Medical Care Survey is a continuing national sample survey of ambulatory medical encounters *outside* of hospitals. The survey covers patient–physician encounters with nonfederally employed physicians. Excluded from the survey are telephone contacts; nonoffice visits; visits to hospital-based physicians; visits to anesthesiologists, pathologists, and radiologists; and physicians involved in research, teaching, or administration. A random sample of office visits to eligible physicians is carried out. In contrast, the National Hospital Ambulatory Medical Care Survey is a continuing annual national sample survey that was initiated in 1992 to examine visits to emergency departments and outpatient departments *inside* nonfederal, short-stay, or general hospitals. Telephone contacts are excluded. Hospital staff is asked to complete patient record forms for a random sample of patient visits during a 4-week reporting period.

The National Health Interview Survey (NHIS) is a continuing nationwide sample survey in which data are collected through personal household interviews. Information is collected on personal and demographic characteristics as well as on illnesses, injuries, impairments, chronic conditions, utilization of health resources, and other health topics. The response rate for the survey has been between 95–98% over the years. In 1985, the NHIS began an oversampling of the African-American population to improve the precision of the statistics.

The National Vital Statistics Program is a major source of national-level vital statistics information that is collected by the NCHS. The NCHS collects and publishes data on births, deaths, marriages, and divorces in the United States. Since 1985, all states and the District of Columbia have participated in the Vital Statistics Cooperative Program (VSCP), sending 100% of their birth and death records to the NCHS. Data are collected using the US standard live birth and death certificates and fetal death reports. The latest revision of these standard certificates was in 1989 when Hispanic ethnicity was added. Among the data on the standard certificates that are collected by some states are maternal education, prenatal care, marital status of mother, Hispanic births, tobacco use, education of the decedent, and Hispanic deaths. Data from the program are available at the county level. An additional source of state or county level data is the Compressed Mortality File, a county-level national mortality and population database. The mortality database is derived from the detailed mortality files of the National Vital Statistics Program. The population database is derived from intercensal estimates and census counts of the resident population of each US county by 5-year age groups, race, and sex. Counties are categorized according to level of urbanization based on the rural–urban continuum codes developed by the Economic Research Service of the US Department of Agriculture (USDA). These data are available at the CDC's WONDER (Wide-ranging OnLine Data for Epidemiologic Research) home page. Refer to Chapter 13 for further information.

In addition to the just mentioned data systems, the NHCS has other comparable data sets available from the CDC Web site including the National Immunization Survey, the Longitudinal Studies of Aging, the National Survey of Family Growth (addressing data on fertility, family planning, contraception, and other related topics), and the State and Local Area Integrated Telephone Survey (SLAITS), a survey tool used to collect state and local data on a variety of health-related issues.

## Other Sources of Data from the CDC

The National Notifiable Diseases Surveillance System provides weekly provisional information on the occurrence of diseases that are defined as notifiable by the Council of State and Territorial Epidemiologists. The system provides summary data on an annual basis. The reporting of the states and territories to the CDC is voluntary. For example, Acquired Immune Deficiency Syndrome (AIDS) surveillance is conducted by health departments in each state, territory, and the District of Columbia. Reporting sources include hospitals and hospital-based physicians, physicians in nonhospital practice, public and private clinics, and medical records systems. The health departments collect data without personal identifiers using a standard confidential case report form.

The National Traumatic Occupational Fatalities Surveillance System is one of several data systems compiled by the National Institute for Occupational Safety and Health (NIOSH) and available on the CDC Web site. This system is based on information taken from death certificates. The following criteria are used to select the death certificates: age 16 years or older, an external cause of death (ICD-9, E800–E999), and a positive response to the "Injury at work?" item on the death certificate. Guidelines have been completed for filling out the injury at work item so the capture of data should improve. Denominator data come from the Census Bureau's county business patterns, supplemented by employment data for agriculture derived from the Census Bureau's 1982 census of agriculture and public administration employment data taken from the Bureau of Labor Statistics' annual average employment data for 1980–1989. Rates are figured for the US civilian labor force. Many other databases about occupational health, such as asbestosis or asthma, are available although there are commonly limitations such as the number of states participating in surveys. Table 11-4 shows select data sources that provide information regarding occupation and other activities or behaviors that can influence health.

From a perspective of community health planning, a number of important health problems (e.g., cardiovascular disease, cancer) have a relatively

**TABLE 11-4   Data for Community Health Planning: Occupational Health and Safety, Substance Abuse, Mental Health/Mental Retardation, Behavioral Risk Factors, and Lifestyle Marketing Data**

| Category | Source | Data Set Name | Smallest Geographic Unit |
|---|---|---|---|
| Occupational health and safety | National Institute for Occupational Safety and Health Bureau of Labor Statistics | National Traumatic Occupational Fatalities Surveillance System | 1. State |
| Substance abuse (e.g., drug-related deaths and emergency room visits, alcohol-related deaths and accidents) | Substance Abuse and Mental Health Services Administration | National Household Surveys on Drug Abuse Drug Abuse Warning Network | 1. Four US regions 2. Metropolitan areas |
| Mental health/ mental retardation (e.g., teenage suicides, serious mental retardation in school-age children) | Substance Abuse and Mental Health Services Administration | Monitoring the Future Survey of Mental Health Organizations | 1. National |
| Behavioral risk factors (e.g., current smokers, sedentary lifestyle, not using seat belts) | Centers for Disease Control and Prevention | Behavioral Risk Factor Survey | 1. State |
| Lifestyle marketing data | Commercial sources (e.g., CACI International or Claritas) | Neighborhood or lifestyle segmentation | 1. Census tract |

*Source:* Reprinted with permission. Lee CV, Irving JL. Sources of spatial data for community health planning. *J Public Health Manage Pract.* 1999;5(4):9–13, Table 1.3.

long latency period. To plan community interventions, information is needed about behavioral risk factors (e.g., smoking habits, physical activity, diet, and health insurance), as well as morbidity and mortality. At the national level, the CDC has collaborated with state health departments since 1981 on a Behavioral Risk Factor Surveillance System (BRFSS), in which each state conducts a telephone survey of a sample of state residents using uniform questions. Similarly, in 1990, the Youth Risk Behavior Surveillance System was developed to address trends in health risk behaviors in youth. Summary data are made available at the state level. Because behavioral risk factor information is quite useful at the local level, some local health departments are now starting to develop behavioral risk factor surveys specific for their jurisdiction. For example, in New York State in 2003, an expanded BRFSS provided data at the local level.

Since 1994, the CDC has administered the National Program of Cancer Registries (NPCR). In 2004, the CDC's NPCR supported central registries and promoted the use of registry data in 45 states, the District of Columbia, and the territories of Puerto Rico, the Republic of Palau, and the Virgin Islands. The CDC also is conducting special research projects such as studies to examine patterns of cancer care in specific populations. The CDC's goal is for all states to maintain registries that provide high-quality data on cancer and cancer care. NPCR complements the National Cancer Institute's (NCI) Surveillance, Epidemiology, and End Results (SEER) registry program. Together, NPCR and the SEER program collect cancer data for the entire US population.

### National Institutes of Health (NIH)

The NIH is one of the world's foremost biomedical research centers and the federal focal point for biomedical research in the United States. The NIH's mission is to uncover new knowledge that will lead to better health for everyone. The NIH works toward that mission by conducting research in its own laboratories; supporting the research of nonfederal scientists in universities, medical schools, hospitals, and research institutions throughout the country and abroad; helping in the training of research investigators; and fostering communication of biomedical information. The goal of NIH research is to acquire new knowledge to help prevent, detect, diagnose, and treat disease and disability.

The NIH has developed the NIH Information Index to provide information on: (1) diseases that are currently under investigation by the NIH or NIH-supported scientists, (2) major NIH research areas, and (3) important health-related topics. Each listing in the index includes the abbreviated name(s) of the NIH institute, center, division, or other component to call for information, as well as the appropriate phone number(s).

One of the most widely used data sources from the NIH is the Surveillance, Epidemiology, and End Results (SEER) Program. The National Cancer Institute contracts with selected population-based cancer registries throughout the United States and Puerto Rico to collect data for the SEER Program on residents who have recently been diagnosed with cancer and to collect follow-up data on persons who were previously diagnosed with cancer. The population estimates used to calculate incidence rates are obtained from the Census Bureau. Sample rates from the collecting centers are used to estimate county rates for the entire country. The SEER Program gathers in-depth data on cancer cases diagnosed in Connecticut, Hawaii, Iowa, New Mexico, and Utah, as well as in six metropolitan areas and several rural and special population areas. The six metropolitan SEER registries and some of the rural and special population registries submit data to the CDC NPCR's state registries. In 2001, SEER began providing additional support to four NPCR-supported state registries (California, Kentucky, Louisiana, and New Jersey).

The National Cancer Institute has developed a cancer mortality maps and graph Web site that provides interactive maps, graphs, text, tables, and figures showing geographic patterns and time trends of cancer death rates for the time period 1950–1994 for more than 40 cancers.

The NIH has also funded studies and surveys that provide important health information such as the Monitoring the Future Study (high school senior survey). This is a large-scale annual survey of drug use and related attitudes that was begun in 1975. Data are collected using self-administered questionnaires that are given out in classrooms. In 1991, the study was expanded to include eighth and tenth graders. The survey tool is administered with the same questions over several years to the same population to determine trends in "behaviors, attitudes and values."[11]

## The Centers for Medicare and Medicaid Services (CMS)

In 2001, the Health Care Financing Administration was restructured into the CMS. The CMS administers the Medicare program and partners with states to administer the Medicaid program and the State Children's Health Insurance Program (SCHIP). The CMS is also responsible for the administrative aspects of the Health Insurance Portability and Accountability Act of 1996 (HIPAA— discussed later in the chapter), quality standards for healthcare facilities, and clinical laboratory standards. The CMS provides data on its Medicare and Medicaid services, which include data on enrollment, spending, and claims data. The CMS' *National Health Expenditures* contains data on spending for health care in the United States by type of service delivered (hospital care, physician services, nursing home care, and so on) and source of funding for those services (such as private health insurance, Medicare, Medicaid, out-of-pocket spending). Expenditure estimates for 1960–2003 are currently available. Similarly, *Health Care Indicators* contains data and analysis of recent trends in healthcare spending, employment, and prices. The National Health Statistics Group tracks trends in healthcare-related industries and presents this information quarterly.

## Health Resources and Services Administration (HRSA)

The HRSA directs national health programs that improve the health of the nation by ensuring quality health care to underserved, vulnerable, and special-need populations and by promoting appropriate health professions workforce capacity and practice, particularly in primary care and public health. The HRSA has developed a geospatial data warehouse to provide access to information about their programs and health resources that HRSA monitors. The health system data includes data on health professional shortage areas (HPSA), medically underserved areas/populations (MUA/P), health workforce composition, health professionals, primary care service areas (PCSA), and healthcare facilities.

## Agency for Toxic Substances and Disease Registry (ATSDR)

The ATSDR was established as an agency of the HHS by the Superfund Act. Examples of sources of data available from the ATSDR include the agency's Hazardous Substance Release/Health Effects Database (HazDat) and environmental exposure registries. HazDat was developed to provide access to information concerning the release of hazardous substances from Superfund sites or from emergency events and to provide information on the effects of exposure to hazardous substances on the public's health. The database includes information on the hazardous waste sites, the contaminants present at the sites, the concentration of the contaminants, the impact on populations, and community health concerns. Environmental exposure registries exist for several chemicals including benzene, trichloroethylene, and dioxin. Persons who have been identified as having environmental exposures to these chemicals are followed through the registries and are given questionnaires to identify any health complaints. Data are available only for the entire registry population and not for local areas.

### Substance Abuse and Mental Health Services Administration (SAMHSA)

The SAMHSA is the federal agency charged with improving the quality and availability of prevention, treatment, and rehabilitation services in order to reduce illness, death, disability, and cost to society resulting from substance abuse and mental illnesses. The National Survey of Substance Abuse Treatment Services (N-SSATS) is part of SAMHSA's Drug and Alcohol Services Information System (DASIS), a cooperative program between the state substance abuse agencies and the SAMHSA to collect data on the location, characteristics, and utilization of services at alcohol and drug abuse treatment facilities (both public and private) throughout the 50 states, the District of Columbia, and other US jurisdictions.

The SAMHSA conducts the National Surveys on Drug Use and Health (before 2002 this was called the National Household Surveys on Drug Abuse) to collect data on trends in the use of marijuana, cigarettes, alcohol, and cocaine among persons 12 years of age and older. The SAMHSA began collecting data for the survey in 1971. The survey covers the civilian, noninstitutionalized population 12 years of age and older in the United States. Persons from 12 to 34 years of age, African-Americans, Hispanics, and individuals in six selected large metropolitan areas are oversampled. Approximately 70,000 people are surveyed annually.

The Office of Applied Statistics at the SAMHSA runs the Drug and Alcohol Services Information System (DASIS), the primary source of national data on substance abuse treatment. DASIS has the following three components:

- The Inventory of Substance Abuse Treatment Services (I-SATS) is a listing of all known public and private substance abuse treatment facilities in the United States and its territories. Before 2000, the I-SATS was known as the National Master Facility Inventory.
- The National Survey of Substace Abuse Treatment Service (N-SSATS) is an annual survey of all facilities in the I-SATS that collects information on location, characteristics, services offered, and utilization. The N-SSATS includes a periodic survey of substance abuse treatment in adult and juvenile correctional facilities. Before 2000, the N-SSATS was known as the Uniform Facility Data Set (UFDS).
- The Treatment Episode Data Set (TEDS) is a compilation of data on the demographic and substance abuse characteristics of admissions to substance abuse treatment facilities. Information on treatment admissions are routinely collected by states. This involves data on almost 2 million admissions reported by over 10,000 facilities to the 50 states, District of Columbia, and Puerto Rico annually.

The Drug Abuse Warning Network (DAWN) is a large-scale, ongoing drug abuse data collection system based on information from emergency room and medical examiner facilities. The system collects information about drug abuse occurrences that resulted in a medical crisis or death. The objectives of the system are to monitor drug abuse patterns and identify trends, identify substances associated with drug abuse episodes, and assess the drug-related health consequences. The system was first developed in 1978 and was redesigned in 1988. In 2003, DAWN was redesigned to expand beyond drug abuse and to function as a public health surveillance system that monitors the following:

- Drug-related visits to hospital emergency departments (EDs)
- Drug-related deaths investigated by medical examiners and coroners (ME/Cs)

The purpose of this surveillance system is to help communities and member facilities identify emerging problems, improve patient care, and manage resources.

## Other Federal Sources of Information

### US Bureau of the Census

The mission of the Census Bureau is to be the preeminent collector and provider of timely, relevant, and quality data about the people and economy of the United States. Its goal is to provide the best mix of timeliness, relevancy, quality, and cost for the data collected and the services provided. The bureau has 12 regional offices with additional processing centers set up temporarily for the decennial censuses. The sole purpose of the censuses and surveys is to secure general statistical information. Replies are obtained from individuals and establishments only to enable the compilation of such general statistics. The confidentiality of these replies is very important. By law, no one—neither the census takers or any other Census Bureau employee—is permitted to reveal identifiable information regarding any person, household, or business.

Accurate and current demographic data (e.g., age, sex, race, ethnic group) and projections are critically important for community planning and for denominators for the computation of rates. The decennial census (e.g., 1990 or 2000) is the gold standard and is available from the Census Bureau to the census block group level.[12]

Selected socioeconomic variables (e.g., poverty, education level, age of housing) are also available from the Census Bureau to the census block group level. Age of housing is of special interest as part of childhood lead poisoning prevention efforts. In some communities, the tax assessor's office may be able to provide information on age of housing in electronic format. If so, then the local health department's childhood lead poisoning prevention program may find it useful to access and link the electronic housing age data with electronic information about new births. Childhood lead poisoning prevention efforts can then be focused on specific individual houses containing an infant and a high likelihood of the presence of lead-based paint.

The Census Bureau's mapping program supports the decennial census through the production of street-level address maps for use by the census enumerators. For the 1990 census, the TIGER (Topologically Integrated Geographic Encoding and Referencing) system was developed. TIGER uses the street segment to form blocks that are the basis of census geography. TIGER was a collaborative effort between the Census Bureau and the USGS. An important feature of TIGER data is that each geographic unit has a unique identifier that links it to the population attribute data in the main census files, allowing the collection of a great deal of population information for a wide variety of areas.

In 1999, the Census Bureau established the American FactFinder Web site to provide individuals access to data tabulations and maps from the available census data sets. Among the data sets that are presently available in the system are the 1990 decennial census detailed files, the 1997 economic census summary files, the American community survey summary tables, and the Census 2000 dress rehearsal summary files. Table 11-5 includes information on data sets related to demographic or socioeconomic factors.

**TABLE 11-5   Data for Community Health Planning: Demographic, Socioeconomics, Health Care Expenditures, and Health Care Resources and Access to Primary Care**

| Category (Examples) | Source | Data Set Name | Smallest Geographic Unit |
|---|---|---|---|
| Demographic data (e.g., age, sex, race, and ethnic distribution) | US Bureau of the Census | 1. Decennial and periodic census | 1. Census block |
| Socioeconomic data (e.g., educational level, poverty level, percent unemployed, age of housing, and number of workers by industry) | US Bureau of the Census  Bureau of Labor Statistics | 1. Decennial and periodic census 2. County business patterns | 1. Census block group 2. County |
| Healthcare expenditures (e.g., number of persons on Medicaid; number of persons in Women, Infants, and Children Program; number of homeless persons; number of food stamp recipients) | Health Care Financing Administration | 1. Estimates of national health expenditures 2. Estimates of state health expendiures | 1. National 2. State |
| Healthcare resources and access to primary care (e.g., number of primary care physicians, community and migrant healthcare centers, uninsured/ underinsured) | Health Resources and Services Administration | 1. Area resource file 2. Physician supply estimates 3. Nurse supply estimates 4. National Health Provider Inventory 5. National Home and Hospice Care Survey | 1. County 2–5. National |

*Source:* Reprinted with permission. Lee CV, Irving JL. Sources of spatial data for community health planning. *J Public Health Manage Pract.* 1999;5(4):9–13, Table 1.3.

## US Bureau of Labor Statistics

The Bureau of Labor Statistics (BLS) is the major federal agency for collect-ing information in the fields of labor economics and statistics. The bureau is an independent national agency that serves as a statistical resource for the Department of Labor. As an independent agency, the BLS must ensure that the data they collect is relevant to current social and economic issues, timely in reflecting the current economic conditions, accurate, and of high statisti-cal quality. In presenting the data, the BLS must be impartial in the selection and presentation of the subject matter. The surveys and programs of the Bureau of Labor Statistics include a wide range of subjects under the general categories of employment and unemployment, prices and living conditions, compensation and working conditions, productivity and technology, employ-ment projections, and international programs. One useful survey is the Non-Farm Payroll Statistics from the Current Employment Statistics, which includes monthly data on employment, hours, and earnings by industry for selected geo-graphic areas.

## US Environmental Protection Agency (EPA)

The EPA was established to protect human health and the natural environment on which human health depends. Table 11-6 provides details of some of the

**TABLE 11-6    Data for Community Health Planning: Meteorological/ Climatological Data and Environmental Hazards**

| Category | Source | Data Set Name | Smallest Geographic Unit |
|---|---|---|---|
| Environmental hazards (e.g., locations of toxic waste sites) | 1. US Environmental Protection Agency | 1a. Envirofacts data warehouse<br>1b. EPA Spatial Data Library System<br>1c. Better Assessment Science Integrat-ing Point and Nonpoint Sources<br>1d. American Indian Lands Environ-mental Support Project | 1.  Local |
| | 2. Agency for Toxic Substances and Disease Registry | 2a. Hazardous Sub-stance Release/ Health Effects Database<br>2b. Environmental exposure regis-tries for selected chemicals (e.g., benzene, trichlor-oethylene, and dioxin) | 2a. Local site specific<br><br>2b. Registry coverage area |

*Source:* Reprinted with permission. Lee CV, Irving JL. Sources of spatial data for community health planning. *J Public Health Manage Pract.* 1999;5(4):9–13, Table 1.3.

data sets for environmental hazards. In 1987, the EPA established a National Geographic Information Systems Program to coordinate the use of spatial data. The EPA also provides information about systems and software used to support mapping of environmental data (www.epa.gov/epahome/Data.html). The EPA Envirofacts warehouse offers access to several EPA databases to provide spatial data from a variety of sources, in several different mapping applications (www.epa.gov/enviro/). Better Assessment Science Integrating Point and Non-point Sources (BASINS) integrates a geographic information system (GIS), national watershed data, and state-of-the-art environmental assessment and modeling tools into one convenient package (www.epa.gov/OST/BASINS/). The EPA maintains a node on the National Geospatial Data Clearinghouse which is a component of the National Spatial Data Infrastructure (NSDI).

## State Sources of Data

### State Vital Statistics

In the United States, responsibility for the certification of vital events rests with the states. Among the items collected by state vital statistics agencies are information on births, deaths, fetal deaths, and induced terminations of pregnancy (abortions). Consistency of the reporting of information is ensured through contracts between the federal government and the states, providing for standardized certification forms that include a standard set of items needed at the federal level.

*Birth Certificate Data*

Birth certificate data can be very useful in healthcare planning. The registration of births is considered essentially complete, with periodic checks showing registration rates for births at more than 99%. Birth registration in this country has been carried out for many years, allowing for time-period analysis of the data. Geographic coverage of births has been complete since 1933. This allows the researcher to use the data for spatial comparisons. Information collected on the certificates can be used for analysis based on maternal age and race. The information is also useful for studying birth weight and some birth defects. Mothers provide demographic information for birth certificates, and hospital records provide health information. One major difficulty in using birth certificate data for local analysis is that actual residence data may not be available in electronic form. Data are generally kept in electronic form for county or ZIP code, but not necessarily for street address. Birth certificate information includes residence at the time of birth, which is not necessarily the residence at the time of the exposure of interest. Some studies have indicated that in certain populations, up to 30% of women may move during their third trimester. Although some information such as birth weight is generally considered reliable, problems have been noted with the information on APGAR score, gestational age, and prenatal history. Problems also arise when using birth defects information contained on birth certificates because some birth defects do not manifest themselves until the child is older and therefore are not noted when the birth certificate is filled out.

## Death Certificate Information

Death certificate information has similar advantages for healthcare planning as birth certificate information. The registration for deaths is considered essentially complete. And, like birth registration, death registration in this country has been carried out for many years, allowing for time-period analysis of the data. Geographic coverage of deaths has been complete since 1933, allowing the researcher to use the data for spatial comparisons. Information collected on the certificates can be used for analysis based on sex, age, and race. Demographic information on the death certificate is provided by the funeral director. Because certain demographic information (race, ethnicity) for the birth and death certificates is provided by persons with different degrees of closeness to the individual (family member vs. funeral director), the possibility exists that the recorded race of an individual may differ from birth to death. Medical certification of the cause of death is provided by a physician, medical examiner, or coroner. Analysis of death certificate data is most useful for rapidly fatal diseases. As with birth certificates, however, a major difficulty in using death certificate data is that the actual residence data may not be available in electronic form. Data are generally kept in electronic form for county or ZIP code, not necessarily for street address. Death certificate information includes the residence at the time of death, which is not necessarily the residence at the time of the exposure of interest. The data are less useful for examining diseases with long latencies or nonfatal conditions.

## Fetal Death Certificates

Fetal death certificates are required by most states for the certification of fetal deaths after 20 weeks gestation. A problem arises because a fetal death is defined as the death in utero of a fetus that weighs 500 grams or more at birth, irrespective of gestational age. Because the certification requirements do not reflect the definition, the certification of fetal deaths is incomplete. For fetuses born after 28 weeks, certification is nearly complete because most of them weigh greater than 500 grams. However, certification is inconsistent for fetuses born between 20–28 weeks gestation and incomplete for those born less than 20 weeks gestation. The problem of data inconsistency and variability of coverage makes the data from fetal death certifications less useful in geographic analysis.

## Abortion Data

Abortion data are used to provide information on fertility, pregnancy rates, and abortion rates. This information can be used to evaluate the effectiveness of family planning programs and programs aimed at reducing teen pregnancies.

## State Disease Registries

Cancers and tumors are the most common groups of diseases for which registries are established. Reporting is generally close to complete for most areas where the registries exist. The data include information on cancer incidence but not mortality. Information from the registries allows for comparisons by age, sex, and race. Residence is considered a personal identifier, and getting such information from the registries at the local level is difficult. The rates of some rare cancers can be very unstable for small areas such as counties. The longer the latency period of the disease, the less useful is the information available on the disease registry.

Congenital malformation or birth defect registries are much less common than cancer registries. Most such registries are passive (do not actively update or confirm information), so the ascertainment rate is not very high for many defects. Residence is considered a personal identifier, and getting information from the registries at the local level is difficult.

Some states, industrial facilities, the NIOSH, and the military have some form of occupational exposure registries for selected chemicals. The information contained in these registries is most useful for identifying some health effects reported by persons who have been exposed to occupational levels of those chemicals.

### State Medicaid Agency

Created in 1965 under Title XIX of the Social Security Act, Medicaid is a jointly funded, federal–state health insurance program to provide medical assistance for certain low-income and needy people. In 2003, it covered approximately 52 million individuals (up from approximately 36 million in 1996), including children; the aged, blind, and/or disabled; and people who are eligible to receive federally assisted income maintenance payments.[13] Federal statutes and regulations provide broad national guidelines for the program. Each state determines its eligibility standards, the scope of services, the rate of payment for services, and how its program will be administered. There are several categorically needy groups that the states must provide services to if they are to receive federal funds. Managed care as an option for Medicaid recipients continues to increase with approximately 60% in 2004.[14] States maintain data on the recipients of services, the scope of services provided, and the cost of the program. In addition to the federal program, several states have "state-only" programs to provide assistance to certain Medicaid-ineligible groups.

### State Department of Transportation (DOT)

The DOT and its predecessors often represent one of the longest tenured line agency functions in state government. The DOT generally coordinates the development of transportation with each mode serving its best purpose. Under its auspices fall the entire transportation network, including the state and local highway system, a rail network, public and private aviation facilities, public transit operators, and major public and private ports.

### State Planning Agencies

Planning agencies deal with development within their boundaries. Most of planning relates to providing a comprehensive guide to the physical, economic, and social environments of communities. Elements of planning include objectives of land development, zoning controls, transportation, strategies for economic revitalization of depressed areas, and guidelines for environmental protection. Many planning agencies can provide a variety of socioeconomic, demographic, and land use data for use by health care planners.

## Local Sources of Data

Much of the information available from state and federal sources of data is not available at the local level. Local public health agencies therefore have information limitations because data from many of these sources are not applicable to the relatively small geographic areas served by local agencies. In addition, vital statistics data and morbidity data collected and available to local health agencies are restricted in scope and may not fulfill a specific information need associated with a health problem or proposed initiative. (Refer to Chapter 15 for further information on community health assessment.)

One way in which public health agencies can obtain additional information for their service areas is by implementing low-cost telephone surveys. Surveys can be designed to meet the needs of local public health agencies in the form of direct questioning, mail, or telephone queries. The advantage of implementing these surveys by a local health agency is that this method works well to obtain information on a particular objective within a defined community. For successful use of this data collection strategy, the following three requirements must be fulfilled:

1. The design of the survey must ensure that individuals interviewed are representative of the community or group of interest.
2. The survey instrument must be acceptable to respondents in terms of length and content.
3. Implementation cost must be relatively low.

### Using a Telephone Survey to Evaluate a Community Folic Acid Intake Campaign

In October 1996, the Onondaga County Health Department (OCHD) launched a campaign to increase folic acid intake among all women of childbearing age in this county of 470,000 people in central New York State. This initiative was based on the US Public Health Service recommendation that all women capable of becoming pregnant consume 0.4 mg of folic acid daily to reduce the risk of having children with spina bifida and other neural tube defects.[15]

Pre- and postcampaign random telephone surveys were conducted to evaluate changes in awareness and use of multivitamins.[16] The first step was to develop a survey tool. This was accomplished through group discussion and a literature review to locate any existing and relevant survey tools. Two instruments were located. One had been created by the Gallup Organization for the March of Dimes and a second was from the Georgia Women's Health Survey.[17,18] With permission of these two organizations, a modified instrument with approximately 20 questions was prepared.

The following three criteria can be applied to a survey tool:

1. Does the survey address key questions that derive from the campaign's goal and objectives?

2. Does it provide information that will inform decisions?
3. Does it permit delineation of populations or geographic areas at risk?

The draft survey tool was field tested with 60 women to assess time for completion, unexpected reactions, and flow. Next, a statistical sample and sampling frame were developed. The overall goal of the sampling methodology was to collect representative, precise information about knowledge and practice regarding folic acid use for women 18–45 years of age. A goal of at least 650 completed surveys was set for each sample, based on a decision to keep the overall margin of error small.

A random sampling design was used with ZIP codes as sampling units. The objective was that the percentage distribution of the completed surveys across ZIP codes would be the same as the percentage distribution of women between the ages of 18–45 years living in these ZIP code areas. However, after meeting these statistical quotas, oversampling was conducted within targeted ZIP codes to increase sample size for racial and ethnic minorities, who make up less than 10% of the overall population. Readily available computer software with all telephone listings on CD-ROM was used as the source of local phone numbers for the call lists in each ZIP code. The size of these call lists took into account an expected "hit rate" of 15 dials to 1 completed interview based on the pilot study results.[16]

A volunteer workforce was used to staff the 36 calling sessions. The total incremental cost for both the pre- and postsurvey was only $2500, which was mostly related to telephone charges and food for the volunteers.[16] The survey results are illustrated in Figures 11-1 and 11-2.

A telephone survey using similar methodology was used in 1997 to ascertain the rate of mammography utilization in women over the age of 50 years.[19] Results of this survey informed local public health officials and healthcare providers about characteristics associated with screening utilization in the community and were important for community-wide efforts to in-

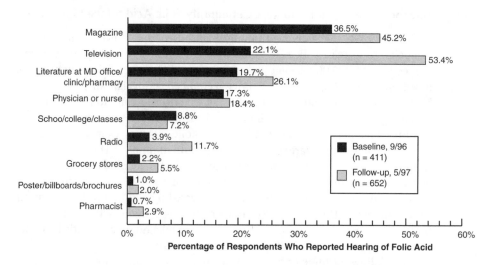

**FIGURE 11-1   Folic Acid Survey, Resident Women 18–45 Years, Onondaga County, NY: Responses to "Where or How Did You Learn About Folic Acid?"**

*Source:* Onondaga County Department of Health, 1997, Onondaga County, New York.

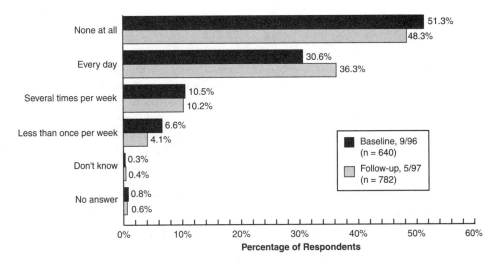

**FIGURE 11-2    Folic Acid Survey, Resident Women 18–45 Years, Onondaga County, NY: Responses to "How Often Have You Taken Multivitamins During the Past 30 Days?"**
*Source:* Onondaga County Department of Health, 1997, Onondaga County, New York.

crease mammography rates. In 2000, a comparable method was used to determine local colorectal cancer screening behaviors. This level of data can be powerful in motivating local policy makers to address identified concerns.

## Other Sources of Data

### Managed Care Data

An increasing proportion of individuals are enrolled in managed care organizations. In addition, many states are enrolling Medicaid recipients into managed care plans for the provision of health services. Data that monitor the receipt of preventive services by managed care organizations are of significant potential importance for public health agencies. Managed care enrollees are a group of individuals who constitute a subpopulation. As enrollment in these plans grows, the aggregate or total of these subpopulations constitutes a substantial proportion of the community population. Data from managed care entities on immunization, blood lead screening, mammography, Pap smear screening, and other factors are important to public health agencies for two reasons: (1) information is provided on the performance of individual plans in delivering preventive services, and (2) information is available on the status of clinical preventive services in a large proportion of community residents.

The opportunity for using this type of data is possible because of the development of the Health Plan Employer Data and Information Set (HEDIS) by the National Committee for Quality Assurance (NCQA). These measures were initially established by representatives from a variety of health plans and employers to respond to employer need: "How to understand what 'value' the healthcare dollar is purchasing and how to hold a health plan 'accountable for its performance.' "[20(p1)] The initial draft document of HEDIS measures was completed in 1991 and incorporated into the NCQA evaluation of health plans.[20] Further information on the NCQA accreditation process may be obtained by contacting the NCQA in Washington, DC (www.ncqa.org).

The standardized performance measures employed by HEDIS include attention to many significant public health issues including cancer, heart disease, smoking, asthma, diabetes, infant mortality, and immunization.[21] The HEDIS Baseline Assessment Tool (2005) has a series of measures related to commercial, Medicaid, and Medicare plans.[21] Some of these measures are used for all these plans, some for two, and others are plan specific. For example, breast and cervical cancer screening is reported for all three plans. Child immunization status, adolescent immunization status, chlamydia screening, and prenatal and postpartum care are reported for both Medicaid and commercial plans, and colorectal cancer screening is reported for Medicare and commercial plans. Similarly, an annual dental visit is reported only for Medicaid, and flu shots for adults age 50–64 is reported only for commercial plans. Items reported only for Medicare plans include glaucoma screening, flu shots for older adults, pneumonia vaccination, and physical activity.

States may have specific quality assurance reporting requirements (QARRs) designed to examine managed care performance. New York State uses measures largely adopted from the NCQA's HEDIS reporting requirements with additional New York State-specific measures needed to address public health issues of particular significance in New York, such as lead screening of children and HIV testing of pregnant women.[22]

Several factors related to the collection and representativeness of the data are important in interpreting managed care data for public health purposes. Two distinct strategies that may be used for obtaining data on specific performance measures include medical record (or chart review) or administrative or transaction information (claims, encounter data, membership data, pharmacy data).[20] Extracting data from medical records is expensive, but this data can be more complete than data in administrative databases. Hybrid methods relying on both strategies are often employed. In examining performance measures of plans, adequacy of the data collection is important in establishing whether plan-specific differences in performance are real or are artifacts of the collection processes.

Another issue facing the local public health agency interested in using managed care data is the lack of congruence between the managed care plan service areas with the jurisdiction of the health department. For example, managed care plans may provide services to enrollees in many counties. Therefore, data on performance measures will be collected for all plan enrollees and not specifically for the individual county jurisdiction of the public health agency. Also, because the sample size for medical records or administrative data is limited, adequate data reflecting performance in the individual county may not be available. This is not a problem for public health agencies where boundaries have significant overlap with managed care plans. However, even where significant overlap does not occur, the performance data of the managed care plan on preventive services is relevant to the public health agency. Poor or questionable performance by the managed care plan throughout its service area is a warning flag that should initiate further inquiry and discussion.

A factor to be considered in interpreting managed care plan performance data is that services provided by the plan are only one of the determinants of the outcomes measured. Other health determinants such as socioeconomic status and education of the enrollees are also operating. Compliance with recommended visits is influenced by both client and plan factors. For some indicators, severity adjustment has been applied. For example, the New York State Department of Health risk adjusts low birth weight (LBW) rates to take into account differences in the demographic profiles of plans' enrollees. Variables included in the risk adjustment for LBW include education, alcohol use, drug use, smoking, level of prenatal care, race/ethnicity, marital status, parity, previous low birth weight, maternal risk factors, and nationality.[22] Similarly, comparing performance rates to a standard such as a year 2010 goal is difficult because of differences between the enrollees of a plan and the *Healthy People 2010* national goal that was developed for the entire US population.

Despite these limitations, managed care data offer significant promise in abetting efforts to improve population health status. In addition to using HEDIS measures, public health agencies with registries containing immunization or lead testing data can match these against Medicaid managed care enrollee files to determine compliance with these preventive measures.

Public health staff can use performance data as indicators of potential problems with preventive services. Discussions of performance with managed care entities are warranted and remediation plans may be requested. Although the data themselves may not be precise measures of performance, they are an important introduction to a quality assurance process. As these data become increasingly available from organized delivery systems, they will become useful community indicators to measure the provision of preventive services.

## Commercial Healthcare Databases

A wide array of data sets that can be used in community health planning is available from commercial vendors.

- CACI International, Inc. offers data on demographics, businesses, lifestyles, consumer spending, purchase potential, shopping centers, traffic volumes, and crime statistics. The data are available in a variety of formats such as reports, maps, electronic media, software, books, and lists. CACI builds on Census Bureau data to create its collection of databases. In addition to the latest census data, CACI also provides current-year updates and 5-year forecasts.
- Claritas produces databases related to health care: DRG/ICD-9 demand, HMAS and hospitals, nursing homes, physicians, and senior life demographics. In addition to data sets, Claritas offers geocoding and point coding services. The geocoding process appends the following information to the records: block group number, census tract assignments, coordinates (latitude/longitude), lifestyle codes from Claritas' neighborhood segmentation system, and ZIP codes.
- Healthdemographics provides healthcare data and analytic systems. It produces packages of coordinated healthcare databases called HealthPacs. HealthPacs include demographic data, population-based models of the incidence of diseases by category, and estimates of the demand for services (such as inpatient, outpatient, physician services).

## Neighborhood Segmentation Data

A neighborhood segmentation system contains neighborhoods that are grouped into clusters, or neighborhood segments, based on demographics and other characteristics (e.g., high proportion of people in the 20–30 age group.) This information could be used by public health officials for targeting interventions (e.g., smoking cessation campaigns) or identifying sites for facilities.

CACI produces a neighborhood segmentation system called ACORN. Similarly, Claritas has a neighborhood segmentation system (PRIZM) based on demographics and lifestyle characteristics (e.g., active travelers).

## Using the Internet to Access Data Sources

Government is increasingly recognizing the power of information technology (IT) to provide information to its constituents. In 1994, the National Performance Review strongly endorsed the use of IT to improve the service of government. Under revisions to the Freedom of Information Act, agencies are required to establish electronic records centers to provide more open access to documents and data. The March 2006 issue of the *Journal of Public Health Management and Practice* provides an excellent overview of how to access electronic data sources for public health purposes.[23] The Census Bureau has developed the Integrated Information Solutions Program to improve data access and dissemination.[24] One goal of the program is to integrate the Census Bureau's geographic, demographic, and economic data sets. The system will serve as a data warehouse with an electronic metadata repository. This will allow users to access focused data sets for their use. In addition to those sources, each state health department maintains an Internet site for data access and querying. In addition, the NCHS provides a link to all state health departments from its Web page.

## Issues in Data Interpretation

### Common Rates Used in Analysis

Data are often presented in the form of a rate. A rate is a type of proportion that includes the element of time. Many of the indicators that are commonly used in public health assessments attempt to determine the frequency of disease in the population (Where do the cases occur?), the pattern of disease occurrence over time (When do the cases occur?), and the effects of that disease on the health of the population (Who in the population gets the disease?). Common measures used to follow this are the incidence rate, prevalence rate, mortality rate, and relative risk[25(p74)]:

- The incidence rate is the number of new cases of a disease in a population over a specified period of time.
- The prevalence rate measures the proportion of people with the disease in the population at a point or period in time.
- The mortality rate measures the number of people dying with the disease in a population over a specified period of time.

- The relative risk evaluates the rate among those individuals with a selected characteristic (exposed) and compares it to the rate of the unexposed. The relative risk is used to provide an indication of the strength of an association.

Rates for populations can be expressed either as crude rates or as adjusted rates. *Crude rates* are based solely on the number of events in the population over a certain period of time. Adjusted rates are statistically transformed to control for the effects of a characteristic that may influence the risk of disease or death.[26] The most common variable that is adjusted for is age because of its profound effects on morbidity and mortality. There are two methods of adjusting rates: direct and indirect. The direct method applies the age-specific rates from the study population to a standard population. The indirect method uses the age-specific rates of a standard population to get an expected number of events in the study population. A standardized mortality (morbidity) ratio (SMR) is then used to relate the number of events observed to the number expected. The SMR is expressed as the total observed events in the study population over the total expected events in that population. An SMR of greater than 1 indicates that there were more of the events in the population than was expected. Thus, adjusted rates attempt to remove the effects of differences in composition between populations, thereby allowing for the comparison of rates.

## Common Biases

Bias is defined as a systematic error in the estimation of an effect. There are three possible sources of bias: selection, information, and confounding. Selection or sampling bias occurs when the control group for the study is not representative of the population. Information, observation, or misclassification bias occurs during the collection phase of a study. Misclassification bias is a problem for environmental and other studies that use surrogates of exposure such as distance to a facility. Observation bias can also arise when either the subjects or the investigators are not blinded to exposure status of the subject. A very important source of bias is that of confounding, which is a mixing of two or more effects. This occurs when the estimate of the effect of an exposure under study is changed because of the effect of an extraneous factor. For a factor to be a confounder, it must have an effect on the occurrence of disease. A confounding factor must be associated with both the exposure and the disease under study. All types of bias must be considered and steps must be taken to deal with them in any study that is undertaken.

## Ecologic Fallacy Issue

The ecologic fallacy problem occurs when it is assumed that results based on grouped data can be applied to individuals who make up the groups under study. The ecologic fallacy occurs because ecologic studies cannot distinguish between associations that are created by the selection of groups or associations that are in the individual data before they are grouped. Ecologic studies are based on measurements from population samples and the data from such studies are averaged over the population. The studies often use proxy measures for both exposure and disease. In addition, it is usually not possible to control for confounding in the analysis.[25] All of these factors make the associations seen in ecologic studies uncertain; therefore, it is difficult to make inferences based on the data.

## Modifiable Units Problem

The modifiable units problem was identified back in the 1930s when it was shown that different results could be obtained by using different areal units for analysis. Correlation between variables is generally higher when areas are aggregated together.[27] When examining the degree of spatial association, one must keep in mind that the association depends on the size and nature of the areal units that are used. The selection of areal units used in many spatial studies is arbitrary and often subject to change. There are no standard guidelines for aggregating data for analysis. The modifiable units problem has two components: a scale problem and an aggregation problem.[28] The scale problem occurs when data that are collected for one scale are aggregated together for analysis at a different scale (one covering a larger area). The aggregation problem occurs when examining the data at the same scale (e.g., counties) but combining the counties together into a different number of zones. Thus, it is important to examine the data using a variety of groupings in order to understand fully the associations that are seen.

## Standardization of Data from Various Sources

When using data from a variety of sources, steps need to be taken to standardize the variables for comparison. Various agencies have different needs for the data that are collected and may define the variables in different ways to meet their needs. The user needs to examine the criteria used to define the variables in the data set, the time period covered by the data, and the quality assurance steps taken in data collection. Certain variables such as race and ethnicity have standard collection requirements for the federal agencies that are established by the Office of Management and Budget. There are also national standards for the collection of spatial data. There are no overriding national standards for the collection of health data, so the user must be mindful that the data may have been collected in a manner that would affect the overall interpretation of combined results. (Refer to Chapter 12 for more detailed discussion of spatial data.)

# Legal Issues Regarding Data Release and Security

Government agencies are creatures of statute or of constitutions that were written before the electronic age. Therefore, the present laws lack guidance for establishing a uniform public policy regarding the ownership of intangible information assets. In 1985, there were more than 400 "information service organizations" in the private sector that repackaged raw government information for resale.

Public access to government information is a fundamental right that operates to check and balance the actions of elected and appointed officials. The Office of Technology Assessment (OTA) reported in 1988 that the federal government spends $6 billion each year on information dissemination (not including the cost of collection, processing, or agency automation).[29] The OTA said at that time that congressional action was urgently needed to resolve federal information dissemination issues and set policy direction for future federal agency activities.

Legal precedent directs custodial agencies to release or withhold records in consideration of the balance between the privacy of individuals and the public's right to know. In a Freedom of Information Act (FOIA) case heard before the Supreme Court in 1989, the court ruled that "FOIA's central purpose is to ensure that the federal government's activities be opened for public scrutiny, not that information about private citizens that happens to be in the federal government's warehouse be so disclosed."[30] The court recognized the difference between a computerized databank and the source records. Unfortunately, the burden for making the distinction between products and records falls on the custodial agencies. The case discussed the possibility that departing from the original purposes of the FOIA could threaten to convert that federal government into a clearinghouse for personal information that had been collected concerning millions of persons under a variety of different situations. The previous interpretations may change because there have been changes in the FOIA that expand it to cover electronic records. The amendment to the FOIA that was passed in September of 1996 requires that computer-based information kept by federal agencies be subject to disclosure and that agencies must comply, if they can, to requests for records in electronic form. This may have a future impact on the type of information kept in computer databases.

Limitations to protect information must be established before the development of the databases. Some courts, in looking at the balance between privacy and the right to know, have reached a compromise that can result in a tremendous burden of resources for some agencies. "When an academic researcher wants information about test scores and income levels, courts have required the custodial agency to perform a statistical analysis of the 'private' data, and provide this analysis in response to an open-records request for otherwise private information. This so-called redaction requirement places a burden on the agency to produce information that did not exist, and was not necessary for agency purposes, to meet the outside request."[31] It was simpler in the preelectronic age to review a specific request and determine whether a privacy issue was involved. When an agency is offering a computer database for public application, the issues become much broader and more obscure. The custodial agency should anticipate what can be done through different forms of access and any privacy invasion that may result. GIS systems are particularly vulnerable to use that results in an invasion of privacy.

Although privacy concerns may limit the use of sensitive information about income or test scores, health information is particularly sensitive and is specifically protected by HIPAA. The law, passed in 1996 with final regulations passed in 2000, addresses the protection of all health information through consumer control (the consumer determines who can see what information), boundaries (healthcare information can be shared for health purposes only), accountability (noncriminal penalties may be imposed for violations), public responsibility (exemptions are made to balance need for security and need to ensure the public's health), and security (places the responsibility of protecting the health on the shoulders of the organizations that have the information, whether on paper records or electronic). Refer to Chapter 13 for further discussion on this topic.

In the related issue of the liability of government agencies for effects from the use of provided goods and services, the use of disclaimer language must be considered. The government has the right not to engage in discretionary functions such as the marketing and selling of GIS and other computer products. Once the decision to engage in a discretionary activity or function has been made, a government agency may be held liable for the negligence of its employees' and agents' actions in the performance of the discretionary activity. Negligence may take the form of incorrect information that is entered into a database that results in the production of an incorrect product. If that leads to damaging results and the information provided by the agency led the injured party to justifiably rely on the information or product, then liability is likely. By issuing and selling information products, the custodial agency assumes a duty to invest sufficient resources that are necessary to achieve what the government and the courts will agree to be proper care in maintaining the database.

There is also a question of whether the Uniform Commercial Code applies. As a general rule, Article 2 of the Uniform Commercial Code applies only to the sale of goods and not to the provision of services. However, courts have found that electricity transmitted over wires and natural gas pumped through pipes are "moveable goods" and therefore subject to the code. It is yet to be seen if electronically transmitted data will be considered similarly.

• • •

Public health officials and health administrators can incorporate a wide variety of types of data as part of community planning efforts. An increasing amount of data is now becoming available online over the Web. In addition, planners potentially could incorporate data from federal programs or, alternatively, available data from local or state sources. The key to success is that data partnerships need to be formed (e.g., to ensure protection of confidentiality and privacy), and the data then need to be collected in such a manner as to be used for a wide variety of community health planning needs. Careful thought should be given to the questions that need to be answered from a community planning perspective and to identify the data that will be most advantageous in answering those questions.

## Chapter Review

1. Collecting data is necessary for the assessment and monitoring of community health and for evaluating the effectiveness of preventive programs.
2. Sources of health data are available at federal, state, and local levels. For each source, a critical parameter is determining the population size and the smallest geographic unit to which the information is applicable.
3. Within the federal government, a broad range of data sets are available from multiple agencies, including the CDC, NCHS, NIOSH, Bureau of Labor Statistics, HCFA, HRSA, and others.

4. At the state level, sources of data include:
   - Vital statistics
   - Disease reporting
   - Disease registries
   - Medicaid information
5. At the local level, additional information can be gathered by surveys for special purposes. Other sources of data can be sought, such as from managed care entities.
6. The Internet is now a readily available method for accessing data sources. Multiple federal data sets are now available electronically, and each state health department maintains an Internet site for data access and querying.
7. To be successful in working with data, queries or hypotheses are structured first, a plan or design to answer these questions is then constructed, and finally, data are sought recognizing potential biases including reporting, measurement, and selection.

## References

1. National Association of County and City Health Officials. Mobilizing for Action through Planning and Partnerships. Available at: http://mapp.naccho.org/mapp_introduction.asp. Accessed June 18, 2006.
2. Weed JA. Vital statistics in the United States: preparing for the next century. *Popul Index.* 1995;61(4):527–539.
3. Mullan F. *Plaques and Politics: The Story of the United States Public Health Service.* New York, NY: Basic Books Inc; 1989.
4. US Department of Health, Education, and Welfare. *Healthy People: The Surgeon General's Report on Health Promotion and Disease Prevention 1979.* Washington, DC: Public Health Service; 1979. DHEW [PHS] Publication No. 79-55071.
5. US Department of Health and Human Services. *Healthy People 2000: The National Health Promotion and Disease Prevention Objectives.* Washington, DC: Public Health Service; 1990. DHHS Publication [PHS] NO. 91-50213.
6. National Center for Health Statistics. *Healthy People 2000 Final Review.* Hyattsville, Md: Public Health Service; 2001.
7. Centers for Disease Control and Prevention. National Center for Health Statistics. Available at: http://www.cdc.gov/nchs/about.htm. Accessed June 16, 2006.
8. National Center for Health Statistics, Centers for Disease Control and Prevention. National Health and Nutrition Examination Survey. Available at: http://www.cdc.gov/nchs/nhanes.htm. Accessed April 25, 2000.
9. Loria CM, Sempos CT, Vuong C. Plan and operation of the NHANES II Mortality Study, 1992. *Vital Health Stat.* 1999;38:1–16.
10. National Center for Health Statistics. Plan and operation of the Third National Health and Nutrition Examination Survey, 1988–1994. *Vital Health Stat.* 1994;1(32).
11. Monitoring the Future. Available at: http://www.monitoringthefuture.org/index.html. Accessed June 18, 2006.
12. US Department of Commerce, US Census Bureau home page. Available at: http://www.census.gov/index.html. Accessed April 25, 2000.
13. US Department of Health and Human Services, Centers for Medicare and Medicaid Services. Medicaid Statistical Information System State Summary

FY 2003. Available at: http://www.cms.hhs.gov/MedicaidDataSources GenInfo/downloads/MSISTables2003.pdf. Accessed June 18, 2006.

14. US Department of Health and Human Services, Centers for Medicare and Medicaid Services. Medicare Managed Care Overview. Available at: http://www.cms.hhs.gov/MedicaidManagCare. Accessed June 18, 2006.

15. US Centers for Disease Control and Prevention. Recommendations for the use of folic acid to reduce the number of cases of spina bifida and other neural tube defects. *MMWR.* 1992;41(RR-14):001.

16. Cibula D, et al. *Obtaining Quality Information on a Shoe-String Budget: A Low-Cost Evaluation of a County-Wide Campaign Promoting Folic Acid.* Syracuse, NY: Onondaga County Department of Health; 1997.

17. March of Dimes Foundation. *Preparing for Pregnancy: A National Survey of Women's Behavior and Knowledge Relating to the Consumption of Folic Acid and Other Vitamins and Pre-Pregnancy Care.* White Plains, NY: March of Dimes Foundation; 1995.

18. Serbanescu F, Rochat R. *Georgia Women's Health Survey—1995: Preliminary Report.* Atlanta, GA: Georgia Department of Human Resources, Division of Public Health; 1996.

19. Onondaga County Health Department. *Breast Cancer and Mammography Utilization in Onondaga County, New York.* Syracuse, NY: Onondaga County Health Department; 1997.

20. National Committee for Quality Assurance. *Health Plan Employer Data and Information Set.* Washington, DC: NCQA; 1993.

21. National Committee for Quality Assurance. HEDIS 2005 information. Available at: http://www.ncqa.org/Programs/HEDIS/2005/index.htm. Accessed July 10, 2006.

22. New York State Department of Health. *Quality Assurance Reporting Requirements, 1997: A Report on Managed Care Performance.* Albany, NY: New York State Department of Health; 1999.

23. Friedman DJ, Parish RG. State Web-based data query systems. *J Public Health Manage Pract.* 2006;12(2):109.

24. Wallace M, Landman CR. Integrated information solutions: the future of Census Bureau data access and dissemination. Paper presented at: National Conference on Health Statistics; August 2, 1999; Washington, DC.

25. Rothman KJ. *Modern Epidemiology.* Boston, Mass: Little Brown and Co; 1986.

26. Mausner JS, Kramer S. *Epidemiology—An Introductory Text.* Philadelphia, Pa: WB Saunders Co; 1985.

27. Green M, Flowerdew R. New evidence on the modifiable areal unit problem. In: Longley P, Batty M, eds. *Spatial Analysis in a GIS Environment.* New York, NY: John Wiley & Sons; 1997.

28. Openshaw S. The modifiable areal unit problem. In: *Concepts and Techniques in Modern Geography,* Vol 38. Norwich, UK: Geo Books; 1984.

29. Antenucci JC, Brown K, Croswell PL. *Geographic Information Systems: A Guide to the Technology.* New York, NY: Van Nostrand Reinhold; 1991.

30. *US Department of Justice v. Reporters Committee for Freedom of the Press.* 489 US, 103 L Ed 2d 774; 109 Sup. Ct. (1989).

CHAPTER 12

# GEOGRAPHIC INFORMATION SYSTEMS FOR PUBLIC HEALTH

Alan L. Melnick

## Chapter Overview

Accurate geographically based data are necessary to improve the health status of communities. Geographic information systems (GIS) integrate several functions, including the incorporation, storage, and retrieval of data with a spatial or geographic component. Analysis and display of the data on maps provide public health practitioners with a tool to assist in understanding disease and the disease risks related to environmental exposures or social demographic data.

## History of GIS in Public Health

As early as 1854, John Snow, the father of modern epidemiology, plotted the geographic distribution of cholera deaths in London, demonstrating the association between the deaths and contaminated water supplies.[1] In doing so, he linked forever the new science of epidemiology with the use of geographic information to reveal relationships between environment and disease.[2]

Of the three core epidemiologic variables of time, place, and person, place has always been the most difficult and time consuming to analyze and depict.[2] In the past, when public health practitioners focused mainly on communicable disease control, pushpins or dots drawn on maps usually proved effective in helping to analyze and control disease outbreaks. Population-based health managers, however, are responsible for analyzing and responding to more complex health issues in a rapidly changing, diverse environment. The social, environmental, and behavioral determinants of health have a strong geographic component. To work effectively with communities in improving health status, modern public health practitioners and their community partners need easy, immediate access to accurate, geographically based data.[3] New developments in GIS technology are making this possible.

### Limitations of Pre-GIS Analysis

For several reasons, local health consumers and health planners have rarely used health data collected routinely by local and state governments. First, the data are not timely. For example, up to 2 years can elapse before states report vital statistics data. Then, the data usually arrive as hard copy, containing limited analysis at the county level. Such hard copy data are not amenable to further analysis, leaving local planners to ask the responsible state agency to make specific data runs, requiring additional time and staff support.[4] Second, many different agencies at the local, state, and federal level collect and maintain health-related data in different formats in different locations, making the data less accessible for consumers, health planners, and local health departments. Third, data analyzed and reported at the county level and above are not useful for assessing the health of diverse communities within large or even medium-sized counties. Such macrolevel data fail to capture the unique essential characteristics of the individual communities, leaving little opportunity for local public health professionals to seek dialogue and strengthen relationships with populations within their counties. By providing easy access to a variety of data that are analyzable at the community level, modern GIS promise to address these problems, enabling public health practitioners to engage diverse communities in a partnership to improve community health.[4]

### Emergence of Modern GIS

Several factors contributed to the development of GIS. Computers became smaller, faster, more accessible, and less expensive. Software became easier to use. Landscape and census data became available in digital format, allowing the linkage of health-related data sets to a geographic map.[5]

## Features of GIS

### Definition

GIS are automated computer packages that are defined more by their functions than by what they are.[5] GIS integrate several functions, including the capture and incorporation of data sets, the storage of data, the retrieval of data, the statistical manipulation of data, data analysis, data modeling, and the display of the data on maps.[5,6] The incorporated data must have a spatial or geographic component. Because much of the data collected today have some geographic reference, such as a street address, GIS have the potential to revolutionize public health practice. With GIS, public health practitioners can map health-related issues such as mortality and birth rates at the neighborhood or even street level.[7] In addition, GIS are tools for understanding and displaying disease or disease risks related to environmental exposures or social demographic data.[2] For example, studies have used GIS to demonstrate the relationship between childhood lead poisoning cases by census block with older housing stock.[8] The public health uses of GIS will be described later in this chapter.

### Data Acquisition and Storage: Creating Spatial Databases

To perform geographic analyses, GIS require a foundation of spatial, or geographic, data. The creation of the US Bureau of the Census' Topologically Integrated Geographic Encoding and Referencing TIGER/Line files as a foundation database contributed to the development of modern GIS.[9] Updated, easily obtainable versions of the TIGER/Line files include detailed street and address range information, along with political and administrative boundaries such as counties, ZIP codes, census tracts, and census block groups.[10] TIGER/Line files are available to order at the Census Bureau TIGER home page at www.census.gov/geo/www/tiger/index.html. Updated geographic data files are also available from commercial vendors, but may be expensive.[7]

The next step in a GIS analysis is to obtain the attribute data and link them to the geographic database.[10] Attribute data relate to any public health issue of interest and can include health, social, and environmental data. Examples of attribute data include the Census Bureau's extensive demographic, economic, and social data sets; state and local vital statistics (perinatal and mortality data); and law enforcement data (reported arrests). To link to the geographic foundation, the attribute data must include a geographic reference, such as an address field. For example, to analyze birth rates by geography, each record in the birth database must include a field with the mother's street address. GIS can analyze any attribute database, such as arrest data, that includes a field with a location.

Geocoding is the process by which GIS software matches each record in an attribute database with the geographic files. The GIS software converts each address in the attribute file to a point on a map. The software then compares each address with the corresponding information in the foundation spatial database. A match occurs when the two agree.[10]

### Map Making and Data Analysis

Once stored and geocoded, the data are ready for analysis and display. The power of GIS technology stems from its ability to allow users to analyze and display health-related data in new and effective ways.[5] The simplest form of display would be analogous to a pushpin depiction—events, such as reported cholera cases, displayed as dots on a map. In one study, local public health planners created a map showing the home locations of children who had high blood lead levels (see Figure 12-1).[10] Areas with larger numbers of children with reported high lead levels show up as clusters of triangular-shaped black dots. Like other epidemiologic studies, this map raised an additional question. Was clustering a reflection of high blood lead prevalence or a reflection of greater screening efforts? A second map, in which circular clear dots displayed all children screened, answered the question, revealing the varying patterns of children with high and low blood lead levels (see Figure 12-2).[10]

Of course, GIS can perform much more complex tasks than a simple mapping of events.[5] The overlay capability of GIS allows the user to display more than one attribute on a map at a time. For example, the Centers for Disease Control and Prevention (CDC) has identified older housing as the most significant risk factor for lead exposure in young children. Local public health planners might be interested, then, in identifying the location of older housing in

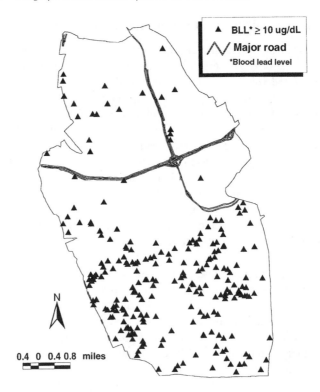

**FIGURE 12-1  Children with Elevated Blood Lead Level**
*Source:* Reprinted with permission. McLafferty S, Cromley E. Your first mapping project on your own from A to Z. *J Public Health Manage and Pract.* 1999;5(2):79.

targeting lead exposure prevention efforts. If the data were available, a map could overlay the triangular black dots of reported childhood lead cases with the location of houses built before 1960. In this case, dots of different colors and shapes could represent older housing. Alternatively, the user could overlay the reported lead cases with a map showing the percentage of homes built before 1960 by census tract or census block group.[10] Each census block group could be colored or shaded based on its range of percentage of housing built before 1960. This type of map, in which a given area, or polygon, is shaded with different colors to depict variations of features such as the percentage of older housing stock, is called a *choropleth* map. Public health planners in Duval County, Florida, used overlays to create such a map. Census block groups were shaded based on the percentage of older housing, with reported childhood lead poisoning cases displayed as black dots (see Figure 12-3).[11] This map was quite useful in focusing blood lead screening efforts.

Buffering is another powerful feature of GIS analysis. Using this feature, GIS can create polygons based on the distance from a target object.[7] Buffers are particularly useful in identifying people at risk of exposure to environmental hazards. A GIS study of childhood lead risk could define a 25-meter zone around main roads to identify areas with potentially high levels of lead-contaminated soil from past use of leaded gasoline (see Figure12-4).[12] The same study could then identify and locate children living within these areas who

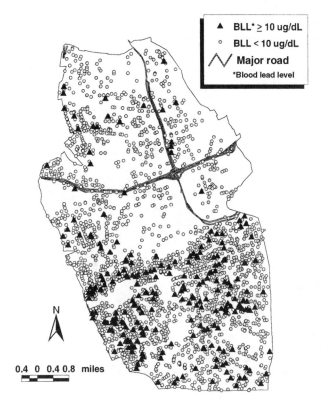

**FIGURE 12-2    Children Screened for Lead**
*Source:* Reprinted with permission. McLafferty S, Cromley E. Your first mapping project on your own from A to Z. *J Public Health Manage Pract.* 1999;5(2):80.

would benefit from lead screening. Another study used buffering to evaluate potential health risks and health risk perceptions of minority populations living within 0.2 miles of businesses that store hazardous chemicals (Figure 12-5).[13] A more recent study used 5- and 15-mile buffers to assess geographic access to supermarkets in metropolitan Detroit.[14]

## Public Health GIS Applications

Given that many determinants of health have strong geographic components, GIS technology has many public health applications. These applications range from epidemiology, including research, to community health assessment and community health planning.

### Epidemiology

Perhaps the most direct use of GIS technology is as a tool for understanding and displaying disease or disease risks that are related directly to environmental exposures.[2] GIS technology can assist in environmental epidemiologic investigations in several ways[15]:

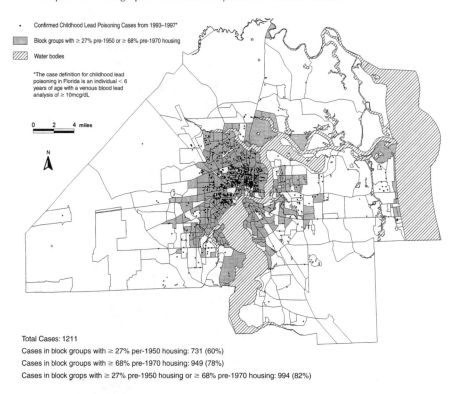

- Confirmed Childhood Lead Poisoning Cases from 1993–1997*

Block groups with ≥ 27% pre-1950 or ≥ 68% pre-1970 housing

Water bodies

*The case definition for childhood lead poisoning in Florida is an individual < 6 years of age with a venous blood lead analysis of ≥ 10mcg/dL

0    2    4 miles

N

Total Cases: 1211

Cases in block groups with ≥ 27% per-1950 housing: 731 (60%)

Cases in block groups with ≥ 68% pre-1970 housing: 949 (78%)

Cases in block grops with ≥ 27% pre-1950 housing or ≥ 68% pre-1970 housing: 994 (82%)

**FIGURE 12-3    Development of Childhood Blood Lead Screening Guidelines: Duval County, FL**
*Source:* Bureau of Environmental Epidemiology, Duval County, Florida.

- By defining the population potentially exposed—for example, cohort studies have used GIS to identify populations with risk of exposure to magnetic fields from high-powered electrical lines and populations potentially exposed to hazardous waste near landfill sites.[12,16,17]
- By identifying the source and potential routes of exposure—for example, GIS studies have depicted nitrate or tricholoroethylene levels in drinking water,[18,19] dioxin in air around industrial plants in Denmark,[20] childhood lead poisoning cases by census block with older housing stock,[8,11] and proximity to highways and point source air pollution emitters in a case control study of asthma.[21]
- By estimating environmental levels of contaminants—for example, a GIS study of Iodine 131 releases from the Hanford Nuclear Reservation estimated the amount of I-131 that might have been present in milk,[22] a Swedish lung cancer study used GIS to estimate air pollutant concentrations,[23,24] and a Durham County, North Carolina, study used GIS and industrial source dispersion monitoring to characterize the spatial distribution and ambient concentration of glycol ethers.[25]

By integrating GIS with statistical methods, epidemiologists can use GIS for modeling, a spatial analysis process that can identify disease risk factors.

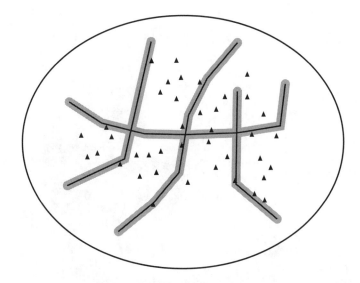

**FIGURE 12-4     25-meter Zones Around Main Roads**
*Source:* Reprinted from Vine MF, Degnan D, Hanchette C. Geographic information systems: their use in environmental epidemiological research. *Environ Health Perspect.* 1997;105(6):598–605.

For example, a study of Lyme disease in Baltimore, Maryland, obtained data for 53 environmental variables at the residence of patients with Lyme disease. Combining GIS with a logistic regression analysis, researchers rapidly identified Lyme disease risk factors over a large area.[26]

Many diseases cluster geographically whether or not they are related to environmental exposure.[2] One of the most useful features of GIS is their ability to identify and analyze space–time clusters or "hot spots" of disease.[5] An early GIS application called the Geographical Analysis Machine (GAM) was used to evaluate whether spatial clusters of childhood leukemia were located near nuclear facilities in Britain.[5,27] More recently, investigators have used GIS to identify spatial cancer clusters in Illinois[28] and spatial clusters of neural-tube birth defects in Shanxi Province, China.[29] Although these ecologic studies do not prove an association between environmental factors and disease, they raise questions useful for follow-up case control and cohort studies.[28]

## Community Health Assessment and Planning

For public health practitioners, the most exciting aspect of GIS technology may be its potential to revolutionize the process of community health improvement by improving access to health-related data. (Refer to Chapter 15 for detailed discussion of this process.) Every community or neighborhood has assets and capacities in addition to needs.[30] GIS will enable communities to assess many of these factors, strengths, and weaknesses related to community well-being and allow communities to evaluate actions they take to improve their health status.[4] This potential is a consequence of several features inherent in GIS.

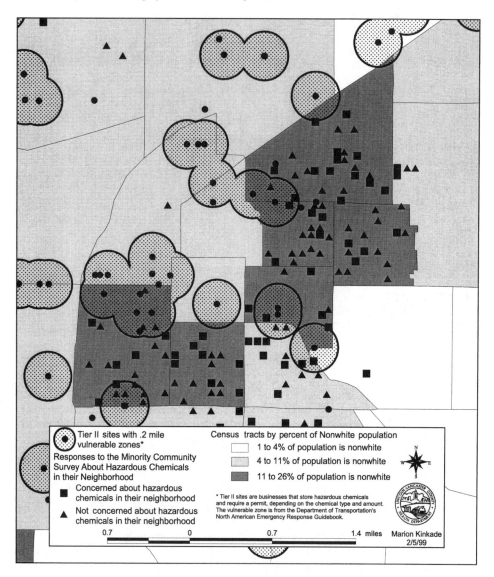

**FIGURE 12-5** **Responses to the Survey of Environmental Health Hazard Risks in the Minority Community, in Relation to the Primary Minority Census Tracts and the Evacuation Zones for Tier II Sites in Lincoln, NE, February, 1999**
*Source:* Lincoln-Lancaster County Health Department, Lincoln, Nebraska.

The relational and overlay features of GIS encourage the rapid incorporation of multiple attribute data sets, including data sets not traditionally viewed as related to public health. Attribute data are available from many sources, both government and commercial.[31] (See Chapter 11 for a more detailed discussion.) Census data, available from the Census Bureau, includes demographic and socioeconomic data at the census block group level. Demographic data, useful as denominator data in calculating rates, contain information on age, gender, race, and ethnicity. Socioeconomic data include educational level, poverty level, employment, and age of housing.[31]

Depending on the state and locality, many data sets are easily obtainable, such as vital statistics data (birth and mortality), healthcare expenditures, access to primary care data, hospital discharge data, and behavioral risk factor data.[31] Table 12-1 lists a few examples of commonly available data sets.

One vision for community health assessment suggests using other data such as high school dropout rates, commuting time, and domestic abuse.[4] Depending on the locality or state, registries not included in Table 10-1 may be available. For example, one study used an Out-of-Hospital Cardiac Arrest registry available through the Rochester, New York, Emergency Medical Services program to identify clusters of out-of-hospital cardiac arrests.[32]

Communities can add data on neighborhood assets, such as local businesses, libraries, social clubs, and religious and cultural organizations.[30,33] Software "data wizards" make it easy for partners to incorporate additional data sets into the system, further encouraging multiple agencies to share data.[4]

The feature of unlimited scale of analysis is particularly helpful when performing community health assessments and program evaluations in densely populated counties. Large counties often contain many diverse and sizable communities with borders that do not necessarily coincide with county boundaries. As a result, summaries based on these boundaries may not accurately capture community characteristics. For example, a large county may have low teen birth rates compared to the state; whereas, several communities within the county may have markedly elevated rates. In this instance, county-level data are not useful in targeting teen pregnancy prevention efforts. Using GIS, public health practitioners and their community partners can analyze and display the data at the local, subcounty, community level. They can compare their teen birth rate measures statistically with state data, national data, and benchmarks. Public health practitioners can also display available resources for teen pregnancy prevention by overlaying physical features such as health and social work facilities, roads, public transit routes, and travel time.[4,34] Over time, they can use the analytic features of GIS to evaluate the outcomes of pregnancy prevention or other public health efforts within their communities.[4]

The flexibility to define community geographically is invaluable in community health planning. GIS software can aggregate census block groups into a variety of community definitions, such as high school attendance areas or legislative districts. Likewise, GIS software can aggregate attribute data, such as vital statistics data, into the same areas for analysis. For example, a GIS prototype application analyzed teen birth rates, teen male arrest rates, and adequacy of prenatal care by high school attendance area, and compared these rates with overall county rates, state rates, and benchmarks.[4] Overlays allow users to look at two variables simultaneously so they can visualize spatial patterns and relationships. In this example, GIS could depict teen birth rates using Youth Risk Behavior Survey (YRBS) results for high school attendance areas. Alternatively, those persons interested in improving prenatal care could evaluate the percentage of first trimester care and income level by legislative district.

GIS programs can be Internet compatible, making them easily accessible. Most communities have access to Internet-capable libraries, where they can create customized maps to meet their needs.[4] GIS Internet packages can be designed for users without formal epidemiologic skills, and tutorials can be added. For example, tutorials can provide explanations of concepts such as

**TABLE 12-1    Types and Potential Sources of Attribute Data**

| Category (Examples) | Source (Varies by State) | Level of Analysis (Varies by State and Locality) |
|---|---|---|
| Demographic data ( e.g., age, sex, race, and ethnic distribution) | US Bureau of the Census | Census block group, county, state |
| Perinatal indicators by age and population subgroups (e.g., births, repeat births, prenatal care, low birth weight) | State vital statistics | Census block group (if address included on birth certificate), county, state |
| Pregnancies; abortions | State vital statistics | County (abortion data do not contain street address), state |
| Mortality (by age and population subgroups) including years of potential life lost | State vital statistics | Census block group if address included on death certificate; otherwise county and state |
| Hospitalization (causes by age and population subgroup) | Depends on state—may be Medicaid agency | Varies (census block group, ZIP code, county, state depending on how residence is reported) |
| Ambulatory encounter data (by diagnosis age and population subgroup for Medicaid population | State Medicaid agency | Census block group, county, state |
| Reportable disease (communicable disease, including sexually transmitted disease, lead poisoning, pesticide exposure) | Local health department, state epidemiologist | Census block group, county, state |
| Immunization of 2-year-olds | Depends on state—may be state health department | Varies |
| Cancer incidence (by age and population subgroup) | State cancer registry | Census block group, county, state |
| Behavioral risk factors | Centers for Disease Control and Prevention | ZIP code, state |
| Youth risk behaviors (Youth Risk Behavior Survey) | CDC, state health department | High school, state |
| Synar reports (reports of tobacco outlet inspections) | Depends on state—agency responsible for alcohol and drug treatment planning | Census block group, county, state |
| Arrests by residence (causes by age and population subgroup) | County law enforcement (e.g., sheriff's office), state justice department | Census block group, county, state |

*Source:* Adapted with permission. Data from Melnick A, Seigal N, Hildner J, et al. Clackamas County Department of Human Services community health mapping engine (CHiME) geographic information systems project. *J Public Health Manage Pract.* 1999;5(2):65. Lee CV, Irving JL. Sources of spatial data for community health planning. *J Public Health Manage Pract.* 1999;5(4):9–13, Table 1.3.

incidence rates, prevalence, confidence intervals, and the need for age adjustment when evaluating mortality rates.[4,35]

Perhaps the greatest strength of GIS technology is that its product is a picture.[2] Epidemiologists often portray analyses in formats that are only comprehensible to other epidemiologists. Program managers, policy makers, and others who must act on results need these results in a way they can digest and therefore believe. GIS take complex data and translate them into easily understandable information. This feature promises to enhance collaboration between all partners involved in community health improvement.

## Lessons Learned and Challenges

Like any other new technology, GIS come with limitations and a potential for problems. Limitations include limited availability of data, inconsistent data quality, lack of a trained workforce, and costs. Potential problems include community definitions, confidentiality, and misinterpretation of results.

### Data Availability and Quality

As with any analysis, useful GIS output is dependent on useful input. Many commonly used databases, such as mortality data or hospital discharge data, frequently lack an address. Public health professionals have to encourage their data-sharing partners to include address fields to make their data useful for community health planning. In addition, public health professionals who decide to contract with commercial vendors for geocoding must be careful to select vendors based on match rates, accuracy, and reliability.[36] Encouraging data producers to geocode the data before release further facilitates incorporation of the data set into effective GIS applications.

Many important data sets are not available, and when they are, users must be careful to evaluate their quality.[2,12] Quantitative information regarding the measured factor, such as environmental hazard exposure, must be present and accurate. Numerator address data may be missing, wrong, or (particularly in rural areas) impossible to match.[2,12] Inaccuracies may exist in denominator data and in the geographic data file, especially if they are outdated. The match rate between geospatial and attribute databases is directly dependent on their quality. Misspellings, empty address fields, and geographic files that are not up to date with the latest road maps lead to low match rates. For example, new housing developments often create new roads that may not be present on an old file. Low match rates, in turn, lead to selection bias in subsequent analyses. Public health professionals need to ensure that GIS users carefully assess and account for these limitations in their analyses. Depending on the quality of the data, unmatched records often need to be evaluated one at a time, a potentially cumbersome process. To solve these problems, agencies, professionals, and commercial vendors using GIS need to incorporate and adhere to standards for currency, quality, and completeness of data. Government and commercial suppliers should provide metadata—data about the data—allowing users to evaluate data quality in relation to these standards.[7,13]

## Trained Workforce and Costs

Many local public health departments will have to invest in hardware, software, and trained staff to apply GIS successfully. In a small study conducted by the National Association of County and City Health Officials (NACCHO) several years ago, the cost to complete relatively small projects was $10,000 to $15,000, beyond the reach of many small, rural health departments.[13] Staff time is required to acquire data sets, geocode the data, check the quality of the data, perform the analyses, and answer questions concerning the data. Increasing the availability of geocoded data would help cut this time.[7] For example, if state health departments released geocoded vital statistics data, they would encourage the use of GIS. At the local level, public health departments can reduce costs and improve collaboration by sharing data sets, trained staff, software, and hardware with other community partners.

## Defining Community

Public health officials and their partners need to be both careful and flexible in defining community when using GIS for community health improvement. (Refer to Chapter 15 for more detailed discussion.) How to portray a community is constrained by the quality of the data and the perceptions of those within the depicted community. Although GIS projects can define communities in many geographic ways—ZIP codes, census tracts, census block groups, high school attendance areas, legislative districts, cities, and counties—in any given situation, all are not equally appropriate.[2] The same data, presented with different geographic boundaries, can result in different interpretations. For example, maps portraying the proportion of homes built before 1950, a risk factor for childhood lead exposure, provide different information when using different geographic levels (see Figure 12-6).[37] Due to the influence of urban areas, compared to the block group and ZIP code scale maps, the county scale map of pre-1950 overlooks many rural areas with older housing.[37] On a case-by-case basis, public health officials can share their community maps with community partners to obtain comments. Then, using GIS, they can easily redraw the community boundaries, selecting the most appropriate mapping strategy.[2]

## Confidentiality

Confidentiality issues pose a significant limitation for public health officials intending to share health-related data with community partners or place data on the Internet. Data containing personal addresses can be as identifying as data with names. Without appropriate, clear laws, guidelines, and standards regarding confidentiality and data release, health agencies and consumers may be unwilling to provide needed information.[9] Those persons responsible for maintaining the data files should ensure appropriate precautions in order to prevent unauthorized access. Great care and thought must precede the depiction of address data linked to confidential information. (Refer to Chapters 10, 13, and 24 for more detailed discussion on protected health information.)

One possible solution is to remove identifiers such as name or address, presenting aggregated data only. State and federal agencies have traditionally reported data aggregated at the county, state, and federal level. Public

**Block groups**  **ZIP codes**  **Counties**

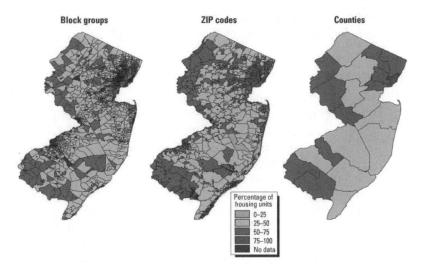

Percentage of
housing units
0–25
25–50
50–75
75–100
No data

**FIGURE 12-6    Percentages of Homes Built Before 1950 in New Jersey Based on US Census Data Reported at the Block Group Level of Resolution. The Three Major Maps Depict the Same Data at Three Different Scales: US Census Block Group, ZIP Code, and Counties.**
*Source:* Reprinted from Elliot P, Wartenberg D. Spatial epidemiology: current approaches and future challenges. *Environ Health Perspect.* 2004;112(9):998–1006.

health officials can do the same for geocoded community-level data by aggregating it into any selected community definition. For example, public health officials could share GIS data wizard software with hospitals unwilling to release discharge data. Local hospitals could then use the wizard to geocode the personal health data and aggregate it by legislative district boundaries. Then, they could remove the personal identifiers such as name and address and release the aggregated data to the public health officials for incorporation into the Web-based GIS. In this way, public users would only view data that was aggregated at the legislative district level.

When small numbers (numerator or denominator) are involved, the possibility exists that aggregated data could still be ascribed to individuals. This is particularly true when GIS users stratify their community health analyses by multiple demographic variables, such as gender and ethnicity. To avoid this, public health officials must develop safeguards, built into the software, that restrict the analysis, reporting, and depiction of very small numbers.[4] For example, standards could prohibit the release of a health statistic, such as teen birth rate, if the population denominator (teenage females) were less than 50. If the denominator were a cohort defined by an event, such as all births, a standard could prohibit release of percentage of outcomes (e.g., first trimester care) for a community with fewer than 10 events (births). Alternatively, GIS applications can allow users to analyze data aggregated over two or more years when rates for a single year are unstable due to small numbers.

Even if GIS studies do not identify individuals, group disclosure, especially in studies of environmental exposure, can lead to financial risk for individuals in an exposed community, including decreased property values and increased insurance cost.[37,38] GIS technology is just one more reason to develop a nationally uniform framework of information sharing that protects privacy while permitting public health practice.[2]

## Misinterpretation of Results

Ironically, the strength of GIS technology may be its biggest shortfall. The elegance of GIS is that they integrate many complex data sets into an easily understandable picture—a map. Because of this, GIS technology is becoming available to a diversity of users, many with little understanding of public health and epidemiologic principles. Many determinants of health, such as age, ethnicity, socioeconomic status, and education, cluster geographically. Consequently, most GIS analyses find an association between geography and health outcomes. Usually, however, these outcomes cluster geographically because of underlying population characteristics, not because of the geography itself. Users without epidemiologic training may be tempted to misinterpret why geographic clustering is occurring, often as proof of a pet theory.[2]

The conflicting analyses of the London 1854 cholera epidemic provide a perfect example. For John Snow, geographic analysis of cholera death clustering implicated the Broad Street pump. However, using the same data, the England General Board of Health was convinced that nocturnal vapors from the Thames River were responsible.

As GIS technology becomes more widely available, inexperienced users, including those in policy-making positions, may be tempted to make individual-level inferences from ecologic data and make false assumptions concerning the nature of associations between exposure and health.[2,12] The job of public health officials is to ensure that any interpretation of geographically referenced health data looks beyond maps to a wider range of analytic tools. For example, a superficial analysis of the geographic variation in childhood asthma hospitalization rates could have led to the conclusion that different populations have different burdens of illness. Closer study revealed that geographic variation in hospital bed supply and hospital proximity, not asthma itself, were independent predictors of admission.[39]

Public health officials can help prevent these mistakes by building safeguards into Internet-based GIS applications. For example, pop-up help screens could contain messages discussing the concept of ecologic fallacy and the need for caution about drawing conclusions when cause-and-effect relationships have not been established previously.[4,35] In addition, built-in links to appropriate county health officials would allow inexperienced users to obtain consultation.

## Getting Started with GIS

Before a local health department invests in a GIS application, it should determine whether it really needs the application or if other, cheaper alternatives might suffice.[40] For example, a small jurisdiction with limited resources and small numbers of residents may not benefit from a detailed geographic analysis. In many cases, other local government or private agencies may have already developed a GIS application and would welcome partnership with the local health department.

The basic components of GIS include appropriate hardware and software. Hardware recommendations change rapidly but should at least include the basic components listed in Table 12-2.[40] Over the past few years, the variety of GIS software products has markedly increased. Each easily obtainable product has its own advantages and disadvantages, as shown in Table 12-3.[40]

## Future of GIS and the Role of Public Health Officials

As GIS technology evolves and becomes more widely available, the role of public health officials will undoubtedly evolve with it. Many more data sets—containing information on a broad range of social, demographic, and health-related data—will be available on the Web. The same information now available only to public health officials will be available to the public.[41]

Rather than posing a threat, the new technology poses incredible opportunities for public health officials and their communities. GIS technology is eminently compatible with the core public functions of assessment, policy development, and assurance.[42] Public health managers will have many important roles to play, such as building data systems, mobilizing community partnerships, serving as resources, inserting (and teaching) science, and ultimately facilitating community health improvement.

### Building Data Systems and Mobilizing Community Partnerships

GIS can encourage public health officials and communities to form partnerships to assess community health status. Through dialogue with their public health partners, communities can decide what data are relevant for commu-

**TABLE 12-2    Minimum Hardware Needed for Basic GIS Applications**

| Device | Speed or Capacity |
|---|---|
| Hard drive | 10 GB or more |
| CD-ROM | 48X or faster |
| Backup capability (Iomega ZIP drive, CD writer, Flash drive, or LAN (local area network) backup | |
| Processor (Pentium 4 or equivalent) | At least 1 GHZ, preferably 2 GHZ or more |
| Random access memory (RAM) | At least 512 MB, preferably 1 GB or more |
| Video card | 64 MB memory |
| Color monitor | 17 inches; minimum of 1024 × 768 pixels resolution |
| Color printer (laser or inkjet) | At least 600 × 1200 dots per inch (dpi) resolution |
| Internet connection | Broadband connection |
| Optional: Color scanner with optical character recognition capability | |
| Optional: Digital video disk (DVD) drive and writer | |

Adapted with permission from Thrall SE. Geographic information system (GIS) hardware and software, *J Public Health Manage Pract.* 1999;5(2):83.

**TABLE 12-3 Selected GIS Software Products: Advantages and Disadvantages**

| GIS Software | Advantages | Disadvantages |
|---|---|---|
| ArcView GIS<br>http://www.esri.com/software/arcgis/arcview/index.html | • Works with ARC/INFO<br>• Excellent tutorials and documentation<br>• Many established users | • Modules priced separately |
| Autodesk MAP<br>http://usa.autodesk.com/adsk/servlet/index?siteID=123112&id=3081357 | • Reads/writes popular GIS and database formats | • Limited documentation<br>• No geographic or demographic data included |
| EpiInfo<br>http://www.cdc.gov/epiinfo/<br>http://www.cdc.gov/epiinfo/maps.htm | • Public domain<br>• Simple to use<br>• Written by CDC | • Limited GIS features |
| Geomedia<br>http://www.intergraph.com/geomedia/ | • Open GIS enterprise solution | • Limited documentation<br>• No geographic or demographic data included |
| MapInfo<br>http://www.mapinfo.com/ | • Excellent documentation<br>• Many established users<br>• Much aftermarket data | • Few branch offices<br>• Quality of resellers may vary |
| Maptitude | • Inexpensive<br>• Bundled with abundance of data<br>• Exports data in variety of GIS formats | • Small user base<br>• Limited documentation |

Adapted with permission from Thrall SE. Geographic information system (GIS) hardware and software. *J Public Health Manage Pract*. 1999;5(2):87.

nity health improvement. (Refer to Chapter 16 for detailed discussion on constituencies.) Public health officials can then help obtain the data sets and incorporate them into an effective assessment system. This essentially creates a "one-stop" shopping data system, eliminating the need for users to search for data from multiple sources.

An early prototype GIS application is one example of how this may work. Figure 12-7 is a map of teen male arrest rates by high school attendance areas in Clackamas County, Oregon.[4]

Historically, local law enforcement agencies had used the location of crime and arrest events rather than incident rates in determining where to deploy resources. With public health input, the Juvenile Crime Subcommittee of the Local Public Safety Coordinating Council became interested in looking at juvenile arrest rates as a measure of community health and safety. Their interest increased when they found that they could use GIS to map and analyze juvenile arrest rates, and associated risk factors, at the subcounty, community level.

On the sample map, the case definition for a teen male arrest is age (10–17), male gender, and an arrest report by law enforcement agencies. The GIS application calculated rates based on the residence of the arrested teen. Public health officials selected high school attendance areas as a community definition because of the potential to design interventions and educational

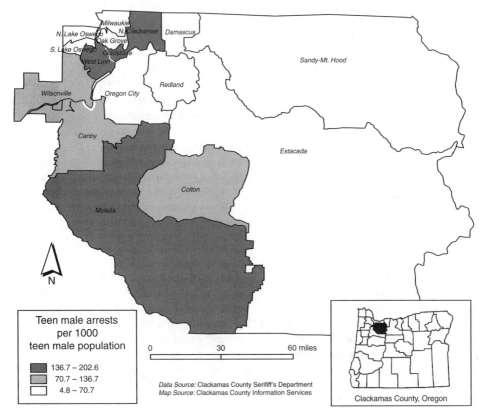

FIGURE 12-7    Teen Male Arrest Rates, Ages 10–17, by High School Attendance Area: Clackamas County, OR, 1995
*Source:* Clackamas County Information Services Clackamas County, Oregon.

messages targeted at high school teachers, students, and parents. Public input through several focus groups confirmed high school attendance area as a reasonable definition of community. Using census block group aggregations, local health officials and their partners analyzed and mapped (on choropleth maps) juvenile arrest rates for each high school attendance area in the county. The application enabled communities to calculate confidence intervals around these rates to determine whether community juvenile arrest rates were significantly above or below benchmark rates.

As the system is developed, it could help community members visualize patterns of juvenile arrests in relationship to demographic factors, specific crimes committed, and community health indicators, such as the poverty rate.[4] In addition, by obtaining other data sets such as the YRBS data, health officials could help communities examine relationships between juvenile arrest rates and behavioral risk factors. With a time trend statistical analysis feature, future applications could enable community partners to evaluate the effectiveness of neighborhood-level juvenile crime prevention initiatives over time.

### Diffusing the Technology, Serving as Resources, and Inserting the Science

Public health officials wanting dialogue and strengthened relationships with local communities, and wanting to develop policy through collaboration, will have to make health information readily available. The information will have to be of high quality and adequately referenced. Health officials at all levels—local, state, and federal—will have to work with their public and private partners to develop guidelines for metadata. These guidelines should include standards for geocoding and data quality. In addition, health officials at all levels will have a responsibility, with their public and private partners, to develop guidelines on data sharing and confidentiality. Adequate guidelines should lead to the development of new and improved data sets, such as morbidity data, that will be relevant to every community.

Once data become readily available, public health officials will have an additional responsibility to work with their partners in teaching the basic concepts in epidemiology and ensuring that the data is used appropriately. Fortunately, GIS are compatible with existing community planning tools, such as Mobilizing Action Through Planning and Partnership (MAPP) and the Assessment Protocol for Excellence in Public Health (APEXPH).[43] (See Chapter 15 for a more detailed discussion.) In many communities, a major issue has been how to assess community health given the chaotic location of health-related data. APEXPH98 software integrated with GIS can provide communities with a tool to organize the process of health assessment at the subcounty level.[4] The most recently developed planning tools, such as the Protocol for Assessing Community Excellence in Environmental Health (PACE-EH), are compatible with GIS.[44]

Several states and communities have developed interactive Internet sites allowing community partners to analyze health issues at the county, and in some cases, neighborhood level. Each of these sites has strengths and weaknesses, as indicated in Table 12-4.*

*The author would like to acknowledge Mandy Green, MPH, GIS/Community Health Assessment Analyst for Clackamas County, Oregon, Community Health Division, for her contribution to this table.

**TABLE 12-4    Interactive Internet Sites for Community Health Issues**

| Jurisdiction | Description |
|---|---|
| South Carolina Department of Health and Environment, Division of Biostatistics and Health GIS. http://scangis.dhec.sc.gov. Accessed 12/29/05. | User can select from births, deaths, cancer, teen pregnancy, childhood lead poisoning, fetal deaths, hospital discharge, infant mortality, health disparities initiative, etc., using multiple combinations of variables. Output is table with options for a variety of charts. The output appears as a pop-up window, taking some time to generate. Users can create choropleth maps by Zip code, county, or DHEC (Dept. Health and Environmental Control) region. The user specifies quartiles or quintiles. The legend title includes rate denominator, interstates, and county boundaries shown—user may add senate or house districts. Map prints with legend and title, but does not save as image. |
| Florida Department of Health Community Health Assessment Resource Tool Set (CHARTS). http://www.floridacharts.com/ charts/CensusTractMap. aspx. Accessed 12/29/05. | Users create maps of vital statistics data and census data. The user interface is a bit clunky, and users can map only one variable at a time. The application provides good labeling and user tools. Vital stats are available in 5-year aggregations. User can choose entire state or county. Map shows variables down to tract level. Identify tool shows Census profile for a selected county. Map can be saved as HTML including title, legend, disclaimers, and printed up to 34″ × 44″. |
| King County, WA (White Center & Boulevard Park neighborhoods). http://www.metrokc.gov/ health/datamaps. Accessed 12/29/05. | MetroKC White Center and Boulevard Park mapping application includes census data layers, which can be mapped one at a time (this displays the data in a bar chart comparing to the county and state as well as the table of the indicator by block group). Maps include detailed labels (e.g., African-American population percent of total population, 2000 by Census block group). Maps saved as 3″ × 4″ GIFs at 96 ppi but do not include labels or the legend. |
| Washington State Department of Health VistaPH. http://www.doh.wa.gov/ EHSPHL/CHS/Vista/ default.htm. Accessed 12/29/05. | Users can request information on cancer incidence; abortion, pregnancy, and fertility rates; birth risk factors; communicable disease incidence, including sexually transmitted disease rates and tuberculosis rate; hospitalization rates; mortality, including infant death rates and causes; divorces; marriages; and life expectancy, population tables, and social and economic status. Data are displayed in table format. "NR" is shown if events $<$ 5 for rates or $<$ 30 for cancer stage at diagnosis or NA if data are not available; for county-level cancer rates and incidence, 3- or 5-year aggregations are available. User can download software and data for running statistical analyses re: WA State. |
| Baltimore City Data Collaborative. http://www.baltimorekids data.org/htdocs/maps/ interactive.html. Accessed 12/29/05. | Application contains data on children's health by community/neighborhood or census tract for Baltimore, MD. User can get a profile for each community listing indicators such as infant mortality, child abuse, school performance, teen births, families in poverty, and overall demographics compared to the same info for the whole city. User can choose a variety of health indicators or resources for children to map, but only one at a time. Maps created are PDF files, which include title and legend, but can not be manipulated or changed by the user.              *(continues)* |

**TABLE 12-4 (continued)**

| Jurisdiction | Description |
|---|---|
| CERP (Community Environmental Resource Program) of St. Louis, MO. http://stlcin.missouri.org/cerp/data.cfm. Accessed 12/29/05. | Interactive mapping of environmental hazards (lead, brownfields, vacant buildings, refuse/waste, and EPA regulatory data maps) for St. Louis and East St. Louis, MO. User can select topic area with one specific indicator at a time and map by neighborhood or ward. Indicators are not well defined and user interface could use improvement. |
| DataSource: The Franklin County, Ohio, Community Data System. http://www.datasource columbus.org. Accessed 12/29/05. | User can define neighborhood to analyze by selecting block groups, or can look at entire county by tract, block group, ZIP code, elementary school attendance area, school district, county child services district, opportunity center service area, or neighborhood liaison area. User may create choropleth by equal intervals, quantiles, or standard deviation and may select the number of classes. Data are available on childcare, child welfare, census data, property values, land use, public assistance, student achievement, student attendance, student population, and water service, but only one variable at a time. User interface is a little slow and frustrating. |
| Baltimore, MD, Neighborhood Indicators Alliance. http://www.bnia.org/mapping/index.html. Accessed 12/29/05. | Data are available for 55 community statistical areas (CSA). Clusters of Baltimore neighborhoods have been created along census tract boundaries to form 55 CSAs. This clustering was necessary for the creation of statistical areas since most of the 270+ neighborhoods in Baltimore City do not have boundaries that fall along census tracts. User can choose choropleths of indicators (one at a time) for census data, crime data, births, housing, sanitation, etc. Some summary measures of community health are available as static maps. The application allows some customization of data classes and variables, but map navigation and overall design of Web interface could use improvement. |

## Facilitating Community Health Improvement

Like other analytic tools, the greatest promise of GIS technology lies in raising additional questions rather than in coming up with answers. The map begins or advances, but not ends, the process of community health improvement. In this way, the development of GIS and other new technologies may change the fundamental roles of public health officials. The public health professional of the 21st century can work closely with his or her community partners to ask questions about community health at the neighborhood level. Together, they can use the new technology to develop neighborhood-based programs that rely on community strengths and meet community needs. Public health officials should serve as resources and facilitators in gathering data, ensuring data quality, and inviting their partners to the community health improvement table. As the technology and information become more available, public health officials can lead the way in promoting assessment, policy development, and assurance as community responsibilities rather than government responsibilities.

## Chapter Review

1. GIS require a foundation of spatial or geographic data. Easily obtainable geographic data files are available from the Census Bureau with detailed street and address information and administrative boundaries including census tract, ZIP codes, and county boundaries.
2. The next step is to obtain attribute data and link them to the geographic database. Examples include vital statistics and law enforcement data. GIS can analyze any attribute database, such as arrest or birth data, that includes a field with a location. Confidentiality issues pose a significant limitation because data with personal addresses can identify individuals. One possible solution is to present aggregated data.
3. Geocoding is the process by which GIS software matches each record in an attribute database with the geographic file. The GIS software converts each address in the attribute file to a point on the map. The data are ready for analysis and display.
4. The overlay capability of GIS allows the user to display more than one attribute on a map at a time.
5. Misinterpretation of results can occur if the GIS user regards associations between geography and health outcomes as causally related. Usually, outcomes will cluster geographically because of underlying population characteristics and not because of the geography itself.
6. GIS encourages public health officials and communities to form partnerships to assess community health status.

## References

1. Snow J. *On the Mode of Communication of Cholera.* 2nd ed. New York, NY: Commonwealth Fund; 1936.
2. Melnick AL, Fleming DW. Modern geographic information systems—promise and pitfalls. *J Public Health Manage Pract.* 1999;5(2):viii–x.
3. Roper WL, Mays GP. GIS in public health policy: a new frontier for improving community health. *J Public Health Manage Pract.* 1999;5(2):vi–vii.
4. Melnick A, Seigal N, Hildner J. Clackamas County Department of Human Services community health mapping engine (CHiME) geographic information systems project. *J Public Health Manage Pract.* 1999;5(2):64–69.
5. Clarke KC, McLafferty SL, Tempalski BJ. On epidemiology and geographic information systems: a review and discussion of future directions. *Emerg Infect Dis.* 1996;2(2):85–92.
6. Tim US. The application of GIS in environmental health sciences: opportunities and limitations. *Environ Res.* 1995;71:75–88.
7. Rogers MY. Getting started with geographic information systems (GIS): a local health department perspective. *J Public Health Manage Pract.* 1999;5(4):22–33.
8. Wilkinson S, Gobalet JG, Majoros M, et al. Lead hot zones and childhood lead poisoning cases, Santa Clara County, California, 1995. *J Public Health Manage Pract.* 1999;5(2):11–12.
9. Croner CM, Sperling J, Broome FR. Geographic information systems (GIS): new perspectives in understanding human health and environmental relationships. *Stat Med.* 1996;15:1961–1977.
10. McLafferty S, Cromley E. Your first mapping project on your own: from A to Z. *J Public Health Manage Pract.* 1999;5(2):76–82.

11. Duclos C, Johnson T, Thompson T. Development of childhood blood lead screening guidelines, Duval County, Florida, 1998. *J Public Health Manage Pract.* 1999;5(2):9–10.

12. Vine MF, Degnan D, Hanchette C. Geographic information systems: their use in environmental epidemiologic research. *Environ Health Perspect.* 1997;105(6):598–605.

13. Bouton PH, Fraser M. Local health departments and GIS: the perspective of the National Association of County and City Health Officials. *J Public Health Manage Pract.* 1999;5(4):33–41.

14. Zenk SN, Schulz AJ, Israel BA, et al. Neighborhood racial composition, neighborhood poverty, and the spatial accessibility of supermarkets in metropolitan Detroit. *Am J Public Health.* 2005;95(4):660–667.

15. Nuckols JR, Ward MH, Jarup L. Using geographic information systems for exposure assessment in environmental epidemiology studies. *Environ Health Perspect.* 2004;112(9):1007–1015.

16. Dolk H, Vrijheid M, Armstrong B, et al. Risk of congenital anomalies near hazardous-waste landfill sites in Europe: the EUROHAZCON study. *Lancet.* 1998;352(9126):423–427.

17. Fielder HMP, Poon–King CM, Palmer SR, Moss N, Coleman G. Assessment of impact on health of residents living near the Nant–Y–Gwyddon land-fill site: retrospective analysis. *BMJ.* 2000;320:19–22.

18. Ralston M. Elevated nitrate levels in relation to bedrock depth, Linn County, Iowa, 1991–1996. *J Public Health Manage Pract.* 1999;5(2):39–40.

19. Reif JS, Burch JB, Nuckols JR, Metzger L, Ellington D, Anger WK. Neurobehavioral effects of exposure to trichloroethylene through a municipal water supply. *Environ Res.* 2003;93(3):248–258.

20. Poulstrup A, Hansen HL. Use of GIS and exposure modeling as tools in a study of cancer incidence in a population exposed to airborne dioxin. *Environ Health Perspect.* 2004;112(9):1032–1036.

21. Oyana TJ, Rogerson P, Lwebuga-Mukasa JS. Geographic clustering of adult asthma hospitalization and residential exposure to pollution at a United States-Canada border crossing. *Am J Public Health.* 2004;94(7):1250–1257.

22. Henriques WD, Spengler RF. Locations around the Hanford Nuclear Facility where average milk consumption by children in 1945 would have resulted in an estimated median iodine-131 dose to the thyroid of 10 rad or higher, Washington. *J Public Health Manage Pract.* 1999;5(2):35–36.

23. Bellander T, Berglind N, Gustavsson P, et al. Using geographic information systems to assess individual historical exposure to air pollution from traffic and house heating in Stockholm. *Environ Health Perspec.* 2001;109(6):633–639.

24. Nyberg F, Gustavsson P, Jarup L, et al. Urban air pollution and lung cancer in Stockholm. *Epidemiology.* 2000;11(5):487–495.

25. Dolinoy DC, Miranda ML. GIS modeling of air toxics releases from TRI-reporting and non-TRI-reporting facilities: impacts for environmental justice. *Environ Health Perspect.* 2004;112(17):1717–1724.

26. Glass GE, Schwartz BS, Morgan JM, et al. Environmental risk factors for Lyme disease identified with geographic information systems. *Am J Public Health.* 1995;85(7):944–948.

27. Openshaw S, Charlton C, Wymer C, et al. A Mark 1 geographical analysis machine for the automated analysis of point data sets. *Int J Geogr Inf Syst.* 1987;1:335–358.

28. Wang F. Spatial clusters of cancers in Illinois 1986–2000. *J Med Syst.* 2004;28(3):237–256.

29. Wu J, Wang J, Meng B, et al. Exploratory spatial data analysis for the identification of risk factors to birth defects. *BMC Public Health.* 2004; 18(4):23.
30. McKnight JL, Kretzman JP. *Mapping Community Capacity. The Asset-Based Community Development Institute.* Evanston, Ill: Institute for Policy Research, Northwestern University; 1996.
31. Lee CV, Irving JL. Sources of spatial data for community health planning. *J Public Health Manage Pract.* 1999;5(4):7–22.
32. Lerner EB, Fairbanks RJ, Shah MN. Identification of out-of-hospital cardiac arrest clusters using a geographic information system. *Acad Emerg Med.* 2005;12(1):81–84.
33. Mason M, Cheung I, Walker L. Substance use, social networks, and the geography of urban adolescents. *Substance Use Misuse.* 2004;39(10–12): 1751–1777.
34. Gordon A, Womersley J. The use of mapping in public health and planning health services. *J Public Health Med.* 1997;19(2):139–147.
35. Morgenstern H. Ecologic studies. In: Rothman KJ, Greenland S, eds. *Modern Epidemiology.* 2nd ed. Philadelphia, Pa: Lippincott-Raven Publishers; 1998:459–480.
36. Whitsel EA, Rose KM, Wood JL, Henley AC, Liao D, Geiss G. Accuracy and repeatability of commercial geocoding. *Am J Epidemiol.* 2004; 160(10):1023–1029.
37. Elliot P, Wartenburg D. Spatial epidemiology: current approaches and future challenges. *Environ Health Perspect.* 2004;112(9):998–1006.
38. Cox LH. Protecting confidentiality in small population health and environmental statistics. *Stat Med.* 1996;15:1895–1905.
39. Goodman DC, Wennberg JE. Maps and health: the challenges of interpretation. *J Public Health Manage Pract.* 1999;5(4):xiii–xvii.
40. Thrall SE. Geographic information system (GIS) hardware and software. *J Public Health Manage Pract.* 1999;5(2):82–90.
41. Thrall GI. The future of GIS in public health management and practice. *J Public Health Manage Pract.* 1999;5(4):75–82.
42. Institute of Medicine, Division of Health Care Services. *The Future of Public Health.* Washington, DC: National Academies Press; 1988.
43. National Association of County and City Health Officials. Mobilizing Action Through Planning and Partnership (MAPP). Available at: http://www.naccho.org/topics/infrastructure/MAPP.cfm. Accessed November 20, 2005.
44. National Association of County and City Health Officials. Pace EH demonstration site project: Communities in Action. Available at: http://www.naccho.org/topics/environmental/documents/PACE_EH_proof.pdf. Accessed November 20, 2005.

# CHAPTER 13

# USING INFORMATION SYSTEMS FOR PUBLIC HEALTH ADMINISTRATION

James Studnicki*
Donald J. Berndt
John W. Fisher

> Where is the Life we have lost in living?
> Where is the wisdom we have lost in knowledge?
> Where is the knowledge we have lost in information?
> —T.S. Eliot, *Choruses from the Rock*

## Chapter Overview

Public health organizations require well-designed information systems in order to make optimal use of the mounting supply of health-related data. Organizations rely on these systems to inform managerial decision making and improve operations in areas such as epidemiologic surveillance, health outcomes assessment, program and clinic administration, program evaluation and performance measurement, public health planning, and policy analysis. Key design considerations in developing information systems include service-based and population-based application objectives, units of analysis, data sources, data linkage methods, technology selection and integration strategies, and information privacy protections. A growing collection of models and resources now exists for developing effective information systems for public health organizations.

Information systems have emerged as an essential public health tool. Today, information systems provide real-time data to guide public health decisions. The rise in importance of health information systems (HISs) has three fundamental sources: (1) the expanding breadth of data available from multiple public and private sources, (2) advances in information technology (IT), and (3) the growing recognition of the power of information in public health decision making. Administrative data from public and private health service providers as well as insurers contain an electronic history of healthcare cost

---

*The authors wish to acknowledge the work of Stephen Parente, the author of the previous version of this chapter.

and use. Government surveys provide an unprecedented level of detailed information on health status, functional status, medical care use and expenditures, nutrition, sociodemographics, and health behaviors.

HISs support a wide variety of public health system objectives, including the following:

- Epidemiologic disease and risk factor surveillance
- Medical and public health outcomes assessment
- Facility and clinic administration (billing, inventory, clinical records, utilization review), cost-effectiveness, and productivity analysis
- Utilization analysis and demand estimation
- Program planning and evaluation
- Quality assurance and performance measurement
- Public health policy analysis
- Clinical research
- Health education and health information dissemination

IT has now advanced to the point that one year of the Medicare program's entire claims history—roughly 200 million observations—can be analyzed on a high-end personal computer (PC) workstation. Advances in IT are dramatically influencing public health organizations and their historical roles in collecting and disseminating data. Vital statistics and disease registries—critical functions of public health departments at both the local and national level—are being transformed by IT and its emphasis on evidence-based decision making. Yet, HIS resources remain difficult to develop and manage in addressing current public health challenges. Data sets are located in a balkanized array of separate computing platforms with little interconnectivity. For HISs to be effective, public health administrators must assess available data sources, design blueprints for extracting information and knowledge, and evaluate the benefits derived from these systems.

This chapter examines concepts, resources, and examples of HISs for public health organizations. Issues and implications for public health management are explored in the following five areas:

1. Contemporary concepts and applications of HISs in public health
2. Information systems architectures
3. Available databases
4. Operational models
5. Privacy and security

## Contemporary Concepts and Applications

What is public health information? A more telling question may be what is *not* public health information, because the scope of data required to examine scientifically the multiple and overlapping health, social, and environmental factors that affect a population can be enormous. Traditionally, public health or epidemiologic data consist of vital statistics, disease registries, and other surveillance-based resources. However, these resources are often limited in scope because they only record natality, morbidity, mortality, and perhaps some measure of environmental and behavioral influences. Managing health resources effectively at the population level requires a much broader scope of data resources to measure the effectiveness and cost of health interventions and policies.

An examination of public health applications of HISs is facilitated by an understanding of the two most common applications of these systems in practice. First, information systems are used to store and make available service data that reflect activities performed by public health organizations and other health-related entities. Second, information systems store and make available population-based data that are important for surveillance, program evaluation, policy making, and priority setting in public health. These two common applications are not separate but interact extensively.

For example, routinely collected service data by local public health agencies often include the results of blood lead screening of children under 5 years of age, immunization status, and encounter data recording the results of client visits for tuberculosis (TB) and sexually transmitted diseases (STDs). Other routinely collected service data include records of individual client encounters in the federal Special Supplemental Food Program for Women, Infants, and Children (WIC) and other early intervention programs. These service data are important for the effective management of individual care by public health and ambulatory care providers. Importantly, these data reflect individual transactions and can be used to monitor program performance and to describe a group of users at a particular facility—but they do not necessarily offer information about an entire community or population.

An important practical distinction exists between the service-based application of HISs and the population-based application, which offers information about defined communities and population groups of interest. To support this latter application, information systems must integrate data from major population-wide sources such as vital statistics registries and disease surveillance systems. In some cases, service data may also contribute to population-based information.

For example, the National Notifiable Diseases Surveillance System (NNDSS), formed more than a century ago, serves as a major source of population-wide data. This system captures information on disease incidence for approximately 50 diseases, which require accurate and timely information for effective prevention and control. The Centers for Disease Control and Prevention (CDC) receives reports of disease from the 50 states, two cities (New York City and the District of Columbia), and five territories.[1] This database is most useful to public health agencies because of its ability to analyze trends and conduct comparisons of disease incidence among communities.

Population-based information systems may also be constructed from service-level data. The immunization registries recently implemented by many state and local public health agencies provide an excellent example of this use. These registries record immunization status and vaccinations provided to all children residing within a defined geographic area so that this information is available not only to the initial provider, but also to other providers, health plans, and schools. Many of these registries incorporate birth certificate data for children born in the community, adding a population denominator. This is an example of an information system that provides service-level information that is helpful to individual providers and their patients, while also providing population-level information that is helpful to public health organizations for surveillance, program evaluation, and policy making. A key qualification, however, is that a large proportion of the children in the community must be captured by such information systems in order for population-based information to have validity and reliability.

Drawing on the successes of immunization registries, a growing number of local public health organizations are developing computerized information systems for other purposes. For example, some local systems track the results of blood lead screenings performed at public health clinics, thereby producing important service information regarding the number of children screened, those with elevated blood lead levels, and those receiving follow-up treatment and lead abatement services. This information is based on service data, but if the systems can capture data on all children in a defined community, then valuable population-based information can become available.

The relatively recent availability of state-of-the art computing technology has enabled public health organizations to collect health data rapidly and extract meaningful information about community health status.[2] The major challenge is to integrate data sources and develop networks that make this information optimally available to public health organizations at all levels of government as well as to appropriate entities in the private sector. New service-oriented computing architectures are intended to build these types of networked information systems. The current impetus to have a surveillance capability supported by a national network of public health HISs is fueled by concerns about bioterrorism and emerging infectious diseases, resulting in sizeable investments by the CDC for constructing linked information systems. (See Chapter 23 for more information on the use of public health information in managing disasters.)

Major practical goals for the future development of HISs for public health organizations include the following:

- Integrate the multiple data sources available for public health purposes.
- Network information systems to make interaction and information flow between different entities feasible.
- Use health care delivery information systems to produce public health information regarding preventive services, preventable diseases, and quality of care.

## Integration

Government public health agencies have historically designed computer-based information systems for single programs. For years, the same data were entered and maintained in many different, often incompatible, systems that supported different public health programs.[3] This duplicative and fragmented information infrastructure hindered the ability of public health managers to know what data existed and how to access them. For example, most local public health agencies maintain multiple programs for children, including lead toxicity prevention, immunization, WIC, and early intervention services. Meanwhile, the local departments of social services enroll families in Medicaid. Despite the fact that Medicaid and public health programs serve client populations that overlap substantially in most communities, the databases used to manage these programs are entirely separate in most cases, reflecting the categorical mechanisms that support these programs. Information systems integration can offer opportunities for improved service delivery and enhanced population-based decision making and management.

Linkage of data sets is often an effective method to obtain information across programs. For example, linkage of WIC records with Medicaid, birth and death, and hospital discharge files has enabled program analysts to document the effectiveness of the WIC program in reducing infant death and costly neonatal hospitalizations. Similarly, linking lead screening registries, Medicaid eligibility files, and managed care plan enrollment files can enable public health organizations to monitor compliance with lead screening by health plans. These linkages for special-purpose studies are often highly customized and assembled only for the duration of particular studies. The ongoing surveillance and community assessment activities that represent core public health functions require HISs to accumulate and integrate data for continuous use. (For more detailed discussion on community assessment, refer to Chapter 15.) This is a data warehousing problem. Data warehousing technologies are widely available and should become a key technology in the public health arena. Data warehouses organize data as cubes that can be "sliced and diced," providing a flexible environment to pursue analyses. Vital statistics, hospital discharge data, and disease registries can be integrated with demographic and economic data to populate public health data warehouses. For example, the Comprehensive Assessment for Tracking Community Health (CATCH) data warehouse integrates Florida data for use by health planners.[4] The warehouse has been used to generate more than three dozen assessment reports, along with many more targeted research projects.

Public health agencies are also beginning to innovate by using unconventional data sources such as market research databases. For example, electronic information compiled from grocery and drug store sales can be used as part of an HIS to identify the purchase of cigarettes concomitantly with products associated with pregnancy or infants, such as diapers. This information by ZIP code can help target or evaluate public health intervention programs, such as efforts to prevent tobacco use in the perinatal period.

## Networks

Another major function of HISs in public health is to create linked networks of information that can strengthen public health operations by: (1) facilitating communication among public health practitioners throughout the United States, (2) enhancing the accessibility of information, and (3) allowing swift and secure exchange of public health data.[5] As a prominent example, the CDC initiated the Information Network for Public Health Officials (INPHO) in 1992. The CDC has been the major supporter of efforts to create networks that link public health information from localities and states with that of federal agencies. Information networks of this type are increasingly indispensable for disease surveillance activities, particularly in cases of local disease outbreaks that have the potential to spread regionally and nationally. In this way, HISs can help to create and sustain effective interorganizational relationships among public health organizations.

## Utilization of Health Care Delivery Systems

Public health organizations can also benefit from timely access to health care services information from providers of personal healthcare services.[5] For example, immunization registries must acquire information on immunization status from multiple community providers who deliver vaccinations. In a growing number of communities, public health organizations are able to obtain relevant and timely information from the systems that are maintained by health care delivery organizations. Large delivery systems can offer information on the delivery and utilization of preventive services (including missed opportunities for prevention), the incidence of preventable diagnoses and co-morbidities, and the quality of healthcare facilities and providers (such as rates of medical errors, mortality, and hospital infections).

These types of resources drive the contemporary development of HISs among public health organizations, and they reflect a basic change of thought regarding the delivery of medical and public health services subsequent to the 1993 federal health reform initiative. This initiative accentuated the need for informed decision making by consumers, providers, employers, and governments. For example, the Clinton administration reform plan relied solely on analyses of the 1987 National Medical Expenditure Survey (NMES) to draw conclusions about the future demand for and cost of health care in the United States. Between the time the NMES was fielded and 1993, the dominance of fee-for-service gave way to managed care as the primary health financing mechanism for the private and public insurance market. As a result, the 1987 NMES could not reliably estimate the impact of the administration's health-care reform proposal without significant and possibly questionable assumptions. The limitations of the data increased the administration's interest in an annual survey that could provide better estimates of a rapidly changing market. In 1996, the Agency for Health Care Policy and Research fielded the Medical Expenditure Panel Survey (MEPS), providing a national annual survey instrument to track changes in health care use and cost as well as health status and insurance coverage. A similar demand for information came from employers, who wanted health plans to provide standardized information on the value of their products. The result was a cooperative effort between employers and health insurers to develop a common set of health plan performance measures known formally as the Health Plan Employers Information Data Set (HEDIS), developed by the National Committee for Quality Assurance. Some of the HEDIS measures were prevention oriented (e.g., immunization) and thus illustrated the principle of obtaining public health information from a health care delivery information system.[5] (See Chapter 11 for more information on data and Chapter 18 for more information on the evaluation of public health information.)

Building new databases for multiple purposes such as MEPS and HEDIS required a clear identification of HIS objectives as well as knowledge of the strengths and weaknesses of established data structures. This knowledge is essential in determining which structures can be recycled in building a new database, such as using existing health insurer records for HEDIS, and which structures need to be newly constructed, such as designing medical record abstraction protocols for obtaining disease and outcomes data for HEDIS. With appropriate design, medical encounter data (service data) can be used for several population-based purposes, including community health assessment, surveillance, and evaluation.

## Information Systems Architectures

A common misperception in developing HISs for public health applications is the expectation that such systems are analogous to their counterparts in IT-intensive industries such as banking or manufacturing. Health is a combination of many uncertain inputs. These inputs range from the unique biologic and behavioral characteristics of the individual patient or population under study, to health insurance characteristics and the accessibility of health resources, to the practice styles of physicians and other health professionals, as well as to thousands of possible diagnoses, comorbidities, risk factors, and interventions. In combination, these inputs generate millions of possible outcomes for a given health episode. Consequently, the HISs used to support public health applications and decision making may need to be more complex and costly than the systems supporting applications in other industries and professions.

In building an HIS, the field of health informatics constitutes a multidisciplinary core of expertise, including specialists from the following fields:

- Computer science
- Electrical engineering
- Medicine, nursing, and allied health management
- Finance and accounting operations research
- Economics
- Sociology
- Survey design
- Epidemiology
- Statistics

These disciplines work in combination to produce HISs to serve the public health system objectives described above. In designing and managing HISs, public health administrators require the ability to: (1) distinguish between data, information, and knowledge; (2) define units of analysis for the level of data aggregation; and (3) understand the health IT architecture of system(s) to be used.

### Data vs. Information vs. Knowledge vs. Wisdom

There have been endless discussions on the differences between data, information, and knowledge. Although the boundaries seem somewhat blurred, the distinction can be helpful at a more abstract level. The current conception of the data, information, knowledge, wisdom (DIKW) hierarchy can be traced in part to T.S. Eliot's poetry that started the chapter. *Data* are raw facts and statistics that are collected as part of the normal functioning of a business, clinical encounter, or research experiment. *Information* is data that has been processed in a structured, intelligent way to obtain results that are directly useful to managers and analysts. This is often the case once data has been organized in a database management system. *Knowledge* is obtained by using information to explain the context of a problem or situation. Finally, *wisdom* is knowledge tempered by experience.

In public health, data are obtained from a variety of sources ranging from patient history at a clinical visit to health insurance claims to bacteriology laboratory reports. To be valuable for generating information and knowledge, data must be readily accessible and reliable. Generally, electronic data in standardized formats are most efficient. However, data that are easy to obtain may not be the most accurate or precise. For example, electronic health insurance claims data can identify a specific immunization on a particular date but do not indicate the child's overall immunization status. For that information, medical records or reports from a computerized immunization registry are needed. Thus, the cost of obtaining accurate and precise knowledge concerning a child's immunization status may be outside the scope of existing data collection processes. Ethical questions also arise if immunization data had to be transferred from another source and parental consent had not been given. (See Chapter 5 for a more detailed discussion on ethics.)

## Service-Oriented Computing

Healthcare planners and administrators are likely to interact with large-scale information systems both as end users and participants on implementation teams charged with the responsibility of deploying new technologies. Even direct providers of care can use an increasingly integrated set of information systems to capture patient-level data in electronic medical records, as well as more general knowledge for clinical decision support systems. This section explores the architectural considerations of large-scale information systems as computing power continues to dramatically improve with each new release and the growth of networking provides increasingly reliable interconnections.

Among the most interesting and promising trends in information systems architecture is the growing body of technologies and standards for service-oriented architectures. In the past, software engineering involved building monolithic systems from customized single-use components. Although the components might be well built and offer sophisticated capabilities, the number of dependencies between components is a source of failure in such highly customized complex systems. Newer programming language extensions and object-oriented approaches emphasize the encapsulation of component details and more explicit programming interfaces to better manage growing software complexity. These evolving software development tools support servicelike approaches based on reusable components. More current service-oriented architectures continue this trend, providing standards for defining and using Web-based services.

Service-oriented computing (SOC) is not new, but maturing standards support the approach and make implementing complex service-based systems practical. As many traditional software engineers observed, it is possible to adhere to the principles of encapsulation and other good programming practices in any language, but explicit support makes the task much easier. Service-oriented computing standards such as the Extensible Markup Language (XML), Simple Object Access Protocol (SOAP), and Web Service Description Language (WDSL), govern the structure, transmission, and description of services. Registry standards such as the Universal Description, Discovery, and Integration

(UDDI) protocol provide a method for publishing and finding services as components of complex systems. These standards allow developers to implement high-quality, tightly focused computing services that can be published and serve as components in large information systems.[6]

Among the most important goals of well-designed information system architectures are scalability to meet growing demands, flexibility to meet changing demands, and reliability or fault tolerance so systems are continually available to meet all demands. Being an agile organization places a premium on the flexibility to change business processes and supporting information systems by adding or modifying components. This is particularly challenging given the number of independent or quasi-independent providers that coordinate to deliver health services. A key advantage of service-oriented computing is the loose coupling between components. No detailed knowledge of the internal operation of a service is required and all coordination is managed through standardized protocols. Using this approach, services can be reused, rearranged, and new services can be added, as systems are adapted in the pursuit of new opportunities.

## Computer Networking

Computer networking and communication technologies provide the glue that binds the different components or services that form complex, distributed information systems. Typically, networking tasks are separated by the general nature of the connection and the underlying technologies used to handle the communications (see Figure 13-1). The major technology classes are wide area networking (WAN), local area networking (LAN), and storage area networking (SAN), although this latter category receives much less attention in the popular press.

*Wide area networking* is the term applied to the task of interconnecting large numbers of geographically dispersed computers. This is typically accomplished in piecemeal fashion by interconnecting smaller networks to create more global connectivity—the Internet being the quintessential example. Internetworking relies on standard protocols or rules of engagement that allow data to be routed through cooperating networks. Although there have been many competing proposals, the current standard that governs the Internet is the Transmission Control Protocol/Internet Protocol (TCP/IP). The Internet Protocol provides for routing or message delivery through cooperating networks, with the most basic service being best-effort delivery of a message (with no guarantees). The Transmission Control Protocol provides a reliable end-to-end delivery service that costs a bit more (computationally speaking). So the services are much like the dilemma that faces any physical mail user, cheap delivery with no guarantees and such premium services as return receipt and package tracking. These wide area networking protocols provide the foundation for the emerging service-oriented computing approaches discussed above.

A local area network (LAN) spans an office, the floor of building, or similarly restricted geographic area. There can be many computers in this small area that are typically interconnected by shared media. That is, devices compete for access to a wire or other means of communication, but the sporadic nature of traffic means overall performance is reasonable. Not every computer needs access to the network at the same time. Ethernet is the dominant

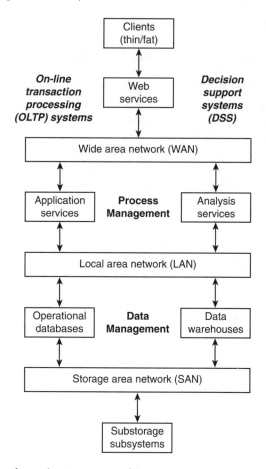

**FIGURE 13-1  Information Systems Architecture**

technology in this arena because of its very low costs, wide availability, and continually improving speeds. In a clinical environment, local area networks are likely to interconnect departmental devices, including handheld wireless devices that are becoming increasingly important.

Storage area networking (SAN) technologies provide an infrastructure for the lower levels of tiered architectures. Database systems, file transfers, document handling, and image storage and retrieval all require the transmission of large amounts of data. Storage area networks provide a high-performance alternative for such demanding tasks. SAN technologies allow storage to be centralized and flexibly reallocated through network addressing.

## Tiered Architectures

Figure 13-1 presents an architectural framework that illustrates some of the major logical functions that are embodied in complex information systems, from the interfaces with the ultimate end users to the storage subsystems that protect very large collections of data. The arrangement of subsystems in separate tiers or layers provides more flexibility as whole systems need to be reconfigured to meet new demands. The ability to meet larger demands is also enhanced by allowing bottlenecks to be isolated and removed by improving computer performance or having several computers focus on a single task. Finally, tiered architectures separate tasks and thereby reduce the dependencies that often cause system failures. These tiers are viewed as logical functions that might physically reside on a single server in the case of a small system or on many machines in complex distributed systems.

## Storage Management

Anchoring tiered architectures are storage subsystems, the actual data repositories. This is shown as a separate tier as there have been many advances that allow storage to be more centrally managed and shared across different information systems. The total cost of ownership for storage is dominated by management costs, with a current rule of thumb estimating that for every dollar spent buying storage, 10 dollars is spent managing that storage. Therefore, effectively allocating and managing storage has become an important architectural goal. The high-performance storage area networking infrastructure just discussed has given system designers both the freedom to centralize storage for management and the flexibility to deploy and dynamically reallocate storage as demands change. Storage subsystems can be as simple as redundant arrays of independent (or inexpensive) disks (RAID) that combine two or more disks for fault tolerance and performance gains. In most configurations, redundant data spread across the disk drives allows the storage system to recover from disk failures, as a hot-swappable spare can be rebuilt from surviving drives. This technology has been widely adopted and is now available on even very low-cost servers. The use of networking also allows the storage to be physically separated from servers running databases or other applications. Network attached storage (NAS) uses existing network capabilities to make storage accessible to many computers as a network resource. For demanding applications, dedicated storage area networks can be used to attach advanced subsystems that offer large storage sizes, dynamic performance tuning, and integrated backup capabilities. These enterprise-class storage systems seem well suited to healthcare applications that must be highly reliable and meet stringent security demands. These devices also support backup and disaster recovery strategies that are critical in the healthcare industry.

## Data Management

The database management systems market has seen considerable consolidation with a few major vendors holding substantial market shares, along with some interesting open source alternatives. Most products are based on relational database technologies, with extensions that make most systems object-relational database management systems. Relational database systems allow users to query large collections of data without knowledge of the detailed storage structure. A high-level query language, such as the structured query language (SQL), is used to express the desired result. The detailed execution plan for actually retrieving the data is automatically constructed by a query optimizer in the database engine. Users of relational database systems need not be overly concerned with the physical storage characteristics and are largely isolated from changes as specific databases evolve.

An important distinction is made between operational systems that support the day-to-day operations of an organization and decision support systems that provide analytic services. Data warehouses are very large collections of data accumulated over time that allow decision makers to better understand trends and conduct "what-if" analyses. The typical operations in a data warehouse are retrievals or "reads" that summarize large subsets of data. The predictable nature of these retrievals has led to the development of many online analytic processing (OLAP) tools, which allow users to easily navigate and visualize the data, creating customized reports for specific decisions. Data warehouses are populated through fairly complex extraction, transformation, and loading (ETL) processes that collect data from the operational systems and ensure data quality.

## Process Management

The next tier focuses on business processes or workflow management, often on dedicated application servers. There are many tools available for designing and implementing workflows that allow systems to handle many contingencies. A workflow is typically a mixture of human and computer activities coordinated through a process model. There are many examples of workflows or processes in the healthcare industry. For instance, the admission process to a hospital can be formally modeled and embedded in an information system. The individual tasks that makeup a workflow may or may not be dependent on previous tasks, so some can be pursued in parallel, while others must await the completion of prior tasks. Each step may also produce data that is passed to the data management tier. In the case of hospital admissions, it is clearly an operational system that captures newly created data as a patient arrives at the hospital, provides insurance coverage details, and is examined by staff. As an example of service-oriented computing, imagine a Web service provided by health plans that allows the hospital to obtain up-to-the-minute details of insurance coverage without bothering the patient with paperwork. Other excellent examples of healthcare workflows are care guidelines that can be embedded in information systems. As patients undergo specific regimens, departures from accepted care guidelines could be more carefully monitored.

## The Client Side

The upper tier of an information system is concerned with the presentation of any results to the ultimate end users of an information system and should thus reflect the needs of the end user. The software complexity and computing demands reside on the end-user's or client's computer. At one extreme is a computer that uses nothing but a Web browser to interact with a large information system through a Web portal (a very thin client). Though the services might be quite sophisticated and require substantial computing resources, the burden is on the collection of servers that are used to build the core information system, not on the end user's computer. An alternative, somewhat "heavier" client is a computer with a traditional statistical package installed locally that might be used to analyze a large data set from a network accessible database. The data are shipped to the end user's computer where all the analyses are conducted.

Of course, the end users (or their support staff) are responsible for correctly configuring the statistical package, upgrading to newer versions, and ensuring the computer is powerful enough to handle the demanding tasks. Therefore, many corporate computing policies attempt to control and minimize the burden of complex software installed locally on client computers.

In many cases, interaction with the client uses the ubiquitous Internet protocols to deliver content through a Web browser or portal environment. If the system is designed as a true Web service, the protocols discussed above can be used to provide a public interface. Therefore, the presentation tier typically includes a Web server listening for connections from client computers over a wide area network.

### Putting the Pieces Together

As examples of information system architectures consider the Florida healthcare data warehouse cited earlier along with the many operational systems that serve as primary data collection points. In Florida, the Agency for Healthcare Administration (AHCA) requires that all acute care hospitals report standardized data after patients are discharged. This data is originally collected using hospital information systems, complex commercial systems that are typically tiered architectures with storage subsystems that provide a high degree of reliability for electronic medical record applications. Data is extracted from hospital systems on a quarterly basis and reported to the state, where various data quality procedures are used to verify the data. The hospital discharge data and many other data sets, including vital statistics and specific disease registries, are loaded into the data warehouse and integrated for decision support activities. The data warehouse itself is a tiered system, accessible to health planners through a Web portal. A middle tier provides analysis services based on data cubes that can be filtered and aggregated as needed, allowing analysts to select an appropriate unit of analysis. The data cubes are constructed from a base tier that includes a large relational data warehouse, where all the data quality and integration procedures are implemented. These types of systems will become standard public health tools, integrating conventional and unconventional data for evidence-based public health.

## Sources of Data for Information Systems

The heart of any public health information system is the data that it contains. Understanding the fundamental characteristics of databases is essential for effectively structuring and employing database technologies. Public health information databases share many characteristics with business enterprise data warehouses. That is, the systems are generally "subject oriented, integrated, nonvolatile, time variant collection[s] of data in support of management's decisions."[7]

Dimensional model data warehouses are constructed of two main components—*fact* tables and *dimension* tables. Facts are most often numeric, continuously valued, and additive measures of interest. For instance, a hospital discharge record includes such fields as length of stay and charge data that can be summed or averaged across various population groupings. Most commonly, however, the discharge counts are aggregated to compute event rates for specified demographic population segments.

Dimensions, on the other hand, are textual and discrete, providing a rich query environment for investigating associations between the dimensions and outcomes. Common hospital discharge dimensions include race, age, gender, physician, diagnosis, procedure code, payer, and so on. To facilitate analysis, many of these dimensions are refined to create *hierarchies* for aggregation. For instance, instead of comparing the hospitalizations for every different age by individual years, records are "rolled up" or aggregated by age bands, which are simply predefined age groupings. Similarly, a geographic hierarchy (ZIP code, community, county, state, region, or nation) identifies multiple levels of aggregation for comparing hospitalization rates.

## Data Characteristics

*Grain*

Data granularity refers to the level of aggregation, or distance from individual events, of the fact tables. The finest grain data is the individual transactions themselves, such as birth or death certificates or individual hospital discharge records. As data is aggregated or summarized, there is a commensurate loss of information. For instance, death records are commonly rolled up geographically (to the county or state level), temporally (quarterly or annual rates), by gender (separate rates for males and females), race (rates for black, white, Asian, etc.), and causes (combining various ICD-9 or -10 codes). Virtually all reports are aggregated data. Although these aggregates are useful for comparing rates, they can not be later disaggregated without access to the underlying transaction records.

In general, the finer the grain of the fact tables, the greater the flexibility in aggregating and analyzing it. On the other hand, finer granularity also increases the number of records that must be maintained and accessed, and increases the complexity of queries that must be formed to create reports. Moreover, as the grain of the data gets smaller, so do the cell sizes, particularly for uncommon events. As cell size declines below approximately 30 events, statistical significance becomes a serious concern. When dealing with multiple data sets, it is important to ensure that the granularity definitions match and have not changed over time. For instance, annual data may reflect an average value over a calendar year, a single beginning, mid-, or end-year value, or even a fiscal year average.

Determining the granularity in a data warehouse is one of the critical design decisions, providing a lower bound on subsequent analyses. Therefore, designers typically err on the side of more rather than less detail. Data warehouses provide a flexible query environment by allowing users to "roll up" or summarize data, enabling a decision maker to choose a *unit of analysis*. The unit of analysis determines a level at which data is aggregated and analyzed in order to generate information. The four most common units of analysis in public health are the following:

1. Person/patient
2. Vendor/supplier
3. Program
4. Region/population

For example, an average diabetic patient is associated with 200 billing records in a year. The information can be bundled at the person/patient level by building a set of counts for the frequency of a certain service that is vital to recommended diabetic care, such as the number of hemoglobin A1c or diabetic retinopathy screening tests. Once completed, a database with one observation per diabetic patient is created to compare patient-level variation in quality of care. This type of bundled procedure can be completed for a variety of different levels of analysis.

Generally, the unit of analysis should correlate to the population of interest for a management decision. For example, if the principal focus of an evaluation is patient compliance with a disease management program, then the correct unit of analysis is the patient. If, however, the goal of the analysis is to compare how different disease management programs perform to improve the health of the population, the appropriate unit of analysis is the program. Vendors or suppliers in health care can be physicians, hospitals, group practices, public health clinics, health insurers, or any other health-related organization. Regions can be defined in a variety of ways, including state, interstate regions (e.g., the Midwest), metropolitan statistical area, county, and ZIP code. Populations can be defined by residence within a given geopolitical subdivision, by sociodemographic characteristics such as age and ethnicity, or by health conditions such as diagnoses or behavioral risk factors. Other health-related units of analysis are defined by diseases, medical procedures, or other health interventions.

## Scope

Scope is a measure of breadth of coverage across any of the dimensions. For instance, geographic grain describes the unit of coverage, such as, census tract level data, and geographic scope is the coverage of all tracts in a county or state. Temporal grain reflects the finest unit of time, and temporal scope reflects the total units available (e.g., monthly or annual data covering the last 5 years).

## Source Type

Public health data can be gathered from a variety of source types, with a correspondingly broad spectrum of reliability. Vital statistics and hospital discharges (and their derived aggregations) are generally among the most accurate, as their sources are individual events recorded by objective individuals and subject to postcollection cleansing efforts by official agencies. Moreover, the formatting and coding systems are often standardized across the states to facilitate ease of reporting to the CDC, which compiles state data into national reports. Similarly, state registries most commonly collect information through questionnaires completed in real-time by third parties at the point of service and are generally validated for accuracy and completeness before entering the database.

In contrast, data sets such as the Behavioral Risk Factor Surveillance System (BRFSS) are collected using survey instruments that are completed by individuals with varying levels of commitment to completeness and accuracy. Moreover, surveys are, by their very nature, partial samplings of the total populace and results must be projected to include the whole population. This necessarily introduces sampling error and the potential for selection bias (respondents may selectively opt out of embarrassing questions).

Finally, some data, such as demographic changes between census years or estimates of per capita income, are simply estimated based on observations of proxy events, such as school registrations, vehicle registration changes, and voter rolls. Different agencies use different methods for arriving at their estimates with necessarily different results. It is important that estimate sources not be mixed in the database.

Regardless of the source of the data, however, it should be checked for completeness and consistency before being added to the data repository. A clear policy for handling missing or inconsistent data elements must be thought out and enforced, unit definitions understood and reconciled, and records containing clearly erroneous data flagged or removed.

## Metadata

Central to the maintainability of the data repository is keeping a clear record of its contents. This record is called *metadata*, or data about the data. Elements such as sources of the data and the agencies responsible for its collection, definitions of each of the fields, the date the data set was last updated, and the number of records each update contains can be invaluable for performing data quality checks, as well as providing needed context for end users. Making such metadata available to end users should be an integral part of any information system, but it is particularly important for health information systems, where timeliness and context are critical for proper interpretation.

## Integration

Although individual databases can be used to investigate simple count or rate questions, tapping the real power of information involves integrating the information from multiple datasets. This is accomplished by linking the tables through *key fields*. In database design, a *primary key* (PK) is a value that can be used to identify a particular row in a table. A *foreign key* (FK) is a field or group of fields in a database record that point to a key field or group of fields forming a key of another database record in some (usually different) table. Usually a foreign key in one table refers to the primary key of another table. For instance, a vital statistics data set can be queried to determine the number of deaths due to cervical cancer in a given county over a given period of time. To calculate a rate, however, requires linking this count with the demographic table for the same county and same period. Fields used to link the numerator (death count) to the denominator (population) necessarily include the county, the time period, and the gender (since only females are susceptible to cervical cancer).

## Common Data Problems

Not all data is created equal, and the prudent investigator choose's sources carefully. Fuzzy data element definitions, inconsistent collection and screening processes, changing variable definitions or scales, and intentional hiding of data values are simply a few of the threats to data quality that must be considered and addressed before bringing new data sources into the data warehouse.

Race is a particularly problematic dimension because it is generally self-reported and poorly understood. Many individuals responding to surveys or questionnaires confuse race with ethnicity or nationality and may classify themselves as multiracial or other if their nationality is not listed as a racial option. This confusion was magnified by the significant expansion of racial and ethnic categories offered in the 2000 census. From the single selection from the relatively simple four racial categories offered in the 1990 census, respondents in 2000 could select from an expanded list of over 30 options. Moreover, since this same smorgasbord of racial options is generally not duplicated in most event data collection instruments (e.g., hospital discharge records or vital statistics forms), reconciling event data with demographics requires careful conformation of racial definitions. That is, the demographic value categories must be conformed to the definitions used in the event records. The CDC has created a bridging methodology for reconciling the different race categorization schemes (see the full description at http://wonder.cdc.gov/wonder/help/bridged-race.html); however, this issue promises to grow significantly with time as more racial, national, and ethnic groups assert their distinctiveness.

A related, more general, data concern is the tendency of data collection agencies to change the definition of data elements or the circumstances of collection. For example, ZIP code boundaries change frequently, with 5–10% of the codes changing each year. Besides the obvious problem of aligning the numerator (event) values with the denominator (population estimates) for rate calculations, the creation and deletion of ZIP codes each year presents challenges when trying to trend data over time.

More serious are changes to definitions of the data itself. ICD-9/10 changes most often involve additions or deletions of codes, rather than changes in definitions themselves; however, aggregations based on these codes often do change. Communicable disease reports, for instance, may simply report hepatitis C incidence one year, and then split the data out to report acute, chronic, and congenital incidences the next year. Unless the change is detected and the new subcategories aggregated, the data warehouse values will be in error.

A more subtle problem with public-use data sets may arise from privacy concerns. Many government agencies responsible for collecting and distributing event level data will mask one or more of the fields that may be used to identify individuals. Masking simply replaces the actual value of the masked field(s) with one or more placeholder values for some predetermined percentage of the records. The most commonly masked fields are ZIP codes, age, gender, and race. For instance, in the case of California hospital discharge records, the public use data set masks the gender of approximately 18% of the records, 26% of the race values, 30% of the ethnicity values, and over 46% of the ages. Although the masking process should not affect comparison of rates between geographical entities within the state (since all entity rates should be reduced similarly), any rates calculated for comparison with other states or national statistics must account for the artificial diminution of the numerator values. Unmasked data may be available, but is generally provided only for specific, defined research projects and requires formal oversight by an approved institutional review board (IRB).

## Common Databases Available for Public Health

A solid understanding of health IT and data structure is required for the optimal design of public HISs. Fortunately for public health managers, there are rich data resources available at federal and state levels. This section provides an overview of the most common databases available to health managers and researchers in developing HISs (more details are available in Chapter 11). Most of the databases described here are federal or state specific in their focus. Although a federal focus may be too broad for local and regional health policy issues, federal surveys can still provide two significant benefits. First, national databases provide field-tested survey instruments or data abstraction tools that can be applied to a more focused information system. Second, federal surveys can provide a comparison database for information systems that also use state and local data sources in order to gauge the effectiveness of local initiatives.

It is worth noting the distinction between health statistics databases and health reports. Web sites that serve as data sources, such as the US Census (http://www.census.gov) and some state departments of health allow users to execute relatively broad queries that return fine grain data across the full scope of one or more dimensions. Report sites, on the other hand, provide either preformatted reports, often in fixed formats such as Adobe PDF files, or point queries that return aggregated data for a limited scope. The census site, for instance, allows end users to generate very comprehensive queries covering a large number of available indicator statistics, grouped by the full spectrum of gender, race, age, and geographical groupings. The data is downloadable as spreadsheet or comma separated value (CSV) files that can be directly imported into database programs for end-user manipulation.

At the other end of the spectrum is the Florida Department of Children and Families Youth Substance Abuse Survey reports (http://www.dcf.state.fl.us/mentalhealth/publications/fysas/countyreports04.shtml) that present aggregated county data in individual PDF files, without benefit of race, gender, or grade-level breakdowns. This requires manual conversion of the data tables into spreadsheet format and even then precludes any end user reaggregation of the data or creating different dimensional views.

Most sites fall between these two extremes. For example, the Florida Community Health Assessment Resource Tool Set (CHARTS) at http://www.floridacharts.com/charts/chart.aspx allows users to return statewide incidence counts and rates for hundreds of diseases and injuries, grouped by county, ZIP code, gender, race, or age bands and formatted in spreadsheets for easy importation into a database. A comprehensive view of the health status of communities across the state can be generated very quickly using this system, although the data is grouped by only one dimension at a time, preventing end-user crossing of the demographic variables.

## Government Survey Data

The federal government collects a broad array of data that may be used by public HISs. The US Department of Health and Human Services (HHS) has the largest health data collection responsibility. However, other federal government departments such as defense, labor, and commerce also collect critical health data.

The phrase "national probability sample" describes a survey instrument that has been deliberately designed to reflect the US national population's sociodemographic variation in age, gender, race, income, and education. If a state-level analysis was attempted, the survey could produce misleading estimates if survey respondents were over- or underweighted to reflect their proportional representation within the nation.

Another important concept is the panel survey. In this design, a panel or cohort of survey participants is followed during several rounds of the questionnaire. For example, some surveys such as the MEPS and the Medicare Current Beneficiary Survey (MCBS) follow participants for at least 2 years to track health status and cost. Panel surveys are valuable to assess long-term impacts in health care, such as a lack of health insurance or follow-up from a massive heart attack.

Most federal surveys are collected on an annual basis and are generally available as public use files 1 to 2 years following the completion of the data collection period. These data are available for a small fee to cover the cost of producing the databases. A list of nearly all of the government surveys used for health is available on the Internet at http://www.cdc.gov/nchs/.

Several examples of government-sponsored survey data are provided in the following paragraphs.

## Current Population Survey (CPS)

This survey is completed monthly by the Census Bureau for the Department of Labor and updated annually. It contains basic information in healthcare use and can be queried online at http://www.census.gov/hhes/www/cpstc/cps_table_creator.html. It is often available before any other federal survey with health data. The sample consists of approximately 52,000 housing units and the persons in them. The survey's primary goals are to provide estimates of employment, unemployment, and other socioeconomic characteristics of the general labor force, of the population as a whole, and of various subgroups of the population.

## National Health Interview Survey (NHIS)

This survey, collected by the National Center for Health Statistics (NCHS) within the HHS, is a national probability sample of the health status of the population. A two-part questionnaire is used with a sample size of approximately 49,000 households yielding 127,000 persons. The NHIS has had continuous data collection since 1957 for national estimates through household interviews by US Census Bureau interviewers. The NHIS provides the sampling frame for other NCHS surveys and is linked to the National Death Index (discussed later). Both a core survey of demographic and general health information and a supplement focusing on different populations are deployed.

## National Health and Nutrition Examination Survey (NHANES)

The NHANES is sponsored jointly by the CDC and the NCHS as part of the HHS. The primary goal of the NHANES is to estimate the national prevalence of selected diseases and risk factors. Target diseases and areas of special interest include (but are not limited to) cardiovascular disease, chronic obstructive pulmonary disease, diabetes, kidney disease, gallbladder disease, osteoporosis, arthritis, infectious diseases, substance abuse, tobacco use, child health, mental health, environmental health, and occupation health. Public use files from the NHANES are currently available.

## NCHS Medical Care Use Surveys

The NCHS has several annual surveys of healthcare services designed to profile the use of services regardless of public or private payer. The surveys are specific to inpatient, ambulatory care, home care, and other types of services. These are excellent surveys for national comparisons of changes in the use of ambulatory and inpatient care. However, they are not able to generalize to any area smaller than a multistate sample (e.g., the northeast United States).

## Administrative/Claims Data

The use of administrative data in public HISs has dramatically increased as the cost to work with the data has been reduced and the quality of data, relative to its past quality, has improved significantly. Administrative data are defined as the data elements that are generated as part of a healthcare organization's operations. For example, health insurers generate claims data to record the services that are reimbursed by the insurer. There are three significant advantages to using administrative data. First, the data cover a large breadth of services ranging from inpatient services to prescription drug use and immunizations. Second, administrative data are an inexpensive source of data when contrasted to other forms of health service data such as medical records. The third advantage is the timeliness of availability when compared with government surveys and other data sources. The most commonly used administrative databases are described to illustrate the range of data available for use in information systems.

## Medicare National Claims History File (NCHF)

The NCHF is more of a database architecture than a single file. Generally, it includes two file types. One file type is an annual 5% sample of the roughly 40 million Medicare beneficiary population. This file is sold as a public use file by the Centers for Medicare and Medicaid Services.

The second file type includes specialized data extracts of the NCHF across the Medicare population. An example of this type of file is any patient who received either a coronary artery bypass graft procedure (CABG) or angioplasty in 1990 and their claims for the next 5 years. Within these data, one can track health outcomes, such as repeat hospitalizations for cardiac conditions as well as mortality. Reimbursed services included in the claims file are inpatient, outpatient, hospice, medical equipment, provider services (e.g., physician), home health care, and skilled nursing care. The key identifying variables for the NCHF data extracts are inpatient diagnosis-related groups (DRGs), physician procedure codes, and diagnosis codes. Unlike survey data, the NCHF can be used to develop state-, county-, and possibly even ZIP code-level analysis, depending on the prevalence of the condition or treatment under investigation. See http://www.cms.hhs.gov/data/default.asp for a listing of Medicare data available.

## State Hospital Discharge Records

Over half of all states maintain annual hospital discharge summary records. These data are valuable for examining changes in inpatient service use and cost. For example, changes in the use of CABGs and angioplasty over several years can be assessed by different age, gender, and health insurance payer categories. The principal advantage of using hospital discharge records for health policy purposes is that they contain data on all payers, whereas the NCHF only provides data on Medicare. Hospital discharge data can be obtained directly from a state's government or from the AHRQ Healthcare Cost and Utilization Profile (HCUP) standardized databases. HCUP databases include the following:

- The Nationwide Inpatient Sample (NIS) contain inpatient data from a national sample of over 1000 hospitals.
- The State Inpatient Databases (SID) contain the universe of inpatient discharge abstracts, including over 100 structured clinical and nonclinical data elements, from 36 participating states. The advantage of the SID is that it allows an analyst to obtain data from 16 of the 36 states in a standardized format from AHRQ; the other 20 states provide the data directly in roughly similar formats.
- The Kids' Inpatient Database (KID) is a nationwide sample of pediatric inpatient discharges, drawn from the SID database and is the only all-payer inpatient care database for children in the United States.

For more information on the HCUP databases, refer to http://www.ahrq.gov/data/hcup/.

## State Medicaid Claims Data

Most states maintain claims data for reimbursements from their Medicaid programs. The states with more advanced Medicaid systems include (but are not limited to) California, Maryland, Pennsylvania, and Wisconsin. As with the Medicare claims data, Medicaid claims include data on inpatient, outpatient, physician, pharmacy, and skilled nursing services. Also available are provider data and Medicaid-eligible beneficiary data. It is vital to secure the eligibility file to properly account for truncated beneficiary enrollment periods. For example, one Medicaid recipient may have been enrolled for one month, whereas another may have been enrolled for one year. If both recipients received an equal number of physician services during a calendar year, the absence of applying the denominator of enrolled months leads to faulty conclusions on service use. The quality of these data varies widely. For example, managed care capitation contracts may not require the collection of encounter information. Therefore, an analyst seeking to complete a multistate Medicaid study is faced with the task of understanding each state's claims data idiosyncrasies.

## National and State Vital Statistics (Births, Deaths)

The NCHS makes available for purchase the complete event-level records of all births and deaths in the United States. To prevent disclosure of individuals and institutions, NCHS excludes (a) geographic identities of counties, cities, and metropolitan areas with less than 100,000 population, and (b) exact day of birth and death, although data with these fields populated may be requested for specific research projects. These data are also generally available directly from the appropriate state health department for a nominal copying fee.

## HIS Applications in Public Health Administration

There are several operating public HISs of note. These initiatives range in scope from federal to local sponsorship. Some provide a general database for a full range of public health issues, while others are designed for specific disease tracking or program evaluation.

### The CDC's INPHO

The INPHO system was developed as a framework for public health information and practice based on a state-of-the-art telecommunications network.[5] The INPHO is part of a strategy to strengthen public health infrastructure. The three concepts of the INPHO are linkage, information access, and data exchange. First, the CDC works with state and local area health agencies to build local and wide area networks. Second, the CDC has expanded "virtual networks" through the use of CDC WONDER. This is a software system that provides access to data in the CDC's public health databases. Third, the CDC has encouraged each state to connect with the Internet to have access to information.

Georgia (discussed in more detail later in the chapter) pioneered the program in early 1993. By 1997, 14 more states made the INPHO vision integral to their public health information strategies: California, Florida, Illinois, Indiana, Kansas, Michigan, Missouri, New Jersey, New York, North Carolina, Oregon, Rhode Island, Washington, and West Virginia. A second round of INPHO projects was funded through a cooperative agreement program, with awards made in the spring of 1998. The program promotes the integration of information systems, with special emphasis on immunization registries. The cooperative agreements were funded as either implementation projects (Florida, Georgia, Missouri, and New York) or demonstration projects (Iowa, Maryland, Montana, Nevada, and Texas). More information on the initiative is available at http://www.phppo.cdc.gov/PHTN.

### CDC WONDER

CDC WONDER was designed by the CDC to put critical information into the hands of public health managers quickly and easily. Originally a PC-based system, it is now available from any computer with an Internet connection, solving the problem of dedicating workstations to a specific database. As such, it is one of the few truly national public health data resources available with real-time access to anyone in the world. With CDC WONDER, one can do the following:

1. Search for and retrieve *Morbidity and Mortality Weekly Review* articles and prevention guidelines published by the CDC.
2. Query dozens of numeric data sets on the CDC's mainframe and other computers via fill-in-the blank request screens. Public use data sets about mortality, cancer incidence, hospital discharges, AIDS, behavioral

risk factors, diabetes, and many other topics are available for query, and the requested data can be readily summarized and analyzed.

3. Locate the name and e-mail addresses of the CDC staff and registered CDC WONDER users.
4. Post notices, general announcements, data files, or software programs of interest to public health professionals in an electronic forum for use by CDC staff and other CDC WONDER users.

For more information on CDC WONDER, refer to http://wonder.cdc.gov.

## State Public HISs

States have multiple public HISs mirroring the complicated array of categorical programs with different funding sources. Commonly maintained information systems include computerized immunization registries, lead toxicity tracking, early intervention databases for children with a disability, congenital disease registries, in addition to vital statistics data, Medicaid utilization, and disease reports. The need for integrated information systems and the support of the INPHO project has spurred models in a number of states. The next sections describe efforts in Missouri, Georgia, Illinois, and New York.

### Missouri

The Missouri Department of Health had a problem with 67 information systems that ran on different platforms and could not communicate with one another.[3] To solve this problem, the Missouri Health Strategic Architectures and Information System (MOHSAIC) was developed. An integrated client service record was an important component of this initiative. From the client's perspective, it was irrelevant if the services were labeled WIC, prenatal care, diabetes, Maternal and Child Health Services block grant, or local funding. Considerable effort and staff resources were committed to develop this system. Also, integrated systems magnify concerns about confidentiality. Benefits include increased capability for community health assessment, coordination of services, outreach, and linkages to primary care delivered by larger networks.[3]

### Georgia

Georgia was the first site of the CDC INPHO initiative. Georgia was able to develop quickly as a demonstration site through a unique consortium of state agencies with academic health partners and IT partners. For example, members of the consortium included the Medical College of Georgia as well as the Georgia Center for Advanced Telecommunications Technology and the Emory University School of Public Health. The program also had initial funding from the Robert Wood Johnson Foundation.[2] The infrastructure includes 81 clinics and 59 county health departments.

The Georgia INPHO system includes local and wide area computer networks, office automation and e-mail, a public health calendar, an executive HIS, and electronic notification of public health emergencies. Before the project began, the state public health office operated 13 small unlinked local area networks. With the INPHO project, hardware and software were consolidated into one integrated network system.

### Illinois

Cornerstone is a management information system developed in Illinois to integrate maternal and child health services. The design expands on the existing WIC program PC-based computer system.[8] This system is an example of a state information system integrating several related programs as compared with wide integration pursued by Missouri, Georgia, and New York State. Risk assessment and demographic information are captured once and used for multiple programs. Exchange of information, risk assessment, assurance of follow-up, and referral are assisted by this information system.

### New York

New York State is implementing an ambitious and far-reaching plan for the integration of public health information. Development of this information system was assisted by funding from the CDC. The New York State Department of Health has developed an enterprise-wide infrastructure for electronic health commerce. This effort has three major components.

- A public Web site (http://www.health.state.ny.us/) of health information serving as an Internet portal with an average of 850,000 hits per week and provider of data to consumers, researchers, and providers on health issues and data
- The Health Information Network (HIN), a public and private health data interchange of information
- The Health Provider Network (HPN) targeted at private data information interchange between state and healthcare providers including clinical laboratories, managed care plans, pharmacies, hospitals, and continuing care facilities

The New York health e-commerce initiative is using the Internet and Web page interface to connect users and databases in a secure environment. For the HIN, the Web-based interface functions as a closed intranet where Web encryption of secure socket layers is established (though transparent to the user) to protect the security and confidentiality of data.[9]

A large effort has been undertaken to ensure information security on the HIN because of the confidential nature of data transactions between state and local public health departments. Organizational and individual security agreements are required for HIN access.[10] Very narrow access is provided for highly confidential items such as case reports for notifiable disease. Particular restrictions and security arrangements are in place for HIV reporting. More broadly defined access exists for statistical data queries.

## Future Public Health Information Systems

The broad range of public HIS applications developed over the past 10 years demonstrates how managers are seeking to improve the scope and quality of their data systems. HIS experts consistently state that the future lies in building an infrastructure that is both easy to use and able to demonstrate value for its investment.[11,12] To build such an infrastructure requires data standards as well as translators for different standards to help bridge the transition from the current system.[13]

One of the most promising developments is the use of the Internet as the platform to collect data, turn data into information, and monitor the health of the population. The development of Internet-based software that is not dependent on operating systems or statistical computing software represents one less barrier to building an infrastructure. (The Internet's ease of software deployment through the use of a simple connection and a Web browser will lead to faster dissemination of standard data translation tools.) Even more powerful is the transition of the medical profession from an arcane paper-based data collection world toward e-commerce for business-to-business applications where new standards can be applied from the beginning of data collection and management activity, not retrofitted. Public concerns about the privacy of health-related information in this new environment are motivating new policies for information use that, it is hoped, will build the public's trust in emerging health information applications while preserving the ability of public health organizations to use health data for essential surveillance, research, and management activities.

Amid the opportunities for developing HISs, substantial barriers remain, but these barriers are becoming less technical and more political. Public health managers seeking to develop and use the IT infrastructure must be prepared to demonstrate its value to society constantly.

## Privacy Issues

The public's concern for the privacy of personal health information has become a major policy issue. Unfortunately, this concern is not easily addressed. At the heart of this issue is the paradox that health data must be identifiable if they are to be valuable for public health interventions. Complicating the issue is that even an encrypted personal identifier still yields a personal identifier. HISs must remain responsive to these evolving data privacy and confidentiality issues.

The public's desire for health data privacy appears to exceed its desire for public health and biomedical research. In a 1993 Lou Harris survey on the public's attitudes on health data privacy, 64% of the sample responded that they did not want medical records data used for biomedical research unless the researchers obtained the patient's consent. When asked if they favor the creation of a "national medical privacy board" to hold meetings, issue regulations, and enforce standards for protecting medical information privacy, 86% responded favorably.[14]

Two recent developments advanced the privacy debate. The first development was the passage of the Health Insurance Portability and Accountability Act (HIPAA) in 1996, which created a timetable for the adoption of national medical privacy legislation by the year 2000. The combination of HIPAA and privacy laws was adopted to ensure health coverage after leaving employment, while also creating the first national policy to prosecute those persons who breach the medical privacy of an individual. The penalties can range from fines to prison. The compliance date for the privacy rule was April 2003.

Protected health information (PHI) is individually identifiable health data that is transmitted or maintained in electronic media and related to the physical or mental health of an individual, the healthcare services provided to an individual, or the payment for those services provided to the individual. For covered entities using or disclosing PHI, the Privacy Rule establishes a range of health information privacy requirements and standards, including procedures for notification of individuals, internal policies and procedures, employee training, and technical and physical data security safeguards.

Public health practice and research uses protected health information to perform many of its required functions, including public health surveillance, outbreak investigation, program operations, terrorism preparedness, and others. Public health authorities have a long history of protecting the confidentiality of individually identifiable health information, and were given significant latitude in the Privacy Rule, which expressly permits PHI to be shared for specified public health purposes. Covered entities may disclose PHI to a public health agency legally authorized to collect information for the purpose of preventing or controlling disease, injury or disability, without separate authorization. It should be noted, however, that in addition to using PHI from covered entities, a public health agency may itself be a covered entity, providing services and producing covered electronic transactions.[15]

Of particular interest for both research and population level assessment are the use of deidentified information and limited use data sets. Deidentified data (stripped of individual identifiers rendering it "impossible" to associate a record with any individual) require no individual privacy protection and are not covered by the Privacy Rule. Deidentification can be accomplished by using accepted analytical techniques to conclude that the subject of the information cannot be identified or by removing 18 specific identifier fields (the "safe harbor" method) to render identification infeasible. Limited data sets may contain some of the 18 identifiers, as long as other safeguards are provided to prevent subject identification.

Ultimately, data are provided to public health managers and researchers as an act of trust. If one individual or organization violates that trust, the public's confidence may erode immediately. The Harris poll results show consistently that health data confidentiality and security issues are an important public concern.[12]

• • •

In developing and using HISs, public health administrators and researchers must demonstrate that the public's trust is deserved. To do so, contemporary HISs must ensure that society receives an optimal return on its public investments in data resources—a return that ultimately must be realized through more effective public health interventions and improved community health status.

## Chapter Review

1. Public health organizations rely on information systems to support a number of key operations, including:
   • Epidemiologic disease and risk factor surveillance
   • Medical and public health outcomes assessment

- Program and clinic administration (billing, inventory, client tracking, clinical records, utilization)
- Cost-effectiveness and productivity analysis
- Utilization analysis and demand estimation
- Program planning and evaluation
- Quality assurance and performance measurement
- Public health policy analysis
- Clinical research
- Health education and health information dissemination

2. Two of the most common types of applications for information systems in public health organizations are:
   - Service-based applications that track encounter-level information on the users and providers of specific services. These applications are useful for program administration and management of services for individual clients.
   - Population-based applications that track information on defined populations of interest. These applications are useful for surveillance, program evaluation, planning, and policy development.

3. To build the public health information systems of the future, data must be extracted from many operational systems, integrated for analysis, and disseminated using multiple technologies such as Web portals. Service-oriented computing is an emerging information systems architecture that supports the construction of networked systems that are flexible, scalable, and reliable. There are many evolving standards to support the development of loosely coupled components that can be assembled into complex systems.

4. Data warehouses are "subject-oriented, integrated, nonvolatile, time-variant collection[s] of data in support of management's decisions." Data warehousing technologies have matured and found wide application in many industries. In the healthcare domain, these technologies offer a powerful method of integrating data for community health assessment, surveillance, clinical decision support, and outcomes review.

5. A variety of data sources can be integrated within a public HIS. Common data sources include survey data, administrative claims data, program administration data, regional and geographic data, registry data, and private industry data. Common data structures include transactional data, cross-sectional data, time series and panel data, and relational databases.

6. Well-designed public HISs must provide strong protections for the privacy and confidentiality of information derived from person-specific health-related data. These protections must cover data acquisition, storage, and linkage and retrieval activities, as well as analytic and reporting activities. Information systems must be responsive to the privacy provisions of recent federal and state legislation.

# References

1. Koo D, Wetterhall SF. History and current status of the National Notifiable Diseases Surveillance System. *J Public Health Manage Pract.* 1996;2(4):4–10.

2. Chapman KA, Moulton AD. The Georgia Information Network for Public Health Officials (INPHO): a demonstration of the CDC INPHO concept. *J Public Health Manage Pract.* 1995;1(2):39–43.

3. Land GH, Stokes C, Hoffman N, Peterson R, Weiler MJ. Developing an integrated public health information system for Missouri. *J Public Health Manage Pract.* 1995;1(1):48–56.

4. Berndt D, Hevner A, Studnicki J. The CATCH data warehouse: support for community health care decision making. *Decision Support Syst.* 2003; 35:367–384.

5. Corrigan JM, Nielsen DM. Toward the development of uniform reporting standards for managed care organizations: the Health Plan Employer Data and Information Set. *J Joint Commission Qual Improv.* 1993;19(12): 566–575.

6. Huhns M, Singh M. Service-oriented computing: key concepts and principles. *IEEE Internet Comput.* 2005;9(1):75–81.

7. Inmon W. *Building the Data Warehouse.* 3rd ed. New York, NY: John Wiley and Sons; 2002.

8. Nelson JR. Cornerstone: Illinois' approach to service integration. *J Public Health Manage Pract.* 1996;2(1):71–74.

9. Gotham I. Personal communication, NYS Department of Health, August, 1999.

10. Baker EL, Friede A, Moulton AD, Ross DA. CDC's Information Network for Public Health Officials (INPHO): a framework for integrated public health information and practice. *J Public Health Manage Pract.* 1995;1(1):43–47.

11. Baker EL Jr, Ross D. Information and surveillance systems and community health: building the public health information infrastructure. *J Public Health Manage Pract.* 1996;2(4):58–60.

12. Milio N. Beyond informatics: an electronic community infrastructure for public health. *J Public Health Manage Pract.* 1999;1(4):84–94.

13. Lumpkin J, Atkinson D, Biery R, Cundiff D, McGlothlin M, Novick LF. The development of integrated public health information systems: a statement by the Joint Council of Governmental Public Health Agencies. *J Public Health Manage Pract.* 1995;1(4):55–59.

14. Lou Harris and Associates. *Health Information Privacy Survey, 1993.* New York, NY: Harris; 1993.

15. Centers for Disease Control and Prevention, Epidemiology Program Office. HIPPA Privacy Rule and public health. *MMWR.* 2003;52:1–12.

## CHAPTER 14

# PUBLIC HEALTH SURVEILLANCE

Benjamin Silk
Theresa Hatzell Hoke
Ruth Berkelman

## Chapter Overview

Surveillance is a primary mechanism through which public health organizations acquire information concerning population health. Surveillance approaches vary widely in both structure and function. Consequently, the optimal system design is contingent on an organization's specific information needs and resources as well as the characteristics of the populations and health issues under study. In developing and maintaining surveillance systems, public health administrators must use current epidemiologic knowledge in tandem with effective managerial strategies.

Public health surveillance is a primary mechanism through which health agencies generate and process information for use in management, policy, and practice. Effective public health management requires an iterative cycle of formulating objectives, designing and implementing interventions, measuring the impact of programs, and using that information to revise program interventions and objectives. Described as the "continuous and systematic collection, analysis, interpretation and dissemination of descriptive information for monitoring health problems,"[1(p435)] surveillance provides essential input for this cycle. Public health surveillance data allow organizations to measure the prevalence of risk factors and healthy behaviors, monitor the effects of interventions, and assess trends in disease and other health outcomes.[2] Conclusions drawn from this information process are used for decision making and action at multiple levels of the public health and health care systems.

This chapter provides an overview of surveillance systems and strategies that are relevant to the public health administrator. The first section describes the various functions that surveillance systems serve in public health and the common forms of surveillance. This is followed by an overview of key design and operation considerations, including administrative and managerial activities to maintain surveillance programs. Readers seeking a more detailed discussion of public health surveillance are directed to other texts written for epidemiologists and others responsible for surveillance operations.[3-8]

## Function and Form of Public Health Surveillance Systems

### Functions: What Purpose Does Surveillance Serve?

Although surveillance originally signified monitoring contacts of persons with communicable diseases for onset of symptoms,[9] public health surveillance applications expanded dramatically in the second half of the 20th century.[10] Surveillance systems now monitor infectious and chronic disease, injury and disability, occupational health and safety, environmental exposures, maternal and child health, health awareness and behavior, and the use of healthcare services.

Surveillance activities support public health management at many levels, beginning with the establishment of health objectives. Health officers rely on surveillance data to select targets for public health action, including populations at higher risk for morbidity and mortality and associated risk factors (e.g., tobacco use, physical inactivity, microbial infection, and exposure to toxic agents). Further, public health officers use surveillance to monitor the effects of changes in healthcare practice and policy.[11] For example, documented underutilization of preventive health services, such as immunization or early disease detection through screening, may point to the need for public health intervention to increase the use of these services. Once officials establish priorities for public health interventions, they continue to rely on surveillance data to design and direct specific programs. Surveillance provides information about the characteristics of people most affected by health conditions and the communities to which they belong. Programs can be formulated to reach targeted populations and address health priorities. With interventions operationalized, surveillance data can also be used to measure program impact. By analyzing trends in specific outcomes, policy makers evaluate whether their program is achieving its desired effect. Surveillance data can then support programmatic decision making about whether interventions should be continued, modified, expanded, or terminated.

Surveillance systems often identify emerging public health problems and epidemics, triggering more intensive surveillance, public health investigation, and disease-control interventions. A 1999 outbreak of salmonellosis in the United States serves as an example.[12] (*Salmonella* infection can cause diarrhea, abdominal cramping, fever, and dehydration.) Health officials in Washington state were notified of 85 cases of salmonellosis that occurred between June 10 and July 9, 1999. An investigation revealed that 67 cases had consumed a particular brand of unpasteurized orange juice. Meanwhile, in Oregon 57 cases of salmonellosis were identified by health officials; all had occurred in the latter half of June. Thirty-nine cases drank the same brand of orange juice. After collaborative investigations by the two states and discussions with the US Food and Drug Administration (FDA), the manufacturer voluntarily issued a recall of the juice. Further investigations identified *Salmonella* in samples of the juice, dispensers in restaurants, and the juice factory. Smaller outbreaks among individuals who drank the juice during the same period were reported in 13 other states.

Surveillance systems can monitor large cohorts over time, producing databases that contain longitudinal information on disease occurrence and revealing issues that warrant in-depth investigation through formal epidemiologic research. The US Renal Data System (USRDS), which tracks outcomes related to end-stage renal disease (ESRD) in the United States, exemplifies the broad scope of surveillance (www.usrds.org). The goals of the USRDS include monitoring trends in the frequency of ESRD-related morbidity and mortality and providing a foundation for research through the provision of national datasets.[11] To achieve these goals, the system integrates data from the Centers for Medicare and Medicaid Services (CMS), the United Network of Organ Sharing (UNOS), the Centers for Disease Control and Prevention (CDC), the ESRD networks, and special USRDS studies.[13] Data on demographics, clinical measures, biochemical laboratory testing results, dialysis and transplantation, and all other medical services reported as Medicaid claims are used to generate a comprehensive *Annual Data Report*, also known as the *Atlas of End-Stage Renal Disease in the United States*.[14] The report demonstrates that inclusion of data on both incident (new) and prevalent (existing) diseases and conditions may be important for monitoring chronic disease trends (Figure 14-1). The number of incident dialysis patients increased gradually from 1988 to 2003 in the United States. Because the number of prevalent patients is a function of the incidence and duration of the condition, prevalence increased markedly in the same period.

## Surveillance System Forms

Surveillance systems take on a variety of forms depending on the health-related events being monitored, the availability of resources, and each system's intended purposes. Several references (including Chapter 11) have characterized sources of health-related information that are either obtained from surveillance systems or used for public health surveillance.[2,15] Major types of surveillance approaches and their strengths and weaknesses are described in the following sections.

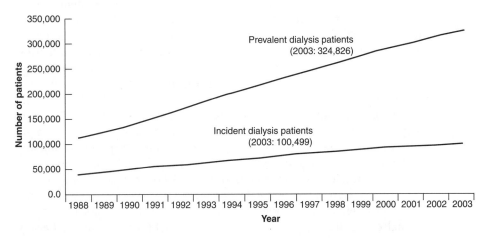

**FIGURE 14–1    Trends in Incident and Prevalent Dialysis Patient Counts for the United States, 1988–2003**
*Source:* Adapted from the US Renal Data System (USRDS). 2005 ADR/Atlas. Available at: http://www.usrds.org/atlas.htm. Accessed January 25, 2006.

*Notifiable Disease Reporting*

Public health agencies monitor diseases, conditions, and events of importance by designating them as notifiable, thereby requiring persons with knowledge of their occurrence to report. Most notifiable diseases are communicable, though other occurrences, including animal bites, birth defects, cancer diagnoses, elevated blood lead levels, poisonings, and illness clusters, are often reportable.[16] Typically, clinicians, infection control professionals, and laboratories report patients whose clinical descriptions and laboratory diagnoses meet case definitions for the diseases under surveillance.[17] In the United States, states have the legal authority to mandate reporting of notifiable diseases.[18] Although each state's list of notifiable diseases varies in accordance with local public health priorities, the majority of states and territories require reporting of most nationally notifiable diseases. In collaboration with the CDC, the list of nationally notifiable diseases is revised yearly by the Council of State and Territorial Epidemiologists (CSTE), whose members include the state epidemiologists responsible for collection and use of notifiable diseases data within their jurisdictions.

Infectious disease reporting operates through collaborations at multiple levels. At the local level, public health officials maintain communication with reporting sources and use disease reports to initiate prevention and control measures (e.g., chemoprophylaxis of close contacts and outbreak investigation). States' organizational structures vary, but state health departments generally support local surveillance activities and consolidate notifiable disease reports from city, county, or district public health agencies as well as directly from reporting sources. Since 1925, all states have voluntarily transmitted notifiable diseases data to the US Public Health Service; the CDC currently oversees the National Notifiable Diseases Surveillance System (NNDSS). The CDC disseminates the NNDSS data from the states, territories, and large metropolitan areas via the *Morbidity and Mortality Weekly Report (MMWR)* and yearly summaries of notifiable diseases (www.cdc.gov/mmwr).

With few exceptions,[19] notifiable disease surveillance systems collectively encompass the United States in its geographic entirety. The systems link public health agencies to healthcare providers who may be the first to become aware of problems in the surveillance system's jurisdiction. For example, the disease that came to be known as acquired immunodeficiency syndrome (AIDS) was first reported in the United States by clinicians with ties to the Los Angeles County Department of Public Health.[20] The notifiable disease reporting approach also has recognized weaknesses. Reporting completeness varies considerably because many diseases are treated empirically without etiologic diagnosis (such as community-acquired pneumonia) and because systems often rely on voluntarily reporting by participants.[21,22] The CDC's burden of illness pyramid illustrates how reported cases of foodborne illnesses are a small fraction of the total number of illnesses under surveillance (Figure 14-2). Reporting is the culmination of a series of conditional events (e.g., laboratory confirmation, laboratory testing). Because each event is dependent on preceding events, absent or delayed events imply that receipt of morbidity and mortality reports will also be absent or delayed.

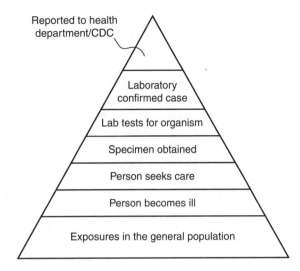

**FIGURE 14–2    CDC's Burden of Illness Pyramid: Underascertainment of Foodborne Illness in Notifiable Diseases Surveillance**
*Source:* Adapted from Centers for Disease Control and Prevention. FoodNet Surveillance—Burden of Illness Pyramid. Available at: http://www.cdc.gov/foodnet/surveillance_pages/burden_pyramid.htm. Accessed January, 25 2006.

*Sentinel Surveillance*

Sentinel surveillance commonly refers to convenience sampling of data that are designed to characterize the magnitude of a public health problem in a larger population. Two components of influenza surveillance in the United States demonstrate how sentinel reporting can be useful.[23] The US Influenza Sentinel Providers Surveillance Network monitors weekly morbidity through state-based networks of clinicians who report age group-specific counts of influenza-like illness (ILI) and corresponding denominators (i.e., total number of clinic visits). Proportions of patient visits for ILI have been a useful surrogate for reporting of confirmed influenza cases. The CDC compiles these morbidity data weekly, monitoring influenza activity regionally and nationally by tracking deviations from baseline levels. The CDC tracks weekly influenza mortality via the 122 Cities Mortality Reporting System. By reporting the number of deaths due to pneumonia and influenza and the total number of deaths occurring in 122 cities and metropolitan areas, sentinel data are used to monitor mortality patterns and assess the severity of circulating influenza virus strains.

The generalizability of the sentinel reporting data depends on how closely the populations served by the sentinel providers represent the general population. Public health agencies can increase generalizability by selecting participants who serve diverse geographic and demographic population strata. Although population-based incidence and prevalence rates cannot be obtained, sentinel surveillance may provide timely and cost-effective data. Sentinel networks can also facilitate acquisition of clinical specimens and isolates, which has been particularly valuable for infectious disease programs. Applications in the United States have included tracking drug-resistant gonorrhea, determining relatedness and relative frequencies of tuberculosis (TB) strains, and matching annual influenza vaccines to circulating viral subtypes.

Sentinel surveillance has another form. A *sentinel health event* refers to a disease or condition for which the occurrence of even a single case warns that improvements in preventive measures are warranted.[1,24] Sentinel health events include illness or injury considered avoidable, death deemed "untimely," and rare disease with a known, specific risk factor. In the United States, a single case of polio or a maternal death are sentinel events that warrant close scrutiny. The CDC's National Institute of Occupational Safety and Health (NIOSH) uses sentinel surveillance to monitor the occurrence of selected serious injuries, exposures, illnesses, and deaths in the workplace.[25] The sentinel health event approach shares the timeliness and cost-effectiveness advantages of sentinel reporting, but also requires motivated reporters. As with notifiable disease reporting, sentinel health reporting can trigger public health investigations.

## Syndromic Surveillance

A primary aim of syndromic surveillance has been early outbreak detection, which can create the opportunity for rapid intervention to interrupt infectious disease transmission and prevent morbidity and mortality. Rather than monitor specific clinical diagnoses (the essence of notifiable disease reporting), syndromic surveillance is intended to identify early signals of increased illness frequency within a population. A syndromic surveillance system may track behavioral data (e.g., absenteeism, over-the-counter medicine purchases) or prediagnostic, clinical data (e.g., emergency department chief complaints, requests for laboratory testing). The term *syndromic surveillance* originates here; many syndromic systems tally sets of signs and symptoms into defined syndromes (e.g., gastrointestinal, respiratory, and neurologic illnesses). Syndromic surveillance is based on the notion that patients' signs and symptoms, such as fever, cough, and fatigue, will manifest and cluster in data captured by the system, triggering a public health investigation before a subset of patients with rapid symptom onset following infection are diagnosed and reported (Figure 14-3).[26] This rationale also recognizes that infectious diseases are frequently treated without assigning etiologic diagnoses (a noted weakness of notifiable disease reporting).[27] In fact, syndrome surveillance has been used for many years in settings where laboratory diagnosis is not generally sought.

Like all surveillance approaches, syndromic surveillance requires collection, processing, analysis, and interpretation of health indicator data.[28] Each step has alternatives, so syndromic surveillance systems are diverse in form. Technology has made automated data transfer and real-time monitoring of electronic health information a hallmark of many syndromic surveillance systems. Connecting information systems, however, requires expertise, stakeholder support, and privacy and security safeguards. Processing indicator data often entails consolidation of data sources and standardization of data elements. The analyst focuses on detection of *aberrations*, which exist when the frequency of observed events differs statistically from an expected frequency; analysis and aberration detection are frequently aided by mapping and graphical display of the data. Event frequencies that exceed a statistical threshold within a defined time period, geography, or time and space are deemed significant, and sound an "alarm." Interpretation of the alarm may

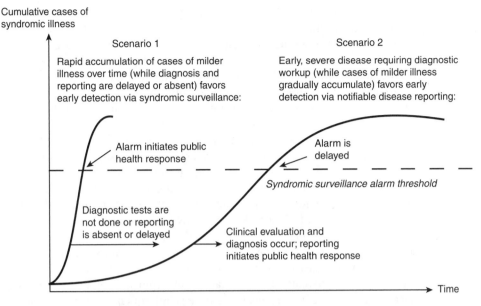

**FIGURE 14–3    Number of Cumulative Cases of Syndromic Illness by Time for a Hypothetical, Unrecognized Infectious Disease Outbreak: Two Scenarios for Early Detection**
*Source:* Adapted from Buehler JW, Berkelman RL, Hartley DM, Peters CJ. Syndromic surveillance and bioterrorism-related epidemics, *Emerg Infect Dis.* 2003;9:1197–1204.

require further analysis before initiating an investigation. In other words, a true outbreak may or may not be occurring when an aberration is detected.

Federal funding, including CDC cooperative agreements for state and local bioterrorism preparedness, as well as technology-driven opportunities to transport and manipulate large amounts of health-related data,[29] have contributed to a proliferation of syndromic surveillance systems in the United States. Meanwhile, the relative merit of this surveillance approach has been disputed. Calibrating statistical thresholds to detect outbreaks with sensitivity, while reducing false alarms, has been a major challenge facing operational systems. Other concerns include the costs and resource diversions associated with implementing and maintaining syndromic surveillance when alternatives for enhancing infectious disease surveillance exist,[30] the large number of factors that influence how a covert attack of bioterrorism would initially be detected (e.g., natural history of the disease),[26] and the need for more critical research and evaluation.[31] Syndromic surveillance systems have detected naturally occurring outbreaks (e.g., diarrheal illness), have provided assurance that outbreaks are not occurring, and may be useful for monitoring known outbreaks. The growing collective wisdom of established systems (www.syndromic.org) and innovation invested in these systems have brought the field closer to real-time, integrated public health surveillance.[29]

## Registries

Disease registries are often a rigorous and resource-intensive surveillance approach by which all cases of a disease, or type of disease, are ascertained for a defined population (typically a geographic area). By compiling information from multiple sources and linking data for individuals over time, registries can produce useful, detailed information. This feature has been valuable for supporting efforts to increase childhood immunization in the United States, where cumbersome and often incomplete paper-based vaccination records are being replaced by electronic childhood immunization registries.[32] States can enter children into a registry at birth (often by linkage with electronic birth records) and registry records are updated each time healthcare providers deliver an immunization. Registries are also valuable tools for chronic disease control programs, allowing disease stages (e.g., diagnosis, treatment) and outcomes (e.g., survival, mortality) to be tracked over time for individuals.[33] For example, the National Cancer Institute's Surveillance, Epidemiology, and End Results (SEER) Program and the CDC's National Program of Cancer Registries (NPCR) monitor cancer incidence throughout the US population.[34] In addition to detailed data collection for several geographic areas, the SEER program shares data with and supports the NPCR state registries. The NPCR registries are similar to notifiable disease reporting systems in that state-level reporting requirements exist. Because immediate public health action is infrequently needed, however, clinical facilities and their healthcare providers report to centralized, statewide registries. The national network of central cancer registries produces an annual publication of cancer incidence and mortality for the United States.[35] Cancer registries are also a key data source for epidemiologic and health services research.[36]

Mandatory data recorded at the time of birth, death, marriage, divorce, and fetal death are a form of registration known as *vital statistics*. In the United States, the National Vital Statistics System tracks these vital events through contractual agreements between the National Center for Health Statistics (NCHS) at the CDC and states' vital registration systems, which have statutory authority to record these events.[37] These agreements are the foundation for data sharing; NCHS collects and disseminates national vital statistics (e.g., race-specific vital rates). Agreements also facilitate standardization of systems' data collection procedures and mechanisms across jurisdiction (e.g., revision of birth, death, and fetal death certificates). Like other registries, near complete coverage of the population and the ability to calculate rates are primary advantages offered by vital statistics. Although vital records are available at local, state, and national levels, time may be needed for the compilation and release of population-based data. In addition, the validity and reliability of these data is often a concern. Despite these limitations, vital records are a key data source for surveillance in several areas, such as maternal and infant mortality, birth defects, and cause-specific mortality (e.g., cancer).

### Health Surveys

Surveys that periodically or continuously collect information can serve as a surveillance mechanism, providing data on health conditions, risk factors, or health-related knowledge, attitudes, and behaviors for the time period in which the surveys are conducted. Although other surveillance approaches are population-based (e.g., notifiable disease reporting) or may not be representative (e.g., sentinel surveillance), sampling is usually a key consideration for the design and use of health surveys. Probability sampling, where survey participants are chosen via a random selection process, allows the survey results to be extended to the larger population from which the participant sample was drawn. To target specific groups for intervention, such as racial or ethnic minority groups experiencing health disparities, survey designs are often complex (i.e., oversampling via stratification and multiple stages).[38]

As discussed in Chapter 11, in the United States, the NCHS sponsors several surveys and data collection systems. By traveling with a mobile examination center (a moving medical clinic), the National Health and Nutrition Examination Survey (NHANES) has periodically combined data from physical exams and diagnostics with personal interviews for a random sample of noninstitutionalized Americans.[39] NHANES results have been vital in monitoring a number of health and nutrition issues. The survey has evolved and now collects data continuously for a wide range of public health areas.

The Behavioral Risk Factor Surveillance System (BRFSS) is the world's largest telephone survey,[40] continuously monitoring American adults' health-related behaviors by using a random-digit dialing protocol. The system is state-based and designed to have flexible content. Questionnaires have multiple components (sets of questions) that allow certain topics to be tracked nationally in a "core component," while other components are either designed by the CDC and optionally added by states or directly designed and added by the state when the topic is of particular importance for a state. Table 14-1

**TABLE 14-1    Assessment of Progress Toward *Healthy People 2010* Targets Using Behavioral Risk Factor Surveillance System (BRFSS) Data for Selected Indicators**

| Objective[§] | State-Specific Median Proportion (Range) | | | Target for Year 2010 |
|---|---|---|---|---|
| | 1992/1993[±] | 1996/1997[±] | 2002 | |
| Current cigarette smoking by adults aged ≥ 18 years | 23.0% (15.7–30.7%) | 23.2% (13.8–30.7%) | 23.1% (16.4–32.6%) | <12% |
| Adults (aged ≥ 18 years) who engage in no leisure-time physical activity | 27.4% (17.1–48.1%) | 27.8% (17.1–51.4%) | 24.4% (15.0–33.6%) | <20% |
| Adults (aged ≥ 18 years) who engaged in binge drinking in the preceding month | 14.3% (5.4–24.5%) | 14.5% (6.3–23.3%) | 16.1% (7.9–24.9%) | <6% |

[§]Respondents were classified as current smokers if they had smoked ≥100 cigarettes during their lifetimes and reported smoking every day or some days during the 12 months preceding the survey. Leisure-time physical activity was measured by the respondent's indication of any participation in exercise, other than their regular job, during the preceding month. Binge drinking was defined as having five or more drinks on at least one occasion during the preceding month.
[±]Physical activity data are for 1992 and 1996; cigarette smoking and binge drinking are for 1993 and 1997.
*Source:* US Centers for Disease Control and Prevention. *MMWR* Surveillance Summaries: past volumes. Available at: http://www.cdc.gov/mmwr/sursumpv.html. Accessed January 27, 2006.

shows another application of BRFSS, measuring states' progress toward meeting *Healthy People 2010* targets.

### Combined Approaches

A combination of surveillance methods and data sources may be required to obtain a complete picture of health conditions. Veterinary surveillance and its application to monitoring of human health illustrate a combined surveillance approach. Following the emergence of West Nile virus (WNV) in the Western Hemisphere in 1999, for example, public health agencies began tracking its spread across the United States by monitoring avian, equine, and human disease. Surveillance for WNV in trapped mosquitoes also has been an important indicator of WNV activity, suggesting the potential for WNV-related human disease locally. One requirement makes this combined approach exceptional; experts from several disciplines (e.g., entomology, geography, veterinary medicine) have collaborated in surveillance efforts.

Surveillance for chronic diseases demonstrates how data on multiple risk factors and outcomes are brought together.[10] In 1996, the CSTE recommended for the first time nationwide surveillance of an avoidable risk factor, adult cigarette smoking. This action raised awareness of the need for a standardized approach to chronic disease surveillance across states. States' chronic disease program directors have worked with the CDC and the CSTE to develop and revise 92 chronic disease surveillance indicators.[41] States monitor these indicators as a means of evaluating disease control programs and measuring progress toward national health priorities. The suggested indicators are drawn from the entire range of surveillance data sources, including BRFSS and the Youth Risk Behavior Surveillance System (a BRFSS analogue focusing on adolescents), US Census Bureau labor statistics, state-level data on tobacco use and prevention and control, the US Renal Data System, cancer registries, hospital discharge data, and death certification systems. Eventually, the surveillance system may include community-level indicators reflecting environmental and policy changes associated with chronic disease control, such as the number of miles of walking trails, sales volumes for fruits and vegetables, and proportion of restaurants with nonsmoking areas.[42]

While individual-level data may be available to a surveillance program, many of the indicators described earlier are summary measures of demographic or geographic groups. The distinction is noteworthy because investigations involving group-level units of analysis are *ecologic*, which implies that data cannot be linked at the individual level. Ecologic investigations are subject to an important inference constraint: only associations at the ecologic level can be correctly examined.[43] For example, suppose a state's summary of vital statistics contains substantial chronic liver disease mortality and BRFSS data indicate that heavy alcohol use among adults in the state is prevalent. Whether the deceased themselves were heavy drinkers, and the extent to which chronic liver disease mortality in the state can be attributed to alcohol use alone and not other contributing risk factors (e.g., infection with hepatitis B or C viruses), remain unknown. On the other hand, demonstrating an ecologic association may be of primary importance. A rapid decrease in average alcohol consumption would likely be accompanied by a substantive decrease in liver cirrhosis mortality in a relatively short time.[44] Furthermore, a *multilevel analysis* (or hierarchical model) that examines individual-level and group-level determinants of morbidity and mortality simultaneously may be accomplished through a combined surveillance approach.[45]

Linkage of individual-level data from two or more discrete sources, or *record linkage*, is a combined surveillance approach that has several applications for surveillance. Examples can be found when expansion of existing data is necessary (e.g., generating comprehensive databases of healthcare services), when longitudinal data are of primary interest (e.g., creating reproductive histories), when exposures or outcomes are related (e.g., linking AIDS and TB registries), when individuals are related or the same (e.g., linking of birth and fetal death certificates), and when independent data are used to evaluate surveillance systems (e.g., completeness of disease reporting studies). Although manual linkage of smaller datasets may be possible, electronic linkage methods are typical. The success of a linkage project depends on the availability, completeness, accuracy, and discriminatory power of the overlapping, identifying information (matching variables). Combinations of name, birth date, and record numbers are commonly used, but coding algorithms can also convert text data into more useful forms. When available matching variables are complete and accurate, a *deterministic* approach would assign linkages exactly, as all or none. Frequently, data sources' identifiers are not entirely complete or accurate. In these situations, linkages may be assigned *probabilistically*. Linkage decisions are based on a total "weight" (i.e., a score obtained from the sum of functions of variables' match probabilities) and a cut-off weight assigned for the linkage decision.

# Surveillance System Design and Operations

This section reviews key steps in the design and operation of surveillance systems. Based on system objectives, managers select and define health-related events and a source population during the system design phase. To implement a surveillance system, managers must consider mechanisms for collection, analysis, interpretation, and dissemination of surveillance data. Training for surveillance personnel, attention to evolving data standards, and periodic evaluations to strengthen the surveillance system are important maintenance requirements. General oversight responsibilities as well as management-related decisions that affect surveillance activities are described throughout the section.

## Establish System Objectives

Surveillance system design begins with the specification of system objectives. In the United States, surveillance policies and practices are established through intergovernmental alliances at the federal, state, and local levels. The CDC distributes recommendations for the development of national disease control strategies that include the collection and use of specific forms of surveillance data. State health departments then receive financial support from federal grants to establish surveillance mechanisms in compliance with CDC guidelines. Close collaboration is required among the different tiers for this system to be successful in achieving disease control objectives. Surveillance requirements need to be sufficiently systematized across jurisdictions for data to be comparable and meaningful at the national level. At the same time, reporting requirements should be flexible enough to permit adaptation to local public health priorities.

Within this context, planners at the state and local levels must delineate the purposes they expect the system to serve. As part of establishing a surveillance system, it is recommended that one engage stakeholders, that is, the data suppliers and eventual data users. A common approach is to form an advisory committee to guide the implementation and operation of the surveillance system. Intended consumers of information, particularly those represented on the advisory committee, should be consulted when surveillance system objectives are being established to help ensure that surveillance data will be used appropriately and optimally. Typically, surveillance data will serve one or more of the following objectives[11,46]:

- Monitor the frequency and distribution of a health problem in a community.
- Describe the clinical and epidemiologic features of a disease.
- Examine the source causes of morbidity and mortality.
- Generate etiologic hypotheses.
- Assess healthcare delivery, quality, and safety.
- Assess the effects of changes in healthcare practice.
- Direct the development, implementation, and evaluation of interventions and policies.
- Prioritize resource allocation.
- Project future trends.
- Identify and support clinical and epidemiologic research needs.

Because surveillance systems are intended to produce information to support public health action, the process of delineating system objectives must include careful consideration of the expected follow-up activities. The public health manager can play an important role in ensuring that the agencies or individuals expected to use surveillance data will actually use them in public health planning and programming.

## Select and Define Health Events to Be Monitored

Each step of surveillance implementation requires substantial resources, and the total cost of surveillance rises incrementally with each additional event that is monitored. Consequently, the selection of health-related events to be tracked by the surveillance system must involve prioritization in order to meet the surveillance objectives of primary public health importance. Various criteria have been proposed for assessing the relative importance of health-related events to be included in a system.[11,46,47] Criteria (and examples of their corresponding indices) include the following:

- Morbidity (case counts, prevalence and incidence rates)
- Mortality (case fatality ratio, mortality rates, and potential years of life lost)
- Risk (transmission modes, communicability)
- Severity (bed-disability days, hospitalization and disability rates)
- Preventability (preventable fraction, existing prevention measures)

- Catastrophic potential (societal costs, vulnerability)
- Direct and indirect economic costs (loss of productivity, health care expenditures)
- Public interest (media attention) and stakeholder opinion (consensus)

The World Health Organization (WHO) has collaborated with the World Bank and the Harvard School of Public Health to estimate the Global Burden of Disease (http://www.who.int/en/).[48] The project uses relevant, available data plus assumption and inference to calculate disability-adjusted life years (DALYs), a single measure that summarizes population health. DALYs measure the difference between a perfect health scenario, where the entire population lives disease free until old age, and the populations' actual life with years lost to disability and premature mortality. DALYs are available for grouped and specific causes of morbidity and mortality and are stratified by geographic region, age group, and sex. Thus, the project offers a metric for prioritizing health events internationally. A notable limitation of the metric is that the health effects of socioeconomic disruption following civil wars, disasters, and epidemics (e.g., SARS) are not included.

Different surveillance approaches result from selection of health-related events for monitoring. Data produced by each surveillance approach may have the strengths and weaknesses described in the previous section. Where capacity exists, compatible surveillance data sources can track a group of health-related events to gain a comprehensive understanding of the larger public health problem. The aforementioned chronic disease indicators illustrated how behaviors (e.g., prevalence of smoking among adults, cigarette sales) and disease stages (e.g., cancer diagnosis, hospitalization, death) can be correlated through combined approaches. Alternatively, a public health agency may only monitor an antecedent of disease or a specific disease stage. It has been suggested, for example, that vital event registration is the most important form of public health surveillance that a developing country can add to its health statistics.[49]

For many forms of surveillance, a *case definition* must be developed to clarify the health-related event being monitored and improve the comparability of reports from different data sources.[11] A case definition may have several components, including clinical (e.g., signs and symptoms, diagnostic results), epidemiologic (e.g., person, place, and time), and behavioral (e.g., risk factors) information. Case definitions may also distinguish between confirmed, probable, and suspect occurrences according to their degree of conformity with the event of interest. If the clinical presentation of a disease is indeterminate (such as viral hepatitis, cancer), laboratory confirmation is often a necessary case definition component. In the United States, the CDC works with the CSTE to publish *Case Definitions for Infectious Conditions Under Public Health Surveillance*,[17] which define the nationally notifiable infectious diseases via clinical, epidemiologic, and laboratory criteria.

The development and revision of a surveillance case definition has important considerations. Components of the definition must be devised with attention to both the system's objectives and the utility of data to be collected. A broad definition will be more *sensitive*, increasing the probability that the system ascertains the event when it occurs, but may require effort in discerning true cases from false positives.[46] A relatively sensitive definition might be appropriate when completeness of reporting is important or when reporting of false positives does not detract from the system's objectives.[1] The influenza-like illness monitored by sentinel providers in the United States uses a simple, broad case definition (temperature of >100°F plus either a cough or a sore throat). Although other respiratory diseases produce these signs and symptoms, the system is useful. A narrower definition, on the other hand, is generally more *specific*. Specificity increases the probability that the events detected by the system are true events of interest, the *predictive value positive*. A relatively specific definition might be appropriate when complete case ascertainment is not necessarily important or when valid diagnostics, such as laboratory tests, are available for inclusion in the case definition. Notably, when laboratory tests or other diagnostic procedures are included as components of the case definition, the sensitivity and specificity of the tests or procedures themselves impact the sensitivity, specificity, and predictive value of the surveillance case definition. US surveillance for influenza-associated pediatric mortality has required laboratory confirmation of influenza because data from precise case ascertainment are needed to identify pediatric groups at risk for severe influenza and any consequent revision of vaccination policies.

Increased scientific understanding, availability of new diagnostics or therapies, and changing information needs may prompt case definition revisions. These definitions may, in turn, affect surveillance sensitivity and specificity. For example, in 1982 the CDC initiated AIDS surveillance in the United States using a set of opportunistic diseases, Kaposi's sarcoma (KS), *Pneumocystis carinii* pneumonia (PCP), and other serious opportunistic infections (OOI), that were definitively diagnosed in the absence of other known causes of immunodeficiency.[50] With the availability of HIV-antibody testing, surveillance specificity improved and a wider spectrum of HIV-related disease was recognized. The CDC revised its case definition in 1987 to include these diseases, which were presumptively diagnosed in persons testing positive for HIV infection.[51] As further knowledge was gained, the CDC changed its case definition again in 1993 to include direct evidence of immunodeficiency. Individuals who were HIV-positive and had CD4+ T-lymphocyte counts less than 200 cells/mm$^3$ (or a CD4+ proportion under 14%) were "counted" as AIDS.[52] This change immediately impacted US AIDS case counts; case reports increased 111% in 1993.[53] In contrast, many developing nations initially relied on clinical diagnoses of AIDS (e.g., weight loss) because laboratory capacities were inadequate for diagnosing KS, PCP, or OOI.[54] Clinical diagnosis was simple and universally applicable, but surveillance specificity was low. Until the late 1990s, most developing countries' case definitions for AIDS relied less on the HIV test because testing was not widely conducted. Although HIV surveillance has begun in many parts of the world, surveillance is not satisfactory for following trends in health outcomes, since most persons are asymptomatic and do not seek HIV testing. *Serosurveys* (serologic surveys) have been implemented in part to monitor transmission patterns.

### Establish the Population Under Surveillance

Although public health surveillance relies on records of individuals, the unit of interest is the population. Therefore, how the population is targeted for surveillance must be explicitly defined. Health surveys and sentinel surveillance sample the population; notifiable disease reporting and registries are *population-based* methods (i.e., they relate to the general population, often as defined by a geographic area).

Surveillance activities may focus on populations defined at geographic levels, which can range from a neighborhood to a nation or the entire world. Within a geographic domain, surveillance may be specifically directed toward an entire population or toward special subgroups that share demographic characteristics or risk factors for disease. Often the case definition reflects the population under surveillance. Residency within a geographic public health jurisdiction, for example, may be incorporated into a case definition to help define the surveillance population. Surveillance systems with populations delineated by geography have a special consideration. A decision to include cases based on where health-related events occurred or to include cases based on residency must be made.[1] When residency data are not readily available from reporting sources, inclusion based on where events occurred is a simple alternative if reports originate directly from eligible source locations. Diagnoses reported by a hospital located within the geographic area are an example. However, this approach will count events among nonresidents who are diagnosed in the area and may miss events among residents diagnosed outside the area.

## Establish Reporting Procedures

Surveillance programs must delineate specific types of data that should be collected, recognizing that different information types may require different forms of surveillance. Health surveys, for example, may be the only source of data on knowledge, attitudes, and behaviors. Clinical events typically occur in the context of health care, so corresponding data are likely to be obtainable through health information systems or directly from healthcare providers. Depending on the event of interest and setting where care or services are likely to be provided, a variety of surveillance approaches may be appropriate.

*Laboratory-based surveillance* systems seek information from clinical laboratories where testing of samples or specimens is necessary to establish or confirm a diagnosis. In the United States, the emerging infections programs (EIPs) have created surveillance networks within 11 geographically defined sites (states, metropolitan areas, or counties).[55] The EIPs maintain ongoing communication with microbiology laboratories, where invasive bacterial diseases and food-borne illnesses that require culture confirmation for diagnostic and surveillance purposes can be tracked. The CDC also coordinates PulseNet, which is a laboratory-based network for molecular subtyping of food-borne bacterial pathogens (e.g., *E. coli* O157:H7, *Salmonella*).[56] The program uses a standardized pulsed-field gel electrophoresis (PFGE) methodology across a network of laboratories in state and local health departments as well as federal public health and food regulatory agencies. Using PFGE, pathogens' DNA "fingerprints" (patterns obtained from genetic material) can be electronically uploaded to a database for comparison amongst PulseNet participants. This *molecular epidemiology* capacity has been particularly helpful in identifying geographically dispersed, common source outbreaks.

Systems and procedures for obtaining data also must be established. Depending on the application, a data collection form may be simple or complex and can exist either on paper or electronically. Often forms use a standard-ized coding system to increase the efficiency of data collection, entry, and storage. Manual (paper-based) data collection can be implemented relatively quickly and easily, but may be labor intensive and unsustainable in the long-term. Electronic reporting procedures have multiple applications for public health surveillance; investments in surveillance information technology are well worth consideration. In the United States, progress has been made in two areas, developing systems for automated, electronic laboratory reporting (ELR) and Internet-based case reporting.[57] ELR systems can greatly improve completeness and timeliness of notifiable disease reporting. In 1998, Hawaii implemented the first statewide automated laboratory reporting system.[58] By es-tablishing data transmission linkages with three commercial laboratories that provided approximately two thirds of all laboratory-based notifiable disease reports, the state health department more than doubled the number of *Giar-dia, Salmonella, Shigella,* invasive *S. pneumoniae,* and vancomycin-resistant *Enterococcus* reports relative to the conventional (paper-based) system. Elec-tronic reports were received 3.8 days earlier, and 12 of 21 data fields (57%) were significantly more likely to be complete when transmitted electronically. In the Netherlands, Internet-based case reporting has fully replaced the paper-based system for data transmission from municipal public health serv-ices to national public health authorities.[59] The change resulted in a 9-day improvement of median reporting timeliness and an 11% increase in the com-pleteness of data fields. Figure 14-4 is a screen capture of the initial data entry screen for another Internet-based, notifiable disease case reporting sys-tem, the State Electronic Notifiable Disease Surveillance System (SendSS) at the Georgia Division of Public Health.

Reporting an epidemic of communicable disease is often critical. Table 14-2 presents an overview of select surveillance networks for detecting and re-sponding to outbreaks and public health emergencies both in the United States and globally. The objectives, scope, and reporting procedures of these and other systems vary widely. Pro-MED, for example, facilitates worldwide dis-semination of information on human, veterinary, and plant disease outbreaks via moderated, daily e-mail communications in multiple languages (www.promedmail.org). Information from any source is eligible for inclusion, which is both a strength and a weakness of the system. The emergence of severe acute respiratory syndrome (SARS) was first publicly reported in Pro-MED in 2003. The WHO/Health Canada Global Public Health Intelligence Network (GPHIN) also detected early signs of the SARS epidemic. GPHIN software scans the Internet to identify infectious disease outbreaks through media and other electronic sources. The WHO investigates and verifies potential epidemics de-tected through the system (Table 14-2). To further strengthen epidemic surveil-lance, the WHO adopted revised International Health Regulations (IHR) in 2005, which provide a legal basis for sharing of critical epidemiologic data across borders.[60] The revised IHR legally obligate reporting and verification of "all events that may constitute a public health emergency of international con-cern" by WHO member and nonmember states that agree to be bound by the IHR. Compliance with the regulations can protect against international spread of disease while minimizing impediments to travel and trade.

Optimizing completeness of reporting and maintaining a consistent flow of accurate data are major challenges for surveillance programs[21]; incomplete, in-

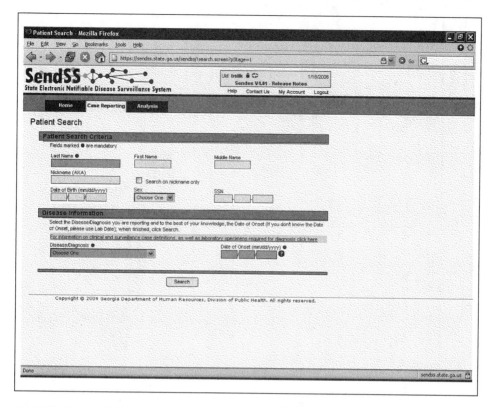

**FIGURE 14-4    Initial Screen for Internet-Based Notifiable Disease Case Reporting to the State Electronic Notifiable Disease Surveillance Systems (SendSS), Georgia Division of Public Health**
*Source:* Georgia Department of Human Resources, Division of Public Health.

consistent, or inaccurate data can introduce case ascertainment and information biases within surveillance data.[47] For example, cases detected in public-sector facilities may be more likely to be reported to health authorities than cases diagnosed by private clinicians, leading to higher reporting completeness for individuals seeking care in public clinics. Data on the incidence of sexually transmitted diseases tend to be more accurate in states with laws requiring that positive tests be reported.[61] Even at a single time and place, surveillance data can be biased. For example, respondents' faulty recall or reluctance to disclose stigmatizing conditions can lead to underreporting in surveillance surveys that rely on self-reporting.[62] Thus, surveillance system managers should be keenly aware of the potential for bias, assess its possible influence when detecting patterns of health-related events, and strive to base analyses on data sets that are as complete, comparable, and representative as possible. National programs often define minimally acceptable standards for data collection and processing. Funds for the field work associated with the operation of an active surveillance system (e.g., for quality control reviews, case-finding audits, etc.) are sound investments for a reliable surveillance database.

To maintain health care professionals' participation in surveillance activities, a multifaceted approach may be needed. The surveillance program manager must provide necessary support for meeting reporting responsibilities.

**TABLE 14-2 Select Surveillance Systems for Detection and Reporting of Infectious Disease Outbreaks in the United States and Globally**

| Name | Sponsor | Objectives | Scope | Description |
|---|---|---|---|---|
| BioSense | US Centers for Disease Control and Prevention | Early detection of public health emergencies, including naturally occurring outbreaks and bioterrorism, by federal, state, and local officials | Visits at federal medical facilities, national laboratory test orders, and over-the-counter retail in major metropolitan areas in the United States | National syndromic surveillance system, compiles data from various electronic sources |
| Enter-net | European Commission | Detect clusters of enteric pathogens, research antimicrobial resistance, standardize data collection and laboratory protocols | National reference laboratories and surveillance programs in European Union countries and beyond (Australia, Canada, Japan, and South Africa) | International surveillance network for salmonellosis and Vero cytotoxin-producing *E. coli* (VTEC) O157 |
| Epidemic Information Exchange (Epi-X) | US Centers for Disease Control and Prevention | Secure communication between public health officials, share preliminary information on health investigations, peer discussions, assistance, and coordination | Over 3900 users at all levels of US public health agencies in 2006 | Secure Internet-based communication system for public health |
| Global Outbreak Alert and Response Network (GOARN) | World Health Organization and partners | Coordination in investigating, tracking, and responding to international disease outbreaks | WHO member countries, government and nongovernment organizations, scientists and technical experts worldwide | Global partnership for detection and response to internationally significant outbreaks |
| Global Public Health Intelligence Network (GPHIN) | World Health Organization/ Health Canada | Identify possible infections disease outbreaks and other significant public health events | Worldwide media and Internet information sources in multiple languages | Software searches Internet-based sources globally for possible outbreaks |
| Laboratory Response Network (LRN) | US Centers for Disease Control and Prevention | Enhance laboratory infrastructure and capacity, including tests for identifying biological and chemical agents | Public health, military, and international laboratories conducting specialized testing from human, veterinary, and environmental sources | Integrated network of public health and clinical laboratories |
| National Electronic Disease Surveillance System (NEDSS) | US Centers for Disease Control and Prevention | Integrated, interoperable surveillance systems; efficient, confidential, and secure data transmission | US public health agencies and surveillance partners | Development of architecture and data standards for Internet-based surveillance |

*Source:* US Government Accountability Office. Emerging infectious diseases: review of state and federal disease surveillance efforts. Available at: http://www.gao.gov/htext/d04877.html. Accessed December 16, 2005; Fisher I. The Enter-net International Surveillance Network—how it works. *Euro Surveill.* 1999;4:52–55; and systems' websites.

Clinicians may be greatly aided by procedural manuals that specify the list of notifiable conditions, case definitions, information recording requirements, and reporting schedules. Other ideas for encouraging reporting compliance include simplifying reporting procedures, conducting seminars or onsite visits to emphasize reporting, and providing multiple reporting modalities (e.g., 24-hour toll-free numbers and Internet-based case reporting systems).[22,33]

Efforts to obtain surveillance data can be described along a spectrum of activities, ranging in intensity from passive to active. In the case of *passive* surveillance, public health officials rely on healthcare providers to report the occurrence of a health-related event voluntarily, as mandated by state law. With *active* surveillance, health officials routinely contact reporting sources to inquire about occurrences and review medical and laboratory reports to identify unreported occurrences. Relative to passive surveillance, active surveillance generally achieves more complete and accurate reporting (i.e., surveillance sensitivity is increased), but active surveillance is more resource intensive for the public health agency.

## Analyze and Interpret Surveillance Data

Before investing in the analysis and interpretation of surveillance data, the analyst needs to be oriented to the surveillance system itself. Intricacies arise from the specifics of how health-related events and the underlying population are defined and, in particular, from how the data are reported.[63] Knowledge of how various factors have influenced reporting may become relevant when findings from the analysis are interpreted (e.g., when and why a case definition was revised, diagnostic and reporting procedures were changed, or media attention fluctuated).

Analysis of surveillance data should start simple.[63] The basic epidemiologic parameters *person, place, and time* provide a framework. Depending on the specific objectives of the surveillance activities, an epidemiologist can apply a variety of analytic techniques that focus on one or more of these descriptors. Surveillance approaches that use sampling may lend themselves to statistical testing, which may be used for testing hypotheses and addressing random variation from the sample. Data from surveillance systems that ascertain all events in the population of interest may be directly described since observed variation is what has occurred in the population.

Descriptions of the persons experiencing the event under surveillance are frequently organized by demographic (e.g., age group, sex, race, and ethnicity) and epidemiologic characteristics (e.g., mode of transmission, disease type). Analysis could begin by tabulating event frequency distributions for each relevant characteristic. Interactions between these characteristics also may need to be assessed. When stratified by race, for example, vital statistics data for the 1990s indicate that two minority populations, American Indians/Alaska Natives and African-Americans, experienced higher mortality rates from traumatic brain injury (TBI) than other racial groups (Figure 14-5).[64] *External cause-of-injury codes* ("E codes"), which provide circumstantial and environmental information on injury causes, showed that motor vehicles were involved in half (49%) of the TBI deaths among American Indians/ Alaska Natives and firearms were involved in half (49%) of the TBI deaths among African-Americans.

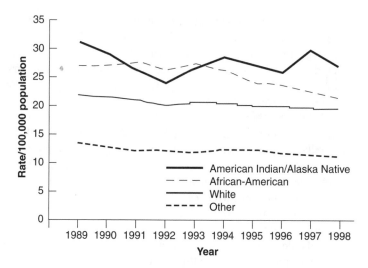

**FIGURE 14–5    Age-Adjusted Traumatic Brain Injury Mortality Rate (Per 100,000 Population), By Race and Year—United States, 1989–1998**
*Source:* US Centers for Disease Control and Prevention. Surveillance for traumatic brain injury deaths—United States, 1989–1998. *MMWR Surveill Summ.* 2002;51:1–16.

Analyses by place can be based either on where health-related events occurred or based on residency of those experiencing the events (though this decision may have been made while establishing the population under surveillance).[1] Simple comparisons and displays of event counts by geographic areas (e.g., neighborhoods, cities, nations) can be useful, particularly when the area's population size is sufficient to yield stable estimates of event frequencies. Event *rates* allow for comparisons of frequency for a given time period across areas with varying population sizes. Depending on the event under surveillance, a variety of rates (e.g., disease attack rate, birth rate, cause-specific mortality rate) can be obtained by carefully specifying the numerator, denominator, and time interval. Within a defined area, the first step is to divide the number of events for a designated time interval (numerator) by an estimate of the population at risk during the same time interval (denominator).[63] Often this yields a fraction that is difficult to interpret. Suppose 2 maternal deaths in the year 2000 were recorded in a state's vital statistics for 78,123 live births. Two divided by 78,213 equals 0.0000256. The next step is to multiply this fraction by some factor of 10, where the choice of an appropriate factor may depend on the frequency of the event, the size of the population at risk, and convention. In the example, a rate of 2.56 maternal deaths per 100,000 live births (0.0000256 × 100,000) helps characterize the frequency of maternal deaths in the state. This rate also can be compared to maternal death rates in other states (using the same 100,000 multiplier). Most epidemiology texts discuss rates in general and *standardization* of crude rates to control for confounding bias.

The high concentration of stroke mortality in the Southeastern United States (the so-called "stroke belt") during the 1990s is readily apparent in Figure 14-6. In this *choropleth* map, degree of shading corresponds to quan-

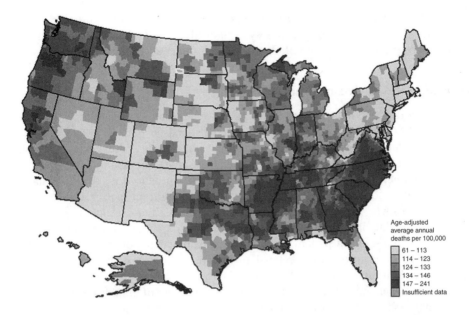

Age-adjusted
average annual
deaths per 100,000

61 – 113
114 – 123
124 – 133
134 – 146
147 – 241
Insufficient data

**FIGURE 14–6    United States Total Population Ages 35+, Stroke Death Rates, 1991–1998**
*Source:* US Centers for Disease Control and Prevention. Heart disease and stroke maps: interactive state maps. Available at http://www.cdc.gov/cvh/maps/statemaps.htm. Accessed January 25, 2006.

titative information (stroke mortality rates) for specific areas (US counties). The map exemplifies how rates help make comparisons across the counties' populations. Annual rates are averaged and categorized for the time period. Standardization allows for comparing rates after accounting for differences in the populations' age structures. *Geographic Information Systems (GIS)* applications are another important tool for spatial analyses of surveillance data. By geocoding (locating latitude and longitude from street address), precise event locations can be correlated with other area attributes. Maps can display these correlations by layering events and attributes. Chapter 12 describes the application of GIS to public health.

Time is significant because surveillance systems often monitor temporal trends within defined geographies. An analysis might begin simply by comparing the number of events in one time period to those of an equivalent time interval (e.g., season, year, week) in the past. Event counts could be tabulated for a table or graphically displayed, with time on the X axis. Building on findings from simpler analyses, a number of more complex methodologies are available for detecting aberrations, whether temporal, spatial, or in time *and* space.[8,63] For outbreak detection systems, such as syndromic surveillance, specialized statistical methods are described in other texts.[7,8]

Analyses involving time can either use dates when health-related events were reported or dates when health-related events occurred.[1] If reporting delays are considerable, report date may be an imprecise measure of when events actually occurred. The use of dates closer to the occurrence of the health event, such as diagnosis date, also needs to be interpreted carefully. When tracking chronic diseases with long latency periods, recent disease counts may underrepresent the current disease frequency. If either reporting delay or timeliness of diagnosis varies systematically, temporal imprecision may be differential across strata of the population under surveillance.

## Disseminate and Apply Surveillance Findings

Reporting of surveillance findings to appropriate stakeholders, including health authorities, policy makers, clinicians, and the general public, is a critical component of surveillance activities. Individuals and agencies that contribute data to the surveillance system are most compliant with reporting requirements when they see the value of data produced by the surveillance program. Ongoing feedback is a particularly important incentive for the clinicians who participate in surveillance activities. Clinicians are motivated by the availability of information on local health conditions, especially in forms that are useful for patient care. In Germany, practicing physicians most often (85%) cited information related to infectious disease outbreaks when surveyed on preferences for feedback of notifiable disease reporting data.[65]

Depending on what merits emphasis, a number of graphical display alternatives (graphs, tables, and maps) are available to help the audience to understand the data and appreciate their significance. If, for example, proportions are important, then a pie chart might be a good format for displaying surveillance data. General recommendations for visual display of quantitative information include the following[63]:

- Explain the graphic in the title, including when and where data were collected.
- Explain variables by labeling rows and columns (tables) or axes (graphs), including how variables were measured and the scale.
- Provide pertinent summary measures for the reader (e.g., row or column totals).
- Use a legend or a key to make categories or codes explicit.
- Define abbreviations with footnotes.
- If data are excluded or qualified, describe accordingly with footnotes.

A good rule of thumb is to imagine the table or figure alone (without accompanying text) and assess whether it remains self-explanatory to a reader who is unfamiliar with the data. Other references provide detailed considerations for how to display data effectively.[66]

A variety of mechanisms exist for publicizing surveillance findings and releasing surveillance datasets. In the United States, the CDC and its partners publish national data from a multitude of surveillance systems (http://www.cdc.gov/mmwr/mmwr_ss.html). At the state and local levels, public health agencies also disseminate information via newsletters, electronic bulletins, press releases, news conferences, and public meetings. Frequently, surveillance programs (e.g., disease registries, health surveys) publish a concise report and then periodically publish a more detailed report with extensive analysis and interpretation.

The dissemination strategy must correspond to the purpose of the surveillance activities. Particular attention should be focused on establishing a message that is readily comprehensible and relevant for the intended audience. Effective communication may be accomplished during public hearings or small group discussions with key individuals. The media can also be an ally for information distribution by judicious use of prepared statements and carefully planned content. Public health managers are encouraged to keep lines of communication with the media open in times of "no news" in order to promote broader, less sensational messages such as cancer screening. Wherever possible, system managers should target informed reporters (e.g., scientific writers) for directed information releases. Cultivating credibility is always a sound policy.

To balance the principles of access to data with confidentiality, surveillance systems must establish protocols and procedures to make determinations on requests for information for scientific research.[67] The data release protocol should include a clearly defined prioritization scheme to promote equal treatment of data requestors and data providers, expedite the release process, and encourage the release of a broad spectrum of data elements without compromising confidentiality.[68] Many states have legislated mandates to establish advisory boards or scientific review committees to oversee the use of surveillance data. Committee membership should include experts from appropriate disciplines who are experienced in the analysis of health data, disease coding, registry operations, and bioethics.

The ultimate objective of public health surveillance is to collect information for action. Therefore, surveillance data should be transformed into useful information concerning the prevalence of risk factors and healthy behaviors, the effects of interventions, and the direction of trends in disease and other health outcomes.[2] Accordingly, public health officials must determine the implications of their surveillance data; often these determinations are made on a regular basis. A committee composed of agency consultants (e.g., clinicians, academic epidemiologists, policy experts) can be formed to support an analysis of the data and assist with the formulation of and support for public health recommendations. Thresholds for public health action can be set so that unusual distributions of health events are identified and appropriate interventions can be implemented. Just as surveillance activities have expanded into various public health domains, the needs for interpretation of surveillance data have diversified as well. The National Program of Cancer Registries, for example, recommends that states allocate resources for epidemiologic guidance, especially for interpreting and applying cancer registry data. Similarly, greater attention has been placed on the interpretation and use of data derived from vital records for monitoring interventions aimed at reducing infant mortality and ensuring children's access to health care.

## Maintain and Evaluate Operations

The public health manager must provide ongoing support to ensure consistent and effective surveillance operations. To do so, surveillance programs require trained personnel, attention to evolving standards for use and management of surveillance data, and periodic evaluation to strengthen the surveillance system itself.

Public health administrators must ensure effective communication and collaboration across the diverse disciplines that contribute to surveillance systems. Epidemiologists and statisticians frequently manage surveillance programs.

Typically they compile, analyze, report, and interpret results from surveillance systems as well as design and refine systems that support valid, reliable, and relevant results. Other important professionals often include database programmers and persons with expertise in database design, linkage, and maintenance. Maintaining a qualified staff is an important consideration for good surveillance. For example, advances in information technology, including increased availability and standardization of electronic health information and expanding applications of the Internet, require a modern surveillance manager to be technologically savvy. The US progress in electronic reporting described above (reporting procedures) requires knowledge of controlled vocabularies, particularly HL7 to apply syntax to data, LOINC (Logical Observation Identifiers, Names, and Codes) to describe tests, and SNOMED (Systematized Nomenclature of Medicine) for test results.[69] Funds for continuing education and professional organization memberships for professional development are important budget considerations for surveillance programs. Chapter 8 details the public health workforce, including training for public health workers.

Surveillance programs and their personnel have ethical standards and legal requirements to maintain. Ethical responsibilities associated with public health practice include seeking information for devising policies and programs that assure health, while protecting the privacy and confidentiality of information, which, if released, could bring harm to an individual or community.[70] In fact, public health has a long history of safeguarding the privacy and confidentiality of individuals' health information while accomplishing their duties.[71] At the same time, legal and ethical responsibilities evolve and public health managers should be aware of necessary measures for compliance as well as the implications of legislation for their surveillance data sources (e.g., use of hospital discharge databases). For example, the US Privacy Rule of the Health Insurance Portability and Accountability Act (HIPAA) provided the first national *Standards for Privacy of Individually Identifiable Health Information*. (Individually identifiable health information is also known as protected health information, or PHI.) Although HIPAA privacy directly relates to "covered entities" (health plans, healthcare providers, and healthcare clearinghouses with PHI), public health authorities work with covered entities to ensure that surveillance activities are allowed to continue and may be considered covered entities themselves. Sharing of PHI for public health is expressly permitted by HIPAA privacy law.[71] (Refer to chapter 13 for more discussion on HIPAA.)

Surveillance programs at the local level require personally identifying information for a number of functions, including public health follow-up and investigation and identification of duplicate reports.[1] The CDC recommendations for security and confidentiality of HIV/AIDs surveillance data are a particularly useful resource.[72] Examples of these minimum standards include encryption during electronic data transfer, removal of identifying information with data transfer, record storage in physically secure areas with computer encryption and coded passwords, restricting data access to authorized staff who have signed confidentiality agreements that include penalties for data disclosure, and reporting for statistical purposes in formats that do not permit direct or indirect identification of individuals. This CDC resource has additional practices that can also be applied.

The distinction between public health research versus practice often arises.[73] Surveillance is a cornerstone of public health practice. As its primary intent is not to produce generalizable knowledge, typically it is not considered research as defined by federal laws for the protection of human research participants (known as the Common Rule).[74] However, distinguishing research and practice from among surveillance-related activities with multiple objectives can be ambiguous. A generic example is when surveillance identifies a public health problem; questions that may be considered research often can emerge from investigating the problem. Chapter 24 provides information on public health research, protection of human research participants, and the role of institutional review boards (IRBs).

Public health surveillance systems require periodic monitoring and evaluation to ensure that desired objectives are being met and operations are efficient and effective. An evaluation begins by identifying and engaging stakeholders in the evaluation process itself.[75] In doing so, the evaluation results are more likely to be both useful and credible to the persons most invested in the surveillance system. Next, a process of describing the systems' objectives and operations can help clarify expectations, increase understanding of the system's nuances, and guide the evaluation through subsequent steps. Several resources offer guidelines for evaluating surveillance systems, including systems focusing on early outbreak detection.[11,31,47,76] The resources include sets of system attributes—criteria with which to assess the utility, efficiency, and effectiveness of the system. The following common criteria are for evaluating surveillance system performance:

- *Sensitivity*—Likelihood that health-related events under surveillance are identified when they occur
- *Predictive value positive*—Likelihood that events identified are true events under surveillance
- *Representativeness*—Degree to which characteristics of persons experiencing identified events are distributed consistently with characteristics of all persons experiencing events in the population
- *Data quality*—Completeness, reliability, and validity of information
- *Timeliness*—Duration of time intervals between event occurrence, event reporting, and report completion as well as information analysis, interpretation, and dissemination
- *Simplicity*—Ease of use for persons participating in all steps of system operation
- *Flexibility*—Adaptability of the system to changing objectives and circumstances

Evaluation culminates in the formulation of recommendations for system-strengthening interventions. To assess the utility of surveillance functions, evaluators are also encouraged to verify that surveillance activities are integrated into the overall public health system and verify that their results are routinely received, understood, and applied by appropriate policy makers.[11]

•    •    •

Surveillance is a primary mechanism for generating and processing information in the cycle of formulating public health objectives, implementing interventions, measuring program impact, and refining interventions. Evaluation should assess whether the information produced by the surveillance system is useful for public health programming and policy making.

## Chapter Review

1. Surveillance systems produce data that support the following:
   - Planning and priority setting
   - Intervention design and targeting
   - Program and policy evaluation
   - Detection and response to emergent public health needs
   - Epidemiologic and health services research
2. Primary surveillance system design formats include the following:
   - Notifiable disease reporting
   - Sentinel surveillance
   - Syndromic surveillance
   - Registries and vital statistics
   - Health surveys
   - Combined approaches
3. The following are major design and operational aspects of surveillance:
   - Establishing system objectives
   - Selecting and defining the health events to be monitored
   - Specifying the population under surveillance
   - Developing reporting procedures
   - Analyzing and interpreting data
   - Disseminating and applying data as information
4. Key managerial strategies for sustaining surveillance systems include the following:
   - Retaining and coordinating appropriately trained personnel
   - Ensuring adherence to legal and ethical standards
   - Implementing evaluation to improve the quality and efficiency of surveillance

## References

1. Buehler JW. Surveillance. In: Rothman KJ, Greenland S, eds. *Modern Epidemiology.* Philadelphia, Pa: Lippincott-Raven Publishers; 1998:435–457.
2. Stroup DF, Brookmeyer R, Kalsbeek WD. Public health surveillance in action. In: Brookmeyer R, Stroup DF, eds. *Monitoring the Health of Populations: Statistical Principles and Methods for Public Health Surveillance.* New York, NY: Oxford University Press; 2004:1–35.
3. Halperin W, Baker E, eds. *Public Health Surveillance.* New York, NY: Van Nostrand Reinhold; 1992.
4. Menck H, Smart C, eds. *Central Cancer Registries: Design, Management and Use.* Chur, Switzerland: Harwood Academic Publishers; 1994.
5. Fritz AG, Hutchison CL, Roffers SD, eds. *Cancer Registry Management: Principles and Practice.* Dubuque, Ia: Kendall/Hunt Publishing Co; 1997.
6. Teutsch SM, Churchill RE, eds. *Principles and Practice of Public Health Surveillance.* New York, NY: Oxford University Press; 2000.
7. Brookmeyer R, Stroup DF, eds. *Monitoring the Health of Populations: Statistical Principles and Methods for Public Health Surveillance.* New York, NY: Oxford University Press; 2004.

8. Lawson AB, Kleinman K, eds. *Spatial and Syndromic Surveillance for Public Health*. Chichester, England: John Wiley & Sons; 2005.

9. Thacker SB. Historical development. In: Teutsch SM, Churchill RE, eds. *Principles and Practice of Public Health Surveillance*. New York, NY: Oxford University Press; 2000:1–16.

10. Remington PL, Goodman RA. Chronic disease surveillance. In: Brownson RC, Remington PL, Davis JR. *Chronic Disease Epidemiology and Control*. Washington DC: American Public Health Association; 1998:55–76.

11. US Centers for Disease Control and Prevention. Updated guidelines for evaluating surveillance systems: recommendations from the guidelines working group. *MMWR Recommendations and Reports*. 2001;50:1–35.

12. US Centers for Disease Control and Prevention. Outbreak of *Salmonella* serotype muenchen infections associated with unpasteurized orange juice–United States and Canada, June 1999. *MMWR*. 1999;48:582–585.

13. US Renal Data System Coordinating Center. Researcher's Guide 2004. Available at: http://www.usrds.org/research.htm. Accessed December 9, 2005.

14. US Renal Data System. *USRDS 2005 Annual Data Report: Atlas of End-Stage Renal Disease in the United States*. Bethesda, Md: National Institute of Diabetes and Digestive and Kidney Diseases; 2005.

15. Parrish RG, McDonnell SM. Sources of health-related information. In: Teutsch SM, Churchill RE, eds. *Principles and Practice of Public Health Surveillance*. New York, NY: Oxford University Press; 2000:30–75.

16. Council of State and Territorial Epidemiologists. NNDSS Assessment 2004. Available at: http://www.cste.org/nndssmainmenu2004.htm. Accessed November 28, 2005.

17. US Centers for Disease Control and Prevention. Case definitions for infectious conditions under public health surveillance. *MMWR Recommendations and Reports*. 1997;46:1–55.

18. Roush S, Birkhead G, Koo D, Cobb A, Fleming D. Mandatory reporting of diseases and conditions by health care professionals and laboratories. *JAMA*. 1994;282:164–170.

19. Kaufman JA, Reichard S, Walline A. Survey of HIV, sexually transmitted disease, tuberculosis and viral hepatitis case reporting practices in tribally operated and urban Indian health facilities. Council of State and Territorial Epidemiologists. Available at: http://www.cste.org/publications.asp. Accessed December 1, 2005.

20. US Centers for Disease Control and Prevention. First report of AIDS. *MMWR*. 2001;50:429.

21. Doyle TJ, Glynn KM, Groseclose SL. Completeness of notifiable infectious disease reporting in the United States: an analytical literature review. *Am J Epidemiol*. 2002;155:866–874.

22. Silk BJ, Berkelman RL. A review of strategies for enhancing the completeness of notifiable disease reporting. *J Public Health Manage Pract*. 2005;11:191–200.

23. US Centers for Disease Control and Prevention. Overview of influenza surveillance in the United States. Available at: http://www.cdc.gov/flu/weekly/pdf/flu-surveillance-overview.pdf. Accessed December 3, 2005.

24. Seligman PJ, Frazier YM. Surveillance: the sentinel health event approach. In: Halperin W, Baker E, eds. *Public Health Surveillance*. New York, NY: Van Nostrand Reinhold; 1992:16–25.

25. Rustein DD, Berenberg W, Chalmers TC, et al. Measuring the quality of medical care: a clinical method. *N Engl J Med*. 1976;294:582–588.

26. Buehler JW, Berkelman RL, Hartley DM, Peters CJ. Syndromic surveillance and bioterrorism-related epidemics. *Emerg Infect Dis*. 2003;9:1197–1204.

27. Reingold A. If syndromic surveillance is the answer, what is the question? *Biosecurity Bioterrorism: Biodefense Strat Pract Sci.* 2003;1:1–5.

28. Mandl KD, Overhage JM, Wagner MM, et al. Implementing syndromic surveillance: a practical guide informed by early experience. *J Am Med Inform Assoc.* 2004;11:141–150.

29. Koo D. Leveraging syndromic surveillance. *J Public Health Manage Pract.* 2005;11:181–183.

30. Hopkins RS. Design and operation of state and local infectious disease surveillance systems. *J Public Health Manage Pract.* 2005;11:184–190.

31. US Centers for Disease Control and Prevention. Framework for evaluating public health surveillance systems for early detection of outbreaks. *MMWR Recommendations and Reports.* 2004;53:1–11.

32. US Centers for Disease Control and Prevention. Immunization information system progress—United States, 2003. *MMWR.* 2005;54:722–724.

33. Birkhead GS, Maylahn CM. State and local public health surveillance. In: Teutsch SM, Churchill RE, eds. *Principles and Practice of Public Health Surveillance.* New York, NY: Oxford University Press; 2000:253–286.

34. US Centers for Disease Control and Prevention. Cancer registries: the foundation for cancer prevention and control. Available at: http://www.cdc.gov/cancer/npcr/about2004.htm. Accessed December 5, 2005.

35. US Cancer Statistics Working Group. *United States Cancer Statistics: 2002 Incidence and Mortality.* Atlanta, Ga: Centers for Disease Control and Prevention, National Cancer Institute; 2005.

36. Sankila R, Black R, Coebergh JW, et al. *Evaluation of Clinical Care by Cancer Registries.* Lyon, France: International Agency for Research on Cancer; 2003. IARC Technical Publication No. 37.

37. US Centers for Disease Control and Prevention. National Vital Statistics System. Available at: http://www.cdc.gov/nchs/nvss.htm. Accessed December 6, 2005.

38. Kalsbeek WD. The use of surveys in public health surveillance: monitoring high-risk populations. In: Brookmeyer R, Stroup DF, eds. *Monitoring the Health of Populations: Statistical Principles and Methods for Public Health Surveillance.* New York, NY: Oxford University Press; 2004:37–70.

39. US Centers for Disease Control and Prevention. National Health and Nutrition Examination Survey. Available at: http://www.cdc.gov/nchs/nhanes.htm. Accessed December 5, 2005.

40. US Centers for Disease Control and Prevention. Behavioral Risk Factor Surveillance System. Available at: http://www.cdc.gov/brfss/. Accessed December 5, 2005.

41. US Centers for Disease Control and Prevention. Indicators for chronic disease surveillance. *MMWR Recommendations and Reports.* 2004;53:1–6.

42. Meriwether R. Blueprint for a national public health surveillance system. *J Public Health Manage Pract.* 1996;2:16–23.

43. Greenland S. Ecologic inference problems. In: Brookmeyer R, Stroup DF, eds. *Monitoring the Health of Populations: Statistical Principles and Methods for Public Health Surveillance.* New York, NY: Oxford University Press; 2004:315–340.

44. Berkelman RL, Buehler JW. Public health surveillance of non-infectious chronic diseases: the potential to detect rapid changes in disease burden. *Int J Epidemiol.* 1990;19:628–635.

45. Bingenheimer JB, Raudenbush SW. Statistical and substantive inferences in public health: issues in the application of multilevel models. *Annu Rev Public Health.* 2004;25:53–77.

46. Teutsch SM. Considerations in planning a surveillance system. In: Teutsch SM, Churchill RE, eds. *Principles and Practice of Public Health Surveillance*. New York, NY: Oxford University Press; 2000:17–29.
47. Romaguera RA, German RR, Klaucke DN. Evaluating public health surveillance. In: Teutsch SM, Churchill RE, eds. *Principles and Practice of Public Health Surveillance*. New York, NY: Oxford University Press; 2000:176–193.
48. Murray CJL, Lopez AD, eds. *The Global Burden of Disease: A Comprehensive Assessment of Mortality and Disability from Diseases, Injuries, and Risk Factors in 1990 and Projected to 2020*. Cambridge, Mass: Harvard University Press; 1996.
49. White ME, McDonnell SM. Public health surveillance in low- and middle-income countries. In: Teutsch SM, Churchill RE, eds. *Principles and Practice of Public Health Surveillance*. New York, NY: Oxford University Press; 2000:287–315.
50. US Centers for Disease Control and Prevention. Current trends update on acquired immune deficiency syndrome (AIDS)–United States. *MMWR*. 1982;31:513–514.
51. US Centers for Disease Control and Prevention. Revision of the CDC surveillance case definition for acquired immunodeficiency syndrome. *MMWR Supplement*. 1987;36:1S–15S.
52. US Centers for Disease Control and Prevention. 1993 revised classification system for HIV infection and expanded surveillance case definition for AIDS among adolescents and adults. *MMWR Recommendations and Reports*.1992;41:1–19.
53. US Centers for Disease Control and Prevention. Current trends update: impact of the expanded AIDS surveillance case definition for adolescents and adults on case reporting–United States, 1993. *MMWR*. 1994;43:167–170.
54. World Health Organization. AIDS and HIV case definitions: overview of internationally used HIV/AIDS case definitions. Available at: http://www.who.int/hiv/strategic/surveillance/definitions/en/. Accessed January 11, 2006.
55. Pinner RW, Rebmann CA, Schuchat A, Hughes JM. Disease surveillance and the academic, clinical, and public health communities. *Emerg Infect Dis*. 2003;9:781–787.
56. Swaminathan B, Barrett TJ, Hunter SB, Tauxe RV; CDC PulseNet Task Force. PulseNet: the molecular subtyping network for foodborne bacterial disease surveillance, United States. *Emerg Infect Dis*. 2001;7:382–389.
57. US Centers for Disease Control and Prevention. Progress in improving state and local disease surveillance–United States, 2000–2005. *MMWR*. 2005;54:822–825.
58. Effler P, Ching-Lee M, Bogard A, et al. Statewide system of electronic notifiable disease reporting from clinical laboratories: comparing automated reporting with conventional methods. *JAMA*. 1999;282:1845–1850.
59. Ward M, Brandsema P, van Straten E, Bosman A. Electronic reporting improves timeliness and completeness of infectious disease notification, The Netherlands, 2003. *Euro Surveill*. 2005;10:27–30.
60. World Health Organization. International Health Regulations of Diseases (IHR). Available at: http://www.who.int/csr/ihr/en/. Accessed December 29, 2005.
61. Cates W. Estimates of the incidence and prevalence of sexually transmitted diseases in the United States. *Sex Trans Dis*. 1999;26:S2–S7.
62. Anderson JE, McCormick L, Fichtner R. Factors associated with self-reported STDs: data from a national survey. *Sex Trans Dis*. 1994;21:303–308.

63. Janes GR, Hutwagner L, Gates W, Jr., et al. Descriptive epidemiology: analyzing and interpreting surveillance data. In: Teutsch SM, Churchill RE, eds. *Principles and Practice of Public Health Surveillance.* New York, NY: Oxford University Press; 2000:112–167.
64. US Centers for Disease Control and Prevention. Surveillance for traumatic brain injury deaths—United States, 1989–1998. *MMWR Surveillance Summaries.* 2002;51:1–16.
65. Krause G, Ropers G, Stark K. Notifiable disease surveillance and practicing physicians. *Emerg Infect Dis.* 2005;11:442–445.
66. Tufte ER. *The Visual Display of Quantitative Information.* Chesire, Conn: Graphics Press; 1983.
67. Storm HH, et al. *Guidelines on Confidentiality for Population-based Cancer Registration.* Lyon, France: International Association of Cancer Registries; 2004. IARC Internal Report No. 2004/03.
68. Havener LA, ed. *Standards for Cancer Registries.* Vol III. Standards for Completeness, Quality, Analysis, and Management of Data. Springfield, Ill: North American Association of Central Cancer Registries; 2004.
69. Wurtz R, Cameron BJ. Electronic laboratory reporting for the infectious diseases physician and clinical microbiologist. *Clin Infect Dis.* 2005;40:1638–1643.
70. American Public Health Association. Principles of the ethical practice of public health. Available at: http://www.apha.org/codeofethics/ethicsposter.pdf. Accessed December 14, 2005.
71. US Centers for Disease Control and Prevention. HIPAA Privacy Rule and Public Health. *MMWR Supplement.* 2003;52:1–24.
72. US Centers for Disease Control and Prevention. Guidelines for national human immunodeficiency virus case surveillance, including monitoring for human immunodeficiency virus infection and acquired immunodeficiency syndrome. *MMWR Recommendations and Reports.* 1999;48:1–28.
73. Council of State and Territorial Epidemiologists. Public health practice vs. research: a report for public health practitioners including cases and guidance for making distinctions. Available at: http://www.cste.org/publications.asp. Accessed December 14, 2005.
74. Office for Human Research Protections. Public welfare: protection of human subjects, 2005. [45 CFR 46]. Available at: http://www.hhs.gov/ohrp/humansubjects/guidance/45cfr46.htm. Accessed December 14, 2005.
75. US Centers for Disease Control and Prevention. Framework for program evaluation in public health. *MMWR Recommendations and Reports.* 1999;48:1–40.
76. European Commission. Protocol for the evaluation of EU-wide surveillance networks on communicable diseases. Available at: http://europa.eu.int/comm/health/ph_projects/2002/com_diseases/fp_commdis_2002_frep_18_en.pdf. Accessed December 15, 2005.

## CHAPTER 15

# ASSESSMENT AND STRATEGIC PLANNING IN PUBLIC HEALTH

Lloyd F. Novick
Cynthia B. Morrow
Glen P. Mays

## Chapter Overview

Public health organizations use assessment processes to transform information into knowledge that guides administrative and policy decision making. The community health assessment process involves a comparative analysis and interpretation of health information to determine priorities and strategies for addressing the health needs of a defined population. Managing an effective assessment process requires skills in data analysis, group process facilitation, negotiation, interorganizational relations, and consensus development.

Population-based management of health requires a thorough understanding of current as well as potential health needs of the community. Through the activity of assessment, public health organizations transform information into practical knowledge about population health needs. Assessment involves collection of data from multiple sources followed by a critical, comparative analysis and interpretation of health information in order to determine the relative importance and priority of multiple public health issues facing a defined population. Both quantitative and qualitative analytic skills are used to carry out this function.

This chapter reviews definitions and the history of health assessment before detailing the administrative processes used by public health professionals to assess health needs in the population. The public health professionals can then develop appropriate policies and interventions to address these needs. The methods, opportunities, and challenges public health organizations face when implementing the assessment process will be described. Organizational tools and protocols developed over the past two decades to facilitate public health assessment activities and contemporary assessment tools that have led to strategic planning approaches will be examined. The latter include an indicator methodology tied to *Healthy People 2010* objectives and Web-based query systems. These illustrate the changing needs and processes of public health assessment in an information age that provides current, easily available population data. Finally, the chapter will examine the widely accepted strategic planning tool known as MAPP (Mobilizing for Action through Planning and Partnerships). This promising and tested approach to community health improvement is a useful template for both assessment and strategic planning in public health.

## Definition and Overview of Assessment

In the context of public health, assessment is the beginning of the continuum of problem identification, priority setting, strategic planning, intervention, and evaluation. Assessment can be either *internal,* addressing processes within an organization, or *external*, addressing processes within the community. This chapter will focus on the latter, or the community health assessment.

Community health assessment (CHA) involves obtaining and interpreting information to determine the health status of a specific community. Community health assessment is central to the understanding and planning for improvement of the community's health. Definition of the community is therefore a basic element of the assessment process. A community can be defined by geographic area, geopolitical boundaries, or by a group of individuals who share common characteristics (attendance at a university, religion, common healthcare need, race, age, occupation, etc.).

One author defines this assessment process as follows:

> First, public health agencies must identify health needs by monitoring the health status of the population in the community. Second, public health agencies must ascertain the public's ability to deal with needs by identifying available public health resources and by evaluating their effectiveness. Third, the results of these efforts must be presented to public health managers, policy makers, and the public in ways that enable them to decide what action to take.[1]

*The Future of Public Health,* the 1988 Institute of Medicine (IOM) report, identified three core public health functions that every public health agency should perform: assessment, assurance, and policy. The IOM report further recommended that local public health agencies "regularly and systematically collect, assemble, analyze, and make available information on the health of the community, including statistics on health status, community health needs, and epidemiologic and other studies of health problems." Furthermore, the report described a fully developed assessment function as "an absolutely essential part of the ideal public health system" as well as a responsibility that governmental public health agencies "could not delegate."[2]

Subsequent work by the Centers for Disease Control and Prevention (CDC) led to the delineation of three specific practices that make up the assessment function as defined by the IOM.[3] These practices, which were identified by a working group of public health experts convened by the CDC during 1991–1992, include the following:

- *Assess* the health needs of the community.
- *Investigate* the occurrence of health effects and health hazards of the community.
- *Analyze* the determinants of identified health needs.

In 1994, the Public Health Functions Steering Committee released the *Ten Essential Public Health Services*. Most of these services involve assessment or the strategic planning that is indicated by assessment findings. Examples include: (1) monitor health status to define community health problems; (2) diagnose and investigate health problems and health hazards in the community; (3) inform, educate, and empower people about health issues; (4) mobilize community partnerships to identify and solve community health problems; and (5) develop policies and plans that support individual and community health efforts.[4]

As described above, once community health needs are identified, specific public health interventions can be developed and their effectiveness evaluated using a similar approach. Information necessary for performing a community health assessment (e.g., data on mortality rates or behavioral risk factors such as smoking) is available from multiple sources. (Refer to Chapter 11 for detailed discussion on data.)

Two principles are key to an effective community health assessment that contributes to strategic planning. The first is that the assessment and analysis are designed prior to data collection and should use specific objectives, indicators, or queries. "Fishing" expeditions beginning with unstructured collections of data are to be avoided. The second is that the assessment ideally incorporates input from a wide range of stakeholders within the defined community. Although an assessment may be initiated by the public health agency, the process can not be implemented in isolation from the public health system and public. In addition to these fundamental principles, two other points are critical to the understanding of public health assessment: (1) determinations of objectives for assessment must be distinguished from the processes of reporting, automation, and other data collection tools; and (2) the agenda for assessment is continually in flux because of evolving and new public health challenges.[5]

Institutional, provider, and public perspectives also play a powerful role in shaping the processes and outcomes of public health assessment. Public health organizations therefore have the responsibility to determine the extent to which various organizations and individuals are allowed a voice in the assessment process. Managing an effective assessment process requires a diverse set of skills not only for the analysis and interpretation of health information, but also for group process facilitation, negotiation, interorganizational decision making, and consensus development.

Prioritization of health issues is ideally followed by strategic planning including the identification of resources and capacities to bring about health improvement. Broad community involvement is needed in these stages as well. This includes public, private, and voluntary organizations as well as members of the community. Various strategic planning models have been used for this purpose. The 1997 IOM publication *Improving Health in the Community: A Role for Performance Monitoring* is one such framework for community health improvement.[6] This framework includes two major cycles: problem identification and prioritization (similar to community health assessment) and the analysis and implementation cycle. A more recent strategic planning model developed by the National Association of County and City Health Officials (NACCHO) and the CDC is Mobilizing for Action Through Planning and Partnerships (MAPP).

## Historical Roots of Public Health Assessment

In 1662, John Graunt published his *Natural and Political Observations Mentioned in a Following Index and Made Upon the Bills of Mortality.* Graunt analyzed London data on mortality and fertility in the human population, noting the excess of male births, the high infant mortality, and seasonal variation in mortality.[7] William Farr, Compiler of Abstracts at the London General Register Office, analyzed occupational mortality by employing census data and used the findings to advocate for reform. Analysis identifying the most hazardous occupations contributed to the effort for improving working conditions in Victorian Britain.[8]

Edwin Chadwick, secretary to the Poor Law Commission in England and Wales, demonstrated that disease was related to physical and social factors, notably sanitation and socioeconomic status. This particular work formed the basis for the earliest community health assessment activities in the United States by Lemuel Shattuck in Massachusetts and John Griscom in New York State.[9] (Refer to Chapter 1 for more further discussion.) Today, the US Census Bureau has population data available that describes communities and their health since 1790. Birth and death records have been maintained for centuries by churches, families, and states and have been a source for counting individuals and providing information on health status. State and local health departments collect data through surveillance and surveys such as the Behavioral Risk Factor Surveillance System (BRFSS) and the Youth Risk Behavior Survey (YRBS), as discussed in Chapter 11.[10]

## The Role of Public Health Organizations in the Assessment Process

Through a successful assessment process, public health organizations and other entities progress from awareness of a problem to identification of a potential solution, to implementation and evaluation of the solution and, finally, to institutionalization of the solution. Public health organizations may assume roles in any or all of these stages in adopting the assessment activities. Furthermore, the degree of involvement of a public health organization can vary at each stage in the process. For internally focused assessment activities, such as quality improvement activities, the assessment stages may all occur within the public health organization. For externally focused assessment activities, focusing on population or community-based problems, other organizations may play critical roles in the adoption process.

Initial awareness or highlighting of a community health concern may be initiated because of a noted increase in the incidence of disease or may be brought to attention by the public, a legislator, a health provider, or a public health agency. Availability of resources or dedicated funding for specific public health interventions may also stimulate interest in a particular health concern. Public health organizations may play an *initiating* role for assessment efforts by raising awareness about a public health problem, only to let other organizations assume responsibility for implementing and institutionalizing an assessment process around the problem. Public health organizations may also play a *convening* role in assessment efforts by bringing organizations and individuals together for the purpose of designing and implementing an assessment process.

During the stage of assessment implementation, public health organizations may choose among several alternative levels of involvement, including the following:

- A *governing* role, wherein the public health organization assumes primary responsibility for directing and managing the assessment process
- A *participatory* role, which entails shared responsibility for managing the assessment process with other organizations
- A *contributing* role, which involves providing information, resources, and expertise to an assessment process that is actively managed by other organizations

The public health organization's role in assessment activities depends on its own mission, skills, and resources as well as those of other interested organizations. By engaging community partners in public health efforts, public health organizations benefit from the additional expertise and resources contributed by these other organizations. Collaborative assessment processes also offer public health organizations opportunities for gaining new knowledge about assessment methods and tools from organizations already skilled in these approaches, including hospitals, managed care plans, medical practices, and laboratories. For example, in a case study analysis of a local public health system, a private hospital assumed primary responsibility for implementing a process aimed at assessing barriers to routine health care for community members.[11] In this case, the local public health agency participated extensively in the assessment process, but the hospital assumed primary responsibility for the core activities of conducting surveys and focus groups with community residents and convening local providers to assess their perceptions on access to care. The challenge associated with encouraging other organizations to assume key responsibilities in public health assessment efforts is that public health organizations sacrifice some measure of control over these efforts.

## Levels of Analysis and Authority in the Assessment Process

Public health organizations vary not only in the degree to which they participate during an assessment process but also vary with respect to the levels of analysis that is used in conducting assessment activities. Government public health functions are carried out at federal, state, and local levels, with overlapping jurisdictions of authority existing for many public health activities. Assessment efforts reflect these different levels of authority. An important task for public health organizations therefore entails identifying the most appropriate level for implementing an assessment effort and encouraging assessment activities to be performed at that level. Some public health issues are addressed most effectively through interventions at state or national levels rather than at the local level, such as tobacco control or seat belt use. Enhanced legal authority or political will may exist at these higher levels, and greater resources may be available to address the problem. Many public health problems extend beyond the boundaries of a single local community and therefore require broader governmental authority to carry out effective assessment activities. Moreover, the problem under study may stem from a characteristic of a state or federal program, rather than from local activities.

For example, environmental health problems such as water quality and hazardous waste disposal often fall into this category because many state governments exercise regulatory authority over these issues. Rather than attempting to lead an assessment effort at the local level, local public health agencies may achieve better results by contributing to state-level or federal-level assessment initiatives.

Conversely, other public health issues involve primarily local populations, resources, and health needs. Often, these issues can be addressed most effectively through community-level efforts rather than large-scale state or national interventions. For example, the task of improving the accessibility of family planning services within a community is likely to be best informed by a local assessment effort. In this case, the processes of service delivery, outreach, and education are implemented primarily by local community organizations and are therefore amenable to local information about community health needs. In other cases, local assessment efforts may be implemented because larger-scale state or national efforts are not feasible because of the lack of political will. Some local communities, for example, have initiated assessment efforts around the task of improving health insurance coverage for the uninsured, in part because state and federal initiatives to address this problem have historically failed to be implemented.[12] As discussed earlier, assessment efforts are sensitive to political will and change accordingly. In the case of this insurance example, the governor of Massachusetts approved "An Act Promoting Access to Affordable, Quality, Accountable Health Care" in April 2006.[13] If successful, renewed efforts for assessment and subsequently at policy change regarding access to care may occur in other states.

Assessment activities may also involve public health organizations at multiple levels of authority. Local assessment efforts may be implemented as components of larger state or national assessment efforts, with linkages maintained through communication and information flows among the various levels of public health authority. These approaches are designed to inform public health activities simultaneously at these multiple levels of authority and are particularly relevant in cases where performance at one level of the public health system has substantial influence on performance at another level. For example, Florida's state health agency maintains a state-level assessment process designed to improve public health outcomes in areas such as infant mortality, adolescent pregnancy, and the incidence of communicable diseases.[14] As part of this effort, individual assessment processes are implemented at each local public health unit within the state. These local assessment efforts identify strategies designed to improve the delivery of public health services at the community level. These efforts also generate information about local resource needs and priorities that inform the state-level assessment process. The state assessment effort uses this local information to improve decision making regarding state budget allocations, policy making, and program development.

The administrative relationships that exist among local, state, and federal public health organizations play important roles in assessment implementation. In states such as Florida, local public health agencies are organized as centralized administrative units of the state public health agency. The state agency maintains direct authority for all public health activities within the state. In other states, local public health organizations are decentralized and operate under the direct authority of local governments and local boards of health. In still other states, local public health agencies operate under state authority for some public health functions (e.g., communicable disease control and environmental health protection) and under local authority for other functions (e.g., health promotion and disease prevention activities and community health assessment). *Centralized* public health jurisdictions may offer state agencies enhanced authority for organizing and coordinating assessment processes at the local level, whereas *decentralized* jurisdictions may offer greater opportunities for incorporating local needs, priorities, and values in the assessment process. Public health organizations therefore face the need to tailor their assessment activities to the specific interorganizational and intergovernmental context in which they operate.

Federal public health agency relationships with state and local public health organizations also help shape assessment efforts. Federal agencies interact with state and local organizations primarily through the provision of public health funding, technical assistance, and regulatory oversight. Much federal public health funding is now disbursed through block grants and similar "pass-through" arrangements to state health agencies, rather than through categorical grants made directly to local public health organizations. Increasingly, federal agencies use these funding vehicles to encourage assessment activities at state and local levels. For example, the Maternal and Child Health Services block grant administered by the US Health Resources and Services Administration (HRSA) requires state grantees to conduct formal needs assessment processes and to develop performance objectives and measures for their programs based on this assessment.

Federal agencies may also encourage assessment implementation through their regulatory authority. Agencies such as the US Environmental Protection Agency (EPA) use their regulatory authority to enforce compliance with federal public health standards such as those concerning air quality, water quality, and solid waste disposal. State and local public health organizations that do not meet these standards are required to adopt remediation processes, which offer opportunities for the application of assessment methods. Since 1995, the EPA's Reinventing Environmental Protection initiative requires the use of assessment methods as part of community-based strategies to achieve and exceed federal environmental health standards.[15]

Federal public health agencies also encourage the implementation of assessment methods by providing technical assistance to state and local public health organizations. The CDC carries out a technical assistance role in partnership with professional associations such as the NACCHO and the Association of State and Territorial Health Officials. Through these partnerships, the CDC has been instrumental in developing several resources to support assessment processes, which are discussed in the following sections. Other federal agencies such as the HRSA provide similar types of technical assistance to public health organizations for assessment activities.

A critical issue with respect to the level of analysis that can occur during the assessment process is the unit or level for which data is available. For example, if data is only available at the state level, assessment specific to that data is likely to occur at the state level. This will be described more fully later in the chapter. A 2002 study by Garland Land examined to what extent data to track the *Healthy People 2010* (*HP 2010*) objectives are typically available at the state and local level.[16] Only 56% of the relevant *HP 2010* objectives were available at the state level and only 33% at the county level. Although there has been some improvement in local data availability since 2002, this remains a major problem related to feasible levels for assessment. Land refers to the well accepted axiom—all public health response is local: "The *HP 2010* objectives will only be met if they can be tracked at all jurisdictional levels."[16]

## Public Participation in Assessment

Public and stakeholder participation is an essential attribute of a successful public health assessment process. Organizations at all levels of the public health delivery system face the need to remain responsive to community needs, values, and priorities. Some public health organizations ensure this responsiveness through direct involvement of community representatives in public health decision making and governance. These organizations may operate under governing boards consisting of community representatives, or they may appoint community members to serve on public health task forces empowered to address specific community health issues. Other public health organizations rely on indirect approaches for ensuring responsiveness and accountability to the public, such as governing boards consisting of publicly elected officials who are accountable to public interests through the electoral process.

These same levels of public participation are often extended to assessment activities conducted by public health organizations. Some organizations directly involve community representatives in their assessment processes. For example, organizations may field community surveys and focus groups designed to elicit community perceptions concerning public health issues. The community health assessment process maintained by a local health department and local United Way chapter in California uses this strategy for identifying priority health issues within their community.[17] Another approach involves appointing community representatives to working committees that are charged with analyzing, interpreting, and prioritizing health information collected through the assessment process. This approach was used in a series of community demonstration projects supported through the W.K. Kellogg Foundation's Community-Based Public Health Initiative.[11] Each of the seven demonstration projects brought together public health organizations, academic institutions, and community-based organizations to form collaborative processes for identifying community health needs, developing and implementing interventions, and evaluating outcomes. Representatives from community-based organizations—including churches, neighborhood associations, and other local groups—shared responsibility for problem identification, intervention, and evaluation with the governmental public health organizations and academic institutions. Steering committees made up of representatives from each participating organization used consensus-driven processes to make decisions about how to evaluate and prioritize public health issues within the community. This approach was designed to ensure that improvement processes were focused on issues of high importance to community members and that they involved organizations and individuals with substantial knowledge of and experience with community health problems. Although foundation support for these projects officially ended in 1996, most of the projects continued to operate successfully. A demonstration effort launched jointly by Kellogg and the Robert Wood Johnson Foundation, entitled "Turning Point: Collaborating for a New Century in Public Health," retains the emphasis on direct community participation in public health assessment and improvement processes. This is discussed in greater detail in Chapter 16.

Other public health organizations employ assessment processes that involve more indirect mechanisms for community participation. These processes rely on community representatives to identify community health needs; however, they often do not directly involve these representatives in the decision-making processes that determine the prioritization, implementation, and evaluation of public health improvement efforts. For example, many public health organizations invite community participation and comment in the early phases of a community health assessment process. During the early phases, organizations assess community perceptions regarding the most pressing public health issues and elicit opinions about the most promising strategies for addressing these issues. In many of these efforts, direct community participation is limited to the task of problem identification. Decisions regarding which issues should receive priority, which interventions should be implemented, and how interventions should be evaluated remain the direct responsibility of public health organizations.

The degree of community participation may have important implications for the effectiveness of public health assessment efforts. An advantage of direct forms of community participation is that it may help ensure that the assessment process maintains a high degree of visibility and responsiveness to public health problems as experienced by community members. Unfortunately, the challenge is that it may also add substantial time and resource commitments to the assessment process because community members must learn about assessment concepts and build trust and familiarity with other participants in the process. Furthermore, assessment processes involving direct community participation may experience difficulties in reaching consensus about key public health issues and potential interventions, given the diversity of opinion and perspective that is likely to exist among participants. In choosing among alternative strategies for community participation, public health managers must balance the trade-offs among responsiveness, feasibility, and efficiency.

## Methods Used for Assessment

Public health assessment efforts vary widely in the methods used to measure and evaluate public health issues. This variation results, in part, from the alternative ways that public health organizations define the scope of public health practice. This variation also stems from the alternative types of information that are available for a given public health issue in a given population and the alternative analytic techniques that are available for evaluating this information. Public health assessment activities may also rely on information concerning the structural dimensions of public health practice, the clinical and administrative processes used in practice, and the health outcomes that result from practice. Moreover, assessment activities may use measures that reflect elements of public health need as well as attributes of public health practice, including its technical quality, effectiveness, appropriateness, comprehensiveness, accessibility, and efficiency.

In addition to variations in methods used to measure public health issues during the assessment process, it is crucial to understand the limitations of the data. When analyzing the data and developing policies for implementation, it must be understood that such health outcomes may not be directly or even be significantly related to the effectiveness of public health practice. For example, infant mortality or lead toxicity rates are typically more related to socioeconomic status and demographics of the population than to the specific public health programs or medical care services. Conversely, the proportion of children immunized or screened for lead toxicity may be more directly related to the effectiveness of public health practice. Thus, the extent to which an indicator reflects public health practice varies greatly.

Although methods for evaluating health information also vary substantially, they uniformly entail comparisons.[18] Objectives or standards that are selected typically have an a priori importance because of their prevalence, functional contribution to health status, and opportunities for prevention. These objectives need to be related to one or more measurable objectives with availability of data. Public health assessment initiatives rely on comparisons with a priori standards and goals that are preidentified by those doing the assessment. Typically standards can include *Healthy People 2010* national goals and objectives for health promotion and disease prevention, national or state data, and data from similar communities. Data on objectives (also called indicators) can be compared between the current time of analysis and a preceding time for the same community (before and after study). Comparisons with these types of goals have the advantage of being relatively simple to carry out once data are available and of being widely recognizable and understandable.

These comparisons, however, have the disadvantage of focusing on only a single level of performance, so that continued improvement is deemphasized once the standard is met (a phenomenon known as a "ceiling effect"). Some assessment initiatives use comparisons over time—also called trend analysis—so that changes in performance can be detected and measured for a given indicator. This method addresses the problem of ceiling effects, but it is limited in its ability to evaluate how much improvement is adequate and desirable over a given period of time. Continued improvement can also be deemphasized if assessment results are considered satisfactory as long as they compare favorably to the surrounding communities or the national experience. If differences in local programs, experience, expertise, or resources are not taken into account, optimal success of the public health initiative may not be realized. This is particularly true for rates of chronic disease in a community that may not be elevated with respect to other geographic areas, but that may be higher than could be achieved through wider implementation of preventive initiatives. Most successful community assessments use a combination of comparison standards and objectives with trend analysis and benchmarking. This combined strategy can be particularly powerful for assessing public health needs and motivating continuous improvement in public health performance.

## Assessment Methods and Tools for Public Health Organizations

Over the past decade, many different public health assessment and improvement activities have been implemented within the field of public health at local, state, and national levels. Performance improvement activities are further discussed in Chapter 17. These efforts reflect the concepts and methods of assessment employing somewhat different alternatives and achieving varying degrees of success. More importantly, these activities provide models, tools, and insight for public health organizations to use in designing and managing their own assessment efforts. Several of these alternatives are models not only for assessment but also for strategic planning and community health improvement. The most prominent of these is the recent development of MAPP (Mobilizing for Community Action through Planning and Partnership), which was released by the CDC and the NACCO in 2001.[19]

Activities relevant to assessment activities undertaken by public health organizations include the following:

- Indicator-based assessment methods
- Web-based data queries
- Assessment initiative partnerships with public and private community task force groups
- Internal appraisal of health department services or activities (quality improvement)
- Community planning and priority-setting tools: MAPP
- Community health report cards

Other areas with relevant and important input to community health assessment are addressed in other chapters including public health information networks (discussed in greater detail in Chapter 13) and performance-based measurement (discussed in greater detail in Chapter 17).

## Community Assessment and Planning Tools

Any discussion of recommended planning tools for community health assessment must include a brief review of some of the tools that have been historically important to this field. A number of tools and protocols have been developed to help public health organizations identify and assess community health problems within their jurisdictions and in planning strategies to address these problems. These tools may serve as important foundations and frameworks for implementing assessment activities within specific institutional contexts. Most importantly, these prior tools have established the basis for community health assessment and strategic planning methods now utilized in contemporary public health practice.

## National Health Objectives

Perhaps the most prominent public health planning tools of the past two decades have been those developed by the US Public Health Service to identify measurable national health objectives. These efforts identified a set of high-priority health issues, formulated national improvement goals for each issue, and specified measurement criteria and data sources to be used in assessing improvement. Objectives were identified for the years from 1980 to 1990 in the document entitled *Healthy People,*[20] and from 1990 to 2000 in the document entitled *Healthy People 2000.*[21] Objectives are now available for the *Healthy People 2010* document that cover the period from 2000 to 2010.[22] (Refer to Chapter 2 for more detailed discussion.) In each area, three types of health objectives are identified: those that target *health status outcomes* for the health issue, those that target *health services and interventions*, and those that target *health risk factors.* For example, an *HP 2000* outcome objective in the area of child health states: "Reduce the infant mortality rate to no more than 7 per 1000 live births."[21] In contrast, the *HP 2010* objective in this area of "no more than 4.5 per 1000 live births" clearly demonstrates that progress has been made in this area.[22]

*Healthy People 2010* was developed through a broad consultation process built on the best scientific knowledge and designed to measure programs over time. The leading health indicators can be used to measure the health of the country over the next 10 years. Each of the 10 leading health indicators has one or more objectives from *Healthy People 2010* associated with it. As a group, the leading health indicators reflect the major health concerns in the United States at the beginning of the 21st century. The leading health indicators were selected on the basis of their ability to motivate action, the availability of data to measure progress, and their importance as public health issues. Of importance is that the selection of these indicators is predicated on the availability of data for measurement purposes.

These national objectives have assisted many public health organizations in their assessment processes by identifying a set of priority health issues in need of attention and by offering measurable goals against which performance may be judged. As a tool for public health improvement, however, these objectives are limited in that they are not sensitive to public health problems of local and regional interest that may not be reflected in broad national trends and priorities. Additionally, these national objectives identify specific performance levels to be achieved rather than establish a process for continuous improvement. To complement the national objectives and address some of their limitations, several additional community health planning tools have been developed in conjunction with the US Public Health Service's efforts.

## Health Planning Tools

One of the most prominent health planning tools, the Planned Approach to Community Health (PATCH), was developed by the CDC in 1985.[23] The PATCH protocol outlines a standard process that public health organizations can follow for analyzing a few selected health issues, determining their root causes and key intervention points, and planning effective strategies for addressing the issues. Expanding on this effort, the American Public Health Association (APHA) developed a protocol to assist public health organizations in creating community health planning and monitoring systems that address a comprehensive range of health-related problems. This protocol, named *Healthy Communities 2000: Model Standards,* was developed in 1991 and was explicitly designed to link with the *Healthy People 2000* national objectives.[23,24] Using this protocol, public health organizations can develop a plan based on measurable public health objectives that target specific public health outcomes, processes, and population groups. Both process and outcome objectives are emphasized in the protocol. The Texas Department of Health, for example, used this protocol in developing performance-based objectives for local public health departments within the state.[26] Objectives were constructed so that the time frame and quantity of improvement could be specified by each local agency, as in the following outcome and process examples:

- The rate of bicycle-related injuries in children ages 5–14 in [name] County will be reduced from [number] per 100,000 in FY [year] to [number] per 100,000 in FY [year].
- By end of FY [year], secure passage of a local ordinance requiring mandatory use of bicycle helmets.

Another assessment and planning tool, the Assessment Protocol for Excellence in Public Health (APEXPH), was developed in 1991 by the NACCHO with sponsorship from the CDC to serve as a self-assessment workbook for public health officials.[27] The workbook includes components for assessing the internal capacity of public health organizations as well as the external capacity of other organizations serving the community. The workbook relies on an array of process indicators, including those addressing public health authority, community relations, community health assessment, policy development, financial management, personnel management, program management, and governing board procedures. A later version of this protocol, the Assessment and Planning Excellence through Community Partners for Health (APEXCPH) aligns the indicators in APEXPH with the 10 essential public health services and expands the community capacity indicators to include a broader array of community organizations and activities.[28] Drawing on these efforts, the US Agency for Health Care Policy and Research (now the Agency for Healthcare Research and Quality) developed a planning tool designed specifically to assist local health departments in responding to managed healthcare systems. This workbook, entitled *Assessing Roles, Responsibilities, and Activities in a Managed Care Environment: A Workbook for Local Health Officials*, provides guidelines for health departments to use in areas such as assessing budgets, staffing, and service delivery activities; developing managed care contracts and affiliations; assessing community health needs; and monitoring policy and marketplace trends.[29]

### Health Assessment and Improvement Tools

Other assessment tools formally integrate the tasks of collecting and analyzing community health data with the processes of community health planning, priority setting, and intervention. In many communities, the hospital industry has become actively involved in developing and applying these tools. Pioneered by efforts in Pennsylvania, Vermont, and Wisconsin, growing numbers of state hospital associations actively encourage their members to conduct community health assessment and improvement initiatives within their service areas.[30] The Hospital Association of Pennsylvania's assessment process, which has served as a model for many assessment initiatives across the country, involves a five-step sequence involving the following:

1. Compiling a community health profile
2. Identifying priorities for community health needs

3. Developing an action plan
4. Implementing community health interventions
5. Evaluating the interventions[31]

The assessment initiative adopted by the Wisconsin association draws heavily on the Pennsylvania model as well as the APEXPH protocol that was originally developed for public health agencies.[32] Hospitals in California are now required by state law to conduct periodic community health assessments using an established protocol in order to maintain their nonprofit status. Hospitals must also demonstrate involvement in community health assessment as part of the accreditation process conducted by the Joint Commission on Accreditation of Healthcare Organizations (JCAHO).

## The IOM Model

The proliferation of community health assessment and improvement efforts in the public and private sectors led the IOM to convene an expert panel to review the many existing processes and recommend a consensus approach for undertaking these efforts. The IOM's work identified several essential characteristics of an effective community health assessment and improvement effort.[6] These characteristics include the following:

- Use of an iterative process that cycles continuously through the tasks of assessment, action, and evaluation
- Use of a team approach through which decisions are made largely by consensus among community representatives
- Use of an incremental strategy for improvement, whereby progress is accomplished through a series of small steps rather than through major breakthroughs

The IOM proposed a model for community health improvement processes consisting of two related cycles of implementation (Figure 15-1). The first cycle consists of five main activities: forming a community health coalition, collecting and analyzing data for a community health profile, and identifying and prioritizing important community health issues. As part of activities in this first cycle, the IOM proposed a set of 25 indicators to use in assessing community health status (Exhibit 15-1).[33] These indicators are an expanded version of a consensus set of 18 indicators that were recommended in 1991 by the CDC to track progress toward achieving *Healthy People 2000* objectives.[34] Of course, for any specific community, these general indicators may need to be supplemented with additional measures corresponding to the specific problems and needs of that community. Community improvement strategies may be broad based, simultaneously exploring a number of health issues, as in the APEXPH model. Alternatively, strategies may focus on a small number of specific issues, as in the PATCH model.

Once a specific health issue has been targeted by a community, the IOM health improvement process moves on to the analysis and implementation cycle (Figure 15-1). The steps in this second cycle include analysis of the health issue, an inventory of health resources, development of a health improvement strategy, discussion and negotiation to establish where accounta-

**Cycle 1: Problem Identification and Prioritization**

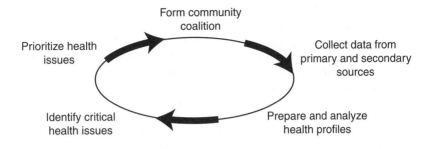

**Cycle 2: Analysis and Implementation**

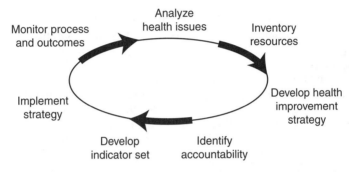

**FIGURE 15-1    The Community Health Improvement Process**
*Source:* Adapted with permission. Committee on Using Performance Monitoring to Improve Community Health, Institute of Medicine. *Improving Health in the Community: A Role for Performance Monitoring.* Washington, DC: National Academies Press; 1997.

bility lies, development of a set of performance indicators for accountable entities, implementation of the health improvement strategy, and measurement to monitor the outcome of efforts by community organizations.

To help identify risk factors for problematic health outcomes, organizations can use the process for cause and effect analysis identified in the APEXPH model.[27] The Florida Department of Public Health and Rehabilitative Services has successfully used this type of analysis to help communities identify promising public health interventions.

A critical step in the community health improvement process is to formulate appropriate action based on the results of a community health assessment. The IOM uses the term *accountable entities* to refer to stakeholders that are expected to achieve specific results as part of the community's strategy for addressing a health issue. Traditionally, communities have viewed the local public health agency as the primary accountable entity. As described earlier, however, solutions to public health problems require action by multiple groups within a community, and accountability should be recognized as an issue of shared responsibility. An important part of the community health improvement process is to designate accountable entities and to establish agreements among entities that specify areas of responsibility, measures of

**Exhibit 15-1    Community Health Indicators Proposed by the Institute of Medicine**

*Sociodemographic Characteristics*
1. Distribution of the population by age and race/ethnicity
2. Number and proportion of persons in groups such as migrants, homeless, and the non-English speaking, for whom access to community services and resources may be of concern
3. Number and proportion of persons aged 25 and older with less than a high school education
4. Ratio of the number of students graduating from high school to the total number of students who entered 9th grade three years previously
5. Median household income
6. Proportion of children less than 15 years of age living in families at or below the poverty level
7. Unemployment rate
8. Number and proportion of single-parent families
9. Number and proportion of persons without health insurance

*Health Status*
10. Infant mortality rate by race/ethnicity
11. Number of deaths or age-adjusted death rates for motor vehicle crashes, work-related injuries, suicide, homicide, lung cancer, breast cancer, cardio-vascular diseases, and all causes, by age, race, and gender
12. Reported incidence of acquired immune deficiency syndrome, measles, tuberculosis, and primary and secondary syphilis, by age, race, and gender as appropriate
13. Births to adolescents (ages 10–17) as a proportion of total live births
14. Number and rate of confirmed abuse and neglect cases among children

*Health Risk Factors*
15. Proportion of 2-year-old children who have received all age-appropriate vaccines, as recommended by the Advisory Committee on Immunization Practices
16. Proportion of adults aged 65 and older who have ever been immunized for pneumococcal pneumonia, and the proportion who have been immunized in the past 12 months for influenza
17. Proportion of the population who smoke, by age, race, and gender
18. Proportion of the population age 18 and older who are obese
19. Number and type of US Environmental Protection Agency air quality standards not met
20. Proportion of assessed rivers, lakes, and estuaries that support beneficial uses (e.g., fishing and swimming approved)

*Health Care Resource Consumption*
21. Per capita healthcare spending for Medicare beneficiaries

*Functional Status*
22. Proportion of adults reporting that their general health is good to excellent
23. During the past 30 days, average number of days for which adults report that their physical or mental health was not good

*Quality of Life*
24. Proportion of adults satisfied with the health care system in the community
25. Proportion of persons satisfied with the quality of life in the community

*Source:* Adapted with permission. From Committee on Using Performance Monitoring to Improve Community Health, Institute of Medicine. *Improving Health in the Community: A Role for Performance Monitoring.* Washington, DC: National Academies Press; 1997.

performance, and rewards for successful performance. Performance gaps should trigger problem analysis and a reformulation of each stakeholder's approach to the health issue.

## Employment of an Indicator Approach for Community Health Assessment

Alice: Would you please tell me which way I ought to go from here?
Cheshire Cat: That depends on where you want to get about any given issue[35]

The indicator approach is a straightforward method used by the author (LFN) and others to assess the health of the community. The advantage of this method is that it employs a relatively small set of indicators that are illustrative of major community health issues to appraise population health status and provide for future direction in improvement activities.

The initial steps to the indicator method community health assessment are shown in Tables 15-1 and 15-2. The community health assessment involves a three-step feedback loop. The first step in such an assessment involves identifying important health indicators. Health indicators are measurable health outcomes, such as death rate, insurance coverage measures, immunization rates, or other data items that are relevant to the health of a community. (Refer to Table 15-3 for types of data that can be used.)

Indicators are thoughtfully selected data points that provide useful information about the health of a community. To organize indicators, it is helpful to identify major areas of focus. For this case, we will refer to these broad categories of public health concerns as *domains.* Please refer to Table 15-4 for examples of domains. For each domain, an example of an indicator is provided.

The second step in the assessment involves matching those indicators with available data. In the third step, the previously designated standards are applied to the data gathered in the first two steps to transform it into useful information about health needs of the population.

Selection of indicators is determined by a set of criteria shown in Table 15-5, which includes data availability and measurability. As previously discussed, *HP 2010* data may not be available at the local level. For example, over 50 of the *HP 2010* objectives where state and county objectives are not available are dependent on national interview surveys such as the National Health Interview Study, National Survey of Family Growth, and others. Indicators dependent on the BRFSS or YRBS may not be available at the county level, although this availability is improving.[16]

**TABLE 15-1    Initiating the Indicator Method for Community Health Assessment**

- Define the community.
- Assemble a community health assessment team to discuss goals, methods, and timeline.
- Look at what has been previously learned through past assessments.
- Find or find out how to obtain information about key issues of health in your community, such as:
  - Immunization rates
  - Economic conditions and indicator
  - High school completion rate
  - Family issues
- Some communities develop a survey to help determine what areas of concern exist.
- Conduct focus groups.
- Initiate discussion with institutions, individuals, and so on in the community.
- Inventory the community's healthcare resources, including who is served, what the availability is (hours), how services are reimbursed (if they are), etc.

In addition, the number of indicators should be kept to a manageable number, and indicators that are redundant should not be used (e.g., low birth weight and infant mortality). Similarly, indicators are of increased value when they are generalizable to several domains. For example, data on immunization rates has significance for communicable disease prevention, maternal and child health, and access to preventive health services. A helpful source for selecting health indicators is the *Healthy People 2010* set of health objectives and in particular the *HP 2010* leading health indicators (See Exhibit 2-6 in Chapter 2).

Consider the following example of an application of the indicator method in central New York. Although county health assessments have been conducted periodically in New York, no regional, multicounty assessment existed for the central New York area until the Commission for a Healthy Central New York was formed and subsequently established a regional community health assessment. Although the New York State Department of Health requires periodic health assessment be conducted and reported by all counties, the available resources to collect such data vary by county. Because of a lack of uniform standards for the collection and reporting of data, comparison across counties is challenging. Beginning in the summer of 2004, the commission

**TABLE 15-2    Stakeholders Invited to Participate in the Community Health Assessment**

- Hospitals
- High schools
- Neighborhood and church groups
- Individuals interested in working on assessment
- Local advocates
- Local businesses
- Civic leaders
- Local health practitioners
- Law enforcement
- Local universities or other educational institutions

**TABLE 15-3   Types and Sources of Data for Indicator Community Health Assessment**

- Types of data:
  - Morbidity
  - Mortality
  - Socioeconomic and behavioral data
  - Demographic data
  - Health care service utilization
- Sources of data:
  - Vital statistics
  - Past or current surveys of the community
  - Hospital discharge data
  - Disease registries
  - Census information

used local community foundation funding support to perform a regional community health assessment. To ensure a way in which counties could compare the health of their residents with that of neighboring counties, the same data was collected for all counties for agreed upon health measures. The focus areas mirror those of *Healthy People 2010*. An example of indicators used for the focus area, access to health care, is shown in Table 15-6. The result was the determination of four priority areas for the region including: access to dental care, access to mental health services, obesity, and stroke care. After having identified these common public health concerns, the commission continues to work together to provide solutions for the identified issues.

## Collaborative Assessment Partnerships

An important new development in community health assessment has been state health assessment activities spurred by CDC funding of the assessment initiative that has built partnerships allowing the development of major data systems. These systems combine information from various public and private systems. In September 1997, cooperative agreement funds were awarded to six states for a 5-year funding cycle: Missouri, Massachusetts, New York, Oregon, Minnesota, and North Carolina. These states built partnerships with private and community organizations, managed care entities, and nontraditional

**TABLE 15-4   List of Domains to Assist Developing an Indicator-type Community Health Assessment**

| Domain: | Example of an Indicator: |
| --- | --- |
| Communicable diseases (including sexually transmitted diseases) | Incidence of gonorrhea |
| Chronic diseases (including cancer) | Incidence of diabetes |
| Injury and violence | Homicide rate |
| Maternal and child health | Childhood immunization rate |
| Environmental health | Rates of lead poisoning |
| Access to health care | Rates of uninsured |

**TABLE 15-5    Criteria for Selection of Indicators**

- Measurable
- Data available
- Prevalent
- Severe
- Amenable to intervention

public health partners such as the state Medicaid bureaus.[36] New York, for example, developed an electronic community health assessment clearing house (CHAC) to collect and disseminate information on health assessment processes, methods, and successful outcomes. The North Carolina Community Health assessment initiative merged the assessment activities of community diagnosis, the state-based biennial assessment process conducted by the State Center for Health Statistics (SCHS) and Healthy Carolinians, a group of community task forces performing community assessments and mobilizing community actions. As of 2006, Healthy Carolinians is completing an assessment documenting midcourse progress on the NC 2020 objectives patterned after the *HP 2010* midcourse review.

## Web-based Data Query Systems

Concurrent with the above described assessment initiatives, the CDC's epidemiology program office embarked on a 3-year project with Opinion Research Corporation company, ORC Macro Inc, to gain a deeper understanding of the extent of states' use of the Internet to disseminate public health data for assessment. The project began in 1999 with an initial abstraction of the Web sites of all 50 states, plus three local jurisdictions to examine the systems and approaches being used.[37] The rapid growth in WDQS (Web-based data query systems) is testimony to the importance of this tool. Only 10 states had WDQS capability in 1999–2000. By 2006, this number had grown to 27 states, most of whom used a Web browser to construct and display the data.[38]

Considerable progress has taken place in the widespread use of the Internet since the CDC developed the first generation of WONDER (Wide-ranging Online Data for Epidemiologic Research) that enabled users to select from a limited number of data sets, specify measures and geographic areas, and submit queries, with query results returned in batch mode later.[39] Contemporary versions of WDQS provides users access through a dynamic interface to data on the World Wide Web pertaining to population health and the determinants of population health.[38] A *dynamic* interface enables the user to customize data queries through selecting data sets, measures, statistics, and formats including tables, graphs, or maps. A *static* interface is also available providing precalculated statistics in preformatted reports.

WDQSs were identified and reviewed at a meeting of 14 users held in September 2005 representing seven states (Arkansas, Massachusetts, Pennsylvania, Rhode Island, South Carolina, and Washington). Further review of WDQSs was conducted in 2005. In addition, a consensus process was employed to develop categorization of the functionalities of WDQSs. The 11 major functionalities that were identified are shown in Table 15-7.[38]

**TABLE 15-6  Focus Area: Access to Health Care**

| HP 2010 Objective number | Objective Title | Onondaga County (%) | 8 County Rate (%) | Upstate (%) | NYS (%) | United States (%) | HP 2010 Target Rate (%) |
|---|---|---|---|---|---|---|---|
| 01-01 | Persons with health insurance coverage, 18–64 years of age | 85 | 87.3 | N/A | 83 | 83 | 100 |
| 16-06a | Prenatal care—Beginning in first trimester | 75.6 | 76.8 | 78.0 | 73.0 | 84 | 90 |
| N/A | Number of primary care providers who accept Medicaid | 5.6 per 1000 | 4.8 per 1000 | N/A | N/A | N/A | N/A |
| N/A | Number of dental providers who accept Medicaid | 0.04 per 1000 | 0.1 per 1000 | N/A | N/A | N/A | N/A |
| N/A | Total percentage of population enrolled in Medicaid | 15.1 | 15.5 | N/A | 21.1 | 15.4 | N/A |
| 01-09a | Hospitalization for ambulatory-care-sensitive conditions: pediatric asthma | 7.9 per 10,000 | 11.9 per 10,000 | N/A | 29.5 per 10,000 | 21.4 | 17.3 |
| 01-09b | Hospitalization for ambulatory-care-sensitive conditions: uncontrolled diabetes | 13.1 per 10,000 | 13.1 per 10,000 | N/A | 16.6 per 10,000 | 7.7 | 5.4 |
| 03-11b | Women 18 years and older who received Pap test within preceding 3 years | 92.4 | 84.6 | N/A | 85 | 81 | 90 |
| 03-12a | Adults 50 years and older who have used home blood stool test w/in past 2 years | 36.6 | 28.8 | N/A | 26.9 | 33 | 50 |
| 03-12b | Adults aged 50 years and older who have ever received a sigmoidoscopy or colonoscopy | 57.3 | 49.2 | N/A | 52.4 | 39 | 50 |
| 03-13 | Women aged 40 years and older who have received mammogram w/in preceding 2 years | 86.5 | 76.3 | N/A | 77.60 | 70 | 70 |

*Source:* Commission for a Healthy Central New York. Available at: http://www.upstate.edu/healthycny/. Accessed on February 6, 2007.

**TABLE 15-7 WDQS Functionalities**

1. Query design: data term geographic area, health topic
2. Geographic level: state, county, city, Zip code, community
3. Statistics: crude, age-specific and age-adjusted with rate ratios, significance tests, confidence intervals, and time trends
4. Tables
5. Graphs
6. Maps and interactive GIS
7. Benchmark and time trend data
8. Custom groupings of data: year, age, geographic level
9. Documentation for individual custom queries: tables, graphs, and maps
10. Online documentation and help: explanation of available statistics, limitations of available data
11. Export to file

*Source:* Adapted with permission. Friedman DJ, Parrish RG 2nd. Characteristics, desired functionalities, and data sets of state web-based data query systems. *J Public Health Manag Pract.* 2006;12(2):119–129.

Daniel Friedman has pointed out that WDQS democratizes the accessibility and use of population health data. Data are now available directly to community users without state and county health department staff acting as intermediaries. WDQSs have both innovative functionalities and are able to store large amounts of population health data leading to potential use by public health agencies and other audiences.[40]

## Community Health Report Cards

Report card systems have become popular strategies for monitoring and improving performance in many areas of health care. Although they vary widely in their structure and content, report card systems typically consist of a set of standardized performance measures that are collected consistently across a group of organizations, individuals, or other entities under study. Using these measures, report card systems employ a metric for comparing and profiling the performance of each entity against its peers on a periodic basis. These systems are distinct from other types of assessment approaches that rely primarily on trend analysis or on comparisons against a priori performance standards and goals.

Report cards are being used in other sectors of health care to monitor performance and encourage improvement through comparison.[41-47] Recent evidence suggests that report card methodologies are also being used to assess community-level health issues in some localities.[48] These existing approaches appear to vary widely in their purpose, scope, and methodology.

Report cards offer several distinct advantages over other assessment approaches, including: (1) encouraging continuous improvement in performance rather than establishing specific floors or ceilings for performance; (2) motivating performance improvement through benchmarking and comparisons with peers; (3) enabling aggregate measures of performance across a group of organizations, individuals, or communities using standardized measures; and (4) creating a framework for identifying best practices among the entities under study. In the medical care field, report card systems are thought to be particularly effective in improving performance among organizations that compete for patients, revenue, or other resources—such as hospitals, physician practices, and managed care plans. In these settings, report cards are used as tools for marketing services to patients, payers, and purchasers. Some evidence suggests that these systems motivate substantial improvements in medical care practice.[41-47]

Report card systems are used at the community level to promote collaboration and information sharing rather than competition. By facilitating comparisons of community-level health measures across local areas, report card systems can serve as tools for mobilizing collaborative, interorganizational efforts in community health improvement. Report card systems can be used to profile the aggregate effects of multiple health organizations and interventions within a community, thereby exposing gaps in performance that need remedy. To be sure, local public health agencies and other community health organizations already have an extensive battery of tools, protocols, and planning guides for conducting community health assessment.[23,25,28,48] Nonetheless, by enabling comparisons among peer groups of local communities, report card systems may offer local public health agencies more meaningful and relevant measures of community health performance than other assessment approaches.

Community health report card systems are attractive tools for organizations other than local public health agencies.[47] If broadly implemented, these systems may assist state and federal health agencies in targeting health resources and services to areas of greatest need and in evaluating the community-level effects of health-related interventions. These systems may be used to integrate the reporting requirements and accountability systems of multiple federal and state health programs, thereby reducing reporting duplication and the respondent burden while enhancing program assessment and evaluation activities. Similarly, report card systems may help to inform the progress toward performance-based contracting initiatives in public health, which are currently taking shape at both federal and state levels.

A frequent criticism of standardized assessment tools and reporting systems in public health is that they fail to account for the unique ways in which public health is organized and administered at local levels.[49] Local public health officials have raised this issue in relation to community health report cards, questioning the local relevance and utility of a standardized system designed for broad implementation. Another issue, previously discussed, is that report card findings may not be related to public health activities but associated with the demographics and broad health determinants in individual communities. Recent studies have begun to explore the extent to which there exists a degree of commonality in the assessment needs and capacities of local public health agencies that might support a standardized report card system.[50,51] These efforts examine whether a core set of community health indicators can be identified that are scientifically sound, locally available, and widely regarded as relevant and useful for measuring community health status. Early results from these efforts suggest that such indicators may be identifiable and useful. A representative survey of the nation's local health agencies during 1997 uncovered that a strong majority of agencies would find comparative assessment data from a national report card initiative to be useful, and that a core set of community health indicators are available at the local level to form the basis of such an initiative.[50]

Additional research and development efforts are needed to identify relevant, reliable, and feasible indicators of community health that can be used to monitor outcomes and practices at the community level. The set of 25 indicators proposed by the IOM provides an appropriate starting point for this work. Ultimately, consensus needs to be reached on a minimum data set that will permit valid comparisons to be made across local and state jurisdictions and that will facilitate progress toward achieving state and national health objectives. The measures included in this set must be readily and uniformly acceptable and understandable, be measurable using easily available data, and indicate specific interventions for public health action as well as broad general measures of community health and program effectiveness. Additionally, strategies are needed for measuring outcomes and practices in small geographic areas, where statistics may not be stable because of small denominators. Valid methods are needed for adjusting community outcomes for the severity of health problems being addressed and the underlying risks that are present in individual communities. Finally, methods must be developed for identifying groups of communities appropriate for comparison and benchmarking purposes, such as groups based on population size, sociodemographic composition, and/or health resources availability.

### Internally Developed Guidelines

Increasingly, public health organizations are engaging in efforts to develop their own practice guidelines—either alone or in combination with other health organizations. These tools are based on evidence and experience amassed by individual organizations in serving specific population groups. One approach to creating local guidelines is to begin with a nationally developed guideline and tailor its specifications to the individual needs and capacities of the organization and the community it serves. The Texas Department of Health used this approach in developing its performance measurement process for district health departments, drawing heavily on guidelines established in the APHA's *Healthy Communities: Model Standards* and the NACCHO's APEXPH. Texas went beyond the generic practices described in these resources by developing specific process objectives tailored to the capacities and policy priorities of its local health agencies.[26]

Similarly, the Denver Health Authority in Colorado developed an internal quality assessment process based on guidelines established for managed care plans in the National Committee for Quality Assurance's *Health Plan Employer Data and Information Set (HEDIS)*. Denver added performance elements that were not included in *HEDIS* but that were perceived as important by key stakeholders, including staff, local and state policy officials, and consumers.[52] The agency also eliminated *HEDIS* elements that did not appear relevant to the organization or that proved to be too difficult to measure accurately. Denver used the resulting process to demonstrate accountability for contract funds received from local and state governmental agencies.

Some public health agencies adopt practice guidelines developed by other organizations with which they interact. Managed care plans are key among those organizations helping to disseminate practice guidelines among public health agencies. Public health agencies that contract with plans for the delivery of personal health services adopt many of the same health plan guidelines used by medical care providers. These may include practices for assessing patient health status, delivering clinical preventive services, and making referrals to other healthcare providers. Agencies participating in health plan provider networks often benefit from the quality improvement processes maintained by these plans, which may allow agencies to compare their own performance in a guideline area with that of other providers.

## Strategic Planning

The history of public health planning in the United States began with sanitary control measures undertaken in response to the epidemiology of communicable disease.[53] Comprehensive Health Planning (CHP) and Regional Medical Planning (RMP) were mandated by federal legislation in the 1960s and 1970s but targeted healthcare services rather than population health issues. The National Health Planning and Resource Development Act of 1974 (PL 93-641) expanded the government's involvement in health planning requiring local health system agencies to develop comprehensive health plans. Federally sponsored health planning remained focused on medical services and resources rather than health status. Planning by public health agencies started with program-focused planning but evolved through more comprehensive approaches discussed earlier in the chapter, including PATCH and APEXH, to the strategic planning today exemplified by MAPP.[54]

Before MAPP, there was no template for public health practice to engage in a public health strategic planning process. Another important concept that has emerged is the public health system that envisions the response to community health problems as not solely the domain of the health department in isolation but as a partnership approach involving all relevant stakeholders (see Figure 2-3 in Chapter 2). MAPP was designed as a method to provide guidance for effective strategic planning for the public health system and the communities they serve.[54]

## MAPP

Mobilizing for Action through Planning and Partnerships (MAPP) was developed through a cooperative agreement between the NACCHO and the CDC. MAPP is a strategic approach to community health improvement intended to result in the development and implementation of a community-wide strategic plan. Broad participation of the community is integral to the process. Creation and strengthening of the local public health system is the goal. The 10 essential public health services are incorporated into MAPP and serve as a link to other initiatives such as the National Public Health Performance Standards Program.[55] (Chapter 17 provides further discussion.)

As shown in Figure 15-2, MAPP implementation proceeds in stages[56]:

- Organization and partnership development—Recruiting stakeholders and community representatives

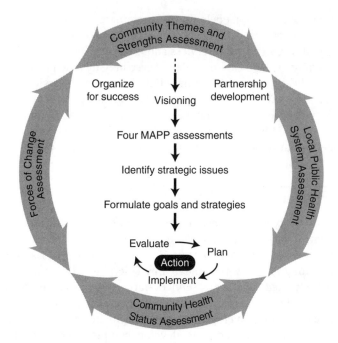

**FIGURE 15-2    The MAPP Model**
*Source:* Developed by the National Association of County and City Health
Officials (NACCHO) in cooperation with the Public Health Practice Program
Office, Centers for Disease Control and Prevention (CDC).

- Visioning—A shared vision and common goals provide a framework to
  achieve long-range goals
- Four MAPP assessments—Community themes and strengths, local public health system assessment, community health status assessment, and
  forces of change assessment
- Identify strategic issues—Participants identify linkages between the
  MAPP assessments to determine the most critical issues that must be
  addressed
- Formulate goals and strategies—For addressing each issue.
- Action cycle—In this final phase, participants plan, implement, and
  evaluate
- In-depth MAPP information, including tools and case vignettes, are
  available at www.naccho.org.

The linkage of MAPP (strategic planning) to community health assessment, as previously discussed, is evident. A community health assessment is a
necessary part of the process in which the indicator approach is used. In this
process MAPP core indicators are utilized that include comparison and trend
data. This method is similar to that outlined earlier in the chapter. Of importance is the MAPP recommendation to monitor the indicators over time.[54]

Strategic issues are identified by a brainstorming process that includes
determining the consequences of not addressing an issue. Issues are priori-
tized to determine which should be addressed first. Strategy alternatives are
considered, and barriers to elimination are enumerated. Finally, implementa-

tion details and plans are drafted. Although the MAPP field guide lists monitoring and evaluation designs as a next step, it is best to design these phases concurrently with implementation planning as this will not only improve evaluation but will also expose weaknesses in the initial implementation design that are amenable to correction.

MAPP has been successfully implemented in a number of communities throughout the nation. The NACCHO selected demonstration sites to implement MAPP. Nine local public health agencies from different states participated serving populations from 35,000 to more than one million. Jurisdictions included a single city, single city-county, multiple cities, and multiple city-counties. A review of this experience can be found in a special issue of the *Journal of Public Health Management and Practice* published in September 2005 describing MAPP activities in Chicago, Northern Kentucky, San Antonio, and other areas.[57]

San Antonio was one of the demonstration sites selected for implementation of MAPP. The San Antonio Metropolitan Health District, under the leadership of one of the nation's most experienced public health directors, Dr. Fernando A. Guerra, agreed to facilitate the process. A core planning team was organized and expanded to a full community working group, the Alliance for Community Health in San Antonio and Bexar County (Alliance). Six strategic issues were identified that became the basis for the San Antonio Community Health Improvement Plan: public policy, data tracking, healthy lifestyles, promoting a sense of community, access to care, and safe environment. The Alliance has leveraged resources and improved public health in San Antonio.[58]

# Activities across Organizational Boundaries: The Public Health Systems Approach

Throughout this text, emphasis has been placed on the need for public health agencies to work within and mobilize a public health system. This approach is necessary for population health improvement as the determinants of health—broad and multifactorial—require more than governmental public health agencies working in isolation of the network of other providers, community-based organizations, and community representatives. Implementation of public health assessment processes are predicated by the fact that in the 21st century public health processes and outcomes are inherently multiorganizational in nature, with no single institution within the community able to monitor and respond to population health needs and outcomes. To be effective in improving health at the population level, assessment methods and improvement strategies often must be implemented across organizational boundaries—a daunting task for many public health organizations. Nonetheless, multiorganizational efforts for public health assessment and improvement have become increasingly common in recent years, fueled in part by marketplace and policy developments that have created shared incentives for improving health at the population level.[59,60] The term *public health system* has recently been adopted and is discussed further in Chapter 2. These developments have also created new opportunities for using assessment methods as part of multiorganizational public health partnerships. To capitalize on these opportunities, public health organizations must actively pursue strategies, such as

MAPP, for building effective interorganizational relationships around assessment processes. Key elements of such a strategy include the following:

- Identifying major internal and external stakeholders that have influence over the public health issues to be addressed through the assessment process
- Facilitating shared interests in assessment among multiple community organizations
- Anticipating the participation constraints faced by key stakeholders and designing appropriate incentives to ensure full participation in the assessment process
- Implementing effective mechanisms of communication and information sharing across organizations
- Developing multi-institutional consensus about the design and operation of the assessment process, including measurement strategies and decision-making and priority-setting mechanisms
- Ensuring appropriate collection and analysis of objective and subjective data measured from multiple institutional perspectives
- Communicating data effectively to all stakeholders using language and concepts understandable to all
- Ensuring an adequate voice for all stakeholders in priority-setting activities
- Developing effective mechanisms for addressing dissenting views and perspectives
- Developing consensus around collective actions that can be taken to address shared assessment interests

The assessment models examined in this chapter by no means represent a gold standard approach for identifying and responding to population health needs. Many different tools and models exist for carrying out this vital activity, each offering unique benefits and limitations. The challenge for public health administrators lies in developing and managing an assessment process that fits the unique capacities and needs within the communities served. An ideal assessment process, therefore, must be tailored to the specific organizations and populations involved. Only through such a process can public health organizations acquire the information and insight necessary for achieving meaningful improvements in population health.

## Chapter Review

1. Assessment is typically defined as the regular and systematic collection, analysis, and dissemination of information on the health of a community, which enables community health needs to be identified. Assessment processes may involve a variety of specific activities, including the following:
   - *Identifying* health needs in the community and among important population groups
   - *Investigating* the occurrence of health effects and health hazards in the community
   - *Analyzing* the determinants of identified health needs in a community or population group

2. Some assessment activities are carried out internally within public health organizations, whereas others are designed to include participation and decision making from multiple organizations serving a population of interest. In choosing the appropriate focus for an assessment effort, public health organizations must consider the following:
   - The nature of the public health problem being targeted
   - The internal strengths and weaknesses of their organization
   - The current and potential roles played by external organizations and individuals in the problem under study
   - The public health organization's current and potential relationships with these external entities

3. Public health organizations may play various roles in an assessment process, including those of *initiating* the process, *convening* major stakeholders, *governing* and managing the process, *participating* in joint management and oversight, and/or *contributing* resources and expertise to an externally managed process.

4. Activities relevant to assessment activities undertaken by public health organizations include the following:
   - Indicator-based assessment methods
   - Web-based data queries
   - Community health report cards
   - Assessment initiative partnerships with public and private community task force groups
   - Internal appraisal of health department services or activities (quality improvement)
   - Community planning and priority-setting tools: MAPP (Mobilizing for Action through Planning and Partnership)

5. Several factors have been found to be important to the successful development and management of public health assessment activities, including the following:
   - Involving the broadest possible range of organizations and individuals in each community that have an interest in the problem under study
   - Ensuring that the assessment process is driven by decisions made by community members themselves, rather than by influences from outside the community (including consultants)
   - Ensuring that the assessment process is highly sensitive to local issues and priorities
   - Focusing the assessment effort on the goal of health improvement through intervention planning

6. Mobilizing for Action through Planning and Partnerships (MAPP) was developed through a cooperative agreement between NACCHO and the Centers for Disease Control and Prevention. MAPP is a strategic approach to community health improvement intended to result in the development and implementation of a community-wide strategic plan. MAPP includes the following various phases:
   - Organization and partnership development—Recruiting stakeholders and community representatives
   - Visioning—A shared vision and common goals provide a framework to achieve long-range goals

- Four MAPP assessments: community themes and strengths, local public health system assessment, community health status assessment, and forces of change assessment
- Identify strategic issues—Participants identify linkages between the MAPP assessments to determine the most critical issues that must be addressed
- Formulate goals and strategies for addressing each issue.
- Action cycle—In this final phase, participants plan, implement, and evaluate.

## References

1. Keppel KG, Freedman MA. What is assessment? *J Public Health Manage Pract.* 1995;1(2):1–7.
2. Institute of Medicine. *The Future of Public Health.* Washington, DC: National Academies Press; 1988.
3. Dyall WW. Ten organizational practices of public health: a historical perspective. *Am J Prev Med.* 1995;11:6–8.
4. Public Health Functions Steering Committee. Adopted Fall 1994, see Exhibit 2-4. Public Health in America.
5. Novick LF. Public health assessment in a new context. *J Public Health Manage Pract.* 1995;1(2):v–vi.
6. Institute of Medicine. *Improving Health in the Community: A Role for Performance Monitoring.* Washington, DC: National Academies Press; 1997.
7. Lillienfeld DE, Stolley PD. *Foundations of Epidemiology.* 3rd ed. New York: Oxford University Press; 1994.
8. Whitehead M. William Farr's legacy to the study of inequalities in health. *Bull WHO.* 2000;78(1):86–87.
9. Rosen G. A *History of Public Health.* New York, NY: MD Publications; 1958.
10. Irani PR. Measuring the impact of a public health data training program. *J Public Health Manage Pract.* 2002;8(4):54–62.
11. Mays GP, Miller CA, Halverson PK. *Local Public Health Practice: Trends and Models.* Washington, DC: American Public Health Association; 2000.
12. Lipson DJ, Naierman N. Snapshots of change in fifteen communities: safety-net providers. *Health Affairs.* 1996;15(2):33–48.
13. The 184th General Court of the Commonwealth of Massachusetts. Available at: http://www.mass.gov/legis/laws/seslaw06/sl060058.htm. Accessed June 14, 2006.
14. Speake DL, Mason KP, Broadway TM, Sylvester M, Morrison SP. Integrating indicators into a public health quality improvement system. *Am J Public Health.* 1995;85(10):1448–1449.
15. US Environmental Protection Agency. *The Changing Nature of Environmental and Public Health Protection: An Annual Report on Reinvention.* Washington, DC: US Government Printing Office; 1998.
16. Land G. Measuring 2010 national objectives and leading indicators at the state and local level. *J Public Health Manage Pract.* 2002;8(4):9–13.
17. Fielding JE, Sutherland CE, Halfon N. Community health report cards: results of a national survey. *Am J Prev Med.* 1999;17(1):79–86.
18. Gerzoff RB. Comparisons: the basis for measuring public health performance. *J Public Health Manage Pract.* 1997;3(5):11–21.

19. National Association of County and City Health Officials (NACCHO). *Achieving Healthier Communities through MAPP: A User's Handbook*. Washington, DC: NACCHO; 2005.

20. US Department of Health, Education, and Welfare. *Healthy People: The Surgeon General's Report on Health Promotion and Disease Prevention*. Washington, DC: US Government Printing Office; 1977.

21. US Department of Health and Human Services. *Healthy People 2000: National Health Promotion and Disease Prevention Objectives*. Washington, DC: US Government Printing Office; 1991.

22. US Department of Health and Human Services. *Healthy People 2010: Conference Edition*. Washington, DC: US Government Printing Office; 2000.

23. Greene LW. PATCH: CDC's planned approach to community health, an application of PRECEED and an inspiration for PROCEED. *J Health Educ*. 1992;23(3):140–147.

24. American Public Health Association. *Healthy Communities 2000: Model Standards*. Washington, DC: American Public Health Association; 1991.

25. American Public Health Association. *The Guide to Implementing Model Standards: Eleven Steps Toward a Healthy Community*. Washington, DC: American Public Health Association; 1993.

26. Griffin SR, Welch P. Performance-based public health in Texas. *J Public Health Manage Pract*. 1995;1(3):44–49.

27. National Association of County and City Health Officials (NACCHO). *Assessment Protocol for Excellence in Public Health (APEXPH)*. Washington, DC: NACCHO; 1991.

28. National Association of County and City Health Officials. Assessment and planning excellence through community partners for health. Available at: http://www.naccho.org/project49.htm. Accessed March 22, 2000.

29. Bartlett L, et al. *Assessing Roles, Responsibilities, and Activities in a Managed Care Environment: A Workbook for Local Health Officials*. Washington, DC: US Department of Health and Human Services; 1997.

30. Gordon RL, Baker EL, Roper WL, Omenn GS. Prevention and the reforming U.S. health system: changing roles and responsibilities for public health. *Annu Rev Public Health*. 1996;17:489–509.

31. The Hospital Association of Pennsylvania. *A Guide for Assessing and Improving Health Status*. Harrisburg, PA: The Hospital Association of Pennsylvania; 1993:25.

32. Mays GP, Halverson P, Miller CH. Assessing the performance of local public health systems: a survey of state health agency efforts. *J Public Health Manage Pract*. 1998;4(4):63–78.

33. Perrin EB, Koshel JJ, eds. *Assessment of Performance Measures for Public Health, Substance Abuse, and Mental Health*. Washington, DC: National Academies Press; 1997.

34. National Center for Health Statistics. Consensus set of health status indicators for the general assessment of community health status—United States. *MMWR*. 1991;40(27):449–445.

35. Caroll L. *Alice's Adventure in Wonderland*. New York, NY: Random House Inc; 1946.

36. Dhara R. Advancing public health through the assessment initiative. *J Public Health Manage Pract*. 2002;8(4):1–8.

37. Schumacher P. Responding to the changing needs of public health assessment in the information age: the evolution of a program. *J Public Health Manage Pract*. 2006;12(2):109–112.

38. Friedman DJ, Gibson Parish RG. Characteristics, desired functionalities, and data sets of state Web-based data query systems. *J Public Health Manage Pract.* 2006;12(2):119–129.

39. Friede A, Reid JA, Ory HW. CDC WONDER: a comprehensive online public health information system of the Centers for Disease Control and Prevention. *Am J Public Health.* 1993;83:1289–1294.

40. Friedman DJ. Envisioning futures for state Web-based data query systems. *J Public Health Manage Pract.* 2006;12(2):196–200.

41. Auerbach S. Report cards found to improve health care. *Washington Post.* January 6, 1998:A08.

42. Longo DR, Laud G, Schramm, et al. Consumer reports in health care: do they make a difference in patient care? *JAMA.* 1997;278:1579–1584.

43. Chassin MR, Hannan EL, DeBuono BA. Benefits and hazards of reporting medical outcomes publicly. *N Engl J Med.* 1996;334(6):394–398.

44. Health care report cards. *New York Times.* July 10, 1995:A12.

45. National Committee on Quality Assurance. *Report Card Pilot Project.* Washington, DC: National Committee on Quality Assurance; 1995.

46. US General Accounting Office. *Report Cards Are Useful but Significant Issues Need to Be Addressed.* Washington, DC: 1994.

47. Pennsylvania Health Care Cost Containment Council. *A Consumer Guide to Coronary Artery Bypass Graft Surgery: Pennsylvania's Declaration of Health Care Information.* Harrisburg, Pa: Pennsylvania Health Care Cost Containment Council; 1991.

48. Fielding JE, Halfon N. Characteristics of community report cards–United States, 1996. *MMWR.* 1997;46(28):647–655.

49. Miller CA, Halverson P, Mays G. Flexibility in measurement of public health performance [editorial]. *J Public Health Manage Pract.* 1997;3(5):vii–viii.

50. Mays GP, et al. Developing a model report card of community health: a proposed methodology? Working paper: Center for Public Health Practice, School of Public Health, University of North Carolina at Chapel Hill, 1999.

51. Mays GP, et al. Identifying indicators for a national community health report card. *Prevention 98 Meeting Abstracts.* Washington, DC: American College of Preventive Medicine; 1998:75.

52. Halverson PK, et al. *Managed Care and Public Health.* Gaithersburg, Md: Aspen Publishers Inc; 1997.

53. Blum HL. *Planning for Health: Development and Application of Social Change Theory.* New York, NY: Human Sciences Press; 1974.

54. Lenihan P. MAPP and the evolution of planning in public health practice. *J Public Health Manage Pract.* 2005;11(5):381–386.

55. National Association of County and City Health Officials (NACCHO). *Achieving Healthier Communities through MAPP: A User's Handbook.* Washington, DC: NACCHO; 2005.

56. NACCHO, CDC. *A Strategic Approach to Community Health Improvement: MAPP Field Guide.* Washington, DC: NACCHO, CDC; 2005.

57. Pullen NC, Upshaw VM, Lesneski CD, Terrell A. Lessons from the MAPP demonstration sites. *J Public Health Manage Pract.* 2005;11(5):453–459.

58. Shields K, Pruski CE. MAPP in action in San Antonio, Texas. *J Public Health Manage Pract.* 2005;11(5):407–414.

59. Institute of Medicine. *Healthy Communities: New Partnerships for the Future of Public Health.* Washington, DC: National Academies Press; 1996.

60. Lasker R. *Medicine and Public Health: The Power of Collaboration.* New York, NY: New York Academy of Medicine; 1997.

## CHAPTER 16

# BUILDING CONSTITUENCIES FOR PUBLIC HEALTH

Michael T. Hatcher
Ray M. Nicola

## Chapter Overview

Public health leaders are challenged to develop effective relationships with the complex constellation of constituents who are involved in or affected by community health issues. An effective constituency-building practice allows public health leaders to develop relationships that facilitate community health improvement. Using this organizational practice, public health leaders identify major public health constituents, delineate participation factors, develop and manage effective interactions with constituency groups, and apply strategies for evaluating and improving constituency engagement in public health initiatives. Each of these tasks requires explicit analytic and management strategies for linking constituency-building processes to community health improvement.

Public health leaders operate within complex institutional environments that include many different types of constituents. The consumers of public health services in any given community are many and diverse, as are the individuals and organizations involved in producing these services. Improving health within communities and populations requires coordinated decision making and problem solving by all of these constituents. Such problem solving occurs most readily and successfully when constituents are actively engaged in addressing health issues that matter to them.[1(p5)]

Problem solving in public health rarely occurs through spontaneous consensus. In a democratic society, change is produced through the tensions of multiple interests and the opinions of differing societal segments. These segments represent constituencies for public health organizations seeking action on community health issues. All too frequently, public health leaders rely on a false dichotomy in developing relationships with constituents—they approach each constituent as either an adversary or an ally. Adversarial situations stimulate defensive responses that stalemate progress. These situations often arise because communication is limited to debate and entrenched positions instead of dialogue, negotiation, and solution development. On the other side of the coin, public health leaders focus on attracting and sustaining the attention of allies and other uninvolved constituents on health issues requiring community-based decisions. Allies are typically sought among individuals and organizations that pursue similar missions and that engage in similar types of activities involving public health issues. However, this dichotomous approach to constituency development can severely limit the actions and outcomes that public health organizations achieve. To transcend this false dichotomy, public health leaders and organizations require an analytic and management framework for linking constituency building with community health improvement goals.

This chapter outlines a practice framework for constituency building in public health that focuses on achieving sustained improvements in community health. Within such a framework, public health organizations identify public health constituencies explicitly and broadly, delineate constituent participation factors, develop and manage effective interactions with constituency groups, and apply models for evaluating and improving the engagement of constituencies in public health issues (Figure 16-1). Each of these tasks requires explicit analytic and management strategies for linking constituency-building activities to community health improvement.

The constituency-building framework begins with the understanding that people need a reason to invest their energy in processes that address community health. If people and the community they are a part of are not motivated and ready to participate, action will not occur. The second aspect of the framework is focused on managing the constituency-building processes and factors for constituent involvement. This segment of the framework addresses the responsibility of public health leaders to manage and enable effective constituent engagement and participation. The third aspect of the framework focuses on approaches or models that facilitate constituent and community involvement and lead to interventions. The fourth aspect of the framework includes public health

| Know | Do | | | Produce | | |
|------|------|------|------|------|------|------|
| Constituent Participation Factors | Organizational Practice | Constituent Improvement Approaches | Public Health Interventions | Health Impacts | Health Outcomes | Quality-of-Life Improvements |
| • Motivations | • Know the community | • PRECEDE PROCEED model | • Clinical | • Clinical | • Decreased morbidity | • Physical |
| • Readiness | • Develop positions and strategies | • MAPP | • Behavioral | • Behavioral | • Decreased mortality | • Mental |
| | | • PATCH | • Systems | • Systems | | • Social |
| | • Build network linkages | • Healthy People in Healthy Communities 2010 | • Environmental | • Environmental | | • Spiritual |
| | • Mobilize for action | | | | | • Environmental |
| | | • Healthy Cities | | | | |

**FIGURE 16-1   Linking Constituency Building to Community Health Improvement**

intervention sciences that are available to produce community-based results. The remaining portion of the framework demonstrates how constituent-based actions are linked to producing behavioral, systems, and environmental impacts, which in turn produce desired health outcomes and quality-of-life improvements. Discussions of the first three aspects of the framework that influence and move constituents and their communities to action are the focus of this chapter. Identifying public health interventions and the resulting health effects such interventions produce is presented in the framework to establish an operational link between constituency building and community health improvement.

## Who is Public Health's Constituency?

A *constituency* (in addition to the meaning of *a body of voters*) is: (1) a group of supporters or patrons, and (2) a group served by an organization or institution; a clientele.[2] By definition, therefore, people who benefit from public health actions and people who support improved health of the public are the constituency. Because public health serves the entire population, everyone in the country is part of the public health constituency. There are, however, certain groups in the constituent population who are in a special position to influence public health outcomes; these include public health workers, policy makers, business leaders, and others.

Building on the concepts of supporters and clients, an operational definition of constituency building can be established. For purposes of this chapter, *constituency building* is the art and science of establishing relationships among a public health agency and the public it serves, the governing body it represents, and other health-related organizations in the community. Relationships are established to generate debate, dialogue, decisions, and actions among constituent groups in addressing community health needs and issues. Key points of this definition acknowledge that sciences such as political science, interpersonal communications, media advocacy, and others can be applied to building linkages and relationships with constituents. Applying the appropriate science at the right time, however, requires artful application. Complicating the simplicity of this definition is the fact that people and organizations are often members of multiple constituencies, and their movement between groups is fluid and frequently based on alignment of issues within the groups.[1,3] Due to the fluid nature of constituent alignment on community health issues, public health leaders must develop a strategic understanding of individual and organizational values, missions, and assets held by constituents affected by or having influence over decisions and actions required to address community health concerns. Such influence may be constituted through a position of power that shapes opinions and directs organizations, controls resources and information, or possesses key technology. Such an understanding is critical in managing constituency relationships.

## Incentives for Constituency Participation

An understanding of why people participate in community activities provides the first guidance for constituency building. Factors include the sociopolitical environment, community needs, community attitudes and beliefs, and existing leadership and organization in the community.[4] The literature from various fields of study and authors such as Brown, Schwartz, Mattessich, and Monsey offer insight on the motivations that move people to act.[4-6] For example, people participate when they feel a sense of community, see their involvement and the issues as relevant and worthy of their time, believe that the benefits of participation outweigh the cost, and view the process and organizational climate of participation as open and supportive of their right to have a voice in the process.[1] The issue itself also influences participation. People are motivated to work for change when conditions of the issue are no longer acceptable to them. The readiness of constituents to take action can be determined by understanding the perception of, and support for, the issue within the community. For example:

- Are there perceptions that a problem or threat that affects health exists?
- Is the issue perceived to be important, achievable, and deserving of community action?
- Is there a science base to resolve the issue?
- Is community collaboration likely due to political and public interest and community history for leadership and collaboration?
- Are resources available for action?
- Is the political and social climate supportive of the constituency's goals?
- Is there a community infrastructure to sustain interest and community action?

Answers to these and related questions are necessary to help public health leaders determine constituent readiness and the level of action that may be possible.[7] Public health leaders who understand the motives for constituent participation and the attributes of readiness can stimulate action with appropriate information and public processes that fulfill individual and group needs for participation.

## Organizational Management for Effective Constituency Interaction

A public health leader who seeks constituent participation on a public health issue can design organizational structure and management processes within his or her agency that facilitate and direct interactions with constituents, for purposes of:

- Knowing the community and its constituents
- Establishing positions and strategies that guide the agency's interaction with constituents
- Building and sustaining formal and informal networks necessary for maintaining relationships, communicating messages, and leveraging resources
- Mobilizing constituencies for community-based decision making and social action

Performance of this organizational practice and its processes is likely to be shared across the agency, with specific roles delegated to organizational units such as an assessment and planning unit, a senior management group, and an education and outreach group. The organizational structures or units tasked with creating or delegating the management and performance of these processes are dependent on existing forms and functions within the agency.

By managing these processes, public health leaders can consistently address factors that produce effective constituent involvement, including the following:[1,5]

- The clarity of initiative goals
- The defined roles for constituent involvement
- Constituent ownership of both initiative process and outcome
- The design of capacity-building elements incorporated into processes and structures used to facilitate individual and group actions of constituents
- The overall feeling of satisfaction, rather than frustration, a process achieves in fulfilling a constituent's reasons for participating in community activities

### Knowing the Community and Its Constituents

Knowing the community and its constituents is more than an epidemiologic assessment. It involves coordinating and directing activities that are necessary to identify constituent groups, analyzing group characteristics and factors that generate constituent involvement, and assessing current and potential assets (including fiscal, physical, informational, and human resources) that constituents and their organizations can direct toward resolving community health issues. The tasks involved in constituent identification and analysis of group characteristics include demographic groupings; individual and organizational beliefs, values, missions, and goals; and organizational and leadership structures of constituent groups as well as their history of working with others. Through this assessment, it is possible to determine the roles and type of support (political, financial, manpower, etc.) constituents can reasonably provide to a public health initiative, as well as possible conflicts of interest that may arise among groups.[8]

To be most effective, public health leaders must determine which constituents are affected by specific issues, assess their probable response to these issues, and use the most effective methods to involve each constituent group in appropriate activities. Constituent skills should match those needed for resolving the public health issue on which the agency is facilitating dialogue and action. If the skills do not match, a determination must be made concerning training and education necessary to increase constituent involvement. In identifying and recruiting a constituent base for public health, the agency must have policies, structures, resources, and leadership to assess community mobilization efforts and assist in developing human and other constituency resources for public health action. Mechanisms that enable the identification and analysis of the agency's constituent base provide essential information concerning potential collaborators on public health issues. From a leadership perspective, knowing the community is essential because social programs tend to fail because of a lack of appropriate management and an oversimplified view of constituent motivations.[9]

## Establishing Positions and Strategies to Guide Interaction with Constituents

Another important process area is focused on organizational decision making that results in the establishment of a position and strategy for bringing a health issue before constituents. The purpose of this decision making and planning is to initiate constituent dialogue and action. Public health leaders must make their decisions based on understanding multiple domains of influence on health such as social, epidemiologic, behavioral, environmental, ecologic, and political factors.[10] Through such analysis in decision making, public health leaders are better equipped to consider the position options available and weigh each option's effect on the different constituencies. Specific attention should be given to the perceived needs of customers served, attitudes of policy-making bodies, application of public health science, public health delivery system capabilities, and appropriate community health data. A position is established against this pool of competing interests. Through this practice element, the agency prepares itself to participate in the democratic process of decision making with constituents. The result is stimulation of community debate, dialogue, and involvement around the health issue, and a determination of the community's expectations. This internal organizational position development is not intended to exclude constituent input. Instead, it provides a starting point for dialogue with constituents and enables the public health leader to communicate clearly.

Once an agency position has been reached, strategy options can be evaluated and selected based on the best chance for achieving dialogue and action. Four organizational strategy types can be considered: authoritative, competitive, cooperative, and disruptive.[11]

1. The *authoritative* strategy applies rules and regulations to require a desired action. It is used when an organization has control over its environment. Successful authoritative strategies demand an ability to monitor and enforce its directives. This strategy was used effectively by the National Highway Traffic Safety Administration in the early 1980s when it was announced that airbags would be required in automobiles unless a specified percentage of the US population was subject to mandatory seatbelt laws requiring occupant restraint use. This prompted policy debate and the passage of vehicle occupant protection laws across the nation.

2. *Competitive* strategies attempt to make an organization's position more desirable and attractive to constituents. The successfully competitive organization attracts adequate support to accomplish its purpose and avoids pressures from others that promote actions that are incongruent with the desired public health goals. Public health officials often apply this strategy when funding is sought and there is competing interest for the same dollars. Success is won by demonstrating why the proposed program spending is needed, the quality and impact of the program over others, and external support for the program.

3. *Cooperative* strategies establish agreements that offer mutual benefits to constituents and their organizations. An organization may use one of three cooperative strategy forms: (1) *contracting,* which is a negotiated agreement between two parties for exchanging resources or services; (2) *coalition,* which is a pooling of resources by several

organizations for a joint venture; or (3) *co-optation,* which is the absorption (or conversion) of representatives from key (opposition or competitive) constituent groups into the leadership or policy-making structure of an organization to moderate or avoid opposition or competition.

4. *Disruption* strategies are "the purposeful conduct of activities which threaten the resource-generating capacities" of an adversary.[11(p79)] The most visible public health example of this strategy is antitobacco initiatives that seek to limit the sales and market base of tobacco companies in an effort to prevent the use of tobacco by children.

Throughout the position development and strategy development process, it is essential to focus on the needs and interests of the agency's constituency. The question of when to enlist direct constituent involvement is of critical concern. Is constituent input advisable during the problem analysis phase or as strategy and objectives are being weighed? Although early constituent involvement is usually indicated, agency time and resource constraints may dictate that constituents are most appropriately brought in during the implementation phase. Some considerations in determining the time most appropriate for involving constituents are the following:

- Operating time frame—How much time is there to achieve the goal?
- Level of constituent knowledge—How much education will constituents need?
- Constituent commitment—How much of a time commitment are constituents willing to make?

Whatever the judgment on a point of entry for constituent participation, public health leaders must establish direction for the interaction and involvement of agency staff with constituents acting on important health issues in the community.

## Building and Sustaining Networks

Network development is the third process area public health leaders must consider in the operations of an agency. Developing networks is focused on establishing and maintaining relationships, communication channels, and exchange systems that promote linkages, alliances, and opportunities to leverage resources among constituent groups. Effective performance results in open channels of communication to constituents, enables active and ongoing interactions, and accelerates resource commitment and community mobilization efforts on service and policy issues. If public health leaders view networking as an ongoing and essential activity in the agency's operations, constituency mobilization can be productive and require minimal effort. If agency leaders only communicate with constituents as a crisis management technique, they may find that communication channels that were once useful no longer exist.

The challenge for public health is to establish ties with a network of diverse constituency supporters that will respond to public health issues. Key to a successful network is identifying and assessing the network structure in place and understanding the effect of structure on the availability of resources for public health. Public health has access to both formal and informal constituent groups. The formal groups or organizations have recognized stability and influence in the community; informal groups may represent less structured and influential constituents who are often very resourceful. Each group brings with it important considerations that public health leaders need to be aware of if true networking potential is to be realized.[12] Thus, the ability of public health leaders to develop and direct networking activities relies heavily on identifying and assessing the existing networking structure.

Assessment of formal ties should reveal interactions of information flow, resource allocation, service delivery, or policy endeavors with influential individuals and organizations serving on boards, committees, coalitions, and governing bodies. If the leader finds that formal ties are weak, he or she may choose to concentrate on strengthening these ties with key partners to improve relationships and increase the agency's influence and its resource potential.

A highly involved constituency base may allow an agency to have several ties with informal and voluntary groups. A lack of ties with such community groups may impede agency outreach performance. Public health leaders may then choose to pursue more informal community ties to enlarge the constituency base and improve service outreach. In this situation, management needs to provide adequate resources to ensure the development, participation, and retention of informal and volunteer organizations.

## Mobilizing Constituencies

Mobilizing constituencies for community-based decision making and social action is the fourth process area. Mobilization is bringing into readiness or organizing people and resources for active service.[2] An agency can prepare or organize the community to act. Making the community ready in this case means organizing constituencies to act through social pressure and community involvement to meet the health needs that exist. Through mobilization, community interest on health issues is stimulated, constituents are prepared to act, and, if necessary, constituents are assisted to respond in resolving the public health issue.

The ability to mobilize the constituents around a particular issue reflects not only the agency's structural capability to mount such an effort, but also the community's ability and readiness to respond. Based on an understanding of the community and its constituents, a public health leader must answer key questions in selecting a mobilization approach. For example:

- Who are the constituents and stakeholders within the community?
- Does the community believe itself capable of affecting its environment?
- Will the community hear and absorb the information that is supplied by the public health agency?
- Does the community have the capability to mount a response?

The answers to these questions provide the framework that the agency can use to analyze its social mobilization options. The mobilization option chosen to bring dialogue and action on a public health issue must support the agency position and be consistent with the strategy selected so as to guide constituent interaction and the constituents' capacity to act. Specific models for mobilization will be discussed later in this chapter.

## Assessing the Effectiveness of Public Health Constituencies

Assessing the effectiveness of a public health constituency means evaluating the group's ability to have a positive impact on the community's health. Because effectiveness in this case means reaching public health objectives, any such assessment should also examine the clarity of the objectives. Clarity of political appeal and intervention science, including mobilization approaches, is central to the assessment.

*Political appeal* is measured against any competing actions that are proposed to achieve the same objective. If the competing actions are equally effective at accomplishing the objective, and one does not cost more than the other, a compromise rather than opposition is appropriate. If the competing action is not built on good public health science, then opposition may be necessary though unfortunate because all involved in a fight become injured. Given the choice between compromise and opposition, it is necessary to apply a competitive strategy to raise the appeal of the advocated action.

*Clarity of science* is achieved with selection and use of effective interventions and mobilization approaches. Appropriate use of science enables identification of measures to establish objective targets and evaluate collaborative actions and intervention outcomes. The health objectives and outcomes require an adequate assessment of the community's health status. Although this chapter is not focused on assessment tools, many approaches described in the following sections are useful in assessing health status. Some of the resources available to aid in establishing objective targets and monitoring progress are *Healthy People 2010,* the National Commission for Quality Assurance's *Health Plan Employer Data and Information Set (HEDIS),* and the National Center for Health Statistics' (NCHS') leading health indicators.[13-15]

Literature is also available that describes methods for assessing the competency and effectiveness of constituency groups based on group interaction and its components of process, structure, and organizational content.[5] These methods describe how effective a constituency is in working together as a group.

## Proven Interventions Improve Health and Build Constituencies

Once there is an understanding of the participation "drivers" of constituents and knowledge of the organizational factors that contribute to effective constituency interactions, it is time to move to action. Public health constituencies become stronger by taking effective action to improve the public's health; that is, the success of group goals in itself provides reinforcement of participation in constituency efforts.

There are different applied public health interventions for specific disease issues and many resources available to provide guidance on interventions. *The Clinical Preventive Services Guidelines* provide the evidence base for the effectiveness of public health interventions in a clinical setting.[16] The

*Guide to Community Preventive Services*, an analogous US Public Health Service project, provides the evidence base for the effectiveness of public health interventions in a community setting with over 100 findings in 15 topic areas.[17] (See Chapter 19 for more detailed discussion.) Several broad cross-cutting interventions are available that facilitate constituent involvement in planning for health actions; examples of these are described in the next section.

### Tools to Mobilize Constituents for Public Health Action

Public health practitioners at local, state, federal, and global levels have developed different tools and initiatives to assist in achieving long-term health improvements in populations. These include *Healthy People 2010*; *Steps to a Healthier US*; Mobilizing for Action through Planning and Partnership (MAPP); Turning Point; the World Health Organization's (WHO's) Healthy Cities; and others initiatives.[13,18–21] These approaches all facilitate constituent involvement.

#### *Healthy People 2010* Tools

*Healthy People 2010* lays out the prevention agenda for the nation and provides direction for local programs as they identify and set priorities and develop health objective targets.[13] The *Healthy People 2010* framework builds on initiatives that have been pursued over the past two decades. *Healthy People: The Surgeon General's Report on Health Promotion and Disease Prevention* provided targets to reduce premature mortality in four life age groups during the 1980s and was supported by objectives with 1990 end points.[22] *Healthy People 2000: National Health Promotion and Disease Prevention Objectives* guided efforts toward health targets for the year 2000.[23] Like its predecessors, *Healthy People 2010* was developed through a broad consultation process characterized by intersectoral collaboration and community participation. It is the action agenda for the first decade of the 21st century. *Healthy People 2010* is the US contribution to the WHO's "Health for All" strategy. (Refer to Chapter 2 for a more detailed discussion.)

The *Healthy People 2010 Toolkit* is a resource developed to support state and local leaders in establishing participatory plans to address priority health objectives over this decade. The toolkit is organized around seven action areas that address building a leadership and structural foundation, addressing resource issues, engaging community partners, establishing health priorities and objectives, addressing measurement issues, managing and sustaining the participatory process, and communicating health goals and objectives to those who can influence accomplishment of the objectives. This toolkit was developed by the Public Health Foundation in cooperation with the US Department of Health and Human Services' Office of Disease Prevention and Health Promotion and Office of Public Health and Science.[24]

*Steps to a HealthierUS* is a 2003 federal initiative from the US Department of Health and Human Services (HHS) that advances a "HealthierUS" goal of helping Americans live longer, better, and healthier lives. The initiative focuses on both personal responsibility for the choices Americans make and social responsibility to ensure that policy makers support programs that foster healthy behaviors and prevention. These steps include promoting health and wellness programs at schools and work sites and in faith- and community-based settings; enacting policies that promote healthy environments; ensuring access to a full range of quality health services; implementing programs that focus on eliminating racial, ethnic, and socioeconomic-based health disparities; and educating the public effectively about their health.[18]

## APEXPH and MAPP

Since 1991, local public health officials have used the Assessment Protocol for Excellence in Public Health (APEXPH) to assess internal organizational capacity and to begin a community process of consensus building around health issues.[25] In 1999, a national work group under the leadership of the National Association of County and City Health Officials (NACCHO) and the US Centers for Disease Control and Prevention (CDC) started developing Mobilizing for Action through Planning and Partnership (MAPP).[19] (Refer to Chapter 15 for further discussion of community health assessment.) This new tool is an evolution of APEXPH and provides community and local health department leaders with a robust tool to guide their creation of a local health system that ensures the delivery of services essential to protecting the health of the public. The MAPP tool offers several new features. One feature provides indicators to measure community capacity for providing essential public health services rather than examining only the capacity of the local health department as APEXPH did. This section of MAPP adopts the local health system measures used by the CDC National Public Health Performance Standards Program. (This is discussed further in Chapter 19.) A second feature presents a strategic planning component and case studies to support this feature. The community health assessment guidance in MAPP supports traditional health status assessment and provides a stronger focus on environmental health, behavioral risk factor data, and health-related quality-of-life indicators.

## Healthy Cities

The original Healthy Cities model began as a demonstration project of the WHO and is used by nations around the world.[21] It has also been adapted and applied in more than 30 states in the United States. California, Indiana, South Carolina, and Massachusetts are states where this model of health and quality-of-life improvement is applied most frequently. The Healthy Cities model uses a broad definition of health. It promotes extensive public–private partnerships through processes of social and environmental change designed to improve the health and quality of life of populations through interventions addressing ecological determinants of health such as education, recreation, employment, health services, transportation, and housing.[26]

The Association for Community Health Improvement,[27] a program of the American Hospital Association's Health Research and Educational Trust, was conceived in 2002 as a successor to three national community health initiatives: the Community Care Network Demonstration Program, the ACT National Outcomes Network, and the Coalition for Healthier Cities and Communities.

These initiatives were approaching the end of their grant cycles or were otherwise ripe for renewal and growth. Each of these three programs had functioned since the mid-1990s and had made complementary contributions to improve community health, focusing on topics that include healthcare delivery and preventive health systems that ensure accessibility and are accountable to local needs; careful planning for and measurement of progress toward defined community health goals; and broad community engagement in resolving systemic challenges to community health and social well-being. The association adopted the key tenets of each predecessor and blended these with additional ingredients of effective community health practice to create a unified professional association with broad values able to serve as a networking hub for continual learning. The association is well informed by experienced advisors and a rich base of members from the health care, public health, and healthy communities sectors.

## Turning Point

Turning Point, started in 1997 and completed in 2006, is an initiative of the Robert Wood Johnson Foundation and the W.K. Kellogg Foundation.[20] Its mission is to transform and strengthen the public health system in the United States by making it more community based and collaborative. The initial idea for Turning Point came from the foundations' concerns about the capacity of the public health system to respond to emerging challenges in public health, specifically the system's capacity to work with people from many sectors to improve the health status of all people in a community. Turning Point's underlying philosophy is that public health agencies and their partners can be strengthened by linking to other sectors (not just the private healthcare sector, but education, criminal justice, faith communities, business, and others) because the underlying causes of poor health and quality of life are tied closely to social issues that are too complex to be approached by disease models of intervention. Turning Point has created a network of 21 public health partners across the country to define and assess health, prioritize health issues, and take collective action.

Local-level Turning Point partnerships are collaborating to gather data on health status, resources, values, and priorities of community members; develop consensus about priority health issues using a broad definition of healthy communities; mobilize local resources to develop action plans to address health priorities; and communicate local needs, priorities, and approaches to elected officials and state agencies to assist in the development of effective health policy. State-level Turning Point partnerships are collaborating to influence good public health policy; expand information technology so data is available to local communities for addressing health concerns; and stimulate state agencies and organizations to develop comprehensive state health plans.

Turning Point partners have formed five National Excellence Collaboratives consisting of state and local members from 5 to 8 states and national constituency representatives who are working to modernize public health statutes, create accountable systems to measure performance, utilize information technology, invest in social marketing, and develop collaborative leaders. (Refer to Chapter 17 for more discussion on Turning Point.)

The Institute of Medicine's report *The Future of Public's Health in the 21st Century* reviews the role of community participation in health improvement processes.[28] It finds that public health leaders have a primary responsibility to engage the community in health promotion and protection activities.[28(p204)] Specific examples of community initiatives using some of the above tools are provided in Chapter 4 of the report. In addition, the above tools and initiatives are frequently incorporated into academic syllabi for public health students and into ongoing practice education such as leadership and management development programs for practicing public health professionals. For example, the Public Health Leadership Institute and many of the state and regional public health leadership development programs require participants to perform an individual project during the life of the program, which uses constituency engagement as a principal feature.

## Initiating the Constituency Building Process

The body of knowledge concerning public health constituency-building continues to grow as does collaboration between public health leaders and the communities they serve.[28(p181-183)] A 1997 publication, *Principles of Community Engagement,* reviews a cross section of social and behavioral science literature and examines the practical experiences of public health practitioners and researchers. From this review, the Committee for Community Engagement identifies the following principles in their CDC publication:[1]

Before starting a community engagement effort:

- Be clear about the purposes or goals of the effort and the populations and/or communities you want to engage.
- Become knowledgeable about the community (Figure 16-1) in terms of its economic conditions, political structures, norms and values, demographic trends, history, and experience with engagement efforts. Learn about the community's perceptions of those initiating the engagement activities.

For engagement to occur, it is necessary to do the following:

- Go into the community, establish relationships, build trust, work with the formal and informal leadership, and get commitment from community organizations to create processes for mobilizing the community.
- Remember and accept that community self-determination is the responsibility and right of all people who make up a community. No external entity should assume that it can bestow to a community the power to act in its own self-interest.

For engagement to succeed:

- Partnering with the community is necessary to create change and improve health.
- All aspects of community engagement must recognize and respect community diversity. Awareness of the various cultures of a community and other factors of diversity must be paramount in designing and implementing community engagement approaches.

- Community engagement can only be sustained by identifying and mobilizing community assets, and by developing capacities and resources for community health decisions and action.
- An engaging organization or individual change agent must be prepared to release control of actions or interventions to the community, and be sufficiently flexible to meet the changing needs of the community.
- Community collaboration requires long-term commitment by the engaging organization and its partners.

•   •   •

The guiding principles presented in this chapter underscore the importance of knowing constituency groups within a community and establishing constituent engagement plans within a health organization. Building constituencies is neither an automatic nor an intuitive process for public health leaders to undertake. Nonetheless, effective constituencies can be formed and sustained through explicit managerial strategies combined with sound evaluation tools. Because constituent interaction is critical for effective organizational performance and community health improvement, constituency building cannot be overlooked as a strategic action for public health leaders and their organizations.

## Chapter Review

1. Constituencies for public health organizations include the *individuals* and *institutions* that benefit from public health actions and that support improved health within the population.
2. Constituency building is the process of establishing relationships between a public health organization and the public it serves, including consumers, governing bodies, and other health-related organizations in the community. Relationships are established to facilitate decision making and action for addressing community health needs or issues.
3. Effective constituency-building practice involves managing organizational units to conduct the following processes:
   - Identify major constituents within the community and their interests.
   - Establish positions and strategies that guide the organization's interaction with constituents.
   - Build and sustain formal and informal network relationships necessary for communication, resource sharing, and joint decision making among constituents.
   - Motivate constituencies to engage in community-based decision making and collective action.
4. Key issues that must be considered in developing strategic relationships with constituents include the following:
   - Operating time frame—How much time is there to achieve the goal?
   - Level of constituent knowledge—How much education will constituents need?
   - Constituent commitment—How much resources are constituents willing and able to commit to the effort?

5. Explicit strategies for evaluating and improving constituency engagement must be used continuously by public health leaders. Assessment and planning tools, such as the *Healthy People 2010 Toolkit,* MAPP, or Healthy Cities, may be helpful to structure some interactions with constituents.

# References

1. US Centers for Disease Control and Prevention. *Principles of Community Engagement.* Atlanta, GA: CDC; 1997. Available at: http://www.cdc.gov/phppo/pce/index.htm. Accessed January 7, 2006.
2. *The American Heritage Dictionary of the English Language.* 3rd ed. [Electronic version]. Boston, Mass: Houghton Mifflin Co; 1992.
3. Institute of Medicine. *Assessing the Social and Behavioral Science Base for HIV/AIDS Prevention and Intervention: Workshop Summary and Background Papers.* Washington, DC: National Academies Press; 1995.
4. Brown ER. Community action for health promotion: a strategy to empower individuals and communities. *Int J Health Serv.* 1991;21(3):448–451.
5. Schwartz RM. *The Skilled Facilitator: Practical Wisdom for Developing Effective Groups.* San Francisco, Calif: Jossey-Bass Publishers; 1994.
6. Mattessich PW, Monsey BR. *Collaboration: What Makes It Work; A Review of Research Literature on Factors Influencing Successful Collaboration.* St. Paul, Minn: Amherst H. Wilder Foundation; 1992.
7. Kar SB, ed. *Health Promotion Indicators and Actions, Indicators for Individual and Societal Actions for Public Health.* New York, NY: Springer Publishing Co; 1989.
8. Public Health Foundation. *Constituency Building: Partnerships for Public Health.* Washington, DC: Public Health Foundation; 1987.
9. Wilson M. The new frontier: volunteer management training. *Train Develop J.* 1984;July:50–52.
10. Green LW, Kreuter MW. *Health Promotion Planning: An Educational and Ecological Approach.* 3rd ed. Mountain View, Calif: Mayfield; 1999.
11. Hasenfeld Y. *Human Service Organizations.* Englewood Cliffs, NJ: Prentice-Hall; 1983.
12. Wellman B. Applying network analysis to the study of support. In: Gottlieb BH, ed. *Social Networks and Social Support.* London, UK: Sage Publications; 1983:173–181.
13. US Public Health Service. *Healthy People 2010.* Washington, DC: Office of Public Health and Science; 2000. Available at: http://www.healthypeople.gov. Accessed January 7, 2006.
14. National Committee for Quality Assurance. *HEDIS-Health Plan Employer Data and Information Set 2006.* Available at: http://www.ncqa.org/communications/publications/hedispub.htm. Accessed January 7, 2006.
15. National Center for Health Statistics, Centers for Disease Control and Prevention. Health, United States, 2005, with chartbook on trends in the health of Americans. Available at: http://www.cdc.gov/nchs/data/hus/hus05.pdf#chartbookontrendsinthe. Accessed January 7, 2006.
16. US Department of Health and Human Services. Guide to clinical preventive services, 2005. Available at: http://www.ahrq.gov/clinic/pocketgd.htm. Accessed January 7, 2006.
17. Task Force on Community Preventive Services, US Department of Health and Human Services. Guide to community preventive services. Available

at: http://www.thecommunityguide.org/default.htm. Accessed January 7, 2006.

18. US Department of Health and Human Services. Steps to a HealthierUS Initiative. 2003. Available at: http://www.healthierus.gov/steps. Accessed January 7, 2006.

19. National Association of County and City Health Officials (NACCHO). *Mobilizing for Action through Planning and Partnership.* Washington, DC: NACCHO; 2000.

20. Robert Wood Johnson Foundation, W.K. Kellogg Foundation. Turning Point (1997–2006). Available at: http://turningpointprogram.org. Accessed January 7, 2006.

21. World Health Organization. *Promoting Health in the Urban Context, Five-Year Planning Framework, A Guide to Assessing Healthy Cities.* Copenhagen, Denmark: World Health Organization Regional Office for Europe; 1988.

22. Public Health Service, US Department of Health and Human Services. *Healthy People: The Surgeon General's Report on Health Promotion and Disease Prevention.* Washington, DC: US Public Health Service; 1979.

23. Public Health Service, US Department of Health and Human Services. *Healthy People 2000: National Health Promotion and Disease Prevention Objectives.* Washington, DC: US Public Health Service; 1990.

24. Public Health Foundation, US Office of Disease Prevention and Health Promotion, US Office of Public Health and Science. *Healthy People 2010 Toolkit: A Field Guide to Health Planning.* Washington, DC: US DHHS; 1999. Available at: http://www.health.gov/healthypeople/state/toolkit. Accessed January 7, 2006.

25. National Association of County and City Health Officials (NACCHO). *Assessment Protocol for Excellence in Public Health.* Washington, DC: NACCHO; 1991. Available at: http://www.naccho.org/pubs/pub_list.cfm. Accessed January 7, 2006.

26. Katz MF, Kreuter MW. Community assessment and empowerment. In: Scutchfield ED, Keck CW, eds. *Principles of Public Health Practice.* Albany, NY: Delmar Publishers; 1997.

27. American Hospital Association, Health Research and Educational Trust. Association for Community Health Improvement. Available at: http://www.communityhlth.org/communityhlth/about/mission.html. Accessed January 7, 2006.

28. Institute of Medicine. *The Future of Public's Health in the 21st Century.* Ch 4. Washington, DC: National Academies Press; 2002. Available at: http://www.nap.edu/catalog/10548.html. Accessed January 7, 2006.

## CHAPTER 17

# PERFORMANCE MANAGEMENT: THE EVOLUTION OF STANDARDS, MEASUREMENT, AND QUALITY IMPROVEMENT IN PUBLIC HEALTH

Laura B. Landrum
Leslie M. Beitsch
Bernard J. Turnock
Arden S. Handler

## Chapter Overview

Public health organizations use performance measurement activities to track the work produced and results achieved through their internal and interorganizational efforts. Increasingly, organizations rely on performance measurement activities both to achieve internal quality improvement goals and to demonstrate accountability to external stakeholders. Public health organizations have begun to focus on using performance measures to actively manage complex public health processes. Performance management integrates an organization's use of standards, measurement, and performance improvement to change institutional capacities, processes, and priorities and to more effectively address the needs of the communities they serve. A growing array of practical tools is available to assist organizations in carrying out performance management activities on a routine basis.

Public health leaders and managers face issues related to performance at many different levels of the public health system, including the performance of individuals, programs, agencies, interorganizational collaborations, and the systemwide enterprise itself. Although these levels represent different aspects of public health performance, each can be assessed using common approaches that focus on the work produced and the results achieved. Performance measurement is an important management tool with an impressive record in improving performance throughout both the public and private sectors. These accomplishments derive from fundamental principles of the improvement science field: to improve something we must be able to control it; to control it we must be able to understand it; and to understand it we must be able to measure it.[1] The link between performance measurement and performance improvement provides a context for understanding the lessons and implications of performance measurement efforts in public health during the 1900s. This chapter examines these lessons, as well as various applications using performance standards to improve the performance of public health organizations and systems, including the accreditation of public health agencies.

The initial development of a performance management framework for use in public health organizations and systems will be described.

## The Elements of Performance Management

Drawing on a growing body of literature and new resources on performance standards, performance measures, and quality improvement, the Turning Point Performance Management National Excellence Collaborative in 2002 articulated the key elements of managing public health performance.[2,3] The collaborative defined performance management as the active use of performance data in making management decisions. The elements of performance management are the following:

- Performance standards
- Performance measures
- Reporting of progress
- Quality improvement process

The Performance Management model illustrated in Figure 17-1 integrates elements of public health practice into a coherent model for understanding and directing complex public health programs, organizations, and systems. The framework also ties together more conceptual and elusive issues in public health policy, such as accountability, effectiveness, and benchmarking, into a practical and feasible model. The forerunner of this new thinking about managing performance began with public health activities focused on performance measurement.[3,4]

### Performance Measurement: A Historical Perspective

Performance measurement, performance monitoring, and performance improvement are topics that are extensively addressed in the literature.[5-7] Although performance measurement is a simple concept, it lacks a simple or single definition. Basically, performance measurement is the selection and use of quantitative measures of critical aspects of activities, including their effect on the public and other customers. Put more simply, it is the regular collection and reporting of data to track work that is performed and results that are achieved.

An effective performance measurement process incorporates stakeholder input; promotes top leadership support; creates a clear mission statement; develops long-term goals and objectives; formulates short-term goals and interim measures; devises simple, manageable approaches; and provides support and technical assistance to those involved in the process. In this light, performance measurement serves several important purposes, providing information concerning the capacity to perform, results of current efforts, and

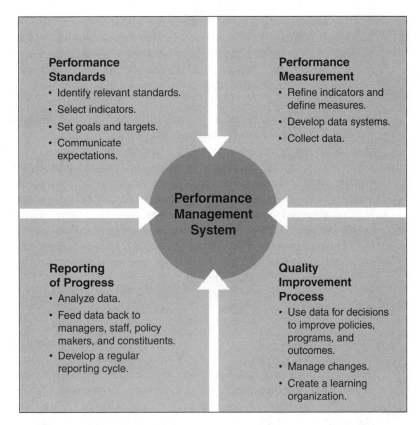

**FIGURE 17-1    The Performance Management Model**
*Source:* Turning Point Program National Office. *From Silos to Systems: Using Performance Management to Improve the Public's Health.* Seattle, Wash: Turning Point; 2003.

effectiveness of current performance. Potential benefits from measuring performance include the following:

- Better goals and objectives
- Identification of strengths and weaknesses
- Opportunities for collaborative approaches
- Clearer lines of accountability
- Improved quality
- Better tracking of progress over time
- More effective communication
- Better resource allocation and deployment

Performance measurement focuses on what is occurring, but it does not extensively address why or how. Evaluative research (sometimes called program evaluation) provides more in-depth assessment of the conceptualization, design, implementation, and utility of social interventions.[8] (See Chapter 18 for a more detailed discussion.) Performance measurement can be viewed as one component of a comprehensive evaluation, but its primary purpose is to inform managers so that changes can be instituted within the life cycle of a set of activities. In sum, performance measurement is a management and oversight tool to facilitate positive change and improvement in performance.

The terminology used in performance measurement is often inconsistent and confusing; the definitions used in this chapter are adapted from several sources.[9,10] In general, a *performance measure* is the specific quantitative representation of a capacity, process, or outcome that is deemed relevant to the assessment of performance. Similar to the concept of prevention, performance measurement requires an object. It is critical to specify what (or whose) performance is being measured. In public health, performance measurement most frequently occurs within the context of a particular program (e.g., childhood immunizations or retail food safety). However, the performance of an agency (e.g., a state or local health department), partnership, community public health system, or even an individual is also an appropriate target for performance measurement. Because the prime focus of this chapter is on measuring and improving performance in organizations and even more complex public health systems, the term *performance measurement* means the selection and use of quantitative measures of public health system capacities, processes, and outcomes to inform public health leaders and managers and the public about critical aspects of the public health system.

Performance measures can take several different forms. A performance measure that takes the form of a generally accepted, objective standard of measurement—such as a rule or guideline against which the level of performance can be compared—is often termed a *performance standard*. In essence, a performance standard is an expectation of what will be done or accomplished. Performance measures that are used to determine whether or to what extent a performance standard is achieved are often called *performance indicators*. For example, a performance standard might call for a comprehensive community health assessment to be completed every three years. Performance indicators for this standard could take one of several forms. The administrator of the local public health agency could be asked whether this standard was met, or perhaps a review team might look for a completed assessment at the time of a site visit. The agency administrator's response (yes or no) and the actual document are both performance indicators in this example.

The definition of performance measurement acknowledges critical dimensions of performance, including capacities, processes, and outcomes. It is important to consider the meaning of these terms as they relate to performance measurement for public health organizations and systems.

- *Capacities* refer to the resources and relationships necessary to carry out the important processes of public health; this capacity to perform is made possible by the maintenance of the basic infrastructure of the public health system, as well as by specific program resources.
- *Processes* refer to what is done to, for, with, or by defined individuals or groups to identify and address community or population-wide health problems. The performance of key processes (e.g., monitoring health status, investigating health hazards, and building constituencies) leads to the development of other processes that can also be viewed as outputs. In public health practice, these outputs take the form of interventions (e.g., policies, programs, and services) intended to achieve outcomes that are important to the system. The formulation known as the essential public health services, which embodies these key processes and outputs, serves as the framework for public health prac-

tice: the identification and addressing of important health problems and the implementation of interventions intended to impact outcomes.

* *Outcomes* reflect the immediate and long-term changes (or lack of change) experienced by individuals and populations as a result of the processes. Measures of outcome reflect the magnitude and direction of the effect of processes on health status, risk reduction, social functioning, or consumer satisfaction outcomes.

The *Public Health in America* framework addresses both the general outcomes and the key processes of public health practice; the link between this document and performance measurement is presented in Exhibit 17-1.[11]

Performance measures provide information concerning the capacity to perform, process performance (including outputs), and ultimate results. Although useful by themselves, performance measures provide richer information when multiple dimensions are measured and related to each other. For example, relating capacities to outcomes (such as the cost-effectiveness or cost per case of disease prevented) is a common approach to assessing effectiveness. Similarly, measures relating capacities to processes (as in the cost per unit of service delivered) provide useful insights into efficiency. Ideally, measuring and relating measures for all of these dimensions provide the most useful information for improving performance.

Performance measurement and performance improvement initiatives proliferated in the public sector in the final decades of the 1900s fueled, in part, by the potential for improving the quality of public programs and services. Federal agencies have been subject to the Government Performance and Results Act since the mid-1990s; state and local governments have adopted a variety of accountability systems.[6,9] Performance measurement has gained widespread acceptance in the health sector, both public and private, as well. Accreditation programs based on principles of performance measurement are in place for a wide variety of healthcare organizations and settings, including community networks providing health services.

Paralleling these developments, specific interest in performance measurement within the public health system matured steadily during the 20th century, especially after the Institute of Medicine's (IOM's) 1988 report, *The Future of Public Health*.[12] This interest is advanced by aspirations of improving quality, enhancing accountability, and strengthening the science base of public health practice.[13-15] The evolution of this interest is a revealing story in its own right.

## Measuring Public Health Performance Through 1990

Over the past century, efforts to measure public health performance have ranged from simple accounting to more sophisticated strategies in which performance is judged against already established expectations or standards.[16] Much of the early activity focused on local public health practice, although the very earliest attempt targeted state health departments. In that 1914 effort, Charles Chapin completed a survey of state health agencies for the American Medical Association (AMA) in order to describe the services of those agencies and their role in fostering the development of local health departments, or local public health agencies (LPHAs). Chapin's report concluded that state public

**Exhibit 17-1** **Links Between** *Public Health in America* **Framework and Performance Measurement**

| *Public Health in America* Elements* | Usefulness for Performance Measurement Activities** |
|---|---|
| *Healthy People in Healthy Communities* Promote physical and mental health and prevent disease, injury, and disability. | Vision Statement Mission statement *Useful for formulating vision and mission statements* |
| Public health: • Prevents epidemics and the spread of disease • Protects against environmental hazards • Prevents injuries • Promotes and encourages healthy behaviors | Broad categories of outcomes affected by public health activities; sometimes viewed as what public health does |
| • Responds to disasters and assists communities in recovery • Ensures the quality and accessibility of health services | *Useful for developing performance measures for public health outcomes* |
| Essential public health services: 1. Monitor health status to identify community health problems. 2. Diagnose and investigate health problems and health hazards in the community. 3. Inform, educate, and empower people about health issues. | Processes of public health practice that affect public health outcomes; sometimes viewed as how public health does what it does |
| 4. Mobilize community partnerships to identify and solve health problems. 5. Develop policies and plans that support individual and community health efforts. 6. Enforce laws and regulations that protect health and ensure safety. 7. Link people with needed personal health services and ensure the provision of health care when it is otherwise unavailable. 8. Ensure a competent public health and personal healthcare work force. 9. Evaluate effectiveness, accessibility, and quality of personal and population-based health services. 10. Research for new insights and innovative solutions to health problems. | *Useful for developing performance measures for public health processes; these can be linked with capacity measures and with outcome measures for more comprehensive assessment of public health performance.* |

*Source:* Data from **authors and from *Public Health Functions Steering Committee. Public Health in America. Available at: www.health.gov/phfunctions. Accessed November 1, 2005.

health agencies were "mostly ill-balanced. Much of what is done counts little for health and much is left undone which would save many lives."[17(p96)] He proposed the use of relative values for various preventive services and rated the state agencies on each service and in the aggregate. This quantitative approach was later incorporated into local public health practice appraisal initiatives orchestrated by the American Public Health Association (APHA).

In 1921, the first report of APHA's Committee on Municipal Health Department Practice called for the collection of information on local public health practice to provide the basis for the development of standards of organization and achievement for LPHAs serving the nation's largest municipalities.[18,19] The committee concluded that "few standards are available to the health officers who would pattern their departments after those which predominate in American practice or achieve most satisfactory results."[18(p7)] A survey instrument was developed and applied to 83 cities through site visits involving various committee members, including public health giants Winslow (committee chairman), Chapin, and Frost.

The committee soon saw the need to examine local public health practice more broadly, and in 1925 the committee was reconstituted as APHA's Committee on Administrative Practice. The new committee developed an appraisal form to be used as a self-assessment tool by local health officers.[20] Both strengths and weaknesses of this initiative are apparent in its aspirations:

> The idea was to measure the immediate results attained—such as statistics properly obtained and analyzed, vaccinations performed, infants in attendance at instructive clinics, physical defects of school children discovered and corrected, tuberculosis cases hospitalized, laboratory tests performed—with the confidence that such immediate results would inevitably lead on to the ultimate end of all public health work, the conservation of human life and efficiency.[20(p1)]

Successive iterations of the appraisal form appeared throughout the 1920s and 1930s; these were well received by LPHAs, although there were occasional concerns that quantity was being emphasized over quality.[21] Using these forms, local health officers were able to compare their ratings with other agencies and submit their assessment to the Health Conservation Contest and its successor, the National Honor Roll. The basis for comparison was a numerical rating score based on aggregated points awarded across key administrative and service areas. Comparative ratings were to be used to improve health programs, advocate for resources, summarize health agency activities in annual reports, and engage other health interests in the community.[20] Agency ratings often attracted considerable media interest, resulting in both good and bad publicity for local agencies. Despite the initial intent to emphasize "immediate results," the major focus of the ratings remained on measuring public health capacity and the intervention or output aspects of public health processes.

In 1947, a new, and still voluntary, instrument, the evaluation schedule, which included capacity, process, and outcome measures and was scored centrally by the APHA Committee on Administrative Practice, replaced the appraisal form (Exhibit 17-2).[21,22] No longer was the focus on good or bad scores; results were presented for health agencies of varying size and type so that individual LPHAs could directly compare their performance in meeting community needs with that of their peers. The use of these tools lost momentum in

**Exhibit 17-2   Measures of Public Health Performance Used in the 1947 Evaluation Schedule**

1. Hospital beds: percentage in approved hospitals
2. Practicing physicians: population per physician
3. Practicing dentists: population per dentist
4. Water: percentage of population in communities over 2500 served with approved water
5. Sewerage: percentage of population in communities over 2500 served with approved sewerage systems
6. Water: percentage of rural school children served with approved water supplies
7. Excreta disposal: Percentage of rural school children served with approved means of excreta disposal
8. Food: percentage of food handlers reached by group instruction program
9. Food: percentage of restaurants and lunch counters with satisfactory facilities
10. Milk: percentage of bottled milk pasteurized
11. Diphtheria: percentage of children under two years given immunizing agent
12. Smallpox: percentage of children under two years given immunizing agent
13. Whooping cough: percentage of children under two years given immunizing agent
14. Tuberculosis: newly reported cases per death, 5-year period
15. Tuberculosis: deaths per 100,000 population, 5-year period
16. Tuberculosis: percentage of cases reported by death certificate
17. Syphilis: percentage of cases reported in primary, secondary, and early latent stage
18. Syphilis: percentage of reported contacts examined
19. Maternal: puerperal deaths per 1000 total births, 5-year rate
20. Maternal: percentage of antepartum cases under medical supervision seen before sixth month
21. Maternal: percentage of women delivered at home under postpartum nursing supervision
22. Maternal: percentage of births in hospital
23. Infant: deaths under 1 year of age per 1000 live births, 5-year rate
24. Infant: deaths from diarrhea and enteritis under 1 year per 1000 live births, 2-year rate
25. Infant: percentage of infants under nursing supervision before 1 month
26. School: percentage of elementary children with dental work neglected
27. Accidents: deaths from motor accidents per 100,000 population, 5-year rate
28. Health department budget: cents per capita spent by health department

*Source:* Reprinted with permission. American Public Health Association, Committee on Administrative Practice. *Evaluation Schedule for Use in the Study and Appraisal of Community Health Programs.* New York, NY: American Public Health Association; 1947:53–54.

the 1950s when APHA's interest in public health performance and its measurement diminished.[23]

Prior to 1990, there were several other efforts to assess public health performance across the entire national public health system. One focused primarily on capacity factors, such as the presence or absence of an LPHA in a jurisdiction and the full- or part-time availability of health officers.[24] The

Emerson report in 1945 advanced several national standards, including one calling for complete coverage of the population by full-time LPHAs (meaning those with full-time health officers).[25] Several other targets established in the Emerson report also provide interesting insights into the capacity of the national public health system at the time. For example, the committee concluded that the nation had 64% of the public health personnel and 63% of the financial resources needed to ensure full coverage of the population with six basic public health services (vital statistics, communicable disease control, environmental sanitation, public health laboratory services, maternal and child health services, and public health education).[25]

Another of these efforts provided extensive information on state health agencies. The Association of State and Territorial Health Officials (ASTHO) established a national public health reporting system, which functioned throughout much of the 1970s and 1980s. Although useful in terms of expenditures and programs for the official state health agencies, these reports had very little information on the public health activities of LPHAs. Information on state-level environmental protection, substance abuse, and mental health services was also incomplete if these services were the responsibility of agencies other than the official state health agency.

In retrospect, a major limitation of the public health performance measurement activities before 1990 was the lack of emphasis on the more fundamental processes of public health practice, such as building constituencies and assessing and prioritizing community health needs, and the inability to link measures of capacities, processes, and outcomes in order to understand their relationships. The lack of a conceptual framework that explicates these relationships was the root cause for this limitation. As a result, the basic assumption expressed in the appraisal form that "immediate results would inevitably lead on to the ultimate end of all public health work, the conservation of human life and efficiency" remained largely untested.[20(p1)]

The 1988 IOM report, which focused on the core functions of public health, was followed by a series of initiatives to facilitate the implementation of this framework. *Healthy People 2000* included, for the first time ever, a national health objective for coverage of the population by an effective local public health presence. *Healthy People 2000* objective 8.14 called for 90% of the population to be served by an LPHA that was effectively carrying out public health's core functions in that community.[26] Despite little consensus as to what was meant by "effectively" addressing the core functions of public health, it was clear that the performance of key public health processes in public health organizations and systems was the focus of this new objective. Subsequent efforts to rally around this national performance measure, however, suggest that the public health community had not learned the lessons of its performance measurement history.

## Measuring Public Health Performance after 1990

Much of what is known concerning current public health performance in the United States has been developed within the context of various initiatives established after the appearance of the IOM report. Unfortunately, many of these experiences remain unpublished, and few can be transported and replicated elsewhere. However, more than a dozen reports on various aspects of public health performance were published during the 1990s. Although these studies used somewhat different panels of performance measures, their contribution to public health performance measurement largely resides in their focus on performance measures for key processes related to the public health core functions and essential public health services (Exhibit 17-1).

Public health practice performance data focused on process performance (including outputs) were reported by the National Association of County and City Health Officials (NACCHO) in its 1990 and 1993 surveys of LPHAs.[27,28] For 48 questions associated with the three core functions from the 1990 NACCHO survey, mean LPHA performance was 50%. For 96 questions linked with the core functions in the 1993 NACCHO survey, mean performance was similar at 46%. Studies using practice measures based on the core functions reported performance scores of 57% performance for 14 LPHAs in 1992, 56% for 370 LPHAs in 1993, and 50% for 208 LPHAs in 1993.[29-33] When similar performance measures were used on a statewide basis in Iowa in 1995, the overall performance score was 61%.[34]

Based on a variety of field tests and performance studies completed in the early 1990s, a consensus set of 20 practice performance measures (Exhibit 17-3) was established by leading researchers in the field. Other investigators have also used these performance measures in published reports, and more than a dozen states have examined public health performance within their state–local public health system using these measures. These studies consistently demonstrate suboptimal performance of key public health practices and considerable variability in the performance of specific measures.

Using the 20 consensus measures with a random sample of 298 LPHAs stratified by population size and type of jurisdiction, an effort was made to assess the extent to which the US population in 1995 was being effectively served by the public health core functions identified in the IOM report (assessment, policy development, and assurance).[35] Performance for these 20 measures ranged from 23% to 94%. The most frequently performed measures were investigating adverse health events, maintaining necessary laboratory services, implementing mandated programs, maintaining a network of relationships, and providing information regularly to the public. The least frequently performed measures were assessing the use of preventive and screening services in the community, conducting behavioral risk factor surveys, regularly evaluating the effect of services on the community, allocating resources consistent with community action plans, and deploying resources to meet identified needs (Table 17-1). The overall weighted mean performance score for all 20 measures was 56%. Subscores for assessment, policy development, and assurance measures were similar to the overall mean. City- and county-based LPHA jurisdictions with populations greater than 50,000 performed these measures more frequently (65%) than other local public health jurisdictions in this study (Table 17-2).

Another study in 1998 using the same 20 measures found similar levels of performance (65%) in 356 jurisdictions with populations of 100,000 or more.[36] Although the performance of the more populous jurisdictions was somewhat higher than the combination of large and small jurisdictions included in the 1995 national study, both the relative rankings and the population size-specific scores were quite similar in these two studies.

Although the various studies conducted throughout the 1990s used somewhat different methods and measures, they consistently demonstrate practice

**Exhibit 17-3   Core Function-Related Measures of Local Public Health Practice Effectiveness Developed Collaboratively by University of North Carolina and University of Illinois-Chicago Investigators: 1995**

Assessment

1. For the jurisdiction served by your local public health agency, is there a community health needs assessment process that systematically describes the prevailing health status and needs of the community?

2. In the past three years in your jurisdiction, has the local public health agency surveyed the population for behavioral risk factors?

3. For the jurisdiction served by your local public health agency, are timely investigations of adverse health events, including communicable disease outbreaks and environmental health hazards, conducted on an ongoing basis?

4. Are the necessary laboratory services available to the local public health agency to support investigations of adverse health events and meet routine diagnostic and surveillance needs?

5. For the jurisdiction served by your local public health agency, has an analysis been completed of the determinants and contributing factors of priority health needs, adequacy of existing health resources, and the population groups most impacted?

6. In the past three years in your jurisdiction, has the local public health agency conducted an analysis of age-specific participation in preventive and screening services?

Policy Department

7. For the jurisdiction served by your local public health agency, is there a network of support and communication relationships, which includes health-related organizations, the media, and the general public?

8. In the past year in your jurisdiction, has there been a formal attempt by the local public health agency at informing elected officials about the potential public health impact of actions under their consideration?

9. For the jurisdiction served by your local public health agency, has there been a prioritization of the community health needs that have been identified from a community needs assessment?

10. In the past three years in your jurisdiction, has the local public health agency implemented community health initiatives consistent with established priorities?

11. For the jurisdiction served by your local public agency, has a community health action plan been developed with community participation to address community health needs?

12. During the past three years in your jurisdiction, has the local public health agency developed plans to allocate resources in a manner consistent with the community health action plan?

Assurance

13. For the jurisdiction served by your local public health agency, have resources been deployed, as necessary, to address the priority health needs identified in the community health needs assessment?

14. In the past three years in your jurisdiction, has the local public health agency conducted an organizational self-assessment?

15. For the jurisdiction served by your local public health agency, are age-specific priority health needs effectively addressed through the provision of/or linkage to appropriate services?

*(continues)*

**Exhibit 17-3    (continued)**

16. In the past three years in your jurisdiction, has there been an instance in which the local public health agency has failed to implement a mandated program or service?

17. For the jurisdiction served by your local public health agency, have there been regular evaluations of the effect that public health services have on community health status?

18. In the past three years in your jurisdiction, has the local public health agency used professionally recognized process and outcome measures to monitor programs and to redirect resources as appropriate?

19. For the jurisdiction served by your local public health agency, is the public regularly provided with information about current health status, healthcare needs, positive health behaviors, and healthcare policy issues?

20. In the past year in your jurisdiction, has the local public health agency provided reports to the media on a regular basis?

*Source:* Reprinted with permission. Turnock BJ, Handler AS, Miller CA. Core function-related local public health practice effectiveness. *J Public Health Manage Pract.* 1998;4(5):28.

(process and outputs) performance in the 50–70% range and paint a picture of less than optimal functioning of the public health system nationally and in many states. Notably, this range is consistent with conclusions of the Emerson report 50 years earlier as to effective public health coverage of the nation based on an assessment of capacity factors. Although the precise status is not known, it is clear that the United States fell well short of its *Healthy People 2000* target of having 90% of the population residing in jurisdictions in which public health's core functions are being effectively addressed. Two studies of practice performance conducted nationally in the 1990s concluded that only approximately one third of the US population in the 1990s was effectively served.[33,35]

These efforts to measure core function performance have served several important purposes. By providing information on both key processes and outputs of public health practice, many state and local systems have initiated public health practice improvement strategies. These efforts also provide the opportunity for measures of public health practice performance to be linked with measures of capacity and outcomes, furthering understanding of the relationships between and among these key dimensions of the public health system.

The relationship between capacity and process performance (including outputs) has been examined in two studies. One study linked practice performance measures from a 1993 national survey with NACCHO profile information for 264 LPHAs.[33,37] Capacity factors linked to higher levels of practice performance included full-time agency head, larger annual expenditures, greater number of total and part-time staff, budgets derived from multiple funding sources, private health insurance as a significant budget component, and female agency heads.

A 1998 study of LPHAs in the most populous jurisdictions identified several capacity factors associated with higher levels of practice performance.[36]

**TABLE 17-1    Percentage of Local Health Jurisdictions (LHJs) Performing 20 Core Function-Related Measures of Local Public Health Practice: 1995 and 1998**

| Core Function-Related Performance Measures | LJHs National Sample, 1995 $n = 298$ | LHJs > 100,000 population, 1998 $n = 356$ |
|---|---|---|
| 1. Community needs assessment process | 53.0 | 71.5 |
| 2. Behavioral risk factor surveys | 29.2 | 45.8 |
| 3. Timely investigations of adverse health events | 93.6 | 98.6 |
| 4. Necessary laboratory services available | 89.3 | 96.3 |
| 5. Analysis of determinants, resources, and populations | 45.0 | 61.3 |
| 6. Analysis of preventive and screening services | 22.8 | 28.4 |
| 7. Network of relationships | 82.6 | 78.8 |
| 8. Inform elected officials | 73.2 | 80.9 |
| 9. Prioritization of community health needs | 52.7 | 66.1 |
| 10. Implemented community health initiatives | 68.8 | 81.9 |
| 11. Community health action plan | 39.6 | 41.5 |
| 12. Plans for resource allocation | 36.6 | 26.2 |
| 13. Resources deployed to meet needs | 37.3 | 48.6 |
| 14. Organizational self-assessment | 50.3 | 56.3 |
| 15. Provision/linkage of services for priority needs | 64.1 | 75.6 |
| 16. Implemented all mandated programs | 82.9 | 91.4 |
| 17. Evaluations of effect of services in the community | 30.5 | 34.7 |
| 18. Programs monitored and resources redirected | 42.3 | 47.3 |
| 19. Public provided information regularly | 78.8 | 75.4 |
| 20. Provide reports to media regularly | 68.5 | 75.2 |
| Average: Assessment measures (#1–6) | 54.9 | 66.7 |
| Average: Policy development measures (#7–12) | 58.2 | 60.2 |
| Average: Assurance measures (#13–20) | 55.4 | 64.4 |
| Average: All activities | 56.1 | 63.8 |

*Source:* Reprinted with permission. Turnock BJ, Handler AS, Miller, CA. Core function-related local public health practice effectiveness. *J Public Health Manage Pract.* 1998;4(5):29.

These were population size, presence of a local board of health, existence of mixed or shared arrangements with a state health agency, and participation in public health activities by managed care plans and universities. This study also documented the substantial contribution (one third of the total effort) to practice performance made by parties other than the governmental health agency in these jurisdictions. The most important contributors to process performance were state agencies, hospitals, local governmental agencies, nonprofit organizations, physicians and medical groups, universities, federally funded community health centers, managed care plans, and federal agencies.

The link between key processes and programs and services (outputs) offered by LPHAs has also been examined. One study linked higher levels of performance of key processes with a greater percentage of services directly provided, as well as with the following specific services: personal preventive and treatment, maternal and child health, chronic disease personal prevention, health education, injury control, dental health, case management

**TABLE 17-2   Mean Performance Score for Local Health Jurisdictions by Population Size and Jurisdiction Type: 1995 ($n = 298$)**

| Local Health Jurisdiction Strata (by Population Size and Jurisdiction Type) | Mean Performance Score (%) |
|---|---|
| City 50,000 ($n = 12$) | 47.9 |
| City > 50,000 ($n = 10$) | 77.0 |
| County 50,000 ($n = 80$) | 56.4 |
| County > 50,000 ($n = 43$) | 66.9 |
| City–County 50,000 ($n = 34$) | 57.1 |
| City–County > 50,000 ($n = 24$) | 59.2 |
| Multicounty 50,000 ($n = 6$) | 60.8 |
| Multicounty > 50,000 ($n = 7$) | 60.7 |
| All other LHDs (all population sizes) ($n = 26$) | 36.9 |
| Jurisdiction unknown ($n = 56$) | 54.8 |
| Weighted sample total | 56.1 |

*Source:* Reprinted with permission. Turnock BJ, Handler AS, Miller CA. Core function-related local public health practice effectiveness. *J Public Health Manage Pract.* 1998;4(5):30.

services, and human immunodeficiency virus (HIV)/acquired immune deficiency syndrome (AIDS) testing.[37] In another study, only the provision of behavioral health services was linked with higher levels of performance of key public health processes.[36]

## Lessons from 20th-Century Efforts

During the 85-year period from 1914 to 1999, an increasing body of information was assembled on various aspects of public health system performance, its capacity (LPHAs, expenditures, health officers, boards of health, state-local relationship, size and type of jurisdiction, agency staff, professional disciplines of staff, organizational structure, etc.), its processes (including key processes and outputs), and its outcomes. However, meaningful comparisons between the findings of the Committee on Administrative Practice's evaluations in the mid-1940s and those from the 1990s are not possible because of differences in approaches, methods, and measures. The earlier studies largely examined capacity, outputs (services), and outcomes, whereas later efforts focused on the essential public health services and emphasized key processes and outputs. These different approaches are evident in Exhibits 17-2 and 17-3, which provide key measures from the evaluation schedule and the 20 public health practice consensus measures described earlier.

Several lessons are apparent. The first is that measurement for the sake of measurement has never been the purpose of these activities. The intent has consistently been to gather information that would be useful for the improvement of local public health practice. However, the early instruments—including the appraisal form and evaluation schedule—placed considerable emphasis on the performance of specific services (outputs) rather than on more basic public health processes, such as community assessment or constituency-building. None of these efforts has comprehensively examined the links between capacity, processes, and outcomes and their relationship to an effective governmental presence. Through more than eight decades of efforts, it has been easier to measure specific aspects of the public health system than to develop consensus as to what these measurements tell us about overall public health performance.

Although the efforts throughout the 1900s included outcome measures, most failed to link capacity and process measures to these health outcomes. Prior to 1990, there was no real effort to do so. After 1990, only one study attempted to relate LPHA practice performance levels to some general community health status indicators.[38] No clear links were found, in part because the study did not focus on health outcomes that were targeted by community needs assessments. It is now possible to perform such an examination in environments where practice performance has been tracked over time and where community needs assessments have led to interventions for high-priority community health problems. Various levels of practice performance can now be related to changes in key outcome measures in order to identify the effectiveness of the various practices. As suggested by the framework depicted in Figure 17-2, performance measurement in the public health system can now begin to measure capacities, processes, and outcomes in ways that allow for changes in one to be linked with changes in others.

## Applications Using Public Health Standards

Public health performance standards, when used prior to 1990, primarily related to capacities and the output aspects of public health practice rather than the key processes necessary to carry out the public health core functions characterized in the IOM report. Standards, or performance expectations, for public health practice developed after 1990 focused on both key processes and outputs and proved useful in a variety of applications, including agency self-assessment for capacity building, measures of performance in state and local public health systems, and state and national surveillance regarding

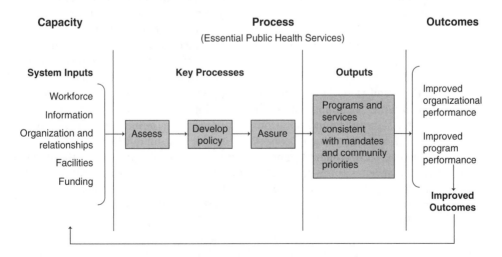

**FIGURE 17-2    Framework for Measuring Public Health System Performance**

*Healthy People 2000* objective 8.14. Still, these standards remain in an early stage of development, with poorly developed links to outcome standards established in national health objectives for the years 1990, 2000, and 2010.

The 1990s witnessed many public health organizations conducting organizational self-assessments, identifying strengths and weaknesses, and channeling this information into organizational capacity-building plans. The panel of performance expectations for local public health practice in the Assessment Protocol for Excellence in Public Health (APEXPH) served as an early blueprint for many public health agencies seeking to focus and strengthen their roles in their communities.[39] APEXPH adoption and implementation experience has been substantial, although not universal. Where APEXPH has been implemented widely, public health practice performance has been found to be substantially higher than where it is less frequently used. Evidence from the most extensive implementation of an APEXPH derivative on a statewide basis showed actual performance nearly doubling in Illinois over a 2-year time frame.[40] However, APEXPH lacked a strategic planning component and a focus on community public health systems.

Although the 1990s saw only modest progress toward the establishment of a framework for continuous quality improvement in public health, the beginnings of a new focus on performance began to take shape. The overall lack of uniformity and consistency among various state and local efforts reflects the different needs, values, and circumstances of the relatively autonomous state and local public health networks across the United States. This diversity and the lack of consistency in public health efforts across the nation were significant factors in the US Centers for Disease Control and Prevention's (CDC) Public Health Practice Program Office shift to promote the development of innovative new public health products for state and local public health agencies and systems interested in improving their effectiveness through systems collaborations. These applications include: (1) Mobilizing for Action through Planning and Partnerships (MAPP), a new strategic approach to community health improvement; (2) performance standards for use in state and local systems; and (3) exploring the feasibility of accreditation of public health organizations.[41] By the late 1990s, this evolving interest in performance measurement, quality improvement, and strategic effectiveness spawned several new tools and resources for the examination of public health practice.[42]

In 1997 increased interest in performance measurement and improvement in public health resulted in expanded community-driven and state-level collaborations focused on improving public health practice. Notable examples of this trend were the local and state partnerships initiated under the innovative program, Turning Point: Collaborating for a New Century in Public Health. Turning Point was prompted in part by the enhanced community health improvement process outlined by the IOM in its 1997 report on performance monitoring to improve community health, promoting the use of performance measures and performance monitoring to link accountable partners to community improvement efforts.[13] The National Turning Point Program funded 21 states and 41 local public health jurisdictions to develop multisectoral partnerships to strengthen and transform the public health mission and practice of public health through the collective effort of systems partners. Funded by the Robert Wood Johnson Foundation and the W.K. Kellogg Foundation, Turning Point emerged from the concern of the foundations about the capacity of the public health system to respond to the challenges of the new century. Core strategies employed by Turning Point grantees were innovative collaborations for the public's health, increased capacity for effective policy development, and alternative structures for improving community health. Underlying the widespread work of state and local public health jurisdictions in Turning Point projects was the recognition that governmental public health alone will not be able to achieve important public health goals in the 21st century.[43]

Another prime example of the turn of the century trend toward strategic effectiveness was the evolution of APEXPH into MAPP, with its increased emphasis on local public health systems rather than on community public health agencies.[44] MAPP, launched in 2001, is a community-wide strategic planning tool promoting broader community health improvement efforts that link public and private community partners to specific performance expectations in addressing priority health needs in the community.[45] Emphasizing the values of strategic planning, systems thinking, and community empowerment, MAPP is a structured but flexible process that at its best will produce collective action at the community level to improve health.

The MAPP process represents an important transition from more traditional or categorical health planning approaches to a model that is grounded in strategic planning concepts. The complex challenges facing public health need a strategic decision-making framework that includes several different analytic phases. The MAPP model supports the identification of strategic community health issues by the findings of four assessments: the community health status assessment, a forces of change (an environmental scan) assessment, a community themes and strengths assessment, and a local public health systems assessment. The assessment of the local public health system grounds MAPP in systems development to stimulate systems changes that link to needed improvements in community health. This is accomplished by integrating the application of the Local Public Health Systems Performance Standards into the community assessment process, a major step forward in the examination and ultimate improvement of public health infrastructure and capacity.[46] (Refer to Chapter 15 for more discussion of MAPP and assessment.)

The National Public Health Performance Standards (NPHPS) program is a CDC-led partnership of national public health organizations (NACCHO, ASTHO, the National Association of Local Boards of Health–NALBOH, the Public Health Foundation, the American Public Health Association, and the National Network of Public Health Institutes) to improve public health systems through the development and application of local and state-based performance standards. Launched in 2002, the NPHPS comprises three performance self-assessment instruments, one for state public health systems, one for local public health systems, and one for local governing bodies. The state and local performance standards are designed for voluntary use by multisectoral systems partners in state and local public health jurisdictions to assess systems strengths and weaknesses as part of a performance improvement process. The NPHPS have undergone validity studies and have been found to have face and content validity as a basis for measuring public health system performance.[47-50]

The NPHPS are framed as optimal standards within the "Ten Essential Public Health Services," and as such constitute a unique resource to examine public health system expectations and measure current performance.[51] Exhibit 17-4 provides examples of performance standards and measures for local and state public health systems used in NPHPS assessments. The local NPHPS instrument examines 32 local model standards for local public health systems, focusing on specific types of activities that should be conducted in all local jurisdictions to carry out each essential service. The state NPHPS instrument establishes 40 state model standards, with performance measures for key state level functions within each essential service; these four key state functions are planning and implementation, technical assistance and support, evaluation and quality improvement, and resources. The governance NPHPS instrument examines one governance model standard for each essential service, examining the oversight functions of boards of health in assuring appropriate legal authority, resources, policy base, community collaboration, and accountability for local public health.[52]

The NPHPS program is a national leadership effort to improve system-wide performance. NPHPS use by state and local public health jurisdictions and local governing bodies has undergirded a noncategorical approach to the examination and management of public health performance. Focused on capacity and processes, the NPHPS enable user jurisdictions to examine key infrastructure elements of their system, identify strengths and weaknesses in their performance and capacity, establish priorities and, through an improvement process, agree on future action.[41] A variety of salutary effects have been cited by the NPHPS program as potential benefits of a nationwide public health performance standards initiative. These include quality improvement in the user jurisdiction; improved accountability; enhanced capacity building for community, state, and national public health systems; widespread use of best practices; and an improved science base for public health practice.[53]

Although the National Public Health Performance Standards represent real progress in establishing optimal expectations of the performance and capacity of public health systems, their widespread use has been slow to develop. Issues related to incorporating these innovations into practice are:

- The voluntary nature of the use of the NPHPS has slowed their adoption. Without financial or regulatory incentives, state and local public health agencies, the natural leaders of these systems-oriented processes, have tended not to consider the use of the NPHPS as an urgent or compelling need.
- Although users of the NPHPS report good results in systems development and strategic planning, achieving those results has been a time-intensive process requiring collaborative leadership skills. Since the launch of the NPHPS, the time and resources of many public health leaders have been devoted to preparedness activities and not overall organization or systemswide performance assessment and improvement.
- Although the NPHPS is incorporated into the MAPP process as the local public health systems assessment, MAPP is not in widespread local use. State NPHPS users have also struggled to develop strategic planning processes as vehicles for using NPHPS results. The lack of strategic planning capacity in public health agencies has been a barrier to effective quality improvement activities.

Exhibit 17-4    Excerpts from the National Public Health Performance Standards

### Essential Public Health Service 3
### Inform, Educate, and Empower People about Health Issues
Local Public Health System (LPHS) Model Performance Standards

**Indicator 3.1: Health Education**
Public health education is the process by which the LPHS conveys information and facilitates the development of health-enhancing skills among individuals and groups in the community. Factual information is provided for informed decision making on issues affecting individual and community health. A broad-based group of entities are involved in public health education, including the local governmental public health agency, healthcare providers, hospitals, and community-based organizations. Education services are provided to assist individuals and groups in the community to voluntarily act on their decisions, establish healthy behaviors, and use knowledge to change social conditions affecting health. Public health education serves to reinforce health promotion messages within the community, ultimately helping to reduce health risk and improve health status.

To provide effective public health education, the LPHS:

- Provides the general public and policy leaders with information on health risk, health status, and health needs in the community as well as information on policies and programs that can improve community health
- Uses appropriate media (print, radio, television, and Internet) to communicate health information to the community at large
- Provides health information to enable individuals and groups, including vulnerable populations and those at increased risk, to make informed decisions about healthy living and lifestyle choices, and sponsors educational programs to develop knowledge, skills, and behavior needed to improve individual and community health
- Evaluates the appropriateness, quality, and effectiveness of public health education activities at least every two years

State Public Health System (SPHS) Model Performance Standards

**Indicator 3.4: Resources**
The SPHS effectively invests, manages, and utilizes its human, information, technology, and financial resources to inform, educate, and empower people about health issues.

To accomplish this, the SPHS:

- Allocates existing resources for informing, educating, and empowering people about health issues to areas of highest need and plans for the development of new resources
- Collaborates with partners to leverage systemwide resources and focus statewide assets on health communication and health education and promotion services
- Provides resources necessary to plan, develop, implement, and evaluate health communication, education, and promotion interventions
- Utilizes the workforce expertise, equipment, and facilities needed for effective health communication services
- Utilizes the resources in workforce expertise, equipment, and facilities needed for effective health education and promotion services

*Source:* Centers for Disease Control and Prevention. National Public Health Performance Standards.

- Despite its importance to achieving public health results, developing multisectoral partnerships at the state and local levels is very hard work. Turning Point projects demonstrated many excellent systems changes, but the state and local collaborative projects have faced numerous sustainability challenges.[54]

There have been few attempts to use performance standards and measures to examine the national public health system on a nationwide basis.[33,35,36] After a decade, there was little attention paid to whether the nation achieved its *Healthy People 2000* national health objective for 90% of the population to be effectively served by a LPHA carrying out the core functions of public health. As a result, the potential for a nationwide performance measurement system to serve as a stimulus for reengineering and systemwide improvement remains yet unrealized. Without national leadership, states have struggled with how best to measure and improve public health practice in the widely varying state and local systems that make up the national public health system. This specific national objective related to effective LPHAs was dropped in the next iteration of national health objectives.

An extensive panel of national health objectives for public health infrastructure was, however, included in *Healthy People 2010* (Exhibit 17-5).[55] Although several of these national 2010 objectives are likely to be withdrawn in the midcourse review, the national health objectives for use of the performance standards and the conduct of performance improvement planning will remain as targets for nationwide public health action and for use in state and community improvement planning.[56] Given this lack of support, critical measures of infrastructure capacity and service availability by effective LPHAs are likely to remain overlooked at the national level and will require advocacy to appear in future documents such as *Healthy People 2020*.

On a more positive note, there have been ongoing efforts at the state and local levels to measure, assess, and improve performance. For example, a 1997 study found that nearly 90% of the states reported some level of involvement in local public health performance assessment, although only one half had an active and ongoing process.[57] Frameworks based on the core functions or essential public health services were used as the basis for these assessments in 22 states. However, few states use these assessments to allocate state funds across program areas and local jurisdictions, inform budget appropriation decisions made by the state legislature, or evaluate public health programs.[57] The 1997 study also found that some states are using various combinations of capacity and process (including outputs) standards as a way to improve performance.

In 2001 the Turning Point Performance Management National Excellence Collaborative (PMC) studied performance management practices in state public health agencies. The PMC found that nearly every reporting state public health agency (n = 46) has some form of performance management process in place and over three quarters of states reported that their performance management efforts have resulted in improved performance. State public health agencies in 2001 most frequently measured, reported, and used performance data related to health status, not focusing on other organizational or systems performance measures. In addition, few state agencies reported having a process to conduct quality improvement or to carry out changes based on performance data for the state public health agency or local public health agencies.[2]

**Exhibit 17-5** *Healthy People 2010* Objectives: Public Health Infrastructure

---

### Chapter 23 Public Health Infrastructure

**Data and Information Systems**

23-1.   (Developmental) Increase the proportion of tribal, state, and local public health agencies that provide Internet and e-mail access for at least 75% of their employees and that teach employees to use the Internet and other electronic information systems to apply data and information to public health practice.

23-2.   (Developmental) Increase the proportion of federal, tribal, state, and local health agencies that have made information available to the public in the past year on the leading health indicators, health status indicators, and priority data needs.

23-3.   Increase the proportion of all major national, state, and local health data systems that use geocoding to promote nationwide use of geographic information systems (GIS) at all levels.

23-4.   Increase the proportion of population-based *Healthy People 2010* objectives for which national data are available for all population groups identified for the objective.

23-5.   (Developmental) Increase the proportion of leading health indicators, health status indicators, and priority data needs for which data—especially for select populations—are available at the tribal, state, and local levels.

23-6.   Increase the proportion of *Healthy People 2010* objectives that are tracked regularly at the national level.

23-7.   Increase the proportion of *Healthy People 2010* objectives for which national data are released within 1 year of the end of data collection.

**Workforce**

23-8.   (Developmental) Increase the proportion of federal, tribal, state, and local agencies that incorporate specific competencies in the essential public health services into personnel systems.

23-9.   (Developmental) Increase the proportion of schools for public health workers that integrate into their curricula specific content to develop competency in the essential public health services.

23-10.   (Developmental) Increase the proportion of federal, tribal, state, and local public health agencies that provide continuing education to develop competency in essential public health services for their employees.

**Public Health Organizations**

23-11.   (Developmental) Increase the proportion of state and local public health agencies that meet national performance standards for essential public health services.

23-12.   Increase the proportion of tribes, states, and the District of Columbia that have a health improvement plan and increase the proportion of local jurisdictions that have a health improvement plan linked with their state plan.

23-13.   (Developmental) Increase the proportion of tribal, state, and local health agencies that provide or assure comprehensive laboratory services to support essential public health services.

*(continues)*

**Exhibit 17-5    (continued)**

23-14.    (Developmental) Increase the proportion of tribal, state, and local public health agencies that provide or assure comprehensive epidemiology services to support essential public health services.

23-15.    (Developmental) Increase the proportion of federal, tribal, state, and local jurisdictions that review and evaluate the extent to which their statutes, ordinances, and bylaws assure the delivery of essential public health services.

**Resources**

23-16.    (Developmental) Increase the proportion of federal, tribal, state, and local public health agencies that gather accurate data on public health expenditures, categorized by essential public health service.

23-17.    (Developmental) Increase the proportion of federal, tribal, state, and local public health agencies that conduct or collaborate on population-based prevention research.

*Source: Healthy People 2010.*

## Critical Issues for Success

Several major issues challenge efforts to improve performance within the public health system through a national public health performance standards initiative. Resolution of these issues will require consensus on the purpose or purposes of the effort, the definition and components of quality, and the ability to effect widespread change. Another major consideration in terms of improving quality is whether performance measurement will be limited or widespread. If limited implementation of quality improvement and performance management tools leads to only scattered local data or piecemeal state and national information, there will be only minimal opportunities to improve quality. It is important to consider mechanisms and incentives for performance standards to be widely used. This may require expanded system-building efforts at the state and local level involving greater use of mandates, such as in statutes and rules. Other incentives, such as grants in aid and direct financial support, or the establishment of professional standards of practice and accreditation initiatives, may also be necessary. Without these kinds of system incentives, goodwill alone may not be enough to improve overall quality in the public health enterprise.

A useful definition of *performance improvement* is positive change in the capacity, process, and outcomes of public health organizations and public health systems (public, private, and voluntary organizations that collectively contribute to the health of the public). This definition utilizes the concepts established early in this chapter to provide a balanced framework of the basic elements of change in public health. The elements of structural capacity, processes, and outcomes were outlined in 2001 as essential components of examining the work of public health systems.[58] These concepts have been used in the NACCHO's efforts to develop its Operational Definition of a Local Public Health Agency (Exhibit 17-6).[59] This landmark project to develop an operational definition of local public health departments describes specific functions of county, municipal, and other local governmental public health agencies and reflects shared opinions about how local public health departments serve their communities. (See Chapter 3.)

Additional work to define reasonable performance expectations for governmental public health agencies is occurring in states. Extensive use of standards, performance measures, and performance improvement processes has been done in Washington, Illinois, Missouri, North Carolina, Michigan, Florida, New Jersey, Ohio, and other states. Using the growing record of experience in these states has stimulated nationwide interest in accreditation of state and local public health agencies as a vehicle to improve public health performance.

## Accreditation of Public Health Organizations

Interest in strategies to accredit public health organizations is long standing and has arisen from several sources.[16] The 2003 IOM *The Future of the Public's Health in the 21st Century* calls for careful study of the feasibility of creating a national voluntary public health agency accreditation system.[60] This recommendation stems from the fact that public health organizations (with the notable exception of academic programs leading to graduate degrees in public health) remain one of the few health-related entities that are not subject to national standards and review from an external accrediting body. In fact, credentialing of both individuals and organizations has become such an accepted means of fostering quality improvement and accountability throughout the health sector that its absence from the public health system is noteworthy. Indeed, this fact has not escaped the notice of policy makers and funders.

Accreditation of educational and healthcare organizations generally involves several steps. Initially, major stakeholders develop an independent entity that establishes the standards and review process to be applied. For example, the Joint Commission on Accreditation of Healthcare Organizations (JCAHO) developed through the efforts of organized medicine and the hospital industry. Institutions of higher learning saw accreditation as a means to facilitate transferring credits earned at one institution to be used toward a degree at another. The Council on Education in Public Health (CEPH) now operates as collaboration between the American Public Health Association (APHA) and the Association of Schools of Public Health. Accreditation of public health organizations would almost certainly require the participation of the ASTHO and the NACCHO, as well as perhaps the NALBOH, the APHA, and possibly other national public health organizations as major stakeholders in the process.

In fact, just such an effort is now underway regarding public health accreditation. Following the recommendation of the IOM report, and the well-traveled pathway of successful predecessors like JCAHO, the CDC and the Robert Wood Johnson Foundation (RWJF) have joined forces to fund an exploration of public health agency accreditation. They convened a national

**Exhibit 17-6  Local Health Department Standards (An Operation Definition of a Functional Local Health Department [LHD]) NACCHO, November 2005**

1. Monitor health status and understand health issues facing the community.
   a. Obtain and maintain data that provide information on the community's health (e.g., provider immunization rates; hospital discharge data; environmental health hazard, risk, and exposure data; community-specific data; number of uninsured and indicators of health disparities, such as high levels of poverty, lack of affordable housing, limited or no access to transportation, etc.).
   b. Develop relationships with local providers and others in the community who have information on reportable diseases and other conditions of public health interest and facilitate information exchange.
   c. Conduct or contribute expertise to periodic community health assessments.
   d. Integrate data with health assessment and data collection efforts conducted by others in the public health system.
   e. Analyze data to identify trends, health problems, environmental health hazards, and social and economic conditions that adversely affect the public's health.

2. Protect people from health problems and health hazards.
   a. Investigate health problems and environmental health hazards.
   b. Prevent, minimize, and contain adverse health events and conditions resulting from communicable diseases; food-, water-, and vector-borne outbreaks; chronic diseases; environmental hazards; injuries; and health disparities.
   c. Coordinate with other governmental agencies that investigate and respond to health problems, health disparities, or environmental health hazards.
   d. Lead public health emergency planning, exercise, and response activities in the community in accordance with the National Incident Management System, and coordinate with other local, state, and federal agencies.
   e. Fully participate in planning, exercises, and response activities for other emergencies in the community that have public health implications, within the context of state and regional plans and in a manner consistent with the community's best public health interest.
   f. Maintain access to laboratory and biostatistical expertise and capacity to help monitor community health status and diagnose and investigate public health problems and hazards.
   g. Maintain policies and technology required for urgent communications and electronic data exchange.

3. Give people information they need to make healthy choices.
   a. Develop relationships with media to convey information of public health significance, correct misinformation about public health issues, and serve as an essential resource.
   b. Exchange information and data with individuals, community groups, other agencies, and the general public about physical, behavioral, environmental, social, economic, and other issues affecting the public's health.
   c. Provide targeted, culturally appropriate information to help individuals understand what decisions they can make to be healthy.
   d. Provide health promotion programs to address identified health problems.

4. Engage the community to identify and solve health problems.
   a. Engage the local public health system in an ongoing, strategic, community-driven, comprehensive planning process to identify, prioritize, and solve

public health problems; establish public health goals; and evaluate success in meeting the goals.

b. Promote the community's understanding of, and advocacy for, policies and activities that will improve the public's health.

c. Support, implement, and evaluate strategies that address public health goals in partnership with public and private organizations.

d. Develop partnerships to generate interest in and support for improved community health status, including new and emerging public health issues.

e. Inform the community, governing bodies, and elected officials about governmental public health services that are being provided, improvements being made in those services, and priority health issues not yet being adequately addressed.

5. **Develop public health policies and plans.**

a. Serve as a primary resource to governing bodies and policy makers to establish and maintain public health policies, practices, and capacity based on current science and best practices.

b. Advocate for policies that lessen health disparities and improve physical, behavioral, environmental, social, and economic conditions in the community that affect the public's health.

c. Engage in LHD strategic planning to develop a vision, mission, and guiding principles that reflect the community's public health needs, and to prioritize services and programs.

6. **Enforce public health laws and regulations.**

a. Review existing laws and regulations on a regular basis and work with governing bodies and policy makers to update them as needed.

b. Understand existing laws, ordinances, and regulations that protect the public's health.

c. Educate individuals and organizations of the meaning, purpose, and benefit of public health laws, regulations, and ordinances and how to comply.

d. Monitor, and analyze over time, the compliance of regulated organizations, entities, and individuals.

e. Conduct enforcement activities.

f. Coordinate notification of violations among other governmental agencies that enforce laws and regulations that protect the public's health.

7. **Help people receive health services.**

a. Engage the community to identify gaps in culturally competent, appropriate, and equitable personal health services, including preventive and health promotion services, and develop strategies to close the gaps.

b. Support and implement strategies to increase access to care and establish systems of personal health services, including preventive and health promotion services, in partnership with the community.

c. Link individuals to available, accessible personal healthcare providers (i.e., a medical home).

8. **Maintain a competent public health workforce.**

a. Recruit, train, develop, and retain a diverse staff.

b. Evaluate LHD staff members' public health competencies,* and address deficiencies through continuing education, training, and leadership development activities.

---

*As defined by the Core Public Health Competencies developed by the Council on Linkages between Academia and Public Health Practice.

*(continues)*

**Exhibit 17-6    (continued)**

---

   c. Provide practice- and competency-based educational experiences for the
      future public health workforce, and provide expertise in developing and
      teaching public health curricula through partnerships with academia.
   d. Promote the use of effective public health practices among other prac-
      titioners and agencies engaged in public health interventions.
   e. Provide the public health workforce with adequate resources to do their
      jobs.
 9. **Evaluate and improve programs and interventions.**
   a. Develop evaluation efforts to assess health outcomes to the extent possible.
   b. Apply evidence-based criteria to evaluation activities where possible.
   c. Evaluate the effectiveness and quality of all LHD programs and activities
      and use the information to improve LHD performance and community
      health outcomes.
   d. Review the effectiveness of public health interventions provided by other
      practitioners and agencies for prevention, containment, and/or remediation
      of problems affecting the public's health, and provide expertise to those in-
      terventions that need improvement.
10. **Contribute to and apply the evidence base of public health.**
   a. When researchers approach the LHD to engage in research activities that
      benefit the health of the community:
      i. Identify appropriate populations, geographic areas, and partners.
     ii. Work with them to actively involve the community in all phases of
         research.
    iii. Provide data and expertise to support research.
     iv. Facilitate their efforts to share research findings with the community,
         governing bodies, and policy makers.
   b. Share results of research, program evaluations, and best practices with
      other public health practitioners and academics.
   c. Apply evidence-based programs and best practices where possible.

*Source:* Local Health Department Standards. National Association of County and City
Health Officials (NAACHO).

---

gathering of key public health organizational stakeholders in December 2004
to gather input and consider whether a voluntary accreditation process was
indeed feasible given the current environment. Consensus was achieved on
the merit of further study. As a result, the CDC and the RWJF agreed to fund
a joint ASTHO/NACCHO-staffed study of accreditation for public health
agencies. The Exploring Accreditation Project (EAP) is a yearlong endeavor,
with its planning committee led by APHA and NALBOH as well as NACCHO
and ASTHO. Guidance for the EAP activities emanated from the steering committee that comprised key public health organizations. The following workgroups were formed to grapple with critical issues:

  • Governance and Implementation will consider governance options for
    a voluntary national accreditation system, its possible structure, and
    points of entry.

- Standards Development is tasked with identifying principles to guide state and local health department standards and to contemplate their relationship with existing standards, such as the NPHPS.
- Financing and Incentives shall construct funding models for a national system while building in incentives for participation.
- Research and Evaluation is assigned the responsibility of establishing a research and evaluation agenda that will sustain and inform the process.

In general, across most fields of endeavor, accreditation activities commence with a self-study or self-assessment by the entity seeking to be accredited. The self-assessment document is submitted to the accrediting body and examined by staff and experts who then perform a site visit of the applicant in order to verify compliance with the standards. Decisions as to full or conditional accreditation are based on the extent to which standards are addressed. Finally, the results are made public. The highest levels of compliance generally result in longer time frames until the next cycle begins. If plans of correction are required, these are generally reviewed on an interim basis or examined at the time of the next review. In this elaborate process, the key elements are the standards and the reviewers. Considerable costs accrue to the applicant organization, which pays a fee to the accrediting body and absorbs the considerable costs of preparation, on-site review, and follow-up.

Although accreditation is considered to be voluntary, in many instances it is anything but that. Both hospitals and schools of public health, for example, perceive accreditation as essential to doing business. Accreditation has its greatest demand where there are multiple parties that value or require it. Third-party payers and governmental regulatory agencies require accreditation of hospitals. A variety of federal grants and contracts can only be awarded to accredited schools of public health. Creating similar incentives to act as drivers for voluntary accreditation may pose a formidable challenge for the public health system. Such concerns are to be addressed by the Financing and Incentives workgroup.

Concurrent with the Exploring Accreditation Project, the RWJF has also funded a Multi-State Learning Collaborative on Performance and Capacity Assessment of Public Health Departments (MLC). The National Network of Public Health Institutes and the Public Health Leadership Society are co-managing this effort to further advance the innovations of states already conducting accreditation and accreditation-like programs within their health departments to further their current efforts and identify and disseminate best practices to the broader public health practice community. The long-term goal is to maximize the effectiveness and accountability of governmental public health agencies.[61] Five states were selected to participate: Illinois, Michigan, Missouri, North Carolina, and Washington. A fundamental intent underlying the project design is for the learning of the MLC to be available to inform the deliberations of the Exploring Accreditation Project.

To date, pioneering state programs have functioned as the laboratories for the study of public health accreditation, with several having embarked upon accreditation or similar processes. Typically, the LPHA is the focal interest. Nonetheless, similar emphasis on state health departments, and even federal agencies, is likewise warranted. In Michigan, LPHAs participate in an accreditation program consisting of a self-assessment and an on-site review.[62] An extensive set of accreditation standards is available in published form addressing requirements for core capacity, cost shared, and categorical services. The on-site review serves to validate and verify self-reported compliance. Although LPHA participation is mandatory, incentives come in the form of linkages to state funding through grants and contracts. An external accreditation commission housed in the Michigan Public Health Institute and based on authority conferred in state statutes coordinates the entire process. Additional information on the Michigan accreditation program is provided in Exhibit 17-7.

The North Carolina Local Public Health Accreditation Program (NCLPHAP) emphasizes capacity within LPHAs. It has foundations in the operational definition of LPHAs as well as standards prescribed in the NPHPS and the 10 essential services. Standards are tied back to state statutes, the administrative code for North Carolina Divisions of Public Health and Environmental Health, and contract and program monitoring requirements. NCLPHAP is a three-part process that includes an agency self-assessment, on-site peer review team visit, and formal determination of accreditation status by the accrediting board. A review team is made up of five members: an LPHA director, a public health nurse, an environmental specialist, a local board of health member, and an accrediting board representative. After the site visit, the team leader prepares a consensus report complete with accreditation status recommendation. The accrediting board reviews the report and votes officially on accreditation. An appeals process is also in place.

Similar to the design found in North Carolina, there are three phases to the Washington standards assessment. Self-assessment prepares the LPHA for the on-site review, utilizing a guide developed by a consultant under the auspices of the Standards Committee. It is sent to the health department before the site visit describing documentation needed to demonstrate that a standard has been achieved. The site visit itself consists of document review and interviews. The reviewer determines whether the documentation provided demonstrates performance of the relevant measure. Most recently site reviewers are a combined team of state and local public health agency staff and contracted external reviewers. In the reporting phase, each agency receives a report detailing performance on each measure, and a listing of the documents reviewed, with annotations of any areas demonstrating exemplary practice. Health departments are expected to utilize the results for quality improvement purposes and to celebrate areas of high achievement. Statewide reports are available to indicate foci meriting further emphasis and resources. Many jurisdictions use the report as part of their strategic plan within a framework of the five domains of the assessment. In contrast to the other state models described, the standards apply to both state and local public health. However, a separate measurement system for state and local practice reflects their differing roles.

Yet another model of "accreditation" is Project Public Health Ready (PHR), with its more program-centered emphasis on preparedness.[63] This collaboration between the NACCHO, the CDC, and the Center for Health Policy at Columbia University School of Nursing was developed to serve as a means for LPHAs to offer concrete evidence of their capacity to respond to terrorism threats and to improve overall preparedness. In many respects PHR is similar to the examples

Exhibit 17-7    Michigan Public Health Institute, Michigan Local Public Health Accreditation Program: Standards and Measures, 2006 Tool

### Administrative Capacity Services

|  | MPRs (Standards) | Indicators (Measures) |
| --- | --- | --- |
| Section I: Powers and Duties | 1 | 7 |
| Section II: Clinical Laboratory | 3 | 3 |

### Local Public Health Operations

|  | MPRs (Standards) | Indicators (Measures) |
| --- | --- | --- |
| Section III: Food Service Sanitation | 26 | 0 |
| Section IV: General Communicable Disease Control | 4 | 14 |
| Section V: Hearing | 6 | 11 |
| Section VI: Immunization | 6 | 15 |
| Section VI: On-site Sewage Treatment Management | 5 | 10 |
| Section VIII: Sexually Transmitted Disease | 9 | 11 |
| Section IX: Vision | 6 | 11 |

### Categorical Grant-Funded Services

|  | MPRs (Standards) | Indicators (Measures) |
| --- | --- | --- |
| Section X: Breast and Cervical Cancer Control Program | 11 | 39 |
| Section XI: Family Planning | 21 | 23 |
| Section XII: HIV/AIDS | 12 | 25 |
| Section XIII: Women, Infants & Children Administration | 12 | 33 |
| Maternal Support Services/Infant Support Services | Not reviewed for the 2006 Tool | Not reviewed for the 2006 Tool |
|  | Total MPRs (Standards): 122 | Total Indicators (Measures): 202 |

Example: Standard
**VIII1. Ensure reporting and follow-up of "venereal disease" and chlamydia.**
Example: Measure

1.1 Reporting and follow-up in compliance with the Michigan Public Health Code and Michigan Communicable Disease Rules.

☐ Fully Met        ☐ Not Met

*Source:* Michigan Public Health Institute. Michigan Local Public Health Accreditation Program: Standards and Measures, 2006 Tool.

cited above. LPHAs that participate are "recognized" by the PHR Oversight Council as "public health ready" if they demonstrate readiness to respond to public health emergencies by documenting compliance with three criteria:

- Goal 1: Preparedness planning: The pilot site's emergency response plan specifies the responsibilities of the public health agency, its relationship with other emergency response plans, and the roles of its staff when responding to bioterrorism.
- Goal 2: Workforce competency: All members of the pilot site's workforce are competent to perform the nine core emergency preparedness competencies.
- Goal 3: Exercise simulation: The pilot site demonstrates emergency readiness by participating in and/or conducting an exercise, or exercises, in which the public health emergency response plan is tested and individual worker emergency preparedness competencies are successfully demonstrated.[64]

Once conferred, recognition is for a 2-year period.

Accreditation programs often must strike a fine balance between minimal and optimal standards. State standards programs and similar initiatives often favor optimal rather than minimal standards. This was certainly the case with respect to the standards adopted in the Washington public health standards program, which were designed to "stretch" the capacity and performance of local and state public health departments.[65,66] Both accreditation and standards programs prefer to focus on clearly accountable entities (e.g., a local public health agency rather than a community public health system).[67] Beyond financial incentives that may be in place, organizations pursuing accreditation must perceive internal value emanating from the process. This was, indeed, reported to be the case in many of the LPHAs undertaking accreditation in MLC states.

Experiences in other fields also suggest that the value of accreditation is derived from how extensively the credential is accepted and used by external stakeholders.[68] For accreditation to be successful, there must be both short- and long-term benefits. Public health goals for a healthier population reflect appropriate long-term benefits. However, short-term and measurable benefits of accreditation to public health organizations must also be articulated, if for no other reason than to provide a reasonable counterbalance to the cost in time, dollars, and political energy needed for the effort.[69] Some potential benefits might include greater accountability, simplified interstate or intrastate transfer of data, legislative exemptions from restrictions on access to confidential data, ability to compete directly for federal funds, contracting advantages with Medicaid and other state agencies, or even a market advantage in competition when directly contracting with the private sector for some services. Also, peer pressure on localities that do not adequately support their public health responsibilities could serve as an inducement. However, even when examining results of accreditation across a number of fields, to date there is limited research data available demonstrating that it improves organizational performance.[68] For public health accreditation to be sustainable, therefore, it must build a solid research and evaluation basis that is able to conclusively demonstrate value and improvement through the process.

Voluntary accreditation of public health organizations could lead to greater interest in the possibility of credentialing various segments of the public health workforce. In one form or another, there are already credentials for some public health workers, including sanitarians, health educators, public health administrators has also grown, with New Jersey licensing local public health administrators and Illinois developing an independent competency-based certification program for public health administrators working in a variety of public and private agencies. Viewed collectively, these burgeoning credentialing initiatives, when combined with the ongoing accreditation efforts described above, hold the potential to produce high-performing public health organizations with a competent workforce, consistently capable of providing the essential services of public health while achieving health outcome goals.

• • •

Performance management leading to performance improvement initiatives were undertaken in many different settings during the 1900s, including the public sector, where they were applied to improving governmental processes, programs, and services. Although only being undertaken in a few locales, its application to improving the performance of public health core functions has been largely positive, suggesting that a national public health performance standards program based on the essential public health services framework could be successful. "What gets measured gets done," is the performance measurement analogy for what is known in research as the Hawthorne effect.[70] Its lesson for the public health community is that the measurement process itself influences the credibility and consistent performance of that which is measured. What we are better able to measure, we will be better able to manage and improve.

With interest increasing inside the public health community and broader participation in public health improvement efforts evolving in many states and localities, the opportunity for a national public health performance standards program emphasizing performance management and quality improvement strategies has never been greater. Similarly, states fulfilling roles as innovative laboratories conducting experimentation in accreditation may guide the national dialogue on its future adoption. Critical factors that must be addressed in order for this effort to be successful include agreement as to the ultimate purpose of performance improvement efforts, delineation of the specific standards and measures to be used, and mechanisms to promote their widespread acceptance. It may prove difficult for any one set of standards and one single process to accomplish all three goals (quality improvement, enhanced accountability, and strengthened science base) of a national public health performance standards or accreditation initiative. Rather, it is likely that different formulations of standards and measures based on the essential public health services framework will be necessary.

Even if a national accreditation system for public health becomes a reality, there will nonetheless remain a continuing need for concerted efforts to improve the performance of public health agencies and systems. Utilizing the Turning Point Performance Management Collaborative framework as well as tools such as MAPP, community health improvement processes linked to *Healthy People 2010* objectives, and leading health indicators in conjunction with performance standards will enable motivated organizations to achieve desired goals.[71,72] Success may also be predicated upon reform of state and local public health systems, organizing them around the core functions and essential public health services rather than categorical programs and services. It is only within this larger context that accreditation initiatives for organizations and credentialing for individuals will be valued and meaningful, especially when combined with grant funding linked to the performance of essential public health services, performance reporting, and commitment to evaluative research activities.

In sum, public health performance standards with accompanying performance management activities will improve quality if they focus on all aspects of the public health system—its capacity, its processes, and the links between them and important community health outcomes—and if the public health community accepts, values, and uses these standards. Early attention to and consensus around these issues will determine the quality and relevance of public health practice in the 21st century.

## Chapter Review

1. Public health leaders and managers face issue related to performance at many different levels of the public health system including the performance of individuals, programs, agencies, inter-organizational collaborations, and system-wide enterprise itself.
2. The elements of performance management are the following:
   - Performance standards
   - Performance measures
   - Reporting of progress
   - Quality improvement process
3. Performance management is the regular collection and reporting of data to track work that is performed and results that are achieved.
4. A *performance measure* is the specific quantitative representation of a capacity, process, or outcome that is relevant to the assessment of performance.
5. A performance measure that takes the form of a generally accepted, objective standard of management is termed a *performance standard.*
6. Integrating the application of the Local Public Health Systems Performance Standards into the community assessment process is a major step forward in the improvement of public health infrastructure and capacity.
7. The National Public Health Performance Standards (NPHPS) are framed as optimal standards with the Ten Essential Public Health Services.
8. Extensive use of standards, performance measures, and performance improvement processes are occurring in a growing number of states.
9. Interest in strategies to accredit public health organizations is also an important trend in public health at both the state and local levels.

## References

1. Harrington HJ. *The Improvement Process: How America's Leading Companies Improve Quality.* New York, NY: McGraw-Hill; 1978.

2. Turning Point Program National Office. *Performance Management in Public Health: A Literature Review.* Seattle, Wash: Turning Point; 2002.
3. Turning Point Program National Office. *From Silos to Systems: Using Performance Management to Improve the Public's Health.* Seattle, Wash: Turning Point; 2003.
4. Landrum LB, Baker SL. Managing complex systems: performance management in public health. *J Public Health Manage Pract.* 2004;10(1): 13–18.
5. Wholey JS, Hatry HP. The case for performance monitoring. *Pub Admin Rev.* 1992;52:604–610.
6. Wholey JS, Newcomer KE. Clarifying goals, reporting results. *New Direct Eval.* 1997;75:91–98.
7. Trott CE, Baj J. *Building State Systems Based on Performance: The Workforce Development Experience, A Guide for States.* Washington, DC: National Governors Association; 1996.
8. Rossi P, Freeman H. *Evaluation: A Systematic Approach.* Thousand Oaks, Calif: Sage Publications; 1994.
9. Perrin EB, Durch JS, Skillman SM, eds. *Health Performance Measurement in the Public Sector: Principles and Policies for Implementing an Information Network.* Washington, DC: National Research Council; 1999.
10. Joint Commission on Accreditation of Healthcare Organizations (JCAHO). *Primer on Indicator Development and Application: Measuring Quality in Health Care.* Oakbrook Terrace, Ill: JCAHO; 1990.
11. Public Health Functions Steering Committee. Public Health in America. Available at: http://www.health.gov/phfunctions. Accessed November 1, 2005.
12. Institute of Medicine. *The Future of Public Health.* Washington, DC: National Academy Press; 1988.
13. Durch JS, Bailey LA, Stoto MA, eds. Improving health in the community: a role for performance monitoring. Washington, DC: National Academy Press; 1997.
14. Perrin EB, Koshel JJ, eds. Assessment of performance measures for public health, substance abuse, and mental health. Washington, DC: National Academy Press; 1997.
15. Northwest Prevention Effectiveness Center, Health Policy Analysis Program SoPHaCM, University of Washington. *Enabling Performance Measurement Activities in the States and Communities.* Seattle, Wash: University of Washington; 1998.
16. Turnock BJ, Handler AS. From Measuring to Improving Public Health Practice. *Annu Rev Public Health.* 1997;18:261–282.
17. Vaughan HF. Local health services in the United States: the story of CAP. *Am J Public Health.* 1972;62:95–108.
18. American Public Health Association. Committee on Municipal Health Department Practice, First Report, Part 1. *Am J Public Health.* 1922;12(2): 7–15.
19. American Public Health Association. Committee on Municipal Health Department Practice, First Report, Part 2. *Am J Public Health.* 1922;12(2): 138–347.
20. American Public Health Association Committee on Administrative Practice. Appraisal form for city health work. *Am J Public Health.* 1926;16(1): 1–65.
21. Walker WW. The new appraisal form for local health work. *Am J Public Health.* 1939;29(5):490–500.
22. Halverson WL. A twenty-five year review of the work of the committee on administrative practice. *Am J Public Health.* 1945;35(12):1253–1259.

23. American Public Health Association. *Evaluation Schedule for Use in the Study and Appraisal of Community Health Programs.* New York, NY: American Public Health Association; 1947.

24. Krantz FW. The present status of full-time local health organizations. *Public Health Rep.* 1942;57:194–196.

25. Emerson H, Luginbuhl M. *Local Health Units for the Nation.* New York, NY: Commonwealth Fund; 1945.

26. US Public Health Service. *Healthy People 2000: National Health Promotion and Disease Prevention Objectives.* Washington DC: US Government Printing Office; 1990. DHHS Pub No. (PHS) 91-50212.

27. National Association of County and City Health Officials (NACCHO). *1990 National Profile of Local Health Departments.* Washington, DC: National Association of County and City Health Officials; 1992.

28. National Association of County and City Health Officials. *1992–1993 National Profile of Local Health Departments.* Washington, DC: National Association of County and City Health Officials; 1995.

29. Miller CA, Moore KS, Richards TB, McKaig C. A screening survey to assess local public health performance. *Public Health Rep.* 1994;109(5):659–664.

30. Miller CA, Moore KS, Richards TB, Monk JD. A proposed method for assessing the performance of local public health functions and practices. *Am J Public Health.* 1994;84(11):1743–1749.

31. Richards TB, Rogers JJ, Christenson GM, Miller CA, Gatewood DD, Taylor MS. Assessing public health practice: application of ten core function measures of community health in six states. *Am J Prev Med.* 1995;11(6 Suppl):36–40.

32. Richards TB, Rogers JJ, Christenson GM, Miller CA, Taylor MS, Cooper AD. Evaluating local public health performance at a community level on a statewide basis. *J Public Health Manage Pract.* 1995;1(4):70–83.

33. Turnock BJ, Handler A, Hall W, Potsic S, Nalluri R, Vaughn EH. Local health department effectiveness in addressing the core functions of public health. *Public Health Rep.* 1994;109(5):653–658.

34. Rohrer JE, Dominquez D, Weaver M, Atchison CG, Merchant JA. Assessing public health performance in Iowa's counties. *J Public Health Manage Pract.* 1997;3(3):10–15.

35. Turnock BJ, Handler AS, Miller CA. Core function-related local public health practice effectiveness. *J Public Health Manage Pract.* 1998;4(5):26–32.

36. Mays GP, Halverson PK, Baker EL, Stevens R, Vann JJ. Availability and perceived effectiveness of public health activities in the nation's most populous areas. *Am J of Public Health.* 2004;94(6):1019–1026.

37. Handler AS, Turnock BJ. Local health department effectiveness in addressing the core functions of public health: essential ingredients. *J Public Health Policy.* 1996;17(4):460–483.

38. Schenck SE, Miller CA, Richards TB. Public health performance related to selected health status and risk measures. *Am J Prev Med.* 1995;11(6 Suppl):55–57.

39. National Association of County and City Health Officials. *An Assessment Protocol for Excellence in Public Health.* Washington, DC: National Association of County and City Health Officials; 1990.

40. Turnock BJ, Handler A, Hall W, Lenihan DP, Vaughn E. Capacity-building influences on Illinois local health departments. *J Public Health Manage Pract.* 1995;1(3):50–58.

41. National Public Health Performance Standards Program, Center for Disease Control and Prevention. Available at: http://www.cdc.gov/od/ocphp/nphpsp/overview.htm. Accessed January 16, 2007.

42. Lenihan P. MAPP and the evolution of planning in public health practice. *J Public Health Manage Pract.* 2005;11(5):381–388.

43. Nicola R, Berkowitz B, Lafronza V. A Turning Point for public health. *J Public Health Manage Pract.* 2002;8(1):iv–vii.

44. National Association of County and City Health Officials. *Mobilizing for Action through Planning and Partnerships.* Washington, DC: National Association of County and City Health Officials; 2001.

45. Corso LC, Wiesner PJ, Lenihan P. Developing the MAPP community health improvement tool. *J Public Health Manage Pract.* 2005;11(5):387–392.

46. Salem E, Hooberman J, Ramirez D. MAPP in Chicago: a model for public health systems development and community building. *J Public Health Manage Pract.* 2005;11(5):393–400.

47. Beaulieu J, Scutchfield FD. Assessment of validity of the national public health performance standards: the local public health performance assessment instrument. *Public Health Rep.* 2002;117(1):28–36.

48. Beaulieu J, Scutchfield FD, Kelly AV. Content and criterion validity evaluation of National Public Health Performance Standards measurement instruments. *Public Health Rep.* 2003;118(6):508–517.

49. Beaulieu JE, Scutchfield FD, Kelly AV. Recommendations from testing of the National Public Health Performance Standards instruments. *J Public Health Manage Pract.* 2003;9(3):188–198.

50. Scutchfield FD, Knight EA, Kelly AV, Bhandari MW, Vasilescu IP. Local public health agency capacity and its relationship to public health system performance. *J Public Health Manage Pract.* 2004;10(3):204–215.

51. Bakes-Martin R, Corso LC, Landrum LB, Fisher VS, Halverson PK. Developing national performance standards for local public health systems. *J Public Health Manage Pract.* 2005;11(5):418–421.

52. Centers for Disease Control and Prevention. *National Public Health Performance Standards: State Public Health System Performance Assessment Instrument.* Available at: http://www.cdc.gov/od/ocphp/nphpsp/TheInstruments.htm. Accessed January 16, 2007

53. Turnock BJ. Can public health performance standards improve the quality of public health practice? *J Public Health Manage Pract.* 2000;6(5):19–25.

54. Mays GP. From collaboration to coevolution: new structures for public health improvement. *J Public Health Manage Pract.* 2002;8(1):95–97.

55. US Department of Health and Human Services. *Healthy People 2010: Understanding and Improving Health.* Washington, DC: US Department of Health and Human Services; 2000.

56. US Department of Health and Human Services. *Healthy People 2010–Midcourse Review.* Washington, DC: US Department of Health and Human Services. Available at: http://www.healthypeople.gov/data/midcourse/default.htm. Accessed June 13, 2006.

57. Mays GP, Halverson P, Miller CA. Assessing the performance of local public health systems: a survey of state health agency efforts. *J Public Health Manage Pract.* 1998;4(4):63–78.

58. Handler A, Issel M, Turnock B. A conceptual framework to measure performance of the public health system. *Am J Public Health.* 2001;91(8):1235–1239.

59. National Association of County and City Health Officials Web site. Operational definition. Available at: http://www.naccho.org/topics/infrastructure/operationaldefinition.cfm. Accessed November 1, 2005.

60. Institute of Medicine. *The Future of the Public's Health in the 21st Century.* Washington, DC: National Academies Press; 2003.

61. National Network of Public Health Institutes. Multi-state learning collaborative performance capacity assessment of public health departments. Available at: http://www.nnphi.org/multistatelearningcollaborative.htm. Accessed October 23, 2005.

62. Michigan Public Health Institute. *Michigan Local Health Department Accreditation Self-Assessment Report.* Lansing, MI: Michigan Department of Community Health; 1997.

63. Estrada LC, Fraser MR, Cioffi JP, et al. Partnering for preparedness: the project public health ready experience. *Public Health Rep.* 2005;120 (Suppl 1):69–75.

64. NACCHO. Project Public Health Ready. Available at: http://www.public-health-ready.org/. Accessed October 23, 2005.

65. Thielen L. *Exploring Public Health Experience with Standards and Accreditation.* Princeton, NJ: Robert Wood Johnson Foundation; October 2004.

66. Beitsch LM, Thielen L, Mays GP, et al. The multistate learning collaborative, states as laboratories: informing the national public health accreditation dialogue. *J Public Health Manage Pract.* 2006;12(3):217–231.

67. Schyve PM. Joint commission perspectives on accreditation of public health practice. *J Public Health Manage Pract.* 1998;4(4):28–33.

68. Mays GP. *Can Accreditation Work in Public Health? Lessons from other Service Industries.* Little Rock, Ark: UAMS College of Public Health; 2004.

69. Greenberg EL. How accreditation could strengthen local public health: an examination of models from managed care and insurance regulators. *J Public Health Manage Pract.* 1998;4(4):33–37.

70. Roethlisberger FJ, Dickson WJ. *Management and the Worker.* Cambridge, Mass: Harvard University Press; 1947.

71. Baker EL, Melton RJ, Stange PV, et al. Health reform and the health of the public. Forging community health partnerships. *JAMA.* 1994;272(16): 1276–1282.

72. Harrell JA, Baker EL. The essential services of public health. *Leadership Public Health.* 1994;3:27–31.

## CHAPTER 18

# EVALUATION OF PUBLIC HEALTH INTERVENTIONS

Michael A. Stoto
Leon E. Cosler

## Chapter Overview

Evaluation encompasses the set of tools that are used to measure the effectiveness of public health programs by determining what works. Traditional evaluations in public health have focused on assessing the impact of specific program activities on defined outcomes. Evaluation is also a conceptual approach to the use of data—as part of a quality improvement process—in public health management. Public health organizations must continually improve upon the standards of evidence used in the evaluation of public health so that results can inform managerial and policy decision making. As public health interventions become more integrated within the community, collaboration in evaluation efforts is a growing imperative.

Evaluation concepts and methods are of growing importance to public health organizations, as well as to education and social services programs. Increasingly, public health managers are being held accountable for their actions, and managers, elected officials, and the public are asking whether programs work, for whom, and under what conditions. Public health decision makers need to know which program variants work best, whether the public is getting the best possible value for its investment, and how to increase the impact of existing programs. These evaluation questions are being asked of long-standing programs, new activities, and proposed interventions. These developments parallel today's emphasis on "evidence-based medicine" in clinical areas and suggest the growing role of "evidence-based management" within public health organizations.

In this context, *evaluation* is, first of all, a set of tools that is used to improve the effectiveness of public health programs and activities by determining which programs work, and also which program variants work most effectively. These tools derive from social science and health services research and include concepts of study design, a variety of statistical methods, and economic evaluation tools. *Evaluation* is also a conceptual approach to the use of data—as part of a quality improvement process—in public health management.

However defined, evaluation can be useful to managers in public health who need, for example, to do the following activities:

- Judge the effectiveness of new approaches to public health service delivery systems that were developed elsewhere, and judge their potential applicability in one's own jurisdiction. For instance, do the immunization registries being tried in a number of US cities actually result in more children being immunized?
- Judge the effectiveness of new approaches to public health service delivery systems that were developed in one's own jurisdiction. For instance, does the new community-based outreach program actually result in more children being immunized? If not, why not?
- Assess how well an intervention is being implemented in one's own jurisdiction. What fraction of children is being enrolled in the community's new immunization registry at birth? Which children are left out? What can be done to improve coverage?
- Ensure accountability of contractors and other entities with a responsibility to the public health agency. Are the managed care organizations with Medicaid contracts in the community ensuring that the children enrolled in their plans are receiving all of the recommended immunizations? Are some plans doing better than others? Why?
- Demonstrate accountability of internal programs to funders or higher authorities. Are federal funds for immunization being used according to the funders' guidelines? Are they achieving the intended effect?

This chapter begins with a primer on evaluation research methods, including economic evaluation, used by public health organizations drawing on examples from immunization programs and needle exchange programs to prevent human immunodeficiency virus (HIV) infection. Special issues in the evaluation of community-based interventions are also covered, as are issues of measurement and data. The second section of the chapter deals with practical aspects of program evaluation in public health, drawing on examples from family violence and other areas, and proposes a process for evaluation in public health settings. The final section focuses on performance measurement—in organizations as well as community settings—as a form of evaluation methodology. An extended example dealing with public health preparedness illustrates the concept of performance measurement.

## Evaluation Methods

### Terminology

All public health programs can be characterized by their inputs, activities, outputs, and outcomes, as illustrated in terms of a childhood immunization program in Exhibit 18–1. *Inputs* are resources dedicated to or consumed by the program. Inputs can, in some settings, include organizational structures and capacities. *Activities* are what the program does with its inputs to fulfill its mission. *Outputs* are the direct product of program activities. Outputs,

Exhibit 18-1    Examples of Program Inputs, Activities, Outputs, and Outcomes

| *Inputs* | *Activities* | *Outputs* | *Outcomes* |
|---|---|---|---|
| Resources dedicated to or consumed by the program | What the program does with inputs to fulfill its mission | The direct product of program activities | Benefits for participants during and after program activities |
| • Money | • Educate consumers | • Number of brochures distributed | • Parental awareness of vaccine benefits |
| • Staff time | • Educate providers | • Doses of vaccines delivered | • Provider awareness |
| • Facilities | • Distribute vaccines to providers | • Percentage of births enrolled in registry | • Changed attitudes |
| • Equipment | • Establish an immunization registry | • Number of providers who establish a reminder system | • Children immunized |
| • Laws | • Provide technical assistance to providers about reminder systems | • Number of providers who monitor immunization coverage | • Reduced burden of vaccine-preventable disease in immunized children |
| • Regulations | • Monitor immunization coverage in the population and health plans | • Program costs | • Reduced prevalence of vaccine-preventable disease |
| • Funders' requirements | | | • Cost per child immunized |

sometimes called intermediate outcomes, can sometimes overlap with outcomes, depending on the stage of the intervention. *Outcomes* are benefits for participants during and after program activities.

Within this framework, a number of different types of evaluations are possible:

- Traditional evaluations in public health have focused on assessing the impact of specific program activities on defined outcomes. For instance, does the new reminder system increase the number of children immunized? Questions may also be asked concerning the impact of resources on outcomes. For example, do laws requiring complete immunization prior to school entry reduce vaccine-preventable disease?

- Economic evaluations combine program effectiveness information with economic resources (i.e., costs and benefits) in quantitative terms. They allow decision makers to prioritize public health activities in the face of finite financial resources. Which program, for example, is most effective in terms of costs per child immunized?

- Process evaluations refer to evaluations that are focused on outputs. Such an evaluation might ask, for instance, whether the change in enrollment procedures increases the number of children enrolled in a registry. In these cases, a relationship is assumed between outputs and outcomes (presumably based on research done elsewhere), and evidence of a change in outputs is taken as indirect evidence of an impact on desired outcomes.

- Formative evaluations refer to efforts to identify the best uses of available resources, prior to a traditional program evaluation. Formative evaluation often employs qualitative methods such as focus groups or structured interviews to understand a process or system and to identify barriers and opportunities for improvement. Project Access in the San Francisco Bay area, for instance, interviewed drug users at needle exchange programs, shooting galleries, parking lots, and drug treatment centers. Researchers discovered a variety of structural barriers that prevented the users from seeking HIV counseling and testing, such as restricted hours of counseling and testing sites, lack of transportation, complications in drawing blood, and insensitive providers.[1]
- Empowerment evaluations involve an approach whereby programs take stock of their existing strengths and weaknesses, focus on key goals and program improvements, develop self-initiated strategies to achieve these goals, and determine the type of evidence that will document credible progress.[2] This approach is discussed in more detail in the following paragraphs.
- Performance measures use statistical methods and other evaluation tools on an ongoing basis to assure accountability for public health programs and to improve performance.

### Efficacy Assessment

Regardless of its ultimate purposes, evaluation is essentially an applied research activity seeking to discover whether a program, in some sense, has beneficial effects for the public's health. The program could be a specific activity in one public health clinic or a comprehensive communitywide activity. The question may be retrospective—Did it work?—before the program is expanded to other venues, or current—Is it working?—to ensure accountability and improve outcomes. The issue may be comparing two or more competing interventions, or assessing whether a particular program is better than nothing. The question may also be whether the program is better in some populations, or under some particular conditions. In every case, however, the central question is one of efficacy: Is some program more effective than some alternative?

Program evaluation thus centers on questions of efficacy, but additional steps are usually necessary in order to make policy decisions about recommendations for individuals and the allocation of resources. Programs shown to be effective in controlled situations, however, may not work in settings where the conditions are different. *Effectiveness* refers to a program's ability to get results in less than optimal situations. A work site smoking cessation program developed by highly motivated and skilled health educators for university employees, for instance, may not be as effective when applied by human resources personnel assigned to a large auto manufacturer. Effective programs employ well-developed materials and training so that they can be generalized, that is, transferred from where they were developed to other settings.

The evaluation of public health interventions requires research directed at estimating the unique effects (or net effect) of the intervention, above and beyond any change that may have occurred because of a multitude of other factors. Such research requires study designs that can distinguish the impact of the intervention within a general service population from other changes that occur only in certain groups or that result simply as a passage of time. These designs commonly involve the formation of two or more groups: one composed of individuals who participated in the intervention (the treatment group) and a second group of individuals who are comparable in character and experience to those who participated but who received no services or an intervention that was different from that under study (the control or comparison group).

To estimate the net effect of an intervention reliably, the following technical issues must be addressed:[3,4]

- The manner in which the control or comparison groups are formed influences the validity of the inference.
- The number of participants enrolled in each group (the sample size) must be sufficient to permit statistical detection of differences between the groups, if differences exist.
- There should be agreement among interested parties that a selected outcome is important to measure, that it is a valid reflection of the objective of the intervention, and that it can reflect change over time.
- Evidence is needed to show that the innovative services were actually provided as planned, and that the differences between the innovative services and usual services were large enough to generate meaningful differences in the outcome of interest.

In clinical medicine, randomization is typically regarded as essential to show that the intervention caused the effect. In public health, however, it is often not possible to randomly assign individuals or populations to interventions for ethical and practical reasons. To make judgments about causality, evaluation researchers have developed a general consensus regarding the relative strength of various study designs, with randomized control trials being the gold standard of evidence and anecdotal case reports being the weakest of the study designs.[3] In addition, a group of statistical methods known collectively as "causal modeling" have been developed to analyze data from nonrandomized experiments and other sources to infer causal relationship when possible.[5]

*Statistical power* is the likelihood that an evaluation will detect the effect of an intervention, if there is one. Two factors affect statistical power: sample size and effect size, a quantitative measure of the program's impact, such as a 10% improvement in immunization rates. Public health evaluation studies are often based on small samples of individuals, and thus lack sufficient statistical power to detect meaningful effects. Power can be increased by increasing the number of subjects or by increasing the number of intervention sites, as long as each site adheres to common design elements and applies uniform eligibility criteria. Evaluators planning a study must consider whether the study size and effect size are large enough to ensure a reasonable probability that the program's impact will be statistically significant. Managers considering the results of a negative study should consider whether the study has sufficient power to detect an effect.

A related criterion is the need for careful implementation of the intervention being evaluated. A careful, randomized assessment of an intervention that is poorly implemented is likely to show, with great precision, that the intervention did not work as intended. Such a study will not distinguish between failures of the theory that is being tested and failures of implementation. Program designers need to identify critical elements of programs to explain why effects occurred and to assist others who wish to replicate the intervention model in a new setting.

## Experimental Designs

The highest level of evidence occurs with *experimental designs* that include randomized controls to restrict a number of important threats to validity. In clinical settings, individual patients are assigned by some random mechanism to a treatment group or a control group, and both groups are observed to see if there is a difference in outcomes of interest. If there is a difference in outcome, it can be assumed to be due to the intervention because the randomization reduces the chance that there are no other differences between the two groups. An additional benefit is that the random allocation per se makes it possible to perform statistical inference, that is, to assess whether the observed differences can be due to chance.

Public health interventions such as immunizations are essentially personal health services, so the randomization model can be used directly. For other programs, the unit of intervention might be social units such as schools, work sites, or even whole communities. In these instances, randomization can still be carried out, but just not on an individual basis.[4,6] Although ethical and political objections are often raised, randomization can be carried out in social settings much more commonly than is currently done. As long as there is equipoise regarding the benefits and harms of the intervention, potential for participants to benefit, and a means of informed consent, randomization is ethically acceptable. Resource constraints that prevent the immediate introduction of a new program to an entire population present an opportunity to randomize which units get the intervention first and concomitantly evaluate the outcome. Waiting lists can be arranged so that every client eventually receives the service, but those who get it first are chosen at random and compared to those who receive it later.[7]

## Quasi-Experimental Designs

In public health, however, random assignment commonly either is not feasible or simply is not done. In such instances, *quasi-experimental designs*, the second level of evidence in the hierarchy, can be used to assess the impact of programs. Included in this group are analyses using existing computerized databases, case-control observational studies, and series based on historical controls. Although these designs can improve inferential clarity, they cannot be relied on to yield unbiased estimates of the effects of interventions because the subjects are not assigned randomly. A before-and-after design, for example, compares some outcome in the same group before and after a program is introduced. Did traffic fatalities go down in the three months after the speed limit was lowered? Designs of this sort, however, are subject to a variety of biases or threats to validity. If fatalities decreased, can it be due to better weather after the speed limit was changed on March 15? Before-and-after designs can be improved by gathering multiple data points before and after the program is introduced, and by careful examination of other factors, such as weather, that may be responsible for the apparent effect.

Another important quasi-experimental design is to have one or more comparison groups that are thought to be similar to the group receiving the intervention. If immunization coverage rates are higher in a community that has received a special program than in a neighboring community with no such intervention, a prima facie case can be made for the efficacy of the program. A slightly more complex design combines the before-and-after and control group approaches: teen birth rates are measured in two communities before and after one community attends a special school-based program. In this approach, a larger decrease in teen birth rate in the school that received the intervention than in the control school is interpreted as evidence of efficacy. The major problem with a comparison-group design is that the treatment control groups may differ in some way other than the intervention that explains the outcome. A selection bias, for instance, occurs when more advantaged population groups are more likely to choose or be chosen for a new program. In either of the examples cited, for instance, the differences may reflect a greater social advantage in the intervention group, which explains both the outcome and why they received the program.

When randomization is not possible or is not performed, statistical methods are available to reduce the effect of selection or other biases. If the experimental and comparison groups differ in some respects that may affect the outcomes, multivariate analysis can be used to "adjust" for these differences and isolate the true effect of the intervention. A work site smoking cessation program, for example, may have been tested in two workplaces that differ substantially in the proportion of male and female workers and in the proportion of blue- versus white-collar positions. Because both sex and kind of job could affect smoking cessation success, evaluators might want to adjust for these factors in their analysis. In clinical settings, where patients with more severe illness seek out academic medical centers and are also at higher risk for failure, evaluators "risk adjust" to account for these differences.

## Nonexperimental Designs

The lowest level of evidence occurs with *nonexperimental designs,* which consist of case series and anecdotal reports. Although such studies can contain a wealth of useful information, they cannot support inference because they cannot control for factors such as maturation, self-selection, historical influences unrelated to the intervention, and changes in instrumentation.

When a difference is detected between treatment and control groups in a study, the first question an evaluator asks is whether the difference could be due to chance (resulting from sampling individuals to be included). Various statistical techniques, depending on the nature of the research design and data, are available to provide answers to this question. If the analysis suggests that the difference is unlikely to be due to chance, it is said to be *statistically significant.* Statistical significance is sometimes assessed through the examination of *confidence intervals* (*CI*). A 95% confidence interval is a range calculated from the data in such a way that there is a 95% chance that the range includes the quantity being estimated. Suppose, for example, an educational program was evaluated in terms of the average difference between the scores of individuals who were in the program and a similar group of controls on a test of knowledge of HIV risk factors. If the average difference was 1.5 points on a 10-point test, and the 95% confidence interval was 0.8 to 2.2 points (0 is not in the range), the difference can be said to be statistically significant.

## Economic Analyses

There are several separate methods commonly employed under the description of economic analyses. These include: cost analysis, cost-minimization analysis (CMA), cost-effectiveness analysis (CEA), cost-utility analysis (CUA), and cost-benefit analysis (CBA). Each method differs in its approach to measuring economic resources, and thus each has applicability to different situations. There are, however, common characteristics important to all of these techniques.

### Cost Analysis

Cost analysis refers to any evaluation that uses the structured collection of costs without regard to evaluating health benefits or outcomes. Costs are frequently categorized into direct costs, indirect costs, and intangible costs. Direct and indirect costs can be subcategorized into medical and nonmedically related costs. Direct medical costs represent the value of the resources used specifically for the healthcare services or interventions being measured. These frequently include all medical services, diagnostic testing, and treatment including medications. Direct nonmedical costs can include necessary expenses that are not healthcare related. These costs may include patient transportation costs, child care, or the costs of advertising related to patient education. Indirect costs attempt to measure the economic value of resources that are lost as a result of contracting an illness or participating in an intervention. Commonly, indirect costs are measured as the value of lost wages or the value of lost leisure time. Intangible costs attempt to quantify costs associated with the pain or suffering associated with disease or its treatment. Intangible costs are extremely difficult to measure, and thus are rarely included in many economic analyses.[8,9]

The cost analysis technique is commonly used to conduct cost-of-illness (COI) studies. These studies attempt to quantify all costs (direct and indirect) associated with a particular illness or condition. Cost-of-illness studies assist public health decision makers in planning interventions and targeting limited research funds. Cost-minimization analysis (CMA) is another common type of cost analysis. CMA requires a thorough assessment of all relevant costs associated with two or more health interventions but further assumes that the health outcomes of each intervention are exactly the same. For example, cost-minimization analysis can be used to compare therapy with brand name versus generic drugs. This method however has been overused because of its simplicity. Frequently, the requirement of identical outcomes is not well established. When health outcomes are not equivalent, another method, such as cost-effectiveness analysis is required.[9]

## Cost-Effectiveness Analysis

When comparing health outcomes that may not be the same, cost-effectiveness analysis (CEA) is a widely utilized method. CEA aggregates all appropriate costs for one or more healthcare interventions and expresses them in terms of health outcomes in their natural (nonmonetary) units. The outcomes may be a very specific single measure (e.g., dollars per life saved or dollars per case of disease prevented) or may be a composite measure that adjusts for quality of life. In situations where the denominator adjusts for quality of life, this technique has sometimes been referred to as a cost-utility analysis (CUA), which is described later.

Results of a cost-effectiveness analysis are commonly reported as two types of ratios, the average cost-effectiveness ratio and the incremental cost-effectiveness ratio (ICER). The average cost-effectiveness ratio is the appropriate summary measure when there are no comparisons between interventions, and the ratio becomes a simple description of the cost per outcome for a single intervention or treatment.[9]

More common is the situation where two or more interventions are being compared, in which case the ICER is the more useful statistic for policy makers. The ICER presents the change in cost per unit change in effect. For example, comparing two interventions (A and B) assuming intervention B is more expensive, the ICER for this comparison can be expressed as:

$$ICER = \frac{\text{Total cost(B)} - \text{Total cost(A)}}{\text{Health outcomes(B)} - \text{Health outcomes(A)}}$$

CEA results present decision makers with quantifiable trade-offs between costs and the health effects of the interventions being compared. This technique can be used for final health outcomes (e.g., patients survived or lives saved), and this technique can also be used for intermediate outcomes (e.g., number of patients who quit smoking). Intermediate outcomes are often easier and more rapidly measured. However, intermediate health outcomes should be clearly and demonstrably linked to final health outcomes to be most useful (e.g., measuring patients who quit smoking can be directly linked to lung cancer cases prevented). CEA is most appropriate when comparing health interventions with similar health outcomes. This technique cannot be used to contrast health interventions with diverse health benefits (e.g., comparing a tobacco cessation program with a prenatal care campaign).[9-12] In these situations, a specialized type of cost-effectiveness analysis utilizing a more complex health outcome is warranted.[13]

### *Example: Cost-Effectiveness Analysis of Smoking Cessation Programs*

A recent study by Secker-Walker et al. used a cost-effectiveness analysis to assess a smoking cessation research project funded by the National Institutes of Health (NIH).[14] The project, called Breathe Easy, was conducted in four counties (two in Vermont and two in New Hampshire) and used community-based interventions targeting women aged 18–64. One county in each state, matched on salient demographic characteristics, served as a control group. Based on telephone surveys, the authors calculated decreases in the number of adult women who smoke and calculated years of life saved from standard mortality tables. Costs were calculated from two different perspectives—intervention costs only and then from a societal perspective including evaluation costs and indirect costs. Because of the duration of the campaign, all costs were adjusted to 2002 dollars using the consumer price index (CPI). The authors computed cost-effectiveness ratios expressed as dollars per life-year saved, using multiple discount rates. Using a discount rate of 5%, the authors reported a cost-effectiveness ratio of $1922 per life-year saved (LYS) using the intervention only perspective, and $6683 per LYS when evaluation and indirect costs were included. Cost-effectiveness ratios computed with no discounting or with a 3% discount rate were not statistically significant. The authors' findings are similar in magnitude to other cost-effectiveness analyses conducted over the previous 20 years.[13]

## Cost-Utility Analysis

Cost-utility analysis (CUA) is a specific type of cost-effectiveness analysis in which the health outcomes are measured in terms of some type of adjusted health utility, the most common measure being the quality-adjusted-life-year (QALY). The outcome of a QALY (and other related measures) requires some assessment of the perceived quality of life, either from a patient or a societal perspective. To use QALYs as an example—living in perceived perfect health would be valued as a health utility of 1.0 while a patient living in severe pain might value this condition as 0.5. In a CUA, an intervention that prevented someone from living for two years of life at this diminished capacity (0.5) would have the same value as one that saved one year of life in perfect health. The advantage of CUA is that different types of health interventions can be compared as long as their outcomes can be expresses in terms of QALYs. The technique combines measures of both morbidity and mortality as well as a quality-of-life assessment of a single condition or disease. As its popularity grows, this type of analysis is becoming more frequently termed a cost-effectiveness analysis in contemporary literature.

Although measuring changes in longevity has been relatively straightforward, the assessment of health-related quality-of-life (HRQOL) represents a more complex and more recent construct in these types of assessments. Quality-of-life measures (i.e., utility values) can be derived by a variety of means; frequently, these must be measured using patient surveys or a variety of role-playing scenarios based on the assumptions of game theory.[10,12,15] These surveys can be either a general index designed to measure several dimensions of health (e.g., physical health, social functioning, and mental health), or they may be disease specific. When the goals of an analysis are appropriate to a national or societal perspective, a broad-based general quality-of-life survey is recommended. Commonly used general survey instruments include the European Quality-of-Life instrument (EQ-5D), Quality of Well-Being scale (QWB), or the Medical Outcome Study Short Form (SF-6D). A recent report of the Institute of Medicine's (IOM's) Committee to Evaluate Measures of Health Benefits for Environmental, Health, and Safety Regulation provides recommendations for the use and selection of HRQOL instruments in a regulatory environment.[13] The committee suggests that (1) general health assessment tools should be used; (2) they should be sufficiently sensitive to detect differences in health status; (3) HRQOL be derived from sufficiently large samples so as to be meaningful; (4) the instrument should be acceptable to users and the public; and (5) the instrument should be practical and inexpensive to use.[13]

### Example: Cost-Utility Analysis of HIV Counseling, Testing, and Referral Programs

A contemporary application of cost-utility analysis was conducted by Paltiel et al. for the evaluation of expanded HIV counseling, testing, and referral (HIVCTR). The authors used simulation modeling to determine the effects of expanded HIVCTR in target populations with different levels of HIV prevalence. Three levels of HIV prevalence were selected:

1. 3.0% prevalence of undiagnosed HIV and 1.2% annual incidence
2. 1.0% prevalence of undiagnosed HIV and 0.12% annual incidence
3. 0.1% prevalence of undiagnosed HIV and 0.01% annual incidence

The second level represents the HIV prevalence at which the CDC had recommended routine HIV testing and the third represents the US general population. The authors use costs and quality-of-life assessments from the national AIDS Cost and Services Utilization Survey and the HIV Cost and Services Utilization Study.[16-17] The authors also use well-established guidelines for HIV testing procedures, testing results, and the effectiveness of pre- and posttest HIV counseling services. Sensitivity analyses were used to test the effects of key assumptions on the cost-effectiveness ratios (reported as dollars per quality-adjusted life-years (QALYs). In the highest risk populations, the addition of one-time screening using enzyme-linked immunosorbent assay (ELISA) for all resulted in a cost-effectiveness ratio of $36,000 per QALY. Testing every 5 years had an estimated cost-effectiveness ratio of $50,000 per QALY. In the CDC threshold prevalence population, the authors estimated a one-time screening with ELISA to result in a ratio of $38,000 per life year gained. In the US general population, one-time screening costs were estimated to be $113,000 per QALY. The authors conclude that in all but the lowest risk populations, both one-time screening as well as periodic screenings may be cost-effective based on their cost per QALY when compared to generally accepted screening interventions for other chronic conditions (e.g., cancer, diabetes, and hypertension).[18]

## Cost-Benefit Analysis

Cost-benefit analysis (CBA) is an economic analysis in which both the costs and the health outcomes are expressed in dollars. The results of a CBA are thus expressed in terms of a *net benefit* representing the difference between all inputs (costs) and all outcomes (both positive and negative health consequences). The benefit/cost ratio can also be computed as the ratio of the value of benefits divided by all appropriate costs. The benefit/cost ratio can be used to rank multiple projects (with positive net benefits). This facilitates prioritization of various inteventions where resources are finite.[9,19]

Both direct and indirect costs may be included in a CBA. Because of the comprehensive nature of this method, CBAs are most often conducted from a societal perspective, particularly when evaluating a public health intervention. The expenses that are avoided because costly health problems are prevented are also included in the valuations of program benefits. The subjective nature of some of these cost categories can sometimes make CBA findings controversial.[20]

Because all costs and outcomes are valued in dollars, CBA has the advantage of comparing vastly different health interventions and allowing decision makers to focus limited resources toward the optimal projects. However, this advantage is also the greatest limitation. CBA, by definition, requires the economic evaluation of morbidity, mortality, and quality of life. The methods used to arrive at these valuations are often debatable, and there is significant variation in the specific methods used. In addition, the evaluation of costs and benefits within a CBA design frequently aggregate data of several years (or decades) for the realization of a program's effectiveness. Thus, this method requires the adjustment of dollar values for inflation and time value (e.g., discounting). The rate selected for discounting can create large variations in a CBA's final results and therefore should be tested in sensitivity analyses.[9,19]

### Example: Cost-Benefit Analysis of Folic Acid Fortification

A recent study by Grosse et al. updated the costs and benefits of folic acid fortification in the United States using both a cost-effectiveness and a cost-benefit analysis.[21] Folic acid fortification of cereal grain products has been required by the Food and Drug Administration (FDA) since 1996 in order to reduce the incidence of neural tube defects (NTDs). The authors present a thorough overview of the various economic studies that have been conducted on folic acid fortification since its implementation. For the most recent cost-benefit analysis, the authors used a cost-of-illness approach that placed a value on NTD deaths based on estimates of lost productivity in the future discounted to present day using a range of discount rates as directed by the recent Office of Management and Budget (OMB) guidelines.[21] The authors also estimate financial benefits based on the direct costs for NTDs that can be averted by folic acid supplementation. The authors estimated the lifetime costs associated with a spina bifida birth at $636,000 with $279,000 representing direct medical costs and the remaining $357,000 indirect costs. For anencephaly, the authors estimate a lifetime cost to be $1,020,000, with $1,014,000 attributed to indirect costs and $6000 the direct costs of hospitalization. For the cost-benefit analysis, the authors estimate a total economic benefit of folic acid fortification to be $422 million per year after adjusting for the cost the fortification (i.e., $3 million per year). The authors conduct a best case and worst case type of sensitivity analysis that adjusted for several of their assumptions. Under their worst-case scenarios, the authors still report a net benefit of folic acid fortification of $312 million per year.[21]

### Measurement Issues Pertinent to Economic Evaluations

Because of the variation in the types of economic analyses, the assumptions and variability of their methodologies and components, researchers have sought to create some standards for economic analyses in order to improve the usefulness to decision makers. One such group was the Panel on Cost-Effectiveness in Health and Medicine, an expert-appointed panel assembled by the US Public Health Service. The panel was charged, in part, with trying to achieve a consensus for standard components of healthcare cost-effectiveness studies and with proposing generally accepted methods for addressing the assumptions inherit in these types of analyses. A few of the most important standards for these analyses are described below.[22]

### Study Perspective

Economic analyses can be conducted from a variety of perspectives or points of view, based on what entity incurs costs or acquires benefits (e.g., hospital or providers, insurers or payers, or society as a whole). The choice of perspective dictates which costs and health outcomes should be evaluated in an analysis. It is thus critical for the study perspective to be selected appropriately for the goals of an evaluation and declared prominently in any published results.[23,24]

The societal viewpoint represents the most comprehensive perspective and includes all direct medical and nonmedical costs, indirect costs, patient and family out-of-pocket costs, as well as costs or benefits that may extend beyond the intended populations. The benefits of an immunization program illustrate this—as a larger proportion of a vulnerable population becomes immunized, economic benefits are realized by everyone, even the remaining unimmunized because of the decreased risk in the entire population (e.g., effect of herd immunity). The benefits of employing the societal perspective is that, in theory, all resources are accounted for, thus controlling for costs that may only be shifted among providers and payers. Some decision makers may select a more narrow perspective for their own organization. However, Gold et al. suggests that any narrow study perspective be combined with an analysis from a societal perspective.[22] The societal perspective is thus the recommended perspective particularly when a healthcare evaluation deals with publicly funded health interventions and prevention activities.[23,24]

### Time Horizon

The benefits of a health intervention often may take months or years to observe, while the costs which are incurred may be immediate. This is most critical in healthcare prevention activities, where benefits may occur far in the future. Thus it is important for economic analyses to use an appropriate time horizon that is sufficient to comprehensively capture all appropriate costs and benefits. For example, a diagnostic assay that predicts breast cancer recurrence over 10 years cannot be measured in an analysis with only a 5-year follow-up. Obviously, any gains in life expectancy would be lost with this truncated time horizon. Experts recommend that changes in life expectancy should be modeled to account for changes in survivals. When the period of potential benefits extends beyond the feasible data collection period, researchers frequently must rely on theoretical modeling.[23,25]

### Discounting

Discounting is commonly used to adjust costs that may accrue over several years in order to present a common basis for comparison. Typically, costs paid in the distant future are valued lower than present costs. It is commonly recommended that costs expended over more than one year be adjusted by using discounting. Discounting however is more controversial when applied to the accrual of health benefits. Some argue that a year of life saved should carry the same value whether it accrues in the present or in the distant future. Most economists, however, have recommended that future health benefits be discounted in the same way that costs are discounted within an economic analysis.[26]

The fundamental issue with discounting is the choice of discount rate at which costs or benefits are adjusted. The choice of discount rate can frequently affect the final results (i.e., whether an economic analysis shows cost savings or cost increases). The Panel on Cost-Effectiveness recommends that the appropriate discount rate be consistent with the contemporary cost of capital, generally between 3% and 5%, but that sensitivity analyses should be used to test rates between 0% and 7% to assess the impact of the discount rate on the final conclusions.[22,27]

### Sensitivity Analyses

Because there are a number of assumptions inherent with many economic analyses, experts recommend that the impact of these assumptions on the final conclusions be tested using sensitivity analyses. This technique requires researchers to identify the plausible ranges for the values of key assumption values and recalculating the study results based on these multiple values. Several types of sensitivity analysis are commonly employed.[22,27]

The most common type of sensitivity analysis modifies one or more variables across reasonable values. Such simple sensitivity analyses can be one-way (e.g., one variable) or multiple-way (e.g., multiple variables). A threshold sensitivity analysis is similar to a one-way sensitivity analysis; however, the values of the assumptions are varied to the point at which the options being compared become equivalent or the point at which the winning strategy changes. Because often several variables need to be examined with sensitivity analysis, the possible combinations can become unwieldy. In this situation, an analysis of extremes can be employed. This type of sensitivity analysis uses a best case and worst case approach whereby all of the lowest cost and highest benefit assumptions are used (best case) and compared to a scenario using the highest cost and lowest benefit assumptions (worst case).

A relatively recent addition to sensitivity analyses is a Monte Carlo simulation. This technique allows researchers to prespecify multiple ranges of values and to describe the underlying mathematical distributions of the variables used in an analysis. Modeling software then randomly selects values from the specified distributions of each variable. Thousands of iterations can quickly calculate results based on these selected values, thus creating confidence intervals around the mean costs and benefits in an economic modeling situation.[22,27]

## Guidelines for the Assessment of Economic Analyses

Several authors have offered specific criteria to audiences of health economic analyses to allow for their assessment of quality and objectivity. Drummond et al. presents a list of 10 questions, the answers to which can be used for the assessment of a published economic analysis.[28] The Panel on Cost-Effectiveness in Health and Medicine designed a checklist for authors of economic analyses that should be addressed in the preparation of their work.[29] Mullins et al. provides a summary of several sets of recommendations cited among major economic analyses in the healthcare setting as a set of the following six principles:

1. An explicit statement of the study perspective should be provided.
2. A detailed description of the benefits of the program or technology should be provided.
3. Researchers should specify what types of costs were used or considered in their analysis.
4. Discounting should be used to adjust for the differential accruals of costs and benefits.
5. Sensitivity analyses should be performed to test important assumptions.
6. In the presence of multiple alternatives, summary measures should be expressed as marginal or incremental ratios.[30]

## Research Synthesis

Because replication is an important part of the scientific process, a systematic review of existing studies—*research synthesis*—can provide a tool for understanding variations and similarities across studies. It can also uncover robust intervention effects. Before implementing a new program, careful public health managers check the evaluation literature to ensure that the intervention has been shown to be effective in other settings. Because such literature reviews often reveal a confusing range of different findings in evaluation studies of varying quality, techniques such as *meta-analysis* and more generally, research synthesis, are increasingly used in public health.[30,31,32,33]

Synthesis of research findings offers the potential to identify areas of agreement and to identify areas needing more research. Synthesis essentially involves a state-of-the-art literature review, presenting and analyzing the available data, and framing results so they can be translated into practice and policy. Meta-analysis is a subset of research synthesis that employs special statistical analyses of a collection of results from individual studies for the purpose of integrating the findings. This analysis can increase the statistical precision of the estimates of a program's effect.

In a research synthesis or meta-analysis, the individual study results are the raw data. Thus, in order to avoid bias, an a priori protocol for the selection of studies to be included and their analyses is needed. Search strategies should include bibliographic sources such as the National Library of Medicine (accessible through a medical library or www.nlm.nih.gov). Searching the bibliographies of review articles and studies at hand, as well as asking experts in the field for additional references, are also effective methods of research synthesis.

Once the relevant studies are identified, they can be presented through a narrative summary of each article or by an evidence table that lays out key aspects of each study, including the publication date, study population, study design and sample size, definitions of the intervention and of outcome measures, and results. When the available studies are sufficiently similar, statistical summaries can be prepared, as illustrated in the following paragraphs.

As part of the efforts of the Community Preventive Services Task Force, for instance, researchers from the Centers for Disease Control and Prevention (CDC) identified and reviewed the effectiveness of population-based efforts to improve vaccination coverage.[34] The interventions studied included efforts to increase community demand for immunizations such as patient reminder/recall systems; programs to enhance access to immunization services by reducing out-of-pocket costs, for example; immunization mandates at school, child care, and college entry; and provider-based strategies such as provider reminder/recall systems and the assessment of immunization rates and feedback for vaccination providers. A systematic literature search yielded 126 studies of such interventions. Following a standard approach, the researchers characterized the body of evidence as strong, sufficient, or insufficient based on the numbers of available studies, the strength of their design and execution, and the size and consistency of reported effects. This analysis then formed the basis for the recommendations of the task force.[35]

### Example: Efficacy and Effectiveness of Influenza Vaccines in the Elderly

In another example, researchers evaluated the efficacy and effectiveness of influenza vaccines in elderly people by identifying 5 randomized, 49 cohort, and 10 case-control studies assessing efficacy against influenza (reduction in laboratory-confirmed cases) or effectiveness against influenza-like illness (reduction in symptomatic cases).[36] Figure 18-1 summarizes the analysis of studies comparing vaccination with no vaccination for prevention of deaths caused by influenza or pneumonia in residents of long-term care facilities. Each line corresponds to one study, labeled by author. The box in the center of each line represents the study's estimate of the vaccine's effectiveness (the size of the box is proportional to sample size); the length of the line represents a 95% confidence interval for the estimate. Because the results might have differed according to the level of virus in circulation and how well the vaccine used matched the circulating viral strain, the studies were grouped according to these variables. In the lines headed "Subtotal" or "Total," the center of the diamonds represents the combined estimate of the studies above it and the width of the diamond represents the 95% confidence interval (CI) on the combined estimate. Although most of the individual studies do not show a significant reduction in risk because the 95% confidence line includes the null value of 1.0, the "Total" analysis suggests that the vaccine has a significant effect on the prevention of deaths caused by influenza or pneumonia. The overall relative risk is estimated as 0.46 with a 95% CI (0.33, 0.63), suggesting a reduction in the risk of death by more than half. Although the results in the four subgroups defined by level of viral circulation and quality of vaccine matching vary, the tests for heterogeneity do not suggest that the differences among them are significant. The results lead the authors of the review to conclude: "In long-term care facilities, where vaccination is most effective against complications, the aims of the vaccination campaign are fulfilled, at least in part. However, the usefulness of vaccines in the community is limited."[36]

In other instances, quantitative combination of results is simply not feasible because the available studies are too dissimilar. A National Research

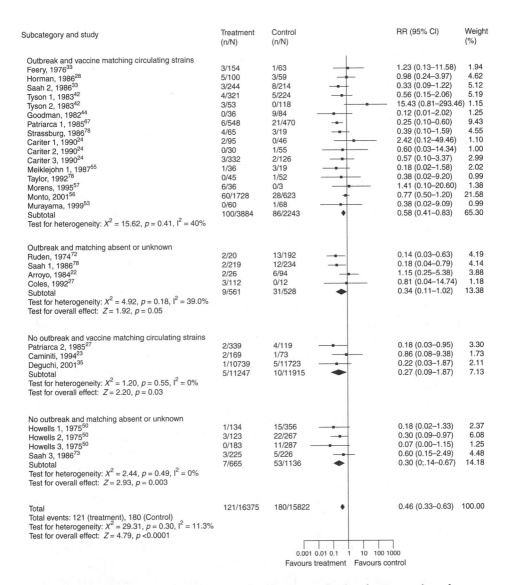

| Subcategory and study | Treatment (n/N) | Control (n/N) | | RR (95% CI) | Weight (%) |
|---|---|---|---|---|---|
| **Outbreak and vaccine matching circulating strains** | | | | | |
| Feery, 1976[33] | 3/154 | 1/63 | | 1.23 (0.13–11.58) | 1.94 |
| Horman, 1986[28] | 5/100 | 3/59 | | 0.98 (0.24–3.97) | 4.62 |
| Saah 2, 1986[33] | 3/244 | 8/214 | | 0.33 (0.09–1.22) | 5.12 |
| Tyson 1, 1983[42] | 4/321 | 5/224 | | 0.56 (0.15–2.06) | 5.19 |
| Tyson 2, 1983[42] | 3/53 | 0/118 | | 15.43 (0.81–293.46) | 1.15 |
| Goodman, 1982[44] | 0/36 | 9/84 | | 0.12 (0.01–2.02) | 1.25 |
| Patriarca 1, 1985[67] | 6/548 | 21/470 | | 0.25 (0.10–0.60) | 9.43 |
| Strassburg, 1986[78] | 4/65 | 3/19 | | 0.39 (0.10–1.59) | 4.55 |
| Cariter 1, 1990[24] | 2/95 | 0/46 | | 2.42 (0.12–49.46) | 1.10 |
| Cariter 2, 1990[24] | 0/30 | 1/55 | | 0.60 (0.03–14.34) | 1.00 |
| Cariter 3, 1990[24] | 3/332 | 2/126 | | 0.57 (0.10–3.37) | 2.99 |
| Meiklejohn 1, 1987[55] | 1/36 | 3/19 | | 0.18 (0.02–1.58) | 2.02 |
| Taylor, 1992[78] | 0/45 | 1/52 | | 0.38 (0.02–9.20) | 0.99 |
| Morens, 1995[57] | 6/36 | 0/3 | | 1.41 (0.10–20.60) | 1.38 |
| Monto, 2001[56] | 60/1728 | 28/623 | | 0.77 (0.50–1.20) | 21.58 |
| Murayama, 1999[53] | 0/60 | 1/68 | | 0.38 (0.02–9.09) | 0.99 |
| Subtotal | 100/3884 | 86/2243 | | 0.58 (0.41–0.83) | 65.30 |
| Test for heterogeneity: $X^2 = 15.62$, $p = 0.41$, $I^2 = 40\%$ | | | | | |
| | | | | | |
| **Outbreak and matching absent or unknown** | | | | | |
| Ruden, 1974[72] | 2/20 | 13/192 | | 0.14 (0.03–0.63) | 4.19 |
| Saah 1, 1986[78] | 2/219 | 12/234 | | 0.18 (0.04–0.79) | 4.14 |
| Arroyo, 1984[22] | 2/26 | 6/94 | | 1.15 (0.25–5.38) | 3.88 |
| Coles, 1992[27] | 3/112 | 0/12 | | 0.81 (0.04–14.74) | 1.18 |
| Subtotal | 9/561 | 31/528 | | 0.34 (0.11–1.02) | 13.38 |
| Test for heterogeneity: $X^2 = 4.92$, $p = 0.18$, $I^2 = 39.0\%$ | | | | | |
| Test for overall effect: $Z = 1.92$, $p = 0.05$ | | | | | |
| | | | | | |
| **No outbreak and vaccine matching circulating strains** | | | | | |
| Patriarca 2, 1985[27] | 2/339 | 4/119 | | 0.18 (0.03–0.95) | 3.30 |
| Caminiti, 1994[23] | 2/169 | 1/73 | | 0.86 (0.08–9.38) | 1.73 |
| Deguchi, 2001[35] | 1/10739 | 5/11723 | | 0.22 (0.03–1.87) | 2.11 |
| Subtotal | 5/11247 | 10/11915 | | 0.27 (0.09–1.87) | 7.13 |
| Test for heterogeneity: $X^2 = 1.20$, $p = 0.55$, $I^2 = 0\%$ | | | | | |
| Test for overall effect: $Z = 2.20$, $p = 0.03$ | | | | | |
| | | | | | |
| **No outbreak and matching absent or unknown** | | | | | |
| Howells 1, 1975[50] | 1/134 | 15/356 | | 0.18 (0.02–1.33) | 2.37 |
| Howells 2, 1975[50] | 3/123 | 22/267 | | 0.30 (0.09–0.97) | 6.08 |
| Howells 3, 1975[50] | 0/183 | 11/287 | | 0.07 (0.00–1.15) | 1.25 |
| Saah 3, 1986[73] | 3/225 | 5/226 | | 0.60 (0.15–2.49) | 4.48 |
| Subtotal | 7/665 | 53/1136 | | 0.30 (0;.14–0.67) | 14.18 |
| Test for heterogeneity: $X^2 = 2.44$, $p = 0.49$, $I^2 = 0\%$ | | | | | |
| Test for overall effect: $Z = 2.93$, $p = 0.003$ | | | | | |
| | | | | | |
| **Total** | 121/16375 | 180/15822 | | 0.46 (0.33–0.63) | 100.00 |
| Total events: 121 (treatment), 180 (Control) | | | | | |
| Test for heterogeneity: $X^2 = 29.31$, $p = 0.30$, $I^2 = 11.3\%$ | | | | | |
| Test for overall effect: $Z = 4.79$, $p < 0.0001$ | | | | | |

0.001  0.01  0.1    1    10  100  1000
Favours treatment    Favours control

**FIGURE 18-1    Influenza Vaccine Compared with No Vaccination for Prevention of Deaths Caused by Influenza or Pneumonia in Residents of Long-Term Care Facilities by Level of Viral Circulation and Quality of Vaccine Matching. Number after Names of Authors Indicates Different Databases.**
*Source:* Reprinted from Jefferson T, Rivetti D, Rivetti A, Rudin M, DiPietrantonj C, Demicheli V. Efficacy and effectiveness of influenza vaccines in elderly people: a systematic review. *Lancet.* 2005; 366:1165–1174.

Council (NRC) evaluation of the evidence surrounding the efficacy of needle exchange programs to prevent HIV transmission provides an example.[37] The logic of this approach is clear—needles are an important vector of transmission among drug users because they are passed among users, so introducing clean needles into circulation should avert new infections. When asked by Congress to review the evidence on this issue in 1995, the NRC found dozens of evaluation studies that had been prepared. Each of these studies, however, addressed different aspects of the problem: how needles can be distributed when state laws prohibit their possession, the costs and logistics of distributing needles and condoms, knowledge of HIV risk factors, various changes in users' needle use and other HIV risk factors, referral to drug treatment, and so on. Other studies examined the concerns of community leaders and individuals living near the needle exchange sites. Only a handful of reports examined HIV infection rates, which are difficult to study because the annual number of new infections in any study group is generally rather small. Moreover, many of the existing studies were of poor quality, which is not surprising given that many of the existing programs were not legally sanctioned.

There were, however, two groups of studies that provided useful information. In New Haven, Connecticut, researchers had been evaluating a needle exchange program run out of mobile vans.[38] One unique aspect of this program was that every needle distributed was marked with an identifying number, and each needle returned was checked using biomedical measures for exposure to HIV. These two pieces of information showed that the program reduced the infectivity of needles in circulation by approximately one third. Coupled with information from a survey of the needle exchange users, the researchers used a mathematical model to show that a needle exchange program could reduce the rate of new infections by approximately one third.

Another series of studies took advantage of the fact that one of the first needle exchange programs in the United States was organized in Tacoma, Washington, which had a preexisting enhanced hepatitis B surveillance program.[39] Hepatitis B is transmitted through blood products and sexual activity, just as HIV, but has a higher infectivity rate and shorter latency period. As a result, a group of studies in Tacoma were able to establish that needle exchange programs were effective in preventing the transmission of a blood-borne virus.

The NRC panel reviewing this evidence used a logic model to synthesize the evaluation evidence. First, a series of process studies showing that needles could be distributed efficiently ruled in the plausibility of the idea. The New Haven studies showed that needle exchange programs can increase the availability of clean equipment and reduce HIV prevalence in needles in circulation. Logically, one expects that decreasing the fraction of needles in circulation that are contaminated will lower the risk of new HIV infections, and the Connecticut model quantified this effect. The Tacoma studies confirmed the logical analysis by showing that needle exchange programs can reduce the incidence of a blood-borne disease. The NRC panel concluded, therefore, that needle exchange programs can reduce the risk of HIV infection.

## Measurement

Measurement is central to evaluation. (Refer to Chapter 17 for detailed discussion of measurement.) Evaluations of program effectiveness can only assess the impact on the outcomes that have been measured, and measures of program inputs are critical for interpreting the results. The importance of measurement in performance improvement is clear from the management aphorism: what gets measured gets done. The development of measures for any evaluation involves the following four steps.

## Clarify the Goals and Purposes of the Evaluation

In general, the goals and purposes of an evaluation determine the types of measures that are needed. Outcome evaluations need measures of health outcomes, whereas feasibility evaluations must focus on costs and barriers to implementation. Evaluations of programs intended to be exported to other venues must include measures of the specific intervention so that it can be replicated. Evaluations based on quasi-experimental designs require careful measures of confounding factors for adjustment purposes. Efforts to ensure accountability often require financial measures.

As illustrated in Figure 18-2, various disciplinary lenses produce different approaches to health promotion and disease prevention. At the micro-level, the *biomedical* lens focuses on biophysiological theories of disease causation and turns to biomedical interventions for solutions. The *psychosocial* lens focuses on the individual, investigating questions about individual and social behaviors such as self-efficacy and control. The *epidemiologic* lens examines disease patterns in populations and identifies differential risk factors, both biologic and environmental. The *society-and-health* lens aims to understand the way that cultural, social, economic, and political processes influence differential risks. The choice of lens underlying the intervention obviously determines the nature of the evaluation: what is measured, and so on.

An explicit "logic model" describing the logical sequence of events that connect an intervention to the desired change can be valuable in evaluating complex interventions or simple interventions in complex causal chains.

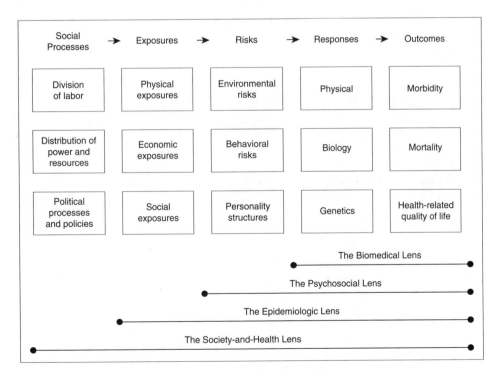

**FIGURE 18-2    Alternative Disciplinary Lenses for Factors Influencing Health Outcomes**
*Source:* Adapted with permission from *Annual Review of Public Health,* Vol 19, © 1998 by Annual Review, www.AnnualReviews.org.

Figure 18-3 illustrates a logic model for a community-based immunization program—part of a larger effort to reduce the impact of vaccine-preventable diseases. The upper component of the figure illustrates the different types of specific interventions that are possible: community-based educational programs designed to increase community demand for vaccinations, interventions to enhance access to healthcare settings, and provider-based interventions to increase the use of vaccines among those who have access to care.

Evaluations of community-based interventions require measures of awareness and access in the community. Evaluations of provider-based interventions, on the other hand, require only measures of covered populations. A beneficial effect of vaccine coverage on vaccine-preventable disease and associated morbidity and mortality is assumed, based on previous clinical studies of the vaccines themselves. Intermediate measures of vaccine coverage, and not of morbidity and mortality, are thus sufficient for evaluations on efforts to improve immunization rates. Other interventions to reduce mortality and morbidity are possible (medical treatment of individuals who contract vaccine-preventable diseases, efforts to reduce contacts between infectious and noninfectious individuals). These are not, however, usually treated in evaluations of immunization programs.

## Identify the Concepts to be Measured

Depending on the nature of the intervention and the purpose of the evaluation, measures should be chosen to reflect the logic of the process. In the immunization example in Exhibit 18-1, for instance, measures need to be developed for each of the major inputs and activities (availability of a registry), as well as the intermediate outcomes (births enrolled in a registry) and final outcomes (in-

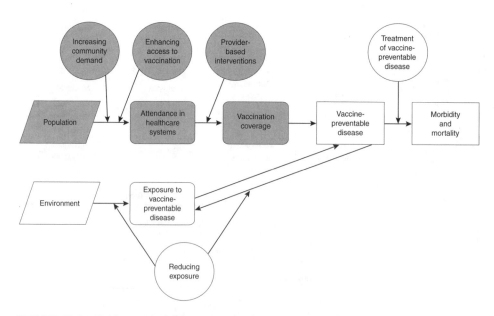

**FIGURE 18-3    Evidence Model for Immunization Program Evaluations**
*Source:* Adapted from US Centers for Disease Control and Prevention. Framework for program evaluation in public health. *MMWR.* 1999;RR-11: 1–40.

creased numbers of children immunized). In performance improvement processes (as discussed later), it is important to identify responsibility for specific activities and to choose measures that enable accountability for performance. It is also important to choose a set of measures that achieves a balance between short- and long-range goals and among levels and types of service.[40]

Complex programs require a variety of measures relating to the logic of the intervention. As a condition of funding, the Health Resources and Services Administration (HRSA) maternal and child health programs, for example, require states to report their yearly performance on a number of measures. States can choose from a variety of standard "health system capacity measures" and "health status indicators" as illustrated in Table 18-1. A group of 18 "national performance measures" covering both process and outcomes is required of all states.[41]

## Develop Specific Indicators for Each Concept

General concepts such as immunization coverage and low birth weight are not sufficient for program evaluation because they can be operationalized in many ways. Careful evaluation requires that each concept be measurable by one or more specific indicators operationally defined in an unambiguous way.

Finding indicators that faithfully represent the critical concepts and that can be calculated in a timely way from available data is often a challenge.

**TABLE 18-1    Examples of Specific Indicators for State Maternal and Child Health Programs**

| Concept | Specific Indicator |
|---|---|
| *National performance measures* | |
| Insurance coverage | The percentage of children with special health care needs age 0 to 18 years whose families have adequate private and/or public insurance to pay for the services they need |
| Insurance coverage | Percentage of children without health insurance |
| Adequate prenatal care | Percentage of infants born to pregnant women receiving prenatal care beginning in the first trimester |
| Immunization coverage | Percentage of 19 to 35 month olds who have received full schedule of age appropriate immunizations against measles, mumps, rubella, polio, diphtheria, tetanus, pertussis, haemophilis influenza, and hepatitis B. |
| *Health system capacity measures* | |
| Eligibility for publicly funded insurance | The percentage of poverty level for eligibility in the state's Medicaid and SCHIP programs for infants (0 to 1), children, and pregnant women. |
| *Health status indicators* | |
| Low birth weight | The percentage of live births weighing less than 2500 grams |
| Very low birth weight | The percentage of live births weighing less than 1500 grams |

*Source:* Maternal and Child Health Bureau. *Maternal and Child Health Services Title V Block Grant Program: Proposed National Performance Measures, Health Systems Capacity Indicators, and Health Status Indicators.* US Department of Health and Human Services. Available at: http://mchb.hrsa.gov/grants/proposal.html.

Mortality, for instance, can be measured through general mortality rates or through disease-specific rates, which are available on a less timely basis. Healthcare costs can be measured by hospital and physician charges, but these may not accurately reflect the opportunity costs of these interventions consistent with economic theory. Quality of health care is sometimes measured through consumer satisfaction surveys, but such measures reflect only part of what policy analysts define as quality.[42] Table 18-1 illustrates the correspondence between some of the HRSA performance measure concepts and specific indicators for state maternal and child health programs.

### Assess the Performance of the Proposed Indicators with Respect to Validity, Reliability, and Sensitivity to Change

Before an evaluation process goes forward, the indicators to be used must be assessed, especially in terms of validity and reliability. *Validity* is an indicator's capacity to measure the intended concept. *Reliability*, on the other hand, assesses whether the indicator consistently measures the concept. The relationship between the two is illustrated graphically in Figure 18-4.

*Sensitivity to change* assesses an indicator's ability to measure change that might be attributed to the intervention being evaluated. Some errors are related to chance fluctuations in epidemiologic rates. For most communities, for example, infant mortality rates fluctuate substantially from year to year simply because the numerator, the number of infant deaths, is small. Statistical measures can be used to assess the degree to which the indicator changes if and only if the concept being measured also changes. A common problem is when service records are used to assess changing disease burdens. Does a decrease in emergency department visits for asthma indicate the success of a prevention program or measures to restrict access to individuals without insurance?

Compromises must generally be made among validity, reliability, data availability, and sensitivity to change. In the area of prenatal care, for example, evaluators often use the receipt of prenatal care in the first trimester, rather than more complex measures based on official recommendations of the US Public Health Service for the frequency and content of prenatal care, because the former measure is available on birth certificates and the latter is not.[43] This is a case of trading validity for increased data availability. In many communities,

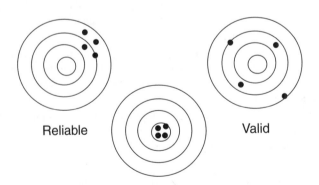

FIGURE 18-4   **Illustration of the Concepts of Reliability and Validity**

annual infant mortality rates are not reliable because of the small number of infant deaths. Instead of annual rates, therefore, epidemiologists commonly calculate running averages by averaging infant mortality rates over three or five years. This is a case in which reliability is gained at the expense of timeliness and responsiveness to change. Another approach that is frequently used to deal with sparse data is to use proxy measures that reflect trends and differences. The percentage of infants born at low birth weight, for example, is used rather than infant mortality because low birth weight has been shown to be strongly associated with infant mortality. This is a case of trading validity for reliability.

### Data Sources

Data for evaluations in public health can be obtained from a wide variety of sources. (See Chapter 11 for an extensive description of various data sources.) The extended tobacco control example at the end of this chapter also illustrates the variety of data sources that can be accessed for evaluation efforts.

Capacity, process, and implementation measures can come from administrative records, existing reports and documents, and persons involved with the program. Administrative records provide good information on resources that are available and expended, the number of service providers assigned to a program, the number of clients served and the nature of services provided, and so on. Data of this sort can sometimes be derived from the management information systems used to run the program itself. In other cases, information can be obtained from clients, program staff, and others through surveys and focus groups. Documents such as grant proposals, newsletters, annual reports, and asset and needs assessments can also provide useful data for evaluations.

Outcome measures can also be derived from a variety of data sources, including vital statistics (birth and death records) and public health surveillance programs. Administrative and medical records from the healthcare system, because they are increasingly computerized and thus accessible, can also provide useful outcome measures. General- and special-purpose population surveys and client surveys can also provide useful information for program evaluation.

## Practical Aspects of Program Evaluation

Improving the standards of evidence used in the evaluation of public health interventions is one of the most critical needs in this field. More rigorous studies are needed to better determine "what works," "for whom," "under what conditions," and "at what cost." According to a National Research Council/Institute of Medicine (IOM) report on family violence programs,[44] which can be generalized to many other areas in public health, the road to improvement requires attention to: (1) assessing the limitations of current evaluations, (2) forging functional partnerships between researchers and service providers, (3) addressing the dynamics of collaboration in those partnerships, and (4) exploring new evaluation methods to assess comprehensive community initiatives.*

---

*This section draws heavily on the contributions of David Cordray to the NRC report *Violence in Families.*[44]

Interventions undergo an evolutionary process that refines theories, services, and approaches over time. In the early stages, interventions generate reform efforts and evaluations that rely primarily on descriptive studies and anecdotal data. As these interventions and evaluation efforts mature, they begin to approach the standards of evidence needed to make confident judgments concerning effectiveness and cost. For instance, current policy discussions are focused on determining the effectiveness or cost-effectiveness of selected programs or strategies, conclusions that require high standards of evidence. Existing evaluation studies, however, consist mostly of nonexperimental study designs, and thus provide no firm basis for examining the impact of programs or for considering the ways in which different types of clients respond to an intervention. Nonexperimental studies, however, can reveal important information in the developmental process of research. They can illuminate the characteristics and experience of program participants, the nature of the presenting problems, and the issues associated with efforts to implement individual programs or to change systems of service within the community. Although these kinds of studies cannot provide evidence of effectiveness, they do represent important building blocks in evaluation research.

A similar developmental process exists on the programmatic side of interventions. Many family violence treatment and prevention programs, for example, have their origins in the efforts of advocates who are concerned about children, women, and the family unit. Over several decades of organized activity, these efforts have fostered the development of interventions in social service, health, and law enforcement settings that program sponsors believe will reduce violent behavior or improve the welfare of victims. Some programs are based on common sense or legal authority; others are based on broad theories of human interaction or theory borrowed from other areas. All of these interventions were preceded by research studies that identified risk factors or critical decision points in the intervention process. As programs mature and become better articulated and implemented, evaluation questions and methods become more sophisticated and complex.

It is difficult for researchers to establish good standards of evidence in service settings because they cannot exert complete control over the selection of clients and the implementation of the interventions. But several strategies have emerged that can guide the development of evaluation research as it moves from its descriptive stage into the conduct of quasi-experimental and true experimental studies. An important part of this process is the development of a "fleet of studies."[44,45] The NRC evaluation of the effectiveness of needle exchange programs discussed earlier provides one example. Although each individual study of a given project was insufficient to support a claim that the needle exchange program was effective, the collective strengths of the studies taken together provided a basis for a firm inference.

To overcome the technical challenges of conducting evaluations in public health service settings, several steps have been suggested.[44] Most importantly, research and evaluation need to be incorporated earlier into the program design and implementation process.[46] The use of innovative study designs, such as empowerment evaluation, described elsewhere in this chapter, can provide opportunities to assess the impact of programs, interventions, and strategies. Drawing on both qualitative and quantitative methods, these approaches can help service providers and researchers share expertise and experience with service operation and implementation.

Integration of the evaluation and practice perspectives requires creative collaboration between researchers and providers who are in direct contact with the individuals who receive services and the institutions that support them. Numerous points in the research and program development processes provide opportunities for such collaboration.[47] Practitioners, for example, have extensive knowledge of the needs of clients and the nature of existing services in the community. Service providers' knowledge of details concerning client flow, rates of retention in treatment, organizational capacity, and similar details are useful in developing new interventions and a logic model that provides the framework for the evaluation. Their participation can highlight differences between new services and usual-care situations, which are often a matter of degree. Practitioners can also help to ensure that the outcomes assessed are the ones of concern. Finally, service providers have knowledge of other services and factors in the community that affect outcomes of interest.

The dynamics of collaborative relationships between evaluators and program managers require explicit attention and team-building efforts to resolve different approaches and to stimulate consensus about promising models of service delivery, program implementation, and outcomes of interest. Creative collaboration requires attention to the following issues:[44]

- Setting up equal partnerships—Tensions between service providers and researchers may reflect differences in ideology and theory about the issues being addressed or mutual misunderstandings about the purpose and conduct of evaluation research. Frontline service providers may resent the time and resources that research takes from the provision of services. True collaborative partnerships require a valuing and respect for the work of all sides. Both sides need to spend time observing each other's domains in order to better their constraints and risks.

  Recent collaborations in the evaluation of family violence interventions illustrate opportunities to address these concerns. Community agencies are beginning to realize that well-documented and soundly evaluated successes will help ensure their financial viability and even attract additional financial resources to support promising programs. Researchers are starting to recognize the accumulated expertise of agency personnel and how important they can be in planning as well as conducting their studies. Both parties are recognizing that, even if research fails to confirm the success of a program, the evaluation results can be used to improve the program.

- The impact of ethnicity and culture on the research process—Ethnicity and cultural competence influence all aspects of the research process and require careful consideration at various stages: formulation of hypotheses taking into account known cultural or ethnic differences, large enough sampling sizes to have enough power to determine differential impact for different ethnic groups, and analytic strategies that account for ethnic differences and other measures of culture. In evaluating family violence interventions, for example, there is a need for researchers who are knowledgeable about cultural practices such as parenting and caregiving, child supervision, spousal relationships, and sexual behaviors in specific ethnic groups.

- Exit issues—The ideal relationship between a research team and the service agency is long term and sustained between large formal evaluations. Such informal collaborations can help researchers, for example, in establishing the publications needed for large-scale funding. Dissemination of findings in local publications is also helpful to the agency. Successful collaboration requires that all partners decide on the authorship and format of publications ahead of time. Thoughtful discussions are also needed before launching an evaluation about what will be released in terms of negative findings and how the findings will be used to improve services.

  Another concern is the continuation of services when research resources are no longer available. Models of reimbursement and subsidy plans are needed to foster positive partnerships that can sustain services that seem to be useful to a community after the research evaluation has been completed.

### Evaluation of Comprehensive Community-Based Interventions

In recent years, public health researchers have developed a series of comprehensive community-based interventions that reflect the growing appreciation of the social determinants of health and health-related behavior.[48,49] (See Chapter 19 for a more detailed discussion of community-based prevention.) These interventions take place in schools, work sites, and even whole communities. They typically address smoking, diet, exercise, and other behavioral risk factors for cancer and cardiovascular disease.[4] Because of their complexity and scale, however, such interventions present special challenges to evaluators.

Moreover, public health interventions increasingly involve multiple services and the coordinated actions of multiple agencies in a community. The increasing prevalence of coexisting problems such as substance abuse and family violence or child abuse and domestic violence, for instance, has encouraged the use of comprehensive services to address multiple risk factors associated with a variety of social problems. In tobacco control, as illustrated below, the range of entities and activities involved is so great that in some senses, the community itself is the proper unit of analysis for evaluations.

As public health programs become a more integrated part of the community, the challenges for evaluation become increasingly complex.[43]

- Because participants receive numerous services, it is nearly impossible to determine which service, if any, contributed to improvement in their well-being.
- If the sequencing of program activities depends on the particular needs of participants, it is difficult to tease apart the effects of selectivity bias and program effects.
- As intervention activities increasingly involve organizations throughout the community, there is a growing chance that everyone in need will receive some form of service (reducing the chance of constituting an appropriate comparison group).

- As program activities saturate the community, it is necessary to view the community as the unit of analysis in the evaluation. Outcomes, however, are typically measured at the individual level. At a minimum, appropriate statistical models are needed to take the different levels into account.[6]
- The tremendous variation in individual communities and diversity in organizational approaches impede analyses of the implementation stages of interventions.
- An emphasis on community process factors (ones that facilitate or impede the adoption of comprehensive service systems), as opposed to program components, suggests that evaluation measures require a general taxonomy that can be adapted to particular local conditions.

Conventional notions of what constituted a rigorous evaluation design are not easily adapted to meet these challenges. Some authors have concluded that randomization is simply not feasible, and that conventional alternatives to randomization are technically insufficient.[50,51] Weiss proposed an alternative evaluation model based on clarifying the "theories of change" that explores how and why an intervention is supposed to work.[51] The evaluation should start with the explicit and implicit assumptions underlying the theory guiding the intervention efforts; this theory is generally based on a series of small steps that involve assumptions about linkages to other activities or surrounding conditions. By creating a network of assumptions, it is possible to gather data to test whether the progression of actions leads to the intended end point.

Other researchers note that the theory of change perspective provides some basic principles to guide collaborative evaluations.[52] First, the theory of change should draw on the available scientific information, and it should be judged plausible by all the stakeholders. Second, the theory of change should be doable—that is, the activities defined in the theory should be able to be implemented. Third, the theory should be testable, which means that the specification of outcomes should follow logically from the theory.

Community interventions are characterized by small relative effects. Strong interventions typically yield a 2% to 5% reduction in the prevalence of risk factors such as smoking or lack of exercise, or a similar percentage reduction in average serum cholesterol or blood pressure. As Geoffrey Rose observed, changes of this magnitude in entire populations are likely to have large effects on disease risk and the burden of morbidity and mortality.[53,54] Thus, from a public health perspective, the impact of an intervention is a product of both its efficacy in changing individual behavior and its reach, meaning the proportion of the population reached either through their direct participation or indirectly through diffusion of intervention messages throughout the community, work site, or school.[55] Anna Tosteson and colleagues, for instance, estimated that population-wide strategies to reduce serum cholesterol are cost-effective if cholesterol is reduced by as little as 2%.[56] Thus, although the effects of community interventions may appear small by standards of clinical research, these interventions can have a substantial public health impact.

Small effect sizes, however, create significant statistical difficulties in the evaluation of community interventions. Although the number of individuals

involved in community trials is often large, the number of units of allocation that are randomized (schools, work sites, or whole communities) is typically very small. Furthermore, the power and precision of statistical tests
depends more on the number of units of allocation than on the number of
individuals.[6] Taken together with small effect sizes, these features of community interventions make it very difficult to achieve statistical significance
in conventional terms. In other words, a true 2% reduction in a risk factor,
which has great public health significance, might not achieve statistical
significance in a study with thousands of individuals in a small number of
communities.

A number of statistical approaches may help resolve this problem. First,
more efficient statistical methods are needed to improve investigators' ability
to detect small differences. This can come through increasing the number of
units of allocation in studies or making better statistical use of the existing
information through, say, the use of appropriate hierarchical statistical models.[57] Alternatively, where separate interventions have used parallel methods
in similar populations, meta-analysis can be useful in increasing statistical
power. Alternatively, future interventions might be planned with enough
parallelism that meta-analysis is appropriate after the individual results are
available.

### Empowerment Evaluation

Empowerment evaluation represents a new use of evaluation concepts, techniques, and findings to foster improvement and self-determination. It has its
roots in education and social services but has many applications to public
health. This form of evaluation draws on empowerment processes, in which
attempts to gain control, obtain needed resources, and critically understand
one's social environment are fundamental. It is designed to help people help
themselves and improve their programs using a form of self-evaluation and
reflection. Empowerment evaluation is necessarily a collaborative group activity, not an individual pursuit.[2]

As illustrated in Figure 18-5, empowerment evaluation involves six steps.
These six steps are described below using the example of coalitions in three
Kansas communities for the prevention of adolescent pregnancy and sub-
stance abuse.[58]

1. Take stock. Determine where the program stands, including strengths
   and weaknesses, and identify community concerns and resources. A
   series of listening sessions—informal public meetings in which individuals identified problems, barriers to addressing the problem, resources
   for change, and potential solutions—were held to engage key leaders,
   people affected by the problem, and people who could contribute to
   addressing the problem. The groups included religious leaders, youth,
   parents, teachers, health officials, and representatives from informal
   neighborhood groups and community organizations.
2. Focus on setting missions and establishing goals. Determine where
   you want to go in the future with an explicit emphasis on program
   improvement. In Kansas, the initial mission and goals were based on
   initiatives that had shown some success in reducing adolescent preg-

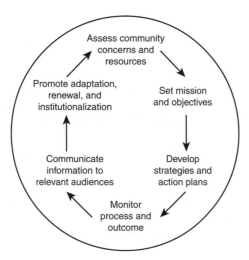

**FIGURE 18-5    Process of Empowerment Evaluation**
*Source:* Adapted with permission. Fawcett SB, Paine-Andrews A, Francisco VT, et al. Empowering community health initiatives through evaluation. In Fetterman DM, Kaftarian SJ, Wandersman A, eds. *Empowerment Evaluation: Knowledge and Tools for Self-Assessment and Accountability.* Thousand Oaks, Calif: Sage; 1996:170.

nancy and substance abuse in other Kansas communities. Following a shooting in one community, the coalition modified its objectives and action plan to reflect community concerns about youth violence associated with substance use.

3. Develop strategies and action plans to accomplish goals and objectives. Each community developed its own action plans, based on the model developed in other communities, consisting of proposed changes in programs, policies, and practices in a variety of sectors. Schools, for example, were to implement a "comprehensive K–12 age-appropriate sexuality education curriculum."

4. Monitor process and outcome measures to document progress toward goals. In Kansas, measurements were based on a monitoring system that was based on logs and administrative records to assess process and intermediate outcomes, constituent surveys of process and outcome, school-based behavioral surveys, community-level indicators such as the pregnancy rate, and interviews with key participants.

5. Communicate information to relevant audiences. Regularly sharing accomplishments and keeping constituents informed of progress are important to maintaining community support, obtaining additional resources, and ensuring accountability. In Kansas, data were shared with the coalition leadership, the community at large, and the Kansas Health Foundation, the primary sponsor.

6. Promote adaptation, renewal, and institutionalization. The monitoring data helped the Kansas coalition recognize accomplishments and redirect energies when necessary. In one community, for example, high levels of substance abuse service provision and low levels of community action indicated that the coalition was becoming a service agency rather than a catalyst for community change.

## The Evaluation Process

A working group from the CDC recently published a set of standards and a framework for effective program evaluation in public health.[59] This framework derives from both the practical experience of the CDC and other public health practitioners and from the published standards and recommendations of practitioners in public health, social services, and education.

To be effective, evaluation efforts must meet the following four standards:

1. Utility—Evaluation must serve the information needs of intended users.
2. Feasibility—Evaluation efforts must be realistic, prudent, diplomatic, and frugal.
3. Propriety—Evaluators must behave legally, ethically, and with regard for the welfare of those involved and those affected.
4. Accuracy—Evaluation must reveal and convey technically accurate information.

The CDC's framework describes evaluation efforts as a cycle consisting of the following six steps (Figure 18-6). Although the steps are logically ordered, all are interrelated, and most actual evaluation efforts require iteration and feedback among the steps.

*Identify and Engage Stakeholders.* A number of different parties have an interest in the outcome of any evaluation; they include persons involved in and affected by the program, as well as the primary users of the evaluation, and especially those who will use it to make decisions about resources or policy. Some stakeholders are obvious: program participants, service providers, and so on. Other stakeholders, however, are less direct. Employers, for instance, may have an interest in a school-based drug prevention program if it increases the productivity of graduates hired by the company.

Engaging these stakeholders means fostering input, participation, and power sharing in the planning and conduct of the evaluation and in the interpretation and dissemination of the findings. This engagement can improve

**FIGURE 18-6   CDC Framework for Program Evaluation in Public Health**
*Source:* Adapted from Centers for Disease Control and Prevention. Framework for program evaluation in Public Health. *MMWR.* 1999;48(AR-11):1–40.

credibility, clarify roles and responsibilities, ensure cultural relevance and understanding, help protect human experimental subjects, and avoid real or perceived conflicts of interest. Ultimately, it helps to increase the chance that the evaluation will be useful and have a positive impact.

*Describe the Program.*   Before a program can be evaluated, it must be described in terms of the needs it is to address and its purpose, activities, resources, and expected effects. Placing a program in a larger context and clarifying why program activities are believed to lead to the expected changes improves the evaluation's fairness and accuracy. It also permits a balanced assessment of strengths and weaknesses and helps stakeholders understand how program features fit together and relate to a larger context. A clear description of the program as actually implemented is especially important for new activities, which may be implemented in very different ways in different localities. Such descriptions are essential in assessing why interventions work in some settings and not in others.

*Focus the Evaluation Design.*   If an evaluation is to be useful, it is important to clarify at the outset its purpose and uses, as well as the potential users of the results. Assessing the effectiveness of a new program may require different research designs than ensuring the accountability of contractors. Different users are interested in different research questions, depending on their interests, authority, and responsibility. Consider, for example, a community-wide campaign to educate people about the need to call 911 immediately after chest pains begin, and specifically to educate them not to worry about being embarrassed if the pain turns out not to be a heart attack. The local chapter of the American Heart Association, which may have been responsible for getting out the word through the media, would want to know how many people saw the ads and whether they understood and recalled the message. Emergency room staff would focus on how individuals were treated after they arrived, and look specifically at those individuals without heart attacks. Managed care organizations might look at the pretreatment approval process. Specific research methods for evaluation are discussed above.

*Gather Credible Evidence.*   To ensure accuracy and meet the needs of users, evaluation efforts must be based on credible quantitative and qualitative indicators. Indicators are specific measures of program attributes or outcomes that pertain to an evaluation's focus or questions. An evaluation of an educational program to prevent teen violence would require, for example, information on the intensity of the intervention as well as the outcome. Specific indicators of program intensity might be the number of hours of student contact time in the ninth grade or the number of minutes of airtime on a specific group of radio stations that teens favor. Outcome indicators could be the percentage of students who recall the basic message of the program and the number of violent incidents in the targeted schools in the year following program implementation.

Data that are timely must be identified or developed, and steps must be taken to ensure the credibility of the data to the intended users of the evaluation. If data are provided by an agency with a stake in the outcome of the evaluation, auditing or other steps to ensure accuracy may be necessary. Often, compromises must be made between validity, reliability, timeliness, and credibility.

*Justify Conclusions.*   The conclusions of an evaluation are justified when they are based on evidence that is credible to the stakeholders and that addresses their values and concerns. Standards are explicit statements of stakeholders' values that are operationalized in a way that allows evaluators to judge an intervention's success. A program to reduce the consequences of sexually transmitted disease (STD), for example, might be evaluated in terms of its feasibility in public health clinics and managed care organizations, sensitivity to public values about sexuality, and reduction of disease burden in the population.

The conclusions and recommendations of an evaluation are the product of statistical analysis appropriate to the design of the evaluation and the synthesis of all of the available data, comparing indicators to appropriate standards. An STD evaluation might include an examination of the number of gonorrhea cases reported to the public health department before and after the intervention. This analysis, however, must be interpreted in context. Does a drop in reported cases reflect a decrease in disease, or in individuals getting treatment in private settings or not at all? Is a shift of cases from public clinics to private clinics a desired outcome? Analyses of this sort generally require a substantial amount of professional judgment by evaluation specialists.

*Ensure Use and Share Lessons Learned.*    Evaluation results do not translate into informed decision making and appropriate action without deliberate efforts to ensure that the findings are appropriately disseminated and called to policy makers' attention. Evaluations must first be carefully designed with the concerns and interests of the stakeholders in mind, as discussed above. Dissemination efforts must be planned to ensure that the evaluation results are brought to the attention of those persons or organizations that are in a position to use them in a form that is understandable and useful to that audience. Evaluations must follow up with stakeholders to ensure that the results are understood and not misused. Finally, opportunities for feedback can be useful to evaluators in creating an atmosphere of trust among stakeholders and in refocusing future evaluation efforts, if necessary.

Some managers in public health say, as a point of pride, that they always evaluate every program that they implement. Indeed, some federal agencies and private foundations require evaluation of all funded projects. How does this square with clinical medicine, where physicians do not "evaluate" every procedure that they perform? Having once shown that a procedure works, there is no need to evaluate it every time. The answer is that there are many forms of evaluation, and there is usually one appropriate for any situation in public health. If an intervention has been shown to work in another community, for instance, health officials might want to check that it is being properly implemented and works under the conditions in their communities. Evaluation techniques can also be useful to ensure that a program continues to be properly implemented, an approach known as *performance measurement* as discussed in Chapter 17.

## Performance Measurement and Improvement Processes

In recent years, public health and healthcare policy makers have come to realize the importance of population-based data on health status and the determinants of health for effective policy determination, especially for improving the accountability of managed care organizations, public health agencies, and other entities that can contribute to the public's health. Part of this realization is due to the nature of public health and the emerging importance of preventive medicine: their impact can only be seen in statistical terms such as declining rates of lung cancer attributed to smoking reductions many years earlier. There are no grateful patients or families who know that they have been "saved" by the intervention of a particular physician or hospital. Managed care organizations and the purchasers of their services, moreover, have come to realize that performance measures based on data from the covered populations can be used to hold plans accountable for providing quality services. Similar approaches are beginning to be applied in public health settings as well.[60,61]

In response, a wide range of health data systems and approaches have been developed at the national level. *Healthy People, Healthy People 2000,* and *Healthy People 2010* have clarified the importance of specific, quantitative, population-based health measures for setting public health policy.[62-65] Other examples include the model standards developed by the American Public lic Health Association and others; Mobilizing for Action through Planning and Partnerships (MAPP), developed by the National Association of County and City Health Officials; the measures used in a Planned Approach to Community Health (PATCH); and the measures proposed by the National Civic League's Healthy Cities/Communities project.[66-70] Taking this approach further, and consistent with the Government Performance and Results Act (GPRA), the US Department of Health and Human Services (HHS) proposed a series of Performance Partnership Grants—to include specific performance measures for states receiving the funds—to replace a number of current block grants.[70] Although this specific approach has not been implemented, performance measurement has become increasingly common in the public health sector.[70] The HRSA's Maternal and Child Health Services block grants, for instance, now require annual performance measures at the state level, as discussed earlier.[41] After September 11, 2001, new federal funding for state and local efforts in relation to bioterrorism, and more recently pandemic influenza, has also come with requirements for performance measures, as discussed below.

At the local level, many communities currently prepare community report cards for health, based in part on one or more of these efforts, but generally uncoordinated with their neighbors.[40,71] The availability of appropriate data is one of the common weaknesses of these approaches. The basic demographic and epidemiologic data available in communities, on which many of these report cards draw, often do not reflect the full spectrum of the dimensions of health or its determinants. Difficult technical problems with the existing measures and lack of data availability (especially for small geographic areas) have further limited the applications of population-based health assessment measures in public health practice.[72]

## Performance Improvement in Managed Care

Managed care organizations and other organized healthcare delivery systems are increasingly using performance measures or report cards based on their defined populations to hold themselves accountable to members and purchasers. In recent years, the federal Health Care Financing Administration (HCFA), the Joint Commission on Accreditation of Healthcare Organizations

(JCAHO), the National Committee for Quality Assurance (NCQA), the Institute of Medicine, and other groups have developed a variety of performance measures for hospitals, providers, health plans, and managed care organizations.[73-76] Because it is responsible for delivering care to a defined group of enrollees, managed care makes possible, for the first time, accountability in terms of quality of care for populations, including access to care and health outcomes.[77] Going beyond current practices, David Kindig has proposed that population-based health outcome measures should be the driving force in the market-based management of health plans, and that the health care for entire populations eventually should be managed with these measures.[78]

This trend presents an important opportunity for public health organizations as guarantors of the public's interest in the accessibility, content, and quality of health services. Rather than provide childhood immunizations directly through their own clinics, for example, public health organizations can work with branches of government responsible for the oversight of Medicaid and the regulation of health insurance to ensure that managed care immunization rates are audited and available to purchasers and the public.

The NCQA's *Health Plan Employer Data and Information Set* (HEDIS) is a prominent set of performance measures that deserves some attention, in particular because of its increasing use in Medicaid and other publicly funded managed care.[74] (See Chapter 11 for a more detailed discussion on HEDIS.) HEDIS is a set of 22 standardized performance measures designed to ensure that purchasers and consumers have the information they need to compare the performance of managed healthcare plans reliably. The performance measures in HEDIS are related to many significant public health issues such as cancer, heart disease, smoking, asthma, and diabetes. The NCQA finds that managed care plans that consistently monitor and report on quality are showing significant improvements in quality, resulting in a substantial positive effect on the health of the American public.[74] Some of the measures most relevant to public health are shown in Table 18-2.

The partial list of HEDIS indicators in Table 18-2 illustrates two important points regarding performance measurement. First, there is a substantial overlap between the HEDIS measures and other public health performance measures. Childhood immunization and prenatal care measures, for example, are also included in the HRSA Maternal and Child Health block grant performance measures discussed above. The specific form of the indicators, however, can vary by application. The HEDIS but not the HRSA measures, for instance, calls for one dose of chickenpox vaccine. The HRSA measure applies to all children in the state aged 19–35 months; the HEDIS measure applies only to 2-year-old children enrolled in a health plan. Lack of immunization associated with lack of access to health care, therefore, appears in the HRSA measure but not in the HEDIS measure.

Second, the breast cancer screening and cholesterol management measures illustrate two different approaches to incorporating clinical practice guidelines into performance measures. The US Clinical Preventive Services Task Force currently recommends biannual mammography for women over age 40. HEDIS focuses its indicator on "women between the ages of 52 and 69 who have had at least one mammogram during the past two years."[72] The cholesterol management measure, on the other hand, takes a tertiary prevention approach, focusing on people who have already had a cardiovascular event.[72]

**TABLE 18-2   Examples of Specific Performance Measures in HEDIS 3.0**

| Concept | Specific Indicator |
| --- | --- |
| Timeliness of prenatal care | Percentage of women beginning their prenatal care during the first trimester or within 42 days of enrollment if already pregnant at the time of enrollment |
| Childhood immunizations | Percentage of children who turned 2 years old during the measurement year and received the following vaccinations: 4 doses of diphtheria-tetanus-pertussis, 3 doses of polio, measles-mumps-rubella, 3 doses of *Haemophilus Infuenza* type b (Hib), 3 doses of hepatitis B, and 1 dose of chickenpox |
| Advising smokers to quit | Percentage of smokers or recent quitters age 18 and older who received advice to quit smoking from a health professional |
| Breast cancer screening | Percentage of women between the ages of 52–69 who have had at least one mammogram during the past 2 years |
| Cholesterol management | Percentage of health plan members 18–75 years of age who had evidence of an acute cardiovascular event and whose LDL-C was screened and controlled to less than 130 mg/dL or less than 100 mg/dL in the year following the event |

*Source:* National Committee for Quality Assurance. *The State of Managed Care Quality 2005.* Washington, DC: National Committee for Quality Assurance; 2005. Available at: http://www. ncqa.org/Docs/SOHCQ_2005.pdf.

## Community Health Improvement Processes

The IOM has proposed a community health improvement process drawing on the existing use of evaluation tools in a community health setting.[40] Other authors describe similar processes using somewhat different terms, but the basic ideas and issues are typically the same: ownership by communities, a broad definition of health, a cross-disciplinary approach to intervention, and sharing of responsibility among stakeholders for both decision making and accountability. The IOM's model also can be thought of as an example of em- powerment evaluation.*

The rationale for the community health improvement process (CHIP) model is that because a wide array of factors influence a community's health, many entities in the community share the responsibility of maintaining and improving its health. Responsibility shared among many entities, however, can easily become responsibility that is ignored or abandoned. At the level of actions that can be taken to protect and improve health, however, specific en- tities can and should be held accountable, with assignments made through a collaborative process. Because resources and concerns of communities differ, each will have to determine its own specific allocation of responsibility and accountability. Once accountability is assigned, communities can use per- formance monitoring to hold community entities accountable for actions for which they have accepted responsibility.

---

*This section draws heavily on the IOM report, *Improving Health in the Community: A Role for Performance Monitoring*.[40]

Growing out of this perspective, a CHIP that includes performance monitoring can be an effective tool for developing a shared vision and for supporting a planned and integrated approach to improve community health. A CHIP offers a way for a community to address collective responsibility and marshal resources of its individuals and families, the medical care and public health systems, and community organizations to improve the health of its members. A CHIP should include two principal interacting cycles based on analysis, action, and measurement (Figure 18-7). The overall process differs from standard models primarily because of its emphasis on measurement to link performance and accountability on a community-wide basis.

The health assessment activities that are part of a CHIP's problem identification and prioritization cycle should include production of a community health profile that can provide basic information to a community regarding its demographic and socioeconomic characteristics and its health status and health risks. This profile would provide background information that could help a community interpret other health data and identify issues that need more focused attention.

For example, the set of indicators for a community health profile might include the following:

- Sociodemographic characteristics, such as the high school graduation rate and median household income
- Health risk factors, such as child immunization coverage, adult smoking rate, and obesity
- Healthcare resource consumption, such as per capita healthcare spending
- Health status, such as the infant mortality rate by race/ethnicity, numbers of deaths due to preventable causes, and confirmed child abuse and neglect cases
- Functional status, such as the proportion of adults in good to excellent health
- Quality of life, such as the proportion of adults who are satisfied with the health care system in the community

Within the CHIP framework, performance monitoring takes place in the analysis and implementation cycle. A community may have a portfolio of health improvement activities, each progressing through this cycle at its own pace. A prototype performance indicator set for vaccine-preventable diseases is shown in Exhibit 18-2. Measures such as these can be further articulated to clarify the accountability of individuals and families, the medical care and public health systems, and community organizations.

To make operational the concept of shared responsibility and individual accountability for community health, stakeholders need to know, jointly and as clearly as possible, how the actions of each potentially accountable entity can contribute to the community's health. Thus, a CHIP should include the development of a set of specific, quantitative performance measures that link accountable entities to the performance of specific activities expected to lead to the production of desired health outcomes in the community. Selecting these indicators will require careful consideration of how to gain insight into progress achieved in the health improvement process. A set of indicators should balance population-based measures of risk factors and health outcomes and health systems-based measures of services performed. Process measures (such as availability of insurance coverage for immunizations) might be included, but only to the extent that there is evidence that links them to health outcomes. To encourage full participation in the health improvement process, the selected performance measures should also be balanced across the interests and contributions of the various accountable entities in the community, including those whose primary mission is not health specific.

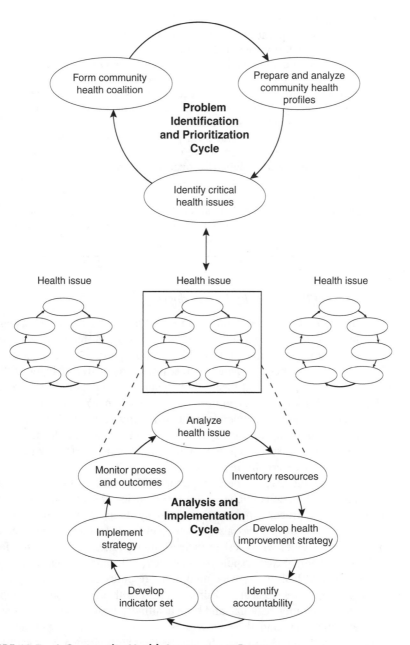

**FIGURE 18-7    A Community Health Improvement Process**
*Source:* Reprinted with permission. Institute of Medicine. *Improving Health in the Community: A Role for Performance Monitoring.* Washington, DC: National Academy Press; 1997.

**Exhibit 18-2    Sample Prototype Indicator Set: Vaccine-Preventable Diseases**

- Immunization rate for all children at 24 months of age.
- Immunization rate at 24 months of age for children currently enrolled in managed care organizations.
- Immunization rate at 24 months of age for children currently enrolled in Medicaid.
- Existence in the community of a computerized immunization registry that provides automated appointment reminders; if available, the percentage of children in the community included in the registry.
- Among children with commercial health insurance coverage, percentage with full coverage for childhood immunizations.
- Percentage of Medicare enrollees who received an influenza immunization during the previous calendar year; percentage who have ever received a pneumococcal pneumonia immunization.
- Pneumonia and influenza death rates for persons age 65 and older.
- Existence in the community of an active childhood immunization coalition involving health service providers, the local health department, parents, and interested parties.

*Source:* Adapted with permission. Institute of Medicine. *Improving Health in the Community: A Role for Performance Monitoring.* Washington, DC: National Academy Press; 1997.

*Example: Indicators of Public Health Preparedness*

The anthrax attacks in 2001 and the threat of bioterrorism, as well as emerging infectious diseases such West Nile virus and SARS, have raised concerns about the public health system's ability to respond to emergencies. (See Chapter 23.) Since then, the federal government has distributed almost $5 billion to strengthen state and local public health, as well as hospital preparedness.[79] An additional $350 million was invested in FY 2006 to help these departments prepare for pandemic influenza.[80] Investments of this magnitude demand accountability measures. In addition, many state and local health departments want measures to guide quality improvement efforts, whether they are internally or externally initiated.

Measuring the preparedness of public health systems faces a number of challenges. First, serious public health emergencies are rare, so outcomes (no matter how construed) can not be assessed by direct observation. The infrequency of such emergencies also makes it difficult to learn from experience about what activities work best to increase preparedness. Second, an effective public health emergency response is complex and multifaceted. In any given situation it is difficult to say what an optimal response is, and certainly to capture it in objectives measures. Third, public health systems are fragmented. There are city, county, regional, and state health departments and offices as well as federal agencies, and these structures vary from state to state and often within states. Public health systems also include partner agencies such as hospitals and physicians, emergency medical services (EMS) agencies, agricultural and environmental protection agencies, police, and others. Many of these do not think of themselves as public health agencies, and they are certainly not under the control of a local or state health official. As a result, accountability for preparedness is diffused. Finally, it should be noted that unlike agencies such as fire departments whose primary purpose it to respond to emergencies, very few people in public health have preparedness as a full-time job.

In response to the need for accountability, four basic types of performance measures have emerged. Perhaps the simplest approach is *informal assessment*: health departments or other knowledgeable parties simply judge how well prepared they are for various public health emergencies. Another approach is embodied in detailed *standards-based assessments* asking whether health departments or other community agencies have undertaken various preparedness activities or meet specified functional standards. Systematic reviews of public health functions during *proxy events* such as major disease outbreaks can also serve to measure aspects of preparedness. Finally, *drills and exercises* of various types are frequently used to raise awareness and for planning and training and less commonly to assess preparedness; they also represent a way to assess preparedness, as discussed below. For the remainder of this chapter we will focus on measures appropriate for measuring functional capacities through drills and exercises.

To develop meaningful and useful measures of public health preparedness for any of these approaches, a logic model that specifies the critical goals and objectives of public health preparedness, as well as how various functions, processes, and resources contribute to meeting them, is needed. One such logic model (Figure 18-8) specifies the goals and objectives of public health preparedness, as well as the functional capabilities and capacity-building activities intended to assure those goals and objectives.[81] In particular, this model helps analysts to distinguish between (1) what the public health system needs to be able to do (the capabilities it needs) during an emergency, and (2) what must be done before an emergency occurs to build capacities. Clearly these two are related, but the tools and approaches needed to measures each are quite different. As discussed below in more detail, inventories and checklists are commonly used to measure what a community has done to build capacity (i.e., has it done what is recommended). On the other hand, proxy events, drills, and exercises can be used to assess how well it did respond or might respond to future emergencies.

The logic model suggests that the overall *goal* of public health preparedness is to mitigate the morbidity and mortality as well as the psychological, social, and economic consequences of a biological attack, a naturally occurring disease outbreak, or other similar disaster (right hand side of model). This goal assumes that effective actions can greatly reduce the health and social consequences of a disease outbreak (especially if a contagious agent is involved), but that 100% prevention is not possible. As such, this goal leaves out other public health activities, such as childhood immunization, that deal with ongoing health problems. Leaving this goal out of this logic model does not imply that these public health activities are any less important than preparedness. Indeed, reductions in performance in these areas can be seen as a cost of public health preparedness efforts.

For a community to meet this goal, in the event of an emergency, it must meet the following objectives: (1) identify and characterize the nature of the outbreak or attack as quickly as possible; (2) mount an early and effective response including providing health care to those affected, taking action to

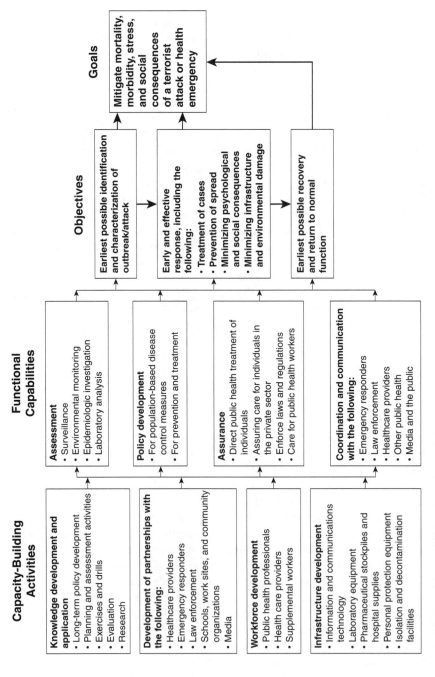

**FIGURE 18-8   Public Health Preparedness Logic Model**

prevent spread, and minimizing the psychological and social consequences; and (3) enable the earliest possible recovery and return to normal function. Of course, depending on the emergency, some objectives will be more important than others. The evidence for the connection between these objectives and the goals is based on logic and general experience with public health emergencies and other natural disasters, especially infectious disease outbreaks in the past.

If a community is to meet the objectives above during an attack or emergency, it must be capable of carrying out certain functions. Some of these *functional capabilities*, such as surveillance, must operate on a continuous or ongoing basis, and others must be available or enhanced in an emergency. To the extent that these capabilities also relate to other ongoing public health responsibilities, they are more likely to be ready and effective in an emergency because those responsible have experience and the systems have been tested. The functional capabilities in the logic model—the building blocks of a public health response—are categorized according to the Institute of Medicine's three core public health functions—assessment, policy development, and assurance.[82] In addition, coordination and communication have been added because of their prominence in emergencies. *Assessment* includes disease surveillance, environmental monitoring, epidemiological investigation, and laboratory analysis. In this context, *policy development* refers to the ability of public health systems to develop and implement policies during a public health emergency covering population-based disease control activities such as quarantine, isolation, mass prophylaxis, vector control, as well as develop and communicate clinical policies relating to infection control, prevention, and treatment. *Assurance* covers care provided by official health departments to affected individuals (mass immunization clinics, for instance) as well as the enforcement of laws and regulations in support of population-based disease control activities such as isolation and quarantine. Assurance also includes health department involvement in assuring private-sector care for affected individuals through the activation of surge capacity and the Strategic National Stockpile (SNS) and special care for public health or other healthcare workers if needed. *Coordination and communication* within public health and with a variety of other organizations are in support of the first three functional capabilities, but are important enough to merit special consideration.

Many of the *capacity building activities* that states and local health departments are currently undertaking with federal funding support are intended to build the functional capabilities identified in the previous section. *Knowledge development and application* includes the development of policies and protocols in advance of an emergency, planning and assessment activities, exercises and drills, evaluation, and research. Because an effective public health response requires more than the health department per se, the second category of capacity-building activities is focused on the *development of partnerships to support emergency operations*. The partners could include hospitals, physicians, and other healthcare providers, including mental healthcare providers; emergency responders; law enforcement agencies; schools, worksites, and other community organizations; and the media. *Workforce development* activities include the recruitment, training, and preparation of public health professionals, including the designation and prevaccination of smallpox response teams, and of healthcare providers including mental health care providers in the private sector who might be called upon in a public health emergency. This category also includes the identification and training of a supplemental workforce, such as nurses and volunteers willing to participate in mass immunization efforts. Other *infrastructure development* activities focus on information and communications technology, laboratory equipment, pharmaceutical stockpiles and hospital supplies, personal protection and decontamination equipment, and isolation and decontamination facilities.

## Using Tabletop Exercises to Measure Preparedness

In a public health tabletop exercise, public health officials and others who would be involved in responding to a public health emergency are assembled in a room (around a table) and are asked by a facilitator to respond to a fictional scenario as they themselves or their organizations would respond if the conditions were real. This is followed by a "hot wash" during which participants are asked to evaluate the response and to suggest changes that are needed to respond more effectively in the future. An after-action report focusing on observed strengths and weaknesses is prepared by the facilitators.

The emergency response community has long used tabletop exercises to motivate and train, and to develop, test, and evaluate emergency response plans. More recently, public health agencies and healthcare providers have adopted this approach for the same purposes. Going beyond these uses, tabletop exercises can also be used to assess the level of a public health's preparedness. In one such approach, individuals from the local health department and other governmental (e.g., police) and private-sector entities (e.g., hospitals, Red Cross) were assembled, presented with information suggesting a serious disease outbreak such as smallpox, and in one or more stages were asked how they would respond.[83]

Another application used a possible smallpox attack. Seven counties in California exhibited a wide variation in their readiness to detect and respond to this attack. Common sources of variation included: initial steps in beginning an epidemiologic investigation, ability to communicate with most of the doctors and hospitals in the community to initiate active surveillance, practices regarding isolation and quarantine, communication with the public, procedures for collection and testing of biological specimens, beliefs about smallpox vaccination, and understanding of legal authority. Commonly identified gaps included: lack of information systems, significant training needs for public health workforce, inadequate numbers of public health professionals, lack of knowledge of potentially vulnerable or difficult-to-reach population subgroups, and lack of community involvement in planning.[84]

To illustrate this approach in more detail, consider the avian influenza tabletop exercises developed by the Harvard School of Public Health.[85] Should a pandemic influenza virus emerge and reach the United States, its impact on health and well-being, as well as the social and economic disruption it causes, will depend on how well health departments, other government agencies, and the private sector are prepared to respond effectively to a public health emergency. Addressing this concern, federal, state, and local pandemic flu plans are currently being developed, and exercises are being employed to evaluate communities' level of preparedness. To effectively judge public health system performance in an exercise, it helps to begin with a logic model such as the one described above. This model can help clarify which functional capabilities implemented by a variety of public and private community organizations can contribute to overall public health preparedness. More importantly, the model helps evaluators distinguish between (1) what the public health system needs to be able to do during an emergency (the functional capabilities that will be assessed during the exercise), and (2) what must be done before an emergency occurs to build capacities.

In the form of a checklist, Table 18-3 illustrates measures of preparedness that exercise evaluators can use to judge the performance of avian influenza

**TABLE 18-3    Preparedness Domains and Indicators for a Pandemic Influenza Tabletop Exercise**

Surveillance and Epidemiology

- Receive and respond to urgent case reports.
- Investigate and track reported cases.
- Track information (i.e., newly hospitalized cases, newly quarantined cases) for policy makers.
- Build laboratory capacity (i.e., rapid identification of unusual influenza strains), including ability to ship specimens to state or CDC lab.
- Link with and share data among different surveillance systems (e.g., state DOH, CDC, other communities and states, local hospitals, etc.).
- Step up surveillance capacity in time to initiate containment protocols.

Disease Control and Prevention

- Determine the legal authorities regarding isolation and quarantine.
- Make available procedures to manage isolation and quarantine.
- Have the capacity to support people in quarantine (e.g., preidentified sites, support for home quarantine).
- Develop infection control policies and disseminate them to hospitals and healthcare providers.
- Implement community interventions such as school closings.
- Conduct mass screening.
- Distribute limited medical supplies (including vaccines) to priority groups.
- Control population movement in and out of the community.

Mass Care

- Ensure continuity of healthcare operations.
- Assure health care for all cases that meets relevant standards of care.
- Protect healthcare workers with personal protective equipment (PPE) and infection control practices.
- Increase hospital capacity (including ventilators and other equipment) when necessary.
- Activate and use the Strategic National Stockpile (SNS).
- Prioritize the use of limited medical supplies.
- Provide security within healthcare facilities and at mass point-of-dispensing (POD) sites.
- Coordinate medical reserve.
- Ensure the provisions of mortuary services.

Communication Within Public Health (broadly defined)

- Provide current information (i.e., newly hospitalized cases, newly quarantined cases) to decision makers.
- Disseminate infection control policies to hospitals and healthcare providers.
- Communicate with public health agencies in neighboring communities and the state.
- Communicate within the local public health system (including other government agencies).
- Communicate with hospitals and healthcare providers.

*(continues)*

**TABLE 18-3 (continued)**

Communication with the Public

- Communicate with the general public up-to-date outbreak information, disease control requirements, individual risk reduction, and when and where to seek medical care.
- Communicate with the public to minimize fear.
- Communicate with marginalized population groups through trusted sources.

Leadership and Management

- Initiate and use the incident command system.
- Identify activities that will be performed at a state, local, or coordinated level.
- Interact with local, state, and federal officials with regard to the delegation of legal and law enforcement responsibilities.
- Identify the authority for declaring a public health emergency.
- Gather resources in support of implementing action.
- Assess and manage local resources.
- Address and respond to cross-jurisdictional needs.
- Assist special needs populations.
- Respond flexibly, in proportion to the magnitude and severity of the scenario and available resources.
- Anticipate psychosocial needs and activate appropriate services.
- Integrate community-based organizations in the response.

tabletop exercise participants. The checklist is organized into six preparedness domains, and each domain has 3 to 11 specific indicators. Numerical scores could be assigned, say using a 5 point scale ranging from 1 (response not sufficient) to 5 (response exceeded expectations) for each domain and a three point scale for each indicator as follows: 1: not sufficient; 2: sufficient; 3: exceeds expectations. Numerical scores of this sort are of course arbitrary, but knowledgeable and sufficiently trained assessors can use them effectively to evaluate the community's response to the scenario and hence provide a measure of preparedness.[86]

Based on feedback from the participants, we found that tabletop exercises of this sort were generally effective in helping a community assess the level of preparedness of its public health systems. The scenarios presented were seen as realistic and elicited critical areas of public health system response. Observations that the participants made in the workshop and the after-action reports helped health departments to identify areas of strength and weakness, and many indicated that they planned to take action to address weaknesses. Some of the critical elements of this approach seemed to be (1) assembling the appropriate participants from the local public health department and representing partner agencies, (2) a realistic and challenging outbreak scenario, tailored to the local situation (i.e., including local institutions such as hospitals and reflecting existing capabilities and responsibilities), (3) simulation of actual decision making through built-in stops during which participants are asked what they would do, and (4) facilitation and evaluation by knowledgeable individuals from outside the community being assessed, using a structured framework such as Table 18-3.

• • •

A large and growing set of evaluation methods now exists to assist public health organizations in measuring and improving their programs and operations. These tools can be used to monitor the quality, outcomes, and efficiency of public health activities carried out by single and multiple institutions. These tools can also be used to examine the effects that interventions outside the domain of public health have on community health. Public health organizations must continually work to improve the standards of evidence used in evaluating public health interventions, so that results can inform managerial and policy decision making. Moreover, as an increasing share of public health interventions are carried out through multi-institutional partnerships, public health organizations must meet the growing imperative for collaboration in evaluation efforts. By doing so these organizations can move closer to the goals of evidence-based management and the gains in population health that it promises.

## Chapter Review

1. Evaluation addresses the following questions:
   - Which programs work, for whom, and under what conditions?
   - Which program variants work best?
   - Is the public getting the best possible value for its investment?
   - How can the impact of existing programs be increased?
2. All public health programs can be thought of in terms of *inputs, activities, outputs,* and *outcomes.*
3. Economic evaluations include costs and benefits in quantitative terms—for example, which program is most effective in terms of dollars per child immunized?
4. Formative evaluation refers to efforts to identify the best use of available resources, prior to a traditional program evaluation. Formative evaluation often employs qualitative methods such as focus groups or structured interviews.
5. *Statistical power* is the likelihood that an evaluation will detect the effect of an intervention, if there is one. Two factors affect statistical power: sample size and effect size, which is a quantitative measure of the program's impact.
6. Research synthesis—systematic reviews of existing studies, including meta-analysis, is increasingly used in public health to uncover robust effects.
7. The goals of an evaluation determine the types of measures that are needed. Outcome evaluations need measures of health outcomes, whereas feasibility evaluations focus on costs and barriers to implementation.
8. A CDC framework for evaluation consists of a six-step cycle:
   - Identify and engage stakeholders.
   - Describe the program.
   - Focus the evaluation design.
   - Gather credible evidence.
   - Justify conclusions.
   - Disseminate evaluation results to improve the program.

## References

1. DeCarlo P. Project Access: Research That Feeds Back into the Community. *CAPS Exchange.* San Francisco, Calif: Center for AIDS Prevention Studies; 1999.
2. Fetterman DM. Empowerment evaluation: an introduction to theory and practice. In: Fetterman DM, Kaftarian SJ, Wandersman A, eds. *Empowerment Evaluation: Knowledge and Tools for Self-Assessment & Accountability.* Thousand Oaks, Calif: Sage; 1996:3–46.
3. Green SB, Byar DP. Using observational data from registries to compare treatments: the fallacy of omnimetrics. *Stat Med.* 1984;3:361–370.
4. Sorensen G, Emmons K, Hunt MK, Johnston D. Implications of the results of community intervention trials. *Annu Rev Public Health.* 1998;19:379–416.
5. Little RJ, Rubin DB. Causal effects in clinical and epidemiological studies via potential outcomes: concepts and analytical approaches. *Annu Rev Public Health.* 2000;21:121–145.
6. Murray DM. *Design and Analysis of Group-Randomized Trials.* New York, NY: Oxford University Press; 1998.
7. Hoaglin DC, Light RL, McPeek B, Mosteller F, Stoto MA. *Data for Decisions: Information Strategies for Policymakers.* Cambridge, Mass: Abt Books; 1982.
8. Sloan FA, ed. *Valuing Health Care: Costs, Benefits, and Effectiveness of Pharmaceuticals and Other Medical Technologies.* Cambridge, Mass: Cambridge University Press; 1995.
9. Understanding and using the economic evidence. In: Zaza S, Briss PA, Harris KW, eds. *The Guide to Community Preventive Services: What Works to Promote Health?* Oxford, UK: Oxford University Press; 2005:449–463.
10. Haddix AC, Teutsch SM, Corso PH, eds. *Prevention Effectiveness: A Guide to Decision Analysis and Economic Evaluation.* 2nd ed. Oxford, UK: Oxford University Press; 2003.
11. Muennig P. Introduction to cost-effectiveness. In: Muennig P, Khan K, ed. *Designing and Conducting Cost-Effectiveness Analyses in Medicine and Health Care.* San Francisco, Calif: Jossey-Bass; 2002:1–32.
12. Russell LB, Siegel JE, Daniels N, et al., Cost-effectiveness analysis as a guide to resource allocation in health. In: Gold MR, Siegel JE, Russell LB, Weinstein MC, eds. *Cost-Effectiveness in Health and Medicine.* Oxford, UK: Oxford University Press; 1996:3–24.
13. Miller W, Robinson LA, Lawrence RS. *Valuing Health for Regulatory Cost-Effectiveness Analysis.* Washington, DC: National Academies Press; 2006.
14. Secker-Walker RH, Holland RR, Lloyd CM, Pelkey D, Flynn BS. Cost effectiveness of a community based research project to help women quit smoking. *Tob Control.* 2005;14:37–42.
15. Torrance GW, Feeny D. Utilities and quality-adjusted life years. *Int J Technol Assess Health Care.* 1989;10:559–575.
16. AIDS Cost and Services Utilization Survey (ACSUS). Public Use Tapes 4 and 5 [Database]. Springfield, Va: National technical Information Service; 1992.
17. Bozzette SA, Berry SH, Duan N, et al. The care of HIV-infected adults in the United States. *N Engl J Med.* 1998;339:1897–1904.
18. Paltiel AD, Weinstein MC, Kimmel AD, et al. Expanded screening for HIV in the United States—an analysis of cost-effectiveness. *N Engl J Med.* 2005;352:586–595.
19. Parasuraman S, Salvador C, Frick KD. Measuring economic outcomes. In: Pizzi LT, Lofland J, eds. *Economic Evaluation in US Health Care: Principles and Applications.* Sudbury, Mass: Jones and Bartlett; 2006:15–40.

20. Nichol KL, Lind A, Margolis KL, et al. The effectiveness of vaccination against influenza in healthy, working adults. *N Engl J Med.* 1995;33: 889–893.

21. Grosse SD, Waitzman NJ, Romano PS, Mulinare J. Reevaluating the benefits of folic acid fortification in the United States: economic analysis, regulation, and public health. *Am J Public Health.* 2005;95(11):1917–1922.

22. Gold MR, Siegel JE, Russell LB, Weinstein MC, eds. *Cost-Effectiveness in Health and Medicine.* Oxford, UK: Oxford University Press; 1996.

23. Farnham PG, Haddix AC. Study design. In: Haddix AC, Teutsch SM, Corso PS, eds. *Prevention Effectiveness: A Guide to Decision Analysis and Economic Evaluation.* 2nd ed. Oxford, UK: Oxford University Press; 2003:11–27.

24. Luce BR, Manning WG, Siegel JE, Lipscomb J. Estimating costs in cost-effectiveness analysis. In: Gold MR, Siegel JE, Russell LB, Weinstein MC, eds. *Cost-Effectiveness in Health and Medicine.* Oxford, UK: Oxford University Press; 1996:176–213.

25. Torrance GW, Siege JE, Luce BR. Framing and designing the cost-effectiveness analysis. In: Gold MR, Siegel JE, Russell LB, Weinstein MC, eds. *Cost-Effectiveness in Health and Medicine.* Oxford, UK: Oxford University Press; 1996:54–81.

26. Garber AM, Weinstein MC, Torrance GW, Kamlet MS. Theoretical foundations of cost-effectiveness analysis. In: Gold MR, Siegel JE, Russell LB, Weinstein MC, eds. *Cost-Effectiveness in Health and Medicine.* Oxford, UK: Oxford University Press; 1996:25–53.

27. Armstrong EP. Sensitivity analysis. In: Grauer DW, Lee J, Odom TD, eds. *Pharmacoeconomics and Outcomes: Applications for Patient Care.* 2nd ed. Kansas City, Kan: American College of Clinical Pharmacy; 2003:231–245.

28. Drummond MF, O'Brien B, Stoddart GL, Torrance GW. *Methods for the Economic Evaluation of Health Care Programmes.* 2nd ed. Oxford, UK: Oxford University Press; 1997.

29. Siegel JE, Weinstein MC, Torrance GW. Reporting cost-effectiveness studies and results. In: Gold MR, Siegel JE, Russell LB, Weinstein MC, eds. *Cost-Effectiveness in Health and Medicine.* Oxford, UK: Oxford University Press; 1996:276–303.

30. Mullins CD, Flowers LR. Evaluating economic outcomes literature. In: Grauer DW, Lee J, Odom TD, eds. *Pharmacoeconomics and Outcomes: Applications for Patient Care.* 2nd ed. Kansas City, Kan: American College of Clinical Pharmacy; 2003:246–273.

31. Louis TA, Fineberg HV, Mosteller F. Findings for public health from meta-analysis. *Annu Rev Public Health.* 1985;16:1–20.

32. Egger M, Davey Smith G, Altman D, eds. *Systematic Reviews in Health Care: Meta-analysis in Context.* 2nd ed. London: BMJ Books; 2001.

33. Mosteller F, Colditz GA. Understanding research synthesis (meta-analysis). *Annu Rev Public Health.* 1996;17:1–23.

34. Shefer A, Briss P, Rodewald L, et al. Improving immunization coverage rates: an evidence-based review of the literature. *Epidemiol Rev.* 1999; 21:96–142.

35. Task Force on Community Preventive Services. Interventions to improve vaccination coverage in children, adolescents, and adults. *Am J Preventive Medicine.* 2000;18(1S):92–96.

36. Jefferson T, Rivetti D, Rivetti A, Rudin M, DiPietrantonj C, Demicheli V. Efficacy and effectiveness of influenza vaccines in elderly people: a systematic review. *Lancet.* 2005;366:1165–1174.

37. Institute of Medicine, National Research Council, Normand J, Vlahov D, Moses LE. *Preventing HIV Transmission: The Role of Sterile Needles and Bleach.* Washington, DC: National Academy Press; 1995.

38. Kaplan EH, Heimer R. HIV incidence needle exchange participants: estimated from syringe tracking and testing data. *J Acquired Immune Deficiency Syndromes.* 1994;7:182–189.
39. Hagan H, Des Jarlais DC, Friedman SR, Purchase D, Alter MJ. Risk for human immunodeficiency virus and hepatitis B virus in users of the Tacoma syringe exchange program. In: *Proceedings, Workshop on Needle Exchange and Bleach Distribution Programs.* Washington, DC: National Academy Press; 1994:24–34.
40. Institute of Medicine. *Improving Health in the Community: A Role for Performance Monitoring.* Washington, DC: National Academy Press; 1997.
41. Maternal and Child Health Bureau. *Maternal and Child Health Services Title V Block Grant Program: Proposed National Performance Measures, Health Systems Capacity Indicators, and Health Status Indicators.* Rockville, MD: Health Resources and Services Administration; undated.
42. Donaldson MS. *Measuring the Quality of Health Care.* Washington, DC: National Academy Press; 1999.
43. US Public Health Service Expert Panel on the Content of Prenatal Care. *Caring for Our Future: The Content of Prenatal Care.* Washington, DC: US Department of Health and Human Services; 1989.
44. Chalk R, King PA. *Violence in Families: Assessing Prevention and Treatment Programs.* Washington, DC: National Academy Press; 1998.
45. Cronbach LJ, Snow RE. *Aptitudes and Instructional Methods: A Handbook for Research on Interactions.* New York, NY: Irvington Publishers; 1981.
46. Reiss AJ Jr, Roth JA, National Research Council. *Understanding and Preventing Violence.* Washington, DC: National Academy Press; 1993.
47. Cordray DS, Pion GM. Psycho-social rehabilitation assessment: a broader perspective. In: Glueckauf R, Sechrest LB. *Improving Assessment in Rehabilitation and Health.* Newbury Park, Calif: Sage; 1993:215–240.
48. Evans RG, Stoddart GL. Producing health, consuming health care. In: Evans RG, Barer ML, Marmor TR. *Why Are Some People Healthy and Others Not? The Determinants of Health of Populations.* New York, NY: Aldine De Gruyter; 1994.
49. Patrick DL, Wickizer TM. Community and health. In: Amick BC, Levine S, Tarlov AR, Walsh DC, eds. *Society and Health.* New York, NY: Oxford University Press; 1995:46–92.
50. Hollister RG, Hill J. Problems in the evaluation of community-wide initiatives. In: Connell JP, Kubisch AC, Schorr LB, Weiss CH, eds. *New Approaches to Evaluating Community Initiatives.* New York, NY: Aspen Institute; 1995:127–172.
51. Weiss CH. Nothing as practical as good theory: exploring theory-based evaluation for comprehensive community initiatives for children and families. In: Connell JP, Kubisch AC, Schorr LB, Weiss CH, eds. *New Approaches to Evaluating Community Initiatives.* New York, NY: Aspen Institute; 1995:65–92.
52. Connell JP, Kubisch AC. *Applying Theories of Change Approach to the Evaluation of Comprehensive Community Initiatives: Progress, Prospects, and Problems.* New York, NY: Aspen Institute; 1996.
53. Rose G. Sick individuals and sick populations. *Int J Epidemiol.* 1985;14:32–38.
54. Rose G. *The Strategy of Preventive Medicine.* New York, NY: Oxford University Press; 1992.
55. Abrams D. Conceptual models to integrate individual and public health interventions: the example of the work-place. In: Henderson M, ed. *Proceedings of the International Conference on Promoting Diet Change in*

*Communities*. Seattle, Wash: Fred Hutchinson Cancer Research Center; 1991:173–194.

56. Tosteson ANA, Weinstein MC, Hunink M, et al. Cost-effectiveness of population-wide educational approaches to reduce serum cholesterol levels. *Circulation.* 1998;95(1):24–30.

57. Murray DM. *Design and Analysis of Group-Randomized Trials.* New York, NY: Oxford University Press; 1998.

58. Fawcett SB, Paine-Andrews A, Francisco VT, et al. Empowering community health initiatives through evaluation. In: Fetterman DM, Kaftarian SJ, Wandersman A, eds. *Empowerment Evaluation: Knowledge and Tools for Self-Assessment & Accountability.* Thousand Oaks, Calif: Sage; 1996: 161–187.

59. US Centers for Disease Control and Prevention. Framework for program evaluation in public health. *MMWR.* 1999;RR-11:1–40.

60. Perrin EB, Koshel JJ. *Assessment of Performance Measures for Public Health, Substance Abuse, and Mental Health.* Washington, DC: National Academy Press; 1997.

61. Perrin EB, Durch J, Skillman SM. *Health Performance Measurement in the Public Health Sector: Principles and Policies for Implementing an Information Network.* Washington, DC: National Academy Press; 1999.

62. US Department of Health, Education, and Welfare. *Healthy People: The Surgeon General's Report on Health Promotion and Disease Prevention.* Washington, DC: US Government Printing Office; 1979.

63. US Department of Health and Human Services. *Promoting Health/ Preventing Disease: Objectives for the Nation.* Washington, DC: US Government Printing Office; 1980.

64. US Department of Health and Human Services. *Healthy People 2000: National Health Promotion and Disease Prevention Objectives.* Washington, DC: Office of the Assistant Secretary for Health; 1991.

65. US Department of Health and Human Services. *Healthy People 2010: Understanding and Improving Health.* Washington, DC: US Government Printing Office; 2000.

66. American Public Health Association, CDC, et al. *Healthy Communities 2000: Model Standards.* Washington, DC: American Public Health Association; 1991.

67. National Association of County and City Health Officials. *Achieving Healthier Communities through MAPP: A User's Handbook.* Washington, DC: NACCHO; 2004.

68. Kreuter MW. PATCH: its origin, basic concepts, and links to contemporary public health policy. *J Health Educ.* 1992;23:135–139.

69. US Centers for Disease Control and Prevention. *Planned Approach to Community Health: Guide for the Local Coordinator.* Atlanta, Ga: 1995.

70. National Civic League. *The Healthy Communities Handbook.* Denver, CO: National Civic League; 1993.

71. Fielding JE, Halfon N, Sutherland C. Characteristics of community report cards—United States, 1996. *MMWR.* 1997;46:647–649.

72. Stoto MA. Public health assessment in the 1990s. *Annu Rev Public Health.* 1992;13:59–78.

73. Joint Commission on Accreditation of Healthcare Organizations. Evolution of *Performance Measurement at the Joint Commission 1986–2010.* Oakbrook Terrace, Ill: Joint Commission on Accreditation of Healthcare Organizations; undated. Available at: http://www.jointcommission.org/ NR/rdonlyres/333A4688-7E50-41CF-B63D-EE0278D0C653/0/Evolution ofPM.pdf. Accessed August 22, 2006.

74. National Committee for Quality Assurance. *The State of Managed Care Quality 2005.* Washington, DC: National Committee for Quality Assurance; 2005.
75. Institute of Medicine. *Performance Measurement: Accelerating Improvement.* Washington, DC: National Academy Press; 2006.
76. Darby M. *Health Care Quality: From Data to Accountability.* Washington, DC: National Health Policy Forum, George Washington University; 1998.
77. Stoto MA, Abel C, Dievler A. *Healthy Communities: New Partnerships for the Future of Public Health.* Washington, DC: National Academy Press; 1996.
78. Kindig DA. *Purchasing Population Health: Paying for Results.* Ann Arbor, MI: University of Michigan Press; 1997.
79. Schuler A. Billions for biodefense: federal agency biodefense budgeting, FY2005–FY2006. *Biosecurity Bioterrorism: Biodefense Strat, Pract, Sci.* 2005;3:94–101.
80. US Department of Health and Human Services. HHS announces additional $225 million for state and local pandemic influenza preparedness efforts [Press release]. July 11, 2006. Available at: http://www.hhs.gov/news/press/2006pres/20060711.html. Accessed July 19, 2006.
81. Stoto MA, Dausey D, Davis L, et al. Learning from experience: the public health response to West Nile virus, SARS, monkeypox, and hepatitis A outbreaks in the United States. *Rand Corporation Technical Report.* 2005.
82. Institute of Medicine. *The Future of Public Health.* Washington, DC: National Academy Press; 1988.
83. Dausey DJ, Diamond A, Meade B, et al. Preparedness training and assessment exercises for local health departments. *RAND Health.* 2005. TR-261-DHHS.
84. Lurie N, Wasserman J, Stoto MA, et al. Local variation in public health preparedness: lessons from California. *Health Aff.* 2004; Suppl Web Exclusives: W4-341-53.
85. Harvard School of Public Health, Center for Public Health Preparedness. Toolkit to assist public health in conducting preparedness exercises. Available at: http://www.hsph.harvard.edu/hcphp/products/exercises/HSPHCPHP%20Avian%20&%20Pandemic%20Influenza%20Tabletop.pdf. Accessed August 22, 2006.
86. Stoto MA, Biddinger P, Cadigan R, Savoia E. Using tabletop exercises to evaluate a community's preparedness for pandemic influenza. Presented at the annual meeting of the American Public Health Association, Boston, Mass, November 2006.

# CHAPTER 19

# COMMUNITY-BASED PREVENTION

Elizabeth A. Baker
Ross C. Brownson

## Chapter Overview

Community-based programs and policies differ from other health interventions in that their development, implementation, and evaluation are informed by both community perspectives and professional expertise. To develop and sustain community-based programs, public health organizations should use an evidence-based approach to mobilize and engage community members in collaborative processes to design, implement, and evaluate interventions. In doing so, public health organizations use existing resources, skills, and relationships with the community, while also cultivating new capacities and partnerships among organizations and individuals. Community-based strategies offer opportunities for public health organizations to improve both the effectiveness and the efficiency of individual-level health interventions.

Public health has traditionally taken a population-based approach to health promotion and disease prevention, with its main functions being recently defined as assessment, policy development, and assurance.[1] Because of the complex web of individual, social, and environmental factors that influence health, these public health functions have been performed by individuals in a variety of public agencies and private organizations.[2] However, for public health practitioners to fulfill these functions, the Institute of Medicine has suggested that practitioners learn to be more responsive to the public's needs, to be more inclusive of community expertise, and to work in interdisciplinary teams with individuals from multiple agencies.[3,4] Public health practitioners and administrators have moved toward community-based prevention programs and policies as a way to accomplish these tasks.

Community-based programs and policies are distinguished from other types of programs because their development, implementation, and evaluation are informed by both community and scientific expertise. This chapter describes two broad areas necessary to gather and use this expertise (community and agency coalition development and evidence-based planning), and points to specific tools or resources that can assist practitioners in their efforts to create community-based prevention programs.

## Defining Key Terms: Community and Coalition

Before discussing community-based prevention efforts, it is important to define and distinguish the important concepts of *community* and *coalition*. For some, a *community* may be defined as a geographic area or neighborhood. For others, in order to be considered a community, members of the community must have a sense of shared identity with other members of the community, a sense of belonging and emotional connection to the community, and a set of shared values and norms.[5] Lastly, some people consider communities to be defined by formal and informal collective associations or organizations.[6] Therefore, many practitioners consider themselves to be working with "the community" when they are working with community-based organizations (CBOs) or other related associations. For purposes of community-based prevention efforts, it is critical to involve both members of the community itself as well as representatives of organizations that work with, or benefit, members of the community. (Refer to Chapter 16 for further discussion of constituencies.)

A *coalition* is defined as a group of community members and/or organizations that join together for a common purpose.[6] Coalitions may differ considerably in the roles and responsibilities of each coalition member, and in the types of activities they wish to engage in (level of integration). Some coalitions are focused on categorical issues, such as breast cancer, diabetes, or arthritis coalitions.[7] Alternately, coalitions may form to address broader public health issues. For example, the North Carolina Community-Based Public Health Initiative was formed to: (1) improve minority health, (2) make public health education programs and services more responsive to the needs of African-American communities, and (3) ensure a key role for CBO partners in shaping public health services and working with health professionals in their communities.[8] The processes of developing and building relationships among coalition partners and meeting the most urgent needs as defined by the community members were considered the primary objectives of the coalitions. Other outcomes of the coalitions included the development of a playground, a neighborhood center to offer health and economic development services, and citizen drug patrols.[8]

### Community and Agency Coalition Development

To be responsive to the public's needs and to garner and use community expertise, it is necessary to define who is to be included from the community and bring these community members and agencies together in a coalition that creates effective programs and policies. In doing so, it is important to use already existing skills, capacities, and relationships among individuals and organizations in the community and to build new ones. Some of these tasks occur prior to the coalition development (preformation), some issues need to be considered in the initial mobilization of the coalition, and others need to be addressed in the development of coalition structures.

*Preformation*

Too often, public health practitioners go into community-based prevention efforts with the belief that they are going where "no man has gone before." Although everyone would like to believe that they are breaking new ground, the reality is that they are working with fields that have been planted several times and with soil that may have either been polluted with toxins or well fertilized and ready for planting. Even with their best efforts to plant healthy plants and provide plenty of sun and water, the fruits of their labor will be affected by the conditions that existed before they began. Therefore, before even beginning to develop community coalitions, it is essential to understand the history of community relations, previous experiences with health projects, intergroup relations, and interorganizational relationships (particularly the levels of trust and respect among these individuals and groups), as well as community resources and values. These have been listed as factors that are part of what has been called *community capacity* or *social capital*.[9,10]

Those persons who are interested in learning more about the types of things to consider prior to initiating a collaborative effort should consult Goodman et al. and Kreuter et al.[9,10]

*Initial Mobilization*

In considering who to include in community-based public health efforts, there are several issues to consider, including breadth versus depth and agency versus community member involvement.

In terms of breadth, one type of coalition might bring together individuals who have multiple points of entry into public health. This might include individuals who work in agencies that address family violence, housing, sanitation, and access to care for the elderly, as well as healthcare providers. Alternately, one might be more interested in bringing together individuals concerned about youth. In that case, a coalition might include individuals from schools, religious organizations, social services agencies, smoking cessation programs, housing and family violence centers, and healthcare providers who work with youth. The first is more appropriate if the intent is to develop broad-based community support, determine overall community needs and assets, and plan community programs and policies based on community-defined issues and concerns. The second is more appropriate if the effort is more categorical. These are critical decisions to make at the beginning of coalition activities. If what is needed is a broad understanding of community needs, then developing a coalition with individuals who are all focused on a single issue will limit input and creativity. Alternately, if the effort is categorical and a broad-based coalition is developed, individuals will feel frustrated at being limited in the types of programs and policies that can be developed. In both cases, community support will be lessened rather than enhanced, and this will carry over to, and influence, future endeavors.

In addition to considering issues of breadth versus depth, it is important to consider the inclusion of representatives from CBOs versus community members themselves. Community members offer different perspectives than agency members. It is important to remember that a single community member's voice is not sufficient, rather inclusion from the multiple groups and subgroups in communities is needed. Individuals of different gender, age, abilities, class, race, ethnicity, and religion can provide different perspectives that can add to coalition activities. Inclusion of community members themselves is important, but more is needed than just an invitation. It is important to ensure that all members of the coalition have similar opportunities to influence the processes and outcomes of the coalition. To do this, the coalition structures must be jointly defined and established by coalition members.

### Developing Coalition Structures

Once individuals have agreed to be part of a coalition, the next step is to decide how members will relate to each other. This step entails developing roles, decision-making structures, and group processes. In considering this, it is important to remember that individuals from different agencies and different community members each have different ways of engaging in these processes. Therefore, any choices regarding policies and procedures must consider the range of possibilities and include training opportunities so that all members of the coalition have the skills necessary to participate in whatever processes are decided on. These skills include cultural competence, conflict resolution, group facilitation, minute taking, agenda development, and communication structure development.

Suggestions for coalition building (including how to enhance these skills) can be found in the University of Kansas Workgroup on Health Promotion and Community Development's Community Toolbox, which can be accessed at http://ctb.lsi.ukans.edu. Johnson et al. and Wolff and Kaye also provide helpful hints as well as worksheets to enhance community efforts at this stage.[11,12]

### Deciding the Level of Integration with Other Agencies

One of the first decisions a coalition must make is to decide the level of integration it wants to have with the other agencies. This can be thought of as a continuum of integration.[8,13] On one end of the continuum is the desire of agencies and individuals to work together to identify gaps in services, avoid duplication of services, and exchange information to allow for appropriate client referral. The next level of integration involves agencies maintaining their autonomy, agendas, and resources, but beginning to use these resources to work on an issue that is identified as common to all agencies. The next level of integration involves each of the agencies lessening their level of autonomy and beginning to develop joint agendas, joint goals, and joint resources.

The level of integration that is appropriate depends on the desires of the agencies and the length of time that the coalitions have worked together. Some coalitions may decide to start at a low level of integration and move to higher levels of integration over time; others may start with attempts to engage in projects that require full integration. What is most crucial is that all agencies agree on the level of integration and jointly define their common goals as well as objectives to reach these goals.

If the decision is to move toward the more integrated involvement, the next step is to determine the appropriate issue to address and the appropriate public health actions to take. The following description of evidence-based planning is one approach to planning that incorporates community expertise with scientific expertise.

## Evidence-Based Planning in Community Settings

Once individuals and agencies have agreed to work together to address a public health issue, the next step is to determine if there is sufficient evidence for public health action (in the form of a specific program or policy) and what specific action should be taken.[14] In taking this next step, a coalition should conduct a complete community assessment as well as consider two types of evidence. (Refer to Chapter 15 for detailed discussion of community health assessment.) The first, type 1 evidence, is used to examine the importance of a particular health condition and its link with some preventable risk factor. The second type of evidence focuses on the relative effectiveness of specific actions to address a particular health condition (type 2 evidence). A third type of evidence recently has been introduced focusing on how to carry out type 2 interventions, focusing on issues such as implementation, context, and how an intervention is received by the target audience.[15]

### Community Assessment

Community assessments are important for several reasons. First, an assessment can provide insight into the community context and ensures that interventions will be designed, planned, and carried out in a way that maximizes benefits to the community. Coalitions can use these assessments to make decisions about where to focus resources and interventions. A community assessment also helps to ensure that all members of a coalition have an understanding of the relationships of interest. Information from a community assessment can influence others in the community to provide support or resources for the intervention efforts. Lastly, a community assessment can be used to understand where your coalition is starting, and what kinds of things you want to track along the way in order to determine how your efforts are contributing to change. A community assessment is more local than the data typically collected as type 1 evidence, and is considered more comprehensive than the more traditional "needs assessment" because it assesses not only the challenges and needs of the community but also the resources and strengths of the community. Coalitions may want to consider assessing the strengths and assets of a community, including infrastructures, the built environment, and social networks and organizations. These data may be qualitative or quantitative. Community assessments may also include a review of morbidity and mortality, health and risk behaviors, and social indicator data (e.g., poverty level, business development, unemployment rates, graduation rates, housing stock). These latter data sets are more likely to be quantitative data, and some may also form the basis of risk identification, or type 1 evidence.

### Type 1 Evidence: Risk Identification

Risk identification is a process that allows community-based coalitions to review what is known about a specific issue or problem and provide information to determine if some broad action might be warranted. For example, an epidemic of lung cancer might be suspected and preventable risk factors (e.g., smoking, certain occupations) might be examined.

*Issue Quantification*

One of the first steps in understanding a public health problem is to examine existing data, often categorizing a problem in epidemiologic categories of person, place, and time. Such descriptive data may be available from ongoing vital statistics data (birth/death records), surveillance systems, special surveys, or national studies. (See Chapter 7 for a more detailed discussion of types of public health data.) Data may be available at the national, state, or even community level, and each type of data provides different information that can increase understanding of the extent and nature of the health concern. For example, US census data are one type of national data set that can be helpful because they provide information by ZIP code on a wide variety of factors that may influence health such as housing, income, employment status, and age. WONDER is another example of a national data set that may be useful to local communities. WONDER can be accessed at http://wonder. cdc.gov. This Web site contains information on the prevalence of chronic disease, cancer, and human immunodeficiency virus/acquired immune deficiency syndrome. Data on numerous other health concerns and issues including maternal and child health, sexually transmitted disease, tobacco use, occupational morbidity, injury, and tuberculosis are also available through this Web site.

In terms of statewide systems, some states have developed systems that enable community groups to assess data regarding the major health concerns in their area and determine if their area has a higher or lower rate of this health concern in comparison to the state as a whole. Similarly, some community groups have begun to either connect with state systems or develop their own systems for tracking the existence of health issues and concerns, as well as list services available to assist community members to cope with these health issues. Examples can be found at the Missouri Department of Health and Senior Services Web site at http://www.health.state.mo.us/MICA/ or the Washington State Department of Health at http://www.doh.wa.gov/Data/data.htm.

One of the challenges of quantifying a health issue or concern is to integrate the multiple sources of data available. There are several tools and processes that can assist public health practitioners in sorting through data to determine if a public health action is warranted. The next few paragraphs provide a very brief overview of some of these tools.

*Public Health Surveillance.* Public health surveillance involves the ongoing systematic collection, analysis, and interpretation of outcome-specific health data, closely integrated with the timely dissemination of these data to those individuals who are responsible for preventing and controlling disease or injury.[16,17] (See Chapter 14 for a more detailed discussion on public health surveillance systems.) A viable surveillance system can provide a wealth of valuable information for decision making in public health. Public health surveillance systems should have the capacity to collect and analyze data, disseminate data to public health programs, and regularly evaluate the effectiveness of the use of the disseminated data. For example, documentation concerning the prevalence of elevated levels of lead (a known toxicant) in blood in the US population has been used as the justification for eliminating lead from gasoline and for documenting the effects of this intervention.[18]

*Risk Assessment. Quantitative risk assessment* is a widely used term for a systematic approach to characterizing the risks posed to individuals and populations by environmental pollutants and other potentially adverse exposures.[19,20] Risk assessment has been described as a "bridge" between science and policy making, and it has become an established process through which expert scientific input is provided to agencies that regulate environmental or occupational exposures.[21] In the United States, its use is either explicitly or implicitly required by a number of federal statutes, and its application worldwide is increasing. There has been considerable debate concerning US risk assessment policies. The most widely recognized difficulties in risk assessment are due to extrapolation-related uncertainties, specifically, extrapolating low-dose health effects from higher exposure levels.

*Economic Evaluation.* Economic evaluation, commonly through studies of cost-effectiveness, should be an important component of evidence-based decision making.[22] These methods provide information to help assess the relative appropriateness of expenditures on public health programs and policies. Cost-effectiveness compares the net monetary costs of an intervention with some measure of health impact or outcome, such as years of life saved.[23,24] (See Chapter 18 for more on evaluation.)

An example of a cost-effectiveness analysis in relation to a public health intervention was shown by Hatziandreu et al. when they assessed the benefits of regular exercise among a cohort of 1000 35-year-old men.[25] They estimated that regular exercise would result in 78 fewer coronary heart disease deaths and 1138 quality-adjusted life-years (QALYs) gained in this cohort. The cost per QALY was favorable compared with other preventive or therapeutic interventions. In public health practice, a continuing challenge is the difficulty in measuring cost-effectiveness for community-based interventions because cost data are often not reported and indirect costs, such as lost work productivity, are difficult to measure.

### Making National and State Data Sets Relevant to Local Communities

Although these surveillance systems and descriptive and analytic studies provide evidence of public health issues and concerns, it is important to note that these systems may not provide all of the information necessary to engage in community-based prevention actions. In particular, community groups may feel that these data do not accurately reflect the reality of their community because of the biases inherent in such systems. For example, some data are collected via the telephone, thus providing information only on those individuals with phones. Other information is collected via a review of hospital and health provider data, and again there are several individuals who may be ill or have health concerns who are not seen until the problem becomes acute. Hence, the data set may not reflect the importance of the issue because it is "silent" to the data collection activities.

A second concern with the validity and utility of these systems, particularly national surveillance systems, is that they focus solely on health problems, not on community assets and other aspects of the community context that may positively or negatively affect these health concerns and the ability of groups to work together to create change. The community context was discussed earlier in terms of preformation activities but is important to revisit at this stage as well. For additional information on these concepts (which have been called *social capital, collective efficacy, community competence,* and *community capacity*), see Goodman et al., Kreuter et al., Sampson et al., and Eng and Parker.[9,10,26,27]

One way to address these weaknesses in existing data is through the collection of local data through quantitative and qualitative methods including questionnaires, individual or group interviews, and content analysis of local publications. These data should focus on assessing the local context, the needs of community members, and the positive social factors that enhance health and the ability of community members to work together. Coalition members can assist in ensuring that the information gathered and the methods used to gather these data are appropriate for the populations of interest.

Additional information on how to collect local data can be found in Johnson et al., Kretzmann and McKnight, and the University of Kansas Workgroup on Health Promotion and Community Development's Community Toolbox, which can be accessed at http://ctb.lsi.ukans.edu.[11,28,29] Goeppinger and Baglian, Interhealth Organizations, and the National Civic League *Civic Index* may also be helpful at this stage.[30-33] State and local data (e.g., http://health.state.mo.us) may also cover some contextual data that could be useful. For example, there may be information available concerning the number of civic organizations, churches, and recreational facilities in an area.

## Type 2 Evidence: Develop Program and Policy Options

Type 2 evidence provides suggestions as to what specifically should be done to address the issue of concern.

### Develop an Initial, Concise, Operational Statement of the Issue

The first step in deciding the specific steps that should be taken to address an issue is to clearly articulate the public health issue of interest. The key components of an issue statement include the health condition or risk factor being considered, the population(s) affected, the size and scope of the problem, prevention opportunities, and potential stakeholders.

An example is provided for an issue that is commonly encountered in public health practice—breast cancer.

- Background of the public health issue—Based on epidemiologic data, only 45% of women aged 40 years and older in state X are receiving mammography screening each year. Rates of screening have remained essentially constant over the past 5 years and are lowest among lower-income women.
- Programmatic issue—The state health department has been charged with developing a plan for increasing the number of women who receive mammography screening, with a special emphasis on increasing rates among low-income women.
- Solutions being considered—Program staff, policy makers, and advisory groups have proposed numerous solutions, including: (1) increased

funding for mammography services; (2) a mass media campaign to promote screening; (3) education of healthcare providers on how to effectively counsel for mammography screening; and (4) use of lay health advisors to work within their own communities to identify reasons for lack of compliance with screening recommendations and creation of programs and policies to address these concerns.

### Determine What Is Known Through the Scientific Literature, Expert Reviews, and Community Expertise

Once the issue to be considered has been clearly defined, the practitioner needs to become knowledgeable about previous or ongoing efforts to address the issue. This should include a systematic approach to identify, retrieve, and evaluate relevant reports on scientific studies, panels, and conferences related to the defined topic of interest. This may include conducting a review of the written scientific literature, or the use of existing reviews (either written or Internet based) and community expertise.

*Conducting a Literature Review.* The most common method for initiating this investigation is a formal literature review. There are many databases available to facilitate such a review. Most common among them for epidemiology and public health purposes are MEDLARS, MEDLINE, PubMed, Current Contents, HealthSTAR, and CancerLit. These databases can be subscribed to by an organization, can selectively be found on the Internet, or sometimes can be accessed by the public through institutions (such as the National Library of Medicine [http://www.nih.nlm.gov], the Combined Health Information Database [http://chid.nih.gov]), universities, and public libraries. There are also many organizations that maintain Internet sites that can be useful for identifying relevant information, including many state health departments, the US Centers for Disease Control and Prevention, and the National Institutes of Health. The methods for conducting a formal literature search can be found elsewhere.[17,41,42]

Once relevant articles and reports have been identified and retrieved, an evaluation of the information should be conducted. Depending on the specific purpose of the review, this evaluation may take the form of a systematic analysis and synthesis.[34-36] Such a synthesis can be primarily qualitative, in which the analytic results are carefully reviewed with respect to the validity of the studies, the generalizability of the results beyond the study populations, and the applicability of the findings in the context of the specific problem definition that originated the review. As described earlier, the synthesis can also be quantitative, in the form of a meta-analysis.

*Use of Existing Reviews.* Most governmental agencies, in both executive and legislative branches, as well as voluntary health organizations, use expert panels when examining scientific studies based on explicit criteria and determining their relevance to health policies and interventions.[37] Ideally, the goal of expert panels is to provide scientific peer review of the quality of the science and scientific interpretations that underlie public health recommendations, regulations, and policy decisions. When conducted well, peer review can provide an important set of checks and balances for the regulatory process. One of the successful outcomes of expert panels has been the production of guidelines for preventive medicine.[38] In related work, the Council on Linkages between Academia and Public Health Practice has concluded that "The potential benefits of public health practice guidelines are immediate and far reaching."[39,40(p5)] These recommendations have helped to stimulate a recent systematic effort to develop the *Guide to Community Preventive Services.*[41,42] The *Guide to Community Preventive Services* documents the effectiveness of a variety of population-based interventions and is considered to be the gold standard of programmatic reviews (http://thecommunityguide.org). The *Community Guide* documents the effectiveness of a variety of population-based interventions in public health through systematic review and evaluation of the scientific evidence. This review begins by convening a review team. The members of the review team develop a conceptual framework that lays out the specific determinants thought to influence the health outcome or behavior of interest. These include individual determinants (e.g., knowledge, attitudes, and behavior) as well as "broader social and environmental determinants of health such as education, housing, and access to health care."[42,43] The review team then identifies, and critically evaluates, programs and policies that have been designed to create changes in these determinants and ultimately the health outcome of interest. The body of evidence for a particular approach to change is then assessed based on a number of factors including: the research design, the execution of the study, the number of studies available to evaluate, the consistency of the findings across studies, the effect size achieved in the studies, and possible harms. Once the information has been summarized the review team determines if the evidence for disseminating the intervention (program or policy) is strong, sufficient, or insufficient. It is important to recognize that a label of strong evidence for a particular program or policy does not mean it should be immediately implemented as is across multiple communities. Rather, it implies that consideration for adaptation to other contexts and population is warranted. In other words, it is assumed that each population and context may have unique characteristics that require intervention adaptation, not simply intervention adoption. Similarly, a program or policy that currently has insufficient evidence to support widespread dissemination may warrant future research and adaptation to different contexts and populations prior to determining that the intervention should not be used to create the desired changes.

The topics completed to date and those currently in progress include the following:

- Vaccine-preventable diseases
- Tobacco use prevention and control
- Reducing motor vehicle occupant injury
- Diabetes
- Physical activity
- Oral health
- Sociocultural environment
- Prevention of injuries due to violence
- Cancer
- Pregnancy
- Violence prevention
- Work site health promotion
- Nutrition and obesity prevention

- Alcohol
- Mental health
- Sexual behavior

Additional information and updates regarding the *Community Guide* and its current state of development can be accessed at http://thecommunityguide.org.

While the *Community Guide* is considered the gold standard, there are other resources available to assist coalitions in deciding on which interventions may be appropriate for them, including Cancer Control Planet (Plan, Link, Act, and Network with Evidence-based Tools) and Intervention MICA (http://cancercontrolplanet.cancer.gov/ and http://www.health.state.mo.us/InterventionMICA/). Some of these other resources provide information not only on interventions that others have used and scientific evidence suggests are effective but also some links to tools to enable coalitions to translate this evidence into practice. Although these evidence-based reviews are very useful, it is important to consider not only which interventions have been effective in other settings, but the extent to which these programs can be transferred and adapted to the population and context of interest and achieve comparable effectiveness. There are a variety of criteria to consider in determining the transferability and adaptability of a particular intervention to the population and context of interest including: resources available (technology, space, funding), community interest and support, organizational and governmental support, complexity of implementation, as well as access to the partners and skills required to successfully implement the intervention. It is also important to recognize that there are some limits to reviews of previous interventions. One concern is that the structure of the review process may limit representation of studies conducted in communities that have traditionally been underrepresented in large research projects (including many racial/ethnic minority and rural communities). It is important to recognize the impact this may have on intervention transferability and adaptability. It may also be appropriate to consider interventions that have not yet been reviewed in these previous systematic assessments when working in communities that have been traditionally underrepresented in large research studies. Coalitions that include representatives from the community to be served by the intervention are critical in assessing and weighing these various criteria.

## Community Expertise

In addition to reviewing existing literature and data sources, it is essential to make use of the community expertise that exists in the coalition. One step that is important to take at this point is to determine what already exists in the community to address the chosen health issue or concern. Such a review can show gaps in programs and services and illuminate policies that can assist or hinder other programmatic plans. In addition, community members and community agencies that are part of the community coalition may have many ideas about possible program and policy options. Several techniques can be used to elicit this expertise, including the nominal group process or the Delphi technique. Further description of how to use these processes can be found in the book, *Needs Assessment Strategies for Health Education and Health Promotion*.[44]

The initial review of the scientific literature can sometimes highlight various options. More often, expert panels provide program or policy recommendations on a variety of issues. The development of these options is typically influenced by political/regulatory, economic, social, demographic, and technological considerations.[45,46] Of these, the assessment and monitoring of the political process is one of the most important considerations when developing policy options. Stakeholder input may be useful to understand fully the political ramifications of various policy options. The stakeholder for a policy might be the health policy maker; the stakeholder for a coalition-based community intervention might be a community member. In the case of health policies, supportive policy makers can frequently provide advice regarding the timing of policy initiatives, methods for framing the issue, strategies for identifying sponsors, and ways to develop support among the general public. In the case of a community intervention, additional planning data may include key informant interviews, focus groups, or coalition member surveys.[47] Several of these planning issues are also a part of the science of policy analysis.[48]

### Develop an Action Plan for the Program or Policy

In considering possible program and policy options, it is important to consider interventions at all levels of what has been described as the ecologic framework. Many community-based health promotion programs use ecologic frameworks to guide the development of their program activities. Ecologic frameworks suggest that it is important to incorporate efforts to address individual, interpersonal, community (including social and economic factors), organizational, and governmental factors because of the effect these factors have on individual behavior change, and because of their direct effect on health.[5,49,50]

Programs focused on changing individual behavior may provide information and/or teach skills to enable individuals to change their behaviors. These programs may focus on changing knowledge, attitudes, beliefs, and/or behaviors. These different approaches are likely to be more or less useful depending on the individual's readiness for change.[51,52]

To address interpersonal factors, many programs include strategies to strengthen social support. As described by Israel, these programs may act to strengthen existing networks or develop new network ties, or the building of social ties may be a secondary aim of programs focusing on other types of community-based activities.[53,54] For example, a program aimed at strengthening existing networks to enhance individual behavior change might invite family members to join fitness facilities or take cooking classes together. Programs may also seek to enhance the total network through lay health advisors.[53,54] Lay health advisors are "lay people to whom others normally turn to for advice, emotional support, and tangible aid."[55(p26)] Lay health advisors may provide specific health information and information about services available to address different health needs, assist clients in improving their communication skills, or establish linkages with health and human service agencies for efficient and appropriate referral.[55,56]

In addition to addressing interpersonal factors, community-based health promotion programs may attempt to create changes in community factors, including social and economic factors. These efforts often focus on creating changes in community structures, processes, and policies. In terms of policy changes, these programs may, for example, focus on creating work site smoking policies or smoke-free restaurants to support changes in individual smoking behavior and to attempt to alter community norms around smoking. Alternately, efforts may be focused on creating organizational or governmental policy changes in other social, community, or economic factors such as housing, jobs, education, and the environment.[57] Program activities focused on these more social and environmental factors are thought to be beneficial in that they can assist in changing community norms and create changes that persist over time.[58]

Ecologic frameworks suggest that because these factors (intrapersonal, interpersonal, organizational, social, and economic) are interrelated, programs that address one level are likely to enhance outcomes at the other levels, and that programs that incorporate interventions at multiple levels are likely to be more effective. It is important to note that ecologic frameworks are useful whether the program is categorical (e.g., focused on a particular disease process) or broadly defined (e.g., community development). For example, programs that focus on a disease category (e.g., breast cancer) and receive categorical funding to change individual behavior (e.g., mammography) can enhance their ability to influence this behavior if they consider the impact of other factors (e.g., interpersonal, economic) and intervene accordingly. This may entail providing low- or no-cost mammograms, changing the policy in the state so that more women are eligible for low- or no-cost mammograms, or developing a lay health advisor approach to enhance breast cancer screening. These different programmatic activities may occur simultaneously or sequentially.

In developing options, it is useful to remember that many public health interventions are founded on the notion that action at the level of a social unit can improve health outcomes at the individual level. This notion is embodied in an overall *causal framework*—one that leads from program inputs (programs and resources) to health outputs (changes in health behaviors or health status) if the program works as intended, and that guides program planners in designing interventions.[59] It is important for evaluation purposes that what has been termed this "small theory" of the intervention be made explicit early in the planning process.[60] The causal framework should lead toward explicit determination of mutable and immutable factors, assisting in program option development. This aspect of the process deals largely with strategic planning issues. Key issues are briefly covered here, with more extensive discussions by others.[61-63]

Once an option has been selected, a set of goals and objectives should be developed. A *goal* is a long-term desired change in the status of a priority health need, and an *objective* is a short-term, measurable, specific activity that leads toward achievement of a goal.[62,63] The course of action describes how the goals and objectives will be achieved, what resources are required, and how the responsibility of achieving objectives will be assigned. Excellent examples exist showing how to construct logic models that lay out the goals, objectives, and activities with a "fill in the blank" format.[64] (See Figure 19-1.)

It is important that objectives are the following:[62]

| Goal: | | | | | Evaluation of goal: |
|---|---|---|---|---|---|
| Objective: | | | | | Evaluation of objective: |
| **Activities:** | Action | By When? | By Whom? | Cost | Evaluation |
| 1. | | | | | |
| 2. | | | | | |
| 3. | | | | | |
| 4. | | | | | |
| 5. | | | | | |
| 6. | | | | | |

**FIGURE 19-1    Simple Logic Model**

- Performance, behavior, or action oriented
- Precise in their language (do not use general or vague verbs)
- Measurable
- Results oriented, with stated outcomes
- Clear in their description of content and performance
- Tied to specific timetables for completion

*Evaluate the Program or Policy*

A logic model should also have embedded specific steps to enable an assessment of the accomplishment of various activities, objectives, and goals. In simple terms, evaluation is the determination of the degree to which program goals and objectives are met. (See Chapter 18 for a more detailed discussion on different evaluation methods.) Most public health programs and policies are evaluated through quasi-experimental designs—that is, those lacking random assignment to intervention and comparison groups.[65]

More complete descriptions of research designs can be found elsewhere.[62,63] In general, the strongest evaluation designs acknowledge the importance of both quantitative and qualitative evaluation. Furthermore, evaluation designs need to be flexible and sensitive enough to assess inter-mediate changes, even those that fall short of changes in behavior. Genuine change takes place incrementally over time, in ways that often are not visible to those persons who are too close to the intervention. Several important considerations for evaluating community-based interventions are shown in Table 19-1.[59]

Measuring the impacts of a program or policy should commonly rely on three interrelated levels of evaluation: process, impact, and outcome. Potential contributions of each type of evaluation will be presented, with a more comprehensive discussion available elsewhere.[66–68]

Initially, one should seek to determine which (if any) changes have occurred as the result of a particular intervention through process and impact evaluation. *Process evaluation* is the analysis of inputs and implementation experiences (activities) to track changes as a result of a program or policy.[66,68]

Process evaluation occurs at the earliest stages of a public health intervention and is often helpful in determining "midcourse corrections." *Impact evaluation* can be considered a subset of outcome evaluation that assesses whether intermediate objectives have been achieved. Indicators may include changes in knowledge, attitudes, or risk factor prevalence.[66,68] The long-term measures of effects rely on *outcome evaluation* such as changes in morbidity, mortality, and quality of life. As discussed earlier, *economic evaluation* is often an important component of an overall evaluation plan. Worksheets to assist communities in developing evaluations of community-based prevention efforts can be found in Johnson et al.[11]

The usual sources of measurement error should be considered when developing and implementing an evaluation plan—that is, validity and reliability. The most useful community-based interventions show high *internal validity* (i.e., can the observed results be attributed to the program or intervention?). Further, *external validity* relates to whether the observed results can be generalized to other settings and populations. *Reliability* (or reproducibility) refers to the extent to which the same measurement is obtained on

**TABLE 19-1    A Summary of Evaluation Principles and Tools**

| Principle | Tool |
| --- | --- |
| Community programs should include an assessment of program theory. | Logic models |
| Instruments that are used to measure community programs must be contoured to each individual community. | Questionnaires and surveys<br>Social indicators |
| Approaches should be guided by the questions asked and often require both a quantitative and qualitative orientation. | Experimental and quasi-experimental designs<br>Qualitative designs |
| Evaluation should be informed by social ecology and social system concepts. | Ecology and systems designs |
| Community evaluation should involve local stakeholders in meaningful ways. | Participatory planning |

*Source:* Adapted with permission from Goodman RM. Principles and tools for evaluating community based prevention. *J Public Health Manage Pract.* 1998;4:39.

the same occasion by the same observer, on multiple occasions by the same observer, or by different observers on the same occasion. An additional source of error in community-based interventions may result from inadequate implementation (so-called type III error).[69] It is also important to acknowledge that it is often difficult to tease out specific effects when multiple intervention strategies are used.[58]

• • •

Community-based prevention is an iterative process involving the formation and management of community coalitions that develop, implement, and evaluate programs and policies to determine if the chosen activities should be continued, modified, or discontinued in the communities served. A flowchart and program example of these activities can be found in Figure 19–2 and Exhibit 19–1, respectively. One of the factors that makes community-based prevention distinct from more traditional programs and policies is the acknowledgment that dissemination of the program or policy can not occur without regard to community context. Thus, this is a process that occurs within and across communities, and it must be repeated as

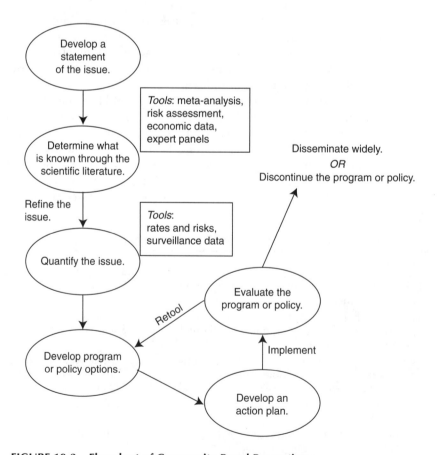

**FIGURE 19-2   Flowchart of Community-Based Prevention**
*Source:* Reprinted from Brownson RC, Gurney JG, and Land G. Evidence-based decisions making in public health. *J Public Health Manage Pract.* 1999;5(5):86–97.

Exhibit 19-1   Detroit's East Side Village Health Worker Partnership

**Goal of coalition:** To promote and conduct collaborative, community-based prevention research that strengthens the ability of communities to address and expand the knowledge base of public health regarding the health of women and children

**Steering committee members (coalition):** Detroit Health Department, a managed care organization, the University of Michigan School of Public Health, community organizations (see citations for descriptions of initial mobilization and establishment of organizational structure)

**Risk identification—determining what is known through the scientific literature:**
- Context assessment (preformation): population descriptives including migration patterns, housing patterns, and economic base; history of union and neighborhood organizing; policy-community relationships; and past racial tensions
- Review of secondary data including crime statistics and agency referral information
- 700-household face-to-face survey developed and implemented jointly by members of the coalition and others in the community
- In-depth interviews with village health workers, health department staff, and community-based organization staff
- Analysis of newspaper clippings

**Program goals:**
- To design, implement, and evaluate a collaborative village health worker intervention to address the factors associated with women's and children's health in the targeted area within east side Detroit
- To identify personal, interpersonal, organizational, community, and policy factors associated with poor health outcomes for women and children on Detroit's east side
- To increase village health workers' and community members' knowledge about and participation in strategies to modify risk and protective factors to improve the health of women and children

**Activities at multiple levels of ecologic framework:**
- Dissemination of survey findings to community members
- Training of village health workers
- Implementation of village health worker program
- Determining policy changes that can be made at the local and state level

**Evaluation of activities:**
- Field notes at meetings
- Pre/post-testing or training of village health workers
- Focus group interviews
- Documentation records by village health workers

*Note:* The above outline is organized according to the constructs presented in this chapter, and is not necessarily using the language used within the project materials themselves. For additional information about this project, see Parker E, Schulz AJ, Israel BA, Hollis R. Detroit's East Side Village Health Worker Partnership: community-based lay health advisor intervention in an urban area. *Health Educ Q.* 1998;25(1): 24–25, and Schulz AJ, Parker EA, Israel BA, et al. Conducting a participatory community-based survey. *J Public Health Manage Pract.* 1998;4(2):10–24.

definitions of the community change (e.g., change in racial group, religious group, or geographic location).

Many public health practitioners are beginning to recognize the importance of developing community-based prevention programs. These programs require the development of skills to work in interdisciplinary teams and with community members who represent a variety of subgroups in the population of interest, skills in collecting and interpreting data from a variety of sources, and program and policy development skills. The types of data and information that are available to assist practitioners in these tasks are at their fingertips as never before. Population health practitioners should be forewarned, however. The tools and skills suggested in this chapter are necessary but not sufficient. Developing community-based prevention programs requires practitioners to not only build skills, but also to build relationships in ways that are new in the field of public health. These programs often necessitate changes in traditional public health systems such as communication systems and financial accountability systems. The blending of community and scientific expertise entails learning from each other and developing common agendas and processes to reach joint goals.

## Chapter Review

1. Community-based prevention efforts should involve both members of the community and representatives of organizations that work with, or benefit, members of the community.
2. In developing community coalitions to address public health issues, it is important to identify and use existing resources in the community, as well as to build new capacities and relationships among individuals and organizations in the community. Some of these tasks must occur prior to the coalition development (preformation), some tasks need to be considered in the initial mobilization of the coalition, and others need to be addressed during the development of coalition structures.
3. One of the first decisions a community coalition must make is to decide the level of integration it wants to have with the other organizations and individuals in the community. The level of integration that is appropriate depends on the preferences of the participants regarding autonomy and control, the extent of familiarity and trust among participants, and the degree to which participants face shared objectives, incentives, and constraints.
4. Before developing a community-based intervention it is important to conduct a complete community assessment.
5. In developing community-based interventions to address health issues, three types of evidence should be considered by decision makers within the community coalition.
   - The first type of evidence, risk identification, is based on data showing the importance of a particular health issue and its link with some preventable risk factor.
   - The second type of evidence, program and policy development, focuses on the relative effectiveness of specific interventions to address a particular health issue.

- A third type of evidence examines how interventions are implemented and maintained.

6. Key actions to be performed by the community coalition in developing programs to address health issues include the following:
   - Develop an operational statement of the health issue.
   - Identify what is known about the issue through a review of scientific literature.
   - Determine what resources and expertise already exist in the community to address the health issue.
   - Identify all possible program and policy options to address the issue. Evidence-based reviews of the effectiveness of previous interventions, such as the *Community Guide,* can be helpful in identifying options, as long as consideration regarding the criteria for transferability and adaptability are considered.
   - Develop an action plan to address the issue, which identifies preferred options and performance objectives.
   - Develop a strategy for evaluating the program or policy.

# References

1. IOM Committee for the Study of the Future of Public Health. *The Future of Public Health.* Washington, DC: National Academy Press; 1988.
2. Fielding J, Halfon N. Where is the health in health system reform? *JAMA.* 1994;272:1292–1296.
3. Institute of Medicine. *The Future of the Public's Health in the 21st Century.* Washington, DC: National Academies Press; 2003.
4. Institute of Medicine. *Linking Research to Public Health Practice. A Review of the CDC's Program of Centers for Research and Demonstration of Health Promotion and Disease Prevention.* Washington, DC: National Academy Press; 1997.
5. Israel BA, Checkoway B, Schulz A, Zimmerman M. Health education and community empowerment: conceptualizing and measuring perceptions of individual, organizational, and community control. *Health Educ Q.* 1994;21(2):149–170.
6. McKnight J. Redefining community. *Social Policy.* 1992;23:56–62.
7. True S. Community-based breast health partnerships. In: Brownson RC, Baker EA, Novick L, eds. *Community-Based Prevention: Programs That Work.* Gaithersburg, MD: Aspen Publishers Inc; 1999:173–181.
8. Parker EA, Eng E, Laraia B, et al. Coalition building for prevention: lessons learned from the North Carolina Community-Based Public Health Initiative. *J Public Health Manage Pract.* 1998;4(2):25–36.
9. Goodman R, Speers M, McLeroy K, et al. Identifying and defining the dimensions of community capacity to provide a basis for measurement. *Health Educ Behav.* 1998;25(3):258–278.
10. Kreuter M, Lezin N, Koplan A. *Social Capital: Evaluation Implications for Community Health Promotion.* Commissioned Paper for the WHO-EURO Monograph on Evaluating Health Promotion Approaches. Geneva, Switzerland: World Health Organization;1997.
11. Johnson K, Grossman W, Cassidy A. *Collaborating to Improve Community Health: Workbook and Guide to Best Practices in Creating Healthier Communities and Populations.* San Francisco, CA: Jossey-Bass; 1996.

12. Wolff T, Kaye G. *From the Ground Up! A Workbook on Coalition Building and Community Development.* Amherst, Mass: AHEC/Community Partners; 2002.

13. Alter C, Hage J. *Organizations Working Together: Coordination in Interorganizational Networks.* Newbury Park: Sage Publications; 1992.

14. Brownson R, Baker EA, Leet T, Gillespie K. *Evidence-Based Public Health.* New York, NY: Oxford University Press; 2003.

15. Rychetnik L, Hawe P, Waters E, Barratt A, Frommer M. A glossary for evidence based public health. *J Epidemiol Community Health.* 2004;58(7): 538–545.

16. Thacker SB, Stroup DF. Public health surveillance. In: Brownson RC, Petitti DB, eds. *Applied Epidemiology: Theory to Practice.* 2nd ed. New York, NY: Oxford University Press; 2006.

17. Thacker SB, Berkelman RL. Public health surveillance in the United States. *Epidemiol Rev.* 1988;10:164–190.

18. Annest JL, Pirkle JL, Makuc D, et al. Chronological trend in blood lead levels between 1976 and 1980. *N Engl J Med.* 1983;308:1373–1377.

19. Samet JM, White R, Burke TA. Epidemiology and risk assessment. In: Brownson RC, Petitti DB, eds. *Applied Epidemiology: Theory to Practice.* 2nd ed. New York, NY: Oxford University Press; 2006.

20. World Health Organization. *Assessment and Management of Environmental Health Hazards.* Vol 89.6. Geneva, Switzerland: WHO/PEP; 1989.

21. Hertz-Picciotto I. Epidemiology and quantitative risk assessment: a bridge from science to policy. *Am J Public Health.* 1995;85:484–491.

22. Gold MR, Siegel JE, Russell LB, Weinstein MC. *Cost-Effectiveness in Health and Medicine.* New York: Oxford University Press; 1996.

23. Petitti DB. Economic evaluation. In: Brownson RC, Petitti DB, eds. *Applied Epidemiology: Theory to Practice.* New York, NY: Oxford University Press; 1998:277–298.

24. Weinstein MC, Stason WB. Foundations of cost-effectiveness analysis for health and medical practices. *New Engl J Med.* 1977;296:716–721.

25. Hatziandreu EI, Koplan JP, Weinstein MC, Caspersen CJ, Warner KE. A cost-effectiveness analysis of exercise as a health promotion activity. *Am J Public Health.* 1988;78(11):1417–1421.

26. Sampson R, Raudenbush S, Earls F. Neighborhoods and violent crime: a multilevel study of collective efficacy. *Science.* 1997;277:918–924.

27. Eng E, Parker E. Measuring community competence in the Mississippi delta: the interface between program evaluation and empowerment. *Health Educ Q.* 1994;21(2):199–220.

28. Kretzmann J, McKnight J. *Building Communities from the Inside Out: A Path Toward Finding and Mobilizing a Community's Assets.* Chicago, Ill: ACTA Publications; 1993.

29. Kretzmann J, McKnight J. *A Guide to Capacity Inventories: Mobilizing the Community Skills of Local Residents.* Chicago, Ill: ACTA Publications; 1993.

30. Goeppinger J, Baglian A. Community competence: a positive approach to needs assessment. *Am J Community Psychol.* 1985;13:507–523.

31. Interhealth Organizations. *A Guide to Community Health Needs Assessment Tools.* Atlanta, Ga: Interhealth Organizations; 1992.

32. National Civic League. *Civic Index Workbook.* Denver, CO: National Civic League; 1987.

33. National Civic League. *Civic Indicators Handbook.* Denver, CO: National Civic League; 2005.

34. Petitti DB. *Meta-Analysis, Decision Analysis, and Cost-Effectiveness Analysis: Methods for Quantitative Synthesis in Medicine.* New York, NY: Oxford University Press; 1994.

35. Goldschmidt PG. Information synthesis: a practical guide. *Health Serv Re.* 1986;21:215–237.
36. Rundall TG. Conducting and writing research reviews. *Med Care Res Rev.* 1996;53(Suppl):S132–S145.
37. Brownson RC. Epidemiology and health policy. In: Brownson RC, Petitti DB, eds. *Applied Epidemiology: Theory to Practice.* New York: Oxford University Press; 2006:349–387.
38. US Preventive Services Task Force. *Guide to Clinical Preventive Services.* 2nd ed. Baltimore, Md: Williams & Wilkins; 1996.
39. Novick LF. Public health practice guidelines: a case study. *J Public Health Manage Pract.* 1997;3(1):59–64.
40. Council on Linkages Between Academia and Public Health Practice. *Practice Guidelines for Public Health: Assessment of Scientific Evidence, Feasibility and Benefits: A Report of the Guideline Development Project for Public Health Practice.* Washington, DC: Council on Linkages Between Academia and Public Health Practice; 1995.
41. Pappaioanou M, Evans C. Developing a guide to community preventive services: a US Public Health Service initiative. *J Public Health Manage Pract.* 1998;4:48–54.
42. Briss P, Brownson R, Fielding J, Zaza S. Developing and using the guide to community preventive services: lessons learned about evidence-based public health. *Annu Rev Public Health.* 2004:281–302.
43. Zaza S, Briss P, Harris K. *The Guide to Community Preventive Services: What Works to Promote Health?* New York, NY: Oxford University Press; 2005.
44. Gilmore GD, Campbell MD. *Needs Assessment Strategies for Health Education and Health Promotion.* 2nd ed. Madison, WI: Browns & Benchmark; 1996.
45. Ginter PM, Duncan WJ, Capper SA. Keeping strategic thinking in strategic planning: macro-environmental analysis in a state health department of public health. *Public Health.* 1992;106:253–269.
46. Ginter PM, Swayne LM, Duncan WJ. *Strategic Management of Health Care Organizations.* 3rd ed. Malden, Mass: Blackwell Publishers Inc; 1998.
47. Florin P, Stevenson J. Identifying training and technical assistance needs in community coalitions: a developmental approach. *Health Educ Res.* 1993;8:417–432.
48. Ham C, Hill M. *The Policy Process in the Modern Capitalist State.* New York, NY: St. Martin's Press; 1984.
49. McLeroy KR, Bibeau D, Steckler A, Glanz K. An ecological perspective on health promotion programs. *Health Educ Q.* 1988;15:351–377.
50. Simons-Morton BG, Greene WH, Gottlieb NH. *Introduction to Health Education and Health Promotion.* 2nd ed. Prospect Heights, Ill: Waveland Press; 1995.
51. Prochaska JO, DiClemente CC. Stages and processes of self-change of smoking: toward an integrative model of change. *J Consult Clin Psychol.* 1983;51(3):390–395.
52. Prochaska JO, Velicer WF. The transtheoretical model of health behavior change. *Am J Health Promot.* 1997;12(1):38–48.
53. Israel BA. Social networks and health status: linking theory, research, and practice. *Patient Couns Health Educ.* 1982;4(2):65–79.
54. Israel BA. Social networks and social support: implications for natural helper and community-level interventions. *Health Educ Q.* 1985;12(1):65–80.
55. Eng E, Young R. Lay health advisors as community change agents. *Fam Community Health.* 1992;151:24–40.

56. Eng E, Hatch J. Networking between agencies and black churches: the lay health advisor model. *Prev Human Serv.* 1991;10(1):123–146.

57. Milio N. Priorities and strategies for promoting community-based prevention policies. *J Public Health Manage Pract.* 1998;4(3):14–28.

58. Thompson B, Coronado G, Snipes S, Puschel K. Methodologic advances and ongoing challenges in designing community-based health promotion programs. *Annu Rev Public Health.* 2003;24:315–340.

59. Goodman RM. Principles and tools for evaluating community-based prevention and health promotion programs. *J Public Health Manage Pract.* 1998;4(2):37–47.

60. Lipsey MW. Theory as method: small theories of treatment. In: Sechrest L, Perrin E, Bunker J, eds. *Research Methodology: Strengthening Causal Interpretations of Nonexperimental Data.* Washington, DC: Government Printing Office; 1990. DHHS Pub. No. (PHS) 90-3454.

61. Bryson JM. *Strategic Planning for Public and Nonprofit Organizations. A Guide to Strengthening and Sustaining Organizational Achievement.* San Francisco, CA: Jossey-Bass Publishers; 1995.

62. Timmreck TC. *Planning, Program Development, and Evaluation. A Handbook for Health Promotion, Aging and Health Services.* Boston, Mass: Jones and Bartlett Publishers; 1995.

63. Turnock BJ. *Public Health: What It Is and How It Works.* 2nd ed. Gaithersburg, MD: Aspen Publishers Inc; 2001.

64. American Public Health Association. *Healthy Communities 2000: Model Standards. Guidelines for Community Attainment of the Year 2000 Health Objectives.* Washington, DC: American Public Health Association; 1991.

65. Shadish W, Cook T, Campbell D. *Experimental and Quasi-Experimental Designs for Generalized Causal Inference.* Boston, Mass: Houghton Mifflin; 2002.

66. Green LW, Kreuter MW. *Health Promotion Planning: An Educational and Ecological Approach.* 3rd ed. Mountain View, Calif: Mayfield; 1999.

67. Rossi PH, Freeman HE. *Evaluation. A Systematic Approach.* Newbury Park, Calif: Sage Publications; 1993.

68. Israel B, Cummings K, Dignan M, et al. Evaluation of health education programs: current assessment and future directions. *Health Educ Q.* 1995;22(3):364–389.

69. Goodman RM, Wandersman A. FORECAST: a formative approach to evaluating community coalitions and community-based interventions. *J Community Psychol.* 1994:(CSAP Special Issue)6–25.

## CHAPTER 20

# COMMUNICATION AND MEDIA RELATIONS

Cynthia B. Morrow
Douglas Hirano
Brad Christensen

## Chapter Overview

Developing and managing successful public health activities requires the ability to communicate effectively with the variety of stakeholders involved in these efforts. Increasingly, public health organizations rely on explicit communication strategies to manage relationships with the media, policy makers, and the public. Key channels of communication include press releases, press conferences, Internet-based communication, radio, television, pamphlets, posters, and town meetings. Media relationships can be especially helpful in advancing population-wide health promotion and disease prevention interventions. External communication strategies should be coordinated with internal communication processes to ensure optimal organizational performance.

## Communication in Public Health

Clear and effective communication is critical to the ability to improve health locally, nationally, and globally. In the United States, recent attention to public health with the anthrax attacks in 2001, sudden acute respiratory syndrome (SARS) and monkeypox in 2003, and the health system's response to Hurricane Katrina in 2005 demonstrated how risk communication is an essential component of population-based management of health at times of crises. As important as communication is during emergencies, it is also a fundamental element of routine efforts to improve the health of a community.

Although the science of public health continues to advance, the concomitant success of communicating results and accomplishments has lagged behind. This is one reason why public health practice—for all its success in improving life expectancy over the past 100 years—continues to toil in relative obscurity compared with organized medical practice. As a result, population-based approaches to health improvement continue to suffer from poor funding and limited advocacy. It has been estimated that health promotion and disease prevention expenditures constitute only 3% of healthcare expenditures.[1]

An added challenge is that public health activities such as the prevention of epidemics, assurance of safe water and food, and maintenance of health statistics are largely transparent to the general public and, consequently, undervalued. Thus, although former Surgeon General C. Everett Koop's well-known comment, "Health care is vital to all of us some of the time, but public health is vital to all of us all of the time," resonates with public health professionals, it may fall on deaf ears when aimed at the public, the media, and policy makers.

Fortunately, the realization that "good communication equals good public health" has been growing. There are now dedicated centers for health communication at such institutions as Johns Hopkins and Harvard School of Public Health. Despite advances in this field, one of the greatest challenges to health communication is the pervasive problem of inadequate health literacy. Given the importance of communication in public health and the scope of inadequate health literacy, ideally all academic institutions and continuing education programs addressing public health should offer pragmatic training in effective communication strategies to improve public health practice. Modern public health organizations use marketing and entertainment education techniques to encourage lifestyle changes, media advocacy to transform health policy making, and risk communication to better characterize health risks.[2]

In the long run, the ability to develop and carry out a strategic communication plan at program, organization, and population levels will go a long way toward strengthening public health practice and also toward providing public health professionals with the visibility and credibility that are needed to lead health system change. The field of communication is broad in scope, and a large body of literature is available on the topic. This chapter describes principles and channels of health communication as well as strategies for public health administrators to improve organizational performance through enhanced communication, including a major focus on relations with the media, as well as strategies for effective communication with policy makers, the public, and stakeholders within the organization.

## Functions of Public Health Communication

Communication is the foundation of almost all of public health practice. Health communication can be incorporated into each of the 10 essential public health services as shown in Exhibit 20-1. In addition, health communication is identified as one of the 28 focus areas for *Healthy People 2010*.[3] Public health communication can serve multiple functions if effectively managed. Listed below are some examples of intended outcomes of such communication. This listing is not meant to be comprehensive, but instead demonstrates the scope of the role of communication in public health practice.

- Increased service utilization—To ensure that available services target at-risk populations, outreach is necessary. Examples of services requiring publicity include immunizations, primary care, family planning,

Exhibit 20-1   The Role of Communication in Performing the Essential Public Health Services

1. Monitor health status and solve community health problems.
   *Communication role:* Deliver relevant health status information to communities, particularly changes in rates that suggest the need for intervention; provide an opportunity for communities to voice concerns about perceived health problems.
2. Diagnose and investigate health problems and health hazards in the community.
   *Communication role:* Notify individuals and communities of potential health hazards (e.g., issue traveler's advisories in areas with known vector-borne disease transmission).
3. Inform, educate, and empower people about health issues.
   *Communication role:* Use multiple levels of communication, including social marketing and community education, to bring about healthy lifestyles.
4. Mobilize community partnerships and action to identify and solve health problems.
   *Communication role:* Assist in the development of coalitions and partnerships that will lead to collaborative action.
5. Develop policies and plans that support individual and community health efforts.
   *Communication role:* Inform the public about new laws that affect health, such as laws protecting the confidentiality of human immunodeficiency virus/acquired immune deficiency syndrome information; share draft planning documents with stakeholders as a means to receive input and to generate investment in outcomes.
6. Enforce laws and regulations that protect and ensure safety.
   *Communication role:* Share information with the regulated community to facilitate the adherence to proper licensing and safety standards; ensure easy access (e.g., Web site availability) to the required forms and rules relating to licensing and regulation.
7. Link people to needed personal health services and ensure the provision of health care when otherwise unavailable.
   *Communication role:* Inform medically underserved populations about opportunities for health care and the need for preventive services.
8. Ensure a competent public health and personal health care workforce.
   *Communication role:* Inform public health practitioners and health care providers about training opportunities, such as satellite video-conferences.
9. Evaluate effectiveness, accessibility, and quality of personal and population-based health services.
   *Communication role:* Inform policy makers about the efficacy of population-based health services.
10. Research for new insights and innovative solutions to health problems.
    *Communication role:* Publish results of applied research in peer-reviewed journals so that other agencies can translate findings into more effective public health practice.

*Source:* Essential Public Health Services Work Group of the Public Health Functions Steering Committee.

and tobacco cessation. Targeted communication regarding service availability can ensure that populations access these services appropriately.

- Healthier lifestyles—Public health organizations play critical roles in informing the public about the important role of personal lifestyle and behaviors in determining health status. Tobacco use, poor diet, lack of physical activity, and alcohol consumption contribute to 885,000 premature deaths a year in the United States.[4,5] Effective communication strategies can convey the risks of such activities.
- Improved organizational performance—Public health organizations, like other bureaucratic institutions, require effective internal and external communication strategies to ensure that the organization functions at optimum efficiency and effectiveness and that employee morale remains high.
- Strengthened community partnerships—The public health system involves partnerships with many other organizations within the community. Effective communication is critical for the success of such partnerships.
- Supportive health policies—Effective public health policy development requires regular communication with the media, elected officials, lobbyists, and community groups, among others.
- Effective management of public health emergencies—The threat of public health emergencies (e.g., natural disasters, bioterrorist activities, and communicable disease epidemics) requires a strong and rapid emergency communication system among public health organizations, emergency care providers, public safety agencies, medical care providers, and many others.

## Health Literacy

Although there are many applications for health communication, the leading barrier to effective health communication, including public health communication, is inadequate health literacy. The Office of the Surgeon General has identified improving health literacy as one of seven public health priorities.[6] *Healthy People 2010*'s definition of health literacy is "The degree to which individuals have the capacity to obtain, process, and understand basic health information and services needed to make appropriate decisions."[3] In 2004, the Institute of Medicine released the report *Health Literacy: A Prescription to End Confusion*, using this definition.[7] This report, which identified that 90 million Americans were at risk for inadequate health literacy, notes that the healthcare system, public health, schools, health consumers, and the media need to work together to improve health literacy to allow for optimal achievements in efforts to improve the quality of life, to reduce disparities in health outcomes, and to reduce healthcare costs in the United States.[7]

## Channels of Communication

The practice of public health offers a variety of ways to communicate information, called *channels* of communication (the term *media* is also used). A channel defines the route or method by which communication occurs. A channel of communication can be in writing (e.g., news release, newsletter, a scientific manuscript, or a memorandum), by verbal means (e.g., news conference, radio inter-view, or conference call), or by Internet-based technology (e.g., Web pages or Web applications, video teleconferencing, or electronic mail with associated functions such as list serves). Advances in communication technology have also provided other opportunities such as automated public notification systems that allow urgent messages to be relayed to residents and businesses in defined areas. More traditional channels include health fairs, pamphlets, and posters. Each mode may have certain advantages in certain situations. Table 20-1 includes a list of typical communication purposes with channels and intended audience.

The choice of an appropriate channel depends both on content and on the audience. Certain audiences prefer certain communication channels. For instance, adolescents and young adults may be more receptive to short, visu-ally oriented messages. In contrast, technical audiences may prefer written documents, with oral explanation available.

Channels can be used to receive information as well as to transmit infor-mation. Town halls, advisory groups, focus groups, and customer satisfaction surveys are means to gather information. Receiving useful information from a number of sources is often as critical as sending information.

## Principles of Effective Communication

The purpose of this section is to describe the key characteristics of good com-munication and to stimulate further research and practice in this area. Listed below are several key principles of communication that are particularly rele-vant to public health practice.

- Keep messages and language simple. There are few reasons to try to communicate information in a manner that is complex. In general, complexity only obscures the central message and important support-ing points. Simple and short messages are more memorable and easily understood. Plain language is best. One state epidemiologist, in de-scribing an outbreak of a fecal-orally transmitted disease, used the term *poop* in numerous television and radio interviews. This may not have sounded scholarly, but it communicated effectively. In developing written materials, it must be remembered that almost half of the popu-lation reads at very basic levels—approximately eighth grade or below.[8]

**TABLE 20-1    Typical Communication Purposes with Channels and Intended Audience**

| Purpose | Communication Channel | Intended Audience |
|---|---|---|
| Disease outbreak announcement | News media | General public |
| Research study results | Scientific journal | Public health practitioners |
| Policy recommendation | Newspaper (co-ed piece) | Policy makers |
| Behavioral change/ social marketing | Television spots/ commercials | General public |
| New program initiative | Press conference | General public |
| Outreach | Lay health workers | Ethnic communities |
| Strategic planning | Community meeting | Community members |
| General health information | Health fair | Community members |

- Ensure cultural competency. Society is becoming increasingly diverse. Estimates suggest that by the year 2050, the majority of Americans will be racial/ethnic minorities. Conceptually, cultural competence is expressed by communicating acceptance, deep understanding, and responsiveness to the needs and concerns of members of special populations.[9] This requires "the willingness and ability to utilize community-based values, traditions, and practices in developing and evaluating interventions, communication, and other activities."[10(pg4)] In 2002, the Institute of Medicine released the report: *Speaking of Health: Assessing Health Communication Strategies for Diverse Populations.*[11]
- Strike while the iron is hot. Sometimes, timing is everything in effective communication. For example, during the 1996 outbreak of bovine spongiform encephalopathy, otherwise known as "mad cow" disease, Hawaiian health officials staved off cuts to the state laboratory by emphasizing the need for strong laboratory capacity to detect emerging pathogens such as that causing "mad cow" disease.[12]
- Use multiple communication channels. Studies indicate that messages provided in multiple ways (e.g., radio, television, newspapers) are more likely to be remembered than those provided through a single medium. Studies indicate that people retain 20% of what they read; however, if they read and hear, they retain 65% of the message.[13]
- Listen. Communication efforts that include an opportunity for interactive dialogue can be effective. This is true for town halls, forums, and other types of meetings where input is the main goal. The purpose of the interaction is to receive useful information from policy makers, constituents, and others to shape policies and programs and to establish a relationship based on openness and shared understanding.

## Target Audiences

One of the most critical factors in effective communication is knowing to whom you are trying to communicate. Although this seems a simple principle, it is violated on almost a daily basis in the field of public health. All too frequently, one-size-fits-all messages are crafted for broad delivery to the public. Thinking of the general public as an audience may make sense conceptually, but it makes little sense for many communication strategies.

As in business marketing, customizing communication strategies to smaller subgroups (i.e., audience segments) of a larger population often pays dividends in terms of information dissemination. Audiences tend to vary by factors (e.g., race/ethnicity, socioeconomic status, age, and educational level) that affect communication effectiveness. Examples of potential public health target audiences include healthcare providers, women of childbearing age, older adults, individuals with disabilities, monolingual individuals, policy makers, other public health practitioners, and the media.

Audience segmentation involves breaking a larger group into smaller, more homogeneous audiences and targeting those audiences with appropriate messages, using appropriate channels. Segmentation avoids sending the same message through the same channel to a large heterogeneous group, resulting in inefficiency and suboptimal communication. For instance, in developing its tobacco prevention campaign, the Arizona Department of Health

Services used focus groups to gather information from adolescents regarding potentially effective media messages targeted at teens. The result was a media campaign that led to a 96% statewide prompted recollection among adolescents of the campaign slogan: "Tobacco: tumor-causing, teeth staining, smelly, puking, habit."[14]

Segmentation can also help avoid information gaps caused by selective attention. For instance, audiences who are better informed about and more favorably inclined toward good nutrition are more likely to be reached by community education programs than those who are less informed, less favorable, and less likely to seek out, receive, or retain nutrition information. Community education campaigns can inadvertently widen the information gap unless uninformed populations are targeted and specific media and messages are tailored for hard-to-reach individuals.

## Building Constituency and Visibility

Public health practitioners have made great strides in improving communication effectiveness, but there are still areas in need of further improvement. This section will discuss strategies for communicating with three separate constituencies: stakeholders within the organization itself, policy makers, and the communities they serve. Although numerous other constituencies must be engaged, these three are important to effective public health practice in any setting. For further detail about this topic, refer to Chapter 16 on Building Constituencies for Public Health.

### Information Technology and Communicating Within Public Health Agencies

Many analysts have examined communication in the workplace. This literature consistently emphasizes that good internal communication is key to good employee morale and to peak operating efficiency in any organization. It is certainly true within a small or large public health organization or program. However, little attention has traditionally been given to this area of public health practice.

From a management perspective, it is important to maintain contact with staff. In addition to standard staff meetings, there are a number of strategies to promote staff interaction. Informal activities such as brown-bag lunches can be effective. One state public health agency instituted a Monday morning informal coffee that allowed all members of the staff to chat, network, and raise issues in a nonthreatening, nonbureaucratic atmosphere. One state health department uses the "employee communique" as a less formal mechanism to provide employee-based human interest updates (e.g., news on employee-related births, retirements, awards). This weekly update is a single sheet that is strategically placed on the walls of the restroom stalls, thus ensuring that all employees have a chance to review the latest edition. Similarly, a department newsletter can serve as a means to communicate internally and also to inform constituencies such as the medical community, service providers, local health organizations, and policy makers about important department activities.

Information technology, particularly electronic mail and Web pages, has assisted greatly in sharing information among and within organizations. For example, Epidemic Information Exchange, Epi-X, is a Web-based communication systems operated through the Centers for Disease Control and Prevention (www.cdc.gov/epix) that allows public health officials at the local, state, and federal level to quickly and securely communicate with each other about disease outbreaks or other health concerns, particularly those that have the potential to affect more than one community. Similarly, the CDC's Health Alert Network and the newer Public Health Information Network are tools that will continue to enhance communication across the field, enabling the public health workforce across the nation to have access to consistent, up-to-date information.

In addition to the above tools for communication, advances in technology with respect to video teleconferencing have allowed for greater interaction among public health workers who work or reside in different locations. This is particularly helpful when funding levels significantly limit travel. Video teleconferencing also provides greater flexibility for "just-in-time" communication in urgent situations.

Unfortunately, despite the advantages afforded by information technology, there are numerous examples of situations in which critical information was not effectively communicated, typically during crises. (Refer to section on risk communication during public health emergencies later in this chapter.)

## Communicating with Policy Makers

A review of the nation's public health system more than a decade ago concluded that "Public health agency leaders should develop relationships with and educate legislators and other public officials on community health needs, on public health issues, and on the rationale for strategies advocated and pursued by the health department."[15(p14)] This observation came from the IOM's groundbreaking 1988 report *The Future of Public Health* and serves to emphasize the importance of effective communication with policy makers. The 2003 follow-up report, *The Future of the Public's Health in the 21st Century*, notes that while some progress has been made, "There has been no fundamental reform of the statutory framework for public health in most of the nation."[16(p100)]

Communication with policy makers can be daunting for several reasons: policy makers are generally busy people with numerous issues to confront; policy makers also hear from the "other side" (e.g., the tobacco industry); and policy makers must take into account public opinion and partisan concerns. These difficulties however, do not provide a reason to avoid communication with policy makers. On the contrary, positive and productive communication with policy makers can reap great benefits for public health agencies. Regular communication is essential. Some suggestions for maintaining open channels with key policy makers are listed below:

- Put legislators and other relevant policy makers on the mailing list for the program or agency newsletter.
- Invite policy makers to attend ceremonies (e.g., new program launches, groundbreaking ceremonies, etc.); this will provide opportunities to both educate the policy makers and to associate them with successful public health programs.
- Be open to accepting invitations to attend important events that have public health ramifications.

- Place periodic phone calls or visit the offices of elected officials to bring them or their staff up to date and to keep the agency's agenda part of their agenda.
- Provide reports, both written and oral, of how citizens complaints referred to the agency have been handled.
- To the extent possible, put a personal face on issues; personal stories should be culled from successful population-based program activities.

In general, it is important to be responsive to requests from policy makers. Competent and timely responses from public health agencies are greatly appreciated and can enhance agency credibility.

## Communicating with Communities

Communicating with the community is one of the most rewarding and yet one of the most difficult challenges in the practice of public health. Successful communication ideally results in protection or promotion of the health of the community the agency serves. Most communities are diverse, with wide ranges of health literacy and cultural attitudes and beliefs amongst their residents; therefore, public health practitioners must be skilled in communicating a message that is acceptable to different audiences. In addition, in any given community, there may be many health advocacy groups, nonprofit associations, healthcare providers, professional associations, and neighborhood groups representing different sectors within the community. Some community members may be suspicious of governmental agencies. The IOM addressed this in *The Future of the Public's Health in the 21st Century* with the recommendation "that all partners within the public health system place special emphasis on communication as a critical core competency of public health practice . . . To do so effectively, such communication must be culturally appropriate and suitable for the literacy levels of the communities they serve."[16(p125)]

If a public health agency needs to communicate a specific health concern to a geographically defined group of residents or businesses, automated notification telecommunication messages may be utilized. For example, in 2005 biohazard detection systems (BDS) were installed in many United States Postal Service centers. After such a system was installed in Syracuse, New York, an automated notification system was used to inform residents who lived in proximity of the postal distribution center that a drill was going to take place and to alert them to expect road closures and multiple emergency response vehicles in the area. This same system will be employed should a real alarm occur at the center. There are many examples in which such a notification system can enhance communication of health messages to the public.

In addition to the above, a word should be added regarding community meetings. Town halls, regular public forums, open meetings, public advisory groups, and other types of group processes all present opportunities to gather input from community stakeholders. In implementing these processes, there are a few keys to success.[17] These may seem self-evident, but are frequently overlooked by public health practitioners. Exhibit 20-2 illustrates some of tips for holding a successful community meeting.

An example of the important role that communicating with the community plays involves a variety of communication strategies used during an

Exhibit 20-2    Keys for a Successful Community Meeting

- Ensure that the process has objectives and a specific target audience.
- Select a time, date, and meeting location consistent with the meeting objectives and audience. Public hearings often exclude people who work during normal business hours.
- Notify target audiences of the meeting or hearing through appropriate, multiple media. Notification should include this basic information: who the meeting affects and why; purpose of the meeting; what is likely to result from the meeting; date, time, and place of the meeting; and directions to the site.
- Make sure the meeting site is ready; select an alternate location in case the audience is too large or small, or in the case of sound, lighting, or other problems.
- Use a carefully planned agenda; this ensures that the meeting does not exceed available time or attention span and also that certain information is provided before deliberations begin.
- Clarify meeting ground rules. This includes issues such as time limits for speakers, acceptability of written transcripts in testimony, and use of Robert's Rules of Order when appropriate.
- Follow through after a meeting to ensure that results and feedback are forthcoming. Important steps include scrutinizing the minutes or transcripts to identify promises, requests, or issues that require follow-up.

investigation of a potential cluster of chronic disease along the border of United States and Mexico.[18] In this particular situation, which was highly charged and politicized, the Arizona Department of Health Services coordinated the conduct of an epidemiologic study of potential cancer and lupus clusters in the community of Nogales, Arizona. There was community suspicion that these illnesses were the result of environmental pollution. Within this process, the Arizona Department of Health Services met with key community members and identified community needs. In the short term, an identified need was medical care for community members with lupus and cancer. The department director personally participated in these meetings.

The department also supported community-based education through a contract with a local nonprofit agency. In collaboration with the state environmental quality agency, the department held environmental health open houses and health fairs. Lastly, upon completion of the health study, the department ensured that the community was the first to receive and review the study. The department maintained its credibility throughout this process while drawing attention to the health problem along the border of Arizona and Mexico. Strategic communication was the key to resolving this potentially explosive situation.[18]

It is also important for public health practitioners to be visible within the community. This includes being routinely present at relevant community health meetings, as well as attempting to build bridges with nonhealth organizations, such as seeking opportunities to speak with organizations. Physician managers and directors should consider joining the local medical society.

A recent published overview of the Massachusetts Tobacco Control Program (MTCP) illustrates how successful a comprehensive communication strategy can be if all of the above elements are taken into account. The MTCP mounted an extensive campaign to decrease tobacco consumption across the state. The strategy included a media campaign to educate the public, an emphasis on treatment of tobacco addiction, and financial support for local boards of health and health departments with all efforts coinciding with an aggressive approach to changing statewide tobacco control policies (e.g., the Clean Indoor Air law, increases in taxation on tobacco products, and more stringent regulations on tobacco product labeling). This intensive organized effort to control tobacco contributed to a 48% drop in adult per capita tobacco purchases over a time period of 11 years, which far exceeded the decreases seen nationally over the same period of time.[19]

Much public health communication occurs through the media. The rest of this chapter will be devoted to discussion of the media as a partner in public health. Specific functions of health communication regarding the community are addressed in chapters on health education and health promotion (Chapter 21) as well as on public health marketing (Chapter 22).

## Media Relations

With advances in information technology, the influence of the media has broadened enormously. Today, many children spend more time with media (such as Internet, mobile phones, television, and music) than they do at school. As news has become more readily available and perhaps simplified, the world has grown ever more complex. As a result, the job of the public health communicator has become more critical and much more difficult.

The first step to success is to embrace the fact that interaction with the media is desired and often necessary for the effective communication of a health message. News correspondent Daniel Schorr once said, "If you don't exist in the media, for all practical purposes, you don't exist."[20] In the recent past, some public health professionals seem content to limit public health information to public service announcements (PSAs) or brochures to be distributed at health fairs or healthcare provider offices. But how often are PSAs aired at suboptimal times? And how many brochures are actually read? PSAs, brochures, and other message carriers can certainly be useful, but they need to be augmented whenever possible with other opportunities, especially the evening news when appropriate.

In Arizona, the state health department's efforts to engage the press at every opportunity on the issue of lead poisoning clearly demonstrate that the news media offer the cheapest and most effective means of reaching the public *and* influencing public policy.

Separate news releases were issued to alert the public about discoveries of dangerous levels of lead in bulk water storage tanks, crayons from China, folk remedies called *azarcon* and *greta*, Mexican candy wrappers, two brands of pool cue chalk, and imported plastic miniblinds. All of the releases prompted radio, television, and print coverage throughout the state. The crayon and miniblinds news releases sparked media inquiries from coast to coast, effectively warning a nation and spurring the federal Consumer Product Safety

Commission (CPSC) into action. A dozen brands of Chinese crayons were recalled and vinyl miniblinds manufacturers were required by the CPSC to discontinue the use of lead as a stabilizer. It was estimated that at least 25 million sets of the leaded miniblinds were being imported annually from China, Taiwan, Mexico, and Indonesia.[21]

The total printing, postage, and fax cost of producing and distributing all six of the lead-warning news releases was approximately $500. Consider how many PSAs and brochures would have been needed—and at what cost—to have even a fraction of the impact.

Once the decision has been that it is appropriate to engage the news media to communicate a public health message, one of the toughest tasks is to reach the media's overloaded radar screen. The two major tools used to proactively engage the media are press releases and press conferences.

## Press Releases

Newspapers, television, and radio stations often are flooded with hundreds of news releases each day. Only a few manage to get incorporated into the main news. Those releases that do get noticed contain a headline and lead paragraph that grab the attention of a harried assignment editor or reporter—a task sometimes akin to capturing lightning in a jar. Please refer to Exhibit 20-3 for tips on writing a successful release.

In addition to the above tips on writing a press release, other strategies to improve having a press release noted by the media include the following:

- Faxing or e-mailing the news release to the appropriate channels. A faxed or e-mailed news release stands a better chance of coverage than a mailed news release. These methods convey a greater sense of immediacy than mailing a release.
- Avoiding firing off releases too frequently because there will be a diminution of overall interest.

Exhibit 20-3    Tips for Writing a Successful Press Release

- Know where to send the release.
- Provide a date and instructions ("For immediate release").
- Have a powerful headline.
- Be factual, accurate, honest, and short—preferably one page.
- Write in third-person news style using direct quotes from trustworthy source.
- Write in clear, simple language; avoid technical complexities, medical terminology, and bureaucratic jargon.
- If noting success of a program, be succinct and positive but not overly enthusiastic.
- Do not use exclamation marks.
- Provide all pertinent contact information for a point person including, at minimum, a phone number.
- Signify end of press release (commonly ### is used).

## What Constitutes News Worthy of a Press Release?

What constitutes what is and is not "news"? The announcement of virtually any grant is news, as long as the press release explains why the grant is important to the public. The launching of any public health outreach or advertising campaign or promotion is also news. Or an enforcement action against a licensed facility such as a child care center, nursing home, or hospital. The introduction or passage of a public health legislative proposal or budget item can prove worthy fodder. The release of any statistical report is news, too, as long as the report's major points are summarized and presented in a compelling manner.

For example, here is how a news release announcing the completion of a statistical report on playground equipment safety began:

> Thousands of trips to emergency rooms and doctors' offices and more than 6000 days of absenteeism are caused each year by playground-related injuries at Arizona elementary schools, according to a new study by the Arizona Department of Health Services.
>
> The study indicated that reportable injuries are occurring at rates of 275 per week and 10,500 per academic year, and that more than 1 out of every 50 elementary school students is injured each year. The study's report called the findings "alarming," especially since schools reported only those injuries severe enough to require hospitalization, restricted activity, absenteeism, or visits to a physician or clinic. The report described the situation as an "injury epidemic."[22]

The release sparked enormous news coverage, including segments on all four major Phoenix television stations and a report on the front page of the state's major daily newspaper that included a bar graph and a photo of a child on a swing set. Most of the reports used the hot-button terms "alarming" and "injury epidemic," both of which had been extracted from deep within the statistical report for the news release. Suddenly the issue of playground safety existed, and the ensuing interest of state, city, and school administrators and policy makers sparked quite a run for copies of the report.

What, then, does not pass muster as news? It is often impossible to stir much interest with a news release announcing a conference on any health topic. In general, conferences are educational, not newsworthy, and reporters generally do not have time to sit through them.

Breast Cancer Awareness Month, by itself, is not news. Neither is National Nutrition Month, Infant Immunization Week, Child Health Day, or any of the other special days, weeks, and months. The problem is that there are more than 9000 special days, weeks, and months each year, according to *Chase's Annual Events*.[23] They include everything from Humpback Whale Awareness Month to National Baked Beans Month.

The media are overwhelmed to the point that no special occasion is special. A news release touting a celebratory cause will head straight for the assignment editor's wastebasket unless the release contains, and is dominated by, an actual news hook. Below is an example of a news release that did inject news into a celebratory event:

SAFETY STRESSED IN
FOOD CODE REWRITE

To help set the stage for September's Food Safety Education Month, the Arizona Department of Health Services today announced it is rewriting the state's Food Code, a reference that guides restaurants, grocery stores, and institutions such as nursing homes on how to prevent food-borne illness.[24]

The release went on to say that the new Food Code "will address the most critical risk factors that cause food-borne illness—unsafe food temperatures, cross-contamination, and poor hand-washing practices." Information specific to Food Safety Education Month began in the sixth paragraph.[24]

## Press Conferences

Unlike press releases, press conferences involve in-person interviews, usually with multiple reporters representing multiple media agencies. If planned and conducted properly, press conferences can prove extremely useful for elevating the importance of an issue such as a public health warning or the notification of a new campaign, an important accomplishment, or enterprise.

Press conferences are economical in terms of the interviewee's time requirements, and they allow the conveyance of a consistent message to a group of broadcast and print reporters. This decreases the risk of miscommunication or misinterpretation of the information by any single reporter. In addition, press conferences typically achieve much broader coverage than press releases because they offer television reporters an interesting, colorful, and relevant visual setting. In short, a press conference can provide the perfect forum to present the public health agency's side of the story to a captive audience.

Press conferences are commonly used to educate the public about a potential immediate health threat. For example, most outbreaks of reportable communicable diseases, such as measles in a camp or unresolved water- or food-borne outbreaks warrant a press conference. Similarly, if routine testing of a public water supply demonstrates significant contamination of the water supply, a press conference is the most efficient way to rapidly inform a large number of people.

In addition to being useful for rapid and widespread dissemination of urgent health messages, press conferences may be useful in facilitating health campaigns. Press conferences proved tremendously valuable during the startup of a massive, tobacco-tax-funded tobacco-prevention campaign in Arizona that initially targeted youth.

The planned ad campaign employed intense visual images, humor, and stomach-turning grossness to reach the MTV generation. In one ad, a boy's date absentmindedly takes a swallow from his spit-tobacco cup at a movie theater. In another, a teenage girl transforms into a rotting apparition as she puffs away. In a radio ad, a boy tells a graphic tale about how pus from a dead bird reminds him of spit tobacco. The word *puking* is featured prominently in the campaign's slogan.[20]

Because Arizona is among the most conservative states in the Union, it would have been political suicide to simply unleash a campaign of this nature on an unsuspecting public without justifying its cost and tactics.[25] The solution was to educate the media (and by extension adults and policy makers) concurrently about the severity of the youth tobacco problem and the strategy behind the ad campaign. Eleven news conferences were held during the first 16 months of the campaign. Every new wrinkle in the campaign, from the latest commercial to the startup of a merchandise center selling T-shirts and other antitobacco gear, offered another opportunity to repeat two points:

1. Tobacco use is the nation's number-one killer, and it begins almost all the time as a childhood addiction.
2. The ads and other elements of the campaign are geared toward capturing the attention of teens and are not intended to appeal to adults.

The news conferences produced massive positive news coverage—more than 200 newspaper articles and 226 minutes of television news in the first 10 months alone. The coverage fostered an understanding of the campaign by the general public, and it spawned fawning editorials in many newspapers, including the major Phoenix and Tucson dailies.

The editorial support and public goodwill that had been established helped enable the campaign to weather a storm that erupted 15 months into the effort when "Maggot," the most controversial and intense of all the ads, aired. It featured a teenage girl going through her morning ritual of brushing her teeth and putting on her makeup. All the while she is smoking, and her beautiful face transforms into a grotesque sight of rotting flesh. Worms appear on her toothbrush, in the sink, and in her mouth. The spot closes with a stylized shot of somebody spewing green vomit.

Within two days, 100 telephone calls were received about the ad, and almost all were critical. The spot, however, was defended editorially and by a columnist for the *Tribune*, a major Phoenix-area newspaper. Already on the wane, the negative phone calls then dropped to a trickle when a written statement was added to the beginning of the commercial warning parents that the contents may be offensive to young children.

Now that the value of a press conference as a communication tool has been established, how does one go about setting up a successful conference? Some of the recommendations are similar to those for a successful press release; however, additional considerations include the following:

- Attract the media's attention—Make the headline and first paragraph compelling, but do not reveal so much information that reporters feel they have all the details. If the press conference is planned well in advance, fax the media advisory no more than two days before the event to reduce the chances it will be lost or forgotten. Make sure a copy is sent to the local Associated Press (AP) bureau, which enters such information in a "daybook" calendar of activities that is sent to broadcast and print media outlets.

  An example of how to attract reporters to the announcement of a campaign to promote folic acid among women of childbearing age is shown in Exhibit 20-4. The advisory went on to list the date, time, and location of the event. Six television cameras, four radio stations, and three print reporters came to the event.
- Start and end on time—Remain in charge throughout the press conference. This starts with being on time and designating a set time to end the conference.
- Think visually—Provide a backdrop that will enhance the message and will appeal to the media. For example, consider using a neonatal unit

Exhibit 20-4   Birth Defects Targeted by New State Campaign

A major campaign will be launched to encourage women in Arizona to greatly reduce their risk of having a baby with a disabling or deadly defect of the spine or brain. The campaign will urge all women of childbearing age to consume folic acid. Sufficient amounts of folic acid can reduce the risk of a neural tube birth defect by up to 70%. However nearly half of all women of childbearing age in Arizona—about half a million women—are unaware of the critical role played by folic acid.[26]

of a hospital for the announcement of a campaign to promote folic acid or having a healthy cooking demonstration in a grocery store's produce department to launch a campaign to promote fruit and vegetable consumption.

- Package the information in sound bites—Prepare a brief statement. Television and radio reporters rely exclusively on sound bites, which encapsulate a key thought in one or two sentences often running less than 10 seconds. Some reporters even cut the bite to a "sound bark" of two or three words. Print reporters like quotes that are colorful, clever, and to the point. Therefore, determine what the primary message is before the press conference and state that message at least once in a clear, honest, and concise manner. The spokesperson can elaborate on other points as long as there is a consistent clear primary message. Throw enthusiasm into the mix, too. If your spokesperson shows no passion for the message he or she is pitching, why should anyone else?
- Be prepared—Preparation is the key to avoiding embarrassment. Make sure the main speaker's knowledge of the news conference topic extends well beyond his or her written text. It is also wise to have a bona fide expert on the subject on hand if possible. Otherwise, even a simple question-and-answer session might call the speaker's credibility into question.
- Provide time for questions—Answers should be clear and brief.
- Provide backup materials—Have a press release and other backup materials available at the news conference. These might include fact sheets, written texts of prepared speeches, reports, graphs, videos, and other documents. Such materials help reporters flesh out the details and background of a topic that might only be glossed over at the news conference. They also seem to add a sense of legitimacy to the news conference.

## Media Interaction Guidelines

Public health officials may have contact with the media in many situations other than press releases or press conferences. Reporters often initiate contact with a public health agency, requesting information for a particular story. Examples include media following up on "tips" from the public or the media may approach a public health official at a public meeting such as open legislative meetings or public budget presentations. Regardless of the forum, the following guidelines will help you get your point across effectively and earn the reporter's respect:

- Accuracy—It is paramount. If you do not know the answer to a question, say so and offer to get back to the reporter with the answer as quickly as possible. Also, do not use words or phrases that make you appear uncertain. These include *apparently*, *it seems*, and to *the best of my knowledge*.

- Preparation—Never risk being ill-prepared in an interview with the news media. If a reporter calls, interview the reporter—for example, ask what the story is about, who else has been interviewed, what other sources are being used. If you are not prepared or are caught off guard, buy yourself some time—even if it is just five minutes—by saying you need to pull a file or obtain relevant information and will call him or her right back.

- Promptness—Remember that reporters operate under strict deadlines. Return their phone calls promptly. One of the performance measures for the public information office at the Arizona Department of Health Services is the percentage of reporters' calls that are returned within five minutes.

- Completeness—Answer questions fully and offer to provide copies of relevant documents. Tell the whole story. Take the time to provide background and be sure to explain the factors that led to a certain situation, condition, or controversy.

- Honesty—Do not shade the truth because in the long run, the truth always prevails. Remember that half-truths and errors of omission can place the credibility of your agency and yourself at risk. Also, never downplay or overplay the severity of a disease threat or outbreak. The former may provoke angry reactions of government cover-up, insensitivity, and inaction; the latter may prompt complaints of scare tactics and grandstanding.

- Clarity—Use simple and clear language, avoiding technical terms, acronyms, or abbreviations that are not familiar to the general public. Try to present a consistent key message.

- Appearance—If the interaction is on camera, remember that how a person looks and sounds can often be more important than what he or she says. Maintain steady eye contact with the reporter, speak confidently, smile whenever you can, and stay away from gaudy jewelry, loud colors, and checkered or striped patterns in your wardrobe. If you can, avoid wearing eyeglasses and never wear dark glasses. Vests also should be avoided.

- Admit a mistake—Do not be afraid to admit to a mistake or to say that a program or service could have been operated better or more efficiently, if that is the case, but be sure to emphasize efforts to correct a problem.

- Never say "No comment"—Explain why you cannot disclose information. If barred by privacy laws, for example, explain that fact and fax the reporter a copy of the statutory restriction.

- Avoid unforgivables—The public will not forgive arrogance, indifference, or incompetence. The price for failure to avoid the unforgivables can be steep.

- Playing defense—Although proactive relations with the media should keep reporters from dwelling on the negatives, there will be times when an action, inaction, or error by a public health organization will raise questions. In responding to such questions, it is possible to simply touch on the answer and then use a bridging phrase such as "it's also important to know" to get back to your message. Prepare beforehand for the toughest questions and for the "bridges" you may use. Finally, when you've answered a question, stop talking. Do not feel compelled to fill silence with sound.

## Risk Communication During Public Health Emergencies

Effective public health communication is exceptionally important in messages relaying a potential threat to the community's health. Such messages may either reassure and empower the community or, if not effective, may contribute to fear and social disruption. There are several useful guides that explore this field in greater depth including the CDC's "Crisis and Emergency Risk Communication by Leaders for Leaders" and the Department of Health and Human Service's "Terrorism and Other Public Health Emergencies: A Reference Guide for Media."[27,28]

There are several common factors that are essential for leaders, including public health officials, to take into account when communicating the risks of a public health emergency. The following suggestions are adapted from the CDC's guide:

- Execute a solid communication plan—With whom will you need to communicate? How will you do so? Where will you meet with them? How often? Having as much information in advance as possible will help your communication in an emergency. For example, if the emergency is likely to last more than one day, establish a set time to update the media on a daily basis or more often if needed.
- Be the first source of information with a simple message—The first message heard is the one that usually receives the most attention and is the one that is remembered, often even if incorrect. Keep this message simple and short. The message should provide action steps that provide the public with something to do, thereby alleviating anxiety and hopelessness. For example, ask people to check on their neighbors or donate blood. Simple instructions should be positive ("Stay calm" or "Stay indoors") rather than negative ("Don't panic" or "Don't go outside").
- Express empathy early—A sincere expression of empathy early in your communication will allow people to settle down the noise in their minds and actually hear what you have to say.
- Demonstrate competence and expertise—People will respond more positively to the message if they trust the spokesperson.
- Remain honest and open—Provide information about what you know, but be honest about what you do not know. Not knowing is often worse than knowing. Rudolph Guiliani's now famous answer to reporters on September 11, 2001, "Whatever it (the loss of lives) is, it will

be more than we can bear," is a striking example of a leader who was able to honestly respond to an unanswerable question while expressing heartfelt empathy.

## Building a Model Public Information Office

Given the wide array of ways in which good, effective communication is essential for optimal public health, public health agencies are well-served by having a communication office. The ideal structure and responsibilities of a model communication/public information office depend on whom you ask. However, the National Public Health Information Coalition (NPHIC), which is an affiliate of the Association of State and Territorial Health Officials and is funded through a grant from the CDC, has developed a model communication office for a state health department.

According to the NPHIC model, the communication/public information office should be established as a branch of the office of the agency's chief executive administrator "so that any and all consultation offered and/or instructions given carry the necessary weight."[29] The NPHIC further recommends that the director of the communication/public information office be directly answerable and have direct and complete access to the agency's chief executive administrator. According to the NPHIC, "Dangerous breakdowns in communication are a given with every layer of administrative responsibility created between the agency's top policy maker and the staff person(s) responsible for communicating those policies internally or externally."[29]

The NPHIC recommends that the director of communication/public information be considered a member of the first team of advisors to the chief executive administrator.

> Involved daily in contacts with agency staff, external publics, and inquiring reporters, the insight offered and queries posed by the director of public information/communication can be invaluable in spotting the strongest approach, as well as the weakest links, in a public policy issue. The importance of direct and frequent access to and briefing of the chief executive administrator can not be overemphasized. As much as any element of a successful management team, the top spokesperson must be able to anticipate the needs of the top policy maker to get the message out, and in many cases, must carry, as an advisor, that very need to the policy maker.[29]

Responsibilities of the model communication/public information office, again according to the NPHIC, should include the following:[29]

- Press releases
- Press conferences
- Agency photographic services
- Media interview requests relating to agency policy
- Speech consultation and/or writing
- Employee newsletter
- Design development and content consultation for all brochures, booklets, posters, and other graphics art materials that are not of a staff training nature

- Production and content consultation for all audio/video materials that are designed for the general public or specific segments of the population
- Public education/awareness campaigns, including planning of campaign scope, materials, timing, and target audiences

To perform the above responsibilities, the communication/public information office should ideally be composed of a director; public information writers; a photographer, videographers, and graphic design personnel; and at least one administrative support person for every five total staff in the unit, according to the NPHIC.[29] In terms of overall numbers, one public information office staff member for every 200 employees of an agency may be sufficient to handle all of the above responsibilities adequately.

• • •

Throughout the past century, public health organizations have played key roles in extending the quality and quantity of life in the United States. Public health administrators need to communicate effectively with a wide variety of constituencies, including healthcare providers, policy makers, the community at large, and the media. In particular, effective relationships with the media can be helpful in promoting healthy behaviors and marketing program efforts and policy decisions. Further progress in developing effective programs and policies depends on health communication strategies such as media advocacy, social marketing, entertainment education, and risk communication. Public health administrators must stay abreast of information technology to maximize communication effectiveness and efficiency.

## Chapter Review

1. The effective use of communication in public health practice is essential to improving the public's health.
2. There are a number of ways to communicate information, called *channels* of communication denoting the route or method used. Each mode may have certain advantages in certain situations. Innovations in informational technology greatly enhance communication at all levels.
3. Principles of communication include the following:
   - Keep the method simple.
   - Ensure cultural competency.
   - Strike at the best opportunity.
   - Use multiple channels keyed to the target audience.
4. Good communication with communities should be maintained by seeking opportunities to gather input at meetings in town halls, regular public forums, and open meetings.
5. Strategies for communicating with staff to improve employee morale and increase operating efficiency should be devised.
6. Press releases and press conferences should be developed in a manner that will engage the media proactively with a newsworthy subject presented in a clear and compelling manner. Relationships with media contact representatives are important.
7. Effective media-interaction guidelines emphasize honesty, clarity, preparation, and completeness. Never appear arrogant, indifferent, or incompetent.

8. The communication/public information office should be structured so that it relates directly and frequently to the organization's chief executive and is continuously available to the media.

## References

1. Brown R, Elixhauser A, Corea J, Luce B, Sheingold (Battelle) S. *National Expenditures for Health Promotion and Disease Prevention Activities in the United States.* Atlanta, Ga: Centers for Disease Control and Prevention; 1991.
2. Maibach E, Holtgrave DR. Advances in public health communication. *Annu Rev Public Health.* 1995;16:219–238.
3. US Department of Health and Human Services. *Healthy People 2010.* 2nd ed. Washington, DC: US Department of Health and Human Services; 2000.
4. Mokdad A, Marks J, Stroup D, Gerberding J. Actual causes of death in the United States, 2000. *JAMA.* 2004;291(10):1238–1245.
5. Mokdad AH, Marks JS, Stroup DF, Gerberding JL. Correction: actual causes of death in the United States, 2000 [Letter, Published Erratum]. *JAMA.* 2005;293(3):293–294.
6. Office of the General Surgeon. Public Health Priorities. Available at: http://www.surgeongeneral.gov/index.html. Accessed March 18, 2006.
7. IOM Committee on Health Literacy. *Health Literacy: A Prescription to End Confusion.* Washington, DC: National Academies Press; 2004. Available at: http://www.iom.edu/?id=32784. Accessed March 18, 2006.
8. Kirsch IA, Jungeblut A, Jenkins L, Kolstad A. *Adult Literacy in America.* Princeton, NJ: Educational Testing Service; 1993.
9. Castro FG. Cultural competence training in clinical psychology: assessment, clinical intervention, and research. In: Bellack AS, Hersen M, eds. *Comprehensive Clinical Psychology.* Oxford, UK: Pergammon; 1998:127–140.
10. Arizona Department of Health Services. *Cultural Competency in the Administration and Delivery of Behavioral Health Services.* Phoenix, Ariz: Arizona Department of Health Services; 1995:4.
11. IOM Board on Neuroscience and Behavioral Health. *Speaking of Health: Assessing Health Communication Strategies for Diverse Populations. Committee on Communication for Behavior Change in the 21st Century: Improving the Health of Diverse Populations.* Washington, DC: National Academies Press; 2002. Available at: http://www.nap.edu/catalog/10018. html. Accessed March 18, 2006.
12. Levy B. Communicating public health challenges for the 21st century. Presentation at: University of Texas, School of Public Health; Houston, TX; February 1997.
13. Maude B. *Practical Communication for Managers.* White Plains, NY: Longman; 1974.
14. Eisenberg M, Lee H, Burgoon M, Beach B, Alvaro E, Givens R. *Evaluation of the TEPP Media Campaign: Report No. 1 (October 1998): Historical Impact of the TEPP Media Campaign.* Tucson, Ariz: University of Arizona Cancer Center; 1998.
15. Institute of Medicine. *The Future of Public Health.* Washington, DC: National Academy Press; 1988:14.
16. Institute of Medicine. *The Future of the Public's Health in the 21st Century.* Washington, DC: National Academy Press; 2003.
17. Garnett JL. *Communicating for Results in Government.* San Francisco: Jossey-Bass Publishers; 1992.

18. Dillenberg J, Hirano D. Confronting a border health crisis: a comprehensive approach. *J Public Health Manage Pract.* 1997;3:12–19.

19. Koh HK, Judge CM, Robbins H, Cobb Celebucki C, Walker DK, Connolly GN. The first decade of the Massachusetts Tobacco Control Program. *Public Health Rep.* 2005;120:482–495.

20. Communications Consortium Media Center. *Strategic Communications for Nonprofits: Strategic Media—Designing a Public Interest Campaign.* Washington, DC: Benton Foundation and the Center for Strategic Communications; 1991:7.

21. US Consumer Product Safety Commission, Office of Information and Public Affairs. *CPSC Finds Lead Poisoning Hazard for Young Children in Imported Vinyl Miniblinds.* Washington, DC: US Consumer Product Safety Commission; 1996, June 25:#96–50.

22. Christensen B. *ADHS Study Finds School Injury Epidemic* [News release]. Phoenix, Ariz: Arizona Department of Health Services; 1998, November.

23. Chase HM, Chase WD. *Chase's Annual Events.* Lincolnwood, Ill: NTC Publishing Group; 1999.

24. Simeri P. *Safety Stressed in Food Code Rewrite* [News release]. Phoenix, Ariz: Arizona Department of Health Services; 1999, August.

25. Dominy A. *Pus* [Radio commercial]. Phoenix, Ariz: Riester-Robb Advertising and Public Relations; 1996.

26. Christensen B. [Media advisory]. Phoenix, Ariz: Arizona Department of Health Services; 1999, January.

27. Centers for Disease Control and Prevention. Crisis and Emergency Risk Communication Course (CERC). Available at: http://www.bt.cdc.gov/erc/cerc.asp. Accessed January 16, 2007.

28. US Department of Health and Human Services. Terrorism and other public health emergencies: a reference guide for media. Available at: www.hhs.gov/emergency/mediaguide/PDF/. Accessed March 18, 2006.

29. NPHIC Executive Board. *Model Communications/Public Information Office.* Atlanta, Ga: National Public Health Information Coalition; 1994.

## CHAPTER 21

# PUBLIC HEALTH EDUCATION AND HEALTH PROMOTION

Lawrence W. Green
Judith M. Ottoson

## Chapter Overview

Public health organizations use health education strategies to facilitate voluntary adaptations of behavior that are conducive to health. *Health education*
influences behavior such as participation in health-promoting activities, appropriate use of health services, health supervision of children, and adherence
to appropriate medical and nutritional regimens. *Health promotion* encompasses a broader set of educational, organizational, environmental, and economic interventions to support behavior and conditions of living that are
conducive to health. Designing and managing successful health education and
health promotion interventions require strong institutional capacities in applied behavioral science, community assessment, and program administration.

The health of populations varies with the interaction of behavior, environment, human biology, and community organization. Various scientific and
professional subspecialties and academic subdisciplines have emerged to address these complex interactions. These subspecialties include environmental
epidemiology, behavioral ecology, behavioral medicine, health psychology,
social medicine, medical geography, and social epidemiology. Application of
the scientific knowledge and technologies developed within these subspecialties falls largely to health workers in the community, especially through the
vehicle of health education.

Public health education employs a combination of methods designed to
facilitate voluntary adaptations of behavior that are conducive to health. It
too has subspecialties such as patient education, school health education,
population education, environmental education, sex education, family planning education, nutrition education, dental health education, mental health
education, and occupational health education.[1] The broader efforts of community or population health promotion may go beyond voluntary changes in
behavior. These broader efforts may include regulatory and environmental

control strategies designed to channel, restrain, or support behavior that is conducive to health or quality of life for the person, the community, or a population.[2] Nonetheless, health education strategies are a core element of most health promotion efforts that target communities and population groups. Without the health literacy and informed electorate that health education helps create, many health laws would never be passed, would be rescinded, or would not be enforced.

This chapter examines the health education and health promotion strategies used by public health organizations to improve community health. The first part of this chapter focuses specifically on the design and management of health education approaches directed at voluntary changes in behavior. The second part of the chapter examines linkages between health education strategies and the larger field of health promotion, with attention given to policy, regulatory, organizational, and environmental factors that enable health education strategies to achieve health promotion goals.

## Public Health Education

Public, community, or population health education interventions are designed to inform, elicit, facilitate, and maintain positive health practices in large numbers of people. The practices in question may be those of individuals whose health is at risk, or those whose behavior influences the health risks faced by other individuals and populations, such as through exposures to environmental threats. *Inform, elicit, facilitate,* and *maintain* refer to the processes of change supported by increasing the understanding, predisposition, skills, and support that motivate individuals to undertake and sustain voluntary actions conducive to their health. These actions reflect the efforts of health education to affect three broad categories of factors that (1) predispose, (2) enable, or (3) reinforce behavior that is related to health. For purposes of this chapter, *health education* is defined as any combination of learning opportunities designed to facilitate voluntary adaptations of behavior conducive to health.

Whether in populations or with individuals, health education addresses current behavior such as the participation in health-promoting activities, appropriate use of health services, health supervision of children, and adherence to appropriate medical and nutritional regimens. Health education also addresses issues in child and youth development that create the cognitive and behavioral foundation for future health. Within their families and with peers at school, children form predispositions—knowledge, attitudes, and values—that can prevent or promote many of the health problems associated with later adult life. Good planning in health education ensures that programs combine these channels of influence appropriately to support voluntary patterns of behavior that are conducive to health.

### A Focus on Health Behavior

Human behavior relates to health in both direct and indirect ways, as shown in Figure 21-1. The direct effect of personal and social behavior on health (arrow a) occurs when behavior exposes an individual, group, or population

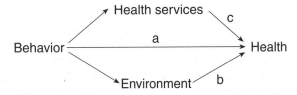

**FIGURE 21-1    Behavior of Lifestyle Can Have a Direct Effect (A) or An Indirect Effect on Health Through Exposure to the Environment (B) or on the Use of Health Services (C).**
*Source:* Green LW, Kreuter MW. *Health Promotion Planning: An Educational and Ecological Approach.* 3rd ed. Mountain View, CA: Mayfield Publishing Co.; 1999:155.

to more or less risk of injury, disease, or death. Sometimes, the exposure is subtle, as with small but repeated doses of a substance that may become addictive or cumulative in their effect. Drugs and fatty food are examples of this type of exposure. At other times, behavior may pose an immediate and excessive risk, such as eating a poisonous or infected food. Acute risks to health in food production, distribution, and consumption have been minimized by the environmental and regulatory controls that are administered by public health agencies.

Behavior influences health indirectly through the environment (arrow b) to the degree that people will plan individual or community actions to bring about changes in the environment. Examples of behavioral influences on health through environment include the following:

- Participating in efforts to control toxic waste disposal
- Organizing a lead paint removal program in the neighborhood
- Voting on referenda or for elected officials in support of community water fluoridation
- Advocating drunk driving laws or other automobile safety provisions
- Writing letters to the editor concerning food and drug labeling
- Signing a petition on air and water pollution controls
- Boycotting stores that sell cigarettes to minors

Behavior also influences health indirectly through health services (arrow c). This can happen in at least three ways. Individuals, groups, or organizations can do the following:

- Influence the distribution and delivery of services through action in the legislative and health planning process.
- Use (or not use) available services in a timely and appropriate way.
- Follow (or fail to follow) the medical or preventive regimens prescribed by their health service providers.

## Voluntary Behavior

Beneficial voluntary health behavior in both children and adults can result from health education if it provides for a combination of planned, consistent, integrated learning opportunities and reinforcement. To achieve these ends, community or population health education systematically applies theories and methods from the social and behavioral sciences, epidemiology, ecology, administrative science, and communications. These approaches are informed by scientific evaluations of health education programs in schools, at work sites, in medical settings, and through community organization and the mass media. Further, indirect evidence is borrowed from experiences outside of the fields of health and education. Community development, agricultural extension, social work, marketing, and other enterprises in human services and behavior change all contribute to the understanding of planned change at the community level and in various populations.

*Planned* learning experiences that can influence voluntary changes in behavior, as distinct from *incidental* learning experiences, link the educational approach to community and population health. Health education is also distinguished from other change strategies that may be excessively manipulative or coercive. Behavioral changes resulting from education are by definition voluntary and freely adopted by people, with their knowledge of alternatives and probable consequences. Some behavioral change strategies may have unethical components. Behavior modification techniques, for example, qualify as health education only when people freely request them to achieve a specific behavioral result that they desire, such as controlling eating or smoking habits. Principles of planning for community health education call for the participation of consumers, patients, or citizens in the planning process.

Mass media qualify as educational channels for community or population health up to the point that commercial or political interests control the messages strictly for profit or propaganda. The regulation of advertisers and the media may be necessary as a more coercive, economic, or legalistic strategy to protect consumers from, for example, deceptive advertising claims concerning the health value of food products. Such was the case when communities took action to restrict the advertising of certain foods and toys on Saturday morning television programs directed at young children. Several countries restrict the advertising of tobacco and alcohol in the mass media. Third world nations took action to restrict the marketing of powdered milk formula for bottle feeding of babies because it was leading the public to use unsanitary water and bottles in place of breast feeding.

## Planning for Public Health Education Programs

Public health administrators and practitioners require a comprehensive planning process to achieve sound health education programming and effectiveness.[3] An understanding of the stages and components of health education planning is therefore requisite for public health administrators. The PRECEDE model on which planning phases discussed here are based has been applied in more than 950 published applications (www.lgreen.net). These include, for example, applications in community diabetes[4] and arthritis self-management in native populations;[5] breast and cervical cancer screening in low-income populations[6,7] and in rural populations;[8] encouraging bicycle helmet use among children;[9] reaching mothers of preschool-aged children with a smoking cessation program;[10] prevention of diarrhea infant mortality in rural Mexico;[11] prevention of heart disease in Quebec;[12,13] parent education for self-management of cystic fibrosis[14] and asthma;[15] a nutrition program for low-income mothers of preschool children[16] and for Vietnamese mothers;[17] and increasing Medicaid child health screenings.[18]

*Phases of Planning for Public Health Education*

An educational plan for community health or population health ideally begins with the following analysis of social issues or quality-of-life concerns:

- Phase 1 begins with a social assessment (Figure 21-2, bottom) of the
  ultimate community concerns or outcomes and the social assets they
  have or need, rather than with an administrative assessment to choose
  educational interventions (Figure 21-2, top).
- Phase 2 is an epidemiologic assessment to identify the incidence,
  prevalence, and cause of the health problems associated with the
  quality-of-life concerns in a given population, and an etiological
  assessment of the priority health problem to determine specific behavioral and environmental determinants of the health problem.
- Phase 3 is an analysis of the factors influencing each behavior implicated in the cause of each health problem. Health education based
  more on favorite techniques than on systematic analysis of behavior
  and of the learning problems influencing the behavior will tend to be
  inefficient if not ineffective.
- Phase 4 involves matching behavioral priorities with adequate
  methods.

*Social Diagnosis.*   The ideal starting point in planning is an assessment of
the social concerns and assets of the community or population. Starting with
social or quality-of-life issues rather than with health problems ensures that
the health planners appreciate the broader context of issues that are paramount in the community. This step requires an understanding of the subjective concerns and values of the community, as well as objective data on social
indicators such as unemployment, housing problems, teenage pregnancy, violence, and poverty.[19] Consideration of varying community perceptions should
take place early in program development. Health programs are not likely to
be successful without community support and participation in the planning
process.

*Epidemiologic Diagnosis.*   The social concern or quality-of-life issues in the
community or population can be analyzed for priority health problems embedded within them. Once the priority health problem is analyzed, addressing
and solving that problem becomes the overall program goal for a community
health or population health program.[20] The agency sponsoring the program
should use the most recent available demographic, vital, and sociocultural
statistics to define the characteristics of the subpopulations experiencing the
health problem. Planners can review the problem from the perspective of related agencies, a review of previously published reports, and the US Department of Health and Human Services objectives for the nation.[19] They can
gain perspective on the experience of the community with the health problem by reviewing similar data from other cities, states, or regions.

Citizens or lay participants in the planning process at this stage can help
identify population subgroups within the community, such as adolescent
mothers and preschool youth, who may have special problems and needs.[21]
Information on these subpopulations can include geographic distribution;
occupational, economic, and educational status; age and sex composition;
ethnicity; health indicators, including age-specific morbidity; and service

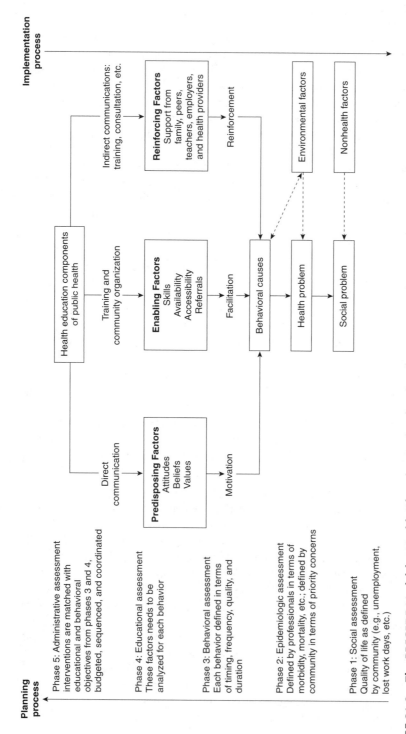

**FIGURE 21-2    The PRECEDE Model for Health Education Begins the Planning Process at the End of a Presumed Causal Chain (Bottom Left) with Social Assessment. Subsequent Phases Work "Backward" Through the Causal Links to the Development of a Health Intervention. Evaluation Criteria are Embedded in Each of These Phases as Objectives. The Implementation Process Reverses the Planning Process by Working from the Educational Program Toward Amelioration of the Health Problem and Toward Quality-of-Life Concerns.**

*Source:* Green LW, Kreuter MW. *Health Promotion Planning: An Educational and Ecological Approach.* 3rd ed. Mountain View, CA: McGraw Hill; 1999:35.

utilization patterns. Once the health problem has been defined and the program goal and high-risk subpopulations have been identified, the behavioral problems or barriers to the community solution of the problem can be specified (Figure 21-2, phase 2). The following guidelines should be considered when performing the behavioral assessment:

- Specify the behaviors that are presumably contributing to the health problem as concretely as possible. Make an inventory of as many possible behavioral determinants as one can imagine.
- Identify the nonbehavioral factors (environmental, biologic, and technological factors) contributing to the problem as determinants for which strategies other than health education must be developed.
- Review research evidence that shows that the behaviors identified as possible causes are amenable to change through educational interventions and that such change will improve the health problem in question.
- For each health problem, identify one or more of the relevant dimensions of health behavior. For example, in prenatal care, one behavioral dimension is the timing or promptness of the care, which should begin with the first trimester of pregnancy.

An assessment should lead to the selection of specific behaviors that will be the target of the educational interventions. Rarely, if ever, does an agency have the resources necessary to influence all the behaviors contributing to a health problem. Therefore, an initial selection of some of the behaviors should be made. The selection are often influenced by policies governing required services of the agency. Priorities might also consider legal and economic factors affecting the desired behaviors, agency resources and expertise available, political viability of the educational interventions, the possibility of continued funding, and the probability of quick program success. The reasons for selecting specific behaviors as the priority focus of the educational interventions should be justified.

The two most important objective criteria for the selection of priority behavioral targets for health education are: (1) evidence that the behavioral change will make a difference in the reduction of the health problem, and (2) evidence that the behavior is amenable to voluntary change.

*Educational and Ecological Assessment.*    Once the behaviors have been selected, they can be subjected to further analysis for assessment of their causes (Figure 21-2, phase 3). The following sets of factors should be considered as *causes* of each behavior:

- Predisposing factors—Knowledge, attitudes, beliefs, and values that motivate people to take appropriate health actions
- Enabling factors—Skills and the accessibility of resources that make it possible for a motivated person to take action
- Reinforcing factors—The attitudes and climate of support from providers of services, families, and community groups who reinforce the health behavior of an individual who is motivated and able to adopt the behavior but who will discontinue the behavior if it is not rewarded

Planners should consult representatives of the various segments within the agency and community who are potentially affected by the program.

Failure to assess some of these factors and to develop a community health education program addressed to all three sets of these factors would seriously limit the impact of the program. Selecting the health education methods for a community health program follows almost automatically from a thorough identification and ranking of predisposing, enabling, and reinforcing factors influencing the health behaviors.

*Administrative Diagnosis.*    The final phase of the process includes the alignment of educational interventions with the predisposing, enabling, and reinforcing factors, and an assessment of available resources to support the selected educational methods. The process of selecting or developing educational interventions to align or match with predisposing, enabling, and reinforcing factors calls first on evidence-based practices identified in systematic reviews of previous studies.[22] But there will never be sufficient evidence to cover all of the combinations of population characteristics, settings, and needs,[23] so theory must come into play as a second source for selecting and mapping interventions onto predisposing, enabling, and reinforcing factors.[24] Gaps will still remain in the certainty with which interventions match and map with the needs identified, so a third source of intervention candidates comes into play with the time-honored method of pooling ideas from other practitioners and health administrators who have planned similar programs for similar populations.[25] Woven through all of these considerations is a participatory patching process of filling gaps in the matching and mapping of interventions onto local population characteristics and circumstances with the advice and guidance of local residence and practitioners who have first-hand, indigenous experience in the locality.[26]

Resources required to deploy the chosen combination of interventions that will make up the program can be identified and obtained from organizations and agencies at national, state or provincial, and local levels, or developed locally for the specific program. Some examples of extant resources include citizens' groups, industry, labor organizations, religious groups, colleges, advertising agencies, drama groups, pharmacies, local facilities (e.g., libraries, health centers, hospitals, training centers, town halls, gathering places), personnel (e.g., volunteers, agency staff, social workers), communications resources (e.g., numbers of telephones and use of radios, billboards, local television and radio stations, newspapers, newsletters, organization bulletins, Internet and World Wide Web sites), and funding sources available for the educational program through the health service agency itself and related organizations. This identification and assessment of available resources should lead to the further refinement of objectives, strategies, and methods. Advocacy for the reallocation of resources or the changes in policy required to support the program may be necessary at this phase of the planning process.

The coordination and budgeting of resources into a timetable that corresponds to the community health program is the next step in the administrative assessment. Both require constructive participation by staff, other organizations, and area residents. By including other organizations and community members in the planning, one obtains their personal commitment to realizing program success, which can help eliminate duplication of services. Most importantly, their participation enables program planners to incorporate the interests, perspectives, and values of various stakeholders into the educational activities of the program. The principle of participation usually applies to representatives of related agencies, institutions, and organizations in the community; to the agency staff who will implement the program activities; and to community residents in the target.

It should be noted that the assessment process used as part of health education planning is analogous to assessment processes that public health organizations may undertake for broader program purposes. (See Chapter 15 for a discussion of these purposes and processes.) Indeed, public health organizations increasingly undertake health education assessment efforts as part of larger public health assessment processes, and the public health program planning process has incorporated many of the behavioral and ecological concepts of health education and health promotion planning, just as health education planning has incorporated the concepts of social, epidemiological, and administrative diagnosis.[2]

### Components of Planning for Public Health Education

The following discussion concerning assessment in health education planning contains a number of cross-cutting concerns at issue in all phases of planning, including the identification of the target population, writing of clear objectives, and the use of health education methods and theories. These issues weave through the assessment phases discussed earlier and continue through organizational implementation and program evaluation in an iterative way, requiring the planner and practitioner to back and fill with new knowledge and understanding as experience with the community or population grows. This process makes planning both a technical and a socially negotiated process.

*Priority Target Populations.*   An early program planning task is the identification of the populations who are at risk, or those who are most affected by the health problem. These populations are the target for, and the intended beneficiaries of, most of the educational interventions, and thus constitute the primary target group that planners should consult. It is the understanding of this group that focuses the social assessment and is deepened in subsequent rounds of epidemiologic, behavioral, educational-ecological, and administrative assessments. An iterative and deep understanding of the target population sidelines an ineffective "one size fits all" approach to packaged educational interventions.

The primary target population should receive direct communication designed to influence members' predisposition to accept the recommended health practices. Planners need to describe the primary target population by their geographic, occupational, economic, educational, age, sex, and ethnic distributions. Planners should consult or collaborate with representative persons from the described population and cooperating agencies in the assessment of needs and the further development of the educational plans. The characteristics of the target population that provide the basic analysis for the specification of community health programs are also the basis for the development of educational interventions.

Education must also be directed toward populations who are not affected by the health problem but who are in a direct position to influence those who are. These "gatekeepers" and social reinforcers, such as parents, spouses, teachers, peers, employers, and opinion leaders, are often an intermediate or additional target population for educational programs. To develop the enabling factors for health education programs, planners can direct educational interventions toward these intermediate target groups. For example, one intermediate target group for community organization efforts would be directors of other agencies who control resources that would enable or facilitate the health behavior. Another intermediate target group might be employers, friends, or family members who would receive training, consultation, or supervision in reinforcing the recommended health behavior.

*Objectives as Planning Tools.* At each of the assessment phases previously discussed, clear statements of objectives serve as a guiding tool not only for the planning, but also for the eventual evaluation of public health education programs. To exemplify the components of objectives, we focus here on the development of behavioral objectives (Figure 21-2, phase 3).

The objectives for behavior change derive from the findings of the behavioral assessment. The proper statement of the objectives should lend purpose to the program plan and direction to its implementation.

Because education appears to be more abstract and difficult to define or measure than some of the other activities of community health programs, time spent on the formulation of objectives in educational planning is especially important. Objectives should be expressed as intended outcomes. They may apply to providers and to the organization or system, as well as to the consumers. Each objective should answer the following question: *Who* is expected to achieve or become *how much* of *what* by *when* and *where*?

The desired behaviors (what) should describe what the participants will do or not do as a result of the program that they could not or did not do (to the same extent) before the program. The conditions of the action should be stated in the following way:

- Who—Some logical portion (percentage) of the target group who is expected to change
- How much or to what extent—An amount of behavioral change that will depend on available resources
- What—The action, change in behavior, or health practice to be obtained
- When, or how soon, or within what time period—Determined by the urgency of the health problem in the population and by the rate of change that can be expected from the amount and type of effort that is devoted to the program
- Where—Geographic, political, or institutional boundaries derived in part from the original description of the health problem

In most community health or population-based programs, *how much* refers to the number of people or percentage of the population expected to change their behavior as a result of the program. For individuals, *how much* would refer to the level of accomplishment (e.g., number of monthly prenatal visits). Planners should word their objectives in such a way as to imply their assessment criteria. They should state the objectives in concrete terms with at least an implied if not stated scale of measurement that can be used to evaluate progress and achievement of the objective.

The test of good objectives is their ability to communicate expected results. Lucidity and precision in their formulation should accomplish several things. First, these objectives should provide limits to expenditure of time and effort on specific educational interventions. Second, they should identify criteria for measurement of program achievement. Third, they should lead to task analyses for selection, training, and supervision of staff. Finally, these objectives, like others, should provide orientation to cooperating agencies and to the general community.

*Health Education Methods and Theories.*    Having set priorities and selected strategies, the next step is to plan for the appropriate educational tools, tactics, and methods. Regardless of the setting in which the community health promotion program occurs, there are three basic types of educational strategies at its core:

1. Direct communications with the target population to *predispose* behaviors that are conducive to health—These include lectures and discussions, individual counseling or instruction, mass media campaigns, audiovisual aids, educational television, and programmed learning. Interpersonal or two-way communication and demonstration processes provide the most favorable environment for learning and generally have greater long-term behavioral effects. One-way communication, such as the use of pamphlets, may be appropriate in the early phases of a program or when other methods with more lasting outcomes are not feasible and when the audience is literate.[27]
2. Training methods to *enable* or *reinforce* behaviors that are conducive to health—These include skills development, simulations and games, inquiry learning, small group discussion, modeling, and behavior modification.
3. Organizational methods to *support* behaviors that are conducive to health—These include community development, social action, social planning, and economic and organizational development. Such methods usually go beyond health education in supporting behavior.

A single educational intervention can not be relied on to have a significant, lasting impact on an individual's health behavior. Only through repeated educational reinforcement by health staff, aides, community leaders, friends, and family, combined with environmental support or the removal of environmental barriers, can health education affect human behavior in the context of today's complex community health problems.

## Implementing Public Health Education Programs

Once the planning operations have been developed and refined, the educational components of the community health program can move toward implementation. At this phase, if involvement of concerned persons has been obtained and detailed written plans are available to staff, volunteers, and cooperating agencies, all will be aware and (ideally) have agreed upon the program's aims and general strategies. Planning participants should be committed to assuming their roles in the educational efforts. Initiating the program will require more specific logistical planning and resource identification, equipment and materials assembly, design of procedures, and training and orientation of staff, volunteers, and cooperating agencies.

*Putting the Educational Plan in Reverse*

Planning for health education programs works backward in the causal chain from the social assessment of ultimate outcomes to the administrative assessment of immediate targets of change, as seen in Figure 21-2. The implementation of plans reverses the flow to work forward from the administrative assessment toward educational interventions that influence behavioral changes that resolve health problems and ultimately meet the social concerns of the population. If the planning process has carefully paved the way from social concerns to educational programs—with adequate assessment, information, and social support—the road back should be a visible and viable one. The health educator or administrator approaches implementation with a well-documented and supported plan in hand. If not, the usual bumps and twists in any implementation path may turn into impassable gaps and crevices.

*Assessing Barriers and Facilitators to Implementation*

To implement the educational plan, an assessment of factors that may impede or facilitate program activities must be conducted. Both the barriers and facilitators to the program should be assessed.

*Barriers.*    Barriers to the achievement of educational objectives can assume several forms. Some examples of social, psychological, and cultural barriers include citizen and staff bias, prejudice, misunderstanding, taboos, unfavorable past experiences, values, norms, social relationships, official disapproval, or rumors. Communication obstacles include illiteracy and local vernacular. Economic and physical barriers include low income, inability to pay for prescribed drugs, means of transportation to medical services, and long distances over difficult terrain to medical or health education facilities. Legal and administrative barriers include residency requirements to be eligible for services, legal requirements that the program operate within defined geographical boundaries, and policies or regulations that restrict program implementation.

*Facilitators.*    Facilitators to the achievement of program objectives go beyond the mere absence of barriers. The predispositions of area residents who are favorable to the implementation of the program may include past and positive experience with similar programs and high credibility of the program's sponsoring agency. Other capabilities facilitating the program might be high education levels of consumers, dynamic and supportive local leaders and organizations, skilled staff with experience, open channels of communication with consumers, and support from other agencies. In addition, some geographic and physical enabling factors may serve as program assets, such as population distribution, density, and access to facilities.

The introduction of new or unfamiliar schemes for promoting awareness and health behavior has its greatest opportunity for success when it is integrated into existing systems of knowledge transfer and influence within the community. Schools, local media, clubs, churches, neighborhoods, and ethnic associations are the most effective channels of communication. In addition, planners should identify barriers in additional objectives that indicate how much and when the program will surmount each of the barriers.

## Priorities for Implementation

Resources are often scarce in relation to the great needs in public health. When budgets are reduced, the first line item to get cut is often the health education component. To ensure the most economical use of the resources available, priorities among alternative educational activities must be considered. Related to this pressing need for efficiency is the need for effectiveness. For an activity to be effective, the most effective combination of educational interventions and activities available must be selected. The first step is to determine which procedures are feasible, given limited staff, services, money, and time, and then to combine these resources to achieve the best support of program objectives.

The following guidelines can be used to set priorities:

- Obtain opinions and contributions from community members on priorities for educational services.
- Delineate the areas that will provide the greatest benefits to the most recipients.
- Phase program activities with a gradual beginning.
- Limit the number and range of activities, with initial emphasis on areas that are most amenable to quick and early success and activities requiring minimum staff training.
- Review the most recent scientific literature on the evaluation of health education methods relevant to the local program to guide these decisions on priorities.
- Develop a contingency plan to aid program survival in the event of future reduction of resources.

Beyond these general principles, the selection of educational efforts in strategic patterns or combinations depends on the particular circumstances of each site, the specific objectives, and the expectations for sustaining or institutionalizing the program.

## Using Educational Methods and Media

Methods, media, and materials can be pretested in the intended target audience to determine their acceptability to the particular group and their convenience (e.g., time demands, personnel requirements, and situational concerns such as light and sound). They should also be selected based on their efficiency and effectiveness. Efficiency relates to fixed costs, continuing costs, space and maintenance requirements, and staff and time needs to convey a message. Presumed effectiveness is based on confidence in the ability to communicate messages, arouse attention and interest, promote interaction, use suitable repetition and message retention techniques, and encourage desired attitudes and the adoption of practices.

## Managing Human Resources for Health Education

Some health workers and allied personnel may be uninformed about the methods of health education; others may feel that educational efforts are too slow, complex, and of dubious efficacy. Training or continuing education for these workers can provide them with time to discuss their concerns and develop their competence and confidence. Training in health education should be differentiated from technical training related to health and medical content. Health education training underscores the attitudinal and behavioral factors essential to long-term health maintenance, the cultural perceptions of the target population, and the necessity of well-planned and properly sustained action. Knowledge of these factors can help health workers achieve the health behavior changes required by the objectives of the community health program.

Although many health professionals are involved in various forms of health education, one group of professionals, the certified health education specialist (CHES), has specialized training in the planning, implementation, and evaluation of public health education. CHES professionals are typically assigned the responsibility for planning, implementing, and evaluating community health education programs because they have specialized training in public health or community health education and experience in a community health agency or institution. Competencies tested for the CHES include the following:

- Planning at the community level, including epidemiologic and socio-logical research methods, community organization, and health services administration
- Assessment and adaptation of communications to attitudinal, cultural, economic, and ethnic determinants of health behaviors
- Educational evaluation within the context of community health (as distinct from formal curriculum evaluation), including biostatistics, demography, and behavioral research methods

When these skills are not available within the staff of a community health agency, consultation for the planning and preparation stages of health education programs may be obtained from other organizations employing CHES professionals. Continuing education and in-service training are important to maintaining up-to-date knowledge and skills in all community health staff.

The CHES may work in a variety of different settings, such as public health departments, hospitals, voluntary agencies, educational institutions, or for-profit organizations. What links educators together in these various settings is their training and intent of facilitating voluntary actions by the public with regard to health. In some organizations, health educators work as part of a team with other health professionals to achieve intended outcomes. For example, a health educator may work as a team member with a physician, nurse, nutritionist, and social worker to develop and implement programs for maternal and child health. In other organizations, health educators may all work in the same department and be loaned to other departments, such as nursing or nutrition, to help plan and implement health education programs. Both models of organization have their advantages and disadvantages; the former promotes collaboration among health professionals, and the latter may allow health educators to support each other, but it isolates them from other health professionals. Careful consideration needs to be given to the placement of health education specialists.

Staff training may include orientation aimed at sensitizing staff members to their educational function and to the general objectives of the education program. It may also include preparation in recognizing educational opportunities, communication skills, and reinforcement techniques; training priorities for those staff members in contact with consumers; and continuing education.

Volunteers are not free of cost. Proper use of volunteers requires continuous, careful supervision and training. These items should be budgeted in the educational plan. A thorough plan for training volunteers might include content designed to foster their interest in health education and in the program's need for their insight into the attitudes, reactions, and daily lives of the target population. It can also include training in communications skills, teamwork roles, and limits of volunteers' responsibility and authority.

## Data Collection and Records

Documenting the implementation process not only provides guidance for present action, but it also provides statistics and financial accounts that are useful for evaluation and future planning. Good records and documentation, supervisor reports on quality control, and other process evaluations can provide immediate feedback on whether things are working satisfactorily. *Records* provide for continuous monitoring of program impact; for supervision, training, and staff development; and for evaluation of program process and outcome. *Peer review* among health professionals helps to maintain quality control, but it must be based on standards and documentation of practice. *Feedback* on patients' or clients' utilization and satisfaction with health services should provide data for program adjustment and redirection. *Population surveillance* will aid in continuous health education planning and evaluation.

Information collection can be integrated into daily routines and may require coordination among various units and sites in order to provide meaningful data for future planning. Information collection that requires additional paperwork must always be weighed against other demands for time. Small additions and checklists may be integrated into existing records with little effort and with staff acceptance. For more intensive narrative reporting and recording, special efforts during limited time periods may be acceptable and may provide sufficient data without generating staff resistance and unmanageable amounts of paperwork. The educational plan should clearly identify the use and purpose of new forms and records.

## Scheduling Implementation

Timing is crucial to the success of the educational plan of action. It requires an analysis of when, where, and who is responsible for implementation. This analysis will provide the starting and completion date required for each activity in relation to the total program. Consideration of the training required, production schedules for material, and staff loads guide the development of timetables. A task analysis and time sequence of activities should integrate the educational implementation with the total program plan. Planners should consider external events when scheduling to avoid conflict with community happenings, school openings, holidays, and related community schedules. The implementation stage is a logical progression from the previous stages of assessment, planning, and organizing.

## Evaluating Public Health Education Programs

Evaluation is the comparison of an object of interest against a standard of acceptability (see Chapter 18 for a detailed discussion of evaluation in public health organizations).[28] The evaluation of a health education program, then, is the systematic assessment of the operations or outcomes of a program against standards for the purposes of improving the program. The evaluation of a program needs to be guided by the standards of program evaluation: accuracy, feasibility, propriety, and utility. That is, evaluation needs to be not only technically well done and ethically conducted, but also feasible in cost and effort and directed toward program improvement.

The various levels of objectives developed in the assessment phases of planning—epidemiologic, behavioral, educational, and administrative—shape the dimensions and standards that are used during evaluation to determine the value (success or failure) of the program or its components. If the objectives were well developed during the planning stage, evaluation can proceed with ease, as compared with programs that have no developed standards for judging their success or failure. The involvement of various stakeholders in determining the dimensions and standards used to judge program value is essential in the highly political context of program evaluation. If stakeholders do not accept the dimensions and standards as those they would use in judging value, they are not likely to accept or use the results of the evaluation.

Program evaluation, at the very least, is an assessment of the worth or merit of a program, a method, or some other object of interest. It may provide an estimate of the degree to which spent resources result in intended activity and the degree to which performed activities attain goals. The determination of whether the program has met its goals is based on criteria indicated by precise statements of objectives along with subjective impressions and reporting. Evaluation can suggest which of several alternative educational strategies is the most efficient and which steps have an effect on the behavior specified. Evaluation provides accountability for time spent. Results usually offer a sense of accomplishment to staff and consumers or sponsors of the program.

### Formative and Process Evaluation

*Formative evaluation* is the earliest phase of process evaluation. Formative evaluation usually refers to preliminary assessments of the appropriateness of materials and procedures before beginning the program. Sources of data for formative evaluation include pretesting of materials, access to planning by relevant stakeholders, and adequate resources. *Process evaluation* refers to continuous observation and checking to see whether the program activities are taking place with the quality and at the time and rate necessary to achieve the stated objective. Process evaluation requires ongoing sources of data that often include budget reports on monthly expenditures in specific categories where rate of expenditures would indicate the amount of program activity relevant to the achievement of objectives.

Professional consensus usually provides the source of the standards of acceptability in formative and process evaluation. The data for process evaluation often come from routine records kept on encounters with consumers, patients, or clients. These might include, for example, clinic attendance records tabulated weekly or monthly for total numbers of patients. Staff can tabulate systematic samples of the records in more detail to estimate progress on such variables as broken appointment rates, sources of referral, and trimester of first visit for pregnant women. Another type of data available for process evaluation is administrative records. Administrators can tabulate personnel records to assess the number of home visits attempted, the number completed, the number of group sessions conducted, and the time allotted for various educational functions. These may become the numerators in evaluations with outcomes as the denominators, where the quotient shows an efficiency measure of, for example, home visits by staff per prenatal visit at the clinic.

Supervisors should conduct periodic reviews of personnel to assess staff performance. Time should be set aside on the agenda of staff and community meetings for consideration of strengths, weaknesses, and adaptation of ongoing programs. There should be a plan for charting records over time or comparing progress statistics with other programs or standards.

## Outcome Evaluation

Outcome evaluation, sometimes referred to as summative or impact evaluation, assesses the achievement of program effects. Intended program effects are contained in objectives that were developed during the planning phase. The more precisely stated the objectives, the more meaningful the evaluation. Outcome evaluation asks the following questions: What are the results of program efforts in the promotion of health behavior? Has there been any change in the attitudes of the clients toward recommended actions, or change in their ability to carry out the recommended actions, or change in the resources and social support for such actions in the community? An outcome evaluation may also assess unintended program effects that may be either beneficial or harmful to intended recipients.

Data concerning program outcomes can be assessed with quantitative or qualitative approaches. *Quantitative* approaches attempt to measure the frequency or prevalence of intended outcomes; *qualitative* approaches are more concerned with explaining why and how outcomes occurred, whether or not they were intended. For quantitative measurement, planners or evaluators should obtain baseline information on a period prior to the program's inception for comparison with similarly gathered data during the program or following the program. The evaluation of a specific educational component (e.g., a pamphlet or a group discussion) should not depend on the comparison of people who receive only that method with people who receive nothing. The comparison should be between a group receiving a comprehensive health education program and another group receiving everything *except* the component to be evaluated. The outcome statistics (knowledge, attitude, and behavioral outcomes) should be better for people who were exposed to the entire program than for those who were exposed to everything except for specific methods or materials of interest. If the evaluation finds no significant difference, it would suggest ways to reduce costs and increase efficiency by eliminating those methods or procedures from the program.

Evaluators should report on outcomes to the affiliated organizations, agencies, and institutions participating in the program and to the clients and general public. Reports can encourage their continued participation by noting their contribution to, or influence on, the program. Finally, practitioners should seek to publish case histories and reports in professional journals and newsletters for use by other departments, programs, or projects and to contribute to the advancement of professional knowledge, practice, and policies.

## Limits of Health Education

People may not truly have the resources or support necessary to make independent decisions and to take voluntary actions when some of the determinants of health are factors beyond their control. Whether they were born in a democratic country to loving parents with access to resources sets some limits on their ability and will to act independently or to control the determinants of their health. These limits must be recognized by public health organizations in designing and managing health education programs.

Such considerations also set limits on how much health education alone can achieve health objectives without placing undue responsibility for change on people who are relatively powerless to make such change. This excessive reliance on health education has been referred to as "victim blaming." Combining health education with policy and regulatory actions that empower the relatively powerless and restrain the more powerful who might exploit them overcomes this risk of victim blaming.

Health education is necessary even when the changes in health risks require regulatory or environmental controls on behavior. For example, health education in a democratic society must precede such controls as drunk driving or seat belt enforcement to gain the public's understanding and support required to pass legislation. It also helps to gain the public's cooperation in abiding by the new regulations. Community health promotion, then, is the combination of health education with related organizational, environmental, and economic supports to foster behavior that is conducive to health.

## Linking Health Education and Health Promotion

Population health and community health promotion require an understanding of health behavior that goes beyond the specific actions of individuals and includes more than educational interventions alone to change behavior. Lifestyle, a broader concept than behavior, describes value-laden, socially conditioned behavioral patterns. This concept has a rich history of study in anthropology and sociology. Only in recent decades has it taken on special significance in epidemiology, population health, and community health promotion. It is a concept that public health administrators need to understand in managing the broad-ranging, complex, and often politically charged interventions of health promotion. This section examines how health education strategies fit within the larger set of health promotion approaches that may be used by public health organizations to improve community health.

### Lifestyle

The midcentury shift from acute infectious diseases to chronic, degenerative diseases as the leading causes of death in Western societies brought a new perspective to epidemiology. No longer could isolation and suppression of a single germ or agent control the predominant diseases. (Refer to Chapter 1 for further discussion.) Now, the causes of most chronic diseases tend to be multiple and elusive. These causes defy simple environmental control measures because they involve people's pleasures and rewards, their social relationships and physical needs, and, ultimately for some, their habits and addictions. They involve lifestyle.

Lalonde identified lifestyle as one of the four elements of his health field concept; the other elements include health services, environment, and human biology.[29] Of these, lifestyle is responsible for more than half of the years of life that are prematurely lost in the more developed nations (Figure 21-3).[30] Tobacco use, diet (in combination with physical activity), and alcohol use are the three leading determinants of the leading causes of death in North America. Together, they account for some 38% of premature deaths. To put these revealing statistics in more positive terms, the greatest gains in preventing premature death and disability can be achieved today through community supports or policies for more healthy lifestyles. Reducing risk means that chances of developing a disease are lowered. It does not guarantee that a disease will be prevented. Because several factors are involved in the development of disease, risk reduction usually involves several strategies or approaches.

## Broad Supports for Lifestyle Change

Health education typically has been called on to alert the public to complex community health problems, but health education by itself can hardly be expected to solve such problems. The lifestyles in question are too embedded in organizational, socioeconomic, and environmental circumstances for people to be able to change their own behavior without concomitant changes in these circumstances. Health promotion combines health education with organizational, economic, and environmental supports for behavior and conditions of living that are conducive to health.

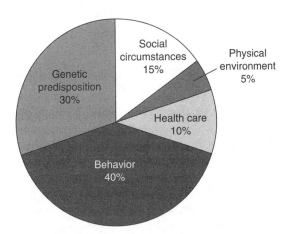

**FIGURE 21-3    Proportions of Premature Mortality Attributable to Genetic Predisposition, Behavior, and Environment (Social, Physical, and Health Care).** *Source:* McGinnis JM, Williams-Russo P, Knickman JR. The case for more active policy attention to health promotion. *Health Aff.* 2002;21(2):78–93.

The entire burden for improved health or risk reduction must not be placed on the individual alone. The responsibility must be shared between individuals and their families; between families and their communities; and between communities and their state, provincial, and national governments. Each level of organizational influence on behavior must assume some responsibility for setting the economic and environmental conditions that will support healthful lifestyles. Families, for example, must set examples for children. Communities must provide facilities and pass local ordinances to encourage, enable, and reinforce healthful behavior. State and national governments and private organizations must assume responsibility for the production, sale, and advertising of foods and other substances that can be either helpful or harmful to health.

## Health Promotion

Any program that has to deal with the complex problems related to lifestyle must address the social, environmental, economic, psychological, cultural, and physiological factors encompassed by the lifestyle in question. In the first part of this chapter, the PRECEDE model of health *education* was introduced. That model will now be expanded to include the additional elements of economic, organizational, and environmental supports for behavior that are conducive to health and applied as the PRECEDE-PROCEED model of health *promotion*.[2] Note that this health promotion model, as shown in Figure 21-4, includes health education at its core along with other types of organizational and regulatory interventions. The combined model has been applied to health promotion programs at international, national, and local levels for planning and evaluating such complex interventions for such complex lifestyle problems.

This section of the chapter begins with a review of the different types of prevention strategies. These levels and strategies are used to compare and contrast health education and health promotion approaches. This understanding paves the way for application of the PRECEDE-PROCEED model.

### Prevention Strategies

Three types of strategies can be used in each of the three prevention levels to accomplish health promotion goals:

- *Educational strategies* inform and educate the public about issues of concern, such as the dangers of drug misuse, the benefits of automobile restraints, or the relationship of maternal alcohol consumption to fetal alcohol syndrome.
- *Automatic-protective strategies* are directed at controlling environmental variables, such as public health measures providing for milk pasteurization, fluoridation of water, and the burning or chemical killing of marijuana crops.
- *Coercive strategies* employ legal and other formal sanctions to control individual behavior, such as required immunizations for school entry, mandatory tuberculosis testing of hospital employees, compulsory use of automobile restraints, and arrests for drug possession or use.

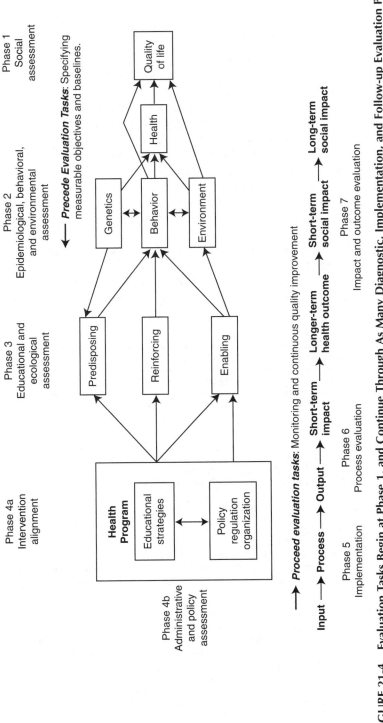

**FIGURE 21-4    Evaluation Tasks Begin at Phase 1, and Continue Through As Many Diagnostic, Implementation, and Follow-up Evaluation Phases as Required**

Table 21-1 provides examples of community health programs and measures classified by level of prevention and category of prevention strategy. The examples illustrate traditional public health strategies and new strategies in community health promotion and drug misuse prevention.

## Planning for Health Promotion Programs

Planning for health promotion programs follows the same phases as those involved in planning for health education programs. One of the differences in planning for health promotion, though, is a broader look at the ecologic influences on health behavior and outcomes and a willingness to consider measures beyond those aimed at voluntary changes in health behavior. To illustrate the use of a health promotion planning and evaluation framework, the following section applies the PRECEDE-PROCEED model to the complex issues of substance abuse. Tobacco, alcohol, and other drug abuse prevention programs incorporating the integrated health promotion approach of educational, organizational, and economic supports for lifestyle conducive to health have a much greater chance of success than programs directed at only one of these categories.

When using the health promotion framework in Figure 21-4 to plan community drug prevention programs, one starts with the final consequences—namely, social problems that are usually defined, in this example, as community drug-related problems but not necessarily as health concerns. One works back

**TABLE 21-1  Examples of Intervention Strategies for Each Level of Prevention of Health Problems, Including Those Associated with Drug Misuse**

| Type of Strategy | Levels of Prevention | | |
| --- | --- | --- | --- |
| | **Primary** | **Secondary** | **Tertiary** |
| Educational | Genetic counseling School health education Public education about drugs | Community hypertension screening education programs Teacher training in recognition of drug problems | Drug education programs for patients in coronary care |
| Automatic-protective | Fluoridation of community drinking water systems Legal control of prescription drugs | Neonatal meabolic screening Requiring medical prescription for drug refills | Referral to community mental health center for counseling following discharge from drug treatment center |
| Coercive | Immunization requirements for school-children Arrests of drug traffickers | Mandatory classes for persons convicted of driving while intoxicated or using illicit drugs | Mandatory treatment for persons having an addiction or a sexually transmitted disease |

*Source:* Green LW, Ottoson JM. *Community and Population Health.* 8th ed. St. Louis, MO: McGraw-Hill; 1999.

from there to the original causes—that is, the causes of the behavior that influenced the health problem or community drug-related social problem.

## Social Assessment

The first phase involves a consideration of the quality of life in a community by assessing the assets and social problems of concern to the various segments of the population. This phase of the model has the same purpose and process as that previously discussed in application of the model for health education. It has the effect of forcing planners to consider the desirable social outcomes of a program before setting priorities on health or selecting program approaches.

It also helps justify a program to the community. This is especially important in the planning of community drug prevention programs because of the relationship between drug-related health problems and the social problems of a community. For example, when a community has a large number of drug-dependent persons, it is likely that there will be high rates of violent and nonviolent crime, school truancy, early dropouts from school, juvenile delinquency, and unemployment (all social problems). Conversely, when a community is experiencing such social problems as high unemployment, inadequate housing, inadequate private and public school programs, or discrimination, a serious drug dependence problem will be present because for some the use of drugs will be a method of coping with the social problems.

By identifying the major social problems of concern to the community, one can select potential outcome evaluation measures and gain an understanding of the community's concerns as they relate to the particular health problem that is the target of the prevention program. A community's social problems can be diagnosed from analyses of existing records, files, publications, and informal interviews and discussions with leaders, key informants, and representatives of various community populations. This is an important first step that should not be undertaken too hastily because its outcome may well affect program scope and quality as well as the extent of community support.

## Epidemiologic Assessment

The objective of the epidemiologic assessment phase is to identify the specific health problems that appear to be contributing to the social problems noted in the preceding phase. Using data from community surveys, hospital admissions, city and county health departments, health systems agencies, and selected state or provincial and national agencies, trends in the drug-related morbidity, mortality, and disability information can be identified.

The incidence, prevalence, distribution, intensity, and duration of each identified health problem should be described. These data can be analyzed to determine the populations that are most affected by the health problem. This process will often reveal and locate a variety of existing health problems such as drug dependence, drug-related psychoses, drug-related depression or anxiety, injuries, and other drug-related problems such as acquired immune deficiency syndrome, serum hepatitis, and endocarditis. The use of spatial maps to depict the distribution of the identified health problems within the city or county is an effective way of presenting data if there is reason to believe that the problems vary by geographic location. Chapter 12 provides more detailed discussion of geographic information systems.

The results of epidemiologic analyses should be used to develop program objectives. The objectives should be stated in epidemiologic terms and answer the following questions: Who will be the recipients of the program? What benefit should they receive? How much of that benefit should they receive? By when or for how long? For example, it has been estimated that in a 6-month period, approximately 1000 persons die of drug overdose in New York City. Therefore, a program objective for a drug prevention program in New York City could be stated as follows: "To reduce the number of drug overdose deaths in New York City by 25% within 1 year and an additional 25% within the next year, until the national average is reached." The major drug-related health problem for most communities would not be death or drug overdose; rather, it would be physiological or psychological dependence.

As an extension of the descriptive epidemiology in this phase, the etiological study of the determinants of the health problems is also examined. This phase of the planning process is where the health education model previously discussed is expanded beyond a behavioral assessment to an environmental assessment, in keeping with the broader health promotion focus. The behavioral and environmental assessment requires the systematic identification of health behaviors that appear to be causally linked to each of the health problems identified in the epidemiologic assessment. The outcome of the behavioral assessment is the generation of a ranked list of specific behaviors to be used as the basis for specifying the behavioral objectives of the program.

The process of identifying the health behaviors linked to the health problems usually relies on the professional literature. The review of the literature can be combined with structured and unstructured interviews of persons who are familiar with the health problem (such as drug treatment personnel), data from observations, and intuition based on personal experiences. In the case of drug dependence, the behavioral causes leading to the health problem are drug use and drug misuse. These should be perceived not as distinct behaviors but, rather, as a continuum of drug use to drug misuse with varying types and amounts of drugs used. Distinct behaviors within the continuum could be specified, such as misuse of prescription medications, use of illicit drugs such as marijuana and cocaine, and use of illicit drugs in a manner that predisposes the user to health problems.

A second part of this phase is the identification of environmental factors that contribute to the health problem. These are the organizational and environmental conditions that influence the health problem and the behavior but that are not controlled directly by the behavior of the target population. Nonbehavioral environmental causes of drug dependence include such factors as the housing situation in the community, the school environment, and the law enforcement activity in the community. Identification of these factors is important because it provides the planners with direction for health promotion activity other than educational measures, such as organizational and economic interventions directed at the regulation of the environment and the availability of services.

## Educational and Ecologic Assessment

The educational and ecologic assessment identifies factors that require change to initiate and sustain the process of behavioral and environmental change. The determinants of health and social conditions identified in this phase will become the immediate targets or objectives of a program.

In this phase, the planner assesses the relative influence of various predisposing, enabling, and reinforcing factors on each of the identified behavioral and environmental causes of the health problem. Figure 21-5 focuses attention on the order of causation of behavior, as indicated by the numbered arrows. People first have an initial motivation to act (predisposing factors). They then deploy their resources and skills to enable the action or acquire them through training and organizational arrangements in the community. Third comes a reaction to the behavior from someone else (or in the case of drug use, the drug effects themselves), which reinforces or discourages the behavior. The reinforcement and strengthening or the punishment and discouragement of the behavior, in turn, affect the predisposing factors by strengthening or extinguishing the motivation to act. Finally, the person has an increased ability to take certain actions, which tends to increase the predisposition or motivation to take such actions.

In the process of identifying and listing factors in the three areas, (1) predisposing, (2) deployment of resource skills (enabling), and (3) reaction to behavior from someone else (reinforcing), one may include factors that seem to encourage the behavior as well as those that seem to discourage the behavior.

After completing the list of relevant factors, the next step is to select those factors that will be most likely to bring about the desired behavior. The factors that should be selected as targets for the program are those that are most changeable and most important. Changeability is assessed from data (evidence-based) or professional judgments. The factors determined to be both important

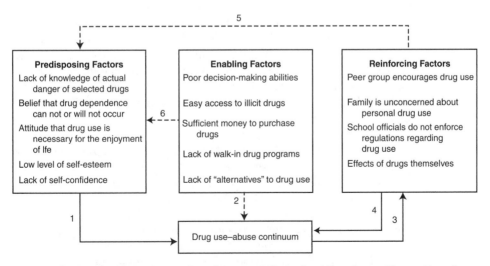

**FIGURE 21-5    The Three Categories of Factors Influencing Lifestyle are Shown Here As Related to Drug Use and Abuse. The Numbered Arrows Indicate the Appropriate Expected Order of Cause and Effect.**
*Source:* Green LW, Kreuter MW. *Health Promotion Planning: An Educational and Ecological Approach.* 3rd ed. Mountain View, CA: McGraw Hill; 1999:155.

and changeable form the basis of the prevention program. This level of specificity helps to use scarce resources in the most appropriate manner as well as to increase the chances of the program being successful. Difficult choices will be made in this phase of the planning process, but in the decision-making process, the level of understanding of the nature of the problem usually increases.

### Administrative Assessment

The administrative assessment phase assesses the resources that are available and the organizational problems that are likely to be encountered as the program becomes operational. Factors such as interagency cooperation, staffing patterns, and budgeting should be thoroughly discussed. This phase of planning analyzes the potential problems within programs, within organizations, and between organizations. A well-conceived program is seldom effective without an implementation plan.

In this phase, the right combination of strategies is selected to affect the priority predisposing, enabling, and reinforcing factors. As a general rule, selected communication methods are effective in altering predisposing factors; organizing resources and training are effective in altering enabling factors; and strategies such as consultation, training, feedback, and group development are effective in altering reinforcing factors. Refer to Table 21-1 for an example of considerations in selecting appropriate educational and other strategies according to the level of prevention.

## Health Promotion Includes Health Education

For purposes of this chapter, health promotion is defined as any combination of educational, organizational, environmental, and economic supports for behavior and conditions of living that are conducive to health. With health education as an integral part of all health promotion interventions, it follows that the interventions should be directed toward voluntary behavior at all levels—individuals, organizations, and communities. At the community, state or provincial, or national level, additional interventions may be legal, regulatory, political, or economic, and therefore potentially coercive. Nevertheless, to be successful, such interventions must be supported by an informed electorate and a consenting public.

Such informed consent requires health education. Ideally, the coercive measures are directed at the behavior of those individuals whose actions may affect the health of others, such as the manufacturers, distributors, and advertisers of hazardous products. Even then, public health education is required to ensure the support of an informed public because taxes, prices, availability of services and products, and jobs may be affected by such regulations of health- or drug-related industries and sources. For example, one part of a health promotion program for drug misuse prevention could target organizational change. Local public leaders could combine health education with various incentives (such as free program consultation services) and persuasion techniques (such as program promotion by local opinion leaders) in an attempt to increase the number of schools offering peer counseling programs for those persons who misuse drugs.

If the program also targeted political change, community organization techniques could be combined with health education activities to develop "concerned parent groups" in neighborhoods and to apply political pressure on local school, law enforcement, and government officials to support drug misuse prevention efforts. If the program directed other efforts toward economic change, health professionals and others could work with representatives of insurance carriers to initiate health insurance reimbursements for counseling and rehabilitation services.

The point is simple: When health education activities are combined with appropriate changes in organizations, political systems, and environmental and economic supports for behavior, the end result is more likely to be favorable than is the result achieved by a series of single, uncoordinated changes. Indeed, uncoordinated changes sometimes make things worse by throwing a community system out of balance and forcing an overreaction or overcompensation by the wrong elements in the community.

The relationships of health education and health promotion activities to the three prevention targets (lifestyle, environment, and health services) and the relationships of these targets to the health or drug misuse objectives set for the community and the nation are depicted in Figure 21-4. The three prevention targets are not isolated. The physical environment and the organization of services continually affect lifestyle. Furthermore, a successful program must effectively integrate and coordinate activities in relation to each of these targets. To facilitate the integration of activities within and between the prevention strategies, a planning framework is needed. The planning framework introduced in the first part of this chapter forces an encompassing and systematic analysis of public health problems in the context of social problems or quality-of-life concerns.

## Organization of Health Education and Health Promotion Activities Within Public Health Institutions

Placing professional health educators and other health promotion specialists within the staffing and organization of public health organizations poses some quandaries. From what has been described here as the tasks of coordinating the necessary components of effective health education and health promotion, it would seem that personnel performing these functions should be distributed to the specific program areas, such as maternal and child health, environmental health, tobacco control, and the like. This would allow each health educator or other health promotion personnel to specialize in and learn the content, resources, and community capabilities of the area in which the work is to be done. However, in recent years, many public health organizations have not been able to afford a sufficient number of health education and other health promotion specialists to have one assigned to every problem area in which they are needed. The usual, preferred staffing arrangement, then, is to centralize or pool the health education and other health promotion staff in a unit that provides planning and organizing services or consultation to the other units within the organization.

The major trap to avoid in centralizing the health education and health promotion staff is turning them into a public relations unit serving the publicity needs of the organization. A separate and distinct public relations officer should serve the purpose of representing the agency to the community and should remain distinct from the health education and health promotion functions of representing the community's needs to the agency, as described in this chapter.

•   •   •

There is no simple solution to such health-related lifestyle problems as tobacco use, alcohol misuse, drug misuse, and obesity. Such complex problems as these may defy even well-planned preventive efforts. Nevertheless, the effects of well-planned and systematically implemented preventive efforts are more likely to be successful than the single-focused, uncoordinated efforts that have typified many of the early attempts to address lifestyle, particularly those at the local level.

Specific measurable objectives for the United States have been set in each of the past three decades in the *Healthy People* initiatives of the federal government. If these objectives were met each decade, the scope and intensity of health problems attributable to lifestyle, the environment, and inadequate health services would be appreciably reduced. These objectives can serve to concentrate the limited resources of communities where they can be most productive. To illustrate how community health programs can work toward the objectives, a planning framework encompassing lifestyle, environment, and services has been presented.

Health education directed at individuals and decision makers has been demonstrated to influence population changes in simple behaviors such as one-time immunizations and more complex behaviors for those segments of the population that are highly motivated, more affluent, and more educated. Health education can enhance its effect on more complex behaviors (lifestyles) and in poorer, less educated segments of a population by combining the best of educational interventions with advocacy and organizational efforts to effect social environments, including political and economic systems. Applying the latest findings from the rapidly developing research in designing and evaluating prevention programs and ensuring the necessary quality and quantity of resources for programs will not guarantee success, but it will increase the probability of reaching the objectives set for a community.

## Chapter Review

1. Human behavior relates to health in both direct and indirect ways, including the following:
   - The direct effect of personal and social behavior
   - The indirect effect of people planning individual or community actions that result in environmental change
   - The indirect effect through health services related to planned distribution, appropriate utilization, and individual compliance with medical and preventive regimens
2. Behavioral changes resulting from education are by definition voluntary and freely adopted by people, with their knowledge of alternatives and probable consequences.

3. The two most important objective criteria for the selection of priority behavioral targets for health education are:
   - Evidence that the behavioral change will make a difference in the reduction of the health problem
   - Evidence that the behavior is amenable to voluntary change
4. Planning sets the foundation for sound health education programming and effectiveness and proceeds through the following stages:
   - Social assessment
   - Epidemiologic assessment, including behavioral and environmental assessment
   - Educational and ecologic assessment
   - Administrative assessment
5. Three types of strategies form the core of health education:
   - Direct communication with the target population to predispose behaviors that are conducive to health
   - Training methods to enable or reinforce behaviors that are conducive to health
   - Organizational methods and indirect communications through families, peers, employers, and others to support and reinforce behaviors that are conducive to health
6. Population and community *health promotion* require an understanding of health behavior that goes beyond the specific actions of individuals and includes more than educational interventions alone to change behavior.
7. Lifestyle, a broader concept than behavior, describes value-laden, socially conditioned behavioral patterns. The greatest changes in preventing premature death and disability can be achieved through community supports or policies for more healthful lifestyles. Planning for health promotion programs follows the same phases as those described for health education, with an added emphasis on environmental determinants and policy, regulatory, and organizational interventions to influence or contain them.
8. Three types of strategies can be used to accomplish health promotion goals for each of the three levels of primary, secondary, and tertiary prevention:
   - Educational—Informing and educating the public
   - Automatic-protective—Controlling environmental factors
   - Coercive—Employing legal and other formal sanctions to control individual behavior

## References

1. Green LW, Ottoson JM. *Community and Population Health*. 8th ed. St. Louis, MO: McGraw-Hill; 1999.
2. Green LW, Kreuter MW. *Health Program Planning: An Educational and Ecological Approach*. 4th ed. New York, NY: McGraw-Hill; 2005.
3. Kok G. Quality of planning as a decisive determinant of health education effectiveness. *Hygiene.* 1992;11:5–8.
4. Daniel M, Green LW. Application of the PRECEDE-PROCEED model in prevention and control of diabetes: a case illustration from an aboriginal community. *Diabetes Spectrum.* 1995;8:80–123.

5. McGowan P, Green LW. Arthritis self-management in native populations of British Columbia: an application of health promotion and participatory research principles in chronic disease control. *Can J Aging.* 1995;14(suppl 1):201–212.

6. Morrison C. Using PRECEDE to predict breast self-examination in older, lower-income women. *Am J Health Behavior.* 1996;20:3–14.

7. Dignan MB, Michielutte R, Wells HB, Bahnson J. The Forsyth County Cervical Cancer Prevention Project–I: cervical cancer screening for black women. *Health Educ Res.* 1995;9:411–420.

8. Earp JA, Altpeter M, Mayne L, Viadro CI, O'Malley MS. The North Carolina Breast Cancer Screening Program–foundations and design of a model for reaching older, minority, rural women. *Breast Cancer Res Treat.* 1995;35(1):7–22.

9. Farley C, Haddad S, Brown B. The effects of a 4-year program promoting bicycle helmet use among children in Quebec. *Am J Public Health.* 1996;86(1):46–51.

10. Keintz MK, Fleisher L, Rimer BK. Reaching mothers of preschool-aged children with a targeted quit smoking intervention. *J Community Health.* 1994;19:25–40.

11. Morrison SD. PRECEDE model as a framework for using health education in the prevention of diarrhea infant mortality in rural Mexico. *Eta Sigma Gamma Monograph Series.* 1994;12(1):41–49.

12. Nguyen MN, Grignon R, Tremblay M, Delisle L. Behavioral diagnosis of 30 to 60 year-old men in the Fabreville Heart Health Program. *J Community Health.* 1995;20:257–269.

13. O'Loughlin J, Paradis G, Kishchuk N, et al. Coeur en Santé St-Henri–a heart health promotion programme in Montreal, Canada: design and methods for evaluation. *J Epidemiol Community Health.* 1995;49:495–502.

14. Parcel GS, Swank PR, Mariotto MJ, et al. Self-management of cystic fibrosis: a structural model for educational and behavioral variables. *Soc Sci Med.* 1994;38:1307–1315.

15. Green LW, Frankish CJ. Theories and principles of health education applied to asthma. *Chest.* 1994;106(suppl 4):219S–230S.

16. Reed DB. Focus groups identify desirable features of nutrition programs for low-income mothers of preschool children. *J Am Dietetic Assoc.* 1996;96:501–503.

17. Reed DB, McCarron Meeks P, Nguyen L, et al. Assessment of nutrition education needs related to increasing dietary calcium intake in low-income Vietnamese mothers using focus group discussions. *J Nutr Educ.* 1998; 30(3):155–163.

18. Selby-Harrington M, Sorenson JR, Quade D, Stearns SC, Tesh AS, Donat PL. Increasing Medicaid child health screenings: the effectiveness of mailed pamphlets, phone calls, and home visits. *Am J Public Health.* 1995;85:1412–1417.

19. Gilmore GD, Campbell MD. *Needs Assessment Strategies for Health Education and Health Promotion.* 2nd ed. Dubuque, IA: Brown & Benchmark; 1996.

20. US Department of Health and Human Services. *Healthy People 2010.* Vol. I and II. Washington, DC: DHHS; 2000.

21. Eakin EG, Bull SS, Glasgow RE, Mason M. Reaching those most in need: a review of diabetes self-management interventions in disadvantaged populations. *Diabetes Metab Res Rev.* 2002;18:26–35.

22. Briss PA, Brownson RC, Fielding JE, Zaza S. Developing and using the *Guide to Preventive Health Services*: lessons learned about evidence-based public health. *Annu Rev Public Health.* 2004;25:281–302.

23. Green LW. From research to "best practices" in other settings and populations. *Am J Health Behavior.* 2001;25:165–178.
24. Glanz K, Lewis FM, Rimer BK, eds. *Health Behavior and Health Education.* 3rd ed. San Francisco, Calif: John Wiley & Sons; 2002:531–544.
25. D'Onofrio CN. Pooling information about prior interventions: a new program planning tool. In: Sussman S, ed. *Handbook of Program Development for Health Behavior.* Thousand Oaks, Calif: Sage Publications Inc; 2001.
26. Kreuter MW. PATCH: its origin, basic concepts, and links to contemporary public health policy. *J Health Educ.* 1992;23:135–139.
27. Maibach EW, Rothschild ML, Novelli WD. Social marketing. In: Glanz K, Rimer BK, Lewis FM, eds. *Health Behavior and Health Education*: *Theory, Research, and Practice.* 3rd ed. San Francisco, Calif: Jossey-Bass; 2002: 437–461
28. Green LW, Lewis FM. *Measurement and Evaluation in Health Education and Health Promotion.* Palo Alto, Calif: Mayfield; 1986.
29. Lalonde M. *A New Perspective on the Health of Canadians: A Working Document.* Ottawa, Canada: Government of Canada; 1974.
30. McGinnis JM, Williams-Russo P, Knickman JR. The case for more active policy attention to health promotion. *Health Aff.* 2002;21:78–93.

## CHAPTER 22

# USING MARKETING IN PUBLIC HEALTH

Lynne Doner Lotenberg
Michael Siegel

## Chapter Overview

The discipline of marketing offers public health organizations a variety of concepts and strategies for understanding and motivating behavior change in specific populations of interest. Public health organizations use these techniques not only to influence individual health behavior, but also to build public support for core public health policies and institutions. Using a marketing approach can therefore enable organizations to improve the effectiveness of specific public health interventions and to strengthen the institutional capacity of the public health system as a whole.

As other authors have noted, many public health efforts have been labeled "marketing" or "social marketing" when in fact they neglect many core marketing concepts.[1-3] This chapter attempts to improve understanding by providing an introduction to the concepts that distinguish marketing from other public health planning processes and to the ways in which these concepts can be applied in a public health environment to help bring about changes in personal health behaviors and in policies affecting public health institutions and practice.

## What Is Marketing?

According to the American Marketing Association (AMA):

> Marketing is an organizational function and a set of processes for creating, communicating, and delivering value to customers and for managing customer relationships in ways that benefit the organization and its stakeholders.[4]

In a public health context, marketing efforts are undertaken to improve societal health, either through influencing changes in the health behaviors of individuals, in policies that impact health behaviors, or in perceptions of and support for public health as an institution. Rothschild conceptualized marketing as one of three primary classes of strategic tools available to public health and noted, "Current public health behavior management relies heavily on education and law while neglecting the underlying philosophy of marketing and exchange."[5(p24)]

- Marketing "attempts to manage behavior by offering reinforcing incentives and/or consequences in an environment that invites voluntary exchange. The environment is made favorable for appropriate behavior through the development of choices with comparative advantage (products and services), favorable cost-benefit relationships (pricing), and time and place utility enhancement (channels of distribution). Positive reinforcement is provided when a transaction is completed."[5(p25)]
- Education is defined as "messages of any type that attempt to inform and/or persuade a target to behave voluntarily in a particular manner but do not provide, on their own, direct and/or immediate reward or punishment."[5(p25)]
- Law is "the use of coercion to achieve behavior in a nonvoluntary manner or to threaten with punishment for noncompliance or inappropriate behavior."[5(p25)] Rothschild noted that law can be used to increase–through price subsidies–or decrease–through taxes–the probability of transactions that might not develop as desired through free-market mechanisms.[5]

Social marketing has played a part in some highly successful efforts to influence personal health behaviors, beginning in 1972 with the formation of the National High Blood Pressure Education Program to increase awareness, prevention, treatment, and control of hypertension. Though it is not possible to measure the direct impact of this program, its implementation is associated with substantial increases in public awareness of high blood pressure and its relationship with stroke, physician visits for hypertension, and hypertension treatment and control rates.[6] Other successful uses of marketing techniques include the US Centers for Disease Control and Prevention's (CDC) VERB program, which garnered a 34% increase in weekly free-time physical activity sessions among 8.6 million children ages 9–10, and the Truth campaign, which contributed to reduced smoking among US teenagers.[7,8]

Public health has been moving toward a broader use of marketing techniques to help bring about policy change or increase support for public health as an institution. As one example, the marketing framework provided a strong foundation for many of the advocacy activities undertaken to support tobacco control, as well as for efforts to preserve or increase public health funding.[9] More recently, there have been efforts to more fully integrate marketing into public health institutions and ways of approaching social change. Turning Point, an initiative of the Robert Wood Johnson Foundation and the W.K. Kellogg Foundation intended to transform and strengthen the public health system in them United States, includes a Social Marketing National Excellence Collaborative.[10] In 2005, the CDC, which had previously called for the application of marketing strategies to promote public support and secure increased funding for public health programs, included being a customer-centric organization as one of the agency's strategic imperatives and created the National Center for Health Marketing (NCHM) as part of their new organizational structure.[11-13] The NCHM is charged with "ensur[ing] that health information, interventions, and programs are based on sound science, objectivity, and continuous customer input."[14(p1)]

## Why Integrate Marketing into Public Health Practice?

Over the past century, the nature and role of public health practice have changed significantly, especially in developed countries. Many basic public health functions became widespread during the 1800s to combat the infectious disease outbreaks that occurred as more and more people moved to urban settings. Although today's public health practitioners continue to address infectious disease, they also confront a medical climate that emphasizes treatment over population-based prevention and a chronic disease epidemic rivaling the infectious disease epidemics of the past. The appropriate use of marketing can help public health practitioners be more effective in today's environment.

### Preventing and Controlling Chronic vs. Infectious Disease

Today, infectious disease control remains a key focus of public health in both developed and developing countries; we can expect new and reemerging infectious diseases to continue to extract a heavy toll on the quality and quantity of life. (Refer to Figure 1-5 in Chapter 1.) However, as life spans in the developed world have increased, chronic diseases have come to pose a major threat as well. Preventing and controlling chronic diseases often requires fundamentally different strategies than those that would be used with infectious diseases, as shown in Table 22-1. (The differences shown will not apply to every infectious or chronic disease.)

As the table shows, preventing and controlling infectious disease are often more straightforward than doing the same for chronic disease. For a vaccine-preventable infectious disease, public health programs can focus on convincing target audiences to get themselves or their children immunized one time, or, at most, periodically. From the consumer's perspective, the action is clear and relatively low cost in terms of money, time (at most, a few trips to the doctor; in some developing countries, immunization campaigns go door to door), psychological (fear), and physical costs (some immunizations cause discomfort). In addition, there is a clear, definite benefit that outweighs the cost: avoidance of a disease that, at the least, will have higher time and physical costs, and, at the most, death.

In contrast, the individual behaviors required to prevent or treat chronic disease generally have higher financial, time, psychological, and physical costs, and the corresponding benefits are less definite and often less immediate. Public health programs must convince consumers to initiate *and maintain* a single behavior change, or, more often, a series of behavior changes (e.g., various changes in diet and physical activity, compliance with monitoring and treatment) in the hopes that these changes might decrease the probability of developing the condition or lessen its severity.

Other factors that differentiate chronic disease control are the lack of public reaction to chronic diseases and the limited tools available to public

**TABLE 22-1 Common Differences Between Preventing and Controlling Infectious Versus Chronic Disease**

| | Infectious Disease | Chronic Disease |
|---|---|---|
| Cause | Straightforward (once infectious agent is discovered) | Complex; often unknown |
| Taking preventive action | Will prevent transmission | May reduce risk of developing condition |
| Availability of one-time preventive behavior versus permanent behavior modification | Depends on disease<br><br>One-time or single-series vaccines available for some; periodic immunization required for others (e.g., influenza)<br><br>Permanent lifestyle modification required for those with no vaccine | If prevention is possible, generally requires permanent lifestyle modification |
| Treatment complexity | Ranges from simple one-time treatment (e.g., course of antibiotics) to ongoing and complex treatment (e.g., HIV/AIDS) | Usually complex and ongoing treatment or monitoring for recurrence is required |
| Force of law | In some instances (e.g., childhood immunizations) | No |
| Public outcry/concern | Spikes when new outbreaks occur | No |
| Possibility of eradication from population | Sometimes yes, if vaccine is available | No |

health practitioners. When there is an unexpected outbreak of infectious disease, especially a relatively uncommon disease, the outbreak generally gets significant media coverage and public attention. People become concerned, often take actions to avoid infection, and expect public health officials to take the necessary steps to limit transmission. In recent years, we have seen examples of this with initial outbreaks of the West Nile virus, Severe Acute Respiratory Syndrome (SARS), and monkeypox, as well as a more virulent than expected influenza season. During the same period of time (1999–2004), many more cases of cancer and other chronic diseases were undoubtedly diagnosed. Yet, because these were expected and not quickly preventable, there was no public outcry, and public health officials were not expected to do anything beyond their usual activities.

## Need for Population-Based Prevention

In general, health resources in the United States are disproportionately allocated to medical treatment rather than prevention, which is fiscally irresponsible and jeopardizes the nation's health in a number of ways:

- There is substantial evidence that the observed decline in mortality in the developed world since the 1700s is attributable largely to public health and not medical interventions.[9,15–18] (See Chapter 1 for the public health accomplishments during this time.)
- Prevention is often cheaper than treatment. For example, an analysis of the US Department of Agriculture's (USDA's) Special Supplemental Food Program for Women, Infants, and Children (WIC) revealed that for mothers and newborns during the first 60 days after birth, the government saves more money on Medicaid than it spends for prenatal care through WIC.[19]
- Treatment advances tend to benefit the socioeconomically advantaged disproportionately, and, as a result, to increase the gap in health status between rich and poor Americans.
- As the CDC noted, "The emergence of drug resistance in many organisms is reversing some of the therapeutic miracles of the last 50 years and underscores the importance of disease prevention."[20(p3)]

Emphasizing prevention, not just treatment, requires changing a wide range of governmental and commercial policies that shape the physical, social, and political environment in which people live, because their behavior is a product of the social conditions and social norms in their community.[21] Because prevention programs must be administered repeatedly, consistently, and over many years (often decades) before the necessary changes in social conditions, norms, behavior, and policy take place, the public health view is inherently long term. A number of trends in the United States are working against widespread adoption of a long-term population-based prevention approach. In particular, although it was initially thought that managed care organizations would be receptive to funding prevention programs because prevention is cheaper than treatment over the long term, the reality is that managed care organizations perceive no financial benefit to funding expensive prevention programs because of high patient turnover and because denying treatment, not expanding prevention programs, is the most effective way to increase short-term profits.[22] Thus, it is critical for public health to increase funding for prevention.

## Key Marketing Concepts

Marketing can be distinguished from other approaches to influencing individual and policy change by its emphasis on the following concepts:

- Exchange
- Self-interest
- Behavior change
- Competition
- Consumer orientation and audience segmentation
- Product, price, place, and promotion

### Exchange

Marketers believe that *exchange* is central to the actions people take: a person gives something in order to get something he or she values in return.

Before entering into an exchange, a person weighs the benefits to be received against the costs (in money, time, or psyche). Only if the benefits are greater than the costs will the person make the exchange—hence the emphasis on creating, communicating, and delivering value as the essence of marketing in the AMA's definition. It is important to understand that the only relevant costs and benefits are those that are important to the person contemplating the exchange. For individual health behaviors, these may or may not be health-related costs and benefits. Immediate tangible benefits usually are more compelling to people than longer-term, intangible benefits. The field of behavioral economics provides a useful framework and body of literature for understanding how people value costs and benefits.[23]

The idea of weighing costs and benefits is not unique to marketing; many models and theories that are used to understand or predict health behavior change incorporate a similar concept. For example, the transtheoretical model of stages of change includes a decisional balance construct that is described as the pros and cons of changing a behavior.[24] Social cognitive theory includes outcome expectancies, which "influence behavior according to the hedonic principle; that is, if all other things are equal, a person will choose to perform an activity that maximizes a positive outcome or minimizes a negative outcome."[25(p63)]

### Self-Interest

> In most situations, people act primarily out of self-interest; in commercial marketing, this self-interest clearly and consistently is acknowledged and pursued. . . . In public health and social issues, managers often ask members of the target market to behave in ways that appear to be opposite of that member's perception of self-interest and are often the opposite of the current manifestation of that self-interest as observed through the member's current behavior. People choose to eat junk food, not exercise, smoke and drink to excess, or engage in unsafe sex because they have evaluated their own situation and environment and made a self-interested decision to behave as they do.[5(p26)]

Self-interest can play a role in education and law as well, though in quite different ways. Educational efforts may include appeals to self-interest (e.g., "If you get 60 minutes of physical activity each day, you will have more energy"), whereas law "offers a self-interested return by promising not to punish those who behave correctly."[5(p27)]

Understanding self-interest is critical to developing and delivering an exchange that target audience members will value.

### Behavior Change

> The bottom line of all marketing strategies and tactics is to influence behavior. Sometimes this necessitates changing ideas and thoughts first, but in the end, it is behavior change we are after. This is an absolutely crucial point. Some nonprofit marketers may think that they are in the "business" of changing ideas, but it can legitimately be asked why they should bother if such changes do not lead to action.[26(p110)]

Depending on the situation in which a marketing approach is being applied, the behavior to be influenced may be colleagues' attendance at a meeting, at-risk individuals coming in for screening for sexually transmitted diseases, or policy makers' support of a new public health initiative. However, the end goal is always getting the audience to take an action, not merely increasing knowledge or changing attitudes. Marketers will increase knowledge to the extent that such activities are precursors to behavior change (i.e., parents are unlikely to get children vaccinated unless they know they need to do so), but the focus is on identifying exactly what is necessary for the behavior change to take place.

Often one challenge is to select a specific behavior to change; a number of behaviors may lead to desired outcomes. Integral to this decision is selecting a behavior that is perceived as "doable" by target audience members. Sometimes this means focusing on one step toward the desired behavior. For example, in its early years the national 5 A Day campaign asked the target audience to *add two* servings of fruits and vegetables each day, even though the program goal was *eating five* servings each day. This decision was made because target audience members were already eating two to three servings a day, and adding an additional two was more reasonable to them.[27] Appropriate models and theories of behavior change can help practitioners make such decisions.

## Competition

> Every choice of action on the consumer's part involves giving up some other action. Thus, campaigns must keep in mind not only what the marketer is trying to get across but also what the customer sees as the major alternatives.[28(p17)]

For a public health initiative, competition can be defined as anything that limits resources, diverts attention from the subject of the initiative, or calls for contrary behaviors. There are three main sources of competition: other organizations conducting programs on the same subject, other behavior changes, and commercial sources.[9] Identifying competition allows planners to identify a niche in which to position a program or activity in regards to the competition. Sometimes, another organization—even a "friend"—may be promoting a product, service, or practice that is in conflict with the public health organization's goals. At other times, a commercial opponent may encourage the very behavior that public health practitioners are trying to stop, such as smoking or ownership of certain types of firearms. More often, commercial advertising, television programs, or magazines emphasize behaviors or choices that have negative health consequences if they are not moderated or balanced by other behaviors, such as having nonmonogamous sex without using condoms or eating only "junk" foods.

## Consumer Orientation

> Social marketing provides a problem-solving process from which behavior change strategies are formulated and translated into discrete and integrated tactics aimed at specific behavior change. The point

of social marketing is that these tactical approaches are selected and implemented based on what has been discovered in the consumer research phase as being most relevant and potentially effective with the target, not what self-designated experts believe to be important for the target population to know or practice.[29(p147)]

An organization's consumer orientation manifests itself in how the organization approaches the exchange and how it approaches the consumer. Andreasen discussed a number of characteristics that are typical of an organization-centered (rather than consumer-centered) mind-set.[28]

- The organization's mission is seen as inherently good.
- Customers are seen as the problem (e.g., assuming they are not doing something they should be doing, rather than determining if in fact they are not doing something and, if so, how that could be fixed).
- Marketing is seen as communications (rather than a broader range of potential solutions).
- Marketing research has a limited role.
- Customers are treated as a mass.
- Competition is ignored.
- Staffers are drawn from those with product (the behavior itself) or communications skills.

In contrast, consumer-oriented organizations analyze the transaction from the consumer's point of view rather than the organization's. They define the "problem" in terms of what the target audience needs and wants, not what the organization would like to provide. "Their mission in life is to know who their customers are, what they want and need, and where and how to reach them."[9(p204)] They do this by following a careful process of audience analysis, and then using this analysis to segment the audience along key dimensions, such as readiness or ability to change behavior. They then select audience segments and determine what is necessary to facilitate behavior change for each segment. In many instances, "fixing" a problem behavior involves much more than communicating with consumers about it. This may require changing any of the marketing variables—the product itself, the price, the experience of getting it, or communication concerning it.

For example, when it became apparent that many child safety seats were improperly installed in the United States, the National Highway Traffic Safety Administration (NHTSA) and many local community and law enforcement agencies worked together to educate parents and caregivers about proper installation procedures and sponsored events where installation could be checked and corrected, if necessary.[30] A product usability study, however, revealed that many safety seats were installed incorrectly because of poor installation technology.[30] Therefore, NHTSA used its educational efforts as an interim approach while it used its policy-making ability to mandate a technological change: a standardized anchorage system in passenger vehicles and corresponding standardized attachments on child safety seats.[31]

## The Four Ps: Product, Price, Place, and Promotion

*Product, price, place,* and *promotion* constitute the marketing mix—the group of variables that a marketer can alter. Understanding these variables is central to understanding the marketing approach. Exhibit 22-1 presents definitions for each variable and key questions that public health practitioners should answer as part of planning marketing strategy and activities.

## Two Other "Ps" To Consider: Partners and Policy

Partners can be other organizations involved with a social change effort or serving as conduits to target audiences. Questions to ask about potential partners include the following:

- What other organizations are conducting activities addressing the social change?
- What organizations are credible to the target audience?
- What are the opportunities to work together with either type of organization?

**Exhibit 22-1    The Marketing Mix (as Applied in Social Change Settings)**

**Product**
The behavior, good, service, or program exchanged for a price—ultimately, the behavior change sought
- What are the benefits of the behavior change to members of the target audience—what needs or wants do they have that the product (behavior change, program, or policy) can fulfill?
- What is the competition for the product?
- What legal, technological, and/or economic policy changes can facilitate individual behavior change?
- What accomplishments can reasonably be expected independent of policy changes?

**Price**
The cost to the target audience member, in money, time, effort, lifestyle, or psyche, of engaging in the behavior
- What will the behavior change "cost" each target audience?
- Do target audience members perceive the cost to be a fair exchange for the benefit they associate with the behavior change?
- How can costs be minimized?

**Place**
The channel(s) through which products are distributed—or situations in which behavior changes can be made
- What are target audience members' perceptions of place?
- What barriers (costs) does the place create, and how can they be overcome?

**Promotion**
Some combination of advertising, media relations, promotional events, personnel selling, and entertainment to communicate with target audience members about the product
- What is the current demand among target audience members for the behavior change?
- What messages can best influence demand?
- What promotional materials and activities are appropriate for the message?
- How can those materials and activities best be delivered to target audience members?

*Source*: Adapted from Siegel M, Doner L. *Marketing Public Health: Strategies to Promote Social Change.* Gaithersburg, MD: Aspen Publishers Inc; 1998:217.

Policy is important because policy changes often are necessary before behavior change can occur or they can support individual behavior change efforts. Two examples of the first situation are the child safety seat issue discussed earlier and exposure to secondhand smoke. Members of the public can not reasonably avoid secondhand smoke in public places, such as restaurants, shopping malls, and airports, without policies that restrict smoking to confined areas. An example of a policy change that facilitates individual behavior changes is the US Food and Drug Administration's (FDA's) rule mandating "Nutrition Facts" labels on most foods, which provides consumers with the information they need to select foods that are lower in fat or sugar. Restaurants that identify lower-fat menu items provide a similar service.

Questions to ask about policy include the following:

- What policy changes *are necessary* for individuals to improve their health behaviors?
- What policy changes *could support* individuals in their efforts to improve their health behaviors?
- What policy changes can this organization bring about?

## Challenges of Public Health Marketing

Public health practitioners confront a number of challenges that commercial marketers often can avoid. Problems that are encountered more frequently by all nonbusiness entities include: "the intangibility of nonbusiness products, the nonmonetary price of purchase, the extreme lack of frequency of purchase, the lack of behavioral reinforcers, the need to market to an entire but heterogeneous society/market, and the extreme levels of involvement varying from very low to very high."[32(p12)] In addition, public health practitioners frequently encounter the following challenges:

- Unfavorable state of demand
- Lack of marketing orientation
- Limited use of branding to build relationships
- Limited professional training
- Better-financed competition
- Limited use of and access to distribution channels

### Unfavorable State of Demand

As Table 22-2 illustrates, there are eight possible states of demand for a product. Public health products are usually in one of the last three (negative, no demand, or unwholesome), although some may experience irregular demand (e.g., influenza vaccines) or faltering demand (e.g., "mature" products, such as HIV/AIDS prevention behaviors, that are no longer as salient due to improved treatment or simply the fact that they are no longer new).

*Unwholesome demand* occurs when an alternative product or behavior is more appealing than the public health product or behavior. On an individual level, tobacco products, alcohol, drugs, and foods of minimal nutrient value are examples of unwholesome demand. At the policy level, the desire for freedom from gun controls is an instance of unwholesome demand. Other public

**TABLE 22-2    States of Marketing Demand**

| Demand State | Marketing Approach |
|---|---|
| Full demand (demand is at desired level) | Maintenance |
| Overfull demand (demand is too high) | Demarket (temporarily or permanently discourage customers without impugning product) |
| Latent demand (people have a strong need for a product that does not yet exist) | Developmental marketing (create and market a product to satisfy existing demand) |
| Irregular demand (seasonal or widely fluctuating) | Synchromarket (synchronize fluctuations in demand and supply) |
| Faltering demand (lower than former level) | Remarket/revitalize (alter the product, the target audience, or the marketing effort) |
| Negative demand (public dislikes the product, does not want it, is not willing to pay a price for it) | Conversional marketing (design a marketing effort to cause demand to rise, perhaps by fulfilling other needs) |
| No demand (no interest in the product) | Stimulational marketing (alter the product or marketing effort to fulfill other existing needs; alter the environment so the product becomes valued; promote in more places in hopes that the problem is actually a lack of exposure) |
| Unwholesome demand (for an alternative product) | Countermarket (designate the product as intrinsically unwholesome) |

*Source:* Data from Kotler P. *Marketing Management: Analysis, Planning, and Control.* 3rd ed. Englewood Cliffs, NJ: Prentice-Hall; 1976.

health programs or products confront a situation of *no demand*—an instance where people are not necessarily against the product, but simply are not interested. Some policies to further chronic disease prevention and control might fall into this category; for example, many employers may not be particularly interested in (or even aware of) policy changes that would help employees get more physical activity during the work day.

Rangan and colleagues outlined the following reasons why social changes are so often in states of *negative demand:*[33]

- The target community opposes the change being advocated (e.g., efforts to reduce family size often conflict with a population's current way of life).
- Adoption costs often exceed tangible benefits.
- Early adopters stand to lose (in the family planning example, if only a few couples choose to have smaller families, they will be at a disadvantage among their peers).
- Benefits accrue only when a large percentage of the target community accepts the proposed change.

For all three unfavorable demand scenarios, the marketer's job is to identify appropriate target audiences and ferret out benefits that they can or do associate with the desired behavior or policy change so that a way can be found to position it as superior to the competing behavior or policy. To do this, solid consumer research—especially in terms of core values and benefits that people can associate with a product or behavior change—is critical.

## Lack of Marketing Orientation

The indicators of an organization mind-set, rather than a consumer/marketing mind-set, were presented earlier in this chapter. This nonmarketing orientation creates a number of difficulties when public health practitioners attempt to market a product or behavior. First, "unlike commercial marketers, who develop products based on what customers are most likely to purchase, public health institutions often allocate resources based on legislative priorities as reflected in mandates or current funding streams (i.e., if tax money or grants are available for tobacco control, then the institution focuses on tobacco control), rather than on an analysis of what behavior changes might best impact a population's health—let alone what changes are most likely to be made by the population served."[9(p205)] Furthermore, those charged with the marketing function within a public health organization are rarely in a position to influence or change the organization's priorities or institute other changes to support the behavior or policy change being sought.

Second, public health practitioners often hesitate to target, or focus on, specific groups of people because of a mandate to serve "the general public." However,

> Trying to appeal to everyone is problematic for a number of reasons. One, it wastes resources because not everyone needs a particular intervention. Often, particular subgroups of the population are reached by other entities, have a very low incidence of the problem the intervention addresses, or have already embraced the behavior being promoted. Two, . . . even if "everyone" needs a particular intervention, some subgroups are likely to be closer to actually changing their behavior, while others are not nearly ready. And different groups will associate different costs and benefits with the behavior in question. Finally, social change resources are often extremely limited. By trying to stretch them to include "everyone," no audience group will be reached with any intensity.[9(p206)]

## Limited Use of Branding to Build Relationships

"In recent years, marketers have come to realize that the best way to influence behavior is not through one-time transactions, but by building ongoing relationships with their customers."[34(p15)] Companies use branding to help them build these relationships. On the surface, a brand is "a name, term, sign, symbol, or design, or some combination of these, which identifies [the goods or services] as the marketer's and differentiates them from competitors' offerings."[26(p374)] Brands originally came about as a way of distinguishing products that otherwise could not be differentiated easily. However, a brand also forms the relationship between the organization or product and its consumer; it has been characterized as a repository, not merely of functional characteristics, but of meaning and value.[35,36] In trying to understand a brand, a fundamental question should be, "What is the significance of this brand in the user's life?"[35(p11)]

Public health is touched by brand identity more than its practitioners may realize, and unfamiliarity with brand management can lead to mistakes and missed opportunities. Every public health institution has an identity in the minds of funding agencies, potential partners, the media, and target audiences. The identity may be fuzzy or clear; positive, neutral, or negative; but it exists. Working through branding exercises can help an organization clarify its core mission, prioritize institutional goals, and reconcile internal versus external perceptions. Actively projecting a clear, consistent, and compelling organizational identity can help a public health institution accomplish its mission by building relationships with supporters, partners, and target audiences.

How do you develop a brand for your institution? Start by gathering information on how internal and external audiences see the institution. Then, determine an appropriate positioning and use it to craft a positioning statement—a two- or three-word message that encapsulates the organizational identity (e.g., the CDC's "safer, healthier people"). The strongest brands are positioned on strong beliefs and values.[37] You can use that information to develop a vision of what the brand must be and do and encapsulate it in a visual identity and tag line. A plan for brand management is critical, to ensure that every contact anyone has with your institution—through materials, Web sites, telephone or interpersonal interactions, or anything else—conveys a consistent brand identity and delivers on all brand promises.

In addition to helping public health institutions position themselves, understanding how commercial marketers use brands to build relationships with target audiences can help practitioners design effective interventions. For example, the *truth*[SM] campaign worked to destabilize the tobacco companies' relationships with their youth customers, offering youth a replacement brand. "In a search to define one's identity, brands (like piercing, haircuts, and even tobacco use) serve as a shorthand way for youth to identify themselves to the world. If we wanted youth to really embrace our antitobacco effort, it would make sense to deliver it just like other successful US youth products, such as Adidas, Fubu, or Abercrombie—in a branded form they understood."[38(p5)] Branding also helps longer-term interventions; as the author of the *truth*[SM] article noted, "Branding has given the Florida effort the benefit of accumulated awareness. Everything we have created builds on the awareness of the marketing components that preceded it."[38(p5)]

Public health professionals often avoid branding because it is so closely associated with commercial applications. However, it is a key component to building—and maintaining—relationships with all of an organization's publics.

## Limited Professional Training in Marketing

Very few public health employees charged with marketing functions have a marketing background, although some have training as health educators or are drawn from communication and public information departments. As might be expected, this lack of experience can lead to poorly conceived marketing efforts, or an excessive dependence on communication when at times adjusting another variable in the marketing mix would accomplish more. For example, if a clinic is underutilized because the hours are inconvenient for clients, all the promotional activities in the world are unlikely to increase usage as much as adjusting the clinic hours to meet client needs.

Similarly, most public health practitioners have limited, if any, training or expertise in advocacy skills, including coalition building, community organizing, media advocacy, and political activity. As the Institute of Medicine (IOM) has noted, "effective public health action for many problems requires organizing the interest groups, not just assessing a problem and determining a line of action based on top-down authority."[39(p122)]

## Better-Financed Competition

The competition may be an unwholesome product, behavior, or policy, but it almost always has more money behind it than the public health effort. This financing often extends beyond the money spent by the product sponsors to create, deliver, and communicate value. For example, tobacco products and alcohol, in particular, make regular appearances in the story lines of television and movie programming; likewise, drug use is often featured in popular music. Although such placements are not always paid for by the obvious competition, they nonetheless create a more pervasive "unhealthy" environment and reinforce the idea that use of such products is normative. In fact, the mass media often portray such product use, particularly cigarette smoking, as far more common than it actually is.

Because public health marketing budgets are often modest at best, when promotional efforts are used it is difficult to attain sufficient reach (percentage of the target audience reached with promotional messages) and frequency (number of times a member of the target audience is reached) to support behavior change.

## Limited Use of and Access to Distribution Channels

The marketing mix variable *place* is often considered inapplicable to social marketing. Yet, many public health and other social marketing efforts underperform or fail precisely because inadequate attention was given to *how* a message, product, or service will reach a target audience member and *where* the person will be when he or she receives a message or needs to engage in the desired behavior—and how aspects of these channels of distribution could facilitate (or impede) the person's ability to take the desired action.

A marketing channel "is a set of interdependent organizations involved in the process of making a product or a service available for use or consumption" and "the route to and relationship with customers."[40(p3)] Channels can disseminate information, handle logistics (transportation, warehousing, delivering products/services at points convenient to customers), and sometimes provide value-added services such as local selling, customization, installation, and so on.[41] Customers engage in a transaction with an expectation of receiving a certain experience (bundle of benefits), and channels of distribution can differentiate a company's offering from a competitor's, thereby providing different customer value. For example, consider buying black coffee at McDonald's versus Starbucks: while the product is somewhat different at each locale, the venues themselves—and therefore the experience—are quite different.

Social marketers (including public health practitioners) need to make greater use of distribution channels to deliver short-term benefits and overcome barriers to behavior change to ensure that healthy behaviors can easily fit into daily lives and to make "good" behaviors available and accessible.[41] For example, someone trying to address childhood obesity might work with elementary schools to ensure that water was always the most available and easily accessed drink; that fruits, vegetables, and other lower-calories, higher-nutrient foods were the most accessible choices at all eating occasions (meals, snacks, parties, extended day programs), and that teachers rewarded students with extra recess or a classroom dance session rather than sweets and sedentary activities—in addition to traditional nutrition education activities and working with school food service to improve offerings.

One of the challenges faced by public health professionals is that they often do not "own" the distribution channels they need to access. However, public health professionals can access channels through judicious use of partnership agreements with public, nonprofit, and private entities.

## The Marketing Process

The marketing process generally follows a defined set of steps, often depicted as a circle to symbolize the iterative nature of the process: everything learned at one stage feeds into the next, and often something learned in a subsequent stage will feed back into an earlier stage. In the example in Figure 22-1, the four major stages of planning, development, implementation, and assessment are depicted, with research and evaluation in the center to illustrate that they play a role in, and provide a strong foundation for, each stage.

**FIGURE 22-1    Stages of Marketing Initiatives**
*Source:* Reprinted from Siegel M, Doner L. *Marketing Public Health: Strategies to Promote Social Change.* Gaithersburg, MD: Aspen Publishers Inc; 1998:200.

Exhibit 22-2 lists the essential activities that take place during each stage. The planning process is extensive because it provides the framework for all subsequent activities. Although portraying marketing as a linear process is the easiest way to present and understand it, the process is not so sequential in practice. For example, planning and development decisions are

**Exhibit 22-2    Planning, Developing, Implementing, and Assessing a Marketing Effort**

---

**Stage 1: Planning**
- Analyze the situation
  - Identify and prioritize problems based on the public health burden.
  - Assess the social change environment, including the competition.
  - Identify interventions most likely to be effective.
- Set goals and objectives; specify behaviors, conditions, or policies to be changed.
- Segment and select target audiences; determine the target populations for each desired social change.
- Understand target audiences.
  - Identify and prioritize basic needs, desires, and values.
  - Identify the current behavior and attributes of the behavior that satisfy those needs, desires, and values.
  - Explore ways of framing the desired behavior to reinforce core values.
- Develop a strategic plan addressing product, price, place, promotion and partners.
  - Redefine the product as offering a desired benefit.
  - Package and position the product as offering the benefit.
- Develop a communication strategy.
  - Frame the communication to reinforce (not to conflict with) the audience's core values.
  - Focus on the promise (the benefit) and support for it.
  - Conduct message concept testing.

**Stage 2: Development**
- Develop product and/or promotion plans.
- Develop prototype products and/or communication materials.
- Pretest with target audience members.
- Refine the products and materials.
- Build in process evaluation measures.

**Stage 3: Implementation**
- Produce the products and materials.
- Coordinate with partners.
- Implement the intervention.
- Conduct a process evaluation.
- Refine the product, materials, and delivery channels as needed.

**Stage 4: Assessment**
- Conduct an outcome evaluation.
- Refine the program.

Source: Reprinted from Siegel M, Doner L. *Marketing Public Health: Strategies to Promote Social Change.* Gaithersburg, MD: Aspen Publishers Inc; 1998:226.

often driven to some degree by limited funds available for development or implementation. Monitoring data may suggest a need to revise the plan or create or revise a tactic, necessitating a return to a previous stage. The following sections discuss fundamental aspects of each stage.

### Planning

A more apt title might be *iterative planning*, because as new knowledge is gained from each planning activity, previous ideas or assumptions often require revision. The major goal of all planning activities is to clearly identify

- The problem that marketing activities will address (e.g., *what* changes need to be made, and *who* needs to make them)
- All possible components of a solution (e.g., *how* changes can be made, and what will facilitate change)
- Of those components, what components the marketing effort will include

One way to do this is to create a model, or map, of how the problem realistically needs to be addressed. This model will help everyone involved identify what individual, social, or policy changes will be necessary to lessen or control the problem. It also helps determine what roles are appropriate for a particular organization and what roles will have to be played by others. The model can be used throughout an initiative to make sure the effort stays focused on the objectives. It is also helpful when crafting evaluation efforts because it provides a blueprint of who is doing what and what the result of each activity should be. Figure 22-2 provides the beginning of such a model for

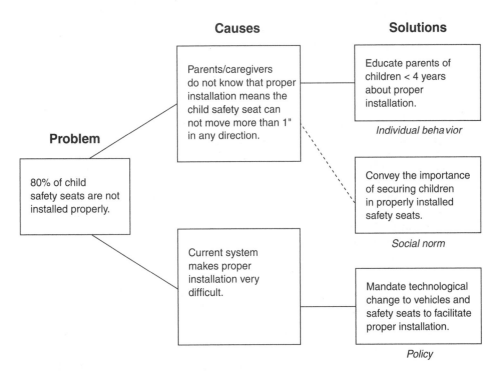

**FIGURE 22-2   Modeling the Child Safety Seat Initiative**

increasing the percentage of child safety seats that are properly installed in passenger cars.

Such a model should begin as a synthesis or depiction of what is learned when the situation is analyzed (see Figure 22-2 and Exhibit 22-3). As the planning process continues, it can be fleshed out and revised: goals and objectives can be added, target audiences can be more carefully defined, and strategies for each component of the solution can be crafted.*

## Problem Definition: Addressing the Real Problem

Many marketing efforts, in public health and in other disciplines, fail because planners do not thoroughly explore and define the problem and its potential solutions. Adequate problem definition requires a thorough understanding of the current behavior, the desired behavior, and the environment—current policies, social norms, and competing behaviors—in which the change will take place.

In the child safety seat example, inadequate problem definition would have occurred if planners had not recognized that two marketing mix variables needed to be addressed: product and promotion. If planners had "blamed" parents and other caregivers for the improper installations without recognizing

Exhibit 22-3    Key Aspects of the Child Restraint System Situation Analysis

---

Problem
- Child restraints are 71% effective in reducing the likelihood of death in motor vehicle crashes. However, actual average effectiveness of restraints in use is 59%, due to
  - Incorrect use
  - Vehicle seat and/or seat belt incompatibility issues
- Consumer frustration with installation and compatibility may lead to eroding confidence in the safety of child restraint systems and decreased usage of the systems.

Causes
- Incorrect use—A 1996 four-state study found that 80% of participants made at least one significant error in installation. Seventy-two percent did not use a locking clip when necessary, or used it incorrectly; 17% used the vehicle seat belt incorrectly.
- Vehicle seat and seat belt incompatibility—Advances in seat and seat belt design features to protect older children and adults have led to increased difficulty with child restraint installation. In consumer clinics (somewhat similar to focus groups) conducted in the United States and Canada, virtually all participants expressed high levels of dissatisfaction with conventional means of attaching child restraints in vehicles.

*Source*: Data from *Federal Motor Vehicle Safety Standards: Child Restraint Systems: Child Restraint Anchorage Systems*. National Highway Traffic Safety Administration; 1999. 64 Fed. Reg. 10785.

---

*More detail on conducting the steps involved in the planning process can be found in other sources.[9,42,43]

that existing product technology made proper installation exceedingly difficult, they might have relied on promotional efforts as a solution. At best, this approach would not be very effective; at worst, it might exacerbate the problem by increasing the number of caregivers who became frustrated or who lost confidence in the safety of existing child restraint systems. In the short term, planners did rely on promotional activities because fixing the product was a multiyear process. (Although one of the initial studies was conducted in 1996, all aspects of the final regulation did not go into effect until 2002, and cars with the pre-2002 technology will remain on the road for years.) Conversely, if they had relied only on changing the product, they probably would not have made as much progress because: (1) not all parents and caregivers have access to the new products, (2) even with the new products, parents and other caregivers still need to know what "properly installed" is, and (3) communicating with parents and caregivers about installing safety seats is likely to influence the social norm regarding their use (e.g., if the target audience constantly hears about the importance of installing the seats correctly, it reminds them to use the seats).

The other half of adequately defining a problem is adequately defining the solutions to the problem—and then determining which of those solutions the organization can actually implement. Ultimately, these solutions become the goals and objectives for the marketing activity. In the child safety seat example, the NHTSA could implement the policy solution (albeit by working with consumer advocacy groups and vehicle and child safety seat manufacturers) and aspects of the individual behavior change and social norm solutions, but the latter require partnerships with many local organizations to be effective. In contrast, an advocacy group would have been wise to concentrate on marketing the policy change to the NHTSA and manufacturers while marketing individual behavior change to parents and caregivers. A local public health agency, on the other hand, might concentrate on promoting individual behavior change through materials, publicity, and local checkpoints.

When selecting approaches to addressing a public health problem, many professionals turn first to communication or education, yet there are many problems that communication or education alone can not solve. Channels of distribution, product/service offerings (if applicable), and means of overcoming barriers also must be considered. If, during the planning process, it is discovered that major policy changes are needed to address the problem adequately, there are three options:

1. Work for the policy changes, or find a partner who can make the policy changes.
2. Proceed with communication and other activities, but carefully limit objectives to what can reasonably be accomplished in the absence of other changes.
3. Allocate resources to a different topic where the organization's efforts can make a greater difference.

When taking the second course, be aware that in some situations promotion will only make matters worse. One example is increasing demand when supply is inadequate, as might have been the case with child restraints: educating consumers about proper installation would drive up demand for it, but the existing child restraint systems could not deliver, ultimately leading to consumer frustration, and potentially, abandonment of the product or efforts to install it properly. Similarly, problems will occur if a local health department wants to promote a new vaccine for children during National Child Health Month, but shipments of it have been delayed. If the promotion effort goes forward as planned, people will be exposed to the promotion and will try to get the vaccine, only to be turned away and told to return when there is more vaccine. They will find the experience frustrating and some will not return, so the promotion will have backfired.

### Understanding How a Behavior or Issue Is Framed

Understanding how the behavior or issue is *framed* in the minds of the target audience(s) is an important aspect of developing useful approaches to solving the problem. Framing involves packaging and positioning an issue to convey a certain meaning.[39,44-47] Frames are

> The broadly shared beliefs, values, and perspectives familiar to the members of a societal culture and likely to endure in that culture over long periods of time, on which individuals and institutions draw in order to give meaning, sense, and normative direction to their thinking and action in policy matters.[45(pxiii)]

Often, frames can be used to define the problem in a different way and suggest solutions to it.[47,48]

It is useful to collect examples of how an issue is being framed and, for each, to identify the core position, metaphor(s), image(s), catch phrases, attribution of responsibility for the problem, implied solutions, and core values being tapped, and then work up alternatives. A similar process can be used to develop possible alternative frames. Table 22-3 presents an abbreviated example; more detail on this process is provided in other sources.[9]

### Role of Theory and Models of Behavior

Once the problem has been clearly defined, theories and models of behavior can be helpful in discerning how best to approach solving it. These theories and models can guide the segmentation and selection of audiences as well as the content of the intervention. Glanz, Rimer, and Lewis's *Health Behavior and Health Education* provides a good overview of many theories and models that can be used to help guide efforts to bring about health behavior change.[49]

Some practitioners shy away from theory, perhaps because the often complex terminology makes it seem inaccessible or inapplicable to the "real world." However, judicious use of theory can keep planners from reinventing the wheel, provide additional support for the recommended approach, and fill in some missing pieces on what to do in a given situation. Applying theory does not have to involve an unfamiliar vocabulary: drawing on various theoretical constructs regarding determinants of behavior, William A. Smith of the Academy for Educational Development argues that the goal should be to make individual behavior changes fun, easy, and popular:[50]

- Fun—Provide perceived benefits the audience cares about.
- Easy—Remove barriers to action; make behavior as simple and accessible as possible.

**TABLE 22-3    Analysis of One Tobacco Industry Frame and One Tobacco Control Frame**

| Frame | "Big Government/ Civil Liberties" | "Nonsmokers' Rights" |
|---|---|---|
| Core position | Big government is interfering with personal lifestyle decisions, taking away smokers' rights. | Nonsmokers have a right to be protected from secondhand smoke in workplaces and public places. |
| Metaphor(s) | Big Brother; prohibition | Environmental toxins; workplace hazards |
| Images | Prohibition era; 1984 | Smoke, hazardous workplaces, chemicals, pollution |
| Catch phrases | Prohibition big government, Big Brother, government off our backs, goes too far, red meat, candy, fat | Nonsmokers rights, health hazard, protection, danger, secondhand, involuntary, passive, smoke-free |
| Attribution of responsibility for the problem | Big government; bureaucracy | Workplace owners, government |
| Implied solutions | Keep government out of tobacco regulation. | Voluntary or legislative policies should restrict smoking in public places. |
| Core values being tapped | Freedom, civil liberties, autonomy, control | Freedom, civil liberties, equality, justice |

*Source:* Adapted from Siegel M, Doner L. *Marketing Public Health: Strategies to Promote Social Change.* Gaithersburg, MD: Aspen Publishers Inc.; 1998:243–244.

- Popular—Influence social norms; help the audience feel that this is something others are doing, particularly others who are important to them.

### Crafting the Plan

As potential solutions (target audiences, the actions they should take, and the means of getting them to take these actions) become clear, a strategic plan can be assembled. Such a plan should be tailored to the situation but typically resembles the outline shown in Exhibit 22-4. The plan closely follows the activities presented in Exhibit 22-2. If multiple approaches are being used (e.g., a policy change and individual behavior changes, as in our example), then separate goals, objectives, target audiences, strategy, and components sections might be developed for each approach. The plan should be used to develop and assess tactics and implementation plans. Also, it (or the executive summary of it) can be shared with partners and other interested parties as a quick way of explaining what the organization is doing.

### Formative Research

"Formative research is foremost. It provides more value for the effort than any other kind of research."[51(p63)]

Exhibit 22-4   Outline of a Strategic Plan

Executive summary
Background and mission
Challenges and opportunities
Goals
Objectives (measurable outcomes)
Target audiences
Core strategy
Components for implementing and monitoring strategy:
   Product and/or service development
   Managing perceived price
   Improving access and channels of distribution (place)
   Promotion (including communication strategy)
   Partnerships
Evaluation

*Source*: Adapted from Siegel M, Doner L. *Marketing Public Health: Strategies to Promote Social Change*. Gaithersburg, MD: Aspen Publishers Inc.; 1998:235.

Marketers place great emphasis on formative research because it underpins how the problem is defined and how strategies to address it are crafted (selection of target audiences, actions they should take, and the approaches that will be used to help them). If a strategy is wrong or incomplete, every tactic can be executed flawlessly, but program objectives are still unlikely to be accomplished. As a result, marketers tend to allocate a large proportion of their research and evaluation dollars to studies that are conducted to understand the problem and the audience, and to develop and assess reactions to proposed strategies, including products, service delivery approaches, messages, and materials.

*Common Marketing Research Methods.*   Marketers tend to rely on a mixture of qualitative and quantitative research. Qualitative techniques typically support the planning and development stages; although as discussed in Chapter 18, they can play important roles in process and outcome evaluation as well. Qualitative research allows the identification of perceived benefits of and barriers to taking a particular action. It is also a good forum for exploring target audience reactions to new or existing products and potential ways of framing messages. Common qualitative methodologies include focus groups and one-on-one, in-depth interviews.[†]

In contrast, *quantitative* techniques provide measures of *how many* members of a population have particular knowledge, engage in a particular behavior, or would be willing to take a specific action. They are particularly useful for obtaining baseline measures and segmenting and selecting audiences; they also can be used to test positioning and messages in some instances. Quantitative methods are most often some type of survey, although observational studies (e.g., observing people and counting how many engage in a particular behavior) or methods such as medical chart review can also fall in this category.

---

[†]Details on qualitative methods and how to use them are provided in other sources.[9,52,53]

Because of the cost and time involved in obtaining solid quantitative data, market researchers often look first to secondary data sources (information that has already been collected for some other purpose). Useful federal and/or state data sources can include the *Behavioral Risk Factor Surveillance System (BRFSS)*, the *Youth Risk Behavior Survey (YRBS)*, the *National Health Interview Survey (NHIS)*, and *the National Health and Nutrition Examination Surveys (NHANES)*.[‡] Useful commercial sources include the annual studies conducted by Mediamark Research Inc. (MRI) and Simmons Market Research Bureau. Some market research companies, such as Claritas Corporation, provide geodemographic segmentation systems that allow neighborhoods to be categorized and mapped according to demographic and lifestyle characteristics. These sources of data are further discussed in Chapter 11.

*Selecting and Understanding Target Audiences.*    Earlier in this chapter, the importance of segmenting and selecting target audiences was presented (see Challenges of Public Health Marketing). Marketers begin selecting target audiences by segmenting the population into groups and then studying each group to determine which one(s) would be the most appropriate target audiences. If possible, it is usually best to segment the population based on its current behavior, or a combination of its current behavior and willingness to make a particular change in it.

One useful exercise is to compare "doers" (those who already engage in the behavior) with "nondoers" (those who do not) to see what other differences exist between the two groups. Often, such an analysis provides insights into the determinants of each group's behavior. These determinants can then be addressed by the marketing initiative. For example, perhaps the child safety seat initiative's program planners discovered that caregivers who install the safety seats properly know that they should not move more than one inch in any direction, and a large percentage of those who install them improperly do not have this knowledge.

Secondary sources may have the necessary variables for a behavioral segmentation; if not, a custom study needs to be conducted. Additional factors to consider when selecting target audience segments are shown in Exhibit 22-5.

It is important to consider the likelihood of progress toward the initiative's objectives when selecting audience segments. For example, the audience

**Exhibit 22-5    Factors Influencing the Selection of Target Audiences**

- Audience size
- Extent to which the group needs or would benefit from the behavior change
- How well available resources can reach the group
- Extent to which the group is likely to respond to the program
- For secondary audiences, the extent to which they influence primary audiences

*Source*: Reprinted from Siegel M and Doner L. *Marketing Public Health: Strategies to Promote Social Change.* Gaithersburg, MD: Aspen Publishers Inc.; 1998:271.

---

[‡]More information on these studies can be found at http://www.cdc.gov.

should be large enough that if a reasonable percentage of the members take action, noticeable progress will be made. Sometimes, practitioners want to choose the group that is most "in need" of a particular action (e.g., their current behavior is farthest from it). But this group may be least likely to respond; choosing a group closer to taking the action may require fewer resources, result in greater progress toward objectives, and positively influence the social norm regarding the behavior.

In the child safety seat example, if only occasional caregivers such as grandparents or baby sitters who have a child safety seat in their vehicle infrequently were targeted, not much progress would be made toward increasing the percentage of child safety seats that are properly installed. Yet this audience might seem to be a logical choice if they are least likely to be familiar with proper installation and therefore most "in need" of the knowledge. Careful selection of audience segments can be particularly critical when the audience is policy makers: persuading those who are undecided, especially if many are, is likely to be far more productive than trying to reach those who are definitely opposed to a change.

Once target audience segments have been selected, they need to be profiled thoroughly to determine the best strategies to help or convince them to take action. In the child safety seat example, the planners took two courses of action: a policy change to improve the product (and therefore make the behavior easier), and education to give people the knowledge they need to engage in the behavior. Next, they needed to figure out how to reach members of the target audience and persuade them to take the action of installing a safety seat correctly. To do this, they needed to understand the benefits and barriers the audience associates with the behavior, where and when to reach the audience, and the types of messages the audience would find compelling. Qualitative research is often used to help craft this understanding.

On the policy side, a consumer preference clinic (somewhat similar to a focus group) was conducted by US and foreign vehicle manufacturers to assess consumer reactions to various technological changes that would enable the seat to attach to an anchorage designed specifically for it. All systems were strongly preferred over existing designs that used vehicle seat belts to attach the restraint to the vehicle. When making its final decision, the NHTSA considered the results of this research, the preferences of vehicle and safety seat manufacturers and other interested parties, cost implications of the various designs, and compatibility with the systems approved or likely to be approved in other countries.

### Framing Messages: Crafting Communication Strategies

Promotional messages are most effective when guided by a carefully crafted communication strategy.

> The communications strategy describes how the behavior or issue will be framed and positioned in the consumer's mind. It spells out the target audience(s), the action they should take and how they will benefit, and how to reach them with messages. It is based on a thorough understanding of the audience and their wants, needs, and values coupled with knowledge of the types of appeals likely to work in a given situation.[9(p312)]

Good communication is focused, specific, personal, and simple. When done properly, it will be compelling to the target audience—whether that audience is some segment of the general public, health professionals, or policy makers. Many professionals recommend drawing a picture (or finding a photograph) to represent the target audience, and then designing communication as though having a conversation with that person. Some version of the following questions helps many commercial and health communicators develop effective communications.[§] Please refer to Chapter 20 for detailed discussion on communication.

- Who should be in the target audience, and what are they like? Demographic characteristics are only the beginning. "What's important to this person? What are his or her feelings, attitudes, and beliefs about the behavior change and its benefits and barriers? What can motivate this person to do something different?"[54(p728)]
- What is the action they should take, and what are they doing now? "Overambition is the pitfall of most strategies."[57(p5)] To select an action, understand the competition (what are they doing now?), and identify from among the possible actions a person could take what the audience perceives to be reasonable.
- What are the obstacles that stand between the audience and the desired behavior? Common barriers include perceived conflicts between the desired action and beliefs, current practice, social norms, or how the issue is typically framed.
- What is the benefit to the audience of engaging in the behavior? Find the most motivating benefit. In most circumstances, personal benefits that will be attained immediately or in the very near future are more compelling than longer-term benefits that may or may not directly reward the target of the communication.
- What is the support for that benefit—what will make it credible to the audience? Support is the reason the benefit outweighs the obstacles. It can take many forms: hard data, demonstrations of how to perform the action (to convey "easy" or increase self-efficacy by showing audience members they can do it), or demonstrations of the valued benefits associated with the action (e.g., a mother feeling like she is "being a good mom" after correctly installing a child safety seat). Executional detail, such as music, colors, design, typeface, and paper stock, or the degree to which people depicted are like target audience members in speech, dress, and action, can all support or detract from the promised benefit.[54]
- What are the best openings for reaching the audience—and are the channels available appropriate for conveying the message? Openings include the times, places, and states of mind when a person is most receptive to a message.[54]
- What image should communication convey? "The symbols, metaphors, and visuals linked to the behavior or positioning of an issue convey image, as do the types of actors, language, and/or music used."[9(p323)] Image tells target audience members whether or not the communication is for them or someone they would like to be.

---

[§]More information on developing effective communications can be found elsewhere.[9,54–56]

When developing a communication strategy, common errors include the following:[9]

- Including multiple actions or framing an issue in multiple ways rather than focusing on one
- Focusing on long-term public health benefits when short-term consumer benefits are more compelling
- Appealing to noncritical values (e.g., good health) rather than core values (freedom, autonomy, control, independence)
- Supporting the message with facts alone when an emotional appeal would be more compelling
- Using mass media to convey complex messages
- Developing strategies for different audiences that conflict or send mixed messages

Activities conducted throughout the planning process (see Exhibit 22-3 and Table 22-3) provide a starting point for determining how an issue or action should be framed and developing the communication strategy. In particular, these activities shed light on how competing behaviors are framed (or on how competitors frame an issue), what the target audience is like, and what openings can be used to reach them. However, some amount of custom formative research (even if it is small and informal due to budget constraints) is generally necessary to determine if audience members think the suggested actions are reasonable, the planners' initial thinking about benefits and barriers is accurate and believable, and the image is appropriate.

## Development, Testing, and Implementation

> In the final analysis, textbooks can offer little on implementation that will improve upon a good plan, an adequate budget, good organizational and policy support, good training and supervision of staff, and good monitoring in the process evaluation stage. . . . The key to success in implementation beyond these six ingredients is experience, sensitivity to people's needs, flexibility in the face of changing circumstances, an eye fixed on long-term goals, and a sense of humor.[42(p205)]

### Selecting Appropriate Tactics

Tactics are the short-term, detailed steps that are used to implement a strategy.[9] Changing a clinic's hours, holding a community event, or producing an ad are all tactics. Selecting tactics for a marketing effort involves considering the model of how change is expected to occur, the marketing strategy, available resources, and the initiative's time line. Because different social change efforts employ a wide range of tactics, it is impossible to review all possible considerations here. However, the following list of questions can be used to help assess the appropriateness of each tactic.

- Is it on strategy? It may be a great idea, but if it doesn't fit with the strategy, save it for another program.
- To what degree does it complement and reinforce other tactics?
- Can it be created and implemented in a time frame that works with the overall time line and with other tactics that may need for it to be in

place before they are put into place (e.g., training staff prior to implementing other program elements)?

- Will the tactic's contribution to achieving objectives be worth its cost?
- For each promotional tactic, what will it contribute to reach and frequency? The goal should be to reach as many target audience members as possible *as often* as possible.
- Does it make sense for the organization to develop or sponsor this tactic, or would it be a better fit for one of the partner organizations?

With complex, multifaceted programs, it is important to have "reality check" meetings periodically to make sure that the various components will work together and reinforce each other conceptually, that nothing has drifted off strategy, that everything can be rolled out in a time line that makes sense, and that each tactic will cost a reasonable amount relative to what it is expected to accomplish.

### Pretesting

Before producing a new product, finalizing a new service, making changes in product or service delivery, or producing messages and materials, pretesting should be conducted with target audience members to ensure optimal results.

*Products and Services.*   If a new product or service will be created, it is desirable to develop a prototype and conduct usability tests prior to production (or, for services, finalizing plans). Usability testing is also a good idea for Internet Web sites. This process can reveal problems, some of which may need to be corrected through design changes; others can be addressed in accompanying instructions. It is wise to test accompanying instructions for any product or service (new or old) included in an initiative, to ensure that directions for use are clear and understandable and that they address common questions and misperceptions.

*Changes in Product or Service Delivery.*   When a new process for obtaining products or services has been designed or an old process has been streamlined, pretesting any forms and pilot testing the process itself can allow areas of confusion or bottlenecks to be identified and resolved prior to wider implementation.

*Messages and Materials.*   Pretesting messages and materials (e.g., advertisements, message points, pamphlets, brochures, instructions, forms, etc.) will not ensure success, but it can identify potential misinterpretations and, for materials, problems with executional details (e.g., readability of typeface or type size, reactions to colors, music, voices, timing, etc.), and can assess the extent to which materials are clear, true to the strategy, and understood by the intended audience. Details on designing, fielding, and analyzing pretests are available in other sources.[9,43]

### Assessment

Evaluation is a critical aspect of marketing. However, marketers use evaluation to *improve* efforts, not just *assess* them. Beyond "How are we doing?" marketers expect evaluation data to help them answer "How can we do better?"

Earlier in this chapter, *formative* research and evaluation were discussed, as was their importance in crafting successful intervention components. This section highlights two additional types of evaluation:

- *Process* evaluation "typically tracks and documents implementation by quantifying what has been done; when, where, and how it was done; and who was reached."[9(p449)] This type of evaluation allows ongoing monitoring and refinement of implementation.
- *Outcome* evaluation (sometimes termed *impact* or *summative* evaluation) examines the degree to which an intervention achieved its objectives or had the effects it was planned to have.

### Importance of Monitoring and Refinement

Marketers use process evaluation data to monitor and refine an intervention constantly once it is in place. Doing so allows tactics to be adjusted in response to changes in audience needs, competitive activities, or environmental factors, thereby maximizing progress toward objectives. Some form of process information should be available for each tactic included in a marketing effort. Ideally, these data will document what was done and also provide information on who was motivated enough to take action as a result. The best way to ensure that adequate monitoring information will be available is to build it into or set it up for each tactic from the beginning. Steckler and Linnan's *Process Evaluation for Public Health Interventions & Research* presents a range of process evaluations and is a useful source of ideas.[58]

### Issues in Evaluating Outcomes

Evaluating the results of public health marketing efforts often is challenging for a number of the following reasons:

- Marketing efforts do not occur in isolation. Because other organizations and secular trends usually address the same social change, it is difficult, and often impossible, to attribute effects to a particular intervention.
- Standard evaluation techniques are not designed to assess interventions that are constantly being refined (e.g., tactics that are not working are altered or dropped, and new tactics may be introduced).
- Measuring statistically significant change may require unreasonable outcome expectations.

How, then, to approach the need to evaluate and assess how well an intervention did or is doing? Consider the following questions when planning an intervention and its corresponding outcome evaluation.[9]

*What Outcomes Are Reasonable to Expect?*    The crucial word here is *reasonable*. Often, public health marketing efforts are expected to attain unrealistically large effects. As Beresford and colleagues noted in discussing population-wide efforts to change eating habits, "The public health model, or population strategy, consists of shifting the entire distribution of a risk factor, including the mean, down. The diminution in risk for a given individual is typically small and may not even be clinically important. Nevertheless, because the entire distribution is affected, the impact on morbidity and mortality can be substantial."[59(p615)]

If large effects are expected, can the intervention be structured so that it is of sufficient intensity and duration to achieve this level of success? Sometimes expectations for large effects have been carried over from expectations for clinical studies. At other times, the power (or lack thereof) of the evaluation drives expectations. For population-wide efforts, measuring statistically significant change can be prohibitively expensive—affordable (smaller) sample sizes have larger margins of error, so larger effects are required before observed changes can be considered statistically significant.

Commercial marketers generally have far greater resources yet expect modest effects. As Fishbein remarked, "Thus, while a condom manufacturer would be more than happy if an advertising campaign increased the company's share of the market by 3% or 4%, a public health intervention that increased condom use by the 3% or 4% probably would be considered a failure."[60(p1075)]

One of the major factors influencing outcome expectations should be the type of intervention. Is it reasonable to expect slow, gradual changes or rapid, large changes? For most public health interventions, an expectation of slow, gradual changes is much more likely.[61] However, it is possible to see large, rapid changes in behaviors that are very easy to change and that result in sharply reduced risks of devastating events (i.e., preventing Reye's syndrome by using an aspirin substitute rather than aspirin, and reducing sudden infant death syndrome by putting babies to sleep on their backs rather than on their stomachs).[62]

*What Type of Evaluation Design is Most Appropriate for the Intervention Setting?*   The gold standard is a randomized controlled trial. That is, target audience members are randomly assigned to treatment and control groups, out-come variables are measured to establish a baseline, the intervention is implemented (usually remaining constant through the implementation period), and outcome variables are measured again. In this way, any differences between the two groups can be attributed to the intervention. Quasi-experimental designs are similar, but assignment to each group is not random. Examples of quasi-experimental designs include community interventions where treatment and control communities are matched on key variables or populations within a community are divided into groups (this approach might be used with a school-based intervention). Chapter 18 provides more discussion on evaluation.

For public health interventions, a frequent problem with any experimental or quasi-experimental approach is what has been termed "the fantasy of untreated control groups."[63(p76)] With many public health initiatives employing communication, education, or marketing techniques, it is very unlikely that members of the control group are receiving no intervention. They may not be receiving a particular organization's intervention, but they are almost certainly receiving something. As Feinlieb observed, "Science does not operate in a vacuum; the forces that operate to justify large, expensive community intervention studies also are operating among the general public to get them to accept the evidence and act on it even before the scientific establishment does."[64(p1697)]

Alternatives to experimental and quasi-experimental designs are designs for full-coverage programs, or programs that are delivered to all members of a target population. Such designs include comparisons between cross-sectional studies (e.g., independent surveys taken at different points in time), panel studies or repeated measures designs (measuring outcomes multiple times among the same group of people), and time-series analyses (taking many measures of outcome variables prior to intervention, using those measures to project what would have happened without the intervention, and comparing the results to repeated measures taken after the intervention). See Hornik's *Public Health Communication: Evidence for Behavior Change* for examples.[65]

*How Will Outcomes be Measured?* The measures should be consistent with what the initiative attempted to accomplish. For example, if the child safety seat intervention was designed to get caregivers to attend a local event where the installation of the safety seat could be checked, the outcome measure should be what percentage of them did that, not what percentage of them have properly installed safety seats.

Measures also need to be sufficiently sensitive to capture progress toward outcomes. Commenting on a community intervention designed to increase safer sex that used as an outcome measure the proportion of young men who engaged in *any* act of unprotected anal sex, Fishbein wrote, "Was it fair to view a person who reduced unprotected sex acts from 100 to 0 as no more of a success than one who reduced such acts from 1 to none?"[60(p1076)]

*What Was Actually Implemented?* A surprising number of outcome evaluations conclude that an approach or program failed when in fact it was not adequately implemented or was not measured as implemented.[66] This disconnect between implementation and evaluation can occur when the evaluation and implementation teams are totally separate and do not communicate well, or when insufficient process evaluation data were collected, so it becomes impossible to determine the degree to which various tactics were implemented.

## Building Marketing Capacity

Elsewhere in this chapter it was noted that few public health practitioners charged with marketing functions have a marketing background. How does a public health professional effectively integrate marketing into public health practice and acquire the necessary training and skills?

To begin, Smith advocates mastering a core of fundamental ideas that can be used to benefit any program of social change:[50]

- Keep the audience and the behavior in the picture constantly (e.g., decide who your audience should be and what you want them to do, then never lose focus of that audience and that behavior).
- Try to make the behavior fun, easy, and popular; using these three words focuses everyone on giving people what they want, in addition to what public health practitioners think they need.
- Base decisions on hard fact, or at least recognize when hard fact is not available, and monitor implementation closely.

Smith calls these core fundamentals *minimalist marketing*, and argues that they can be used to integrate marketing into many of the activities that public health professionals might undertake to support a social change effort, giving the following as examples:[50]

- Organize meetings—Invite members of the audience to meetings; identify and discuss both structural and internal barriers to the behavior to ensure that the real problem is identified.
- Build partnerships—Ask people what they *want* instead of what they *need.*
- Give presentations—Think about the audience, what they expect, and what you want them to do after the meeting.
- Review proposed programs—Focus on the audience and the behavior or action, the benefits that will be offered, and the evidence that the approach is right.
- Speak up—Every interaction is a marketing opportunity if you believe that the person(s) are an audience that you have to understand and offer something to in order to get what you want from them.

Beyond these basic practices, marketing capacity can be built in the following ways:

- Take advantage of opportunities to partner with organizations with more marketing expertise.
- Look for marketing experience when making new hires, including interns, technology transfer fellows, and interagency personnel exchanges.
- Apply for federal or state grants that include training or technical assistance in marketing.
- Look for other relevant training opportunities.
- Require demonstrated marketing experience for appropriate contractors and grantees.
- Invite qualified experts to review grant or contract proposals, or to sit in on strategic planning sessions (get recommendations for such experts from others who are more familiar with marketing whose judgment you trust).
- See if a local college or university class would consider working on an initiative as class project.

For those who are interested in learning more about the marketing process and its applications in public health, the University of South Florida's School of Public Health sponsors an annual conference, Social Marketing in Public Health (held every June), and a variety of training sessions in conjunction with the conference and at other times during the year. In addition, a number of graduate schools include one or more social marketing classes.

## Using Marketing Approaches on Limited Budgets

Planning, designing, implementing, and assessing large-scale, sophisticated marketing initiatives require a lot of training and experience in a variety of disciplines—and a lot of money. But not all public health problems require elaborate, highly expert marketing efforts or vast resources.[50]

Although the importance of adequate formative research has been emphasized, many local and state programs, in particular, do not have the funding to conduct extensive primary research. In such a situation, it is best to look for research that has already been conducted on the topic. Often, other states, the federal government, or other organizations are addressing the same topic and may have conducted studies that will inform your initiative, even if they are not a perfect fit. Involving members of the potential audience(s) in planning and design can be helpful, as long as it is remembered that individual opinions can not be considered representative of an entire population. Audience members can also serve as a "reality check" for tactical ideas and can review materials for cultural and language appropriateness, relevance, and impact. Finally, depending on the target audience, small-scale pretesting can consist of a few intercept interviews conducted where people already gather—for example, a healthcare facility waiting room, senior center, community center, or church. A number of books provide more detailed guidance.[9,43,67]

Local community resources can sometimes provide help with developing tactics. For example, many graduate students are interested in freelance projects. College or university professors of marketing, marketing research, advertising, and public relations often look for real-world class projects, although they often proceed more slowly than paid contractors, and their involvement generally will be confined to a quarter or semester. Some students might be interested in an ongoing internship for the experience it would provide. Another option is local professionals who may be willing to donate some time pro bono, perhaps in exchange for recognition of their contributions.

## Chapter Review

1. Marketing can be distinguished from other strategies for influencing health status and policy change by its emphasis on the following:
   - Exchange
   - Self-interest
   - Behavior and policy change
   - Competition
   - Consumer orientation and audience segmentation
   - Formative and process evaluation
   - Program components beyond communication (e.g., product, price, and place)
2. Product, price, place, and promotion constitute the marketing mix— the group of variables that a marketer can alter to achieve the desired public health outcome of behavior change.
   - The *product* is the specific behavior change, good, service, or program of interest.
   - The *price* is the cost that must be borne by the target audience in terms of monetary expenditure, time, discomfort, inconvenience, and so forth.
   - The *place* refers to channels of distribution, including the outlets through which the product is available or situations in which behavior changes can be made.
   - The *promotion* involves some combination of advertising, media relations, promotional events, advocacy, and entertainment used to communicate with target audience members about the product.

3. Public health organizations confront a number of challenges in marketing interventions and policies to the intended target audience, including the following:
   - Intangible products
   - Nonmonetary costs
   - Extreme levels of audience involvement, from very low to very high
   - Unfavorable states of demand within the target audience
   - Lack of marketing orientation within the organization
   - Limited use of branding to build relationships
   - Limited professional training in marketing within the organization
   - Better-financed competition
   - Limited use of and access to distribution channels
4. The marketing process consists of four major activities: planning, development, implementation, and assessment. Each of these major activities is facilitated and supported by research and evaluation.
5. Marketers rely on information from a combination of qualitative and quantitative research activities to design appropriate marketing strategies. *Qualitative* research activities often involve focus groups and key informant interviews conducted with members of the target audience. *Quantitative* research activities typically involve surveys of the target population and the use of secondary data that reveal attitudes and behaviors of the target population.
6. Understanding how a behavior or health issue is *framed* in the minds of the target audience is an important aspect of developing a successful marketing strategy. Framing involves packaging and positioning an issue to convey a specific meaning.
7. Key steps in developing and implementing a marketing process include the following:
   - Determine what changes need to be made, who needs to make them, and how they can be made effectively.
   - Set realistic marketing goals and objectives.
   - Segment, select, and profile target audience(s).
   - Develop a strategic plan addressing product, price, place, and promotion (including how to frame messages).
   - Develop and pretest prototype products, tactics, and/or materials.
   - Implement intervention, using process evaluation to monitor and refine as needed.
   - Assess outcomes and refine efforts as needed.

# References

1. Grier S, Bryant CA. Social marketing in public health. *Annu Rev Public Health*. 2005;26:319–339.
2. Hill R. The marketing concept and health promotion: a survey and analysis of "recent health promotion" literature. *Soc Marketing Q*. 2001;2:29–53.
3. Maibach EW, Rothschild M, Novelli W. Social marketing. In: Glanz K, Rimer B, Lewis FM, eds. *Health Behavior and Health Education: Theory, Research and Practice*. Indianapolis, IN: Jossey-Bass; 2002:437–461.
4. American Marketing Association. Available at: http://www.marketing power.com/content4620.php. Accessed November 10, 2005.

5. Rothschild ML. Carrots, sticks and promises: a conceptual framework for the management of public health and social issue behaviors. *J Marketing.* 1999;63:24–37.

6. Roccella EJ. The contributions of public health education toward the reduction of cardiovascular disease mortality: experiences from the national high blood pressure education program. In: Hornick RC, ed. *Public Health Communication: Evidence for Behavior Change.* Mahwah, NJ: Lawrence Erlbaum Associates; 2002.

7. Potter LD, Duke JC, Nolin MJ, Judkins D, Huhman M. *Evaluation of the CDC VERB Campaign: Findings from the Youth Media Campaign Longitudinal Survey, 2002–2003.* Atlanta, Ga: CDC; 2004.

8. Farrelly MC, Healton CG, Davis KC, Messeri P, Hersey JC, Haviland ML. Getting to the truth: evaluating national tobacco countermarketing campaigns. *Am J Public Health.* 2002;92:901–907.

9. Siegel M, Doner L. *Marketing Public Health: Strategies to Promote Social Change.* Gaithersburg, Md: Aspen Publishers Inc; 1998.

10. Pirani S, Reizes T. The Turning Point Social Marketing National Excellence Collaborative: integrating social marketing into routine public health practice. *J Public Health Manage Pract.* 2005;11(2):131–138.

11. US Centers for Disease Control and Prevention. Public opinion about public health–California and the United States, 1996. *MMWR.* 1998;47:69–73.

12. Kroger F, McKenna JW, Shepherd M, Howze EH, Knight DS. Marketing public health: the CDC experience. In: Goldberg ME, Fishbein M, Middlestadt SE, eds. *Social Marketing: Theoretical and Practical Perspectives.* Mahwah, NJ: Lawrence Erlbaum Associates; 1997:267–290.

13. Centers for Disease Control and Prevention. Futures Initiative. Available at: http://www.cdc.gov/futures/index.htm. Accessed November 2, 2005.

14. Centers for Disease Control and Prevention. National Center for Health Marketing mission statement. Available at: http://www.cdc.gov/maso/pdf/NCHMfs.pdf. Accessed November 2, 2005.

15. Evans RG, Barer ML, Marmor TR, eds. *Why Are Some People Healthy and Others Not? The Determinants of Health of Populations.* New York, NY: Aldine DeGruyter; 1994.

16. Lee PR, Estes CL, eds. *The Nation's Health.* 5th ed. Sudbury, Mass: Jones and Bartlett; 1997.

17. Levine S, Feldman JJ, Elinson J. Does medical care do any good? In: Mechanic D, ed. *Handbook of Health, Health Care, and the Health Professions.* New York, NY: Free Press; 1983:394–404.

18. Turnock BJ. *Public Health: What It Is and How It Works.* Gaithersburg, Md: Aspen Publishers Inc; 1997.

19. WIC decreases Medicaid costs, USDA study shows. *Nutr Week.* 1990; 20(41):6–7.

20. US Centers for Disease Control and Prevention. Achievements in public health, 1900–1999: control of infectious diseases. *MMWR.* 1999;48: 621–629.

21. Tesh SN. Hidden arguments: political ideology and disease prevention policy. In: Schwartz HD, ed. *Dominant Issues in Medical Sociology.* 3rd ed. New York, NY: McGraw-Hill; 1994:519–529.

22. Mallozzi J. Consumer advocacy in Medicare HMOs. *States of Health.* 1996;6(8):1–9.

23. Bickel WK, Vuchinich RE, eds. *Reframing Health Behavior Change with Behavioral Economics.* Mahwah, NJ: Lawrence Erlbaum; 2000.

24. Prochaska JO, Redding CA, Evers KE. The transtheoretical model and stages of change. In: Glanz K, Rimer BK, Lewis FM, eds. *Health Behavior*

*and Health Education: Theory, Research and Practice.* 2nd ed. San Francisco, Calif: Jossey-Bass Publishers; 1997:60–84.

25. Baranowski T, Perry CL, Parcel Guy S. How individuals, environments, and health behavior interact: social cognitive theory. In: Glanz K, Rimer BK, Lewis FM, eds. *Health Behavior and Health Education: Theory, Research and Practice.* 2nd ed. San Francisco, Calif: Jossey-Bass; 1997: 153–178.

26. Kotler P, Andreasen AR. *Strategic Marketing for Non-Profit Organizations.* 5th ed. Upper Saddle River, NJ: Prentice-Hall; 1996.

27. National Cancer Institute. *5 A Day for Better Health: NCI Media Campaign Strategy.* Bethesda, Md: NCI; 1993.

28. Andreasen AR. *Marketing Social Change: Changing Behavior to Promote Health, Social Development, and the Environment.* San Francisco, Calif: Jossey-Bass; 1995.

29. Lefebvre RC, Lurie D, Goodman LS, Weinberg L, Loughrey K. Social marketing and nutrition education: inappropriate or misunderstood. *J Nutr Educ.* 1995;27(3):146–150.

30. National Highway Traffic Safety Administration. *Patterns of Misuse of Child Safety Seats: Final Report.* Washington, DC: National Highway Traffic Safety Administration; 1996. Rep. No. DOT HS 808–440.

31. National Highway Traffic Safety Administration. *Federal Motor Vehicle Safety Standards; Child Restraint Systems; Child Restraint Anchorage Systems.* 64 Fed. Reg. 10785; 1999.

32. Rothschild ML. Marketing communications in nonbusiness situations or why it's so hard to sell brotherhood like soap. *J Marketing.* 1979;43:11–20.

33. Rangan VK, Karim S, Sandberg SK. Do better at doing good. *Harvard Business Rev.* 1996;74:42–54.

34. Hastings G. Social marketers of the world unite, you have nothing to lose but your shame. *Soc Marketing Q.* 2003;9(4):14–21.

35. Mark M, Pearson CS. *The Hero and the Outlaw: Building Extraordinary Brands Through the Power of Archetypes.* New York, NY: McGraw-Hill; 2001.

36. McDivitt J, et al. Innovations in Social Marketing Conference Proceedings Session II: is there a role for branding in social marketing? *Soc Marketing Q.* 2003;9(3):11–17.

37. Kotler P, Armstrong G. *Principles of Marketing.* 10th ed. Upper Saddle River, NJ: Pearson/Prentice Hall; 2004.

38. Hicks JJ. The strategy behind Florida's 'truth' campaign. *Tobacco Control.* 2001;10:3–5.

39. Chapman S, Lupton D. *The Fight for Public Health: Principles and Practice of Media Advocacy.* London, UK: BMJ Publishing Group; 1994.

40. Coughlan AT, Anderson E, Stern LW, El-Ansary AI. *Marketing Channels.* 6th ed. Englewood Cliffs, NJ: Prentice-Hall; 2001.

41. Strand J, Rothschild ML, Nevin JR. 'Place' and channels of distribution. *Soc Marketing Q.* 2004;10:8–13.

42. Green LW, Kreuter MW. *Health Promotion Planning: An Educational and Environmental Approach.* 2nd ed. Mountain View, Calif: Mayfield; 1991.

43. National Cancer Institute. *Making Health Communication Programs Work: A Planner's Guide.* Bethesda, Md: NCI; 2002. NIH Pub. No. 02-5145.

44. Entman R. Framing: toward clarification of a fractured paradigm. *J Comm.* 1993;43:51–58.

45. Schon DA, Rein M. *Frame Reflection: Toward the Resolution of Intractable Policy Controversies.* New York, NY: Basic Books; 1994.

46. Wallack L, Dorfman L. Media advocacy: a strategy for advancing policy and promoting health. *Health Educ Q.* 1996;23:293–317.

47. Wallack L, Dorfman L, Jernigan D, Themba M. *Media Advocacy and Public Health: Power for Prevention*. Newbury Park, Calif: Sage Publications; 1993.

48. Watzlawick P, Weakland JH, Fisch R. *Change: Principles of Problem Formation and Problem Resolution*. New York, NY: Norton; 1974.

49. Glanz K, Rimer BK, Lewis FM, eds. *Health Behavior and Health Education: Theory, Research and Practice*. 3rd ed. San Francisco, Calif: Jossey-Bass; 2002.

50. Smith B. Notes from the field: marketing with no budget. *Soc Marketing Q*. 1999;5(2):6–11.

51. Balch GI, Sutton SM. Keep me posted: a plea for practical evaluation. In: Goldberg ME, Fishbein M, Middlestadt SE, eds. *Social Marketing: Theoretical and Practical Perspectives*. Mahwah, NJ: Lawrence Erlbaum Associates; 1997:61–74.

52. Krueger RA. *Focus Groups: A Practical Guide for Applied Research*. 2nd ed. Thousand Oaks, Calif: Sage Publications; 1994.

53. Morgan DL, Krueger RA. *The Focus Group Kit*. Vols. 1-6. Thousand Oaks, Calif: Sage Publications; 1998.

54. Sutton SM, Balch GI, Lefebvre RC. Strategic questions for consumer-based health communications. *Public Health Rep*. 1995;110:725–733.

55. Maibach E, Parrott RL, eds. *Designing Health Messages: Approaches from Communication Theory and Public Health Practice*. Thousand Oaks, Calif: Sage Publications; 1997.

56. O'Sullivan GA, Yonkler JA, Morgan W, Merritt AP. *A Field Guide to Designing a Health Communication Strategy*. Baltimore, Md: Johns Hopkins Bloomberg School of Public Health/Center for Communication Programs; 2003.

57. Roman K, Maas J. *How To Advertise*. 2nd ed. New York, NY: St. Martin's Press; 1992.

58. Steckler A, Linnan L, eds. *Process Evaluation for Public Health Interventions and Research*. San Francisco, Calif: Jossey-Bass; 2002.

59. Beresford SA, Curry SJ, Kristal AR, Lazovich D, Fenq Z, Wagner EH. A dietary intervention in primary care practice: The Eating Patterns Study. *Am J Public Health*. 1997;87:610–616.

60. Fishbein M. Editorial: great expectations, or do we ask too much from community-level interventions? *Am J Public Health*. 1996;86:1075–1076.

61. Kristal AR. Choosing appropriate dietary data collection methods to assess behavior changes. In: Doner L, ed. *Charting the Course for Evaluation: How Do We Measure the Success of Nutrition Education and Promotion in Food Assistance Programs? Summary of Proceedings*. Alexandria, Va: USDA Food and Nutrition Service; 1997:39–41.

62. Hornik R. Public health education and communication as policy instruments for bringing about changes in behavior. In: Goldberg ME, Fishbein M, Middlestadt SE, eds. *Social Marketing: Theoretical and Practical Perspectives*. Mahwah, NJ: Lawrence Erlbaum Associates; 1997:45–58.

63. Durlak JA. *School-Based Prevention Programs for Children and Adolescents*. Thousand Oaks, Calif: Sage Publications; 1995.

64. Feinlieb M. Editorial: new directions for community intervention studies. *Am J Public Health*. 1996;86:1696–1698.

65. Hornik RC, ed. *Public Health Communication: Evidence for Behavior Change*. Mahwah, NJ: Lawrence Erlbaum; 2002.

66. Basch CE, Sliepcevich EM, Gold RS, Duncan DF, Kolbe LJ. Avoiding type III errors in health education program evaluations: a case study. *Health Educ Q*. 1985;12:315–331.

67. Andreasen AR. *Marketing Research That Won't Break the Bank*. San Francisco, Calif: Jossey-Bass; 2002.

# CHAPTER 23

# ROLES AND RESPONSIBILITIES OF PUBLIC HEALTH IN DISASTER PREPAREDNESS AND RESPONSE

Linda Young Landesman*
Cynthia B. Morrow

## Chapter Overview

Public health has broad responsibilities to prepare for and respond to disasters. Carrying out these responsibilities effectively requires a multiorganizational response. Key among these responsibilities are disaster epidemiology and assessment, which are used as managerial tools as well as instruments of scientific investigation. Public health organizations also play essential roles in managing the psychosocial effects of disasters and in managing environmental resources to ensure disaster preparedness. The threat of bioterrorism and emerging infectious disease, such as pandemic flu, creates new risks and responsibilities for public health organizations. Although the challenges of managing environmental health threats are greater in developing countries than in the United States, essential elements of public health administration—including the management of food, water, and waste—can be compromised substantially in the most devastating domestic disasters, creating imperatives for disaster preparedness.

Population-based management requires strong public health preparedness. Disasters have significant negative consequences for the community, resulting in increased morbidity and mortality, with both physical and psychological impacts that may be reduced with adequate intervention. Public health professionals should augment their ability to respond to disasters for the following reasons:

- The occurrence of natural disasters is increasing.
- There is a ubiquitous risk across the United States.

*The author wishes to acknowledge the work of the coauthors on the previous version of this chapter: Josephine Malilay, Richard A. Bissell, Steven M. Becker, Les Roberts, and Michael S. Ascher.

**657**

- Disasters have negative impacts on health, but these impacts may be mitigated by a strong public health infrastructure.
- The effects of disasters will escalate, generating an increased need for public health intervention.
- Public health has the expertise to help communities handle the most common health-related problems in the aftermath of a disaster.

Across the globe, mankind is experiencing an increase in natural disasters, as evidenced by events in recent years.[1,2] A disaster a day, on average, occurs somewhere in the world where external international assistance is required. In 2004 alone, 241,400 people died from natural disasters in 123 countries worldwide. As a consequence of these disasters, more than 1.45 million people were affected and $103 billion was lost in property damage.[3] One of the deadliest disasters in modern history occurred on December 26, 2004, when the Sumatra-Andaman earthquake, the world's fifth-largest quake to occur in a century, struck the Indian Ocean. This earthquake, with a magnitude of 9.15 and the second largest ever recorded on a seismograph, generated a tsunami that destroyed coastal areas in Indonesia, Sri Lanka, India, Thailand, and as far away as South Africa, killing more than 225,000 people.[3] Similarly, in October 2005, an earthquake decimated parts of Pakistan. The earthquake and aftershocks have killed over 73,000 people, injured an estimated 75,000, and destroyed the health system, leaving fewer than half of the medical centers functional.[3,4] One of the most devastating natural disasters in US history occurred in August 2005 when Hurricane Katrina claimed approximately 1200 lives. Parts of Louisiana, Mississippi, and Alabama were the hardest hit. Katrina was the most costly hurricane on record with damages estimated at $75 billion in the New Orleans area alone.[5] All of these events resulted in the need for public health intervention with diverse populations for prolonged periods.

Understanding the global need for strong public health preparedness, this chapter will review past and current threats to describe how public health professionals can intervene effectively with both natural and man-made disasters.

## Definitions

Disasters have been defined as ecologic disruptions, or emergencies, of a severity and magnitude resulting in deaths, injuries, illness, and/or property damage that can not be effectively managed by the application of routine procedures or resources and that result in a call for outside assistance. As the field of disaster study evolved, a common set of vocabulary emerged as well, notably distinguishing among hazards, emergencies, and disasters.[6]

- *Hazards* present the probability of the occurrence of a disaster caused by a natural phenomenon (e.g., earthquake, tropical cyclone), by failure of man-made sources of energy (e.g., nuclear reactor, industrial explosion), or by uncontrolled human activity (e.g., conflicts, overgrazing).
- *Emergencies* are typically any occurrence that requires an immediate response.[6] These events can be the result of nature (e.g., hurricanes, tornados, and earthquakes), they can be caused by technological or

manmade error (e.g., nuclear accidents, bombing, and bioterrorism), or
they can be the result of emerging diseases (e.g., West Nile virus in
New York City).

* *Natural disasters* are rapid, sudden-onset phenomena with profound
  effects, such as earthquakes, floods, tropical cyclones, and tornadoes.
  *Man-made disasters* are technological events not caused by natural
  hazards, such as fire, chemical spills and explosions, and airplane
  crashes. A type of man-made disaster, called a complex emergency, includes armed conflict and mass migration. No clear demarcation exists
  between the two categories. For instance, fire may be the result of
  arson, a man-made activity, but may also occur secondarily to earthquake events, particularly in urban areas where gas mains may be
  damaged. With increasing technological development worldwide, a category of disasters known as *natural–technological,* or *na-tech, disasters,* has been described in the literature. Na-tech disasters refer to
  natural disasters that create technological emergencies, such as urban
  fires resulting from seismic motion or chemical spills resulting from
  floods.[7]

The life cycle of a disaster event is typically known as the disaster continuum, or emergency management cycle. In all phases of the disaster continuum (preimpact, impact, and postimpact) the actions taken by public
health, emergency management officials, and the population at risk can reduce or prevent injury, illness, or death. The basic phases of disaster management include mitigation or prevention, warning and preparedness, response,
and recovery. *Mitigation* includes the measures that are taken to reduce the
harmful effects of a disaster by attempting to limit impacts on human health
and economic infrastructure. Although prevention may refer to preventing a
disaster from occurring, such as cloud seeding to stimulate rain in fire situations, in public health terms, *prevention* refers to actions that may prevent
further loss of life, disease, disability, or injury. *Warning* or forecasting refers
to the monitoring of events to look for indicators that signify when and
where a disaster might occur and what the magnitude might be. In *preparedness,* officials or the public itself plan a response to potential disasters and,
in so doing, lay the framework for recovery.

In the United States, the *response* to disasters is organized through multiple jurisdictions, agencies, and authorities. The term *emergency management*
is used to refer to these activities. The emergency management field organizes
its activities by sectors such as fire, police, and emergency medical services
(EMS). The response phase of a disaster encompasses relief and is followed by
recovery and rehabilitation or reconstruction. *Emergency relief* focuses attention on saving lives, providing first aid, restoring emergency communications
and transportation systems, and providing immediate care and basic needs to
survivors, such as food and clothing or medical and emotional care. *Recovery*
includes actions for returning the community to normal, such as repairing infrastructure, damaged buildings, and critical facilities. *Rehabilitation* or *reconstruction* encompasses activities that are taken to counter the effects of the
disaster on long-term development.[8]

Domestically, there are 40–70 presidential disaster declarations per year.
The Stafford Act, passed by Congress in 1988, provides for orderly assistance

by the federal government to state and local governments to help them carry out their responsibilities in managing major disasters and emergencies.[9] A disaster declaration must precede any federal aid whereby states make a request for federal assistance to activate a declaration. Most presidential declarations are made immediately following impact. However, if the consequences of a disaster are imminent and warrant limited predeployment actions to lessen or avert the threat of a catastrophe, a state's governor may submit a request even before the disaster has occurred. Although rarely used, the president may exercise his authority in certain emergencies and make a disaster declaration prior to state request in order to expedite the sending of federal resources. Under the Stafford Act, the president may provide federal resources, medicine, food and other consumables, work and services, and financial assistance.

Disasters pose a number of unique healthcare problems that have little counterpart in the routine practice of emergency health care. Examples include the need for warning and evacuation of residents, widespread urban search and rescue, triage and distribution of casualties, having to function within a damaged or disabled healthcare infrastructure, and coordination among multiple jurisdictions, among all levels of government, and among private-sector organizations. To be effective managers, public health professionals must be knowledgeable about unfamiliar information such as the lexicon of emergency management and the science of engineering and must be competent in a specialized set of skills because disasters pose unique healthcare problems. For example, although temporary deficiencies in resources may occur at certain times in any disaster, resource problems in US disasters more often relate to how assets are used or distributed rather than to deficiencies.[10] In a foundational study of the impact of 29 major mass casualty disasters on hospitals, only 6% of the involved hospitals had supply shortages, and only 2% had personnel shortages.[11]

## Natural Disasters

Residents of the United States share a ubiquitous risk.[12] Across the United States, a massive number of people are at risk from three classes of natural disasters: floods, earthquakes, and hurricanes. There are more than 6000 communities with populations of 2500 or more persons located in flood plains that have been highly developed as living and working environments.[13] At least 70 million people face significant risk of death or injury from earthquakes because they live in the 39 states that are seismically active. In California alone, if a single major earthquake occurs, similar to nine others that occurred in the state over the past 150 years, there could be 20,000 deaths, 100,000 injuries, and economic losses totaling more than $100 billion.[14] Other parts of the country face serious risk because more than 3 million people live within a 75-mile radius of the New Madrid fault in the Midwest.[15] Even in Utah there is a 20% probability that a large earthquake of a magnitude of 7.5 will occur on some segment of the Wasatch front within the next 50 years.[16]

More than a third of the US population live in coastal areas of the United States, including the Great Lakes region. By the year 2010, the coastal population will have grown from 80 million people in 1960 to more than 127 million people–an increase of 60% nationwide.[17] The significance of this shift is evident when the risk posed by hurricanes alone is examined. Because of climatic changes in western Africa, hurricane activity along the Atlantic Coast and the Gulf of Mexico is expected to become as frequent as that which occurred between 1940–1950.[2] During that decade, three category 4–5 hurricanes struck Miami, New Orleans, and the Gulf Coast. The 2005 Atlantic hurricane season was the most active season on record with 28 storms, including 15 hurricanes. Of the seven major hurricanes that were formed during this season, four (Dennis, Katrina, Rita, and Wilma) hit the United States.[18] The National Oceanic and Atmospheric Administration has noted an increasing trend in hurricane activity since 1995, consistent with a multidecadal climate pattern that is predicted to last for many more years.

Many lessons can be learned about the public health role from natural disasters of the past. For example, following the 1993 floods in the Midwest, victims increased their use of primary health care and experienced long-term impediments to their access to health care.[19] Local health departments (LHDs) in Missouri understood the need for involvement in preparedness efforts because they experienced difficulties in collecting and using assessment information, coordination was burdensome, and there were interorganizational impediments to an effective response.[20] The 1995 heat wave in Chicago is another natural disaster where high mortality demonstrated the need for standardized methodologies to enable geographic comparisons across the country.[21]

## Man-made Disasters

Man-made or technological disasters can also have devastating impacts on the public's health. The most shocking US man-made disaster occurred in 2001, with the collapse of the World Trade Center in New York City after a terrorist attack. Over 2600 people died at the World Trade Center, 125 died at the Pentagon, and 256 died on the four planes involved in this coordinated attack.[22] Further, many who witnessed the events or participated in the recovery suffer emotional and/or physical problems even 5 years later. Much about the role of public health has also been learned from earlier man-made disasters. The 1992 civil unrest in Los Angeles caused 53 deaths, more than 2000 injuries, and destruction or closure to 15 county health centers, 45 pharmacies, and 38 medical and dental offices. There were also significant impacts to the quality of water, to hazardous materials and solid waste, and to protecting sources of food. Because widespread burning, as occurred in the civil unrest, can release hazardous materials into the air, almost 3000 sites were surveyed for release of hazardous waste.[23]

The actual and potential effects of man-made disasters will likely escalate, generating an increased need for public health intervention as the world's population grows, as population density increases, and as technology becomes more sophisticated. The need for public health information has spurred the development of readily available guidance.[24,25]

## Public Health Personnel

Worldwide, the growing number of humanitarian emergencies has resulted in an expanding need for skilled public health professionals. The application of public health principles in a domestic response differs from public health practice in an international response, but the competencies required of the profession are the same. The tasks involved in fostering the development of community self-sufficiency are also functionally different in the United States than in international development. In developed countries, the medical response for emergency care is well organized through EMS. In developing countries, that infrastructure often doesn't exist. In developing countries, public health personnel play a key role because virtually all of the problems resulting from disasters are related to the health of the populations. In complex humanitarian emergencies, public health personnel perform the following:

- Conduct initial assessments of health needs.
- Design and establish health activities.
- Plan for the delivery of services.
- Establish refugee camps.
- Provide and monitor food supplies.
- Supervise and monitor environmental health activities.
- Monitor the protection of human rights.

Public health can help communities handle the most common health-related problems. There are four domains where public health expertise is superior to that of other professionals involved in disaster preparedness and response. Public health officials are trained to conduct *assessments,* to survey the impacted site and determine the scope of damage and subsequent impacts on the community and the population. Using the management information systems that public health officials have developed throughout the healthcare industry, public health professionals are well prepared to *share information.* Public health can build on the *triage* procedures used in emergency medicine to help other responders prioritize both medical and public health problems. Finally, public health's knowledge of *casualty distribution* will facilitate the development of procedures for distributing patients needing care and for setting up "point of dispensing" sites.

Disaster preparedness poses the quintessential public health dilemma—how to motivate people to prevent disaster-related health problems. It is human nature to say, "A major disaster will never happen here" and to fail to prepare. Healthcare organizations often do not give high priority to preparing for disastrous events, which are rare, when the general financial environment for health care is fragile. Furthermore, the benefits of preparedness often are not evident until after a disaster has occurred. In addition, economic constraints are often coupled with public apathy. Social scientists have noted that the public's perception of risk is often not correlated with actual risk, and that risks are usually downplayed. Many people continue to live in flood plains, even after repeated floods, and millions of people move to areas that are located on earthquake faults.

However, the benefits of effective prevention are demonstrated in a comparison of the morbidity and mortality statistics of Hurricane Andrew (Florida, 1992) and the hurricane that struck, without warning, off the Gulf Coast of Texas in 1900. Due to successful prediction, warning, and evacuation, actual deaths following Andrew were less than two dozen. By contrast, in Texas 90 years earlier, 6000 people were killed and 5000 were injured.[26] As tragic as the outcomes of Hurricane Katrina were, many deaths were averted because of the warning and mass evacuation that took place in the days preceding the hurricane, again demonstrating the benefits of prevention. Unfortunately, socioeconomically disadvantaged individuals were disproportionately affected by the disaster, in part due to their inability to evacuate because of lack of available resources.

In recent years, there have been numerous opportunities for disaster-related public health interventions. In two examples, strong planning was evident when the Los Angeles Department of Health provided important services following the 1994 Northridge earthquake and the New York City Department of Health and Mental Health was crucial to the recovery of New York City following the collapse of the World Trade Center in 2001. In both cases public health intervened when there were numerous concerns: environmental (e.g., water, air, sewage), clinical (e.g., personal and mental health, healthcare facilities, clinical operations), and educational (public information about safety, health, and environmental concerns).[27,28]

## History of Public Health's Role

Although public health is late in contributing to disaster preparedness and response, epidemiology made an early contribution to the domain of disaster research. Noji first detailed the course of epidemiology's research contribution.[29] In 1957, Saylor and Gordon suggested using epidemiologic parameters to define disasters.[30] Almost a decade later, the Centers for Disease Control and Prevention (CDC) helped develop techniques for the rapid assessment of nutritional status in Nigeria. The 1970s brought the establishment of the Centre for Research on Epidemiology of Disasters in Belgium and specialized units within the World Health Organization (WHO) and the Pan American Health Organization (PAHO). The science of public health has now begun to show that variations in morbidity and mortality from one country to another are often due to differences in building standards and population density rather than the magnitude of an earthquake. This is demonstrated by a comparison of the impacts of recent earthquakes. In California, where antiseismic building and land use codes are well enforced, the Northridge earthquake of 1994 resulted in 57 deaths and almost 9200 serious injuries.[27] In contrast, in Armenia, with poor construction and antiseismic regulations insufficient and poorly enforced, an earthquake of lesser magnitude killed 25,000 people and injured more than 100,000. The August 1999 earthquake in Turkey resulted in a variable rate of collapse of buildings that were built side by side. The standards used for construction were the determinate factor for a structure's survival. Finally, in the tsunami following the 2004 Sumatra-Andaman earthquake, of the 225,000 deaths, it is not known how many could have been saved by warning systems that advise residents to seek higher ground.

The earliest investigations of disaster response were conducted by sociologists who studied organizational behavior under stress. Other contributions have been made by psychologists, management scientists, architects, engineers, economists, and public administrators. Since the early 1980s, there has been increased attention and interest in organizing a public health response to disasters and conducting studies within the public health discipline. The eruption of Mt. St. Helens in 1980 accelerated the involvement of the US federal government in organizing a response.[31,32] The United Nations (UN) declared the 1990s as the disaster decade, International Decade for Natural Disaster Reduction, due to continued human losses across the globe.[33] The declaration for the decade spurred the development of educational and research programs in all phases of disaster management by a broad variety of academic disciplines. The decade came to an end on December 31, 1999, and was succeeded by the International Strategy for Disaster Reduction, as adopted by resolution 54/219 of the General Assembly of the UN.[34]

Prior to the recent US effort to enhance public health preparedness for bioterrorism, the profession has reacted slower than other disciplines in organizing professional activities. In many locales across the country, the medical/health efforts of preparedness were not coordinated as part of the community's disaster response. Health departments were called in as an afterthought to handle problems that were part of their domain, rather than as part of the team planning the response. Federal recognition of the need for public health intervention resulted in directed federal funding for departments of health to improve their core abilities to respond to acts of bioterrorism, bringing public health intervention into the core of disaster preparedness and response. Further, after Hurricane Katrina, there is the broadest recognition of the need for public health to be an integral part of the emergency preparedness effort in every community. Finally, the medical literature regarding disasters is full of anecdotal accounts of response. Reports substantiating the *effectiveness* of the reported preparedness are beginning to be published.[35,36]

## Public Health's Role

Public health has a natural role in disaster preparedness and response. This role is evolving as the emergency management community recognizes the skills possessed by the profession. Through increased recognition of what public health professionals can do, public health professionals are being called on more often to control injury and disease that are caused by both natural and technological hazards and to prevent infectious disease following natural disasters. State departments of health, with responsibility as a major directing unit overseeing the public's health, already work in partnership with LHDs and other appropriate federal, state, and local agencies. Disaster response is more than an extension of daily tasks for public health professionals. In many states and localities, public health professionals coordinate the health response following natural and technological emergencies.[25]

Because of its impact on realms where public health is core, including healthcare infrastructure, Hurricane Andrew demonstrated that public health professionals must be involved in preparedness and response operations. Hurricane Andrew was considered one of the most destructive disasters ever to affect the United States,[37(p243)] leaving 175,000 Floridians homeless and water systems inoperable for at least a week.[26] The infrastructure of the healthcare system was also destroyed—59 hospitals were damaged, more than 12,000 patients needed to be examined, and pharmacies could not dispense medication.[38] To help in this situation, more than 850 public health nurses were deployed during the 2 months following the storm.[39] This lesson was magnified by Hurricane Katrina, where over 400,000 Louisiana residents were displaced because of the mandatory evacuation orders and the flooding that followed the hurricane.[40] Public health activities in response to Hurricane Katrina included investigations of infectious disease, environmental assessments, morbidity and mortality surveillance, shelter-based surveillance, community health and needs assessments, location and follow-up of displaced persons with tuberculosis, and broad utilization of immunization registries for displaced children.[41] In an assessment of the public health response, Greenough and Kirsch state that "The biggest health concern, however, was and will continue to be the inability of the displaced population to manage their chronic diseases."[42]

With the increase in both domestic natural disasters and international complex emergencies, there is greater recognition of the need for intergovernmental experts who understand disasters. Although the calls for widespread training of the public health workforce began relatively recently, there is now mainstream recognition that public health is a key player in disaster preparedness and response.[39] *Healthy People 2010* includes, as part of the core competencies, the enhancement of professional training in preparing for and responding to disasters.[43]

## What Is Public Health's Responsibility in Disaster Response?

The mission of public health in disaster preparedness and response includes responsibility for the following domains, referred to as *functions* within the emergency management field:

- Assessment of the viability of the healthcare infrastructure, including the drug supply
- Assessment of environmental infrastructure (food, water, sanitation, and vector control)
- Assessment and provision of healthcare services (acute, continuity of care, primary care, and emergency care)
- Preventive care
- Assessment of the needs of the elderly and other special populations
- Health surveillance and case identification/verification, including injury surveillance
- Infectious disease control
- Expert assistance in response to chemical, radiologic, or biologic-hazards
- Public health information
- Mental health
- Emergency shelter
- Victim identification/body management

To fulfill these functions, public health has three major tasks:

- One task is the collection, evaluation, and dissemination of information. The other sectors that have traditionally responded to disasters are response oriented, not science oriented. Public health brings a basis for evaluating activities using a scientific method. Public health brings unique resources to the emergency management community. These include assessment and epidemiology and the capacity to analyze, make recommendations, and act on information. As an example, using Stafford Act funds, the state of Iowa established a statewide systematic electronic system for surveillance during the 1993 flood.[44]

- The second task is one of cooperation and collaboration with other disciplines. The responsibilities of public health in disaster preparedness and response are more complicated than in a typical public health response. First, the participants are from "sectors of response" (e.g., fire, EMS, emergency management) rather than from other parts of the healthcare delivery field. Workers have to participate as part of a multidisciplinary team that includes mostly professionals or paraprofessionals with whom they normally do not have interactions and who have little or no knowledge of public health (i.e., engineering, police, and the military/national guard). Further, the process of working together is unique. The other sectors who are involved in disaster response have a lexicon and methods that may be different than those of public health. A typical response incorporates multiple bureaucratic layers of infrastructure working together in a condensed time frame. Public health must often integrate itself into an already established response team whose members have trained together and who have clearly defined roles.

- The third task constitutes the prevention of disease and continuity of care. Public health looks at localities where a disaster has occurred, or is likely to occur, as a diseased or compromised community. No other discipline assesses how or acts to prevent disease following disaster. Public health has a major responsibility in ensuring the continuation of the delivery of all health care.

Being prepared is necessitated not only because of legal mandates, but also because of the devastating consequences if healthcare systems are unable to function. The Joint Commission on Accreditation of Healthcare Organizations prescribes standards and requirements that healthcare facilities must meet in order to remain accredited. These standards ensure that basic disaster plans are in place and that exercises of these plans are held on a regular basis.[45] The public health professional is involved in ensuring that essential health facilities are able to function after the impact of a disaster.[10,25] Essential facilities include hospitals, health departments, poison control centers, storage sites for disaster supplies, dispatch centers, paging services, and ambulance stations. Hurricane Katrina demonstrated the importance of developing advance creative solutions for the maintenance and continuation of home-based services (e.g., dialysis, intravenous antibiotics, visiting nurses services, etc.). Patients in all residential care facilities (long-term care, psychiatric, rehabilitation) may need to be evacuated and placed elsewhere. Public health also initiates arrangements to ensure that routine sources of medical care will be functioning after a disaster. When physicians' offices, mental health clinics, nursing homes, pharmacies, community clinics, and urgent care centers are closed, those individuals needing routine care or medication will seek care from emergency departments based in already stressed hospitals. Following Hurricane Andrew, for example, more than 1000 physicians' offices were destroyed or significantly damaged, greatly adding to the patient load of surviving hospitals.[39]

## Functional Model of Public Health's Response in Disasters

In disaster preparedness and response, public health professionals are providers of service, scientists, and administrators. The core functions of public health have specific application to the organizational model of disaster preparedness and response, providing an opportunity for the breadth of the public health discipline to participate. To enter as full members of the emergency management response team, public health practitioners need to relate the framework of activities defined by the emergency management community to what public health can do. To provide technical assistance to communities, public health professionals must expand their lexicon to include specialized information that may not be directly related to health and seek out modalities for accessing state-of-the-art resources of other scientific fields, such as earth science, engineering, and demography. This interface between the core components of professional training and the matrix of emergency management is called the functional model of public health's response in disasters.

The functional model provides a paradigm for identifying disaster-related activities for which each core area of public health has responsibility. The functional model is composed of six phases that correspond to the type of activities involved in preparing for and responding to a disaster. The paradigm (Table 23-1) identifies the roles and responsibilities, operationalizes a typical disaster response, and categorizes the cycle of activities performed by the public health field. The functional model expands traditional public health partnerships with other disciplines because it requires public health professionals to collaborate with other responding sectors and to work in an integrated fashion with networks whose roles are previously well defined. The public health role for international scenarios has been independently assessed and described as if it were a conceptual seventh core area.

The components of the model follow:

- Planning—The goals of planning are to work cooperatively with other disciplines and understand the resources, skills, and tools that public health professionals bring to the diseased community.
- Prevention—Prevention involves primary, secondary, and tertiary efforts and includes the activities that are commonly thought of as *mitigation* in the emergency management model.
- Assessment—Assessments are both short-term and long-term snapshots that help with decision making and enhance the profession's ability to monitor disaster situations. The goal of conducting assessments is to convey information quickly in order to recalibrate a system's response.
- Response—Response includes both the delivery of services and the management of activities.
- Surveillance—Surveillance includes both data collection and monitoring of morbidity and mortality.
- Recovery—Recovery includes activities of repairing and replacing those elements of a community damaged by the disaster and helping community members recover emotionally. Recovery has policy, political, and social implications that are both short and long term.

**TABLE 23-1 Functional Model of Public Health Responsibilities in Disaster Management**

| | Health Administration | Epidemiology/Biostatistics | Behavioral/Social Sciences | Environment | International |
|---|---|---|---|---|---|
| Planning | • Apply local public health to disaster management<br>• Coordinate with hospital disaster plans<br>• Help develop community disaster plan<br>• Provide training<br>• Determine assets | • Provide training<br>• Analyze hazards and vulnerability<br>• Conduct needs assessment | • Develop health promotion and disease prevention<br>• Conduct training | • Conduct training<br>• Analyze hazards and vulnerability | • Analyze hazards and vulnerability and develop response |
| Prevention Primary | • Provide immunizations<br>• Protect and distribute food<br>• Establish safe water and sanitation | | • Educate community<br>• Train public in first aid | • Protect and distribute food<br>• Establish safe water and sanitation | • Provide emergency nutrition<br>• Protect and distribute food<br>• Establish safe water and sanitation |
| Prevention Secondary | • Detect and extricate victims<br>• Provide emergency care<br>• Manage bystander response | • Conduct care identification and surveillance<br>• Implement infectious disease control | • Detect and extricate<br>• Provide emergency care<br>• Manage bystander response | • Detect and extricate<br>• Provide emergency care<br>• Manage bystander response | |
| Prevention Tertiary | • Reestablish health services<br>• Manage emergency services<br>• Manage injuries | | • Provide long-term counseling | | • Convert response to development |
| Assessments | • Conduct surveillance for disease, behavioral, social, and political impacts<br>• Assess damage to healthcare infrastructure | • Conduct surveillance for disease, social, behavioral, and political impacts<br>• Assess causal factors of disease | • Conduct surveillance for disease, social, behavioral, and political impacts<br>• Collect data for decision making | • Conduct surveillance for disease, social, behavioral, and political impacts<br>• Identify hazards and assess exposure | • Conduct surveillance for disease, social, behavioral, and political impacts<br>• Collect data for decision making |

| | | | | | |
|---|---|---|---|---|---|
| | • Survey assets<br>• Conduct vulnerability analysis<br>• Collect data for decision making | • Conduct vulnerability analysis<br>• Conduct needs assessment<br>• Collect data for decision making<br>• Establish continuous monitoring | | • Conduct vulnerability analysis<br>• Assess damage from radiation, toxins, thermal, and water<br>• Collect data for decision making<br>• Do short-term cluster sampling<br>• Establish continuous monitoring | • Do short-term cluster sampling |
| Service Response | • Administer logistics<br>• Establish command and control, including casualty management<br>• Identify, contain, and provide emergency treatment<br>• Continue provision of primary care<br>• Utilize the Federal Response Plan | | • Educate to prevent illness and injury<br>• Organize mental health services | • Identify, contain, and provide emergency equipment | • Utilize international disaster relief, United Nations agencies, International Committee of the Red Cross, and nongovernmental organizations |
| Management Response | • Establish infection control, safe water, sanitation, and quarantine<br>• Manage dead, biologic hazards, and waste disposal<br>• Manage media<br>• Utilize field skills<br>• Establish security and protection | • Determine risk of delayed effects<br>• Communicate risk | • Establish information systems | • Establish infection and vector control, safe water, sanitation, and quarantine<br>• Reduce postdisaster injury (fire, nails, and electrocution)<br>• Manage dead, biologic hazards, waste disposal<br>• Communicate risk | • Manage dead, biologic hazards, waste disposal |

(continues)

**TABLE 23-1** (continued)

| | Health Administration | Epidemiology/Biostatistics | Behavioral/Social Sciences | Environment | International |
|---|---|---|---|---|---|
| Surveillance | • Establish information systems | • Utilize information systems<br>• Look for sentinel events<br>• Develop passive and active systems<br>• Establish disaster informatics<br>• Trend disease | • Establish information systems | | • Monitor malnutrition |
| Recovery | • Use data for deployment of resources<br>• Conduct evaluations<br>• Plan and direct field-work | • Conduct evaluations<br>• Plan and direct field studies | • Conduct evaluations<br>• Plan and direct field studies | • Conduct evaluations<br>• Plan and direct field studies | • Use data for deployment of resources<br>• Conduct evaluations<br>• Plan and direct field-work |
| Development | | | | | • Build capacity<br>• Mobilize resources<br>• Distribute food<br>• Control injury and communicable disease<br>• Provide population-based immunization<br>• Provide primary health care, reproductive health, and transcultural care |

*Source:* Adapted from L. Landesman 2000.

## Structure and Organizational Makeup of Disaster Response

When the healthcare sector responds to a disaster, it is most efficient to do so with the resources already at hand. However, because disasters overwhelm the local authority's ability to respond effectively in protecting human health, local assets often need to be supplemented by resources from organizations outside the area. Additionally, disasters typically generate needs that are beyond the breadth of any one type of healthcare organization. This tension between need and availability is overcome by planning for and mounting a *multiorganizational* response, one of the key characteristics of disaster operations in the health sector. This section provides a quick overview of the organizations that are typically involved in the health sector's response to disaster, and describes how they interact with each other in disaster situations. Table 23-2 provides a listing of the most important response organizations.

### Structure and Operations of the EMS System

For most sudden-onset disasters, the first medical response is provided by the local or regional EMS system. The potential public health impact that can be contributed by EMS in times of disaster is substantial.[46] In most parts of the United States, EMS is provided by semiautonomous local agencies with regional or state oversight. This service is provided under the authority of the state health department in most, but not all, states, but is not provided directly by the health department. EMS is thought to consist of

- A *public access system* by which the public notifies authorities that a medical emergency exists (In most of the United States, the 911 emergency telephone system is the backbone of this public access.)
- A *dispatch communications system* by which ambulance personnel and other emergency first responders are dispatched to respond to the person(s) in need
- *Trained emergency medical responders*, commonly called emergency medical technicians (EMTs), or the higher-trained paramedics (EMT-Ps). EMTs and paramedics are trained to identify and treat in the field the most common medical emergencies and injuries, and to provide medical support to victims while they are en route to the hospital.
- *Transportation* to definitive medical care, usually in a hospital. Ground ambulances are the vehicle of choice for most transports, but helicopters, boats, and snow cats have also been used.
- *Definitive care*, usually initiated in a hospital emergency department by emergency physicians and certified emergency nurses and followed up in a variety of healthcare settings.

The EMS is often discussed in terms of the prehospital system (e.g., public access, dispatch, EMTs/medics, and ambulance services) and the in-hospital system (e.g., emergency departments, inpatient care, and other definitive care, facilities, and personnel). The kind of medical care provided by EMS is divided into basic and advanced life support. The great majority of EMS providers are trained at the basic life support level. Basic life support includes fairly sophisticated noninvasive first aid and stabilization for a broad variety of emergency conditions, as well as semiautomatic defibrillation for cardiac arrest victims.

**TABLE 23-2   Disaster Response Organizations**

| Organization | Functions and Definitions |
| --- | --- |
| Public Access System | Enables public to communicate response needs, typically through a 911 phone system. |
| Fire Department | Finds and extricates victims; often provides on-scene incident management. |
| Emergency Medical Services (EMS) | Assesses scene for medical needs, initiates triage of patients, assesses individual patients for status and treatment needs, initiates life-sustaining first aid and medical care, determines treatment destination, and transports patients to definitive care. |
| Incident Management Systems (IMS or ICS) | This is a function often provided by an emergency management agency, a fire department, or multiple agencies. |
| Emergency Management Agency (EMA) | A state or jurisdictional agency tasked with preparedness and response for disasters and other emergencies. This is sometimes called the Office of Emergency Preparedness (OEP). |
| American Red Cross (ARC) | Private voluntary national organization tasked by government to provide mass care and shelter to disaster victims |
| Department of Health and Human Services (HHS) | The federal action agency charged with protecting the public's health |
| Emergency Support Function 8 (ESF#8) | The public health and medical function of the National Response Plan provides coordination between HHS operating divisions and ESF#8 interagency partners. |
| National Disaster Medical System (NDMS) | A multiagency response system coordinated by the US Public Health Service-OEP with responsibility for responding to overwhelming medical needs in a disaster-struck state or territory |
| Disaster Medical Assistance Team (DMAT) | A trained unit of medical response personnel available to respond with the NDMS to a disaster scene |
| Private Volunteer Organization (PVO) | A broad range of functions and structures |
| Centers for Disease Control and Prevention (CDC) | One of 13 major operational components of HHS. CDC established the Office of Terrorism, Preparedness, and Emergency Response (OTPER) to coordinate and support CDC's response efforts. |
| Department of Homeland Security | The coordinating agency for all federal level agency responses to disasters. |

Advanced life support, provided by paramedics, includes sophisticated diagnosis of patient conditions followed by initial on-site, protocol-driven medical treatment for conditions that will receive definitive treatment in hospitals.

In responding to a disaster, the function of coordinating and managing the multiple simultaneous activities, as well as managing the effective deployment of incoming resources, is of primary importance. Drabek et al.

found that the coordination of multiple activities, resource inputs, and organizations was among the most difficult and crucial challenges in managing a disaster response.[47] A strong command and coordination system is imperative if emergency health services are to overcome the disruption to the normal operations of the system and to manage additional incoming resources. First published as the FIRESCOPE Program in 1982, the Incident Command System (ICS) is the standard management structure used in disaster response across the United States. Through a system called *sectorization*, the tasks and functions of those responding, and the use of resources, are divided into manageable components. As the size or type of the operation changes, it is those sectors that allow for the ICS to be universally applied.

## Organization of Public Health Emergency Response

The basis for all local public health emergency responses resides in the LHD. However, the public health sector is not nearly as uniformly organized for emergency responses as the EMS system is with its broad variety of system designs. Furthermore, the health department is only one actor in the overall emergency response, which is usually coordinated by a public safety agency such as the emergency management authority, a sheriff's office, or a fire department. The best prepared health departments have well-designed emergency or disaster response plans, complete with a thorough risk analysis, prognostication of probable health effects, and analysis of the resources needed (and available) to provide an appropriate response. The health departments that are well prepared are likely to have coordinated their plans with other response functions in the health sector (EMS and hospitals), and with other public safety efforts.

The public health response to local emergencies and disasters is inevitably a multidisciplinary effort. The American Red Cross (ARC) provides emergency shelter; basic health services for those residing in shelters; food services on-site and in shelters; counseling, including mental health services or referrals; and family reunification. The public works department or a contracted commercial provider most often manages the potable water supply. Social services agencies work with the displaced, attend to psychosocial needs, and ensure that special needs populations such as the older adults, children, and individuals with disabilities receive the care required. Home nursing associations are often integrated into the emergency response plan to assist individuals with chronic diseases or special nursing needs. The health department is responsible, in most jurisdictions, for coordinating the efforts of the above-mentioned agencies on behalf of the public's health.

When the resources of the local jurisdiction are insufficient to meet the needs resulting from the disaster, local authorities have the option to call for additional help. The coordinating agency can seek help from surrounding jurisdictions (often referred to as mutual aid resources) or can escalate a request to the state or federal level, or both. The call for outside aid is often called "escalate upward." All states have an emergency management authority (EMA), sometimes called an office of emergency preparedness (OEP). It is the responsibility of the EMA, under the authority of the governor's office, to coordinate the efforts of all state resources used during an emergency or disaster. These resources may be expansive and include the state's health department, housing and social services agencies, and public safety agencies (i.e., state police). In disasters of this magnitude, certain federal resources are made available to the states, such as the National Guard, the CDC (e.g., Epidemic Intelligence Service), and the US Public Health Service (e.g., the Agency for Toxic Substances and Disease Registry). Local and state emergency management agencies typically convene a command center away from the disaster site whose function is to coordinate the multiorganizational response of representatives of each pertinent response agency. Health departments should plan to participate in the command center activities as a full partner. A local disaster timeline is presented in Exhibit 23-1.

Like a local jurisdiction, states also have the ability to escalate upward if the disaster response requires more resources than the state can quickly provide. States in many regions of the country are forming multistate regional mutual aid compacts, such as that in the lower Mississippi River region, based on the Central United States Earthquake Consortium. These consortia can provide relatively rapid response due to geographic proximity.

### Federal Response

The US Department of Homeland Security, established through the Homeland Security Act of 2002, coordinates federal programs and assists states through operational and/or resource coordination and on-scene incident command structures to respond to those events that rise to the level of national significance. To provide federal, state, and local guidance regarding a national emergency response, the Department of Homeland Security (DHS) created the National Response Plan (NRP) and National Incident Management System (NIMS). The NRP, with an all hazards approach, provides national direction for managing and responding to domestic disasters and combines fundamental principles from previous federal response plans. Using established protocols, the NRP provides guidance for federal coordination with state, local, and tribal governments and with the private sector during incidents.[48] The resources covered by the NRP are normally accessed by a request from a state's governor or the state's EMA to Homeland Security, referred to earlier in this chapter as a presidential declaration. A core concept of the national response plan is that the responding federal resources work at the behest of, and in support of, the local or state jurisdiction that is in charge of managing the disaster response.[48]

#### *National Incident Management System (NIMS)*

To enhance the ability of the United States to manage domestic incidents, DHS established a single, comprehensive model for the national management of major incidents. The NIMS was developed through a collaborative effort by the users of the plan. In a unified structure and standardized management plan, NIMS uses common terminology, concepts, principles, and processes so execution during a real incident will be consistent and seamless. Key elements and features of NIMS include the following:

- Incident Command System (ICS)—ICS is an incident management model with five functional areas: command, operations, planning,

Exhibit 23-1   Disaster Timeline

### Disaster Event

| | Preevent Planning | Emergency Response (0–24 hrs) | Emergency Response (24–72 hrs) | Recovery (>72 hrs) |
|---|---|---|---|---|
| **Tasks** | Develop disaster plan:<br>　Interagency development<br>　Hazard analysis<br>　Resource analysis<br>　Define concept of operations<br>　Establish chain of command<br>　Establish mutual aid resources<br>　Integration of state and federal resources<br>Perform plan drills and exercises<br>Establish disaster training<br>Update and maintain plan<br>Establish resource/equipment caches | Activate emergency operations center<br>Establish communications<br>Conduct damage and needs assessment<br>Search, rescue, and extricate<br>Provide field triage, on-site medical care<br>Establish casualty collection points<br>Transport patients to definitive care<br>Activate mass casualty hospital protocols<br>Request mutual aid resources<br>Mitigate occupational hazards<br>Mitigate ongoing threats and hazards, e.g., HAZMATs, sewage | Integrate state and federal resources<br>Continue rescue and extrication<br>Continue health and medical care<br>If applicable, plan and enact a medical evacuation<br>Begin restoration of public works to essential facilities<br>Establish shelter, potable water supplies, and the delivery of food supplies<br>Ensure the safety of water and food<br>Establish means of sanitation/waste disposal, minimize releases<br>Establish disease surveillance<br>Establish CISM services | Continue medical care<br>Monitor public health and medical care<br>Continue monitoring of food, water, and shelter quality and safety<br>Monitor for disease outbreaks<br>Establish vector control<br>Restore public works<br>Provide disaster grants and loans to families and businesses |
| **Organizations** | Work with<br>• Emergency management agency<br>• City/county council<br>• Local: fire, EMS, police<br>• Social services<br>• Public health<br>• Environmental health<br>• Public works<br>• Hospitals<br>• Nongovernmental/private (e.g., Red Cross, RACES) | Coordinate with<br>• Emergency management agency<br>• City/county council<br>• Local: fire, EMS, police<br>• Social services<br>• Public health<br>• Environmental health<br>• Public works<br>• Hospitals<br>• Nongovernmental/private (e.g., Red Cross, RACES) | Seek help from<br>• Emergency management agency<br>• City/county council<br>• Local: fire, EMS, police<br>• Social services<br>• Public health<br>• Environmental health<br>• Public works<br>• Hospitals<br>• Nongovernmental/private (e.g., Red Cross, RACES)<br>• State and federal resources:<br>　–DMATs, DMORTs<br>　–FEMA, CDC<br>　–Military | Initiate recovery activities with<br>• Emergency management agency<br>• City/county council<br>• Local: fire, EMS, police<br>• Social services<br>• Public health<br>• Environmental health<br>• Public works<br>• Hospitals<br>• Nongovernmental/private (e.g., Red Cross)<br>• State and federal resources: DMATs, DMORTs, FEMA, CDC, Military |

**Disaster Event**

**Local Disaster Timeline**

**Organizations**

- Emergency management agency
- City/county government
- Local fire, police, EMS
- Public health: disease surveillance and control
- Environmental health: provisions for potable water and public sanitation
- Public works
- Hospitals
- Social services
- Nongovernmental/private (e.g.; Red Cross, RACES)
- State and federal resources: FEMA, CDC, military, DMATs, DMORTs

Timeline phases:
- Prevent Planning
- Emergency Response (1–24 hrs)
- Emergency Response (24–72 hrs)
- Recovery (>72 hrs)

**Tasks**

Development of disaster Plan:
- Interagency development
- Hazard analysis
- Resource analysis
- Define concept of operations
- Establish chain of command
- Establish mutual aid resources
- Integration of state and federal resources
- Perform plan drills and exercises
- Establish disaster training
- Update and maintain plan
- Establish resource/equipment caches

- Activation of EOC
- Damage and needs assessments
- Request mutual aid resources
- Integration of state and federal resources
- Search and rescue extrication
- Field triage/on-site medical care
- Establish casualty collection points
- Transport to definitive medical care
- Activate mass casualty hospital protocols
- Consider medical evacuation
- Establish disease surveillance
- Vector control
- Establish shelter, water, and food supplies
- Ensure continued safety of water and food
- Mitigate environmental hazards, establish means of sanitation and waste disposal
- <<Begin restoration of public works to essential facilities, general restoration of public works>>
- Mitigate occupational hazards
- Establish CISM services

Level of Involvement
- Low
- Medium
- High

*Source:* Copyright © R. Bissell, 2000. Used with permission.

logistics, and finance/administration. Through unified command, NIMS coordinates the efforts of all responding jurisdictions.

- Preparedness—NIMS defines the activities necessary to be prepared, such as planning, training, exercises, qualification and certification of responders, equipment acquisition and certification, publication management, and mitigation activities such as public education and enforcement of building standards and codes.
- Communications and information management—NIMS prescribes interoperable communications systems for both incident and information management in order to standardize communications during an incident.
- Joint information system (JIS)—To ensure that all levels of government are releasing the same information during an incident, the JIS provides the public with timely and accurate incident information and unified public messages about the event.
- NIMS integration center (NIC)—The NIC will provide strategic direction and oversight of the NIMS and will develop and facilitate national standards for NIMS education and training, communications and equipment, resources, responder qualifications and credentialing, and equipment standardization.

As of October 1, 2006, all states, territories, local jurisdictions, and tribal entities must be NIMS compliant to be eligible to receive federal preparedness assistance funds.[49]

### Strategic National Stockpile

The Strategic National Stockpile (SNS) Program was established to maintain a stockpile of push packs of medical supplies and equipment to augment state and local resources during a large-scale disaster or bioterrorism event. The push packs are located in 12 sites around the country, each under the care of the state in which it resides. Each pack weighs over 50 ton, fills seven 53-foot trucks, and contains pharmaceuticals, antibiotics, antitoxins, vaccines, medical supplies and equipment, nerve agent antidotes, other emergency medications, intravenous supplies, airway equipment, and so on. Upon request, the SNS Program will deliver materials anywhere in the United States within 12 hours or less.

### Voluntary Agencies

Of considerable importance to the successful provision of good public health response to a disaster is mass care. The ARC is the primary agency responsible for this function, which includes sheltering, feeding, emergency first aid, family reunification, and the distribution of emergency relief supplies to disaster victims. The ARC responds first through its local chapters, then state and regional chapters, which may call on national ARC resources if necessary.

A vast array of other voluntary agencies participate in disaster response with functions that contribute significantly to public health outcome. Many of these are church affiliated, such as the Salvation Army, Mennonite Central Committee, and Catholic Relief Services. Some are dedicated solely to disaster-related functions, but most have more routine public service and emergency functions that are activated according to the needs of a specific disaster.

## International Agencies

A vast array of agencies stands ready to respond to requests for international assistance to protect the public's health after disasters. Multinational United Nations-based organizations include World Health Organization, UNICEF (United Nations Children's Fund), the UN High Commissioner for Refugees, and the World Food Program. The PAHO (WHO's regional affiliate for the Americas) has a highly organized Office for Emergency Preparedness and Disaster Relief Coordination, which helps coordinate international health sector response in the Americas. Many national governments have an agency that provides unilateral foreign disaster assistance, such as the US State Department's Office of Foreign Disaster Assistance. Numerous voluntary agencies have gained considerable expertise in responding to postdisaster health needs across international borders. Examples include Médecins Sans Frontières, World Vision, Oxfam, and Save the Children.

## Assessment in Disasters

Public health, at the local, state, and federal levels, has a major role in assessing and monitoring the nature of disasters and their impacts on communities. These assessments are important managerial tools in preventing morbidity and mortality and in organizing a response.

Assessing the postdisaster situation requires gathering and evaluating information, recovering from the event, and rehabilitating postdisaster conditions as they are restored to "normalcy." The information provided in these assessments helps health officials or emergency managers make informed decisions about response and recovery activities. These processes lead to an identification of: (1) the needs of the affected community after a disaster has occurred, (2) appropriate relief goods or services for that community, (3) epidemic levels of disease or injury if indicated, and (4) resources that may be needed by healthcare services in the disaster zone.

### Measurements of Disasters

Objective measures are used to quantify environmental hazards and human impacts related to natural disasters. To indicate the severity of a disaster event, scales developed by different scientific disciplines such as seismology and meteorology are used to measure and describe the hazard from the public health standpoint. For example, the magnitude of an earthquake is indicated by the Richter scale, which provides a measure of the total energy released from the source of the earthquake. Similarly, the strength of tornadoes is measured by the Fujita scale.

Measuring the physical manifestations of a disaster event can indicate the size and severity of that event. For example, the height of a river can signal the scope of a flood event. Levels of pesticides in drinking water or sediment after severe flooding may lead to questions about acute and chronic exposure to toxic chemicals in na-tech events.

Measures of biologic effects indicate resulting impacts on human health and disease. In earthquake events, age-specific injury and death rates may be calculated in cases where a direct health outcome is associated with the event. Among displaced persons in shelters where an infectious disease outbreak might occur, laboratory typing of organisms in biologic samples such as blood and urine may indicate exposure to a disease-causing pathogen and confirmation of disease. In famine situations, anthropometric measurements, such as height to weight ratios among young children, may indicate the type and degree of malnutrition caused by lack of food.

## Applied Epidemiology

A systematic approach to assessing postdisaster conditions is based on the principles of epidemiology, the cornerstone of public health science. One recent application of epidemiology is the investigation of the public health and medical consequences of natural disasters. Known as *disaster epidemiology*, or *epidemiology in disaster settings*, this discipline evolved as scientists realized that the effects of disasters on health were amenable to study by epidemiologic methods.[50] Epidemiologists identify risk factors with the aim of preventing the occurrence of death. Some of the methods involve a comparison of people who were killed or injured with people who were not in order to learn the ways in which they differed.

The ultimate aim of disaster epidemiology is to determine strategies to prevent or reduce deaths, injuries, or illnesses related to the disaster. Prevention strategies are often grouped into the following three categories:

1. *Primary prevention*, or prevention of the occurrence of deaths, injuries, or illnesses related to the disaster event (e.g., evacuation of a community in a flood-prone area, sensitizing warning systems for tornadoes and severe storms)
2. *Secondary prevention*, or the mitigation of health consequences of disasters (e.g., use of carbon monoxide detectors when operating gasoline-powered generators after loss of electric power, building a "safe room" in dwellings located in tornado-prone areas)
3. *Tertiary prevention*, minimizing the effects of disease and disability among the already ill, is employed in persons with preexisting health conditions and in whom the health effects from a disaster event may exacerbate those health conditions. Examples include appropriate sheltering of persons with respiratory illnesses from haze and smoke originating from forest fires, and sheltering elderly who are prone to heat illnesses during episodes of extreme ambient temperatures.

Applications of epidemiology in disaster settings are conducted for many reasons. Primarily, they are used to describe the health effects of contributing factors, such as demographic characteristics and environmental parameters, and to prevent adverse health effects from occurring in a particular disaster event and in similar events in the future. Epidemiologic investigations may also provide informed advice regarding probable health effects. Following the Mt. St. Helens volcanic eruption, individuals with a history of asthma were found to have a higher risk of contracting respiratory illness when matched to healthy controls.

In the immediate aftermath of a disaster, a critical concern of relief authorities is the identification of the needs of an affected community, and epidemiologic studies help provide that information. With a list of needs, public health authorities or emergency management officials can provide information for emergency planning, provide reliable and accurate information for relief decisions, and ultimately, match resources to requirements. Finally, managers can employ epidemiologic applications to evaluate the effectiveness of programs used to provide relief.

Epidemiologic activities in the impact phase include the following techniques: (1) rapid needs assessment, (2) disease surveillance, and (3) descriptive and analytic investigations.

- *Rapid needs assessment* represents a collection of techniques—epidemiologic, statistical, and anthropological—designed to provide information about an affected community's needs after a disaster.[51] The objective is to obtain a quick and objective snapshot of a disaster-stricken community, so that immediate relief actions may be taken.
- *Surveillance* refers to an ongoing and systematic collection, analysis, and interpretation of information linked to planning, implementation, and evaluation of public health practice, and it is closely integrated with the timely dissemination of these data for decision making by public health authorities.[52] Often, disease surveillance systems are implemented to signal whether outbreaks of infectious diseases are occurring in the community.
- *Descriptive and analytic investigations* may be undertaken by health authorities in situations where assessment and surveillance raise further questions and hypotheses concerning a health condition in the affected population. These investigations are designed to address questions or test hypotheses so that recommendations can be made for the prevention of any adverse health outcomes related to the disaster event.

During each phase of the disaster continuum, public health assessment for a disaster event is conducted by answering the following questions:[53]

- What problems are occurring? Why are they occurring?
- Where are the problems occurring?
- Who is affected?
- What problems are causing the greatest morbidity and mortality?
- What problems are increasing or decreasing?
- What problems will subside on their own?
- What problems will increase if they are left unattended?
- What relief resources are available?
- Where are relief resources available?
- How can relief resources be used most efficiently?
- What relief activities are in progress?
- Are relief activities meeting the relief needs?
- What additional information is needed for decision making?*

---

*Reprinted with permission from Sidel VW, Onel E, Geiger HJ, Leaning J, Foeg WH. Public health responses to natural and human-made disasters. In: Wallace RB, Doebbelong BN, eds. *Maxcy-Rosenay-Last: Public Health and Preventive Medicine.* Stamford, Conn: Appleton & Lange; 1992:1173–1186.

### Emergency Information Systems

Information is critical to any response effort after a disaster has occurred. The need for objective and reliable information is underscored because disasters disrupt physical and social environments, may trigger threats to health, often cause ecologic changes and population displacement leading to overcrowding and situations in which sanitation and hygiene are compromised, and disrupt normal public health programs. Moreover, the potential for communicable diseases increases for vector-borne, waterborne, and person-to-person transmission. As such, accurate and reliable information is needed to aid decisions about immediate relief efforts, short-term responses, and long-term planning for recovery and reconstruction. These emergency information systems facilitate the monitoring of health events, diseases, injuries, hazards, exposures, and risk factors related to a designated event.

Several types of information are collected for decision making, and each type has multiple uses. Mortality data is tracked to assess the magnitude of the disaster event, to evaluate the effectiveness of disaster preparedness and the adequacy of warning systems, and to identify high-risk groups where more contingency planning is required. By reviewing information about casualties or the injured, emergency medical personnel and managers of critical care facilities can estimate needs for emergency care, evaluate predisaster planning and preparedness, and evaluate the adequacy of warning systems. Managers can assess information about morbidity to estimate the types and volume of immediate medical relief needed, to identify populations at risk for disease, to evaluate the appropriateness of relief activities, and to identify areas for further planning.

In addition to information that helps public health professionals understand the health effects of disasters, information concerning public health resources, particularly from LHDs, is important for emergency information systems. Using these data, officials can estimate the types and volume of supplies, equipment, and services required. Finally, information may be compiled about specific events related to and health outcomes associated with community hazards.

### Surveillance

Public health surveillance is described as the following:

> Ongoing and systematic collection, analysis, and interpretation of health data used for planning, implementing, and evaluating public health interventions and programs, closely integrated with the timely dissemination of these data to those who need to know. Surveillance data are used both to determine the need for public health action and to assess the effectiveness of programs. A surveillance system includes a functional capacity for data collection, analysis, and dissemination linked to public health programs.[52(p164)]

In the postdisaster setting, surveillance provides information that can serve as the basis for action during the immediate disaster and also for planning of future activities. (See Chapter 14 for more information on surveillance activities in public health.) For example, measles vaccination campaigns can be launched in shelters if potential outbreaks are identified. Surveillance is also conducted to investigate rumors, such as the occurrence of infectious disease, which commonly arise in the aftermath of a disaster event. Surveillance data can signal whether an outbreak has actually occurred. If unusual increases of disease are observed, public health workers may be deployed to investigate and confirm diagnosis. Finally, surveillance is also conducted to monitor the effectiveness of response activities. For example, cases of acute diarrheal disease would be expected to decline with the use and implementation of water treatment interventions. A surveillance system that monitors diarrheal disease where water treatment has been implemented could indicate, as evidenced by rates of diarrheal disease, whether intervention was effective.[54]

Surveillance systems measure hazards, exposures, and outcomes. A *hazard* surveillance is, by definition, an assessment of the occurrence of or distribution of levels of hazards and the trends in hazardous levels (e.g., toxic chemical agents, physical agents, or biologic agents) responsible for disease and injury. An example of the application of postdisaster hazard surveillance is the tracking of daily variations in respirable particulate matter (i.e., particles with a mass median aerodynamic diameter of $\leq$ 10 microns) after wildland fires. Thresholds can be established for guiding those susceptible to pulmonary disease to take precautionary measures when the particles reach a certain size.

Surveillance may also assess *exposure*. In disaster settings, exposure may be based on physical or environmental properties of the disaster event, such as "ash fall" after volcanic activity or pesticide-contaminated soil unearthed by flood water.[55]

Surveillance most commonly looks for health *outcomes,* defined as a health event of interest, usually illness, injury, or death. Other types of surveillance systems may be based on the characteristics and objectives for establishing those particular systems.

Those establishing a surveillance system determine the variables of potential importance after a specific disaster event (i.e., diseases, injuries, and causes of death). Diseases that were endemic in the affected area prior to the disaster event should be included in the system because these would be expected to rise with increased population density, displacement, interrupted normal public health programs, and compromised sanitation and hygiene.

Facilitating the dissemination of information is critical to a successfully implemented surveillance system. Proper dissemination includes content reported in a format that would alert policy and decision makers, prevention program managers, the media, and the public about the required public health actions.

## Data Collection

Accurate and reliable information is needed for planning relief, recovery, and evacuation activities, and for disaster response. (See Chapter 11 for more information on data sources in public health.) Historical information may be used by emergency managers as a reference against which to compare phenomena exhibited by a given disaster event. Such information originates from a variety of sources, including existing community institutions (e.g., utility companies) and units created specifically to provide immediate response following a disaster. A decision maker will have a better idea about the severity of an event if historical information about the hazards, risks, and vulnerabilities of a particular area has already been gathered. Historical information is available from the local emergency management authority, geologic institutions, or international ministries responsible for natural resources and the environment.

During the relief phase, the following data help gauge appropriate relief efforts by emergency managers and public health officials:

- Demographic characteristics of the affected area and surrounding vicinities
- Casualty assessment, including deaths, injuries, and selected illnesses
- Assessment of the needs of the displaced population
- Coordination of volunteer assistance
- Management of facilities
- Storage and distribution of relief materials
- Communication systems
- Transportation systems
- Public information and rumor control
- Registration inquiry services
- Traffic and crowd control

Data for postimpact surveillance may be extracted from a variety of sources, including: (1) existing data sets (e.g., census and national health information systems); (2) hospitals and clinics (e.g., hospital emergency department and inpatient records); (3) community healthcare providers (e.g., patient records); (4) temporary shelters (e.g., daily shelter census, medical logs at shelter); (5) first responder logs (e.g., DMAT patient logs); and (6) mobile health clinics (e.g., patient logs, records of prescription medications dispensed).

The selection of an appropriate sampling method depends on the objectives of a collection system and the existence of a sampling frame. Population-based sampling techniques, when possible, should be employed. For instance, if all of the households in an affected area are identified and mapped prior to a disaster event, a simple random sample may be appropriate for a community-based needs assessment. If a sampling frame does not already exist, then a cluster design might be more appropriate. Other designs include a systematic or stratified sampling.

# Mental Health Considerations in Disasters: Psychosocial Impacts and Public Health

When most people hear the word *disaster*, they tend to picture the physical destruction—images of injured people and collapsed buildings. As disasters can flatten trees, break bones, and tear houses apart, they can also profoundly affect individual well-being, family relations, and the fabric of community life. The psychosocial impacts of disasters range from mild stress reactions to serious problems such as substance abuse, depression, and post-traumatic stress disorder (PTSD).

The mental health sequelae of a disaster can be quite widespread. In terms of morbidity, the social and psychological impacts of a disaster can greatly exceed the direct toll of physical injuries. Furthermore, these less-visible effects of disasters have historically affected the functioning of individuals and communities years after a disaster struck. Thus, any effort to help restore the health of a community that has suffered a calamity should incorporate mental health into response and recovery efforts.

Public health agencies and public health professionals are heavily involved in addressing the social and psychological impacts of disaster, and attention to these issues represents a core part of the public health profession's response to disaster.[56] In fact, at the federal level, the US Public Health Service is a leader in the field of disaster mental health services. Staff of the Public Health Service's Emergency Services and Disaster Relief Branch in the Center for Mental Health Services (CMHS) helps to ensure that victims of presidentially declared disasters receive immediate, short-term crisis counseling, as well as ongoing support for emotional recovery. Numerous other examples of public health involvement with mental health issues can be found at the federal, state, and local levels.

## Mental Health Effects of Disaster

Disasters are life-changing experiences—these events are highly stressful, disruptive experiences for individuals, families, and entire communities. During a disaster, people may experience such traumatic stresses as loss of relatives, friends, and associates; personal injury; property loss; witnessing death or mass destruction; or having to handle bodies.[57] The period after a disaster can bring additional stresses, such as grieving for lost loved ones, "adjusting to role changes such as widowhood and single-parent status, moving, cleaning and repairing property, and preparing lengthy reports associated with loss."[58(p133–134)] Overall, experiencing a disaster "is often one of the single most traumatic events a person can endure."[56(p101)]

People who have gone through a disaster may experience any of a range of emotional, physical, cognitive, and interpersonal effects, and the numbers of people experiencing stress reactions following a major disaster can be large. A list of common stress reactions to disaster is provided in Exhibit 23-2.

In general, the transient reactions that people experience after a disaster represent a normal response to a highly abnormal situation. People are exposed to situations that are well outside the bounds of everyday experience, and such situations place extraordinary demands—both physical and emotional—on people. According to Young et al., "*Mild to moderate* stress reactions in the emergency and early post-impact phases of a disaster are highly prevalent. Although stress reactions may seem 'extreme,' and cause distress, they generally do not become chronic problems."[57(p15)] As a general rule, most individuals who are exposed to a disaster do not suffer prolonged psychological illnesses.[59]

Importantly, common stress reactions should not be ignored in the planning and implementation of a comprehensive public health response to a disaster. Mental health programs and services should include informational and educational support about normal reactions, ways to handle reactions, and early treatment where indicated,[59] in addition to the many types of services required at family assistance centers and in long-term treatment.[25]

Exhibit 23-2   Common Stress Reactions to Disaster

**Emotional Effects**
Shock
Anger
Despair
Emotional numbing
Terror
Guilt
Grief or sadness
Irritability
Helplessness
Loss of pleasure derived from
   regular activities
Dissociation (e.g., perceptual experience
   seems "dreamlike," "tunnel vision,"
   "spacey," or on "automatic pilot")

**Physical Effects**
Fatigue
Insomnia
Sleep disturbance

Hyperarousal
Somatic complaints
Impaired immune response
Headaches
Gastrointestinal problems
Decreased appetite
Decreased libido
Startle response

**Cognitive Effects**
Impaired concentration
Impaired decision-making ability
Memory impairment
Disbelief
Confusion
Distortion
Decreased self-esteem
Decreased self-efficacy
Self-blame
Intrusive thoughts and memories
Worry

**Interpersonal Effects**
Alienation
Social withdrawal
Increased conflict within relation-
   ships
Vocational impairment
School impairment

*Source*: Reprinted from Young BH, Ford JD, Ruzek JI, et al. *Disaster Mental Health Services: A Guidebook for Clinicians and Administrators.* Menlo Park, Calif: National Center for Post-Traumatic Stress Disorder; 1998.

*Persistent Effects*

Although most stress reactions after disaster tend to be transient, a portion of the population impacted by a disaster may suffer more serious, persistent effects. Research shows that mental health problems can result from exposure to both natural and technological disasters. These psychological problems include acute stress disorder (ASD), post-traumatic stress disorder (PTSD), depression, substance abuse, anxiety, and somatization. Other kinds of problems, including physical illness; domestic violence; and more general symptoms of distress, daily functioning, and physiological reactivity, have also been documented.[56]

ASD is "characterized by post-traumatic stress symptoms lasting at least 2 days but not longer than 1 month post-trauma."[60(p7)] In the aftermath of stressful events that are "both extreme and outside of the realm of everyday experiences," some individuals may experience a prolonged stress response known as PTSD.[61(p29)] Unlike transient stress reactions seen among disaster survivors, PTSD is associated with much greater levels of impairment and dysfunction.[57]

Although PTSD usually appears in the first few months after a trauma has been experienced, sometimes the disorder may not appear until years have passed. Likewise, PTSD's duration can vary, with symptoms diminishing and disappearing over time in some people and persisting for many years in others. It should also be noted that PTSD frequently occurs with— or leads to—other psychiatric illness, such as depression. This is known as comorbidity.[62,63]

Much is known about factors associated with the development of PTSD and about factors that may reduce the likelihood of developing PTSD. A key factor, the nature of the trauma experienced, poses the greatest risk of PTSD, if the persons have had their life threatened or been "exposed to terror, horror, and the grotesque."[59(p9),60] According to Young et al., disaster-related variables associated with long-term adjustment problems include mass casualties, mass destruction, death of a loved one, residential relocation, and toxic contamination.[57] There is evidence that some pretrauma factors have an effect as well, such as a history of prior exposure to trauma.

As might be expected, what happens in a disaster survivor's life after the trauma also appears to affect the risk of developing PTSD.[64] For example, it appears that in many situations, social support may play a role as a protective factor. Although PTSD is usually associated with primary exposure to trauma, people who have not actually experienced a disaster themselves can still develop PTSD and related symptoms, such as spouses and significant others of disaster workers.[65]

In recent years, researchers have focused increasing attention on ethnocultural issues related to PTSD.[66] Although a number of studies of disasters in the United States have found differing rates of PTSD or other disaster-related impairment among groups of different race or ethnicity, the PTSD construct has been found to have a universal dimension that makes it applicable across cultures.[67] As such, "The need for culturally sensitive assessment techniques and the need to identify other post-traumatic expressions of distress may be particularly pertinent to non-Western individuals."[66(p536),68,69]

### Social Impacts of Disaster

In addition to having the potential to produce PTSD, ASD, depression, and other psychological effects, disasters can also profoundly affect the *social* health of communities. Postdisaster efforts must include interventions to restore support networks and the health of the community as a whole. The need for this was dramatically illustrated in Erikson's study of the 1972 Buffalo Creek disaster, where a makeshift dam used by a coal mining company sent millions of gallons of waste and debris-filled flood waters roaring into a mountain hollow known as Buffalo Creek, West Virginia. The Appalachian mountain community was devastated: 125 people were killed, many others were injured, hundreds of homes and other buildings were wrecked, and thousands of people were displaced. Survivors, many of whom had witnessed dead and dismembered bodies, suffered a wide array of impacts including nightmares, numbing, insomnia, guilt, despair, confusion, depression, and hopelessness. In addition to these individual effects, the disaster, plus an ill-conceived relocation effort, effectively destroyed the social support system that held together the formerly tight-knit community.

## Long-Lasting Mental Health Impacts

The extent to which disasters cause serious, long-lasting mental health impacts can also vary by disaster and by community. In some disasters, victims seem to fare well without long-lasting problems. In other disasters, they suffer major mental health problems both immediately and for several years after the disaster. At Buffalo Creek, even 14 years after the West Virginia disaster, the Buffalo Creek survivors still showed significantly higher rates of major depression, general anxiety, and lifetime PTSD as compared to the non-exposed group.[70] Yet, studies of other disasters have come to different conclusions concerning long-term mental health effects after disaster, such as after the tornado in Xenia, Ohio, where 33 people were killed and between 1000–2000 people were injured.[71]

What accounts for the dramatic difference between studies of Buffalo Creek and the Xenia study? One factor may be that whereas Buffalo Creek's tight-knit community network was obliterated by the flood, most of Xenia's extended support networks remained intact despite the damage caused by the tornado. Outcomes may be dependent not only on the highly complex nature of disaster situations but also the enormous variations that often exist between communities and disaster agents.

## Natural Disasters and Technological Disasters

In recent years, there has been considerable discussion in the disaster research community regarding the similarities and differences between natural and man-made disasters. To the degree that natural and man-made disasters can be compared, the two, suggest Green and Solomon, "are probably more alike than different."[70(p164)] Although both have in common an immediate threat and the potential for ongoing disruption, there is a huge difference in perceived and actual human control over the disasters. Natural disasters tend to be seen as part of nature over which we have no control. On the other hand, man-made disasters are, in principle, preventable. Because we expect to be able to control technology, technological disasters often produce higher levels of anger and distrust than natural disasters because blame and responsibility are often ascribed.

## Services Provided After a Disaster

Public health professionals should work with local emergency planning committees to ensure that disaster and emergency plans adequately address potential social and psychosocial issues and that these concerns are appropriately incorporated into a community's disaster plans.

The numerous psychosocially oriented activities and services that are typically provided after a disaster are listed in Table 23-3. Public health professionals should also identify community resources and assets (citizen groups, associations, publications, specialists at nearby universities, etc.) and link them with mental health plans for assistance.[72,73] In addition, public health professionals should build community capacity to address social and psychological impacts.[25,74]

Activities and services provided in the aftermath of disaster need to be tailored to the community being served. This means involving stakeholders,

**TABLE 23-3    Community Behavioral Services Needed Following a Disaster**

Adult, adolescent, and child services
Assessments, crisis interventions, evaluations, and referrals
Bereavement counseling
Business counseling
Crisis counseling
Debriefing groups for health care and emergency workers
Drop-in crisis counseling
Emergency services in medical emergency departments
Family support center
Individual and group counseling
Mobile mental health crisis teams
Multidisciplinary services to designated community sites (police precincts,
    fire departments, temporary business locations)
Multilingual services
Outpatient mental health services and counseling
Ongoing support groups
Outreach to schools for students, parents, and teachers
Outpatient services
School presentations
Short-term treatment
Telephone triage
24-hour emergency psychiatric service
24-hour crisis hotline
Walk-in services
Weekly support groups

*Source:* Reprinted with permission. Landesman LY. *Public Health Management of Disasters: The Practice Guide.* 2nd ed. Washington, DC: American Public Health Association; 2005:201.

community groups, and others in the development and delivery of services.[72] In addition, special services and assistance should be geared towards vulnerable groups of the population and those with special needs, such as children, the elderly, and the disabled.[25,75] Older adults may have more limited support networks, mobility impairment or limitation, or illnesses. Finally, it is important to direct special attention to disaster workers who risk their own lives and their ability to provide for their families while being repeatedly exposed to mutilated bodies and life-threatening situations while doing physically demanding work.[59]

# Public Health Aspects of Environmental Services during Disasters

## General Principles

Assuming that following disasters certain hazards move through the environment and cause harm to humans, postimpact environmental control measures must focus on preventing the hazardous situation, the transport of the hazard, or people being exposed to the hazard once they encounter it. For example, in malaria control, prevention activities would include stopping mosquito breeding by draining stagnant water, spraying for mosquitoes to avert the transport of pathogens, and getting people to use impregnated bed nets or insect repellent to diminish their exposure. Whether the subject is diarrhea prevention or toxic waste control, these three types of preventive measures can apply.

As a general premise, no environmental measure functions perfectly 100% of the time. In developed countries, this is compensated by having multiple sanitary barriers between a hazard and a population. If, on a given day, any redundant measure is not functioning, the others will protect against the hazard. Most waterborne outbreaks in developed countries occur when a series of mishaps cause several of the public health barriers (i.e., filtration and chlorination) to fail.

A second sanitary principle is that distance aids safety. In general, the more dangerous a substance is and the more volume that exists, the more space is required between the substance and populations. Keeping hazardous material at a distance may cut down on human exposure because distance provides time for detection and for protective actions.

Within the context of an emergency situation, where people have been displaced from their homes and are sheltered in overcrowded conditions, these general premises of sanitary engineering become problematic. Resources are usually limited, and services must be established at very short notice. Moreover, where shelter is unavailable, displaced people are often shunted onto land where space to separate people and their nearest hazard is unavailable. Thus, the environmental practice becomes quite crude when applied to displaced populations and refugees. The principal hazard created within these settlements is usually feces. Because its creation is unavoidable, the public health task is to minimize fecal transport and to minimize the population's exposure, which in the case of fecally transmitted illnesses means minimizing oral ingestion.

During natural disasters, the usual task is either to protect or to restart the protective barriers that exist, or to promote changes in behavior that will compensate for the disrupted sanitary barriers. Examples of such messages include orders to boil water, warnings about foods that may have spoiled during electrical outages, or announcements regarding where potable water will be provided. For displaced populations, all basic services usually need to be restarted from scratch. During natural disasters, especially in developed countries, there may be few commonalties between the same types of crises in different locations. Typically, the infrastructure to provide safe water and food is in place; but it may be inoperative.

## Sanitation

Because, during an emergency, the use of latrines or other excreta-containment facilities has been shown to prevent diarrheal illness more than any other environmental measure in undeveloped countries, one of the first disaster response activities should be the establishment of a sanitation system. The appropriate type of facility varies between settings and cultures, although several overriding concepts are relevant.

### Purpose

The purpose of a sanitation system is to contain human excreta so that it is not free to spread throughout the environment. Therefore, getting as many people to use only the excreta-containment facilities is an essential part of all sanitation programs. In some cultures, this may include building separate latrines for men and women or separate latrines for children. In some settings, latrines may be needed in work or gathering areas. Local workers implementing the sanitation program should communicate to the population being served that the goal is for everyone to use proper facilities all of the time.

### Latrines

People's excreta poses little hazard to themselves because families are likely to have common immunologic histories and exchange pathogens on an ongoing basis. Thus, to the extent possible, households should not share latrines or toilets with other households. Because latrine cleaning and maintenance is an unpleasant task in virtually all cultures, having one latrine per household will also increase the likelihood that the facilities will be kept clean. However, the increasing health benefit with increasing coverage needs to be balanced against the time, effort, and expense of building excreta-containment facilities. Populations that are unstable or are expected to be moved within days, such as in complex emergencies in developing countries, are perhaps better served by a communal latrine system. Both UNHCR and UNICEF propose a minimum coverage target of 20 people per latrine, although this level of coverage is rarely achieved in transit and reception centers.

### Initial Response

Mortality and morbidity rates among displaced populations in the first days and weeks of a crisis are often many times higher than rates among the same population once it is stabilized. Thus, providing some sanitation facilities during the first days of a crisis is critical. This means that either latrines of some kind need to be built before the population arrives at a site (which is rare) or defecation fields need to be established. Because defecation fields need to be located away from water sources, not too far from the people who will use them, and in rainy climates downhill from living areas, reserving the proper spaces for defecation fields must be done at the outset of a crisis.

### Children

Young children pose a particular concern for excreta-control programs because children shed the most hazardous feces with a disproportionate amount of diarrhea and because their defecation habits are difficult to control. Two approaches are helpful with children. Educate child-care providers about proper handling of children's feces and about the importance of washing their hands after cleaning the child or handling the child's feces. In addition, by making excreta-disposal facilities more child friendly (not dark, perhaps with no walls and with an opening that is smaller than in an adult latrine), it is more likely that the children will use them.

## Personal Hygiene

The promotion of personal hygiene following a disaster is among the most difficult environmental interventions. Personal habits can influence a population's well-being, regardless of the infrastructure and resources provided, such as the poor hand washing practices among relief workers that caused diarrhea during the Oklahoma City bombing. Not only do cultural practices vary between peoples, but different languages often do not have comparable concepts for notions such as privacy or diarrhea. Therefore, as with sanitation, local professionals are best suited to develop and deliver any hygiene education program. Regardless of the setting, several basic premises are universal, specifically, soap provides protection from diarrheal illness independent of any educational program that may accompany it.[76] As people need to be able to clean themselves after defecating, materials for cleansing (paper, sticks) should be made available along with water and soap.

Hand washing, particularly after defecating and before preparing food, has been shown to be protective against fecal-oral illnesses. No studies examining the impact of personal hygiene that were included in a recent review found health benefits associated with education alone, only with documented changes in behavior.[77] Therefore, any efforts to promote hand washing should have a simple monitoring component to ensure that increased hand washing is actually occurring.

To work, educational messages should be short and focused. All messages included in an educational campaign should promote measures known to prevent the specific health threat at hand, such as "Boil your drinking water" and should focus on behaviors that are not presently practiced by a significant portion of the population.

## Water Quality

Water quality is usually evaluated based on the presence of some bacterial measure, which indicates the possible presence of feces. Because human feces typically contain tens of millions of bacteria per gram, even minute amounts of feces in water are often detectable via bacterial monitoring. Fecal coliforms are a general category of bacteria that are empirically defined to match the characteristics of bacteria found in the stool of warm-blooded mammals. Finding no fecal coliforms in untreated water is a good indication that there are no fecal-oral bacterial pathogens present, although finding fecal coliforms in water does not prove that the water is dangerous. UNHCR considers water with less than 10 fecal coliforms per 100 mL to be reasonably safe, whereas water with more than 100 fecal coliforms is considered to be very polluted. Other indicator bacteria, such as *E. coli,* fecal streptococci, or total coliforms, operate on the same premise that absence implies water safety. Although water sources may be of differing water quality, in many if not most settings, the handling and storing of water by people will be the main determinant in water safety. Studies have shown that the dipping of water from household storage buckets causes considerable contamination and that water quality deteriorates over time after the water is initially collected. The best assurance that clean water will stay clean is to add a chlorine residual to the water. This means that in unsanitary settings, or during times of outbreaks, it may be appropriate to chlorinate safe source water. Exhibit 23-3 provides additional information about surface and ground water.

## Water Quantity

In developing countries, by providing people with more water than they currently have, we can protect them against fecal-oral pathogens better than by

Exhibit 23-3   Getting and Treating Water in a Crisis Situation

---

Surface Water

**Bucket collection:** Where people collect water directly from water bodies in buckets, the only treatment of surface water that can easily be achieved is chlorination. Water can be chlorinated in the home or by health workers at the point of collection. Ideally, enough chlorine should be added to the bucket so that after 30 minutes, there is still at least 0.5 mg/L free chlorine in the water.

**Pipe distribution:** In systems that have many broken distribution pipes or during times of disease outbreaks, attempting to have 0.5 to 1.0 mg/L free chlorine is appropriate. During crises of conflicts, pressure intermittency in pipes allows water to be drawn in through cracks, resulting in cross-contamination responsible for most major waterborne outbreaks. Monitoring of chlorine is recommended to achieve a dose allowing free chlorine throughout the system.

Groundwater

**Spring:** A location where groundwater flows to the earth's surface of its own accord. To protect the water from contamination, build a spring box, which is a collection basin with an outflow pipe at or below the point where the water comes to the surface.

**Wells:** To prevent contamination with surface water, the well usually includes a skirt around the opening of the well, or a plate sealing off the surface at the top of the well. Where there is household water contamination or high risk of a waterborne outbreak, water disinfection of wells and springs with chlorine is advisable.

Wells can be of a variety of sizes and shapes, with a variety of pumps or devices to raise the water. Although many reasons relating to siting and construction errors can cause a well to never come into service, wells that operate for a time typically fail because of lack of maintenance and repair capacity. Thus, groups planning to build wells need to budget from the outset for parts and personnel to maintain the projects until local wealth and economic activity can sustain the water system, or until the wells are abandoned.

---

providing people with cleaner water.[77,78] UNHCR purports that people need at least 15–20 liters of water per person per day (L/p/d) to maintain human health. Because of the importance of water to maintaining health, contaminated water sources should never be closed until equally convenient facilities become available.

During a crisis, water consumption should be estimated at least weekly. Often, the local utility or NGO providing water to a population collects these figures. Note that water consumption means what people receive, not what the water operators produce. Water can be lost or wasted during pumping and transport, and people may be prevented from getting adequate quantities because they do not have containers to hold water, thus leading to discrepancies between estimates of production and consumption. Therefore, sampling that documents people's use of water (such as household interviews) or the actual collection of water at watering points is a preferable method of assessing usage than to divide the water produced at a well or a plant by the number of people served. Cholera outbreak investigations have revealed that not owning a bucket puts families at increased risk of illness or death.[79] Thus, not only should the average water consumption be 15 L/p/d or more, but there should not be anyone with very low water consumption ($<$ 5 L/p/d) in the population.

During natural disasters in areas with piped water, rapid surveys can quickly determine which areas are lacking in water service. Areas where service is expected to be cut for days or weeks are often vacated, or else water is transported to the area by vehicle.

## Specific Outbreak Control Strategies for Epidemic Diarrheal Diseases

For several specific fecal-oral diseases, different combinations of environmental measures have been shown to be more effective than others. This becomes important when trying to choose the one or two messages to be included in a campaign and when available staff and resources limit the environmental programs that can be undertaken. Exhibit 23-4 describes control strategies for four major diarrheal diseases.

## Heating and Shelter

Although often not thought of as a health issue, heating and shelter have been essential components of disaster response. Although cold conditions are widely associated with the medical conditions of hypothermia and frostbite, symptoms of malaise and nutritional shortages probably result in more morbidity. Living in cold conditions, even with proper clothing, requires more caloric intake to maintain the same activity level. In general, approximately 1% more calories is needed for each degree below 20°C. Thus, someone whose house is 10°C requires 10% more food intake to sustain his or her activity level. Since food availability or intake rarely increases when energy is scarce, the metabolic response to cold is for people to slow down. Surveys in Bosnia and Armenia during the early 1990s found that many people were sleeping 18–20 hours per day.

In very cold climates, several things can be done to reduce the hardships associated with cold. High-energy foods such as oil can be made available. Plastic sheeting can be handed out to cover windows and unused doorways. Getting several people or households to share one common heated place can also be useful. In multistory buildings, the temperature in living areas can be dramatically increased by organizing structures so that each floor or apartment heats the same room, causing the heat loss from the floor below to pass into the heated room above. Blankets and sleeping bags can also help people conserve energy while sleeping. Educational messages should warn people about the signs of carbon monoxide poisoning and how to check for gas leaks where fuel is burned as a source of heat.

In warmer climates, sheeting to keep people dry during rainstorms and to provide shade in the daylight can be important for improving the quality of life. Sheeting can allow for the rapid construction of shelter and is often taken by displaced populations when they return home.

## Vector Control

In the United States, mosquito spraying and mosquito monitoring can be a major component of a posthurricane public health program. In developing

**Exhibit 23-4  Control Strategies for Epidemic Diarrheal Diseases**

Cholera: Cholera is perhaps the most waterborne of all diarrheal diseases. Food has also been seen as the main route of transmission in many outbreaks, although food-borne outbreaks are typically less widespread and less rapidly occurring than waterborne outbreaks. Thus, the first task during a cholera outbreak is to make sure that the water people are consuming is chlorinated. In this setting, chlorinated water is considered to be water with a chlorine residual of at least 0.2 mg/L at the moment it is consumed. Where chlorination is not possible, a lemon per liter has been shown to be effective in killing the bacteria that causes cholera (*Virbrio cholerae*), as is boiling water. Because vibrios grow well in unrefrigerated foods, efforts to ensure that people have the fuel needed to heat their food adequately is also called for. Adding acidic sauces such as tomato sauce to foods has been shown to be protective against food-borne cholera. Educational efforts should focus on getting people to consume only chlorinated or boiled fluids and eat only hot, cooked foods or peeled fruits and vegetables. Hand washing practices among those who prepare food for others should also receive attention.

Typhoid fever: Typhoid is also a water- and food-borne disease caused by the bacteria *Salmonella typhi*. Ensuring that the water supply is chlorinated is the best assurance against a massive outbreak, as most large outbreaks are waterborne. Many smaller outbreaks are food-borne, with the hands of the food handlers being the primary hazard. Thus, food hygiene efforts should focus on hand washing among food handlers and ensuring that infected people do not prepare food for others. Although most people, once infected, stop passing the bacteria shortly after regaining their health, 10% of people will still be shedding three months after the onset of symptoms. Therefore, keeping food vendors with typhoid fever away from work until they are noncommunicable takes considerable effort.

Shigella: Outbreaks *Shigella Dysentarie* type I have become quite frequent during periods of civil unrest in recent years. Case fatality rates for this illness can exceed 10%. Other forms of dysentery generally follow the same transmission patterns. Because the infective dose of shigella species tends to be low, perhaps less than 100 organisms, hand-to-mouth or person-to-person transmission is more important than with many other waterborne diseases. Several epidemiologic studies have even linked shigella transmission to flies. Strategies for control need to focus on a comprehensive personal hygiene program (soap and plentiful water made available, hand washing promotion), along with water chlorination and food hygiene efforts. Secondary cases within the households of shigellosis patients are common, so outreach programs should focus education efforts on those households where cases occur.

Hepatitis E: Although hepatitis E is fairly uncommon, it disproportionately strikes refugee populations. During major outbreaks, water has been the main route of transmission, although the most common fecal-oral hepatitis, hepatitis A, is transmitted by food and other routes also. This illness is particularly lethal to pregnant women. Thus, control measures should focus on chlorinating water for the entire population and equipping and educating pregnant women about the need for personal and food hygiene.

countries, rat control (particularly in food warehouses), mosquito spraying and eliminating breeding sites, distributing impregnated bed nets, dipping cows, spraying for housefly and tsetse flies, setting fly traps, and delousing a population have all been done repeatedly among refugee settings. Usually these measures are taken because of a specific health threat. The most common measures are as follows:

- Rat control is usually undertaken primarily to limit food and material losses. Rats destroy food and packaging, chew on the insulation of wires, and are generally seen as unsanitary. Thus, many if not most food warehouses will attempt to control rats with poisons, traps, cats, or some combination thereof. Rats can transmit a myriad of diseases such as plague, leptosporosis, and salmonella, although the cost-effectiveness of health improvements through rat control is largely undocumented.
- Mosquito control is often seen as an essential effort where malaria is a major cause of morbidity. Reducing breeding sites is an inexpensive and safe measure that is often undertaken either formally or informally. Spraying for mosquitoes has been done but is often seen as expensive or environmentally unsound. Mosquito monitoring is widespread in the United States and can be a useful tool following storms and floods for assessing the risks of mosquito-borne illnesses.

### Environmental Surveillance

Planning and organizing environmental surveillance is required before any crisis occurs in order to reestablish the sanitary barriers that previously protected a stricken community. Displaced populations always require food, water, and some type of sanitation services. Establishing these services requires a predictable set of material inputs (e.g., water, latrines, soap, food, fuel) and a set of culturally and socially appropriate messages needed to optimize the use of those materials. Evaluating the effectiveness of these efforts is critical to ensuring the success of an environmental response.

The monitoring process allows for an accurate estimate of how conditions are changing over time. More importantly, having a numeric estimate of service levels or service quality often improves the service either by making the monitored workers more conscientious or by adding political impetus. Often, the process of surveying keeps workers in touch with the people being serviced and enables them to notice ancillary issues to the parameters being measured.

Monitored information should be graphically displayed in a public location to increase everyone's awareness of the efforts underway. Programs for which the level of indicators is favorable will help inspire other programs. Programs that are not meeting their goals may generate suggestions, help, or even prodding from others. Certain parameters, such as fuel and soap availability, need to be monitored only when indicated. In some settings, such as when people are still in their houses and have electricity, people have all of the fuel they need and monitoring the average hours of electrical service is a more demonstrative indicator of their conditions.

## Bioterrorism, Influenza, and Emerging Infectious Diseases

In recent years, there has been a global recognition of the potential peril from bioterrorism and other emerging threats such as severe acute respiratory syndrome (SARS) and pandemic influenza. Terrorist activity both within United States borders and around the world is increasing, and a number of experts suggest that the likelihood of a chemical or biological warfare attack (CBW) is also increasing.[80] Further, the public health and health sector would have difficulty containing a massive infectious disease outbreak.[81] We saw how CBW agents can have an overwhelming impact on public health when on March 20, 1995, members of the Aum Shinriko religious cult released sarin, a nerve gas, in the Tokyo subway. Twelve people were killed, 1000 required hospitalization, and 5000 received medical attention.[80,82] In response to growing concerns for public safety, there has been a decade of federal funding to help the country prepare. Although initial programs were created to bolster nonpublic health preparedness at federal, state, and local levels, later funding specifically addressed the role of public health.

### Bioterrorism Agents

Some understanding of the specific agents that might be employed by terrorists will assist in adequate preparation for a bioterrorist incident.[83] The military weapons displayed in Table 23-4 and Exhibit 23-5 are helpful as a starting point. Of these, anthrax is most formidable in its production of mortality and is the agent of greatest concern (Table 23-5). Smallpox and pneumonic plague can also pose problems of magnitude and are contagious. The CDC has developed a list of critical agents for health preparedness (Table 23-6).[84] Category A has high impact and requires high preparedness. Category B has a lesser requirement for preparedness. Category C can be handled within current public health capacity.

Many of the diseases that may occur as a result of biologic terrorism are rare (inhalational anthrax, pneumonic plague) or have previously been globally eradicated (smallpox).[84] The possibly unannounced dissemination of a biologic agent may go unnoticed at first, with the exposed individuals leaving the scene and not showing signs of illness for hours, days, or weeks. The first response to bioterrorism is at the local level, but subsequent public health management is coordinated at local, state, and federal levels.

**TABLE 23-4   Destroyed US Biologic Arsenal**

| Lethal Agents | Incapacitating Agents | Anticrop Weapons |
|---|---|---|
| *Bacillus anthracis*<br>Botulinum toxin<br>*Francisella tularensis* | Venezuelan equine encephalitis<br>Staphylococcal enterotoxin B<br>*Brucella suis*<br>*Coxiella burnetii* | Wheat-stem rust<br>Rye-stem rust<br>Rice-blast spore |

*Source:* Reprinted from US Department of the Army. *US Army Activity in the US Biological Warfare programs.* Washington, DC: US Department of the Army; 1997. Pub. No. B193427L.

Exhibit 23-5   Rating System (Russian) of Bioagent Distribution According to Probability of Use as BW

- Smallpox virus
- *Yersinia pestis*
- *Bacillus anthracis*
- Botulinum toxin
- Venezuelan equine encephalitis virus
- *Francisella tularensis*
- *Coxiella burnetii*
- Marburg virus
- Influenza virus
- *Burkholderia mallei*
- *Rickettsia typhi*

*Source:* Reprinted from Vorobjev AA, Cherkassey BL, Stepanov AV; Kyuregyan AA, Fjedorov YM. Key problems of controlling especially dangerous infections. In: *Proceedings of an International Symposium: Severe Infectious Diseases: Epidemiology, Express-Diagnostics and Prevention.* Kirov, Russia: State Scientific Institution, Volgo-Vyatsky Center of Applied Biotechnology; 1997.

*The Threat List*

The definition of the threat list depends heavily on who is being threatened and how the threat is perceived. The military definition focuses primarily on bacteriologic agents and toxins that have been weaponized in aerosol form by a nation interested in producing a large number of battlefield casualties. These are the prototypical weapons of mass destruction. The military's threat list is dynamic and depends on intelligence assessment. Thus, it is possible that an organism could be appropriate in theoretical terms as a threat but is not considered a threat because no one has developed a large-scale weapon for containment and dispersion.

**TABLE 23-5   Results of the Hypothetical Aerosol Dissemination of Various Infecting Agents**

| Agent | Downwind Carriage | Deaths | Total Casualties |
|---|---|---|---|
| Venezuelan equine encephalitis | 1 km | 400 | 35,000 |
| Tick-borne encephalitis | 1 km | 9500 | 35,000 |
| Epidemic typhus | 5 km | 19,000 | 85,000 |
| Brucellosis | 10 km | 500 | 100,000 |
| Plague | 10 km | 55,000 | 100,000 |
| Q fever | >20 km | 150 | 125,000 |
| Tularemia | >20 km | 30,000 | 125,000 |
| Anthrax | >>20 km | 95,000 | 125,000 |

*Note:* Casualty figures assume 50 kg of dried agent disseminated along a 2-km line upwind of a population center of 500,000.
*Source:* Data from *Health Aspects of Chemical and Biological Weapons.* World Health Organization; 1970.

**TABLE 23-6   Critical Agents for Health Preparedness**

| Category A | Category B | Category C |
|---|---|---|
| Variola virus | *Coxiella burnetii* | All other biological agents |
| *Bacillus anthracis* | *Brucellae* | may emerge as future |
| *Yersinia pestis* | *Burkholderia mallei* | threats to public health |
| Botulinum toxin | *Burkholderia pseudomallei* | |
| *Francisella tularensis* | Alphaviruses | |
| Filoviruses and | *Rickettsia prowezekii* | |
| arenaviruses | Certain toxins (Ricin, SEB) | |
| | *Chlamydia psittaci* | |
| | Food safety threat agents | |
| | (*Salmonellae, E coli* O157:H7) | |
| | Water safety threat agents | |
| | (*Vibrio colera*, etc.) | |

*Source:* Reprinted from *Critical Agents for Health Preparedness, Summary of Selection Process and Recommendations.* Centers for Disease Control and Prevention, National Center for Infectious Diseases; 1999.

The civilian threat list is much broader because the rapid onset or the effects of the diseases are not critical, and contagious diseases would also be considered effective bioterroristic agents. Many normal public health threats overlap with the agents of bioterrorism, both in the nature of the outbreaks produced, and in the nature of the response to control them. Pneumonic plague is a good example where a naturally occurring case generates a rapid and vigorous public health response to prevent further dissemination.

For purposes of this discussion, it is clear that there are relative priorities among the diseases on the threat list. Of these diseases, only five agents (anthrax, smallpox, plague, botulism, and tularemia) are considered serious threats. The diseases can be categorized in three ways. The first are those diseases that can be spread by an aerosolized release of bacteria producing a respiratory or pulmonary disease. The three agents in this category are anthrax, plague, and tularemia. The second category of illness is where the dissemination is dependent on person-to-person transmission, such as smallpox. Finally, there are diseases that can be caused by contamination of food, water, or other ingested material, such as botulinum toxin.

Anthrax is considered, both in the scientific and popular literature, to be a highly efficacious biologic warfare agent for a number of reasons. First, it forms spores, which give it stability in aerosol. Second, it is relatively easy to disseminate using off-the-shelf technology. Third, if acquired by the respiratory route, the disease is frequently fatal. The US response system was challenged in 2001 when anthrax was mailed to locations in Florida; Washington, DC; and New York City.

Smallpox, as mentioned previously, has the additional feature of being highly contagious in unimmunized populations, with a cycle of 10 to 14 days, an attack rate of up to 90%, and mortality rate as high as 35%. Although an eradication program eliminated the natural illness from the planet and only two samples of live virus were maintained in the United States and Russia, it is thought that smallpox virus is also held by North Korea, injecting uncertainty into any planning.

Plague, a respiratory-acquired illness, is also spread person to person. Because it occurs as and enzootic disease of rodents in the United States, it may be possible to obtain and isolate for use as a terrorist agent. Botulism is likewise an environmental organism that can be easily cultured from soil. Its toxin has the disturbing clinical feature of necessitating intensive supportive care of its victims. Additionally, the treatment for it, in the form of an anti-toxin, is limited in supply and availability.

Tularemia can be disseminated in water. In aerosol form, it produces a severely debilitating pneumonia although it has a lower mortality rate than anthrax. Other agents are on longer threat lists. Q fever and brucella generally produce mild illnesses that would not generate large-scale stress on medical systems or produce large-scale panic. The agents in the next rank of concern are routine public health threats such as viral encephalitis, cholera, salmonella, and staphylococcal enterotoxin B.

## Differences Between Overt and Covert Release

It is unlikely that terrorists would use an overt release, in the form of an announced event or something that is recognized at the time, as their mode for biologic terrorism. This type of release would allow treatment before the onset of disease. In the case of overt releases, an assessment of the threat is made before the response is initiated. In many cases, announced biologic threats are considered hoaxes, and a limited and tempered response is often activated based on an analysis of the situation, thus allowing for resolution of the incident without major difficulties.

A covert release of a biologic agent would present as illness in the community, and its detection would be dependent on traditional surveillance methods. Recent federal programs have enhanced such systems through syndromic surveillance and have increased the sensitivity of frontline medical practitioners to the importance of recognizing and reporting suspicious syndromes. (Refer to Chapter 14 for more detailed discussion.) For some diseases early recognition and diagnosis of the disease is essential for preventing devastating outcomes. For example, with anthrax, treatment is usually only effective before the onset of severe symptoms. Covert release of a contagious agent has the potential for large-scale spread of disease before detection. A release in an airport or in a highly mobile population could disseminate a pathogen such as smallpox throughout most of the world before the epidemic would be recognized. To bring such an epidemic under control, a major multifocal international response would need to be activated.

## The Role of Health Departments and Preparedness

Comprehensive preparedness planning should involve multiple partners within the local, state, federal, and even global community as mentioned above. Because it may take 24–48 hours for regional and federal resources to organize and deploy, the local community must be prepared to respond at the onset. Clearly, LHDs are first-line responders for all incidents involving the health of the community and these principles of preparedness can be used in all hazards, including bioterrorism. In incidents involving suspected bioterrorism, protocols should be developed to deal with the most likely agents. At the local or regional level, public health planning for a bioterrorism event can be modeled after planning models for pandemic influenza because many bioterrorism agents present as flulike illness. There are numerous steps that must be taken to address biologic threats to a community, such as the steps listed on the checklists released by the Department of Health and Human Services (HHS) to guide multisector preparedness for pandemic flu. The following list is a brief overview of the essential elements in planning at a local level, regardless of the threat:

- Readiness and impact assessment—In developing public health preparedness plans, the state or local health department needs to consider both the state of readiness of the community and the potential impact of the threat. In assessing readiness, all other components of planning listed below must be considered.
- Expansion of surveillance and epidemiology capacity—To maximize opportunities to mitigate, community plans should include an ongoing effort to enhance the capacity for surveillance. A surveillance system to track the large numbers of potentially exposed individuals can be designed in accord with the guidance described earlier in this chapter. Strengthened surveillance will ensure (1) the earliest possible recognition of disease, (2) ongoing assessments of the impact of both the threat and subsequent disease, and (3) data to evaluate individual and community responses to population-based interventions.
- Communication—Preplanned strategies for communication with other community agencies and the public are critical. Effective communication, fundamental in any response, is unfortunately often wrought with problems during the crisis as evidenced in the United States both after the September 11, 2001, terrorist attacks and after Hurricane Katrina. Protocols for communication, both internally within the LHD and externally with other response agencies and the public, must have built in redundancy (e.g., Internet, land-based and cellular telephones, radios) and be regularly tested. Templates, such as sample press releases for communicating risk to the public, can be developed in advance. Local health departments should both test the capacity of their Web pages to provide up-to-date information to the public and conduct a drill of their hotline. (See Chapter 20 for further details on communication.)
- Laboratory capacity for identification of the chemical or biologic agent—The LHD should establish linkages with a laboratory capable of identifying agents of concern, the state public health agency, and the CDC in advance of any reported incident. Please refer to the section below on the Public Health Laboratory Network.
- Infection control measures including isolation and quarantine— Isolation and quarantine are among the most complicated infection control measures that must be addressed in the LHD disaster plan. Discussions with local law enforcement and legal authorities to clarify conditions for declaring a public health emergency, or issuing and executing court orders to protect the public's health, should be part of LHD planning. Although LHD may have powers under their normal authority, advance clarification is required about when it might be neces-

sary to establish and use extraordinary legal powers. (See Chapter 4 for more information on public health law.)

- Mass provision of clinical interventions (vaccine or medications)— Depending on the threat facing a community, clinical interventions such as vaccine for smallpox or antibiotics for a bacterial agent may be available to mitigate a biologic threat. Uniform protocols with respect to vaccine distribution or prophylactic antibiotic usage are advisable. This is discussed in greater detail below.
- Coordination and capacity assessment of healthcare delivery system— Communication between the responders and coordination of the healthcare delivery system is essential to minimize the morbidity and mortality associated with a biologic threat. Preparedness plans should include a mechanism for surge capacity, including ongoing assessment of needs, identification of alternate triage and treatment sites, and local capacity for isolation.
- Workforce training and support—In addition to NIMS and ICS training, training plans should include the capacity for "just-in-time" refreshers for the public health workforce and the psychosocial support needed by both responders and the public during the crisis.

In planning a response strategy, LHDs should identify key responders in the community, including emergency medical services, HAZMAT, and police and fire agencies. Discussions about coordinating the response and surveillance should also take place with hospitals and poison control centers. In these incidents, individuals may appear at their local hospital with concerns about potential exposure.

Finally, evaluation of the public health preparedness efforts is important and is discussed in greater detail in Chapter 18.

### The Public Health Laboratory Network*

The Laboratory Response Network (LRN) was established in 1999 by the Association of Public Health Laboratories and the CDC to assist in the US response to biological and chemical terrorism. The LRN is now an integrated national network of about 120 biological and chemical labs with the capacity to respond to bioterrorism, emerging infectious diseases, and other public health threats and emergencies.

The LRN supports surveillance and epidemiological investigations by identifying disease, providing direct and reference services, and conducting environmental, rapid, and specialized testing. Five of the major threats (i.e., botulism, plague, anthrax, tularemia, poxvirus illnesses) occur naturally in the United States, and specimens for these diseases are routinely evaluated by public health laboratories. In addition, the standard techniques for detecting bacterial agents (i.e., gram stain, culture on selective media, visual colony morphology, growth after heat shock and confirmatory methods using phage and direct immunofluorescence) are well recognized for establishing definitive

---

*Section on the Public Health Laboratory Network reprinted with permission from Landesman LY. *Public Health Management of Disasters: The Practice Guide.* 2nd ed. Washington, DC: American Public Health Association; 2005.

diagnosis. Methods such as isolation in cell culture, inoculation of animals, direct fluorescence methods, and electron microscopy are considered definitive methods in virology.

The laboratory response network has three levels of performance designated as sentinel, reference, or national. Designation depends on the types of tests a laboratory can perform and how it handles infectious agents to protect workers and the public. Membership in the LRN is not automatic. State lab directors determine the criteria and whether public health labs in their states should be included in the network. Prospective reference labs must have the equipment, trained personnel, properly designed facilities, and demonstrate testing accuracy.

Sentinel labs (formerly Level A) represent the thousands of hospital-based clinical labs that are on the front lines. In an unannounced or covert terrorist attack, sentinel labs could be the first to identify a suspicious specimen and screen out a presumptive case during routine patient care. A sentinel laboratory's responsibility is to recognize, rule out, and refer a suspicious sample to the right reference lab. They may assess risks for aerosol agents. They use bio safety level 2 (BSL-2) techniques.

Reference labs, (formerly Level B and C) can perform tests to detect and confirm the presence of a threat agent. These labs, also called "confirmatory reference labs," ensure a timely local response in the event of a terrorist incident or other emergency. Rather than having to rely on confirmation from labs at the CDC, reference labs are capable of producing conclusive results. Reference labs can be county, state, or major state public health laboratories that perform direct fluorescence or phage testing such as molecular diagnostics. Using BSL-3 techniques, reference labs have the safety and proficiency to confirm and characterize susceptibility and to probe, type, and perform toxigenicity testing.

National laboratories (formerly Level D) are the network of federal and private partners in the US Public Health Service, Department of Defense, national laboratories, and industry that can perform research on and develop new techniques that are disseminated to the other levels of the network. National labs have unique resources to handle highly infectious agents and are responsible for definitive high-level characterization (seeking evidence of molecular chimeras) or identifying specific agent strains. The CDC and USAMRID national labs, operating at BSL-4, handle the most dangerous agents.

If a covert event occurs that is not recognized immediately, the incidence of disease in the community would trigger public health to submit samples to the laboratory and report to the surveillance network. With an announced threat or an overt event, the situation would be reported to the Federal Bureau of Investigation, which would in turn determine which level of laboratory is required and transport samples to the nearest appropriate laboratory resource in the network.

## Point of Dispensing Sites for Available Countermeasures to Bioterrorist Event

Preventive measures have the distinct advantage of decreasing the potential impact of a bioterrorist event before the threat occurs. In December 2002, in the face of perceived increased threats of biologic terrorism, the US government launched a national smallpox vaccination program in an effort to immunize healthcare providers and thereby decrease the impact of a potential smallpox epidemic. Across the country, health departments and health care facilities stepped up planning for a rapid large-scale immunization program in response to a highly infectious outbreak. This is similar to what was done in the smallpox eradication campaign of the late 1970s. The program resulted in the immunization of far fewer providers than planned, but did set the stage for a response to a reintroduction of smallpox, natural or unnatural.

For the major bacterial threat agents, the administration of antibiotics is the key component of the response. In the event of a release of anthrax, there are several possible scenarios for the large-scale administration of antibiotics. In addition to antibiotics, a vaccine may be administered to at-risk individuals to cut down on the duration of antibiotic administration required. A licensed vaccine for anthrax has been administrated fairly widely to military populations but is not currently available to the public.

Antibiotics are the mainstay of the response to plague and tularemia. The description of the response to these organisms, as well as the others, is found in several resources.[85,86] The public health response to a botulism outbreak is a bit more complicated because the occurrence of paralysis in a number of individuals may overrun the short supply of both ventilators and intensive care beds in pulmonary units. Further, the immune globulin used in the routine treatment of both wound and food-borne botulism is in short supply, and increasing the supply would require a major effort to manufacture a large enough stockpile.

Planning for point of dispensing sites includes preselection of ideal locations and needs assessments for staffing, security, and information technology. There are many considerations in choosing sites including geographic distribution, population density, and the physical layout of the site. Factors to consider include the ability to ensure security at all entrance and exit points, access for parking, and accessibility for persons with disabilities. Performing exercises of point of dispensing plans is critical to identify potential problems, such as bottlenecks in client flow.

Part of the federal public health response has been the earmarking of a national stock of antibiotics and vaccine for the major bioterrorist agents of threat, discussed earlier as the SNS. The long-term strategy for the SNS includes developing a "virtual supply" by contracting with manufacturers to provide large amounts of product on relatively short notice.

## Pandemic Influenza

Influenza, a common but frequently serious disease known as "flu," annually results in more than 200,000 hospitalizations, 36,000 to 40,000 deaths, and $1 billion to $3 billion in direct costs for medical care in the United States.[87] Influenza spreads rapidly and can be transmitted by those who are asymptomatic but infected, leading to the near simultaneous occurrence of multiple community outbreaks in an escalating fashion. Influenza infections are responsible for secondary complications such as pneumonia, dehydration, and worsening of chronic respiratory and cardiac problems. Despite the potential severity of epidemics, the effects of seasonal influenza are usually moderated because most individuals have some immunity to the recently circulating viruses either from previous infections or from vaccination.

Pandemic influenza occurs on average every three to four decades when a new strain of the flu, capable of causing significant morbidity and mortality, emerges. Three pandemics occurred in the 1900s–1918, 1957, and 1968. A key component in pandemics is that the virus be capable of efficient human-to-human transmission. Many infectious disease outbreaks, including SARS, Ebola, or West Nile virus, can have devastating effects. However, these disease outbreaks typically are limited in spread to either localized areas or regions, or to certain at-risk populations because of demographic, climactic, or other factors. Influenza pandemics, by contrast, are explosive global events in which most, if not all, persons are at risk for infection and illness worldwide. Pandemics are expected to begin in the fall to spring seasons and multiple waves are likely 3 to 12 months after the initial outbreak. Such events have the potential to quickly overwhelm countries and their health systems that have not made adequate preparation. Using projection models, public health authorities predict that the next influenza pandemic has the potential to infect 30% percent of the US population, resulting in between 209,000 and 1.9 millions deaths based on mortality data from the 1957 and 1918 pandemic respectively.[88] In addition, the potential cost to the US economy has been estimated at between $71 and $166 billion dollars.[89]

Despite vast improvements in medical technology since the 1918 Spanish Flu epidemic, where 675,000 died in the United States and 20 to 40 million people died worldwide, modern trends increase the potential for illnesses and deaths due to influenza. In past pandemics, influenza viruses spread worldwide within months. The 1957 Asian Flu pandemic caused 70,000 US deaths in an era with much less globalization and spread to the United States within four to five months after being detected in China. The 1968 pandemic spread to the United States from Hong Kong within two to three months, causing 34,000 US deaths. Modern travel patterns will result in quicker spread in the future with increased impact because of the susceptibility to infection in all age groups. Despite the earlier warning that increased surveillance provides, the recent worldwide SARS outbreak was foreboding because it demonstrated that most countries will have minimal time to implement their response plan once pandemic viruses have begun to spread. Importantly, concern has been expressed that planning efforts for pandemic influenza are lagging in the United States when compared to the United Kingdom and Canada.[90]

## Distinguishing Pandemic from Seasonal Influenza

Virologists and epidemiologists predict that new flu pandemics will continue to occur three to four times a century at irregular intervals.[91(p23)] Several epidemiological features distinguish pandemic influenza from seasonal influenza. The infrequency and unpredictable timing of these events is explained by the fact that influenza pandemics occur only when a new influenza A virus emerges for which people have no immunity and then spreads globally infecting the unexposed who are susceptible to infection. By contrast, seasonal influenza virus strain variants are modified versions of influenza A viruses that already are in widespread circulation. Therefore, there usually is some level of existing immunity to strain variants. Because of the frequent appearance of new variants, virus strains contained in influenza vaccines must be updated annually.

## Why Influenza Pandemics Occur

Influenza viruses, negative-stranded RNA viruses classified taxonomically as orthomyxoviruses, are fragile viruses that are primarily divided into two types: A and B viruses. Only type A viruses are known to cause pandemics. Currently, two subtypes of A viruses are in worldwide circulation: H3N2 and H1N1. The emergence in the 1900s of both of these subtypes led to separate pandemics.

Influenza viruses have the ability to modify (drift) or replace (shift) two key viral proteins on the viral surface. Drift and shift have a profound impact on the antigenicity, or the ability to stimulate an immune response, in any given season because these proteins are the main targets for the immune system. Drift, a continuously evolving process of mutation to the virus genome, results in the emergence of variant strains of virus. The amount of change can be subtle or dramatic, but eventually one of the new variant strains becomes dominant, usually for a few years, until a new variant emerges and replaces it. In essence, drift affects the influenza viruses already in worldwide circulation. This process allows influenza viruses to change and reinfect people repeatedly through their lifetime, and it is the reason the influenza virus strains in vaccine must be updated each year. Shift occurs when existing viral proteins are replaced by significantly different proteins.

Pandemic viruses can also arise when some of the genes from animal influenza viruses mix or reassort with some of the genes from human influenza viruses, creating a new hybrid virus. This can occur when a single animal is simultaneously coinfected by both a human influenza virus and an avian influenza virus. In this situation, genes from the human and avian viruses can mix and create a virus with the surface proteins derived from the avian virus (hence, creating a new subtype) and the internal proteins derived from the human virus, enhancing the transmissibility of the hybrid virus. Reassorted viruses have been frequently identified and are thought to have been responsible for the 1957 and 1968 pandemic viruses.

Novel influenza viruses occasionally emerge among humans as part of the natural ecology and biology of influenza viruses. Large reservoirs of influenza viruses circulate among other animal species, notably wild birds. Wild birds are considered the ultimate reservoir for influenza viruses because they usually harbor the virus without becoming sick and readily transmit the virus to domestic chickens or ducks, probably via the fecal-oral route. Normally, animal influenza viruses do not infect humans. However, avian influenza viruses can sometimes "jump" the species barrier and directly infect humans. This was first demonstrated in 1997, when an outbreak of avian influenza A (H5N1) virus infected both domestic poultry and humans in Hong Kong, leading to 18 hospitalizations and six deaths. This virus, known as "avian flu," is currently circulating in Asia, Europe, and Africa, alerting health officials that a pandemic may be brewing. Between 2003 and July 2006, avian outbreaks have occurred in 10 countries with a total of 229 cases and 131 deaths, a case fatality rate of 57%.[92] At the time of publication, there have been limited cases of human-to-human transmission, but no sustained human-to-human transmission has been identified.

### Why Control by Vaccination Is Problematic

Widespread use of influenza vaccine can reduce the burden of mortality and morbidity. However, the availability of sufficient vaccine for seasonal influenza in the US population has been problematic because the industry manufacturing vaccine is shrinking for economic reasons and because of the decentralized distribution system in the United States. Only two companies—Sanofi Pasteur and Chiron Corporation—provide the country with over 95% of our total supply. In the 2004–2005 influenza season, broad vaccination programs became chaotic when the US vaccine supply was cut in half due to manufacturing problems at one of the two suppliers. In addition, while there was not a shortage of vaccine for the 2005–2006 flu season, delays and other distribution troubles presented enormous challenges in the United States.

The challenges facing production and distribution of a vaccine for H5N1 are even greater. First, while a vaccine that effectively protects against the virus commonly referred to as the avian flu has been developed, as of this writing, it has not yet been approved by the Food and Drug Administration. Once approved, its manufacture could strain an already troubled vaccine manufacturing program. Current methods necessitate that manufacturers make advance predictions about both the demand and the type of vaccine to produce. Because the current H5N1 virus has not mutated into a form that is readily transmissible from person to person, vaccine developed today may not match the virus strains that eventually circulate.[93] Should the virus change, vaccine developed today is likely to be less effective, if it protects at all. Further, when a new influenza strain spreads worldwide, sufficient vaccine will not be available for 6 to 8 months due to current manufacturing capabilities. Finally, the annual delivery of vaccine to the United States is unpredictable for the influenza strains currently in circulation, contributing to increased uncertainty that the manufacturers could produce enough vaccine in a pandemic, even if an exact match is found. In an effort to alleviate these concerns, the federal government has earmarked over a billion dollars to develop cell-based vaccine and manufacturing capacity in the United States.

In addition to manufacturing problems, the delivery system for influenza vaccines in the United States is highly decentralized with public health agencies having limited information about ordering by providers in the private sector and manufacturers' distribution of available vaccine. This lack of centralized oversight inhibits advance planning for or providing advanced direction about redistribution during an influenza vaccine shortage.

With respect to antivirals, in February 2005, the World Health Organization recommended that countries stockpile antiviral medications to protect against the avian flu currently circulating in Asia. However, once an epidemic starts, there would be high global demand for the limited supply of antivirals. While the United States[94] has reportedly ordered 5.3 million courses of Tamiflu for the Strategic National Stockpile, this is woefully insufficient as 70 million courses are needed to protect only 25% of the population. In addition, the virus may develop resistance to these antiviral medications, making a control strategy that depends on their use less than ideal.

## Public Health Planning and Preparedness for Pandemic Flu

The goal of *all* preparedness activities is to reduce morbidity and mortality, and minimize social disruption and economic losses. In an influenza pandemic, all categories of responders (first responders, public health, and healthcare professionals) will become ill and the outbreak will be prolonged, occurring over months. For these reasons, planning should address the continuity of operations of essential services in the face of a marked decrease in available workforce. Furthermore, regional and federal assets, usually counted on in a natural disaster, are likely to be limited because of both demand and the difficulty of moving things around the country given widespread outbreaks.

Although much can be done to improve the readiness of communities, pandemic planning must be flexible as assumed widely variable attack rates will drive a specific community's need for federal supplies. Ensuring that your community has robust surveillance and laboratory testing in place is an important step. Laboratories need to be prepared to handle a surge of specimens and to verify that their testing algorithms are adequate. Plans for traditional "shoe leather" public health should include contact tracing and legally vetted procedures for isolation and quarantine.

Vaccine and antiviral distribution will be a massive undertaking. Because of limited supply, procedures have to be established to (1) acquire and take delivery of the drugs; (2) prioritize who will receive available drugs; (3) track supplies, their distribution, and use; (4) conduct mass vaccination clinics; and (5) track adverse events due to vaccination. Further, vaccination to a novel virus may require two doses of vaccine, 30 days apart, to achieve maximum immunity. Thus, any prophylaxis plan should address tracking and recall of individuals receiving novel flu vaccine.

During a pandemic, hospitals should prepare for an increase in inpatient medical care. Even a mild pandemic could produce a 25% increase in demand for inpatient beds, Intensive Care Unit (ICU) beds, and ventilators. With a 30% attack rate, staff absenteeism is expected to be high, and there will be limited availability of critical resources.[83] Hospital preparations should address

- Surge capacity issues
- The role of triage centers, volunteers, and home care
- Guidance for hospital employees
- Infection control guidelines
- Mass mortality issues
- Support for staff and their families
- Tracking hospital resources

Communications will be critical throughout the pandemic. In advance of any case in the United States, strategies for communicating risk reduction behaviors must be shared across all media. These include social distancing, hand washing, and respiratory etiquette. Further, planning should include communications about seeking care and vaccine and/or antiviral distribution. It is critical that key messages be communicated uniformly with one voice.

**Federal Preparedness Activities**

The HHS Web site, www.pandemicflu.gov, provides up-to-date information of national and global activities relating to pandemic flu. Specific planning tools (checklists) are posted, providing consistent preparedness guidelines across the country and across different sectors of society. The CDC, as part of the global preparedness effort, has established cooperative agreements for surveillance in other countries and is supporting World Health Organization activities. To ensure vaccine security and supply, HHS has provided funding to research cell-based influenza vaccine and to promote the expansion and diversification of the US influenza vaccine production. The National Institutes of Health (NIH) is testing pilot lots of H5N1 vaccine, which have been found effective, but as mentioned earlier, the vaccine has yet to be approved by the FDA. Finally, antiviral drugs are being added to the Strategic National Stockpile.

The Federal Pandemic Influenza Preparedness and Response Plan can serve as a foundation for the federal response to seasonal flu vaccine shortages. The federal plan provides guidance on assuring and expanding production capacity for influenza vaccine; increasing the use of influenza vaccination; stockpiling influenza antiviral drugs in the Strategic National Stockpile (SNS); enhancing US and global disease detection and surveillance infrastructures; supporting public health planning and laboratories; and improving healthcare system readiness at the community level.[95]

•   •   •

Public health organizations carry out a broad and complex set of responsibilities in preparing for and responding to disasters and acts of bioterrorism. Carrying out these responsibilities requires a multiorganizational effort. Disaster epidemiology and assessment are important components of the public health response, as these activities support scientific investigation as well as disaster management decision making. Public health organizations also play critical roles in preventing and controlling the psychosocial effects of disasters. The emerging threats of bioterrorism and global disease through pandemic influenza call attention to the importance of public health organizations in disaster preparedness and response initiatives, creating new risks and responsibilities for organizations along the continuum of public health practice settings. The contemporary public health environment demands informed decision making and effective management in response to the health threats posed by man-made and natural disasters.

## Chapter Review

1. Disasters are ecologic disruptions or emergencies of magnitude resulting in deaths, injuries, and property damage exceeding the local capacity to respond and calling for external assistance.
2. The public health role in disaster is broad and includes assessment, sharing information, preparedness, triage, casualty distribution, and preventing outbreaks of infectious disease through surveillance, maintaining healthcare services, environmental interventions, and other measures.

3. Response to disasters are multiorganizational, with the first response at the local level.

4. Information about the acute impacts of disasters may be provided through rapid needs assessments and surveillance systems.

5. Surveillance systems are conducted after disasters to detect illnesses or injuries in the affected population and are usually one of three types.
   - Hazard
   - Exposure
   - Outcome

6. Disasters are highly stressful, disruptive experiences for individuals, families, and entire communities. Mental health sequelae of a disaster can be widespread, exceeding the direct toll of physical injuries.

7. Most stress reactions after disaster tend to be transient. However, a portion of the population may suffer more serious, persistent effects such as PTSD.

8. Mental health measures after disaster include outreach, education, restoration of community services, crisis counseling, and rebuilding support networks.

9. Within the context of an emergency situation, where people have been displaced from their homes and are existing in overcrowded conditions, environmental factors and sanitation are key to health protection.

10. Environmental measures in a disaster situation include the provision of adequate volumes of water free from contamination, facilities to dispose of human excreta, hand washing, protection of food from spoilage, and the provision of housing and shelter.

11. Bioterrorism and emerging infectious diseases are continually evolving threats, requiring preplanning for a coordinated first response at the local level and linkages with state and federal public health and other involved agencies.

## References

1. Nishenko SP, Bollinger GA. Forecasting damaging earthquakes in the central and eastern United States. *Science.* 1990;249:1412–1416.

2. Gray WM. Strong association between west African rainfall and US landfall of intense hurricanes. *Science.* 1990;249:1251–1256.

3. Universite Catholique de Louvain, Brussels, Belgium. EM-DAT: The Office of Foreign Disaster Assistance/CRED International Disaster Database. Available at: http://www.em-dat.net. Accessed June 25, 2006.

4. World Health Organization. WHO calls for more funds for health to avoid 2nd wave of deaths from Pakistan earthquake. Available at: http://www.who.int/mediacentre/news/releases/2005/pr54/en/. Accessed June 14, 2006.

5. NOAA National Hurricane Center. Hurricane History. Available at: http://www.nhc.noaa.gov/HAW2/english/history.shtml. Accessed June 9, 2006.

6. Gunn SWA. *Multilingual Dictionary of Disaster Medicine and International Relief.* Dordrecht, The Netherlands: Kluwer Academic Publishers; 1990.

7. Showalter P, Myers MF. Natural disasters in the United States as release agents of oil, chemicals, or radiological materials between 1980–1989. *Risk Analysis.* 1994;14:169–182.

8. Cuny F. Introduction to disaster management: lesson 2—concepts and terms in disaster management. *Prehospital Disaster Med.* 1993;8:89–94.

9. Robert T. Stafford Disaster Relief and Emergency Assistance Act, Pub L 93-288.

10. Auf der Heide E. *Community Medical Disaster Planning and Evaluation Guide.* Dallas, TX: American College of Emergency Physicians; 1996.

11. Quarantelli EL. *Delivery of Emergency Medical Care in Disasters: Assumptions and Realities.* New York, NY: Irvington Publishers Inc; 1983.

12. National Research Council. *Reducing Disasters' Toll: The US Decade for Natural Disaster Reduction.* Washington, DC: National Academy Press; 1989.

13. L.R. Johnston Associates. *Floodplain Management in the United States: An Assessment Report. Volume 2 Full Report. Prepared for the Federal Interagency Floodplain Management Taskforce. FIA-18/June 1992.* Washington, DC: US Federal Emergency Management Agency, Federal Interagency Floodplain Management Taskforce; 1992.

14. Berke PR, Beatley T. *Planning for Earthquakes.* Baltimore, Md: The Johns Hopkins Press; 1992.

15. Testimony before the Committee on Science, Space, and Technology. US House of Representatives. 101st Cong, 1st Sess (1989) (testimony of Dr. James E. Beavers, member, Scientific Advisory Committee of the National Center for Earthquake Engineering Research, State University of New York at Buffalo, Buffalo, NY).

16. Utah Earthquake Preparedness Information Center. *Earthquakes: What You Should Know When Living in Utah.* Salt Lake City, UT: Federal Emergency Management Agency; 1996.

17. Culliton TJ, Blackwell CM, Remer DG, Goodspeed TR, Warren MA. *50 Years of Population Change along the Nation's Coasts, 1960–2010.* Rockville, Md: National Oceanic and Atmospheric Administration; 1990. Coastal Trends Series, Report 2.

18. National Oceanic and Atmospheric Administration. NOAA predicts very active North Atlantic hurricane season. Available at: http://www.noaanews.noaa.gov/stories2006/s2634.htm. Accessed June 9, 2006.

19. Axelrod C, Killam PP, Gaston MH, Stinson N. Primary health care and the Midwest flood disaster. *Public Health Rep.* 1994;109(5):601–605.

20. Gautam K. Organizational problems faced by the Missouri DOH in providing disaster relief during the 1993 floods. *J Public Health Manage Pract.* 1998;4(4):79–86.

21. Whitman S, Good G, Donoqhue ER, Benbow N, Shou W, Mou S. Mortality in Chicago attributed to the July 1995 heat wave. *Am J Public Health.* 1997;87(9):1515–1518.

22. Nation's Commission on Terrorist Attacks upon the United States. The 9/11 Commission Report: Final Report of the Nation's Commission on Terrorist Attacks Upon the United States. Executive Summary. Available at: http://www.9-11commission.gov/report/911Report_Exec.htm. Accessed June 9, 2006.

23. Evans CA. Public health impact of the 1992 Los Angeles unrest. *Public Health Rep.* 1993;108(3):265–272.

24. Landesman LY. *Public Health Management of Disasters: The Practice Guide.* 2nd ed. Washington, DC: American Public Health Association; 2005.

25. Landesman LY. *Public Health Management of Disasters: The Pocket Guide*. Washington, DC: American Public Health Association; 2005.

26. Lyskowski R, Rice S. *The Big One: Hurricane Andrew*. Kansas City, Mo: Miami Herald Publishing Co; 1992.

27. Carr SJ, Leahy SM, London S, Sidhu S, Vogt J. The public health response to the Los Angeles 1994 earthquake. *Am J Public Health*. 1996;86(4): 589–590.

28. Holtz TH, Leighton J, Balter S, Weiss D, Blank S, Weisfuse I. The public health response to the World Trade Center disaster. In: Levy BS, Sidel VW, eds. *Terrorism and Public Health: A Balanced Approach to Strengthening Systems and Protecting People*. New York, NY: Oxford University Press; 2002.

29. Noji E, ed. *The Public Health Consequences of Disaster*. New York, NY: Oxford University Press; 1997.

30. Saylor LF, Gordon JE. The medical component of natural disasters. *Am J Med Sci*. 1957;234:342–362.

31. Buist AS, Bernstein RS. Health effects of volcanoes: an approach to evaluating the health effects of an environmental hazard. *Am J Public Health*. 1986;76(3 suppl):1–90.

32. Bernstein RS, Baxter PJ, Falk H, Inq R, Foster L, Frost F. Immediate public health concerns and actions in volcanic eruptions: lessons from Mount St. Helens eruptions, May 18–October 18, 1980. *Am J Public Health*. 1986;76(3 suppl):25–37.

33. Resolution 44/236 of the General Assembly of the United Nations, 1989.

34. Resolution 54/219 of the General Assembly of the United Nations, 1999.

35. Bissell RA, Pinet L, Nelson M, Levy M. Evidence of the effectiveness of health sector preparedness in disaster response: the example of four earthquakes. *Fam Community Health*. 2004;27(3):193–203.

36. Qureshi KA, Gershon RRM, Merrill JA, et al. Effectiveness of an emergency preparedness training program for public health nurses in New York City. *Fam Community Health*. 2004;27(3):242–249.

37. Ginzburg HM, Jevec RJ, Reutershan T. The public health services response to Hurricane Andrew. *Public Health Rep*. 1993;108(2):241–244.

38. Lewis P. *Final Report: Governor's Disaster Planning and Response Review Committee*. Tallahassee, Fla: Governor's Disaster Planning and Response Review Committee; 1993.

39. Landesman LY. The availability of disaster preparation courses at US schools of public health. *Am J Public Health*. 1993;83(10):1494–1495.

40. Daley WR. Public health response to Hurricane Katrina. *MMWR*. 2006; 55(2):29–30.

41. Toprani, Ratard R, Straif-Bourgeois S, et al. Surveillance in hurricane evacuation centers—Louisiana, September–October 2005. *MMWR*. 2006; 55(2):32–35.

42. Greenough PG, Kirsch TD. Hurricane Katrina. Public health response—assessing the needs. *N Engl J Med*. 2005;353(15):1544–1546.

43. Office of Disease Prevention and Health Promotion. *Healthy People 2010*. Washington, DC: USDHHS; 2000.

44. O'Carroll PW, Friede A, Noji EK, Lillibridge SR, Fries DJ, Atchison CG. The rapid implementation of a statewide emergency health information system during the 1993 Iowa flood. *Am J Public Health*. 1995;85(4):564–567.

45. Joint Commission on Accreditation of Healthcare Organizations. *Comprehensive Accreditation Manual for Hospitals: The Official Handbook*. (EC 1.6, EC 2.5, EC 2.9, EC-5, EC-6, EC-12, EC-13, EC-25, EC-26, EC-49, EC-50, HR 1.25 (draft), HR 4.35 (draft). Oakbrook Terrace, Ill: JCAHO; 2005.

46. Bissell R, Becker BM, Burkle FM Jr. Health care personnel in disaster response: reversible roles or territorial imperatives? *Emerg Med Clinics North Am.* 1996;14(2):267–288.

47. Drabek TE. *Managing Multiorganizational Emergency Response: Emergency Research and Rescue Networks in Natural Disaster and Remote Area Setting.* Boulder, Co: Natural Hazards Information Center, University of Colorado; 1981.

48. United States National Response Plan. Available at: http://www.dhs.gov/dhspublic/interapp/editorial/editorial_0566.xml. Accessed August 12, 2005.

49. Federal Emergency Management Agency, National Incident Management System. Frequently Asked Questions: NIMS Compliance: What does full NIMS compliance mean? Available at: http://www.fema.gov/emergency/nims/index.shtm. Accessed June 9, 2006.

50. Cuny F. Introduction to disaster management, lesson 1: the scope of disaster management. *Prehospital Disaster Med.* 1992;7(4):400–409.

51. Anker M. Epidemiological and statistical methods for rapid health assessment: introduction. *World Health Stat Q.* 1991;44:94–97.

52. Thacker SB, Berkelman RL. Public health surveillance in the United States. *Epidemiol Rev.* 1988;10:164–190.

53. Sidel VW, Onel E, Geiger NJ, Leaning J, Foege WH. Public health responses to natural and human-made disasters. In: Wallace RB, Doebbeling BN, eds. *Maxcy-Rosenau-Last: Public Health and Preventive Medicine.* Stamford, Conn: Appleton & Lange; 1992:1173–1186.

54. US Centers for Disease Control and Prevention, Epidemiology Program Office. *Training Notes.* Atlanta, Ga: CDC; 1992.

55. Baxter PJ, Ing R. Mount St. Helens eruptions, May 18 to June 12, 1980: an overview of the acute health impact. *JAMA.* 1988;246:2585–2589.

56. Gerrity ET, Flynn BW. Mental health consequences of disasters. In: Noji EK, ed. *Public Health Consequences of Disasters.* New York, NY: Oxford University Press; 1997:101–121.

57. Young BH, Ford JD, Ruzek JI, et al. *Disaster Mental Health Services: A Guidebook for Clinicians and Administrators.* Menlo Park, Calif: National Center for Post-Traumatic Stress Disorder; 1998.

58. Murphy SA. Health and recovery status of victims one and three years following a natural disaster. In: Figley CR, ed. *Trauma and Its Wake: Traumatic Stress Theory, Research, and Intervention.* New York, NY: Brunner/Mazel Publishers; 1986:133–155.

59. Ursano RJ, Fullerton CS, McCaughey BG. Trauma and disaster. In: Ursano RJ, McCaughey BG, Fullerton CS, eds. *Individual and Community Responses to Trauma and Disaster: The Structure of Human Chaos.* Cambridge, England: Cambridge University Press; 1994:3–27.

60. Fullerton CS, Ursano RJ, eds. *Posttraumatic Stress Disorder: Acute and Long-Term Responses to Trauma and Disaster.* Washington, DC: American Psychiatric Press; 1997:3–18.

61. Hobfoll SE, Dunahoo C, Monnier J. Conservation of resources and traumatic stress. In: Freedy JR, Hobfoll SE, eds. *Traumatic Stress: From Theory to Practice.* New York, NY: Plenum Press; 1995:29–47.

62. Karam EG. Comorbidity of posttraumatic stress disorder and depression. In: Fullerton CS, Ursano RJ, eds. *Posttraumatic Stress Disorder: Acute and Long-Term Responses to Trauma and Disaster.* Washington, DC: American Psychiatric Press; 1997:77–90.

63. Hoffman KJ, Sasaki JE. Comorbidity of substance abuse and PTSD. In: Fullerton CS, Ursano RJ, eds. *Posttraumatic Stress Disorder: Acute and*

*Long-Term Responses to Trauma and Disaster.* Washington, DC: American Psychiatric Press; 1997:159–174.

64. O'Brien LS. *Traumatic Events and Mental Health.* Cambridge, England: Cambridge University Press; 1998.

65. Fullerton CS, Ursano RJ. Posttraumatic Responses in Spouse/Significant Others of Disaster Workers. In: Fullerton CS, Ursano RJ, eds. *Posttraumatic Stress Disorder: Acute and Long-Term Responses to Trauma and Disaster.* Washington, DC: American Psychiatric Press; 1997:59–75.

66. Marsella AJ, Friedman MJ, Gerrity ET, Scurfield RM, eds. *Ethnocultural Aspects of Posttraumatic Stress Disorder: Issues, Research, and Clinical Applications.* Washington, DC: American Psychological Association; 1996.

67. Green BL. Cross-national and ethnocultural issues in disaster research. In: Marsella AJ, Friedman MJ, Gerrity ET, Scurfield RM, eds. *Ethnocultural Aspects of Posttraumatic Stress Disorder: Issues, Research, and Clinical Applications.* Washington, DC: American Psychological Association; 1996:341–361.

68. Friedman MJ, Marsella AJ. Posttraumatic stress disorder: an overview of the concept. In: Marsella AJ, Friedman MJ, Gerrity ET, Scurfield RM, eds. *Ethnocultural Aspects of Posttraumatic Stress Disorder: Issues, Research, and Clinical Applications.* Washington, DC: American Psychological Association; 1996:11–32.

69. Gusman FD, Stewart J, Young BH, et al. A multicultural approach and developmental framework for treating trauma. In: Marsella AJ, Friedman MJ, Gerrity ET, Scurfield RM, eds. *Ethnocultural Aspects of Posttraumatic Stress Disorder: Issues, Research, and Clinical Applications.* Washington, DC: American Psychological Association; 1996:439–457.

70. Green BL, Solomon SD. The mental health impact of natural and technological disasters. In: Freedy JR, Hobfoll SE, eds. *Traumatic Stress: From Theory to Practice.* New York, NY: Plenum Press; 1995:163–180.

71. Taylor VA. *Delivery of Mental Health Services in Disasters: The Xenia Tornado and Some Implications.* Columbus, OH: Disaster Research Center, Ohio State University; 1976. Disaster Research Center Book and Monograph Series #11.

72. Leviton LC, Needleman CE, Shapiro MA, eds. *Confronting Public Health Risks: A Decision Maker's Guide.* Thousand Oaks, Calif: Sage Publications: 1998.

73. McKnight JL, Kretzmann JP. *Mapping Community Capacity.* Evanston, Ill: Center for Urban Affairs and Policy Research, Northwestern University; 1990.

74. Bracht N, ed. *Health Promotion at the Community Level.* Newbury Park, Calif: Sage Publications; 1990.

75. Pynoos RS, Goenjian AK, Steinberg AM. A public mental health approach to the postdisaster treatment of children and adolescents. *Child Adolesc Psychiatr Clin North Am.* 1988;7:195–210.

76. Peterson EA, Roberts L, Toole MJ, Peterson DE. Soap use effect on diarrhea: Nyamithuthu refugee camp. *Int J Epidemiol.* 1998;27:520–524.

77. Esrey SA, Ptash JB, Roberts L, Shiff C. Effects of improved water supply and sanitation on ascariasis, diarrhoea, dracunculiasis, hookworm infection, schistosomiasis, and trachoma. *Bull WHO.* 1991;69(5):609–621.

78. Centers for Disease Control and Prevention. Mortality among newly arrived Mozambican refugees–Zimbabwe and Malawi. *MMWR.* 1992;42(24): 468–477.

79. Hatch DL, Waldman RJ, Lungu GW, Piri C. Epidemic cholera during refugee resettlement in Malawi. *Int J Epidemiol.* 1994;22(6):1292–1299.

80. Hood E. Chemical and biological weapons: new questions, new answers. *Environ Health Perspec.* 1999;107(12):931–932.

81. Masci JR, Bass E. *Bioterrorism: A Guide for Hospital Preparedness.* New York, NY: CRC Press; 2004.

82. Okumura T, Suzuki K, Fukuda A, et al. The Tokyo subway sarin attack: disaster management, part I: community emergency response. *Acad Emerg Med.* 1998;5(6):613–617.

83. Cieslak TJ, Eitzen EM. Bioterrorism: agents of concern. *J Public Health Manage Pract.* 2000;6(4):19–29.

84. National Center for Infectious Diseases. *Critical Agents of Concern, Summary of Selection Process and Recommendations.* Atlanta, Ga: CDC; 1999.

85. Weinstein RS, Alibek K. *Biological Terrorism: A Guide for Healthcare Providers and First Responders.* New York, NY: Thieme Publishers; 2003.

86. Veenema TG. *Disaster Nursing and Emergency Preparedness for Chemical, Biological, and Radiological Terrorism and Other Hazards.* New York, NY: Springer Publishing; 2003.

87. Heinrich J. *Infectious Disease Preparedness—Federal Challenges in Responding to Influenza Outbreaks.* Washington, DC: US Government Accountability Office; 2004.

88. US Department of Health and Human Services. Pandemic flu planning assumptions. Available at: http://www.pandemicflu.gov/plan/pandplan.html. Accessed June 9, 2006.

89. Meltzer MI, Cos NJ, Feiji K. The economic impact of pandemic influenza in the United States: priorities for intervention. *Emerg Infect Dis.* 1999; 5(5):659–671.

90. Trust for America's Health. *A Killer Flu.* Washington, DC: Trust for America's Health; 2002.

91. World Health Organization. Avian influenza: assessing the pandemic threat. Available at: http://www.who.int/csr/disease/influenza/WHO_CDS_2005 _29/en/index.html. Accessed June 25, 2006.

92. World Health Organization. Epidemic and pandemic alert response, cumulative number of confirmed human cases of avian influenza A/(H5N1) reported to WHO. Available at: http://www.who.int/csr/disease/avian_influenza/country/cases_table_2006_07_04/en/index.html. Accessed July 6, 2006.

93. Treanor J. Influenza vaccine—outmaneuvering antigenic shift and drift. *N Engl J Med.* 2004;350:3.

94. Gerberding J. US influenza supply and preparations for the future. Hearings before the Committee on Government Reform, US House of Representatives, (2005) (testimony of J. Gerberding on the US influenza vaccine supply and preparations for the future).

95. American Public Health Association. *Developing a Comprehensive Public Health Approach to Influenza Vaccination.* Washington, DC: APHA; 2004.

# CHAPTER 24

## EVIDENCE FOR THE FUTURE

Glen P. Mays

## Chapter Overview

Concerns about the nation's health and health systems have returned to the forefront of public debate in the United States, with rising healthcare costs and persistent gaps in quality, safety, and accessibility dominating the discussion.[1-3] Despite spending more on health services than any other nation, Americans continue to experience higher rates of premature death and preventable diseases and disabilities, and lower life expectancies, than their counterparts in many other industrialized countries.[4,5] At the same time, the threat of terrorism and emerging infectious diseases such as SARS and pandemic influenza have brought increasing public attention to gaps and inadequacies in the basic infrastructure that protects health at the population level. Moreover, the rapidly growing obesity epidemic has highlighted the difficulties faced by the health system in addressing the myriad social, behavioral, physical, and environmental conditions that precipitate disease and injury.

Addressing these problems requires targeted efforts to strengthen the nation's public health infrastructure and ensure that governmental public health agencies can engage effectively with other components of the health system to mount effective, population-based prevention and health protection activities.[6] Historically, such efforts have been hindered by an underresourced and deteriorating public health infrastructure;[7,8] by institutional, professional, and cultural differences between medical and public health settings;[9,10] and by gaps in the evidence base concerning what constitutes effective public health practice.[6,11] To begin to address these issues, the federal government has allocated more than $6 billion in new funding to strengthen public health system preparedness for bioterrorism and other emerging health threats. Along with these new resources, the public health community urgently needs a strong evidence base on how best to allocate and apply these funds. The nation's historical experience with healthcare financing clearly indicates that increased spending alone will not guarantee improved health.

## The Role of Research in Public Health Improvement

Over the past three decades, a growing body of evidence has demonstrated wide variation in the availability and quality of public health services across communities.[7,12-16] Nevertheless, efforts to improve public health systems and public health infrastructure have lagged behind comparable efforts in medical care.[17] A persistent obstacle to public health system improvement has been the lack of information about what constitutes effective public health practice and how best to organize, finance, and implement these activities. Recognizing this problem, the research community has begun to investigate these critical issues of policy and practice through studies of public health systems.

Strengthening the nation's public health systems requires better information on how best to organize, finance, and deliver public health services to achieve improvements in population health. As demand for this information has grown among public health policy makers and administrators, the academic and research communities have responded by applying the concepts and methods of health services research to the study of public health practice. In so doing, the field of public health systems research has emerged as a specialized branch of health services research that focuses on the operation and impact of public health systems.

Public health systems research is a field of inquiry that examines the organization, financing, and delivery of public health services within communities and the impact of these activities on population health.[18] Studies within this field are designed to produce the evidence needed by key public health decision makers—including practitioners, administrators, and policy makers—to improve the effectiveness and efficiency of public health systems. From this perspective, a public health system includes the full complement of public and private organizations that contribute to the delivery of public health services for a given population, including governmental public health agencies as well as private and voluntary entities. Public health systems can be defined at multiple levels of operation, including community, state, regional, national, and international levels. Although some studies examine public health systems in their entirety, others choose to focus on specific components within these systems, such as local health departments, community-based initiatives, and linkages between medical care and public health providers. The public health services examined in this field include the full range of activities undertaken to protect and improve health at the population level, as described by the 10 essential public health services identified by the Public Health Functions Steering Committee in 1994 (see Chapter 2).

Conceptually, public health systems research fits within the larger field of inquiry known as health services research. In practice, however, much of the health services research conducted to date has focused on the organization, financing, and delivery of medical care. That the medical care system has dominated the health services research agenda for much of the past four decades is not surprising, given the fact that medical care accounts for the vast majority of national health expenditures. The field of public health systems research has emerged as a vehicle for applying the concepts and methods of health services research to public health settings. As with studies of the medical care system, public health systems research is a multidisciplinary endeavor that comprises studies from a variety of theoretical and methodological perspectives, including epidemiology, biostatistics, economics, sociology, psychology, political science, information science, and operations research.

In its 2003 report on the nation's public health system, the Institute of Medicine (IOM) recognized the critical importance of public health systems research, finding that this emerging field needs to expand considerably to address the current and future need for evidence in public health practice:

> Research is needed to guide policy decisions that shape public health practice. The Committee had hoped to provide specific guidance elaborating on the types and levels of workforce, infrastructure, related resources, and financial investments necessary to ensure the availability of essential public health services to all of the nation's communities. However, such evidence is limited, and there is no agenda or support for this type of research, despite the critical need for such data to promote and protect the nation's health. CDC, in collaboration with the Council on Linkages between Academia and Public Health Practice and other public health system partners, should develop a research agenda and estimate the funding needed to build the evidence base that will guide policy making for public health practice.[6]

Although studies of this nature do exist and are currently underway, the field of public health systems research is still relatively new and the volume and strength of evidence produced by it are necessarily limited.

## Intervention Research vs. Systems Research

Much of the existing research carried out in public health settings can be classified as intervention research. These studies focus on testing the efficacy of specific public health interventions in improving health-related outcomes. For example, this type of research includes studies of health education programs designed to reduce rates of tobacco use among youth, studies of exercise programs designed to increase the proportion of adults who engage in regular physical activity, and studies of social marketing programs designed to increase rates of influenza vaccination among the elderly. The strongest studies of this type use experimental research designs in which members of the target population are randomly assigned either to the intervention group that is exposed to the intervention of interest, or to one or more control groups that are not exposed. These studies measure the effect of the intervention by calculating the differences in the outcomes observed in the intervention and control groups.

By contrast, public health systems research focuses on identifying ways of implementing and sustaining public health interventions within real-world public health settings (Table 24-1). This type of research seeks to identify the organizational, financial, technical, and human resources needed to operate public health interventions successfully and efficiently. In doing so, this research seeks to explain why there are disparities in the availability and quality of public health interventions across states and communities, and to identify effective strategies for closing these gaps. Unlike intervention research, systems research often must rely on observational research designs

**TABLE 24-1 Comparison of Intervention Research and Systems Research in Public Health**

| Intervention Research | Systems Research |
|---|---|
| Goal is to determine whether a specific public health intervention improves outcomes of interest | Goal is to identify how best to implement and maintain effective public health interventions in real-world public health settings |
| Uses experimental research designs and controlled trials | Uses observational research designs and participatory research approaches |
| Measures of interest typically reflect health, behavioral, and/or economic end points | Measures of interest often reflect elements of public health system performance such as service availability, accessibility, quality, efficiency, and/or equity |
| Comparisons are made between groups that are exposed or not exposed to the intervention | Comparisons are made across different public health settings defined by characteristics such as their organizational, financial, human, and technical resources |

that collect data during the normal course of operations in public health settings. Researchers usually do not have the opportunity or resources to randomly assign communities to different types of public health systems in order to compare the outcomes that result. Rather than comparing outcomes observed in intervention and control groups, systems researchers usually compare outcomes observed in different public health settings and/or across different time periods, using advanced statistical methods to control for factors that may confound the analysis. These methods allow researchers to estimate the differences in outcomes that are attributable to differences in system characteristics such as the organizational, financial, technical, and human resources available within public health settings.

## What Can Be Learned from Public Health Systems Research?

Well-designed research studies can produce many different types of evidence needed for improving the nation's public health systems. Some of the most important areas in which studies are now under way are described below:

- Descriptive studies on the current organization and operation of public health systems—Surprisingly little information exists about the basic characteristics of public health systems, including how many local, state, and tribal public health systems exist across the nation; the range of organizations that contribute to public health systems and the division of labor among them; the range of responsibilities and authorities carried out by public health systems; the organizational structures and financing strategies used by public health systems; and the size, composition, and skills of the workforce that maintains our public health systems. Documenting how these system characteristics vary across communities is an essential first step in identifying both strengths and weaknesses within the nation's public health infrastructure.

- The scope and scale of public health services needed within communities—Public health practitioners and administrators face an ongoing need for information about what services, programs, and activities constitute effective public health practice within their communities, and how to ensure access to these services for the populations that need them. This information is needed to allocate scarce public health resources efficiently among the broad range of programs and interventions maintained by public health systems, and to address disparities in access to public health services. Several initiatives are currently under way to identify existing research and outstanding research needs in this area, including the CDC's *Guide to Community Preventive Services* and the efforts of the National Association of County and City Health Officials to develop an operational definition of what citizens can expect from a functional local health department.

- How organizational and financial characteristics affect the effectiveness and efficiency of public health systems—Studies in this area provide vital insight into how best to organize, finance, and staff public health systems in order to produce the desired services and programs considered essential elements of public health practice. The public health profession currently does not have good evidence about the funding and staffing levels that are required to assure all citizens access to high-quality public health services. Nevertheless, preliminary research in this area has linked public health system effectiveness to a variety of system characteristics including having full-time executive leadership and a governing board of health, health department staffing levels and per capita expenditures, and the size of the public health jurisdiction.

- How public health system performance affects community health—These studies are perhaps the most difficult to conduct given the complex relationships that exist between public health systems and community health outcomes. Preliminary research has begun to explore the cross-sectional relationships between system performance and community health status, but additional work will be required—using longitudinal data and multivariate modeling techniques—to elucidate the mechanisms through which public health systems influence community health.

## Research Opportunities and Priorities

The research needs in public health systems are many and varied, but fortunately, new research opportunities have begun to emerge in the wake of several recent developments in public health. As one of the most promising opportunities, the National Public Health Performance Standards Program was officially launched in June 2002 after several years of development by the CDC, the American Public Health Association, the National Association of County and City Health Officials, the Association of State and Territorial Health Officials, the National Association of Local Boards of Health, and other leading public health organizations. The Performance Standards Program provides a process and set of instruments for collecting valid and reliable measures of public health system performance at local, state, and national levels. Already implemented in more than 10 states, these instruments provide a rich source of data for comparing performance across public health systems and over time, thereby creating opportunities for important new studies in public health systems. Several studies already have been conducted using pilot test data from this program, and additional studies are now under way. As the number of states participating in the Performance Standards Program grows, it is sure to become a valuable new resource for researchers and public health decision makers alike.

As another research opportunity, the CDC and other public health organizations are continuing to develop data and measures to assess progress toward the *Healthy People 2010* national health objectives related to public health infrastructure development. These objectives, described in Chapter 23 of *Healthy People 2010*, have taken on added importance in the wake of the events of 2001; however, considerable work remains to be done in developing valid and reliable measures of progress toward these goals. The field of public health systems research is well positioned to carry this effort forward and, in so doing, to demonstrate the value of this research to a broad audience of public health decision makers.

Finally, the Institute of Medicine (IOM) recently released a new report on the nation's public health system that identifies a number of important roles that the research community can play in strengthening public health. Specifically, public health systems research will be vital for achieving the IOM's recommendations concerning:

- Developing accountability and accreditation systems for public health
- Monitoring and strengthening the competency of the public health workforce
- Strengthening governmental public health infrastructure and partnerships with other sectors
- Making evidence the foundation of decision making in public health.

The CDC and other public health organizations undoubtedly will look to the field of public health systems research for the information and insight needed to implement these recommendations.

## Building Capacity for Public Health Systems Research

Realizing the promise of public health systems research in informing public health practice will likely require developments along several fronts. As the IOM emphasizes, adequate research funding and well-reasoned research agendas are basic and essential ingredients. Other key elements include the following:

- Research-quality data resources to support system-level research—A persistent barrier to conducting research on public health systems is the lack of current and longitudinal data on basic characteristics of the nation's public health infrastructure, including information on the public health workforce, public health spending, and state and local public health agencies. Rather than depending on the current mix of episodic and ad hoc data sources, the public health research and practice communities must find ways of developing standardized, public use data sets on public health infrastructure collected at regular intervals.

- Research-practice partnerships—Public health systems research is a practice-based field of inquiry that requires strong partnerships between researchers and public health practitioners to be successful. Practitioners must be engaged throughout the research process to ensure that studies ask the right questions, collect the right data, interpret the results correctly, and translate the findings appropriately so that the evidence is useful in the real world of public health practice.
- Methodological advancements—The methodological challenges of defining public health systems and measuring what they do are daunting given the enormous diversity that exists in the organization and delivery of public health services at state and community levels. Nevertheless, the long-term success of the field of public health systems research will depend on our ability to make continued progress on this front, building on current efforts such as the National Public Health Performance Standards Program.[19] Although public health systems research is an applied field of study, considerable attention must be given to the development of analytical methods and tools in public health systems measurement before these tools can be applied to answer the questions of interest to policy and practice.
- The pipeline of public health systems researchers—Expanding the evidence base for public health practice requires researchers who have the requisite skills, experience, and motivation to pursue research opportunities in public health. To build this research capacity, training opportunities are needed to attract new researchers into the field and to encourage established researchers to apply their skills to public health problems. Such opportunities will require strong partnerships between the academic and practice communities.

Although these developments will not occur overnight, progress in each of them is critical to the growth and expansion of the field of public health systems research.

## Protecting Human Subjects in Public Health Research

Public health systems research—and the larger field of public health research—may pose risks to the individuals and populations under study. These risks may involve adverse social and economic consequences associated with accidental disclosure of personal health information, as might be the case if a research subject's medical history or disease status became known to coworkers, a prospective employer, or health insurer. In the case of intervention research, research risks may involve adverse health outcomes that result from unintended side effects of the intervention or the research design, such as inflammation caused by receiving an experimental vaccine or anxiety triggered by exposure to a health education program. Public health organizations play key roles in protecting the health and well-being of individuals and communities that participate in public health research. As a result, these organizations need to stay informed about the evolving methods for protecting human subjects in public health research.

Federal regulations require that institutions engaged in the conduct of research maintain institutional review boards (IRBs) to review all proposed research and ensure the protection of human subjects.[20] To protect human subjects, IRBs and the researchers they oversee must assure and document that the following conditions exist throughout the research process:

- Researchers take all steps possible to minimize the risks posed to human subjects.
- Any risks are reasonable in relation to the anticipated benefits of the research.
- Research risks and benefits are distributed equitably among potential research subjects.
- Potential research subjects are fully informed about the research protocol, its risks and benefits.
- Potential subjects are allowed to choose freely whether to participate in the study, and no subjects are vulnerable to coercion or undue influence regarding their participation.
- Researchers have adequate processes in place to monitor the safety of subjects throughout their participation in the study.
- Researchers have adequate provisions in place to protect the privacy of subjects and to maintain the confidentiality of data.

Large public health organizations that frequently engage in research often find it most effective to maintain their own IRB, and in some cases develop multiple IRBs that can each specialize in a different area of research. Smaller organizations that are infrequently engaged in research activities may elect to use the IRB of an affiliated institution such as a university or a professional association.

Human subjects are frequently involved in public health systems research studies to one extent or another. Because these studies rely most often on observational rather than experimental research designs, the risks they pose most often relate to unintentional disclosure of research data. For example, studies may collect data from workers in different public health settings in order to estimate the effects of staff training and experience on the quality of public health services. In this case, public health workers must be protected as human subjects. Alternatively, studies may collect data from community participants in public health programs and activities in order to examine barriers to participation in different public health settings. In this case, the community participants are the subjects to be protected. In these types of studies, research risks can be minimized through the use of strong data security protections and through efforts to purge identifiable information such as names, addresses, and identification numbers from research data sets once this information is no longer needed.

## Research and the Future of Public Health Systems

Public health professionals are far behind their counterparts in the medical profession in having a base of reliable and relevant research on which to base their decisions. However, the emerging field of public health systems research is helping to close this gap. As this field continues to develop, it is important to recognize that it is the public health practice community rather than the scientific community that must lead this progression. Public health administrators, practitioners, and policy makers must articulate the research questions of interest and demand the evidence to inform pressing public health decisions of the day. Continued leadership from the field of practice is essential if public health systems research is to produce relevant answers and insight for the future.

The need for a strong research base for public health practice has become particularly acute in view of the rapid pace of change in public health systems. Public health organizations manage change continuously in the current environment, as very few elements of the contemporary public health environment remain static for any length of time. The health status of communities and population groups evolves in response to emerging disease risks, evolving patterns in human behavior, demographic shifts, and environmental and climactic turbulence. Chronic diseases are now our nation's leading causes of death, but new and resurgent threats such as bioterrorism and pandemic influenza are continuously appearing on the horizon. Meanwhile, the professional knowledge and technology available to prevent and control disease continues to expand as the biomedical and behavioral sciences advance. Public health organizations also navigate a political and economic landscape that shifts rapidly and often unpredictably as public health issues compete with a variety of other interests for resources and public attention. All of these forces interact to create a volatile environment for carrying out public health activities within communities.

Modern public health organizations face an imperative to identify new and better ways of improving population health. Without such innovations, public health organizations can have no hope of keeping pace with the rapid changes in population health needs and health system structures. Research and evaluation provide the engines for developing these innovations. Diffusing these innovations successfully into practice, however, will require the many other ingredients of successful public health administration, including adequate organizational and human resources, responsive laws and regulations, functional surveillance and information systems, and effective communication and marketing capabilities. Research alone will not lead us to the improved public health system of the future.

A fundamental question concerning the public health system of the future involves its capacity to achieve continued gains in population health. Can the earlier public health successes in sanitation and immunization be recast to reduce the behavioral risks now responsible for the bulk of preventable mortality and morbidity? Are complex psychosocial problems such as violence, obesity, racial and ethnic health disparities, and mental illness amenable to population-based public health interventions? The emerging public health system is uniquely positioned to develop population-based responses to these problems. Increasingly, the necessary information, expertise, and organizational capacity exist to develop and sustain such responses. The remaining challenge lies in the ability of public health decision makers to mobilize and manage these resources appropriately at the population level so as to achieve gains in health.

## References

1. Chernew ME, Hirth RA, Cutler DM. Increased spending on health care: how much can the United States afford? *Health Affairs.* 2003;22(4): 15–25.
2. Schoenbaum SC, Audet AM, Davis K. Obtaining greater value from health care: the roles of the US government. *Health Affairs.* 2003;22(6):183–190.
3. Institute of Medicine. *Crossing the Quality Chasm: A New Health System for the 21st Century.* Washington, DC: National Academies Press; 2002.
4. Anderson G, Hussey P. Comparing health system performance in OECD countries. *Health Affairs.* 2001;20(3):219–232.
5. Organization for Economic Cooperation and Development (OECD). *A Disease-Based Comparison of Health Systems: What Is Best and at What Cost?* Geneva, Switzerland: OECD; 2003.
6. Institute of Medicine. *The Future of the Public's Health in the 21st Century.* Washington, DC: National Academies Press; 2002.
7. Institute of Medicine. *The Future of Public Health.* Washington, DC: National Academy Press; 1988.
8. Centers for Disease Control and Prevention. *Public Health Infrastructure: A Status Report to the Appropriations Committee of the United States Senate.* Atlanta, Ga: Centers for Disease Control and Prevention; 2001.
9. Halverson PK, Mays GP, Kaluzny AD. Working together? Organizational and market determinants of collaboration between public health and medical care providers. *Am J Public Health.* 2000;90(12):1913–1916.
10. Lasker RD. *Medicine and Public Health: The Power of Collaboration.* New York, NY: New York Academy of Medicine; 1997.
11. Roper WL, Mays GP. Performance measurement in public health: conceptual and methodological issues in building the science base. *J Public Health Manage Prac.* 2000;6(5):66–77.
12. Handler AS, Turnock BJ, Hall W, et al. A strategy for measuring local public health practice. *Am Prev Med.* 1995;11(Supp. 2):29–35.
13. Miller CA, Moore KS, Richards TB, McKaig CA. A proposed method for assessing public health functions and practices. *Am J Public Health.* 1994;84(1):1743–1749.
14. Richards TB, Rogers JJ, Christenson GM, Miller CA, Taylor MS, Cooper AD. Evaluating local public health performance at a community level on a statewide basis. *J Public Health Manage Pract.* 1995;1(4):70–83.
15. Mays GP, Miller CA, Halverson PK. *Local Public Health Practice: Trends and Models.* Washington, DC: American Public Health Association; 2000.
16. Mays GP, Halverson PK, Stevens R, et al. Availability and perceived effectiveness of essential public health services in the nation's largest communities. *Am J Public Health.* 2003;94(6):1019–1026.
17. Institute of Medicine. *Performance Measurement: Accelerating Improvement.* Washington, DC: National Academies Press; 2006.
18. Mays GP, Halverson PK, Scutchfield DF. Behind the curve? What we know and need to learn from public health systems research. *J Public Health Manage Pract.* 2003;9(3):179–182.
19. Corso LC, Wiesner PJ, Halverson PK, Brown CK. Using the essential services as a foundation for performance measurement and assessment of local public health systems. *J Public Health Manage Pract.* 2000;6(5):1–18.
20. Office for Protection from Research Risks. *Protecting Human Research Subjects: Institutional Review Board Guidebook.* Washington, DC: National Institutes of Health; 1993.

# INDEX

Note: Italicized page locators indicate a figure; tables are noted with a *t*.